ASSEMBLY AND ASSEMBLERS

ASSEMBLY AND ASSEMBLERS
The Motorola MC68000 Family

G. W. GORSLINE

Professor of Computer Science
Virginia Polytechnic Institute
and State University

PRENTICE HALL, Englewood Cliffs, New Jersey 07632

Library of Congress Cataloging-in-Publication Data

Gorsline, G. W.
  Assembly and assemblers.

  Bibliography: p.
  Includes index.
  1. Motorola 68000 (Microprocessor)—Programming.
  2. Assembler language (Computer program language)
  3. Assembling (Electronic computers)   I. Title.
  QA76.8.M6895G67 1988   005.265   87-14403
  ISBN 0-13-049982-X

Editorial/production supervision and
   interior design: David Ershun/Nancy Menges
Cover design: George Cornell
Manufacturing buyer: S. Gordon Osbourne

 © 1988 by Prentice Hall
A Division of Simon & Schuster
Englewood Cliffs, New Jersey 07632

Printed in the United States of America

10 9 8 7 6 5 4 3 2 1

ISBN 0-13-049982-X   025

PRENTICE-HALL INTERNATIONAL (UK) LIMITED, *London*
PRENTICE-HALL OF AUSTRALIA PTY. LIMITED, *Sydney*
PRENTICE-HALL CANADA INC., *Toronto*
PRENTICE-HALL HISPANOAMERICANA, S.A., *Mexico*
PRENTICE-HALL OF INDIA PRIVATE LIMITED, *New Delhi*
PRENTICE-HALL OF JAPAN, INC., *Tokyo*
SIMON & SCHUSTER ASIA PTE. LTD., *Singapore*
EDITORA PRENTICE-HALL DO BRASIL, LTDA., *Rio de Janeiro*

Contents

Contents

Preface

In the fall of 1985, our department started to require all incoming computer science freshmen to purchase a microcomputer for use in classes. This decision was based on the past and probable future impossibility for the university to furnish a centralized system with the requisite languages, realistic response times, and adequate terminal access. I hasten to add that the university had made valiant efforts to provide the necessary service, but a combination of unsatiable and growing demands for service and limited financial resources constituted an insoluble situation. In addition, the technology of microcomputer manufacturing and distribution had resulted in a pricing situation that allowed our student computer purchase decision without causing an impossible financial burden on the individual student or his/her parents/guardians. (To assure this last point, arrangements were made for time payments and for a laboratory of systems to be established for the use of financially embarrassed students and nonmajors.)

After extensive investigations, negotiations, and formal bidding, the computational system finally delivered was based on the Motorola MC68000—with one megabyte of primary memory, a 10-megabyte Winchester disk, a removable minidisk, and a monochrome display. The operating system was UNIX, and the primary languages were Pascal, C, and Assembly. In addition, the proprietary window-oriented operating system of the vendor (Apple Computer), along with various applications packages, was available.

Our undergraduate computer science curriculum is based on ACM Curriculum '78, as modified to accommodate ten-week quarters as well as the experiences of our faculty and other faculties around the country. After one year of experience with the MC68000-based system, we have found the computational system and its use as an educational tool very satisfactory. To the best of our knowledge, the students have had a similar positive reaction. From my viewpoint, the major shortcoming has been the lack of an adequate textbook to assist our students in learning the first principles of computer architecture and organization, using assembly language as the vehicle. As of this date, a suitable text has not been available (or, at least, has not been found).

In 1984, our university made the major decision to change from a 10-week quarter academic calendar to a 15-week semester system in Fall 1988. Besides being the departmental coordinator for designing all of the course syllabi, I was directly responsible for the computer architectural offerings. At the sophomore level, this included two courses: one that introduced computer architecture via learning to implement algorithms in an assembly language, along with the implications, and another that studied the design and required the implementation of a simple assembler and of a linker. In ACM Curriculum '78, these subjects are covered in a single-semester course—CS4. Our faculty decided to follow the overall plan of Curriculum '78; thus, we have combined our two-term course into a single-semester course, with appropriate adjustments in coverage. The adjustments largely consisted of less emphasis on extreme proficiency in using an assembly language for production purposes. But again, the problem of a suitable text was evident. Not only was a suitable Motorola MC68000-based assembly language text not available, but the incorporation of the design and implementation of an assembly and linker into the same course would require that our students purchase two textbooks for a single course—not a desirable situation.

This text, then, is my attempt to make available to our students a single textbook that will furnish them a vehicle for mastering the first principles of computer organization, of assembly language, of the assembly process, and of linking and relocation. From an educational standpoint, it is somewhat superfluous that the learning vehicle uses the Motorola MC68000 as the example architecture from which generalizations are made. Of much more importance are the operating system, the languages, the programming environment, and the text, as well as the approach used by the instructor. That is, although a specific architecture must be learned and used, of equal importance is gaining at least an elementary understanding of the architectural variations that exist, the current place of assembly language in systems and package implementation, and the design principles and implementation techniques that have evolved for an assembler and for a linker, including the all-important aspects of program relocation.

Every student should solve, using assembly language, a series of problems of graduated difficulty. It is suggested that the first three or four such assignments employ I/O routines furnished via the system by the instructor. At Virginia Tech, we furnish I/O routines implemented in C. In my opinion, it is particularly important that these assignments sample the different data types, such as integer and character. At least one or two assignments should include the use of an assembly language subprocedure invoked by a procedural-level language such as Pascal. It is suggested that particular attention be given to the concept and the implication of stack frames.

Some instructors may prefer to delay the study of interrupts, DMA, and channel-based I/O (Chapter 7) until after the study of assemblers (Chapter 8). This would allow the time necessary for the students to design and implement an assembler to be used in lecture for the consideration of interrupts and DMA, with emphasis on an introduction to concurrent parallel processing, semaphores, co-routines, and truly simultaneous multiprocessing. In addition, although I consider the floating-point data type both important and particularly interesting, the time available in a single semester often will prevent an assignment involving this data type in assembly language. For this reason, I have made the chapter on floating-point data and the MC68881 the concluding chapter, with the suggestion that it be studied during the period that the students are concentrating on designing and implementing the linker and/or the implications of relocation.

It is my distinct pleasure to give well-deserved credit to Ned Okie, a doctoral student–instructor here at Virginia Tech, who has had the major responsibility for integrating the Motorola MC68000 processor-based system into our term course on assembly language. He was kind enough to read the entire text, to find many typing errors, and to make many valuable suggestions regarding programming techniques and presentation. Over the past two years, I have learned to treat his suggestions with respect. It is also a pleasure to express my appreciation to the Summer 1986 class of CS2072, who acted as a "test bed" for the approaches and information content of this text. In addition, my wife (Mrs. G to our students) has once again read every word of the manuscript with a critical eye toward spelling and sentence structure while exhibiting a cheerful countenance toward my tyrannical writing hours. Finally, the Motorola Corporation has been kind in making documentation available and in allowing the use of copyrighted materials. Nevertheless, any errors or oversights in the information are, and must remain, my own.

G. W. Gorsline
Blacksburg, Virginia

Additional Note to Preface

To the faculty, students, programmers, and others who will find this book useful: There are no additional words of wisdom I can offer, since Dr. Gorsline died before he was able to go over the final copy of his manuscript; please accept my apologies for any errata you may find. My expertise was in love, encouragement, and proof-reading, and perhaps the latter leaves much to be desired.

I want to extend my thanks to the many people who were supportive through Dr. Gorsline's illness, and for the patience they had in helping me to complete the text. In particular I wish to thank Dr. Sung Chi Chu, a devoted student and friend whose kindness and help in the past and present have been invaluable to Dr. Gorsline and me. I also wish to thank Judith A. Watson, who came to my rescue when I needed help, and the Computer Science Department at Virginia Tech for their loyalty and support.

Anne B. Gorsline

ASSEMBLY AND ASSEMBLERS

1

Assembly Language and the Computer

Over your lifetime, you, as a person, have become a *problem-solving* entity. As you grew and developed, the problems facing you changed in kind, in character, and in difficulty. Concurrently, you changed—not only physically, which allowed you to approach and be successful in solving certain problems involving increased degrees of strength, coordination, and skill, but mentally, which also allowed you to contemplate and be successful in solving a wider range of ever more difficult problems involving skills in arithmetic and mathematics, in logical inference, and in all the other aspects that distinguish us as human beings. That is, you gained skills in and became comfortable in manipulating *abstract objects*.

Along this developmental path of yours over the past several years, you have formed certain habits of classifying and organizing facts as well as methods of drawing conclusions from them. In this process, you have learned to use various tools to assist you—such as paper and pencil; dictionaries, encyclopedias, and reference books; and the modern equivalent of them—a *computational system*. Let us examine this process of problem solution a trifle closer. Recognizing that humans differ—that each of us is a unique individual and that the way my mind works can be assumed to be somewhat different from the way your mind works—I nevertheless submit that we can validly generalize to some extent regarding this universal mental process of problem solving. For a moment, let us assume that you (or Sallie, or Henry, or I) have a problem. How do we, as humans, go about the process of solving it?

THE PROBLEM-SOLVING PROCESS

First, we must become aware that a problem exists. Sometime during this *recognition phase,* we make informal judgments about the problem: (1) Is this problem important enough to us for further consideration, or should we just ignore it? During this somewhat informal consideration, we also ask: (2) Does this problem need solution now, or can we delay? Concurrently, we are also very informally judging: (3) How hard a problem is this to solve? Is it impossible, difficult and time-consuming, moderately easy and fairly fast, trivial? That is, we make a judgment call: Is this problem important enough to me so that I am willing to spend the time and effort even to attempt a solution? In the technical terms of the commercial world, we have performed a very rough and preliminary *cost-benefit analysis.*

Second, after recognizing that a problem exists and that our preliminary informal cost-benefit analysis suggests that it is worthy of proceeding with, we should now refine our viewpoint of the problem to the extent that we can *accurately state the problem* in precise English, using the accepted terminology of the problem area. That is, if this is a problem in accounting, the problem statement should correctly employ accounting terminology; if this is a problem in interpersonal relations, the problem statement should correctly employ psychological terminology; if this is a problem in road construction, the problem statement should correctly employ the terminology of civil engineering. Note that the domain of the problem completely determines the jargon of the problem statement. Computer jargon at this stage is not only wrong, it dangerously suggests possible solution routes before we have defined what the problem is or even whether a problem really exists. This is an extremely important point, as it allows you and me—as professional (paid) problem solvers (for others)—to assure ourselves and our customers that we really do understand what the problem is. At this point, it is most important to consider only what the problem is and to delay all aspects of how to solve it. Our problem statement is sometimes termed the *functional specifications.* Once again, an informal and preliminary cost-benefit analysis is appropriate. Now is the time for the first draft of the user documentation to be prepared.

Third, we can now think of very general problem solution strategies. This level of thinking involves considering *what general types of tools* are appropriate to accomplish the task at hand. Is the task to move a house from 624 Watson Lane to 106 Locust Avenue? If so, certain tools are indicated. The appropriate tools for this job might be heavy-duty jacks, adequate timbers with attachable and strong wheels, motive power, an adequate (width and height) route, a traffic interruption permit, and so on. I don't see a computational system in that list of tools! Fine—not all problem solutions should involve a computational system. On the other hand, a computational system may very well be involved in solving some of the subproblems, such as determining the best route and time, calculating loads, and determining just what constitutes "adequate" timbers and "requisite" wheels, and the like. Note, however, that we suddenly started considering how to use the tools and stopped thinking about what tools are needed. At this stage, confine yourself to what tools are appropriate.

This stage, often termed *technical specifications,* may encompass the legal defini- tions of deliverables and performance. Court cases are not at all unusual if the map- ping from the functional specifications to the technical specifications is imperfect. Of course, court cases also result from inadequate design, sloppy implementation, deficient documentation, and so on, subsequent to this stage.

Fourth, at this time we can transform the overall technical specifications into subproblems and these subproblems into subsubproblems, *ad infinitum.* Recall the rules relative to this phase that you have worked so hard to master: (1) identify mod- ules by working from the top downward toward the details; (2) perform this modu- larization using the criteria of a transformation to the data as they flow and are mapped from the inputs to the outputs; (3) each module should perform a single function at its level of abstraction, as tested by your ability to describe the action in a single simple sentence, with no connectors such as commas or "and"; (4) the ter- mination of this hierarchical modularization process is reached when the descriptive simple sentence changes from describing a data transformation in terms of the prob- lem to using terms in the programming language; and (5) it is extremely important to restrict module definitions to three items of information: inputs with domain limits, outputs with valid ranges, and the transformations. This phase is usually termed the *design phase.* No decisions relative to how to implement a module are made at this stage. (Exception: If the specifications and/or design specifies a particular solution algorithm, then, and only then, is this "how to" requirement a valid fourth piece of information.)

Fifth, now that the modules and their interfaces have been defined, they can be implemented. (Yes, we did define the interfaces when we specified the module in- puts and outputs.) The implementation should employ an appropriate programming language and should include the discipline of restricting oneself to the precepts of commented code blocks, structured programming, indentation, white space, mnemonic names, and all the other habits you have learned and used. If the choice of programming language is not preempted by the specifications or by its availabil- ity, it should be chosen on the basis of necessary data type availability in the lan- guage, including the necessary operations on the data as well as the familiarity of the programmers with the language and the efficiency of the code output by the avail- able compiler. In addition, the language should be as far up the continuum of lan- guages—from circuit notation through instruction step notation (microprogramming) through assembly language to procedural-level languages and finally to problem- oriented languages (or packages)—as is economically cognizant with programmer productivity in the language, necessary execution speed of the code, desirable mem- ory usage, and factors of maintainability and market acceptance. During this *imple- mentation phase,* each module should not only undergo unit testing but should have been constructed taking advantage of any code verification techniques available (such as assertions and loop invariants).

Sixth, as the various modules successfully pass unit testing, they should be combined with other such modules, one or two at a time, and higher-level unit test- ing should be accomplished. In this way, the entire system will finally be constructed and tested; the final stage of this phase is often termed *system testing*. Many installations maintain that the final system test should be performed by people other than the designers and implementors, on the theory that if the authors had thought about a certain possible eventuality, they would have designed the system to be immune. People who do not know the system can presumably give it a more complete and better test.

Seventh, on-time, within-cost *delivery*, adequate user training, and satisfying and effective systems use are always the overall objective of the development team. Using these three criteria, the record of our industry over the long haul is commonly assumed to be somewhat less than spectacular. Although I tend to agree with this overall assessment, in my opinion, it is largely based on hearsay evidence. There are at least some reasons to believe that a valid survey of recently well-defined and realistic systems, designed and implemented by recently trained and experienced professionals using the techniques termed *software engineering*, would be termed successful or near-successful.

Eighth, because the human activities within the business, the government agency, and the like, are continually changing and evolving, the computational needs are also continually changing. Thus, a delivered system must undergo change in order to continue to satisfy the needs of the users. This *maintenance phase* actually involves two kinds of activities: (1) *correction of errors* in design or implementation that are found during use and (2) changes made to the system as the needs of the customer gradually change—that is, changes in the specifications that result in continuing *system augmentation or enhancements*.

Ninth, at some point, some manager (often at the prodding of technical personnel) determines that further maintenance is almost futile. That is, the system has become so unstructured as the result of myriad enhancements and corrections over the years by diverse programmers that it has become impractical, if not impossible, to make further changes correctly. In terms of error corrections, correcting one error very often causes a new error. In terms of system augmentation, adding one new feature not only causes several new errors but is inordinately expensive in terms of both time and money. Note that the symptoms are those of positive feedback—perturbing the system results in a greater perturbation, which results in a greater perturbation, which . . . . At this stage, a new replacement system should be authorized. Upon its delivery, the present system should be retired (killed). This normal and expected stage for all systems is termed *system death*.

As you might imagine, depending on the specific problem and the programming environment, all sorts of minor and major variations exist in practice in the process of solving problems just described. Three variations seem important enough to mention at this time.

Reusable modules. Almost every computational system used for system development has a program library facility and available methods for incorporating previously produced procedures and/or sections of code into new systems. If and only if (iff) these library routines are well designed, expertly implemented, adequately tested, intelligently documented, and useful is it a practical possibility for careful system designers/implementors to use them with minimal worry. Scientific programmers have lived in this type of environment almost since the beginnings of FORTRAN in the late 1950s. The idea and realization of a program library dates to Wilkes at Cambridge (Great Britain) during the early days of the original implementation of a stored-program digital computer—the EDSAC of the very early 1950s.

Prototypes. There is a current tendency in some programming installations to produce a prototype of the contemplated system and to have this prototype used by the customer's operational personnel in an attempt to clarify and solidify their functional requirements specifications (second stage above) as well as their translation to technical specifications (third stage) and design (fourth stage). Any methodology that materially improves the accuracy of communication between the eventual users and the designers/implementors/testers cannot help but result in systems that are more satisfying. Presumably, more satisfied customers indicate better systems.

Object-oriented systems and data encapsulation. One of the more modern methods of increasing the safety of data from inadvertent, unplanned changes is to hide them (Parnas, 1972) within the set of routines that are specifically and deliberately designed and implemented to perform the desired, and only the desired, manipulations. Using languages such as Pascal, PL/I, ADA, and so forth, that provide local/global data knowledge restrictions, it is somewhat easy to accomplish this data encapsulation and data hiding. Among the better recent treatments of this subject, I recommend Fairley (1985) and Myers (1982). Although both of these references are at the postgraduate and professional level, I believe that most serious undergraduate computer science students will find the sections on data encapsulation in Fairley and the section on data objects in Myers both comprehensible and valuable. The approach and style of all three references cited in this paragraph are superior and commendable.

My presentation of the basic thrusts of this dual concept will involve one of several possible and practical methods of implementation and therefore will no doubt be at least somewhat repugnant to at least a few course instructors. In this learning example, we will conceive of a data object as consisting of three portions:

1. A *data container*—the format of the contents is known only to the routines (the operations) that are specifically designed to access or manipulate specified portions of the contents. Each instance of this object (data container) is known and thus only accessible via these operations routines; that is, it is addressed indirectly by a pointer. Note how this technique accomplishes the information hiding of Parnas and the data encapsulation that Fairley so eloquently recommends.

2. A *capability*—a list of users who can legally read, change, or destroy the entire data object instance or a specified portion or portions. Note how this capability list implements rigorous data protection/security. Of course, the key to

breaking the safety feature of a capability is to obtain the ability to change the capability list itself. This security problem can be partially solved by a *change capability operation* that is, itself, protected by a capability list consisting of the owner of the data object only.

3. A *set of operations*—a group of routines that accomplish the needed data accesses/manipulations on the contents of the data object instance only after checking the capability for the legality of this operation by this user.

This viewpoint implies a subsystem for each data object that includes a private data container unknown outside the subsystem, a set of capability lists, and a group of access (operation) routines. Figure 1.1 should clarify these ideas.

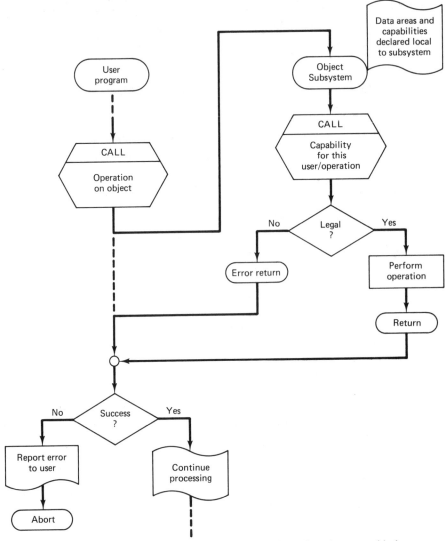

Figure 1.1 The process for accessing data in an object-oriented system with data encapsulation.

LANGUAGE LEVELS

As you have learned in previous course work, the communication of an algorithm to a computational system is accomplished by expressing the algorithm in a programming language. You are also no doubt aware that there are many such languages—some special-purpose, some general-purpose, and some requiring more knowledge of the computational system than others. It is this last differentiation that is of importance to us at this time. That is, it is appropriate for us to consider programming languages from the viewpoint of their orientation toward the problem or, at the other extreme, their orientation toward the computer itself.

Very High Level Programming Languages

The very high level programming languages allow the problem solution to be described in terms of the problem area, and no attention (or only very minimal attention) need be paid to the process of solution, to the operating system, or to the computer itself. For example, the problem solver might specify that the problem to be solved is a payroll system. The language system then might prompt the problem solver with appropriate questions, such as hourly wage or salary? weekly, biweekly, or monthly? United States income tax rules? which state income tax rules? Social Security or not? retirement plan withholding rules? and so on—and the final result would be a working program in the library, ready for appropriate testing (and, as a result, probably an iterative series of retries). There are not too many current examples of this type of very high level programming language at this time, although it is possible to argue that such packages as Visicalc and Lotus 1-2-3 are examples.

Procedural-Oriented (High-Level) Programming Languages

Procedural-level programming languages require that the steps constituting the algorithm chosen for the problem solution be described in terms of the data manipulations on the data containers chosen, and almost no attention need be paid to the operating system or to the computational system itself. Examples include Pascal, PL/I, ADA, COBOL, FORTRAN, Prolog, and many others. This text assumes that you are familiar enough with at least one such language so that you will understand various forms of pseudocode statements used to illustrate points as desirable.

Assembly (Low-Level) Programming Languages

Assembly programming languages require not only that the process of problem solution be specified but that it be described in terms of the available resources furnished by the computer itself, such as memory addresses, registers, primitive operations on scalars (add, move, etc.), condition tests, and so on. Because of the intimate relationship (a one-to-one mapping) of the operations to the facilities of the computer, each different computer of each different vendor will have a unique assembly language and perhaps several different versions (dialects) of that assembly language. The assembly language of the Motorola MC680XY is the main subject of this text, although we will continually call your attention to general principles and important differences between machines in an effort to assist understanding and to allow you to learn and use the assembly language of other computers fairly easily. This text is intended to be more than an assembly language programming text for a single computer family.

Machine Language (Absolute or Relocatable Binary Code)

Machine language consists of the actual bit patterns for each operation and for each associated data address in the problem solution specified. Translating programs, termed compilers and assemblers, transform programs expressed in any one of the foregoing language levels and output machine language for loading into memory for subsequent interpretation by the computer during execution. Among the more important subjects treated in this text is the process of producing relocatable binary machine language from assembly-level code and loading it into memory.

Microprogramming Languages

Microprogramming languages are the short control routines that describe the steps necessary for the actual hardware circuits to accomplish each machine language operation. Such languages are usually used (but not always) to implement the computer itself and are only rarely used to solve applications problems. In this text, we will not examine this subject any more than is necessary to our understanding of the computer itself. The subject of microprogramming is most often reserved for specialized senior and graduate-level courses and tends to be of more interest and utility to computer implementation engineers than to those with interests in software and software systems.

Figure 1.2 summarizes the levels of programming languages. Please note that our discussion has forced us to draw fences on a continuum, forming somewhat artificial classes. Nevertheless, these five language level classes are generally accepted in the fields of computer science and computer engineering.

Language level	Number of language statements per machine language instruction
Very high level languages	One to very many
Procedural-level languages	One to many
Macro-assembly languages	One to many
Basic assembly languages	One to one
Binary machine languages	—
Microprogramming languages	Many to one

Figure 1.2 An overview of programming language levels.

THE MICROCOMPUTER

Because our main interest in studying assembly language programming is to gain a deeper understanding of the tool (the computer) that distinguishes us from other types of problem solvers, we will need to examine the different types of computers and the different types of software that constitute a computational system. In this text we will be accomplishing this learning task using a modern microcomputer—the Motorola MC680XY. Therefore, it seems appropriate to start our learning process by examining microcomputers and then, later, to use them as a basis for comparison.

The microcomputer as a system has as its basis the microprocessor chip. These chips come in various sizes and are implemented in various technologies. When the microprocessor chips are combined with other integrated circuits, a microcomputer system can be constructed. The majority of these have been 8-bit and 16-bit data oriented, although the number of 32-bit devices is increasing. The evolution of both computers and microcomputers is summarized in Figure 1.3.

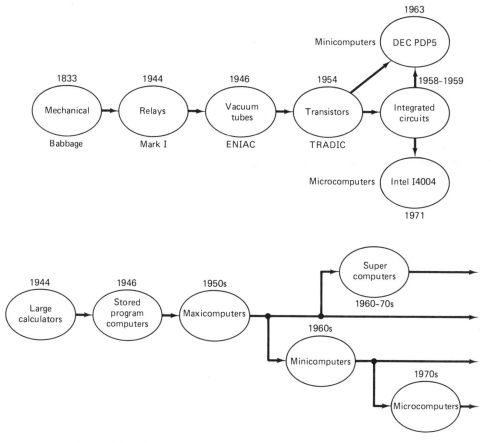

Figure 1.3 Microcomputer evolution. (From G. W. Gorsline, *16-Bit Modern Microcomputers: The Intel I8086 Family.* © 1985, p. 9. Reprinted by permission of Prentice-Hall, Inc., Englewood Cliffs, NJ.)

One of the continually evolving aspects of the physical microcomputer system topology is the number of functions centered on a single chip. Most very large scale integrated circuit (VLSI) chips now available are really microprocessors. For a microprocessor to qualify as a microcomputer requires the addition of enough circuits to allow basic computer functions to take place—usually a basic arithmetic processor that can interact with a memory and also control the input and output of data. Some microcomputers for limited applications, such as carburetion control of an automobile, are self-contained on a single chip.

The *arithmetic-logic unit* is the central element of the entire microcomputer. A typical implementation of the ALU function includes primitive arithmetic operations such as the addition and subtraction of data words. The unit also performs logic operations such as "and," "or," and "exclusive or." Quite often, the majority of the miscellaneous processor operations, such as counting, will all be centralized here. This is advantageous, because the ALU already contains the basic logic pieces used to perform most such operations.

Interfacing is a key problem area in a microprocessor. Interfacing must solve the question of how to handle the interaction between functions on different chips and, more specifically, the connection of the processor functions with the memory and the input/output. An obvious answer to one aspect, the interaction of processor functions, is the emergence of true single-chip processors.

In the first-generation chips (such as the Intel 4004), additional logic was required to interface the various microprocessor pieces, such as the timing and the interfaces to memory and input/output (Figure 1.4*a*). Because of the problems in adjusting timing circuits, it was quite common to have an external clock. In some of the later microprocessors, the timing was placed on the chip itself. The only external connection required was to a crystal oscillator. As the chips evolved, memory addressing was assigned to separate pins so as to eliminate some of the memory interface requirements. This had certain limitations, because the number of memory circuits that could be electrically driven was small. If the memory requirements were extensive, additional "driving" circuits were still required.

Microcontrol is the sequencing of primitive operations within the CPU. Thus, the sequence of steps that constitute the fetching of an instruction from program memory and its subsequent execution is initiated and controlled by this subsystem. The control function may be directly implemented in hard circuits with a permanent information path and step logic. Alternatively, this function may be implemented employing a lower-level microcontrol function and control-program memory that is microprogrammed to implement (to emulate) each step of fetching and executing every instruction of the microcomputer as seen by the applications and systems programmer. An early and excellent tutorial on implementing the control function of computers through microprogramming was published in *Computer Surveys* (Rosin, 1969). Some microprocessors use random logic instead of microprogramming and place the control on the same chip as the ALU (MC 6800), which, of course, requires more logic functions on the chip. The decision on how best to partition the functions is significantly dependent on how the control function is implemented.

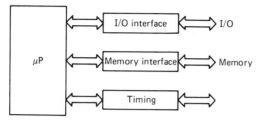

(a) Configuration with support elements

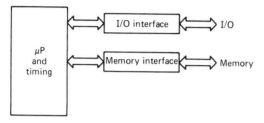

(b) Configuration with integrated clock

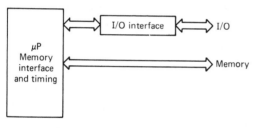

(c) Configuration with integrated clock
and memory interface

Figure 1.4 Trends in microcomputer configurations. (From G. W. Gorsline, *16-Bit Modern Microcomputers: The Intel I8086 Family*. © 1985, p. 11. Reprinted by permission of Prentice-Hall, Inc., Englewood Cliffs, NJ.)

It is often desirable to separate the control function from the other processor functions. This is because read-only memory (ROM) can now be implemented using any standard commercial ROM chip, and thus the CPU chip becomes less dense with a potentially higher yield (Figure 1.5). This technique is used in the DEC LSI-11. It results in additional chips, which are used to microprogram the microprocessor. The flexibility of added functions obtained from the microprogramming technique will quite often offset the cost of the additional control chips. In fact, the additional chips necessary to add functions to nonmicroprogrammed processors will often add more chips to the system than would be required for microprogrammed control.

This fact indicates that the assignment of functions to a chip is not always done with total system minimization as a goal. Further, there is a preoccupation by the manufacturer to market the one-chip microprocessor. This is, of course, quite desirable for controller applications. When used in a systems application, the resulting

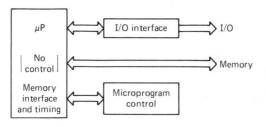

Figure 1.5 Microprogrammed control. (From G. W. Gorsline, *16-Bit Modern Microcomputers: The Intel I8086 Family.* © 1985, p. 12. Reprinted by permission of Prentice-Hall, Inc., Englewood Cliffs, NJ.)

large chip count often comes as a shock and is a reminder of the meaning of *caveat emptor*.

The *register* section of the CPU varies considerably from processor to processor. The number of registers may vary from one to eight or more. Some of the possible uses of the registers are for address modification, for saving subroutine addresses, for the program counter, for auxiliary accumulators, or as a small scratchpad memory. Of course, various combinations of these uses depend on the architectural plan.

The interfacing of the processor with *memory* requires some amount of read/write memory, which is usually random-access memory (RAM). Portions of this can be replaced by a fixed program in read-only memory (ROM). For systems with large amounts of memory, a memory address register must be added. Some processor chips do not have sufficient logic to handle the expansion of memory, so that additional external control circuitry may be necessary.

The *I/O control* section is always the most difficult portion of the computer to standardize. But in general, buffering of data and of control is almost always required between I/O devices and the computer. The effort to place as much of this buffering as possible on the processor chip is a continuing effort. The proper sequencing of I/O data to and from the processor demands that some of this control be incorporated into the microcontrol of the processor. However, this may not be sufficient if there is any expansion of I/O functions, so that additional control with additional circuits will probably be needed.

When all the pieces are put together to form a usable microcomputer, no matter how the manufacturer partitioned the computer, it has become a computer-on-a-board (Figure 1.6). How well the pieces intermesh to form a smoothly functioning computer structure will determine the success of the architectural plan.

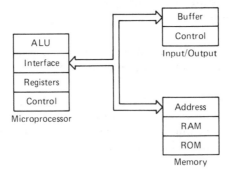

Figure 1.6 Main elements of a microprocessor. (From G. W. Gorsline, *16-Bit Modern Microcomputers: The Intel I8086 Family.* © 1985, p. 13. Reprinted by permission of Prentice-Hall, Inc., Englewood Cliffs, NJ.)

ASSEMBLY LANGUAGE

It is vital always to remember that the MC680XY, as an actual computer, can only execute instructions that are in binary machine code in memory. Thus, the actual running of a program requires that the program be expressed as a linear series of binary instructions. Although it is possible to compose programs in machine language format, it is time-consuming, boring, and extremely error-prone; that is, machine language programming is overly expensive and not at all practical.

As you are already aware, programs have been designed and implemented that will accept a problem solution formulated in a syntax, and associated semantics, that is easier to learn and correctly use than machine language. Generally, if one statement of the language results in several machine language instructions, the translator program is termed a *compiler* and the input would be *source code* statements in a language such as Pascal, FORTRAN, COBOL, and the like. If one statement of the source code results in one binary machine instruction (object code), the translator is termed an *assembler*. Notice that the foregoing implies that an assembly language employs the terminology of, and forces programmers to think at the level of, the computer itself, while the terminology of a procedural-level language is almost always abstracted away from the computer toward the steps of the problem solution. We are also implying that one statement in a procedural-level language, such as Pascal, is usually equivalent to several statements in an assembly language.

Procedural-level language such as Pascal or BASIC can decrease the time required to transliterate a problem solution design into executable code, compared with the time required when an assembly language is used. In addition, these higher-level languages have the advantage of a degree of machine independence that often allows relatively easy transfer of programs from one vendor's computer to those of another vendor. Finally, more people know and have facility in using these languages than have practice in using a lower-level language.

One the other hand, most procedural-level languages do not permit a programmer to access directly many of the unique features provided by the specific computer design. The compilers—the translators—for higher-level languages tend to produce object machine code that is generalized to cover all possible situations, even those situations that are expected to occur very rarely. In addition, most compilers produce object code consisting of a fairly small and restricted subset of the available operand addressing modes. Nevertheless, compilers for such relatively simple languages as FORTRAN and COBOL are available that generate code that usually executes almost as rapidly and occupies only a trifle more space than most assembly language programmers would produce when solving the same problem. For most situations, the optimal solution usually involves implementing most of the problem solution in a procedural-level language while using assembly language for the few lowest-level routines that must solve special strange data manipulations that are either time- and/or space-critical.

It must be noted that certain data manipulations that are cumbersome and difficult to accomplish in a procedural language are often straightforward and easy to implement using an assembly language. In addition, the direct control of most peripherals via device drivers employing the interrupt system of the combined hardware–software interface is best accomplished using an assembly language. Finally, anyone who has the intellectual drive to understand the computer deeply must become intimately familiar with the machine at the instruction–register–memory–device level, a task that is only possible employing assembly language. It should be realized that this human–computer intimacy is not for everyone.

The assembly language designed for the Motorola MC680XY that is available from the Motorola Corporation is a fairly typical example of such language processors available from the manufacturers of most computers and from commercial software suppliers. It is to be expected that the specific syntax of the assembler available from the Motorola Corporation will vary slightly from the syntax employed by the assembler furnished with the Apple Lisa/MacIntosh and that both of these may be slightly different from the syntax required for the assembler available on your specific machine. Nevertheless, the syntax for assembly language programs is almost always so easy and uniform that only slight difficulties should occur.

The group of assembly language statements and comments that are presented to the assembler for transformation into corresponding machine language instructions is called a *module*. The assembler is a program that acts as a translation function for a named module:

$$\text{source module} \xrightarrow{f} \textit{object module}$$

An assembly language module is defined as the set of source statements that are presented as a file to the assembler as input (source module) and as the corresponding set of object code (object module) that results as a file from the successful assembly of a correct source module. The source module is presented to the assembler as an input file with a name—an identifier. The assembler output file—the object module—will have a default name consisting of the name of the source file unless a directive is issued to name it something else. The object file is normally one of the inputs to a program—the *linker*—that combines modules preparatory to loading into physical memory with subsequent execution.

The syntax of a *statement* in the Motorola MC680XY assembler is:

label   OPERATION   OPERAND,OPERAND   comment

where the portions given here in uppercase are required and those in lowercase are (usually) optional.

The optional *label* is a programmer-chosen unique symbolic name for this memory location. It could identify a branch target within the module, a procedure name, or a data container (a declared memory allocation that will later contain a datum value). If present, the label must start with an alphabetic letter (A through Z), must be eight characters or less in length, and must be followed by one or more blanks. Note that many modern assemblers allow longer labels, allow certain specific and limited symbols as the starting character, and sometimes require a colon as the last (terminating) character.

The required *operation* name is the directive for which operation is to be performed. It must be followed by one or more blank characters. It can be of three types:

> *Operation code (opcode)*—the symbolic designation of a legal MC680XY action (as listed in Figure 2.10).
>
> *Assembly directive*—the symbolic designation of an action for the assembler itself, such as declaring (creating) a data container. (We will return to this subject very shortly.)
>
> *Macro name*—the programmer-chosen unique symbolic name of a group of assembly statements to be physically inserted into the module at this point. Among the macros often furnished by the system are those that accomplish simple input/output. The composing and use of macros will be covered in some depth in a later chapter.

The *operand* field contains the designation of the data container whose contents will be manipulated, or it is the target label of a branch. In general, each operand is a self-naming constant, the name of a register, or a label along with the directions (i.e., addressing mode) for calculating the effective address in memory. A few instructions imply the operand, some instructions require one operand, and many instructions require two operands, in which case they are separated by a comma. No embedded blanks are allowed within the operand field—which, again, is followed by one or more blank characters.

The operand field of any statement may be followed by a *comment*. In generally accepted programming practice, comments at the right-hand end of individual statements should be somewhat rare and should occur only when the statement accomplishes some obscure, strange, or unusual action. On the other hand, program sections should always be preceded by comment lines (an asterisk in column 1, although some assemblers employ a semicolon) containing somewhat brief but complete explanations of what the following code section accomplishes, how it accomplishes it, and why. These explanatory signpost comments are usually enclosed within blank comment lines and are often surrounded by comment lines of all asterisks for clarity. At an absolute minimum, each module should be headed by a comment preamble containing the program name, the purpose, the date, the programmer's name, and other explanatory information.

Readability and understanding are vastly improved if a fixed format is employed for source programs. One very common format is

Label—start in column 1.

Operation—start in column 10.

Operand(s)—start in column 16.

Comments—if at statement end, start in column 40; otherwise, start in column 3, with asterisk in column 1.

In addition, the liberal use of blank lines (comment blank) greatly aids comprehension.

The Motorola MC680XY assembler requires the use of certain syntactical notations:

Base 16 (hexadecimal) numbers—$ digits
Base 10 (decimal) numbers—digits
Base 2 (binary) numbers—————— (prohibited)
ASCII characters—' ccc. . .c'
Immediate operands
  Hexadecimal—#$ digits
  Decimal—# digits
  ASCII—#' ccc. . .c'

In addition, in those cases where an arithmetic expression is allowed with the operand, the operators +, −, *, /, and (. . .) are employed with their common and usual meanings in such languages as Pascal, FORTRAN, and BASIC.

A few paragraphs earlier, we stated that the operation field could contain an *assembly directive*. The syntax required by the Motorola MC680XY assembler is

Module Delimitors

ORG   value or expression

The assembler will use this as its starting address during translation. Relocatable programs—the usual applications type—should use zero.

END

Required as the terminating operation of a module.

Data Container Declarations

          B
label   DC.W   value,. . ., value
          L

Create a memory storage space of the specified length containing the specified values in the order given. The value may be given in hexadecimal, decimal, or ASCII. The label is usual but not necessary.

          B
label   DS.W   number
          L

Create a memory storage space of the specified number of bytes, words, or long words that initially contain uninitialized junk. Again, the label is usual but optional.

Symbol Definitions

label	EQU	expression	Evaluate the expression to form a value for use only during the assembly process. Although the label is optional, its use is almost universal.

Listing Printout Controls

LLEN	value	The length of each line in characters. Most often 80, 100, or 120.
LIST		Create an assembly output file of the source and corresponding hexadecimal object code with error notations for eventual printing and/or viewing on the CRT screen.
NOLIST		Do not create a listing file. The system default is most usually LIST.
PAGE		Print the following line on a new page in the listing file.
SPC	value	Skip this number of lines in the listing file.
G		In the define constant (DC.-) print line, include all of the values on the listing. Otherwise, only the first value will be printed. I highly recommend that this assembly directive always be used for clarity.

Certain of the foregoing assembly directives need further comment:

ORG   Unless otherwise indicated by the use of this directive, the assembler will transliterate the module as if the first memory location were to be byte zero in main memory. In the usual case for applications programs that will be executed under the auspices of an operating system such as UNIX, this is desirable. The program will have all of the addresses changed by a *loader* program as it is being placed into memory preparatory to execution. Under certain circumstances, it may be necessary for a module to be located in memory at a very specific and known location as part of the operating system itself. In these cases, and only in these cases, the ORG directive is necessary.

B
DC.W   Initial values are specified. It is important to realize that these ini-
L   tial values may be changed during execution. More than one con-
              stant (initial value) may be defined in a single define constant (DC)
              by separating the values by commas. The effective address in
              memory of a label may be placed in storage by using the syntax:

              LABEL DC.L LABEL

              The define constant (DC) directive enlarges the object file by the
              number of bytes required to contain the constant(s). The define
              storage (DS) directive does not have this effect.

B
DS.W   The storage locations created by the define storage (DS) directive
L   are not initialized but contain the *junk* values that just happened to
              be in those memory locations before the program was loaded. Al-
              though some operating systems employ loaders that violate this
              rule, it is factual often enough that all assembly language pro-
              grammers should always assume that it is true and program accord-
              ingly—that is, initialize all variables before use.

EQU   This assembly directive allows the programmer to employ more ac-
              ceptable and mnemonically meaningful terminology for certain fa-
              cilities in the system. For example, if you desire to refer to the data
              register DO as DREGO and address register A3 as AREG3, then
              employ the statements:

              DREGO EQU DO
              AREG3 EQU A3

              In addition, as the I/O devices in the Motorola MC680XY are
              memory-mapped into absolute memory addresses, you may wish to
              refer to them by device name instead of as an absolute address:

              CRT EQU $7FFF

The general format for a Motorola MC680XY assembly language module is

          LIST
          LLEN   80   ; line length = 80 characters
          G

```
*
*   EXAMPLE OF MODULE FORMAT
*
*   G. W. GORSLINE, 1 SEPTEMBER 1986
*
            ORG   0
CRT         EQU   $7FFF
KEYBRD      EQU   $7FEF
*
*   DATA AREAS
*
ONE         DC.B  1
FIFTEEN     DC.B  F
              .
              .
              .

ADR_WRK     DC.L  ADR_WRK+4
WORK        DS.B  73
              .
              .
              .

*
*   CODE AREA
*
              .
              .
              .
              .
            END
```

The following is an example of the listing output from a trivial program involving absolute addresses:

```
003000 43F81000   LEA.L    $00001000,A1  SOURCE BLOCK STARTS AT $1000
003004 45F82000   LEA.L    $00002000,A2  DESTINATION BLOCK STARTS AT $2000
003008 203C00000010 MOVE.L #16,D0        BLOCK LENGTH EQUALS 16 WORDS
00300E 34D9       MOVE.W (A1)+,(A2)+      MOVE WORD AND POINT TO NEXT WORD
003010 5380       SUBQ.L   #1,D0          UPDATE COUNT
003012 66FA       BNE.S    $00300E        REPEAT FOR NEXT WORD
003014 60FE       BRA.S    $003014
```

Note that the leftmost column contains effective addresses as generated by the assembler and that the second leftmost column is the binary machine language object code equivalent (expressed in hexadecimal) of the source code in columns 3 and 4 that were copied directly from the assembly source module (along with the comments).

THE INSTRUCTION CYCLE

Consider the somewhat generalized microcomputer whose organizational structure is shown in Figure 1.7. The memory subassembly of this and all other conventional computers consists of consecutively numbered cells, each one of which can contain one item of information. This information can represent (1) a portion of a program, (2) a portion of the data that the aforementioned program is designed to manipulate, or (3) undefined or noise contents of a memory cell that has not been deliberately filled with either data or program.

A program for all conventional microcomputers is a fully ordered set of instructions that will be executed in sequential order (except for those instructions that specifically change this execution order—jumps or branches). The address in memory of the instruction currently being executed is contained in the program counter (PC)—one of the addressing registers illustrated in Figure 1.7 (often the only one). To reiterate, the PC contains the address in memory of the instruction currently being executed.

An instruction of all conventional computers consists of two portions: an operations code that specifies the action and an operand address or addresses, each of

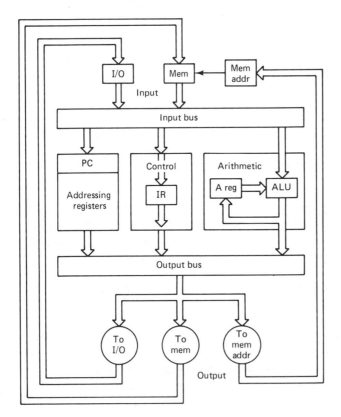

Figure 1.7 Generalized microcomputer structure. (From G. W. Gorsline, *16-Bit Modern Microcomputers: The Intel I8086 Family.* © 1985, p. 14. Reprinted by permission of Prentice-Hall, Inc., Englewood Cliffs, NJ.)

which explicity specifies the address in memory of a datum on which the action specified in the operations code (opcode) is to be carried out. In general, computers are designed with the following instruction types: (1) data manipulation, (2) input/output, and (3) program control flow.

1. Data manipulation instructions:

MOVE	X,Y	[Register(X)] $\longrightarrow$ [Register(Y)]
MOVE	X,MemAddr	[Register(X)] $\longrightarrow$ [Memory(Z)]
MOVE	MemAddr,X	[Memory(Z)] $\longrightarrow$ [Register(X)]
MOVE	#17,X	Datum $\longrightarrow$ [Register(X)]
MOVE	#17,MemAddr	Datum $\longrightarrow$ [Memory(Z)]
ADD	X,Y	[Register(X)] + [Register(Y)] $\longrightarrow$ [Register(Y)]
ADD	X,MemAddr	[Register(X)] + [Memory(Z)] $\longrightarrow$ [Memory(Z)]
ADD	#17,X	Datum + [Register(X)] $\longrightarrow$ [Register(X)]

2. Data input/output instruction:

OUT   X,Device#3   [Register(X)] $\rightarrow$ [Device (3)]

3. Program control flow instructions:

JMP THERE	[PC] $\leftarrow$ MemAddr THERE
JMPZ THERE	IF < last result = 0 >
	Then [PC] $\leftarrow$ MemAddr THERE
	Else [PC] $\leftarrow$ [PC] + 1

In accomplishing the instructions listed above, as well as numerous additional instructions, conventional computers, including microcomputers, must first obtain the instruction from memory and then execute it. As this process is repeated for every instruction in a program, a repetitive process or loop is indicated:

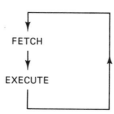

We will illustrate this *instruction cycle* by tracing the details of executing an instruction commonly known as ADD IMMEDIATE. This instruction is often indicated in an assembly language program as

ADD   #17   [Register] + Datum $\rightarrow$ [Register]

and resides in the memory locations whose address is currently contained in the program counter (PC) and in the next consecutive location. Referring to Figure 1.8, it should be realized that our example hypothetical microcomputer possesses only one accumulator register, and therefore its identification is implied in the instruction.

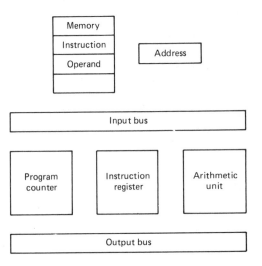

Figure 1.8 Subassemblies of the microcomputer diagrammed in Figure 1.9. Using this structure of subassemblies, Figure 1.9 illustrates the instruction cycle for the Move Immediate Instruction ADD #17, where the operation code is contained in the memory location whose address is contained in the program counter, the data are contained in the next sequential memory location, and the next sequential instruction is the memory location following. (From G. W. Gorsline, *16-Bit Modern Microcomputers: The Intel I8086 Family.* © 1985, p. 16. Reprinted by permission of Prentice-Hall, Inc., Englewood Cliffs, NJ.)

The instruction cycle for this instruction of our hypothetical microcomputer consists of four instruction steps, as illustrated in Figure 1.9. A flowchart of the instruction cycle is given in Figure 1.10. Figure 1.11 illustrates some alternative microcomputer organizational schemes that would affect the details of the instruction cycle. The actions of the execute phase of the instruction cycle of various instructions are illustrated in Figure 1.12.

Particular attention should be given to the method of accomplishing a branch, as shown in Figure 1.13. Recall that the normal flow of program execution is the sequential execution of instructions in the order of their occurrence in memory. Also recall that this is accomplished by incrementing the program counter during the fetch phase of the instruction cycle (and also in the execute phase of many instructions). The typical branch instruction of microcomputers has the form

JMP THERE

where the symbolic operand represents an address within the program in memory. The branch is accomplished by replacing the contents of the program counter with this address, after which the sequential nature of the microcomputer is again in force through incrementing the program counter during the fetch phase (and during the execute phase, if indicated) of subsequent instructions.

The conditional branch instruction is accomplished, as illustrated on the right side of Figure 1.13, by first testing the specified condition flag—overflow, for example—and then either executing the branch in the identical manner described above or

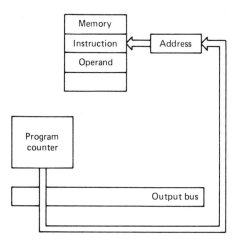

(a) Instruction Cycle — Fetch Phase — Step 1:

[MAR] ← [PC]

Send the contents of the Program Counter to the Memory Address Register.

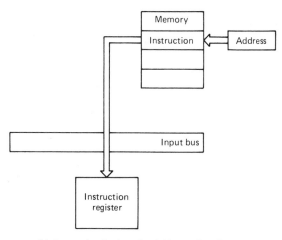

(b) Instruction Cycle — Fetch Phase — Step 2:

[IR] ← [Memory (MAR)]
[PC] ← [PC] + 1

Get the operation code from memory and send it to the Instruction Register (IR). Simultaneously increment the Program Counter so that it points at the next sequential memory location.

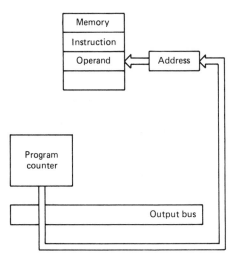

(c) Instruction Cycle -- Execute Phase — Step 3:

Decode Operation Code
[MAR] ← [PC]

After determining, by the bit pattern of the contents of the Instruction Register, that this is an Add Immediate instruction (the data is implied as the contents of the next memory location); contents of the Program Counter are sent to the Memory Address Register.

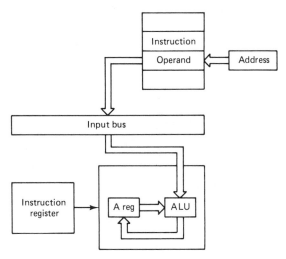

(d) Instruction Cycle — Execute Phase — Step 4:

[A] ← [A] + [Memory (MAR)]
[PC] ← [PC] + 1

Get immediate data from memory and send it to adder-circuits in Arithmetic/Logic Unit; also send contents of Accumulator Register to adder circuits and deliver sum from adder circuits to Accumulator Register. Simultaneously, increment the Program Counter so that it prints to the next memory location — the next sequential instruction. Start Fetch Phase.

Figure 1.9 Execute cycle of an ADD Immediate instruction. (From G. W. Gorsline, *16-Bit Modern Microcomputers: The Intel I8086 Family,* © 1985, p. 17. Reprinted by permission of Prentice-Hall, Inc., Englewood Cliffs, NJ.)

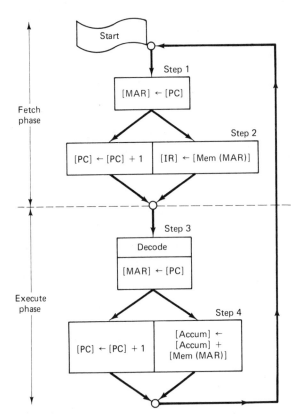

Figure 1.10 Graphical representation of the instruction cycle for the microcomputer instruction ADD Immediate, also illustrated in Figures 1.8 and 1.9. Note the parallelism achieved in instruction steps 2 and 4. (From G. W. Gorsline, *16-Bit Modern Microcomputers: The Intel I8086 Family,* © 1985, p. 18. Reprinted by permission of Prentice-Hall, Inc., Englewood Cliffs, NJ.)

by incrementing the program counter so as to point to the next sequential instruction just beyond the operand address of the conditional branch instruction.

Although it is not certain exactly who invented the closed subprogram, it is a matter of record that Maurice Wilkes made extensive use of this concept in programming the first operational stored-program electronic digital computer, the EDSAC, at Cambridge University in Great Britain during 1948 or slightly earlier. Essentially, a closed subprogram is a logically *and* physically separate entity that is invoked by an instruction such as

JMPSUB   ANYSUB

or

CALL   ANYSUB

After execution of the instructions constituting the closed subprogram, control must revert to the instruction sequentially following the invoking instruction (JMPSUB or

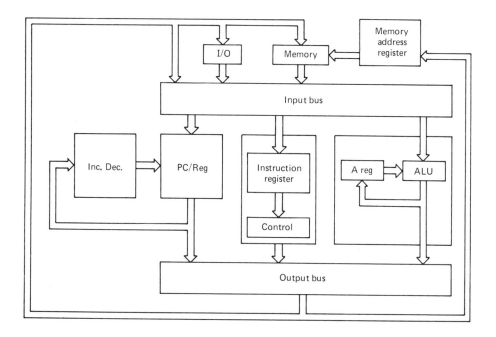

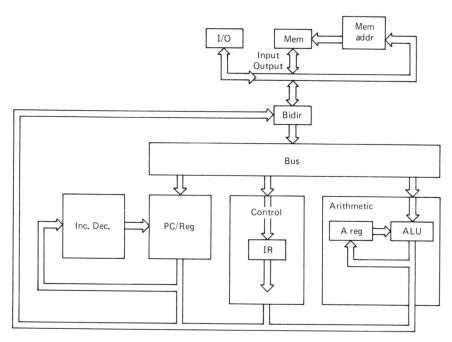

Figure 1.11 Alternative microcomputer organizational scheme examples. Although the details of the instruction cycle would change, the overall principle would remain constant. (From G. W. Gorsline, *16-Bit Modern Microcomputers: The Intel 18086 Family,* © 1985, p. 19 and 20. Reprinted by permission of Prentice-Hall, Inc., Englewood Cliffs, NJ.)

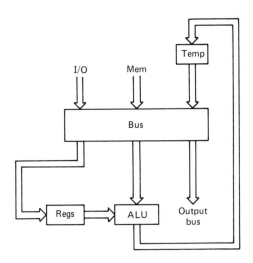

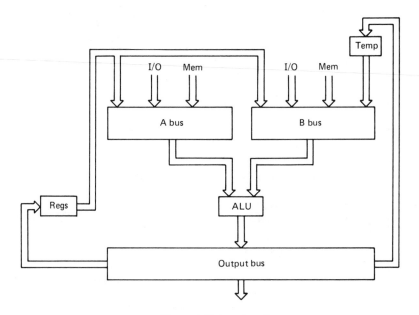

Figure 1.11 (*continued*)

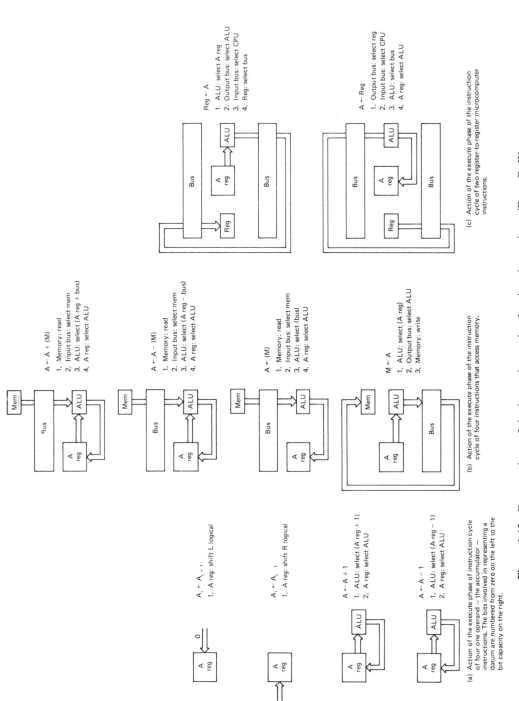

$A_i \leftarrow A_{i+1}$
1. A reg: shift L logical

$A_i \leftarrow A_{i-1}$
1. A reg: shift R logical

$A \leftarrow A + 1$
1. ALU: select (A reg + 1)
2. A reg: select ALU

$A \leftarrow A - 1$
1. ALU: select (A reg - 1)
2. A reg: select ALU

(a) Action of the execute phase of instruction cycle of four one operand — the accumulator — instructions. The bits involved in representing a datum are numbered from zero on the left to the bit capacity on the right.

$A \leftarrow A + (M)$
1. Memory: read
2. Input bus: select mem
3. ALU: select (A reg + bus)
4. A reg: select ALU

$A \leftarrow A - (M)$
1. Memory: read
2. Input bus: select mem
3. ALU: select (A reg - bus)
4. A reg: select ALU

$A \leftarrow (M)$
1. Memory: read
2. Input bus: select mem
3. ALU: select (bus)
4. A reg: select ALU

$M \leftarrow A$
1. ALU: select (A reg)
2. Output bus: select ALU
3. Memory: write

(b) Action of the execute phase of the instruction cycle of four instructions that access memory.

Reg $\leftarrow$ A
1. ALU: select A reg
2. Output bus: select ALU
3. Input bus: select CPU
4. Reg: select bus

A $\leftarrow$ Reg
1. Output bus: select reg
2. Input bus: select CPU
3. ALU: select bus
4. A reg: select ALU

(c) Action of the execute phase of the instruction cycle of two register-to-register microcomputer instructions.

Figure 1.12 Execute phase of the instruction cycle of various instructions. (From G. W. Gorsline, *16-Bit Modern Microcomputers: The Intel I8086 Family*, © 1985, p. 21. Reprinted by permission of Prentice-Hall, Inc., Englewood Cliffs, NJ.)

27

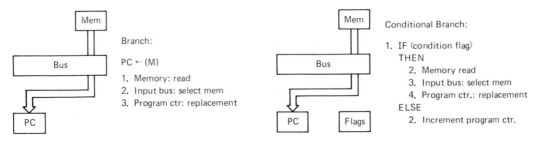

Figure 1.13 Action of the execute phase of the instruction cycle of two microcomputer instructions that change the program flow from sequential to a jump or a branch. (From G. W. Gorsline, *16-Bit Modern Microcomputers: The Intel I8086 Family,* © 1985, p. 22. Reprinted by permission of Prentice-Hall, Inc., Englewood Cliffs, NJ.)

CALL) of the calling routine. Thus, it is necessary that the *return address* be available for placement into the program counter at the execution conclusion of the subprogram. The return address must be preserved by the invoking program in a place known to the subprogram. Figure 1.14 illustrates the three common methods that have been used to solve this problem.

The historically earliest method is shown at the top of Figure 1.14. Note that the return address is placed in the first memory location of the subprogram and that execution starts at the location following this return address. The coding of the subprogram might be

```
ANYSUB    JMP    RETURN ADDRESS IN CALLING PROGRAM
START     -
          -
          -
          -
          -
ENDSUB    JMP    ANYSUB
          END
```

with execution starting at the instruction at memory address START. This scheme necessitates placing the return address in the subprogram. Thus, the subprogram is altered, does not consist of pure code, and cannot execute from ROM. Note that if the subprogram invokes itself, the original return address is covered up and destroyed so that a return to the original calling program is impossible. In effect, the program loses itself. Thus, recursive subprocedure calls are not possible. Nevertheless, subprograms may call—invoke—other subprograms to an arbitrary depth as long as self-calling or calling in circles (recursion or pseudorecursion) are not allowed. This somewhat antiquated method of subprocedure return address preservation is powerful and adequate for all situations not requiring pure code (ROM or PROM memory) or recursive calls. This method is not employed in conventional microcomputers.

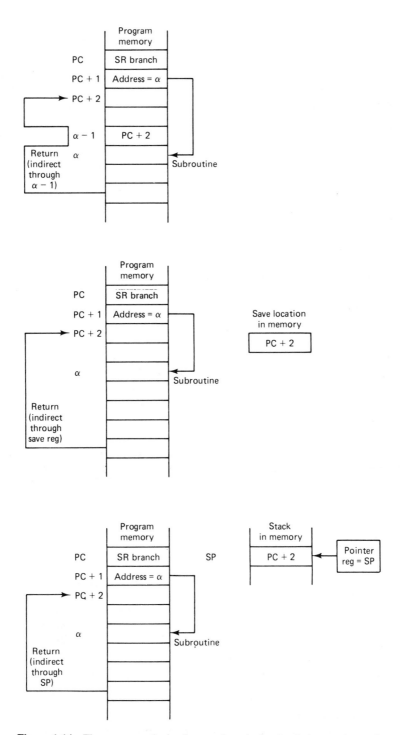

Figure 1.14 Three commonly implemented methods of subprogram invocation and return (From G. W. Gorsline, *16-Bit Modern Microcomputers: The Intel I8086 Family,* © 1985, p. 23. Reprinted by permission of Prentice-Hall, Inc., Englewood Cliffs, NJ.)

A method commonly employed in maxicomputers (IBM/360–IBM/370–IBM 303X extended family) and used in the Texas Instruments microcomputer 99/4 is illustrated in the middle portion of Figure 1.14. In this scheme, the software system assumes that the return address has been placed in a particular register by the calling program (register 14 in both the IBM and the TI conventions). Thus, a return is accomplished by branching to the address in register 14. In the IBM case, this could be

```
BR    14      *BRANCH TO ADDRESS IN REGISTER 14
```

It is further assumed that if a call to a subprogram subservient to the subprogram is made, the called subprogram will save the return address of the calling program in a known place in memory before placing its own return address in register 14. Thus, provisions for calling subprograms to any depth are provided. In addition, as the code of the subprogram is not altered, pure code is achieved. As a last and most important point, the return address is not destroyed (at least not intentionally), and thus recursive and circular subprogram calls are allowed.

The bottom portion of Figure 1.14 illustrates the more usual call/return scheme employed with conventional microcomputers as well as with some mini-, midi-, and maxicomputers (examples: HP3000, B6700, etc.). All conventional microcomputers are designed and implemented with an address register—the *stack pointer* (SP)—which has special execution characteristics when one of the inverse-twin instructions JMPSUB and RET is executed.

For an understanding of this subprogram scheme, it is necessary first to understand the action of a stack. Stacks of return addresses, of data, of playing cards, or of dishes all behave identically—an item may be placed only on top of the stack and an item may be taken only from the top of the stack. Thus, only the last item (or card or dish) placed on the stack is available for retrieval from the stack. The discipline is *last in–first out* (LIFO). With a stack of information in computer memory, we universally term the two complementary actions PUSH and POP and use the terminology "push onto" and "pop from". Also, with a stack of information in contiguous locations in memory, it is necessary to maintain the address of the top of the stack—the address of the place to PUSH to and the place to POP from. In conventional microcomputers, a special *stack pointer register* is devoted to this task and thus contains the memory address of the top of the stack. For historical reasons having to do with memory management, stacks in computer memory always grow toward lower memory addresses—that is, backwards. (We will return to this subject in a subsequent section.) The action of the complementary instructions PUSH and POP are

```
PUSH    DATUM
```
1. Decrement SP contents to point to one place beyond the new stack top (the next empty location).
2. Store DATUM at a location in memory whose address is in SP.

POP   DATUM   1. Retrieve DATUM from stack top.
                         2. Increment SP contents to point to current nonempty stack top (which will be new empty location after POPping).

Note that these actions are complementary and inverse. An examination of the bottom portion of Figure 1.14 should make clear the use of a stack of return addresses:

CALL   ANY   1. PUSH return address to stack from PC.
                        2. Decrement SP.
                        3. Load address of start of subprogram ANY into PC.
                        4. Resume normal instruction fetch.

RET   1. Increment SP.
                        2. POP return address from stack to PC.
                        3. Resume normal instruction fetch.

This scheme allows

1. Calling subprograms to any depth
2. Pure code subprograms
3. Recursive and circular subprogram invocation

MEMORY

Memory in a computational system is any entity that has the ability to retain information over time. As a generality, memory reacts to two instructions:

STORE   Datum at address
RETRIEVE   Datum from address

It must be emphasized that memory is a passive device that preserves information over time but does not change or transform it in any way. Memory may logically be classified in several ways. Among these are those storage locations accessible as operand addresses of simple arithmetic statements such as ADD. There are two kinds: registers and primary memory.

Registers are temporary data and address storage entities. Usually, there are a relatively few registers with numeric or alphabetic identifiers. Some registers may be reserved by hardware or by software conventions for special purposes.

Primary memory, often called *main memory,* consists of program and data storage entities. The amount of primary memory is usually a power of 2, with the maximum number of locations depending on the number of bits available as an operand address. Memory sizes for microcomputers with data entities of length 4

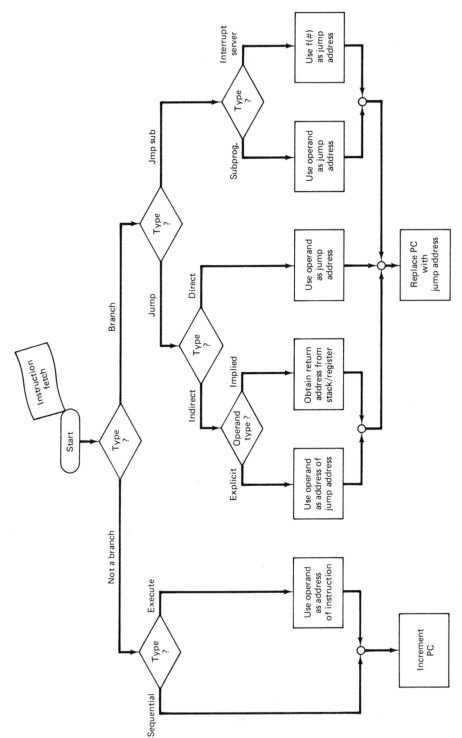

Figure 1.15 Generalized schemata of instruction acquisition, emphasizing the program counter (PC) register changes. (From G. W. Gorsline, *16-Bit Modern Microcomputers: The Intel I8086 Family*, © 1985, p. 27. Reprinted by permission of Prentice-Hall, Inc., Englewood Cliffs, NJ.)

bits (a nibble) tend to have byte-length addresses and thus have a maximum memory size of $256 = 2^8 = \frac{1}{4}$ K nibbles; 8-bit microcomputers tend to use two bytes for operand addresses and thus can access up to $65,536 = 2^{16} = 64$K bytes; 16-bit microcomputers often employ a 16-bit operand address, although the use of additional addressing techniques allows up to 48 million bytes of primary memory with one design. In current conventional microcomputers, primary memory is implemented as random address integrated circuits. Memory for variable data storage must be read/write and is often referred to as RAM; memory for programs and constants of a permanent nature is often implemented as read-only memory (ROM); and semipermanent programs are often stored in programmable (alterable) read-only memory (PROM). Figure 1.15 may be helpful. The term *random-access memory* means that any address may be accessed next and that any address may be accessed in an equal amount of time—that is, access time for RAM is constant. In some microcomputer designs, memory is logically treated as an external device; in other microcomputer designs, external devices are logically and programmatically treated as memory locations. Figure 1.16 helps to explain this.

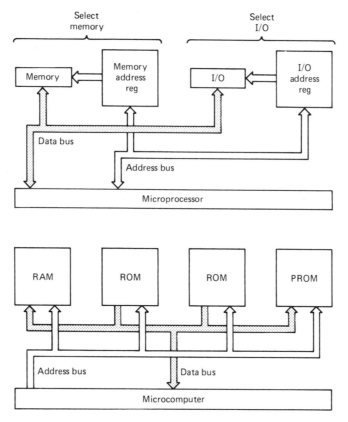

Figure 1.16 Two differing aspects of memory. (From G. W. Gorsline, *16-Bit Modern Microcomputers: The Intel 18086 Family,* © 1985, p. 28. Reprinted by permission of Prentice-Hall, Inc., Englewood Cliffs, NJ.)

INPUT/OUTPUT

Those storage locations accessible as addresses on external devices through the use of input/output instructions and not available as operand addresses of simple arithmetic instructions are known as *secondary memory*. Although RAM secondary memory is sometimes employed with large systems, it is not employed with conventional microcomputers.

The action of the execute phase of the instruction cycle of simple input/output instructions of microcomputers that require I/O through the ALU is illustrated in Figure 1.17. This scheme is enlarged on and given additional detail in Figure 1.18. The top left portion of Figure 1.18 can be interpreted as I/O through the accumulator, as in the Intel 8080/8085, in which the device address is the number of an I/O port that connects with the I/O device. Its control and data buffer are shown in the top right portion of Figure 1.18. Alternatively, the top right portion of Figure 1.18 can be interpreted as memory-mapped I/O, as in the Motorola 6800 and the DEC LSI 11, in which each device is associated with a double-word of memory. In this scheme, the device data buffer is an address in memory and the control/status information is the next sequential address in memory. Thus, the Intel 8080/8085 has a separate READ and a separate WRITE instruction, while the Motorola 6800 and the DEC LSI 11 use memory MOVE instructions to accomplish I/O.

INTERRUPTS

An interrupt is a signal that something has happened. An interrupt will result in some reactive program action (possibly null) in the future. An interrupt usually is posted by some event that is time-unexpected; that is, it is expected, but the exact time of its happening is unknown. The posting of an interrupt will result in the invocation of a software *interrupt servicing routine* at some time in the future (usually very soon). This is accomplished by the hardware forcing the known absolute address of the appropriate interrupt service routine to replace the contents of the program counter and the saving of the original contents of the PC for an eventual return to the previously executing program at the point of interruption. Note the very close similarity to a subprocedure invocation, with the obvious differences that the interrupt branch is externally (not program) caused and that the interrupt branch address is event-controlled. With additional logic external to the conventional microcomputer, it is possible to implement a priority scheme for interrupt servicing. Figure 1.19 may be helpful. Interrupts allow many programs to execute much faster and may allow the attachment of various I/O devices without alteration to the applications programs using the devices.

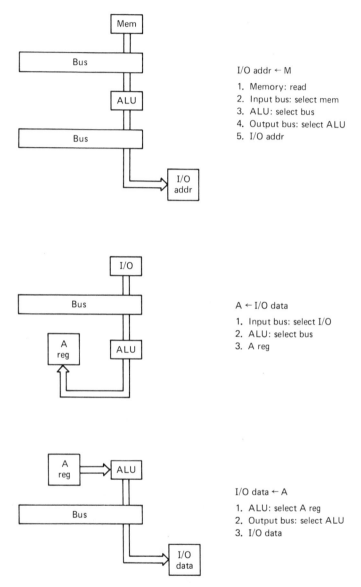

I/O addr ← M

1. Memory: read
2. Input bus: select mem
3. ALU: select bus
4. Output bus: select ALU
5. I/O addr

A ← I/O data

1. Input bus: select I/O
2. ALU: select bus
3. A reg

I/O data ← A

1. ALU: select A reg
2. Output bus: select ALU
3. I/O data

Figure 1.17 Input/output in many microcomputers is through the ALU (arithmetic-logic unit) and effectively prevents simultaneous compute and I/O. The action of the execute phase of the instruction cycle of three I/O instruction is illustrated. (From G. W. Gorsline, *16-Bit Modern Microcomputers: The Intel I8086 Family,* © 1985, p. 29. Reprinted by permission of Prentice-Hall, Inc., Englewood Cliffs, NJ.)

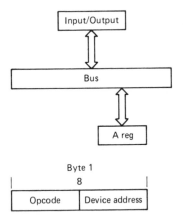

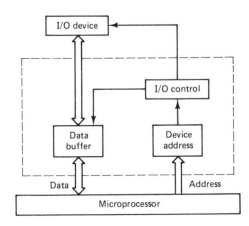

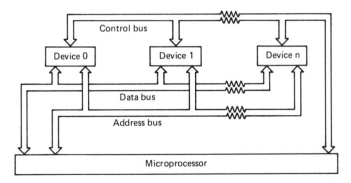

Figure 1.18 The two types of I/O schemes can be interpreted from these diagrams. In those microcomputers with I/O instructions such as the Intel 8080/8085, I/O is required to be to or from the accumulator, from or to an I/O device. In those microcomputers without separate I/O instructions, the devices are assigned nonexistent memory "addresses" and I/O is accomplished by memory MOVE instructions. This "memory-mapped I/O" scheme was pioneered with the DEC PDP 11 and is quite common in microcomputers, including the Motorola 6800. The top right diagram gives additional I/O detail for a single device. In memory-mapped I/O, the data buffer would occupy one memory "address" and the control would occupy the next. The bottom diagram illustrates the use of multiple I/O devices. (From G. W. Gorsline, *16-Bit Modern Microcomputers: The Intel I8086 Family,* © 1985, p. 30. Reprinted by permission of Prentice-Hall, Inc., Englewood Cliffs, NJ.)

INSTRUCTIONS

The *short-word problem* is characterized by a need to specify more information in a computer instruction than there are bits available with which to do so. Figure 1.20 illustrates some aspects of the short-word problem. Although one of the basic characteristics of stored-program computers is the ability of the computer to change or

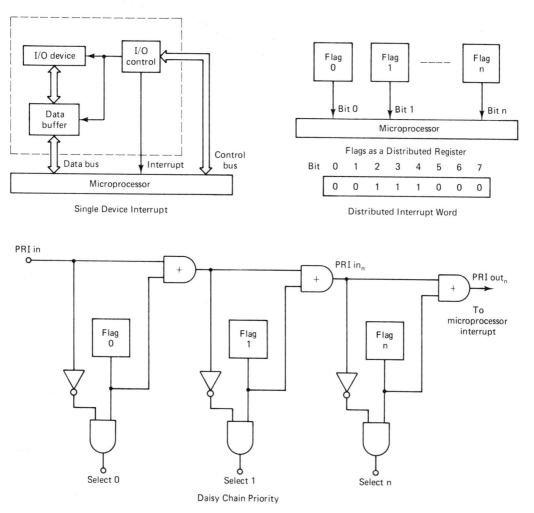

Figure 1.19 An interrupt is a signal that an unexpected event (at least time-expected) has occurred that requires some action (possible null). Thus, an interrupt will result in the invocation of a software service routine at a specific memory location and an eventual return to the original program at the point of interruption. Interrupts may have a priority. (From G. W. Gorsline, *16-Bit Modern Microcomputers: The Intel 18086 Family,* © 1985, p. 31. Reprinted by permission of Prentice-Hall, Inc., Englewood Cliffs, NJ.)

alter its own instructions, long experience by thousands of programmers strongly suggests that self-modifying programs are difficult to understand, are almost impossible to debug, and all in all are a very bad programming technique. Thus, we may claim that there are two kinds of information available to the computer during execution of a program: *instructions* and *data*. The instruction contains two types of information: the operation code (opcode), or what to do, and the operand address(es), or where the datum is that is to be transformed.

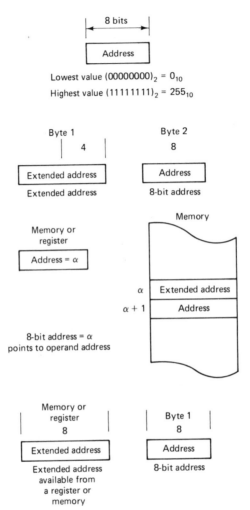

Figure 1.20 The "short-word problem" is exemplified in the top diagram by an 8-bit address that allows a memory size much too small for many applications. Although the second diagram allows for a memory size of 4096 cells, only 16 opcodes are possible—not an attractive solution. The bottom diagram illustrates two methods of providing a 16-bit address to address 64K. The next to bottom address illustrates one form of indirect addressing. (From G. W. Gorsline, *16-Bit Modern Microcomputers: The Intel I8086 Family,* © 1985, p. 32. Reprinted by permission of Prentice-Hall, Inc., Englewood Cliffs, NJ.)

With modern conventional microcomputers, data registers and memory are usually organized and addressable as 8-bit bytes, although a few microcomputers exist with data registers and memory organized and addressable as 4-bit nibbles. The relatively new 16/32-bit microcomputers that we will discuss later in this book have memory organized as 8-bit bytes but addressable as 8-bit, 16-bit, 32-bit, or longer entities. While discussing the problem of incorporating the information necessary to specify a practical number of opcodes, at the same time incorporating the information necessary to specify a memory location of data in a memory large enough to be practical, we will use the very common 8-bit Intel 8080 microcomputer as an example.

Even if all 8 bits of a byte were used as a memory address, allowing a memory with 256 locations, program implementers would have great difficulty in fitting practical problem solutions into the available memory space. Thus, the designers of the Intel 8080 decided to allow for 16-bit memory addresses, or a maximum memory size of 65,536 = 64K bytes. They also decided to provide six 8-bit data registers and one accumulator as well as referring to the use of memory as the use of the nonexistent eighth register (with the address of the data being placed at some other known place). In addition, they provided a group of 16-bit address registers (some of which consist of combining two of the data registers). Their scheme for specifying a usable number of instructions (72), a usable numbers of data registers (seven), and a usable-size memory (64K) not only is interesting in its own right but is instructive as an illustration of an intelligent practical alleviation of the short-word problem.

Instructions in the Intel 8080 are of length one byte, two bytes, or three bytes, depending on the need for information content. Without attempting to be complete, some of the one-byte instructions are of the following form:

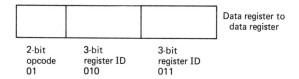

Example: MOV C, D
Meaning: [C] ← [D] , or replace current contents of register C with contents of register D; do not change contents of register D.

Note that the operand order in the Intel family of computers (and in the IBM group) is destination followed by source; in the Motorola family (and in the DEC group), the operand order is source followed by destination. Such bothersome syntax quirks are all too common in assembly languages.

This type of addressing is generically known as *register addressing*. In the Intel 8080, the registers have the following symbolic names and corresponding numerical designation:

B 0   H 4
C 1   L 5
D 2   M 6 (memory)
E 3   A 7 (accumulator)

If one of the registers is specified as M or 6, the 16-bit contents of the address register H (physically, the data registers H and L or the HL pair) is used as an address in memory. This type of memory addressing is generically known as *indirect addressing through a register* and is fairly common in microcomputers. As the hardware facilities to allow memory moves do not exist in the Intel 8080, the memory-to-memory move instruction (01110110) is illegal; this bit pattern is interpreted as a HALT instruction.

As further examples of the instruction formats, consider the following two-byte I/O instruction:

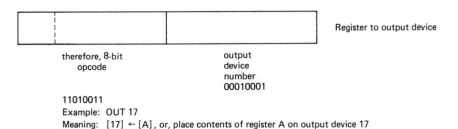

Register to output device

therefore, 8-bit
opcode

output
device
number
00010001

11010011
Example: OUT 17
Meaning: [17] ← [A], or, place contents of register A on output device 17
while preserving contents of register A.

Another two-byte instruction is

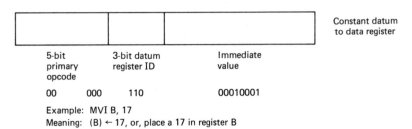

Constant datum
to data register

5-bit
primary
opcode

3-bit datum
register ID

Immediate
value

00   000   110   00010001

Example: MVI B, 17
Meaning: (B) ← 17, or, place a 17 in register B

This type of addressing is known as *immediate addressing*. Note that the datum itself is a portion of the instruction. From another standpoint, this type can be called program counter *relative addressing*.

As a last example, consider the three-byte memory-to-register A instructions:

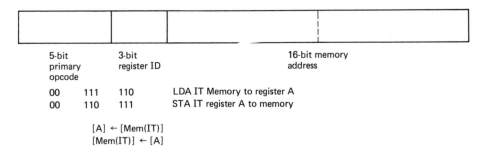

5-bit
primary
opcode

3-bit
register ID

16-bit memory
address

00   111   110   LDA IT Memory to register A
00   110   111   STA IT register A to memory

[A] ← [Mem(IT)]
[Mem(IT)] ← [A]

This type of addressing is known as memory *direct addressing*.

The object of this entire discussion is to give an understanding of the derivation or calculation of the location of the data—be it in a register, in a location in memory, or on an I/O device. If an address in memory must be derived by some calculation or by using the contents of a register pair or two memory locations as an address, such an operation is referred to as *finding the effective operand address* (EOA). Figure 1.21 is a summary of this process.

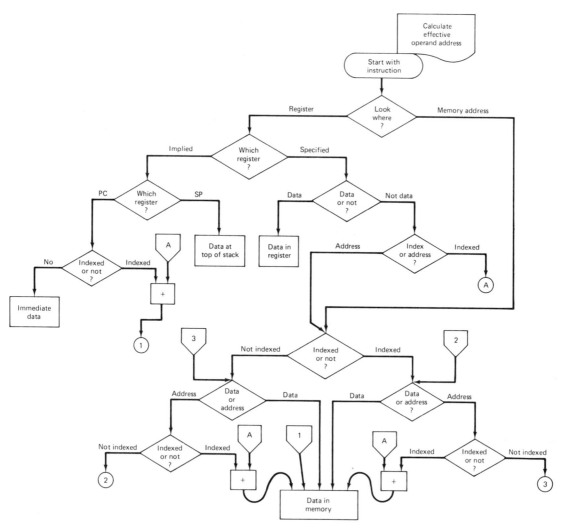

Figure 1.21 Generalized schemata for calculating the effective operand address of data. Note that the EOA may be an offset from the PC (PC-relative) or from another register (array base-relative), that indirect addressing can be to any depth, and that indexing may be pre- or postindirect. (From G. W. Gorsline, *16-Bit Modern Microcomputers: The Intel I8086 Family,* © 1985, p. 35. Reprinted by permission of Prentice-Hall, Inc., Englewood Cliffs, NJ.)

Most conventional microcomputers provide hardware assistance for maintaining data in a stack. Recall that a stack is similar to a cafeteria plate holder. The topmost item is the only one available. If an item is added, the stack drops down, with the new item on top. If the topmost item is removed, the next item pops up. The discipline is *last in–first out* (LIFO).

A possible implementation of a stack would employ a contiguous area in primary memory as the stack receptacle and a register as an address pointer to the current top of the stack. The process of placing a datum on the stack is almost universally termed PUSH and must be preceded by an incrementation of the stack pointer

(SP) register. Care must be taken to avoid PUSHing a datum onto a full stack—that is, beyond the upper limits of the stack area in primary memory—lest other information be overwritten and destroyed. The process of removing a datum from the stack is termed POP and must be followed by a decrementation of the SP register. Again, care must be taken to avoid POPping a datum from an empty stack—that is, below the lower limit of the stack area in primary memory—lest an unwanted datum be used in an incorrect context.

As discussed earlier, and shown in the bottom diagram of Figure 1.14, the subprocedure invocation instruction places the return address on the top of the stack, as pointed to by the address in the SP register. Similarly, the return instruction uses the top of the stack as the return address. Figure 1.15 illustrates the logic of deriving the new value of the program counter (PC), and Figure 1.21 illustrates the logic of determining that the operand is in a memory location whose address is in the SP register. The Intel 8080 provides two one-byte instructions:

2-bit primary opcode	3-bit register ID	3-bit secondary opcode		
11	ID	101	PUSH	register pair
11	ID	001	POP	register pair

where the register pairs are identified by the number of their first register:

BC	000	0
DE	010	2
HL	100	4
A status	110	6

Figure 1.22 should be helpful in understanding the action of these instructions:

	PUSH H	POP H
Step 1	Decrement SP	Load register L from top of stack
Step 2	Store register H at top of stack	Increment SP
Step 3	Decrement SP	Load register H from top of stack
Step 4	Store register L at top of stack	Increment SP

Note that the stack is backward, with the first item at the highest address, and that 16-bit addresses are involved. The programmer is responsible for being sure that the program does not PUSH to a full stack or POP from an empty stack.

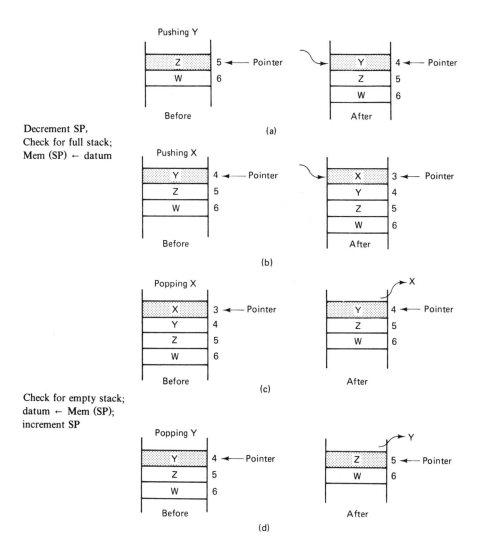

PUSH   Decrement SP,
        Check for full stack;
        Mem (SP) ← datum

POP   Check for empty stack;
        datum ← Mem (SP);
        increment SP

Figure 1.22 A stack acts like a stack of plates, with a datum being able to be "pushed" onto the top or a datum being able to be "popped" from the top. Conventional microcomputers contain a stack pointer (SP) register that contains the address in memory of the current stack top. Note that a stack in a conventional microcomputer has the addresses in reverse order. The access discipline of a stack is first in–last out (FILO) or last in–first out (LIFO). After defining storage space for the stack, the stack pointer register must be initialized to the high address of the stack area. (From G. W. Gorsline, *16-Bit Modern Microcomputers: The Intel I8086 Family,* © 1985, p. 37. Reprinted by permission of Prentice-Hall, Inc., Englewood Cliffs, NJ.)

ACCESSING DATA

The purpose of a computer is to manipulate information; that is, a microcomputer is an information-manipulating machine. Human beings create things. Although it is probable that some things are created idly, with absolutely no purpose in mind, most human creations have a purpose. This purpose may be aesthetic, with the created thing serving the purpose of pleasing the senses; or this purpose may be practical, with the created entity alleviating a felt need by serving a useful purpose. Without a doubt, there is an aesthetic quality—a beauty—in the logical interrelationships of the functional parts of a microcomputer as a mechanism for alleviating the practical problem of rapidly and accurately manipulating symbolic information. Nevertheless, most microcomputers are secured and used as tools in solving the very practical problems of acquiring, storing, transforming, transmitting, comparing, or otherwise massaging information. Without denigrating the aesthetics, we will concentrate on the practical information-manipulating aspects of microcomputers.

Information in a modern microcomputer is represented using one or more of a series of flip-flops, each able to be either on or off. The setting of a single flip-flop may encode the information that is interpreted by the human computer user as a numeric 0 or 1 or, alternatively, as a logical true or false. That is, the meaning of bit patterns within a microcomputer is entirely arbitrary. In a more formal sense, the semantic meaning of a particular bit pattern is arbitrary and is determined by the context of the usage.

Data Types

By convention, microcomputers are designed and implemented with the ability to manipulate correctly groups of bits whose settings are interpreted as one of the data types listed below.

Logical data. The setting of each bit is interpreted as "true" or "false" or as "on" or "off." In some circumstances, it is advantageous to have a single flip-flop known as a *flag*; in other circumstances, it is advantageous to group flags together into a register. The transformations allowed to logical data normally include AND, OR, XOR, NOT, SET, and CLEAR.

Integer data. This type of data is a group of bits that are interpreted as a number. The Institute of Electrical and Electronics Engineers (IEEE) standard interpretation in microcomputers involves the base 2 number system, with the sign being indicated by the leftmost bit. Negative numbers are coded in the two's-complement notation. Figure 1.23 illustrates the bit patterns and their interpretation in this notation. Some standardization of data sizes has occurred within the microcomputer industry:

Nibble: 4-bit item; unsigned range is $+0$ to $+15$, two's-complement range is $+7$ to -8.

Base 2	Base 10	Unsigned	Two's complement	Base 16
0000	0	0	0	0
0001	1	1	1	1
0010	2	2	2	2
0011	3	3	3	3
0100	4	4	4	4
0101	5	5	5	5
0110	6	6	6	6
0111	7	7	7	7
1000	8	8	−8	8
1001	9	9	−7	9
1010	—	10	−6	A
1011	—	11	−5	B
1100	—	12	−4	C
1101	—	13	−3	D
1110	—	14	−2	E
1111	—	15	−1	F

Figure 1.23 Common semantic interpretations of 4-bit integer data items in microcomputers, illustrating both the unsigned integer (assumed positive) interpretation and the two's-complement interpretation. Note particularly that the range is from +7 through 0 to −8 utilizing the two's-complement notation. (From G. W. Gorsline, *16-Bit Modern Microcomputers: The Intel I8086 Family,* © 1985, p. 39. Reprinted by permission of Prentice-Hall, Inc., Englewood Cliffs, NJ.)

Byte: 8-bit item; unsigned range is +0 to +255, two's-complement range is +127 to −128.

Word: 16-bit item; two's-complement range is +32,191 to −32,192, unsigned range is +0 to +65,383.

Double-word: 32-bit item; two's-complement range is +2,147,483,647 to −2,147,483,648.

Quad-word: 64-bit item; two's-complement range is +9,223,372,038,854,775,807 to −9,223,372,038,854,775,808.

While working with numbers represented in base 2, human comprehension tends to be overwhelmed by the mere length of the bit pattern, and mental translation to base 10 is normally impractical. For these reasons, many computer workers have developed the habit of mentally manipulating base 2 numbers in groups of 4 bits—that is, as base 16 numbers. Figure 1.23 illustrates this concept. The use of octal is a historical anachronism and should be discontinued.

It is sometimes convenient and advantageous to represent base 10 numbers directly in a microcomputer. Such a notation has become known as *binary-coded decimal* (BCD). BCD numbers normally have the sign (if a sign exists) designated in a separate nibble and employ the signed-magnitude number representation. Many microcomputers possess an operation to convert unsigned binary representation to the equivalent BCD representation.

Character data.   Almost all microcomputers employ the American Standard Code for Information Interchange (ASCII) for encoding character or alphanumeric data. To be exact, we are referring to Standard No. X3.4-1968 of the American National Standards Institute (ANSI X3.4-1968). ASCII is a 7-bit code with each character occupying an 8-bit byte, with the leftmost bit (the most significant bit) set to zero. Thus, 128 characters may be encoded using ASCII. Programmers should be aware that the leftmost bit (the sign bit) of ASCII characters may be employed for various purposes during data transmission and thus may not be a zero upon receipt and input into a microcomputer. Conservative programming practice would include zeroing out the leftmost bit before using the data, on the philosophy that it is better to be safe than sorry. Figure 1.24 illustrates the encoding pattern of the 7-bit ANSI X3.4-1968 ASCII encoding scheme.

Certain characteristics of the ASCII encoding scheme are worth noting:

1. The numerical difference between corresponding uppercase and lowercase letters is 00100000 (20 base 16), enabling programmatically simple conversions.
2. The uppercase letters start with 01000001 (41 base 16), representing an A, and have a uniform encoding space of one between letters such that 01011010 (5A base 16) represents a Z, while the lowercase letters start with 61 base 16 representing an a and 7A base 16 representing a z.
3. The alphanumeric numerals start with 00110000 (30 base 16) representing a zero and have a uniform encoding space of one such that 00111001 (39 base 16) represents a 9. It must be emphasized that these symbols have no associated numeric semantics in the microcomputer design. Arithmetic operations are meaningless.
4. A single alphanumeric numeral may be converted to BCD encoding by subtracting 00110000 (30 base 16). The conversion of a string of ASCII numerals to BCD and then to binary, or the reverse, requires somewhat complicated but straightforward algorithms that will be presented later in a more appropriate section.

Floating-point numbers.   It is sometimes necessary and often extremely convenient to be able to represent numeric values that include a fractional portion or whose value exceeds the range representable employing integer encoding. In such circumstances, an encoding scheme known as *floating-point,* which is based on scientific notation, is employed in microcomputers. The recently adopted IEEE Floating-Point Standard for Microcomputers has largely been implemented on the Motorola MC68881 floating-point coprocessor described later in this text. This standard provides that a value be interpreted from the syntax

$$\pm \text{significand} \times \text{base}^{\pm \text{exrad}}$$

	Second hexadecimal digit															
First hexadecimal digit	**0**	**1**	**2**	**3**	**4**	**5**	**6**	**7**	**8**	**9**	**A**	**B**	**C**	**D**	**E**	**F**
0	NUL[a]	SOH	STX	ETX	EOT	ENQ	ACK	BEL	BS	HT	LF	VT	FF	CR	CO	SI[a]
1	DLE[a]	DC1	DC2	DC3	DC4	NAK	SYN	ETB	CAN	EM	SUB	ESC	FS	GS	ES	US[a]
2	SP	!	"	#	$	%	&	'	(	)	*	+	,	-	.	/
3	0	1	2	3	4	5	6	7	8	9	:	;	<	=	>	?
4	@	A	B	C	D	E	F	G	H	I	J	K	L	M	N	O
5	P	Q	R	S	T	U	V	W	X	Y	Z	[	\	]	^	_
6	`	a	b	c	d	e	f	g	h	i	j	k	l	m	n	o
7	p	q	r	s	t	u	v	w	x	y	z	{	|	}	~	DEL

Notes:

1. To find the ASCII binary code for a given symbol: (a) Find the symbol on the chart. (b) Read the first hexadecimal digit on the same horizontal line at the left edge of the chart. (c) Read the second hexadecimal digit on the same vertical line at the top of the chart. (d) Convert the two-digit hexadecimal number to binary.

2. To find the symbol for a given binary code: (a) Add a leading zero if necessary and convert the 8-bit binary number into the equivalent two-digit hexadecimal code. (b) Find the first hexadecimal digit on the left edge of the chart. (c) Find the second hexadecimal digit at the top of the chart. (d) The desired ASCII symbol is at the intersection of the first digit row and the second digit column.

[a] Teletype control characters.

Figure 1.24 Seven-bit ANSI X3.4-1968 ASCII encoding scheme used for character data in most microcomputers. (From G. W. Gorsline, *16-Bit Modern Microcomputers: The Intel 18086 Family*, © 1985, p. 41. Reprinted by permission of Prentice-Hall, Inc., Englewood Cliffs, NJ.)

Note that four pieces of information must be available for correct interpretation of the significand and of the exrad (a total of eight pieces of information). The IEEE standard provides that the significand be expressed as a base 2 number between 1.0 and 2.0, with the implied radix point one bit to the right of the extreme left and with no leading-zero bits. The sign of the significand shall be the leftmost bit of the floating-point datum and thus corresponds in position to the sign bit of an integer datum. The magnitude of the significand (the precision) consists of a binary fraction of length 23 bits for single precision, 52 bits for double precision, and at least 63 bits for double extended precision. The latter precision is employed for all temporary intermediate calculation values. The IEEE standard also provides that the exrad be expressed as a base 2 integer, and thus the implied radix point is on the extreme right. The magnitude of the exrad consists of 8 bits for single precision, 11 bits for double precision, and at least 15 bits for double extended precision. Values of the exrad above the midpoint are interpreted as positive by the amount of deviation from the midpoint; values of the exrad below the midpoint are interpreted as negative by the amount of deviation from the midpoint. Note that the terms *significand* and *exrad* are employed to specify the bit patterns or syntax, and the terms *mantissa* and *exponent* are used to specify the interpretation, meaning, or semantics of the components of the floating-point data type, although this distinction is not universally followed.

The IEEE Floating-Point Standard specifies that a floating-point overflow results from an attempt to develop an exponent whose magnitude is too large for the bit pattern of the exrad to represent. An appropriate flag will be set "on" and a special bit pattern signifying either infinity or "not a number" will replace the inappropriate value. An underflow results from an attempt to develop an exponent whose magnitude is less than that allowed for by the bit pattern of the exrad while the binary fractional significand is all zeros. Again, an appropriate flag will be set "on" and a special bit pattern signifying either infinity or "not a number" will replace the inappropriate value. Subsequent arithmetic operation involving an operand whose value is either infinity or "not a number" results in an operand with a similar value. Figure 1.25 illustrates the syntax and specifies the semantic interpretation of the IEEE Floating-Point Standard.

Instructions. The fully ordered sequence of operation code and operand pointer(s) that constitute a program are also data—data of a special kind, but data all the same. The only firm rules for the bit patterns that are interpreted as instructions by microcomputers are:

1. Each instruction must have a unique bit pattern with a unique interpretation. Thus, each bit pattern must have one and only one meaning, and each meaning must have one and only one bit pattern.
2. The operations code must be placed to the left of the operand address pointer(s).

Single. A 32-bit format for a binary floating-point number X is divided as shown below. The component fields of X are the 1-bit sign s, the 8-bit biased exponent e, and the 23-bit fraction f. The value v of X is as follows:

a. If $e = 255$ and $f \neq 0$, then $v = $ NaN.
b. If $e = 255$ and $f = 0$, then $v = (-1)^s \infty$.
c. If $0 < e < 255$, then $v = (-1)^s 2^{c-127}(1.f)$.
d. If $e = 0$ and $f \neq 0$, then $v = (-1)^s 2^{-126}(0.f)$.
e. If $e = 0$ and $f = 0$, then $v = (-1)^s 0$ (zero).

Single-Precision Format

s	e	f

0   8   31

Double. A 64-bit format for a binary floating-point number X is divided as shown below. The component fields of X are the 1-bit sign s, the 11-bit biased exponent e, and the 52-bit fraction f. The value of X is as follows:

a. If $e = 2047$ and $f \neq 0$, then $v = $ NaN.
b. If $e = 2047$ and $f = 0$, then $v = (-1)^s \infty$.
c. If $0 < e < 2047$, then $v = (-1)^s 2^{c-1023}(1.f)$.
d. If $e = 0$ and $f \neq 0$, then $v = (-1)^s 2^{-1022}(0.f)$.
e. If $e = 0$ and $f = 0$, then $v = (-1)^s 0$ (zero).

Double-Precision Format

s	e	f

0   11   63

Single extended. Extended is an implementation-dependent format. An extended binary floating-point number X has four components: a 1-bit sign s, an exponent e of specified range combined with a bias which might be zero, a 1-bit integer part j, and a fraction f with at least 31 bits. The exponent must range between a minimum value $m \leq -1023$ and a maximum value $M \geq +1024$. The value of X is as follows:

a. If $e = M$ and $f \neq 0$, then $v = $ NaN.
b. If $e = M$ and $f = 0$, then $v = (-1)^s \infty$.
c. If $m < e < M$, then $v = (-1)^s 2^e(j.f)$.
d. If $e = m$ and $j = f = 0$, then $v = (-1)^s 0$ (this is normal zero).

Double extended. The double extended format is the same as single extended, except that the exponent must range between $m \leq -16383$ and $M \geq +16384$ and the fraction must have at least 63 bits.

Figure 1.25 Basic formats of the IEEE proposed standard for binary floating-point data. (From G. W. Gorsline, *16-Bit Modern Microcomputers: The Intel I8086 Family*, © 1985, p. 44. Reprinted by permission of Prentice-Hall, Inc., Englewood Cliffs, NJ.)

Data within a microcomputer must exist as bit patterns within a memory that is physically and logically a portion of the microcomputer system. Again, it must be emphasized that memory is passive; that is, memory can preserve bit patterns representing information, but memory cannot cause the change of a bit pattern (barring a rare error). Memory reacts to versions of a single order from logically adjacent portions of a microcomputer:

Move datum to here from there

with no change in the bit pattern (syntax) of the datum. Memory exists in microcomputer systems as several logically distinct entities: flags, registers, main memory, and auxiliary memory.

Flags.   Flags are single-bit flip-flops with an explicit name that are used to record the occurrence of an event. Thus, they record "on" or "off" or, alternatively, "true" or "false." Groups of flags may or may not be grouped together into indicator or condition registers. Instructions are provided to test the setting of flags or condition registers as well as to set or clear them.

Registers.   Registers are specially named groups of flip-flops with the ability to retain information. Often, certain registers of microcomputers are associated with certain operations, while certain instructions may access specific registers by implication. The registers of certain microcomputers are materially faster than program or data memory, whereas the registers of other microcomputers may not possess this access-speed advantage. Even if the registers of a microcomputer have no speed advantage, their existence (or pseudoexistence) is an advantage in that they exist in lower numbers than the cells of program or data memory; therefore, fewer bits are needed in an instruction to refer to a register (recall the short-word problem). The main use of registers is to save data or addresses before and between data transformations or address manipulations.

Main Memory.   Although I prefer the term *primary memory,* many computer vendors employ the term *main memory.* In either case, the term refers to that memory whose addresses occur as operand pointers in ordinary arithmetic-logic instructions such as ADD or AND. Most modern microcomputers have main (primary) memory implemented as random-access memory (RAM), whose addressable quantum of information is the byte with a numeric identifier (address) ranging from zero to (usually) some power of 2 minus 1. The term RAM means that access to any address may be next and that the time to access the data at that address is the same as the time to access any other address—a constant. A very few special-purpose microcomputers have their main (primary) memory in two separately addressed logical and physical spaces, both starting at address zero. In all cases that I have encountered, this situation implies that program memory is not alterable during normal program execution—it is read-only memory (ROM) that is also RAM. Programs stored in ROM cannot alter themselves, cannot contain any variable data areas, and are known as *pure code.*

Auxiliary Memory. There are many forms of relatively large storage capacity auxiliary memory devices, which are accessed by computers as if they were input/output devices. Among these devices are hard disks, floppy disks, cassette and cartridge magnetic tapes, optical disks, magnetic bubble memory (MBM), charge-coupled devices (CCD), as well as other storage media. We will delay our discussion of these secondary memories until later, when we treat I/O.

Main Memory Addressing Modes

As discussed earlier, a computer program is an ordered set of instructions designed and implemented to manipulate data to satisfy a need. Each of the data manipulation instructions must consist of (1) a specification of what manipulation is to be carried out (the opcode) utilizing (2) data residing at some location in main memory, in some register, or on some auxiliary memory device whose designation is a pointer (the *operand address*). The operand address in the instruction often points directly to the location of the datum; alternatively, the operand address must be modified in one or several ways to point to the location of the datum. This process of operand address pointer modification is often referred to as calculating or deriving the *effective operand address* and can be illustrated in general as

effective addresss ← operand address + modifier + · · · + modifier

where the + stands for any functional operation, including substitution, and the term *modifier* implies the contents of any register or location in main memory. Very often, the different methods of deriving the effective address of a datum are termed *addressing modes*.

The various addressing modes and their associated methods of effective operand address calculation can be understood from several considerations.

Direct addressing. The unmodifiable address of the datum is given by the operand address in the instruction. This address can be the identifier (name) of a flag, a register, or an address in main memory. Thus, there is *flag direct, register direct,* and *memory direct* addressing, where the location of the datum is explicitly or implicitly given in the instruction.

Indirect addressing. The unmodified address of the datum in main memory is contained in the register or main memory address pointed to by the operand address in the instruction. Thus, there is *register indirect* and *memory indirect* addressing, where the location of the datum in main memory is explicitly contained in the register or memory location pointed to explicitly or implicitly in the instruction. Some microcomputers provide automatic incrementing or decrementing of the address register either before or after use. Thus, there can be automatic postincrement register indirect, automatic predecrement register indirect, and so on. Included in this group is *stack addressing,* in which the datum is contained in the memory location at the current top of the stack whose address is always contained in the stack pointer (SP) register.

Relative addressing. The operand (a displacement) in the instruction is added to the starting address of a section of memory contained in a register designated explicitly or implicitly in the instruction. Thus, there is *base address relative* and *program counter relative* addressing, where the location of the datum is derived as the sum of the starting address of a memory area in a register and the displacement in the instruction. The common *immediate data* addressing mode can be considered to be program counter relative zero addressing, in that the datum follows the opcode and therefore is pointed to by the PC.

Indexed addressing. The address of the datum in main memory is modified by the contents of an index register. It is common to combine indexing with the other addressing modes, resulting in *indexed memory direct, preindexed register indirect, postindexed register indirect, preindexed memory indirect, postindexed memory indirect,* and *indexed base address relative* addressing. Note that the combination of indexing with indirectness can specify that the indexing be performed before or after the indirectness is accomplished.

A classification of addressing modes. The Motorola MC680XY assembly language uses the following terminology and syntax to specify the semantics of deriving the effective operand address (addressing mode) of both the source and destination operands. Normally, instructions must contain two operands, as follows:

MOVE X,Y: $[X] \rightarrow [Y]$, or replace the current value at location Y with the value at location X while preserving the value at location X.

ADD X,Y: $[X] + [Y] \rightarrow [Y]$, or replace the current value at location Y with the sum of the value at location X and the value at location Y while preserving the value at location X.

The standard for microcomputer assembly language provides for at least 19 different methods of calculating the effective address of both the destination and the source data operands. For convenience in grasping the concepts, we have classified these 19 addressing modes into five groups. Figures 1.26 through 1.32 should be helpful in studying these five groups of addressing modes. A summary of the addressing modes follows.

Direct Addressing.

- **Register direct:** the contents of register D1 Example:

  D1

- **Memory direct:** the contents of the main memory location designated by the identifier THERE with or without displacement. It can be indexed. Examples:

  THERE
  THERE + 17

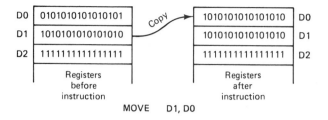

Registers   Registers
before   after
instruction   instruction
                    MOVE   D1, D0

(a) Register direct addressing mode

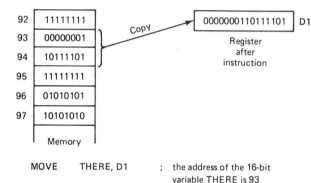

MOVE   THERE, D1   ; the address of the 16-bit
                            variable THERE is 93

(b) Memory direct addressing mode

Figure 1.26   Direct addressing modes.
(From G. W. Gorsline, *16-Bit Modern
Microcomputers: The Intel I8086 Family*, © 1985, p. 48. Reprinted by permission of Prentice-Hall, Inc., Englewood
Cliffs, NJ.)

Indirect Addressing.

- **Register indirect:** the contents of the main memory location whose address is contained in an address register, which could be indexed, or the base of an array with or without displacement. Examples:

  (A1)
  @ A1

- **Memory indirect:** the contents of the main memory location whose address is contained in the main memory location designated by the operand identifier. Displacement is often allowed. Example:

  @ THERE

Relative Addressing.

- **Base address relative:** the contents of the main memory location whose address is derived as the sum of the address in the base address register plus the

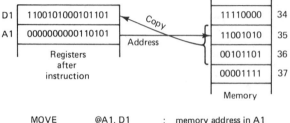

MOVE   @A1, D1   ;   memory address in A1
MOVE   (A1), D1

(a) Register indirect addressing mode

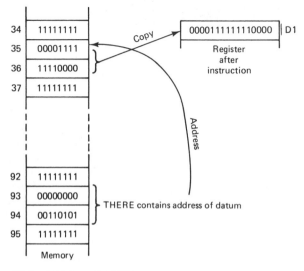

IEEE: MOVE   @THERE, D1

(b) Memory indirect addressing mode

Figure 1.27   Indirect addressing modes. (From G. W. Gorsline, *16-Bit Modern Microcomputers: The Intel I8086 Family,* © 1985, p. 49. Reprinted by permission of Prentice-Hall, Inc., Englewood Cliffs, NJ.)

displacement or offset given as the operand in the instruction. It can have absolute displacement or structure displacement. Examples:

$A1
(A1)
(A1 + 3)
(A1) − ANY

- **Program counter relative:** the contents of the main memory location whose address is derived as the sum of the address in the PC (the address of the current instruction) plus the displacement or offset given as the operand in the instruction. Note the resemblance to base address relative addressing.

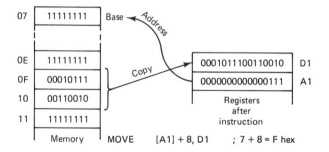

(a) Base address relative addressing mode: $Reg ± offset

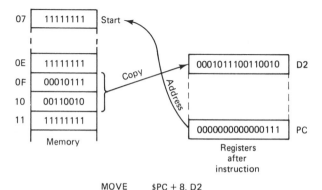

MOVE $PC + 8, D2

(b) Program counter relative addressing mode: $PC ± offset

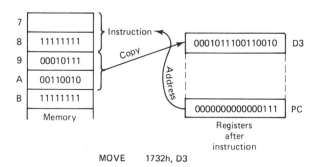

MOVE 1732h, D3

(c) Immediate addressing mode: #Value

```
IT:   MOVE    THERE, D1
      MOVE    1732h, D2
      MOVE    D3, D4
      JMP     * -3              go to third statement preceding
```

(d) Current statement relative branch addressing

Figure 1.28 Relative addressing modes. (From G. W. Gorsline, *16-Bit Modern Microcomputers: The Intel I8086 Family,* © 1985, p. 50. Reprinted by permission of Prentice-Hall, Inc., Englewood Cliffs, NJ.)

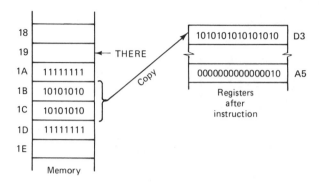

MOVE   THERE (A5), D3   ; address of THERE = 19   ; address of datum = THERE + [A5] = 19 + 2 = 1B hex

Figure 1.29 Indexed direct memory addressing modes. (From G. W. Gorsline, *16-Bit Modern Microcomputers: The Intel I8086 Family*, © 1985, p. 51. Reprinted by permission of Prentice-Hall, Inc., Englewood Cliffs, NJ.)

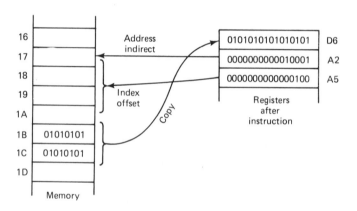

MOVE   [A2] [A5], D6   ; A2 = 17, A5 = 04   ; datum at 1B hex

Figure 1.30 Indexed base register indirect memory addressing mode. (From G. W. Gorsline, *16-Bit Modern Microcomputers: The Intel I8086 Family*, © 1985, p. 51. Reprinted by permission of Prentice-Hall, Inc., Englewood Cliffs, NJ.)

- **Immediate:** the value of the operand field is to be used as the datum. In effect, the datum is pointed to by the PC and the offset is zero. Note that the value cannot start with a hexadecimal A through F. Examples:

123h
OA1h
#123h
#A1h

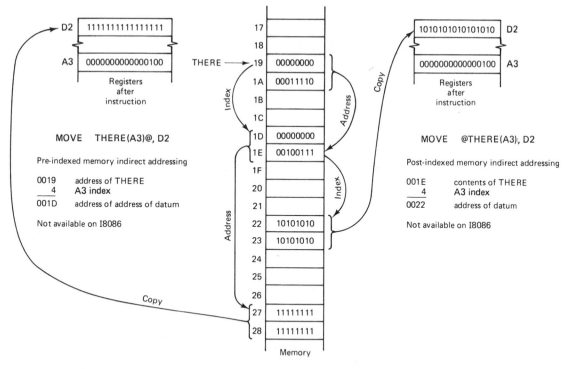

Figure 1.31 Indexed memory indirect addressing modes. (From G. W. Gorsline, *16-Bit Modern Microcomputers: The Intel I8086 Family,* © 1985, p. 52. Reprinted by permission of Prentice-Hall, Inc., Englewood Cliffs, NJ.)

- **Current statement relative:** used in JUMP statements (program flow-of-control statements) to indicate that the next statement to be executed is plus or minus the number of statements from the current jump statement. This form of programming is not recommended, in that later addition or deletion of statements during debugging or maintenance may not always include a correction of the JUMP offset amount, with subsequent disastrous results. Examples:

```
* +7
* −7
```

Absolute Addressing.   Not normally used on the Motorola MC680XY, absolute addressing means that the value of the operand is used directly as an address in main memory to obtain the desired datum. In effect, an absolute address is an offset from the beginning of main memory and thus is computed as zero + offset. Example:

/1234h

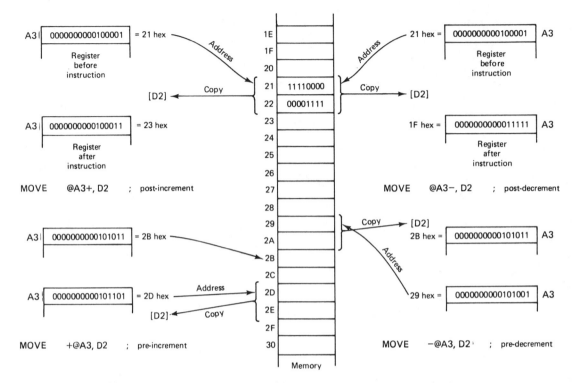

Figure 1.32 Automatic post-increment and post-decrement as well as pre-increment and pre-decrement register indirect addressing modes. (From G. W. Gorsline, *16-Bit Modern Microcomputers: The Intel 18086 Family,* © 1985, p. 53. Reprinted by permission of Prentice-Hall, Inc., Englewood Cliffs, NJ.)

Indexed Addressing.

- **Indexed memory direct:** the contents of the main memory location designated by the sum of the address of the identifier THERE and the contents of the index register SI, with or without a displacement. The Intel and IEEE syntax are identical. Examples:

```
THERE (A2)
THERE (A3 + 3)
THERE (A4) + 3
```

- **Indexed indirect:**
  1. *Indexed base register indirect:* the contents of the main memory location pointed to by the base register BX modified by the contents of index regis-

ter SI. The last example below gives the displacement as the number of bytes into a defined structure of the substructure identifier ANY. Examples:

```
(A1)(A4)
$(A1)(A4)
(A1).ANY(A4)
```

2. *Indexed memory indirect:*
    a. *Postindexed memory indirect* (not available on I8086): uses the contents of the main memory location pointed to the contents of the location THERE modified by the contents of the index register A5.
    b. *Preindexed memory indirect:* modifies the address of the identifier THERE by the contents of the index register A5 and uses the contents of this location as the address in main memory of the datum.

Automatic Increment/Decrement Register Indirect Addressing.

- **Auto-postincrement register indirect:** the contents of the main memory location whose address is contained in a register whose contents are automatically incremented by the width of the datum in bytes after each access.
- **Auto-postdecrement register indirect:** the contents of the main memory location whose address is contained in a register whose contents are automatically decremented by the width of the datum in bytes after each access.
- **Auto-preincrement register indirect:** the contents of the main memory location whose address is contained in a register that has been automatically incremented before use by the width of the datum.
- **Auto-predecrement register indirect:** the contents of the main memory location whose address is contained in register AX, which has been automatically decremented before use by the width of the datum.

THE ABILITY-COST-SIZE TREND

Over the past century and a half, there have been many innovative developments and trends in implementing and programming arithmetic-logic machines. Considering hardware, computers have progressed from the original mechanical logic "engine" of Charles Babbage in the second third of the nineteenth century, through the electromagnetic relay machines of the first third of the twentieth century, to the vacuum tube/acoustic memory of the first electronic stored digital program computer of the mid-1940s. These were followed by the discrete transistor/coincident current core memory computers of the 1950s, through the initial small-scale integrated circuit computers of the early 1970s, to the very large scale integrated circuit (VLSI) microcomputers of the early 1980s. The trend has been toward simplified assembly and repair; smaller physical size and reduced operating energy; greater reliability and lower cost; increased speed, logical complexity, and ability; and more registers with increased abilities together with faster and logically much larger memories.

Similarly, the programming of digital computers—that is, the design and implementation of the ordered set of instructions that constitute the program—originally required expressing the data manipulation process (the algorithm) in the absolute address machine language (a series of binary 1's and 0's). A progression over time occurred through the incorporation of "shop-standardized" input/output sections of absolute machine language code; through the invention of one-to-one symbolic programming systems—that is, assembly languages; to the development of macro-assemblers, conditional assembly, relocating linking loaders, and libraries of subprograms, as well as procedural-level compiler languages such as FORTRAN. Included was the development of monitors that led to operating systems with such current common features as multiprogramming, interactive processing, virtual memory, data base management systems, and job control languages. The trend has been to allow the applications program designer/problem solver to pay less and less attention to the details of the computer while depending on systems of software produced by technical "experts" and thus to approach and solve larger and more complex problems. Programmers have become almost addicted to compiler languages, to libraries of useful procedures, to the services of an operating system, and to expert consultation help. This trend may eventually develop into professionalism when the current large, intense research efforts produce results that finally permeate the education of new generations of computer personnel. This will force the presently practicing personnel to "lift themselves by their own bootstraps" into the world of the near future.

Economically, these past, present, and probable near-future developments have resulted in the establishment, proliferation, and growth of a data processing industry whose gross dollar worth is measured in the several tens of billions and whose operations permeate the daily life of each and every person in "developed countries." The industry is presently vital and absolutely essential to the functioning of Western civilization—that is, the finding, production, and distribution of the human necessities of food, shelter, clothing, and so on. For the computer professional, the most important economic trends are of three kinds:

1. A steady, long-term, and drastic reduction (a dramatic and revolutionary reduction) in the cost of the hardware necessary for performing a data manipulation or transformation.

2. A steady, long-term increase in the cost of the personnel necessary to determine the problem specifications and solution strategies; to design the solution tactics and implement the computer procedures; to collect and build the requisite data bases; to acquire and operate the computer equipment; and to manage the personnel, equipment, and supplies.

3. A steady, long-term, but relatively slow reduction in the cost of computing and outputting a quantum of information.

A consequence of these trends is the relative decrease in cost of the computer itself (produced in a non-labor-intensive environment) compared to the systems software and applications programs (produced in a labor-intensive environment). An approximate graphical presentation of this relationship is shown in Figure 1.33.

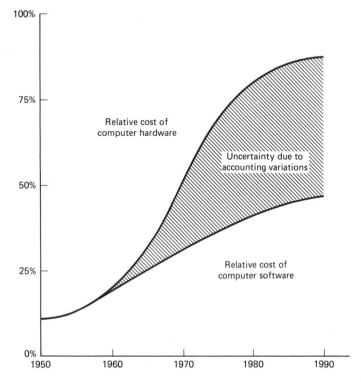

Figure 1.33 Long-term trend in the relative costs of hardware and software. (From G. W. Gorsline, Computer Organization: Hardware/Software, Second Edition, © 1986, p. 59. Reprinted by permission of Prentice-Hall, Inc., Englewood Cliffs, NJ.)

In addition, economists enunciate the *economy-of-scale* "law." In terms of computer technology, it is stated as follows:

> A larger and/or faster computational system will produce applications problem output at a lower cost per quantum than a smaller and/or slower computational system until the expense of coping with the volume of input/output or the overhead of the more complex and larger operating system overcomes the economies of scale.

A graphical representation of this relationship is shown in Figure 1.34. Many years ago, Herbert Grosch formulated the empirical relationship between the price of computational systems and the ability of the same systems:

$$\text{price} \times 2 = (\text{ability})^2$$

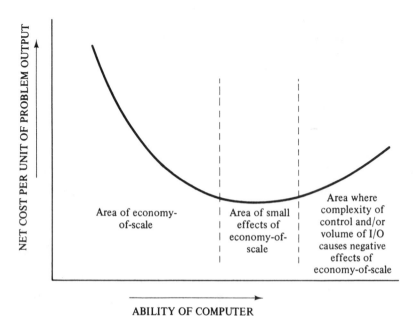

NET COST PER UNIT OF PROBLEM OUTPUT

Area of economy-
of-scale

Area of small
effects of
economy-of-
scale

Area where
complexity of
control and/or
volume of I/O
causes negative
effects of
economy-of-scale

ABILITY OF COMPUTER

Figure 1.34   Rough diagrammatic illustration of the economy-of-scale relationship as it applies to computers within a single technological base. (Reprinted with
permission from G. W. Gorsline, *Computer Organization: Hardware/Software* 2nd
ed., Prentice-Hall., Englewood Cliffs, N.J., 1986.) (From G. W. Gorsline, *16-Bit
Modern Microcomputers: The Intel I8086 Family,* © 1985, p. 54. Reprinted by
permission of Prentice-Hall, Inc., Englewood Cliffs, NJ.)

Note that *Grosch's law* can be derived from the law of economy of scale if only the
left side is considered—that is, if the area of positive economy-of-scale effects is
considered. This is illustrated in Figure 1.34.

Recent work by Ein-Dor (1985) indicates that an approximation of Grosch's
law holds within each of the five present classes of computer systems:

$$P = f * W^{-.55}$$

where P is system cost, W is the relative system performance, and f is a system class
factor as follows: microcomputers = 6.2, minicomputers = 98.5, small mainframes = 303.9, mainframes = 856.8, and supercomputers = 1474.8. On the other
hand, the overall relationship across all five classes of computers did not follow
Grosch's law but rather showed that performance per $100 purchase price was: mi-
crocomputers = 8 MIPS (millions of instructions per second), minicomputers = 0.5
MIPS, small mainframes (midicomputers) = 0.25 MIPS, mainframes = 0.22
MIPS, and supercomputers = 0.25 MIPS.

There are subjective reasons to believe that the introduction of a radical new
technology will cause discontinuities in the law of economy of scale and in that por-

tion of it known as Grosch's law. Among these effects, the following seem important:

Symbolic assembly languages in wide use	1950 approx.
Discrete transistors in computers	1954 approx.
Coincident core memory	1957 approx.
First integrated circuits	1958–1959 approx.
Procedural-level languages in wide use	1960 approx.
Minicomputers	1963 approx.
Families of compatible computers	1964 approx.
Practical transistor memories	1965 approx.
Microprocessor-on-a-chip-based microcomputers	1971 approx.
Microcomputer-on-a-chip-based microcomputers with high ability	1978 approx.

Some of these long-term gross cost effects are illustrated in Figure 1.35.

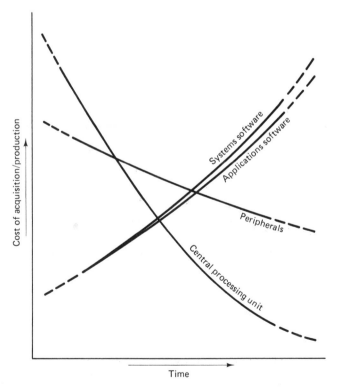

Figure 1.35 Relationship of trends in the costs of the CPU, peripheral devices, systems software (operating system, etc.), and applications programs. (From G. W. Gorsline, *16-Bit Modern Microcomputers: The Intel I8086 Family,* © 1985, p. 5. Reprinted by permission of Prentice-Hall, Inc., Englewood Cliffs, NJ.)

It is strongly suggested that the traditional minicomputer will rapidly disappear over the next very few years from the cost-ability pressure of the 16/32-bit microcomputer. Examples of this class of microcomputer are the Intel 8086/286/386, the Zilog Z8000/Z80000, the Digital Equipment Corporation (DEC) LSI 11/MicroVAX, the National Semiconductor NS16016/32032, the Motorola MC68000/68010/68020, and the AT&T WE32100. It is also very probable that the low-ability end of maxicomputer families will also rapidly disappear (a process now well under way) because of the cost/ability pressure from the midicomputer. Examples of this class of midicomputer are the DEC VAX 780, the PE 32XO, the Prime 750, the IBM 43X1, the IBM System 38, and others.

HISTORICAL PERSPECTIVE

The most volatile technological developments of the contemporary industrial age are in the electronics industry. Since the introduction of the transistor in 1948 and its incorporation into computers in 1954, the physical size of electronic devices has been reduced by an average factor of 2 every year. Until the advent of the transistor, each type of component in an electronic circuit was fashioned from one or more materials possessing the needed electrical characteristics. For example, carbon was used for resistors, ceramics and a dielectric for capacitors, tungsten for the emitters in vacuum tubes, and so on. Such components, with characteristics defined by their composition and construction, were used in creating a circuit with specified characteristics and responses. Circuits were then combined into systems.

The transistor was the first electronic component in which materials with different electrical characteristics were not interconnected but were physically fabricated in one structure. Thus, the transistor obviated the need for separate materials (carbon, tungsten, ceramics, etc.) used in fabricating the circuit components. Nevertheless, the discrete transistor did little to alter the requirement for connecting the individual components—and electronics is a technology of complex interconnections.

The preferred transistor raw material was a single crystal of silicon sliced into round wafers. By suitable masking and "doping" techniques, which selectively altered the electrical behavior of small regions, many transistors could be fabricated on each wafer slice. After sawing them apart, each such transistor was sealed into a three-connection canlike package about 0.25 inch in diameter. The problem of combining these discrete transistors into a complex circuit with many interconnections remained.

A series of standard circuit modules on plastic boards, each with a specific function, were developed and used as logical building blocks for creating subsystems that could be plugged together as needed. As systems became larger and more complex, the fabrication of the complex wiring interconnection networks between boards became very costly as well as a signal speed limit for the system. Thus, as transistor technology increased the switching speed of the circuits, it became increasingly important to decrease both the size of the components and the length of the interconnections.

In October 1958, Jack Kilby of Texas Instruments, Inc., created what is considered the first integrated circuit (IC) by manually connecting in a predetermined pattern, using very fine wires, the many transistors on a single wafer of silicon. This process not only did not reduce the problem of complex interconnections but, as can be imagined, was not very practical. In April 1959, Robert Noyce of Fairchild Semiconductor perfected a method of depositing (evaporating) aluminum as planned interconnections between the many transistors on a silicon wafer. This "planar process" resulted in the first practical integrated circuit and thus was the breakthrough that has solved the long-standing electronics problem of complex interconnections. The special properties needed for the various circuit elements were achieved by selectively diffusing traces of impurities into the silicon or oxidizing it to silicon dioxide. The principles of photolithography were used to expose selected regions of the silicon to diffusion while protecting other regions.

Continued development has raised the number of components contained in such an integrated circuit from about 5 to 20 (small-scale integration, SSI), through several hundred components (medium-scale integration, MSI) to thousands of components (large-scale integration, LSI), and finally to hundreds of thousands of components (very large scale integration, VLSI). Point faults in the semiconductor crystal cause faulty circuits and thus reduce the yield of acceptable units. Such crystal faults are randomly distributed over the surface of the silicon wafer and thus of the chip. Different technologies have different characteristics and costs. An exploration of this subject is beyond the scope of this book. Excellent tutorials, presented at the university student level, are given in Clark (1980) and Tobias (1981). Figure 1.36 traces the developmental trends.

In 1967, a patent was issued for an experimental four-function pocket calculator based on a single integrated circuit (McWhorter, 1976). By 1970, it was practical to market such a device for less than $100, and in 1976, several mass-produced models were available for less than $10. Sophisticated multifunction models that include a wide selection of trigonometric functions and are user-programmable have also become available at higher prices.

The steady increase in integrated circuit component density, complexity, and organization led to the microcomputer, a full-fledged general-purpose machine whose logic and memory circuits could be mounted on a single plastic card. In 1971, the Intel Corporation developed a versatile, programmable, single-chip microprocessor, the Intel 4004 (see Figure 1.37). Logically a central processing unit (CPU), the I4004 manipulated data that were 4 bits wide and had instructions for both binary- and decimal-mode data manipulations. The I4004 had 2250 transistors on a silicon substrate measuring 0.117 by 0.159 inch. Combined with a master clock, a primary memory, and a control memory (for microinstructions), it would be a minimal general-purpose microcomputer priced below $100 (current prices).

A few months later, Intel introduced a microprocessor chip designed to manip-

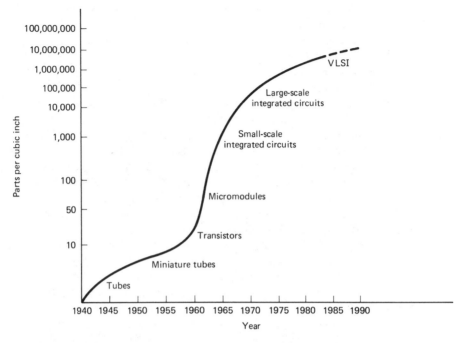

Figure 1.36 Electronics miniaturization trends. (From E. Braun and S. MacDonald, *Revolution in Miniature*, Cambridge University Press, New York, 1978.)

Year	Company	Development
1964	Viatron Computer	Developed first 8-bit LSI microprocessor used to control data terminal
1969	Viatron Computer	Developed first 8-bit LSI microprocessor used as basic element in a minicomputer
1971	Intel	Developed 4-bit 4004 for commercial sales
1972	Rockwell	PPS-4 microprocessor
	Fairchild	PPS-25 microprocessor
	Intel	8008
1973	National Semiconductor	IMP
	Intel	8080
1974	Motorola	6800
	Monolithic Memories	Bit-slice introduction
1975	Texas Instruments	4-bit slice
	Fairchild	F-8

Figure 1.37 Early historical development of the microprocessor. (From G. W. Gorsline, *16-Bit Modern Microcomputers: The Intel I8086 Family*, © 1985, p. 8. Reprinted by permission of Prentice-Hall, Inc., Englewood Cliffs, NJ.)

ulate 8-bit data, the I8008, that had more computing power and flexibility and thus was more suitable for data handling and control applications. Two other early models were designed and manufactured by Rockwell International and National Semiconductor. These microprocessors were quickly incorporated into a wide range of applications, from laboratory/industrial instruments to sales terminals and electronic games. It should be noted that the first known commercial use of an integrated circuit occurred with miniaturized hearing aids in December 1963.

Companies such as Rockwell, National Semiconductor, and Fairchild introduced microprocessors to the market, and these gained sufficient acceptance to encourage further activity. In 1973, the modern microprocessor era began when Intel announced the 8080 microcomputer, which had more capability than prior microcomputers. It was followed a year later by Motorola's 6800, which had such features as index registers, two accumulators, and an input/output system that programmatically looked like memory. The next step, the entry by other semiconductor companies with their microcomputer designs, was quite predictable. The microcomputer had arrived!

EXERCISES

1.1. In your problem-solving experiences over the past several months, you have practiced the process of abstraction. Confirm or correct your understanding of the term *abstraction* via the use of a dictionary. In this context, give five examples of concrete objects and the corresponding abstract objects.

1.2. Use the problem of balancing a checkbook as an example problem-solving process. Consider each of the phases of solving this problem employing a personal computational system and answer the following questions:
   (a) Is this an appropriate problem for solution using a personal computer? Defend your conclusion.
   (b) Succinctly and completely verbalize the problem in terms appropriate to the problem itself; that is, give functional specifications.
   (c) Transform the functional specifications into technical specifications.
   (d) At the module level and in general terms, give a systems design that would satisfactorily encompass the technical specifications.

1.3. Using the computer language of your choice, implement a stack using the concepts of data encapsulation and employing the data object approach.

1.4. Using the concepts illustrated in Figure 1.9, give the instruction cycle for adding the 32-bit contents of a register to the contents of a memory long word, with the result stored in the same memory long word.
   (a) The memory address is contained in address register A2.
   (b) The memory address is contained in address register A2 as indexed by data register D3.
   (c) The memory addressing mode is indexed base register indirect.
   (d) The memory addressing mode is postincrement register indirect.

1.5. In a procedural-level language of your choice, implement a procedure capable of reading N (N not known at programming time) ASCII-encoded integer numbers, including a preceding sign, and printing the corresponding values in base 10, base 2, and base 16. Detect and report any input or conversion errors.

1.6. Extend Exercise 1.5 to include floating-point input encoded in ASCII and include the IEEE binary format in the output as well as the equivalent base 16. In addition, output the value in base 10 scientific notation.

2

The Motorola MC680XY Family

PROCESSOR ORGANIZATION

The Motorola MC680XY family of microcomputers possesses an organization centered on an information bus that is used to communicate both address information (memory location including memory-mapped I/O port identity) and data from various subassemblies to other subassemblies. Figure 2.1 illustrates the clean separation of the information-processing unit from memory and from the input/output portions. This separation is typical of modern microcomputers. In the terminology being employed, the information-processing unit acquires an instruction, updates the address in the program counter, decodes the instruction, calculates the effective address of the datum in memory or on an I/O device, executes the instruction, and finally stores the result, including any exception information.

Employing Figure 2.2, we will first concentrate in some detail on the execution cycle of an instruction. We will employ an ADD instruction in our example. The Motorola MC680XY microcomputer has several different ADD instructions involving signed integer data, with variations involving the possible magnitude as well as the location of the data. In Figure 2.2, note that a datum may be 8-bits, 16-bits, or 32-bits in size and that an address may be 16-bits or 32-bits in size. These different bit capacities control the maximum possible magnitude of the contents. In all cases, the ADD instruction involves acquiring two source, or input, data and results in the production of one destination, or result, datum. This may be illustrated as

[S1] + [S2] → [D]

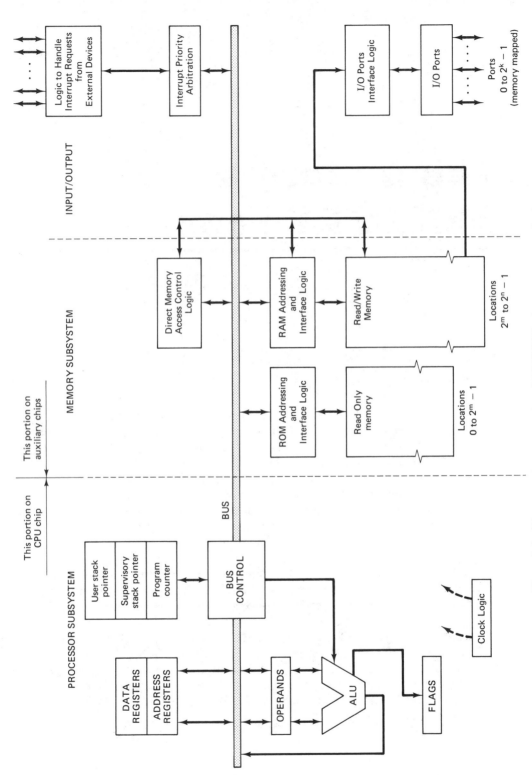

Figure 2.1 Diagrammatic representation of MC680XY microcomputer organization.

70

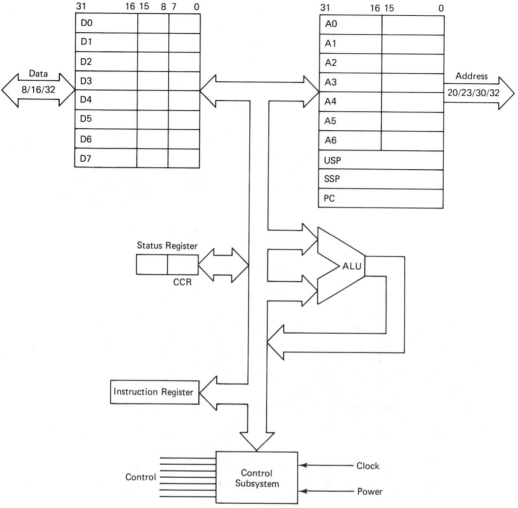

Figure 2.2 MC680XY registers and transfer paths.

where the brackets signify the signed numeric value of the datum contained in the memory location or register with this identifier (or name). The above wording was used for complete accuracy and has the relatively simple meaning: the contents of a named memory location or register. The design of the MC680XY microcomputer specifies that the instructions to accomplish diadic arithmetic-logic operations must explicitly specify two operand addresses or values and that only one of these addresses can be in main memory, with the other being a register or an immediate datum. This is accomplished by implicitly specifying the third operand address. Thus, the ADD instructions have the following symbolic format with designated meaning:

source   destination
 ↙ ↘   ↓
[S1] + [D]   →   [D]
  ↑
 ADD

where the first source operand identifier may refer to any location in main memory
or to a register or, alternatively, may be the actual datum (an immediate); and where
the destination/second-source operand identifier may refer to any location in read/
write (RAM) main memory or to a register. Note that input/output devices are memory-mapped; that is, they are wired into pseudomemory locations and thus are referred to as memory.

Thus, the 32-bit register-to-register integer instruction:

ADD.L   D1,D2

is interpreted as: Replace the contents of the 32-bit register D2 with the sum of the
contents of the 32-bit registers D1 and D2 while leaving the contents of the 32-bit
register D1 unaltered. The overflow flag will be set ON if the value of the sum exceeds the capacity of the register; the sign flag will be set ON if the sum is negative;
the zero flag will be set ON if the sum is zero; and both the carry flag and the extend
flag will be set ON if the sum exceeds the capacity of the register considered unsigned (useful for multiprecision arithmetic).

Similarly, the register-to-register word instruction:

ADD.W   D1,D2

is interpreted as: Replace the contents of the 16-bit data register D2 with the sum of
the contents of the 16-bit data register D1 and D2 while leaving the contents of the
16-bit data register D1 unaltered. The flags will be set as specified above. The high-
order half (bits 16–31) of registers D1 and D2 will neither enter into nor be affected
in any way by the word ADD instruction. The mixture of word with long-word or
with byte-sized operands is not legal.

Also, the byte register-to-register instruction:

ADD.B   D1,D2

is interpreted as: Replace the contents of the 8-bit data register D2 with the sum of
the 8-bit data registers D1 and D2 while leaving the contents of the 32-bit data register D1 and the contents of bits 8 through 31 of the data register D2 unaltered. The
flags will be set as indicated above. The mixture of byte with word or with long-
word operands is not allowed.

In addition, the address register-to-register long-word instruction:

ADDA.L   A1,A2

is interpreted as: Replace the contents of the 32-bit address register A2 with the sum of the contents of the 32-bit address registers A1 and A2 while leaving the contents of the 32-bit address register A1 unaltered. Because the destination is an address register, the flags are not affected. Thus, addresses in memory are always unsigned and assumed positive. Addresses that specify memory locations that are not implemented—that is, larger than existing memory—are illegal and will result either in an error flag being set (it is hoped) or in the access of an unexpected location, usually resulting in a strange and unexpected result.

Finally, the address register-to-register word instruction:

ADDA.W   A1,A2

is interpreted as: Replace the lower half (bits 0–15) of the address register A2 with the sum of the contents of the lower half (bits 0–15) of the address registers A1 and A2 while leaving the contents of the 32-bit address register A1 and the high-order half (bits 16–31) of the address register A2 unaltered. Again, arithmetic is assumed positive (unsigned). Because the destination is an address register, the flags are not affected.

I have been attempting to emphasize that the eight data registers—D0 thru D7—are usable for 8-bit, 16-bit, or 32-bit data operations and storage. Similarly, the seven address registers—A0 thru A6—are usable for full addresses: 20 bits for the MC68008, 24 bits for the MC68000 and MC68010, 30 bits for the MC68012, and 32 bits for the MC68020. In addition, these seven address registers are also usable for the 16-bit address modifiers of more limited magnitude—such as indexes. Also note that the PC (program counter) and the two stack pointers—USP (user stack pointer) = A7 and SSP (supervisor stack pointer) = A7'—have a capacity of 32 bits, allowing them to specify (point to) any address in main memory with all members of the processor family. Figure 2.3 should aid full understanding of this design feature.

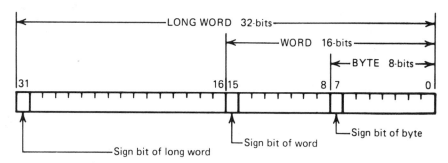

Figure 2.3 Data register format. (From T. L. Harman and B. Lawson. *The Motorola MC68000 Microprocessor Family: Assembly Language, Interface Design, and System Design,* © 1985, p. 88. Reprinted by permission of Prentice-Hall, Inc., Englewood Cliffs, NJ.)

It is interesting that memory in the MC68000 is accessed in 16-bit quanta; that is, two bytes equal one word, always starting at an even address—0, 2, 4, 6, 8, and so on. Thus, the number of address lines in the system bus can be one less than the $\log_2$ of the maximum main memory size, as follows:

	Number of Data Lines	Number of Address Lines	Maximum Memory Size Allowed
MC68008	8	20	$2^{20} = 1$ MB (megabyte)
MC68000	16	23	$2^{24} = 16$ MB
MC68010	16	23	$2^{24} = 16$ MB
MC68012	16	30	$2^{30} = 1$ GB (gigabyte)
MC68020	32	32	$2^{32} = 4$ GB

Note that this memory address restriction is not true for the MC68008, which accesses only one byte per physical access. It is interesting that the MC68020, which accesses four-bytes (32 bits) per physical access, also allows byte addressing via a full 32-bit address bus. Figure 2.4 should be helpful in understanding this.

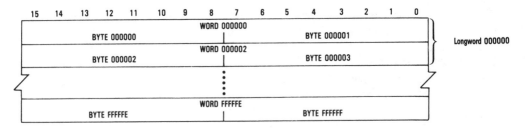

Figure 2.4   Memory organization by address. (Courtesy of Motorola, Inc.)

Consider the following memory-to-register word instruction and the corresponding register-to-memory word instruction employing the memory indirect through a register addressing mode; that is, the address of the datum container in memory is contained in an address register:

```
ADD.W    (A4),D1
ADD.W    D1,(A4)
```

It must be emphasized that direct memory addressing is not available in the MC680XY family of microcomputers, although a few assemblers may allow the syntax of this addressing mode but transliterate it to a displacement from the program counter (PC) during the process of assembling to object code. Two forms of the ADD instruction allow an immediate datum (a constant) to be added to a register or to the contents of a memory location:

```
ADDI.W   #1234,D1
ADDI.W   #1234,(A2)

ADDQ.W #5,D3          ; the immediate value is limited to the
ADDQ.W #2,(A4)        : range +0 through +7
```

TWO STACK POINTERS—WHY?

Previously (and see Figure 2.2), we specified that the MC680XY had two stack pointer registers: one for the user's programs and one for the supervisor. At this time, students should assure themselves that they understand the operation of a stack in memory and the action of the stack pointer during PUSH and POP. (As a suitable reminder, we suggest Figure 1.22.) In addition, because the stack is most often employed as the receptacle for the return address from subprograms (among other uses), it is important that you understand this usage. (The bottom portion of Figure 1.14 provides a suitable review.)

An *operating system* consists of all the programs that control the equipment and software resources of the computer system, such as processors, main memory, I/O devices, secondary storage, files, libraries, and so on. These program modules simplify the use of the system, resolve conflicts in resource usage, and attempt to optimize the performance of the system under a given set of restraints. In effect, the operating system acts as an interface between the applications program and the actual physical computer. In a broader sense, it is a buffer that smooths the interface of the user with the harsh realities of the bare hardware.

An operating system is a program—usually quite complicated and large, with many modules—that controls the operation of the computer. In most, if not all, cases, the operating system accomplishes this function by being the resident main program executing in the computer hardware, with an application program being treated as a subprogram that is CALLed at the appropriate time and allowed to execute, with the RETurn being made to the "main program," the operating system. In this philosophical viewpoint, errors in the applications program with requests for help or services are merely CALLs to existing submodules of the operating system.

Thus, the operating system constitutes and provides a predefined environment in which any of myriad software packages can execute or run. It would be a major catastrophe if an applications program accidentally or maliciously ruined a portion of the operating system, as this would probably result in strange and unanticipated actions. Strange and unanticipated happenings are particularly undesirable with computational systems. The "happening" might be so minor as not to be noticed or it might result in a plane crash or the launching of a nuclear-armed missile. A computer must carry out, in exact order, only those actions specified in its set of programs—and nothing else. Thus, the operating system of the computational system must be protected. The MC680XY family of computers, as well as most others, employs several strategies to accomplish this. Basic among these is the idea of a *supervisory state* and a *user state*. Instructions that could easily contaminate the operating system are prohibited in user state. These *privileged instructions* can be executed only while the system is in supervisory state. (We will discuss this concept and some of its consequences in much more depth at a later and more appropriate time.) In addition, the operating system acts as the only main program in the computer and calls routines within itself, with the return address placed on the supervisory stack (using the SSP), besides initiating each user application program by calling it with the return address on the supervisory stack. Recall that many (most) user application programs will also call other subservient routines, with the return address being placed on the user stack (using the USP). In addition, each routine may or may not use the appropriate stack for other storage, such as local variables. From long and bitter experience, it has been found that the number and frequency of errors in the use of a stack is orders of magnitude higher for user application programs than for the operating system. If the stack usage of these two classes of programs were mixed together into a common stack, the result would have a much higher probability of being chaotic—a most undesirable happening that must be avoided at almost any cost. Thus, the provision for two separate stack pointers implies two separate stacks.

When a user application program requests some service—such as I/O—from the operating system via a call to a specific I/O routine, that routine will immediately place the MC680XY into supervisory mode by changing the S bit in the status register (SR) to ON = 1. (This change from user to supervisory state can be accomplished by any user application program at any time via an attempt to use a privileged instruction, a nonexistent instruction, and the like, or by attempting to address nonexisting memory or read-only memory.) After accomplishing the requested and privileged work requested, the I/O routine will place the MC680XY into user mode by changing the S bit in the status register to OFF = 0. (This change to user state is a legal instruction in supervisory mode.) Figure 2.5 illustrates these changes. Note

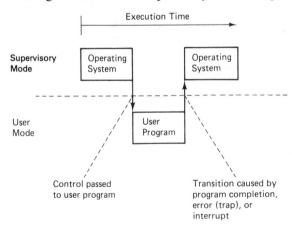

Figure 2.5 Processor states. (From T. L. Harman and B. Lawson. *The Motorola MC68000 Microprocessor Family: Assembly Language, Interface Design, and System Design,* © 1985, p. 35. Reprinted by permission of Prentice-Hall, Inc., Englewood Cliffs, NJ.)

that this dual stack pointer design gives a user application program the ability to contaminate and ruin its own stack, controlled by the USP, but denies the user application program any ability to contaminate and "ruin" the system supervisory stack, controlled by the SSP. Figure 2.6 should be helpful in understanding this feature.

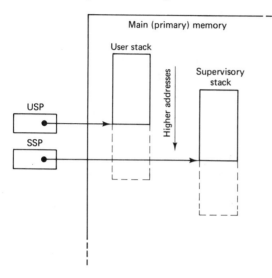

Figure 2.6 The user stack pointer (USP) contains the address of the current top-of-stack of the application (user) program stack of return addresses, local variables, etc. The supervisory stack pointer (SSP) separately contains similar information for the operating system that executes both privileged and nonprivileged instructions in supervisory state.

INSTRUCTIONS

An instruction for a computer must explicitly or implicitly contain two kinds of information: (1) the operation code (opcode), or what to do; and (2) from zero to N operand references (operand addresses, or just operands), or whom to do the operation with or to. Recognizing that the foregoing sentence was not a very pretty way to express the idea, let us recall a few ideas and concepts from Chapter 1:

1. A computer is an information manipulation machine.
2. At the beginning of each such manipulation operation, the source information must already be stored in, and thus be obtainable from, specified memory locations, registers, or I/O buffers within the computer.
3. At the end of each such manipulation operation, the resultant value must be stored in a known memory location, register, or I/O buffer within the computer.
4. The source information may be
   a. A single datum. Example: SET a bit; CLEAR a register; MOVE the contents from.
   b. Two data. Example: ADD two values.
   Some computer designs allow more complicated situations.

5. The destination information often is limited to changing the contents of a specified memory location, register, flag, or I/O buffer but can also include side effects such as SETting or CLEARing an indicator flag. Examples: overflow, zero contents, and the like.

6. The designation of the location(s) of the source information and of the location for the destination (result) are termed the *operands* (often the term *operand addresses* is used). Some instructions of some computers imply certain of these operands, while some instructions of some computers require that all operands be given explicitly. The situations in the MC680XY family are

   a. *Zero-address instructions* (all operand addresses implied). Example: RTS (return from subroutine).

   b. *One-address instructions* (only one operand explicitly given). Example:

   CLR   destination   (replace current contents with all zero bits and
                            appropriately SET status register flag bits).

   c. *Two-address instructions* (two operands explicitly given). Example:

   MOVE   source,destination   (copy the contents of the source into the
                                destination and appropriately set SR bits)

The move multiple registers from or to memory instruction is a two-address instruction, but it may not seem to conform, depending on the syntax required by the specific assembler for specifying the list of registers:

MOVEM   source,destination   (the source or the destination can be a
                                  list of registers, while the other must
                                  be an address in memory)

Earlier, we emphasized that the basic action of a computer is to execute an ordered set of computer instructions (termed a *program*) by fetching and then executing each instruction in the order specified in the program. A review of this concept can be gleaned from Figure 1.10, and a specific example is detailed in Figure 1.9. In Figure 1.9b, note that the instruction is fetched into an instruction register (IR), where it is, in effect, examined (decoded) to determine what actions are necessary, including the acquisition of source operand(s). Although the exact implementation may be different, the IR (instruction register) acts as if it were 16 bits in length, effectively requiring that all of the information vital to decoding be in that portion of the instruction. The general syntax of the binary machine language instructions for the MC680XY family of computers is shown in Figure 2.7.

From Figure 2.8, it can be deduced that the designers of the MC680XY have used the leftmost four bits of the operation word (bits 15, 14, 13, 12) to classify the operations (instructions) into 16 groups. Fourteen of these groups have been imple-

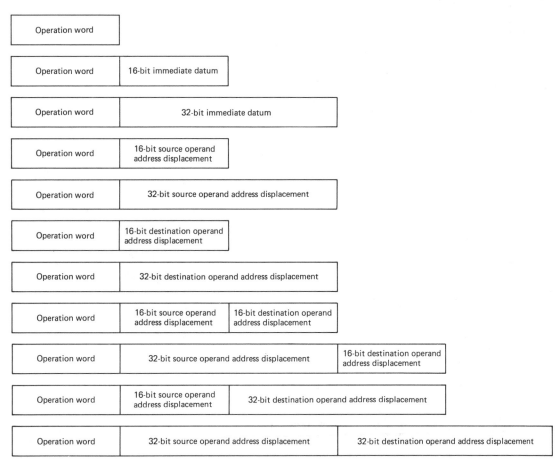

Figure 2.7 The syntax of Motorola MC680XY instructions. The MC68020 also uses two displacements in its memory indirect to memory addressing modes (see Figure 2.13).

mented, while one (1/1/------------) is being used to specify floating-point arithmetic operations that are not implemented on the MC680XY but are available via an additional coprocessor (MC68881) or as interrupt-invoked software. The other not implemented group of instructions (1010------------) is currently reserved for possible future processor augmentations to specify instructions particularly suitable for a possible lucrative future market. One example of such a possible future market might be the area known as word processing. For example, the Intel Corporation has reacted to this marketplace by implementing and marketing the I82730 Alphanumeric Text Co-Processor. It would not be unexpected for the Motorola Corporation to react in a similar manner.

Instructions can also be examined from the viewpoint of the number of operands involved: zero-address, one-address, or two-address. From this viewpoint, the bit patterns of the operation word also exhibit some regularity, as shown in Figure 2.9.

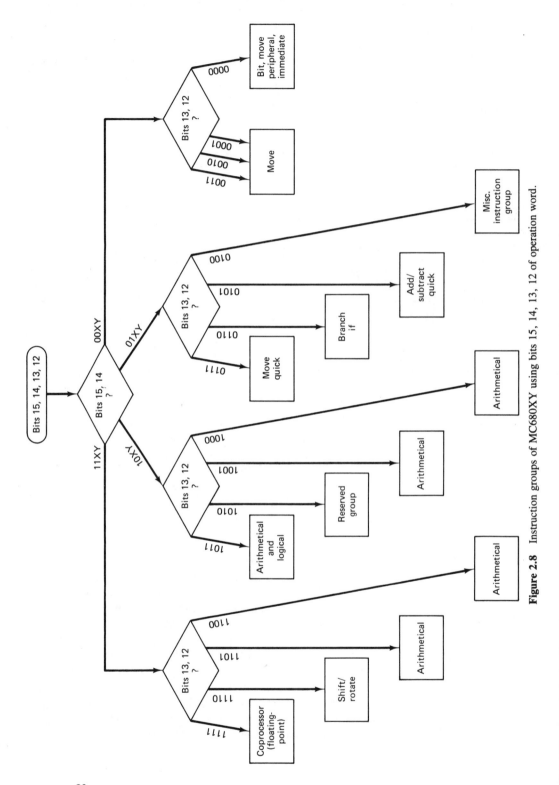

Figure 2.8 Instruction groups of MC680XY using bits 15, 14, 13, 12 of operation word.

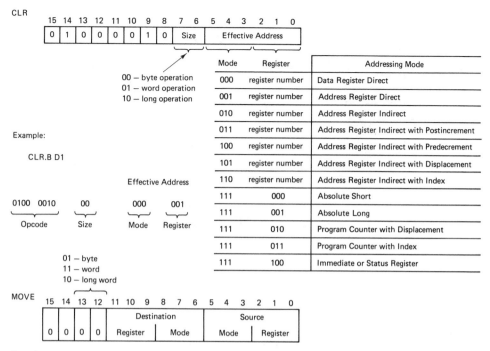

CLR

15	14	13	12	11	10	9	8	7	6	5 4 3 2 1 0
0	1	0	0	0	0	1	0	Size		Effective Address

00 – byte operation
01 – word operation
10 – long operation

Mode	Register	Addressing Mode
000	register number	Data Register Direct
001	register number	Address Register Direct
010	register number	Address Register Indirect
011	register number	Address Register Indirect with Postincrement
100	register number	Address Register Indirect with Predecrement
101	register number	Address Register Indirect with Displacement
110	register number	Address Register Indirect with Index
111	000	Absolute Short
111	001	Absolute Long
111	010	Program Counter with Displacement
111	011	Program Counter with Index
111	100	Immediate or Status Register

Example:

CLR.B D1

Effective Address

0100 0010	00	000	001
Opcode	Size	Mode	Register

01 – byte
11 – word
10 – long word

MOVE

15	14	13	12	11	10	9	8	7	6	5	4	3	2	1	0
				Destination						Source					
0	0	0	0	Register			Mode			Mode			Register		

Example:

MOVE.W D1, D3

	Destination			Source	
0011	011	000	000	001
Opcode	Register	Mode	Mode	Register

ADD

15	14	13	12	11	10	9	8	7	6	5	4	3	2	1	0
1	1	0	1	Register			Op-Mode			Effective Address					

any of the eight data registers

Operation	Byte	Word	Long
$(<Dn>) + (<ea>) \rightarrow <Dn>$	000	001	010
$(<ea>) + (<Dn>) \rightarrow <ea>$	100	101	110

Examples:

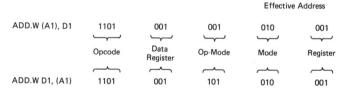

Effective Address

ADD.W (A1), D1	1101	001	001	010	001
	Opcode	Data Register	Op-Mode	Mode	Register
ADD.W D1, (A1)	1101	001	101	010	001

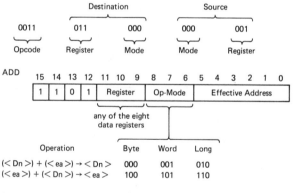

Figure 2.9 Example instruction formats. Note that the one-address CLR instruction (replace contents with zero bits) can involve any data register, any address register, or any memory location; that the two-address MOVE instruction can involve any two data registers, any two memory locations, a data register and a memory location, or an immediate value and a data register or memory location; and that the ADD instruction must involve one data register and a register, memory location, or immediate value.

81

(a) Instruction Set

Mnemonic	Description
ABCD*	Add Decimal with Extend
ADD*	Add
AND*	Logical AND
ASL*	Arithmetic Shift Left
ASR*	Arithmetic Shift Right
Bcc	Branch Conditionally
BCHG	Bit Test and Change
BCLR	Bit Test and Clear
BRA	Branch Always
BSET	Bit Test and Set
BSR	Branch to Subroutine
BTST	Bit Test
CHK	Check Register Against Bounds
CLR*	Clear Operand
CMP*	Compare
DBcc	Decrement and Branch Conditionally
DIVS	Signed Divide
DIVU	Unsigned Divide
EOR*	Exclusive OR
EXG	Exchange Registers
EXT	Sign Extend
JMP	Jump
JSR	Jump to Subroutine
LEA	Load Effective Address
LINK	Link Stack
LSL*	Logical Shift Left
LSR*	Logical Shift Right

Mnemonic	Description
MOVE*	Move Source to Destination
MULS	Signed Multiply
MULU	Unsigned Multiply
NBCD*	Negate Decimal with Extend
NEG*	Negate
NOP	No Operation
NOT*	One's Complement
OR*	Logical OR
PEA	Push Effective Address
RESET	Reset External Devices
ROL*	Rotate Left without Extend
ROR*	Rotate Right without Extend
ROXL*	Rotate Left with Extend
ROXR*	Rotate Right with Extend
RTD	Return and Deallocate
RTE	Return from Exception
RTR	Return and Restore
RTS	Return from Subroutine
SBCD*	Subtract Decimal with Extend
Scc	Set Conditional
STOP	Stop
SUB*	Subtract
SWAP	Swap Data Register Halves
TAS	Test and Set Operand
TRAP	Trap
TRAPV	Trap on Overflow
TST*	Test
UNLK	Unlink

*These instructions available in loop mode on MC68010/MC68012.
See **APPENDIX G MC68010/MC68012 LOOP MODE OPERA-TION**.

(b) Variations of Instruction Types

Instruction Type	Variation	Description
ADD	ADD*	Add
	ADDA*	Add Address
	ADDQ	Add Quick
	ADDI	Add Immediate
	ADDX*	Add with Extend
AND	AND*	Logical AND
	ANDI	AND Immediate
	ANDI to CCR	AND Immediate to Condition Codes
	ANDI to SR	AND Immediate to Status Register
CMP	CMP*	Compare
	CMPA*	Compare Address
	CMPM*	Compare Memory
	CMPI	Compare Immediate
EOR	EOR*	Exclusive OR
	EORI	Exclusive OR Immediate
	EORI to CCR	Exclusive OR Immediate to Condition Codes
	EORI to SR	Exclusive OR Immediate to Status Register

Instruction Type	Variation	Description
MOVE	MOVE*	Move Source to Destination
	MOVEA*	Move Address
	MOVEC	Move Control Register
	MOVEM	Move Multiple Registers
	MOVEP	Move Peripheral Data
	MOVEQ	Move Quick
	MOVES	Move Alternate Address Space
	MOVE from SR	Move from Status Register
	MOVE to SR	Move to Status Register
	MOVE from CCR	Move from Condition Codes
	MOVE to CCR	Move to Condition Codes
	MOVE USP	Move User Stack Pointer
NEG	NEG*	Negate
	NEGX*	Negate with Extend
OR	OR*	Logical OR
	ORI	OR Immediate
	ORI to CCR	OR Immediate to Condition Codes
	ORI to SR	OR Immediate to Status Register
SUB	SUB*	Subtract
	SUBA*	Subtract Address
	SUBI	Subtract Immediate
	SUBQ	Subtract Quick
	SUBX*	Subtract with Extend

*These instructions available in loop mode on MC68010/MC68012.
See **APPENDIX G MC68010/MC68012 LOOP MODE OPERA-TION**.

Figure 2.10 The instruction set of the Motorola MC68000. Note from part b of this figure that many of the instructions have several variations. An extensive set of addressing modes is available for these instructions where such are appropriate. Figure 2.9 contains much of this information. (Courtesy of Motorola, Inc.)

Both the number of different instructions (as shown in Figure 2.10) and the extensive addressing modes (as shown in Figure 2.9) provide conclusive evidence that the MC680XY is an example of a CISC (complicated instruction set computer) and is not a RISC (reduced instruction set computer). An interesting discussion of this current controversy in computer organization can be found in Colwell et al. (1983), which gives references into the RISC research literature. After a somewhat cursory examination of the SR (status register), we will examine each of the addressing modes, including the specific method that is used to derive (calculate) the actual address (location) of the desired datum container.

INDICATOR-STATUS FLAGS

We now consider the status register (SR) of the MC680XY family of microcomputers. From Figure 2.11, note that this word-sized status register is divided into two byte portions: the system byte and the *condition code register* (CCR), or user byte. Also note that three bits are not used in the system status byte; these same three bits are not used in the CCR of the standard MC68000/M68008 but are available to designers of advanced systems such as the MC68020 to indicate additional information. At a more appropriate time, we will consider the use of these bits.

We have already discussed the user state versus the supervisory state with additional privileged instructions for the operating system. Bit 13, the S bit, controls this distinction. We will delay our discussion of bit 15, the T (trace) bit until our discussion of program debugging. Similarly, we will delay our consideration of bits 8, 9, 10 (the I_0, I_1, I_2 or interrupt mask bits) until we discuss interrupts and physical I/O.

The CCR automatically records certain conditions that occur as the result of executing certain arithmetic, logical, data movement, and other instructions. Note that there are only three ways for the setting of any these bits to be changed:

1. As a desirable side effect of an instruction; that is, the Z bit (zero bit), bit 2, will be set to ON = 1 as the result of an ADD, SUB, OR, AND, EOR, and so on, iff (if and only if) the result of the operation is zero (all bits = 0 = OFF). The values of the bits in the CCR will remain unchanged until one of these three conditions is met.
2. The contents of the entire status register or of any portion of it can be replaced (changed) by the MOVE to SR instruction—a privileged instruction that can only be executed in supervisory mode (S bit set).
3. Similarly, the CCR portion of the SR can be replaced (changed) by the MOVE to CCR instruction, which can be executed in either user or supervisory mode.

The main uses of the various bits in the CCR are to allow conditional branches in programs. Thus, the assembly-level instruction Bcc (branch conditionally) tests

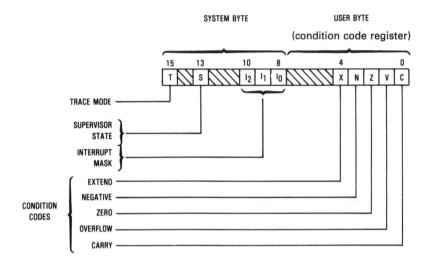

INTERPRETATION OF CONDITION CODES

Name	Symbol	Meaning
Extend	X	Used in multiple-precision arithmetic operations; in many instructions it is set the same as the C bit.
Negative	N	Set to {1} if the most significant bit of an operand is {1}.
Zero	Z	Set to {1} if all the bits of an operand are {0}.
Overflow	V	Set to {1} if an out-of-range condition occurs in two's-complement operations.
Carry	C	Set to {1} if a carry is generated out of the most significant bit of the sum in addition. Set to {1} if a borrow is generated in subtraction.

Figure 2.11 The Motorola MC680XY status register (SR) consists of two bytes: the system byte (bits 8–15) and the user byte, or condition code register (CCR) (bits 0–7). (Courtesy of Motorola, Inc.)

the specific bit of the CCR specified and branches if the bit is set or not set, as specified in the condition (the cc of the Bcc). The foregoing is not true, and would not be useful, for the X bit (extend bit) = bit 4. In Chapter 4, we will examine in some detail the program flow of control instructions and their use in programs.

CALCULATION OF THE OPERAND ADDRESS

In general, the effective operand address is the address of the location of a datum. Five different classes of effective operand addresses occur in the Motorola MC680XY microcomputer, with a plethora of subclasses. A summary is given in Figure 2.12. (Chapter 1 also discusses this topic.)

Mode	Method of Address Generation
Direct Addressing	
Register Direct Addressing	
Data Register Direct	EA = DN
Address Register Direct	EA = An
Memory Direct Addressing	
Absolute Short	EA = (Next Word)
Absolute Long	EA = (Next Two Words)
Indirect Addressing	
Register Indirect Addressing	
Register Indirect	EA = (An)
Implied Register Indirect	EA = (SP); SP = SP + N $\mid$ = SP = SP − N; EA = (SP)
Register Indirect With Offset	EA = (An) + d_{16}
Indexed Register Indirect With Offset	EA = (An) + (Xn) + d_8
Scaled Indexed Register Indirect With Sized Offset	EA = (An) + [(Xn) * N] + $d_0 \mid d_{16} \mid d_{32}$ (MC68020 only)
Postincrement Register Indirect	EA = (An), An ← An + N
Predecrement Register Indirect	An ← An − N, EA = (An)
Program Counter Relative Addressing	
Relative with Offset	EA = (PC) + d_{16}
Relative with Index and Offset	EA = (PC) + (Xn) + d_8
Relative with Scaled Index and Sized Offset	EA = (PC) + [(Xn) * N] + $d_0 \mid d_{16} \mid d_{32}$ (MC68020 only)
Immediate	DATA = Next Word(s) After Operation Word
Quick Immediate	Within Operation Word
Memory Indirect Through Register Indirect Addressing	
Register with Sized Offset Pointing to Scaled Indexed Memory Address With Sized Offset	EA = {(An) + $d_0 \mid d_{16} \mid d_{32}$} + {[(Xm) * N] + $d_0 \mid d_{16} \mid d_{32}$} (MC68020 only)
Scaled Indexed Register with Sized Offset Pointing to Memory Address With Sized Offset	EA = {(An) + [(Xm) * N] + $d_0 \mid d_{16} \mid d_{32}$} + {$d_0 \mid d_{16} \mid d_{32}$} (MC68020 only)
Memory Indirect Through Program Counter Relative Addressing	
Relative With Sized Offset Pointing to Scaled Indexed Memory Address With Sized Offset	EA = {(PC) + $d_0 \mid d_{16} \mid d_{32}$} + {[Xn) × N] + $d_0 \mid d_{16} \mid d_{32}$} (MC68020 only)
Relative With Scaled Index and Sized Offset Pointing to Memory Address With Sized Offset	EA = {(PC) + [(Xm) * N] + $d_0 \mid d_{16} \mid d_{32}$} + {$d_0 \mid d_{16} \mid d_{32}$} (MC68020 only)

NOTES:

EA = Effective Address
An = Address Register
Dn = Data Register
Xn = Address or Data Register used as Index Register
SR = Status Register
PC = Program Counter
All indices can be scaled (1,2,4,8) on MC68020

d_8 = Eight-bit Offset (displacement)
d_{16} = Sixteen-bit Offset (displacement)
N = 1 for Byte, 2 for Words, 4 for Long Words, and 8* for quad words. *(only for MC68020)
( ) = Contents of
← = Replaces
$\mid$ = or

Figure 2.12 Motorola MC680XY addressing modes employed to determine the location of the datum in a register or in memory. As I/O is memory-mapped, a device exists as a pseudomemory location, so these memory addressing modes are also I/O device addressing modes.

It is necessary that we consider and understand several types of addresses and that we be exact in terminology:

Operand address: the operand designation as explicitly given or implied in the instruction. This operand address may or may not be varied by a displacement or by the contents of a register during calculation of the effective address.

Effective operand address: the address in memory (or the name of a register) relative to the start of memory (location 0) or relative to some chosen spot in memory; often termed the *effective address* (EA). In effect, the effective address is a displacement from either (1) the start of memory (absolute addressing) or (2) the start of the program.

Physical address: the actual physical address in memory (or the name of some register) during actual program execution of the program or program portion. We must distinguish three quite different cases as far as memory is concerned:

*   *Absolute addressing:* the effective operand address is the physical address. Absolute addressing should be used only with (1) memory-mapped I/O device addresses in pseudomemory, (2) absolute addresses within the interrupt branch table in low memory, and (3) certain operating system routines. Thus, application programs will not normally employ absolute addressing.

*   *Statically relocatable addressing:* the physical address is the sum of the effective operand address (EA) plus a relocation factor (the physical address of the start of the memory area into which the program is loaded before execution commences). The relocation factor is a constant for any one execution but can be, and probably is, different for each execution. Note that absolute addressing can be thought of as statically relocatable addressing with a relocation factor of zero. If, for any reason, the program is removed from memory during execution, with the expectation of restarting it at a later time, it must be placed back into memory in exactly the same locations. This is the normal mode for user application programs with the MC68000 and the MC68008.

*   *Dynamically relocatable addressing:* The physical address is the sum of the effective operand address (EA) plus a relocation factor, as above, except that the relocation factor may vary during a single execution. This allows a program to be removed from memory during execution and later to be restarted after reloading into a different area in memory. Thus, the relocation factor is a variable.

Although it is not vital at this stage that you fully understand virtual memory as implemented on the MC68010, the MC68012, and the MC68020, it is worth noting that this memory management technique, in effect, creates N different dynamically alterable relocation variables—one for each of *N* different sections (pages or segments) of program and data.

In our discussion of the different addressing modes available on the MC680XY family of microprocessors, we will give a formula for the calculation of the physical address (PA) and accompany it with a diagram. We will approach the different addressing modes from the scheme shown in Figure 2.12 and will not employ the vendor specific classification used in Motorola manuals. Note that both schemes are correct and fully equivalent, but I think that the more general scheme is easier to understand and allows more accurate comparisons between computers of different vendors.

Direct Addressing Modes

In direct addressing modes, the value desired is the contents of the datum container named as the operand in the instruction.

Register direct addressing.   The value desired is the contents of the register named in the instruction.

Data Register Direct Addressing.   PA = EA = Dn (where Dn is D0, D1, . . . , D7):

```
31                15        7        0
┌──────────────────┬────────┬────────┐
│                  ┊        ┊        │ Dn
└──────────────────┴────────┴────────┘
```

Address Register Direct Addressing.   PA = EA = An (where An is A0, A1, . . . , A7):

```
31                15        7        0
┌──────────────────┬────────┬────────┐
│                  ┊        ┊        │ An
└──────────────────┴────────┴────────┘
```

Memory direct addressing.   The value desired is the contents of the memory location(s) named in the instruction.

Absolute Memory Direct Addressing.   The value desired is the contents of memory locations named in the word (short address) or long word (long address) following the operation word of the instruction. Relocation is not possible; that is, the relocation factor is zero. This addressing mode should not be used in normal application programs.

- *Absolute short-memory direct addressing:* PA = EA = operand$_{16bits}$:

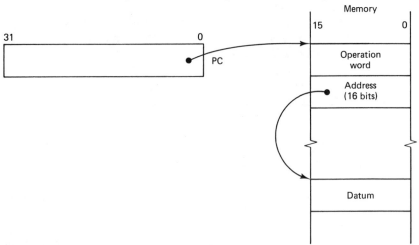

- *Absolute long-memory direct addressing:* PA = EA = operand$_{32bits}$:

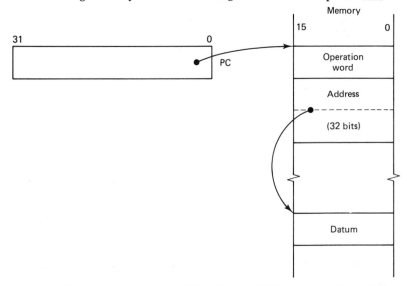

Relocatable Memory Direct Addressing. This mode, either of the static or the dynamic type, is not available on the MC680XY family. Although programming techniques are available and commonly employed in most computers that render this addressing mode unnecessary, I believe that this lack is unfortunate—particularly in my attempts to have beginners learn assembly language programming; it just makes things more complicated for the "raw beginner" even though it is not a major programmatic problem for experienced people. In fact, at least one commercial assembly system simulates this mode by transforming such addresses to offsets from the program counter (PC).

Indirect Addressing Modes

In indirect addressing modes, the value desired is the contents of the data container whose address is contained in the data container named as the operand in the instruction. This indirect address can be varied by a displacement or by the contents of a register (such as an index register).

Address register indirect addressing.   The value desired is in the memory location (including memory-mapped I/O) whose address is in the address register named as the operand in the instruction. PA = (RF + EA) = An (where An is A0, A1, . . . , A6 and RF is the relocation factor.

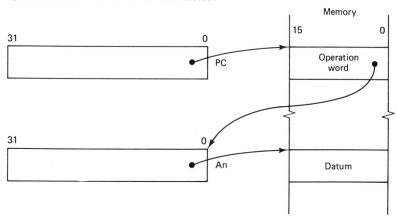

Address register indirect with offset addressing.   The value desired is in the memory location whose address is in the address register named as the operand in the instruction plus the signed 16-bit offset (displacement). The magnitude of the offset can be +32467 through −32468 and includes zero. PA = (RF + EA) = An + displacement:

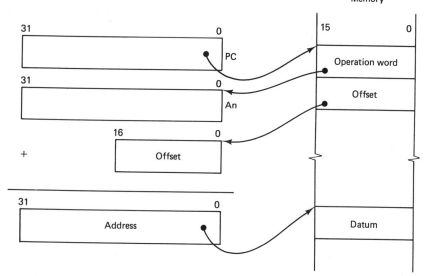

Indexed address register indirect with short offset addressing.   The
value desired is in the memory location whose address is in the address register
named as the operand, as altered by the 8-bit displacement ($+127$ through -128)
and also as altered by the contents of the index register named in the instruction. The
signed index register can be specified as a word (16 bits) or as a long word (32 bits).
It must be emphasized that the index is in bytes. It is the programmer's responsibility to increment the index appropriately by 1, 2, 4, or 8 as needed for byte, word,
long-word, or quad-word data. Exception: the MC68020 allows the incrementation
to be specified as necessary for different data lengths. PA = (RF + EA) = An +
Rm + displacement:

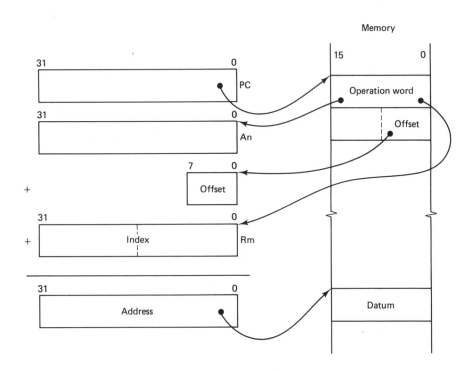

Postincrement address register indirect addressing.   The desired value
is in the memory location whose address is in the address register named as the
operand. *After* this address is dispatched to memory, it is incremented by the amount
appropriate to the data—byte = 1, word = 2, long word = 4—in preparation for
accessing   the   next   element   of   an   array.   PA = (RF + EA) = An   *and*
An = An + increment:

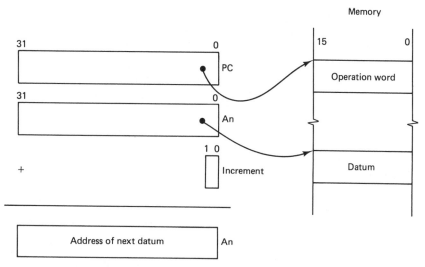

Predecrement address register indirect addressing. The desired value is in the memory location whose address is derived by decrementing the value in the named address register by the width of the datum in bytes. Note that this addressing mode and the previous one are exact mirror images of each other, allowing arrays and any other data structures implemented as arrays to be accessed in serial order from either end. An = An − decrement *and* PA = (RF + EA) = An:

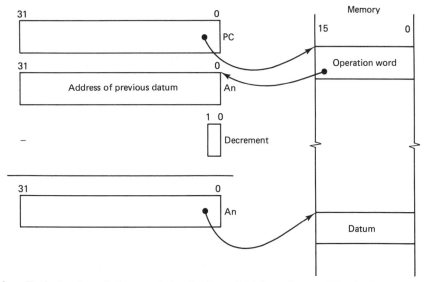

Implied stack pointer register indirect addressing. The desired value is an address that is to be PUSHed onto the stack or POPped from the stack. Recall that the current address of the top of the stack is contained in the USP (user stack pointer) or the SSP (supervisory stack pointer), depending on the current value of the S (supervisory) bit in the SR (status register). The PEA (push effective address) instruction employs the predecrement addressing mode with the appropriate stack pointer register, while the three returns from subroutine instructions (RTE, RTR, RTS) also employ the postincrement addressing mode, with the appropriate stack pointer register. Experienced programmers will note that commonly available PUSH to and POP from the stack instructions are missing from the MC680XY design. Exactly the same action is provided by the predecrement and postincrement address register indirect addressing modes:

PUSH   An@−   or   SP@−
POP   An@+   or   SP@+

which always leaves the address register (stack pointer) pointing to the current top of the stack, with the assumption that the stack grows toward lower addresses in memory.

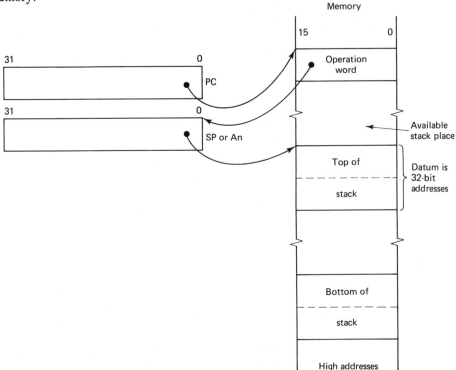

Program counter relative with offset addressing.   The value desired is in the memory location whose address is the current value of the program counter plus the signed 16-bit offset (+32469 through −32466 bytes). This addressing mode may not be used to store a datum into memory; that is, it is only usable as the target of a branch or to obtain a value from memory. PA = (RF + EA) = PC + displacement + 2

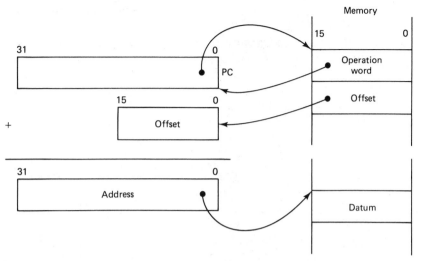

Indexed program counter relative with short offset addressing. The desired value is in the memory location whose address is the current value of the program counter (PC) plus the signed 8-bit offset (+127 through −128) plus the signed value in a specified 16-bit or 32-bit address or data register. Again, this addressing mode, like the previous one involving the PC, cannot be used to store data into memory but is restricted to memory accessing. Also, it must be emphasized that the index registers of the MC680XY family require that the programmer increment them by the appropriate number of bytes for the data type involved (1 for byte, 2 for word, 4 for long-word, or 8 for quad-word). Again, the MC68020 has provisions for specifying this incrementation/decrementation factor in the instruction. It is interesting to note that at least some assemblers convert this addressing mode and the previous one for destination (memory storage) operands to absolute long addresses and mark them to be altered during the static program linkage/relocation process. PA = (RF + EA) = PC + Rm + displacement:

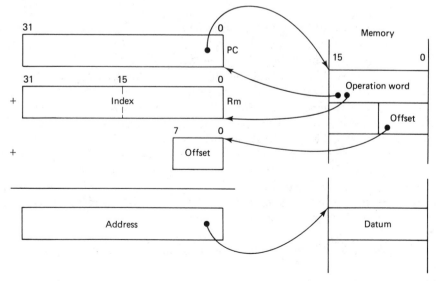

Immediate addressing mode.   The value desired immediately follows the operation word of the instruction and may be byte, word, or long-word in size. Although the Motorola documentation specifies that a byte immediate operand is available, in reality 16 bits are employed, with bits 8 through 15 being zeros. PA = (RF + EA) = immediate:

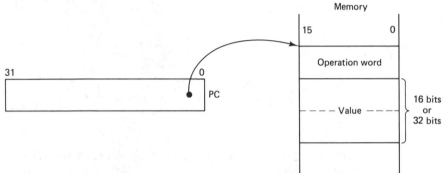

The designers of the Motorola MC680XY family chose not to provide explicit increment and decrement instructions but instead implemented two instructions:

ADDQ   (add quick)
SUBQ   (subtract quick)

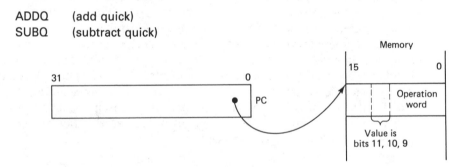

which allow adding or subtracting an unsigned value (range = 1 through 8) contained in the operation word of the instruction. A MOVEQ (move quick) instruction is also implemented that allows a signed 8-bit operand (+127 through −128) value in the second byte of the operation word to be correctly moved with leading zeros or ones to a long-word (32-bit) data register.

The designers of the MC68008, MC68000, MC68010, and MC68012 chose not to provide a memory indirect addressing mode—that is, addressing to memory where the address of the desired value is contained in a long-word of memory addressed using a register to hold its address. In my experience, this makes the construction and use of a table of branch addresses a trifle harder but not impossible, even though the resulting code is longer and slower during execution. Consider the case where it is desirable to have a table of 32-bit addresses in memory, starting at location TABLE. The algorithm could be

1. Load the effective address of TABLE into an address register.

2. Determine the position of the desired address within the table. Move this position * 4 into another address register.

3. ADD the two address registers giving the address of the desired address.

4. Branch to this desired address, using the address register indirect with short offset (=0) addressing mode.

Additional MC68020 Addressing Modes

After the release of the MC68000 microcomputer, when at least a few programmers had gained experience using it to solve real-world problems, comments—almost all at least partially favorable—were common, as is usual within the microcomputer user community. One of the more interesting and favorable reports was that of John Gilmore (1980) in the nonrefereed *SIGARCH News* of the Association for Computing Machinery (ACM). After justifiably starting with, "The MC68000 is an outstanding processor . . . ," he lists 29 specific suggestions for improvements. I haven't the slightest idea whether or not Mr. Gilmore's suggestions had any influence on the specifications of subsequent models, but it is at least true that the MC68010, the MC68012, and the MC68020 all support virtual memory (his point #2) and that the MC68020 does support 32-bit addressing (point #11), a true 32-bit multiply and divide (points #8 and #9), an instruction cache (point #12), scaled indexes by data element size (point #10), and memory indirect addressing to directly support branch tables (point #25). If Mr. Gilmore had an effect, the Motorola designers were attentive to note the validity of his points; if his comments were not noticed, the Motorola designers deserve even more credit for recognizing and correcting shortcomings in the original design.

At this time, it is important to consider four programmatically important improvements in the addressing capabilities of the MC68020 over the previous models:

1. Full 32-bit addresses, allowing 4 GB of main (primary) memory instead of the 16 MB of the MC68000/MC68010 and the 64 KB of the MC68008.

2. Provision for address offsets (displacements) of 32 bits, 16 bits, and 0 bits (no offset).

3. Provision for indexing by data element size when using an index register; thus, the index value in the index register can be forced to be left-shifted before use to automatically accommodate byte data (no shift), word data (shift left one bit = * 2), long-word data (shift left two bits = * 4), or quad-word data (shift left three bits = * 8).

4. Memory indirect addressing, facilitating the use of branch tables—that is, the use of a table of addresses pointing to different sections of code, data, or subprocedures.

These extensions are given in Figures 2.12 and 2.13, and are noted as being limited to the MC68020. It is now appropriate to discuss the six extended addressing modes of the MC68020.

Single Effective Address Instruction Format

15	14	13	12	11	10	9	8	7	6	5	4	3	2	1	0
										Effective Address					
X	X	X	X	X	X	X	X	X	X	Mode			Register		

MC68020, Brief Format Extension Word

15	14	13	12	11	10	9	8	7	6	5	4	3	2	1	0
D/A	Register			W/L	Scale		0	Displacement							

MC68020, Full Format Extension Word(s)

15	14	13	12	11	10	9	8	7	6	5	4	3	2	1	0
D/A	Register			W/L	Scale		1	BS	IS	BD SIZE		0	I/IS		
Base Displacement (0, 1, or 2 Words)															
Outer Displacement (0, 1, or 2 Words)															

Field	Definition
Register	Index Register Number
D/A	Index Register Type:
	0 = Dn
	1 = An
W/L	Word/Long Word Index Size:
	0 = Sign Extended Word
	1 = Long Word
Scale	Scale Factor:
	00 = 1
	01 = 2
	10 = 4
	11 = 8
BS	Base Suppress:
	0 = Base Register Added
	1 = Base Register Suppressed
IS	Index Suppress:
	0 = Evaluate and Add Index Operand
	1 = Suppress Index Operand
BD SIZE	Base Displacement Size:
	00 = Reserved
	01 = Null Displacement
	10 = Word Displacement
	11 = Long Displacement
I/IS	Index/Indirect Selection:
	Indirect and Indexing Operand Determined in
	Conjunction with Bit 6, Index Suppress

IS	Index/Indirect	Operation
0	000	No Memory Indirection
0	001	Indirect Pre-Indexed with Null Displacement
0	010	Indirect Pre-Indexed with Word Displacement
0	011	Indirect Pre-Indexed with Long Displacement
0	100	Reserved
0	101	Indirect Post-Indexed with Null Displacement
0	110	Indirect Post-Indexed with Word Displacement
0	111	Indirect Post-Indexed with Long Displacement
1	000	No Memory Indirection
1	001	Memory Indirect with Null Displacement
1	010	Memory Indirect with Word Displacement
1	011	Memory Indirect with Long Displacement
1	100-111	Reserved

Addressing Mode	Mode	Register
Data Register Direct	000	Reg #
Address Register Direct	001	Reg #
Address Register Indirect	010	Reg #
Address Register Indirect with Postincrement	011	Reg #
Address Register Indirect with Predecrement	100	Reg #
Address Register Indirect with Displacement	101	Reg #
Address Register and Memory Indirect with Index	110	Reg #
Absolute Short	111	000
Absolute Long	111	001
Program Counter Indirect with Displacement	111	010
Program Counter and Memory Indirect with Index	111	011
Immediate Data	111	100
Reserved for Future Motorola Use	111	101
Reserved for Future Motorola Use	111	110
Reserved for Future Motorola Use	111	111

Figure 2.13 Instruction syntax and semantics for the Motorola MC68020. (Courtesy of Motorola, Inc.)

Scaled indexed address register with offset indirect addressing. The desired datum is in the memory location whose address is the contents of an address register, as indexed by a register scaled by the datum width in bytes (1, 2, 4, or 8) and also modified by a signed displacement of length 0 bits (=0), 16 bits (+32467 through −32468), or 32 bits (+2 GB through −2 GB). PA = (RF + EA) = An + (Rm * scale) + displacement

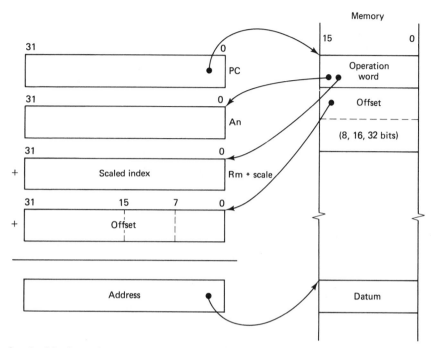

Scaled indexed program counter relative with offset addressing.   The desired datum is in the memory location whose address is the current value of the program counter, as indexed by a register scaled by the datum width in bytes (1, 2, 4, or 8) and also modified by a signed displacement of length 0 bits (=0), 16 bits (+32467 through −32468), or 32 bits (+2 GB through −2 GB). PA = RF + EA = PC + (Rm * scale) + displacement:

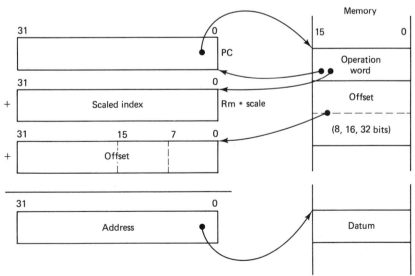

Memory indirect with scaled indexing and offset through address register with sized offset addressing. The desired datum is in the memory location pointed to by the scaled index, with sized offset address in the memory location long word pointed to by an address register as modified by a sized offset. PA = RF + EA = [Memory(An) + Offset#1] + [(RM * scale) + Offset#2]:

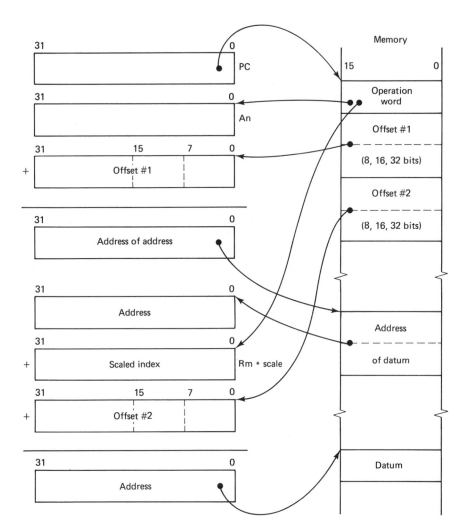

Memory indirect with scaled indexing and sized offset relative to program counter with sized offset addressing. The desired datum is in the memory location pointed to by the scaled index, with sized offset address in the memory location long word pointed to by the program counter (PC) modified by a sized offset. Note the resemblance to the previous addressing mode, with the PC being employed instead of an An. This addressing mode cannot be used to store a datum into memory; that is, it is usable only to obtain an item from memory or to specify a branch address (label). PA = RF + EA = [Memory(PC) + Offset#1] + [(RM * scale) + Offset#2]:

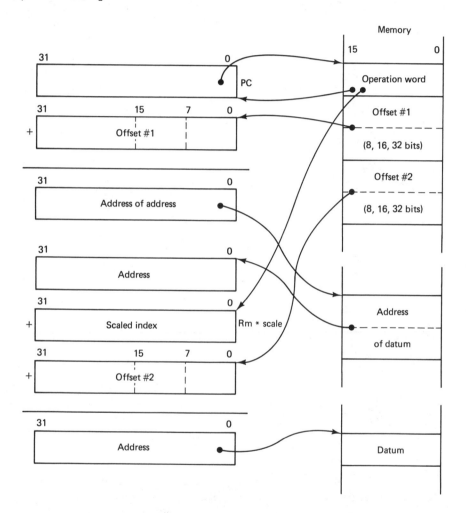

Memory indirect with sized offset through address register with scaled indexing and offset addressing.   The desired datum is in the memory location pointed to by the sized offset address in the memory long word pointed to by a scaled index address register as modified by a sized offset. PA = RF + EA = [Memory(An) + (Rm * scale) + Offset#1] + Offset#2:

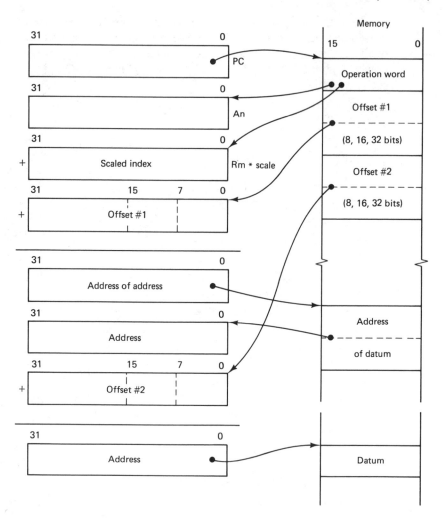

Memory indirect with sized offset relative to program counter with scaled indexing and sized offset addressing. The desired datum is in the memory location pointed to by the sized offset address in the memory long word pointed to by the program counter (PC) as modified by a scaled index register and by a sized offset. Again, note the close resemblance to the previous addressing mode, with the PC being employed instead of an An. As this addressing mode involves the PC, it cannot be used to store a datum into memory but can be used only to obtain a datum from memory or to specify a branch address label. PA = RF + EA = [Memory(PC) + (Rm * scale) + Offset#1] + Offset#2:

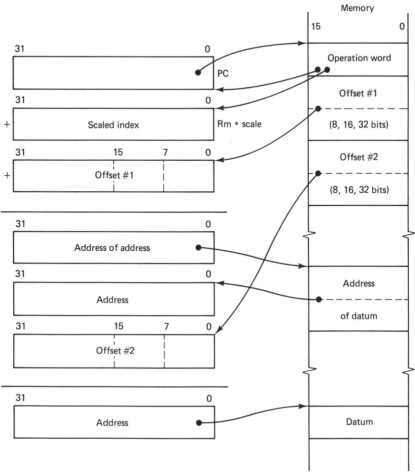

MOTOROLA MC680XY IMPLEMENTATION: MICROPROGRAMMING

Microprogramming is an implementation technique in which a *host computer* is programmed at the level below assembly language to appear to the programmer of assembly or higher-level languages to be a more programmatically desirable *virtual computer*. Each instruction of the host computer is an instruction step of the virtual computer, and each instruction step of the virtual computer is an instruction of the host computer. The concept of instruction steps can be reviewed using Figure 1.12. If the host computer is implemented in hardware with simple instructions that deal directly with the data paths and registers—for example, data registers, address registers, accumulator, MAR (memory address register), MDR (memory data register), IR (instruction register), PC, and so on—we would use the terms *microprogramming* and *emulate*. That is, we emulate the virtual computer by microprogramming the host computer using microinstructions. If the host computer has instructions that include a series of steps—for example, ADD or LOAD or BRANCH—we would use the term *simulate* and not imply microprogramming or microinstructions. The article by Rosin (1969) is an excellent introduction to this implementation technique. In effect, the simple instruction cycle given in Chapter 1 is elaborated as shown in Figure 2.14.

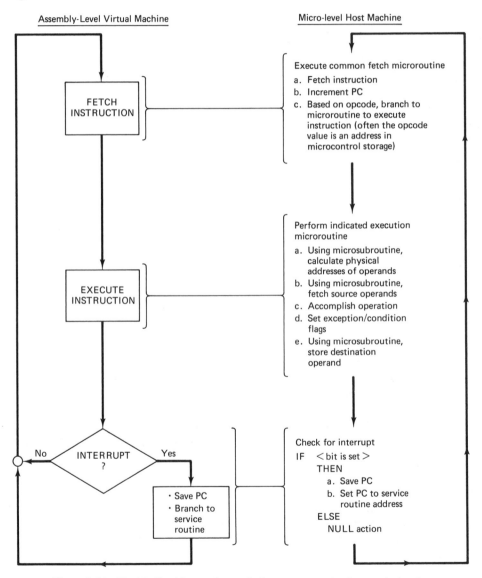

Figure 2.14 The idealized instruction cycle for a computer implemented via microprogramming.

A fairly complete description of the user-apparent Motorola MC680XY can be found in the *User's Manual* (Motorola, 1986). All in all, the MC680XY family of microcomputers forms a superior implementation vehicle for personal computers, small business systems, laboratory control systems, and specialized processors (via microprogramming) with maxi- and midicomputers. At the present time (1986), the commercial acceptance of the MC680XY is second only to that of the Intel I8086 family among the more capable microcomputers, and its popularity is rapidly increasing.

The MC680XY microprocessor is an excellent current example of the two-level control storage concept. The idealized instruction cycle of the host computer shown in Figures 2.15 and 2.16 is sketched in Figure 2.17. Note that the execution of an assembly-level, virtual machine (the MC680XY), programmer-visible instruction is initiated by sending the starting address of the microroutine to the top-level control store, after which instructions from this microcontrol store are executed in sequence (with branches possible). This narrow (10 bits) top-level microinstruction either contains an address of the desired gate settings in the lower-level horizontally encoded wide (68-bit) nanoinstruction *or* contains a branch address within the top level microstore, allowing a branch to the fetch-a-virtual-machine-instruction-routine, for example. Only a single nanoinstruction is accessed via a microinstruction. Note that the execution of a virtual machine (MC680XY) instruction consists of the execution of top-level microinstructions, most of which cause the execution of a single nanoinstruction, although some cause a branch within the microcode. Thus, the execution of an instruction step usually requires two sequential control store accesses, one to the microstore and then one to the nanostore. On the other hand, the total volume of control storage is reduced by employing a two-level control store, because many of the nanoinstructions can be used in multiple contexts (i.e., can be used as a portion of many different virtual machine instructions). The calculations supporting this contention are shown in Figure 2.18. The expenditure of execution time to save memory space is an extremely common trade-off at all levels of computer software and hardware. More detailed information on the MC680XY host microengine can be found in Stritter and Tredennick (1978) and Nash and Spak (1979).

It may assist student understanding of the practical problems often encountered while implementing a microprogrammed computer to cite some of the reasons for the design decisions made by the MC680XY design team. Perhaps the most basic decision concerned the question of whether to use microprogramming as an implementation tool or to use combinatorial logic (i.e., direct hardware circuits). As all previous microprocessor design efforts of Motorola had been with combinatorial logic, the use of microprogramming necessitated a learning process for the design team, with the probable need for different and unavailable software tools and a learning curve to acquire new modes of thinking. During this learning time, errors would probably occur at higher rates than desirable. Thus, this was a major and serious decision, with large economic consequences. As reported by Stritter and Tredennick, the decision was based on a combination of managerial and technical factors, such as the following:

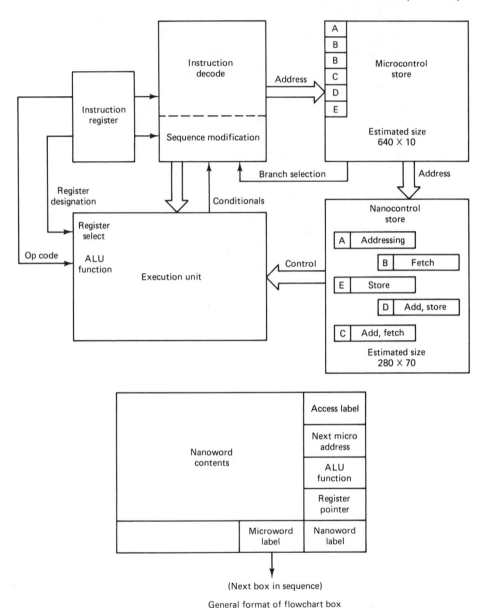

Figure 2.15 The overall organization of the host computer that is micro-/nanoprogrammed to implement the Motorola MC68000. Note that the microinstruction either specifies a branch or the address of a single horizontal nanoinstruction (acts like an EXECUTE). An engineering coding type is used. (Reprinted with permission from *SIGMICRO Newsletter*. © 1979 IEEE.)

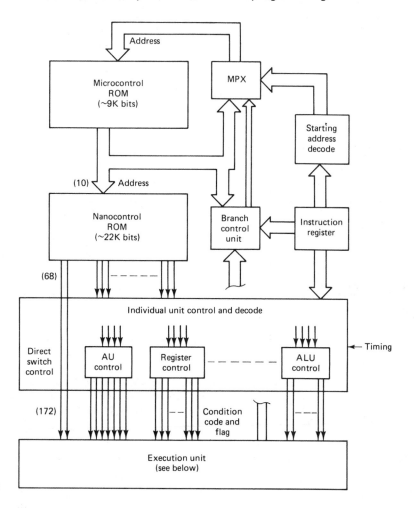

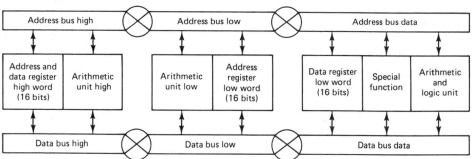

Figure 2.16   Further detail of the MC68000 host computer (also see Fig. 2.15). (Reprinted with permission from *SIGMICRO Newsletter*. © 1978 IEEE.)

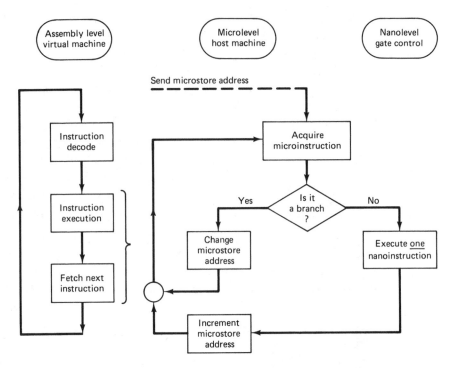

Figure 2.17   The idealized instruction cycle of the Motorola MC68000 computer and its host microengine. (From G. W. Gorsline, Computer Organization: Hardware/Software, Second Edition, © 1986, page 144. Reprinted by permission of Prentice-Hall, Inc., Englewood Cliffs, NJ.)

1. Necessity for a short design schedule.
2. Availability of a relatively small staff.
3. Regularity of control store (repeat of the same basic features), easing and shortening the chip design work while also allowing less complex timing constraints and signal interconnections on the chip.
4. Flexibility that microprogramming allowed relative to design error correction and possible future augmentation for "follow-on" chips such as the MC68020.
5. Practical possibility to allow simultaneous work by multiple teams on different portions of the complete processor design.

Thus, it was expected that a shortening of the "time to market" would ensue through the use of microprogramming as the implementation technique.

The second basic decision involved whether to separate the control storage onto other chips or to place it on the processor chip along with all the other necessary and desirable circuits. The DEC LSI 11 designers chose to use additional chips. The arguments seem to reduce to the question: Is there enough physical room ("real estate") on the silicon chip to allow the microcoding of the desired repertoire of in-

Control store size reduction with a two-level control store.

Assume:

n = number of individually-controlled switches in an execution unit (width of the horizontal control word)

k = total number of control states required to implement all instructions

ρ = proportion of unique control states to total number of control states

Single-level control store

In a simplified model of a single-level control store there are k microinstructions, each containing a control state (n bits) and a next microinstruction address ($[\log_2 k]$ bits).

Total size of single-level control store:

$$S_1 = k(n + [\log_2 k])$$

Two-level control store

A simplified model of a two-level control store has a micro control store of k microinstructions with a nanoaddress ($[\log_2 v]$ bits) and a next microinstruction address ($[\log_2 k]$ bits). The nanocontrol store has $v(= \rho k)$ nanoinstructions, each containing a control state (n bits).

Total size of two-level control store:

$$S_2 = k ([\log_2 v] + [\log_2 k]) + nv$$

where $v = \rho k$

Control store size comparison

Two-level store requires less control store bits than single control store when:

$$S_2 < S_1$$

from the previous:

$$k([\log_2 \rho k] + [\log_2 k]) + n\rho k < k(n + [\log_2 k])$$

Simplifying this gives:

$$[\log_2 k] + [\log_2 \rho] + n\rho < n$$

Solving for n and k gives the result that two-level store is smaller than single-level control store if

$$n > \frac{[\log_2 k] + [\log_2 \rho]}{1 - \rho}$$

or

$$k < \frac{1}{\rho} 2^{n(1-\rho)}$$

Example: The MC68000 microprocessor

$n \simeq 70$
$k \simeq 650$
$\rho \simeq 0.4$
$S_1 = k (n + [\log_2 k]) = 52400$
$S_2 = k ([\log_2 v] + [\log_2 k]) + nv = 30550$
$\frac{S_2}{S_1} = 0.58$
$\Delta S = S_1 - S_2 = 21850$ bits

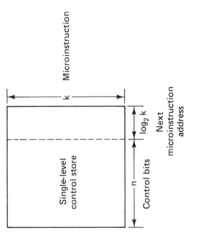

Figure 2.18 Rough comparison of control store sizes required for one-level versus two-level control stores. Speed of execution is completely ignored in this comparison. (Adapted with permission from *SIGMICRO Newsletter*, © 1978 IEEE.)

structions while maintaining a desirable execution rate? Note that this memory space versus execution speed trade-off is a common design choice in almost all, if not all, computer software. The answer to this basic question is intimately intertwined with the next question.

Should the microcode be of the vertical or of the horizontal type or of some combination? Vertical microcode is highly encoded and thus requires a significant amount of combinatorial logic to decode the microinstruction. Fully vertical microinstructions allow only one action per instruction and largely preclude performing two or more actions in one time cycle, usually resulting in more microcycles to accomplish each assembly-level instruction. At the same time, each microinstruction can be encoded into a relatively few bits and thus can be contained in a relatively narrow memory. Fully horizontal microcode necessitates a bit for every control gate (or its inverse). In the MC680XY, there are 172 control points that each require a bit and would have resulted in a horizontal microinstruction of 172 bits. In addition, certain instruction steps (really microinstructions) of one assembly-level instruction are needed in other assembly-level instructions. Fully horizontal microcode would necessitate that these microinstructions be repeated as needed. The designers arrived at two compromises:

1. A two-level control store that required only one copy of each nano-order, which could be used as needed to implement portions of several different assembly-level instructions.
2. Partial encoding of the horizontal nanoinstructions, thereby reducing the number of bits per control word to 68 while necessitating a minimal amount of combinatorial decode circuits.

In addition, not all combinations of these 68 bits are meaningful (if they were, a nanocode store of size $2^{68} \approx 256 \times 10^{18}$ would be needed). Only about 280 distinct bit patterns are actually necessary, allowing for a small control store whose addresses can be expressed in nine bits ($2^9 = 512$). Each nanoinstruction is actually used in about two and one-third assembly-level instructions, as an average. The use of a two-level control store with partial encoding of the nanoinstructions resulted in the need for a small enough control store memory to allow its placement on the single chip that also contains the processor.

The other aspect of using a two-level control store involves the necessity to fetch the top-level microinstruction, examine one bit to see if it is an address in nanomemory (if not, it is a branch address in micromemory), then fetch the low-level nanoinstruction, and finally execute it. Note that two sequential memory accesses are implied and consequently a relatively slow execution rate. A relatively slow execution rate would seriously limit the market for the product—not desirable for a profit-oriented situation. Can a way around this time bottleneck be found? Consider that with almost horizontal nanoprogramming, more than one action can be invoked and accomplished simultaneously if no interferences in the use of registers, memory, or data paths are involved. Thus, the MC680XY designers decided to fetch

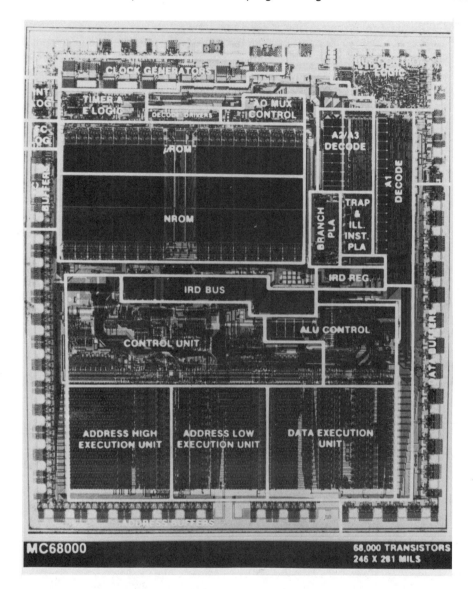

Figure 2.19 The MC68000 microprocessor chip, which contains more than 68,000 transistors, is 246 by 281 mils (6.24 by 7.14 mm) in size. This photo shows the location of the major functions of the chip. "Int. Log." stands for "Interrupt Logic"; "A0 Mux Control", for "Microcode A0 Multiplexer Control"; and "FC Log.", for "Function Code Logic." The labels "μROM" and "NROM" indicate two areas of microcode. "Trap and Ill. Inst. PLA" stands for "Trap and Illegal Instruction Programmable Logic Array"; "IRD Reg.", for "Instruction Register Decode Register"; and "ALU Control", for "Arithmetic and Logic Unit Control." The Data Execution Unit houses the main functions of the arithmetic and logic unit, while the two Address Execution Units perform the arithmetic associated with the calculation of an address. (Courtesy of Motorola, Inc.)

the next microinstruction at the same time (as a part of the nanoinstruction) as they were executing the present nanoinstruction. As a result, one of the control store accesses was effectively time-hidden. But this ideal cannot be fully realized in practice because of the existence of conditional branching. Recall that with a conditional branch, it is necessary to decide which of two instructions is to be fetched and used next, depending on the result of the condition tested. Therefore, time-hiding may not be fully realizable in this situation, even if the most common branch is prefetched during the nanoinstruction that evaluates the conditional test. At least some instances

Figure 2.20   The Motorola MC68020 microprocessor chip. A comparison of this microphotograph with Figure 2.19 emphasizes that the chip design itself is new, even though the architecture of the MC68020 is a proper superset of the MC68000. (Courtesty of Motorola, Inc.)

will occur in which the test necessitates the discard of the already fetched microinstruction and the subsequent fetch of the alternate. Although partial solutions to this design dilemma exist, the Motorola designers did not implement them. Even though we do not really know their reasoning, it could have been that the gains in time performance would not be expected to be great enough to justify the added design and implementation costs.

As a matter of possible interest, microphotographs annotated with function specifications are shown for the MC68000 in Figure 2.19 and for the MC68020 in Figure 2.20.

MC68020 ON-CHIP CACHE MEMORY

The MC68020 incorporates an on-chip cache memory as a means of improving the performance of the processor. The cache is implemented as a CPU instruction cache and is used to store the instruction stream prefetch accesses from the main memory.

Studies have shown that typical programs spend most of their execution time in a few main routines or tight loops. Therefore, once captured in the high-speed cache, these active code segments can execute directly from the cache. Thus, the processor does not suffer any external memory delays, and the total execution time of the program is significantly improved. The performance is also improved by allowing the MC68020 to make simultaneous accesses to instructions in the internal cache and to data in the external memory.

Another of the major benefits of using the cache is that the processor's external bus activity is greatly reduced. Thus, in a system with more than one bus master (such as a processor and DMA device) or a tightly coupled multiprocessor system, more of the bus bandwidth is available to the alternate bus masters without a major degradation in the performance of the MC68020.

The MC68020 on-chip instruction cache is a direct-mapped cache of 64 long-word entries. Each cache entry consists of a tag field made up of the upper 24 address bits and the FC2 value, one valid bit, and 32 bits (two words) of instruction data.

Figure 2.21 shows a block diagram of the on-chip cache. Whenever an instruction fetch occurs, the cache (if enabled) is first checked to determine if the word required is in the cache. This is achieved by first using the index field (A2–A7) of the access address as an index into the on-chip cache. This selects one of the 64 entries in the cache. Next, the access address bits A8–A31, and FC2 are compared to the tag of the selected entry. If there is a match and the valid bit is set, a cache hit occurs. Address bit A1 is used to select the proper word from the cache entry and the cycle ends. If there is no match, or if the valid bit is clear, a cache miss occurs and the instruction is fetched from external memory. This new instruction is automatically written into the cache entry and the valid bit is set, unless the freeze cache bit has been set in the cache control register. Since the processor always prefetches instructions externally with long-word, aligned bus cycles, both words of the entry will be updated, regardless of which word caused the miss.

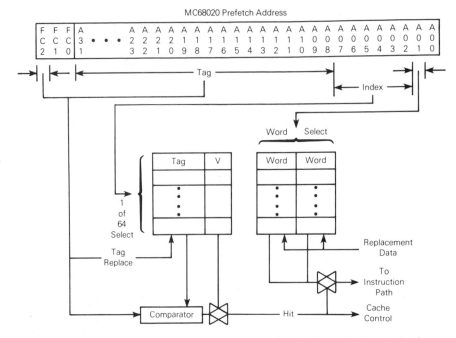

Figure 2.21 MC68020 On-Chip Cache Organization (Courtesy of Motorola, Inc.)

Data accesses are not cached, regardless of their associated address space.

The cache itself is accessible only by the internal MC68020 control unit. The user has no direct method of accessing (read/write) individual entries (tag, data, etc.). To manipulate the cache entries, however, the user does have a set of control functions available in the form of a cache control register.

Access to the cache control register (CACR) is provided by means of the move control register (MOVEC) instruction. The MOVEC instruction is a privileged instruction. The CACR is a 32-bit register, which is organized as shown in Figure 2.22. The unused bits (including bits [31:8], which are not shown) are always read as zeros. The cache control register bits are as follows:

E—Enable Cache: The cache enable function is necessary for system debugging and emulation. This bit allows the designer to operate the processor with the cache disabled. Clearing this bit will disable the cache (force continuous misses and suppress fills) and force the processor always to access external memory. The cache will remain disabled as long as this bit is cleared. The user must set this bit, which is automatically cleared whenever the processor is reset, to enable the cache.

F—Freeze Cache: The freeze bit keeps the cache enabled, but cache misses are not allowed to replace valid cache data. This bit can be used by emulators to freeze the cache during emulation function execution.

CE—Clear Entry: When the clear entry bit is set, the processor takes the ad-

C   = Clear Cache
CE   = Clear Entry
F   = Freeze Cache
E   = Enable Cache

Figure 2.22   Cache Control Register (Courtesy of Motorola, Inc.)

dress (index field, bits 2–7) in the cache address register (CAAR) and invalidates the associated entry (clears the valid bit) in the cache, regardless of whether or not it provides a hit—that is, whether the tag field in the cache address register matches the cache tag or not. This function will occur only when a write to the cache control register is performed with the CE bit set. This bit always reads as a zero, and the operation is independent of the state of the E or F bits or the external Cache Disable (CDIS) pin.

C—Clear Cache: The cache clear bit is used to invalidate all entries in the cache. This function is necessary for operating systems and other software which must clear old data from the cache whenever a context switch is required. The setting of the clear cache bit in the cache control register causes all valid bits in the cache to be cleared, thus invalidating all entries. This function occurs only when a write to the cache control register is performed with the C bit set. This bit always reads as a zero.

EXERCISES

2.1. Although the design of the MC680XY does not accommodate direct memory addressing, a few assemblers allow this syntax by transforming the direct address into an offset from the current value of the program counter (PC relative). Outline a scheme that would allow an assembler to accomplish this address transformation. Are there situations in which a transformation to PC relative would be inappropriate? What solution would you suggest?

2.2. In Chapter 3, locate the details of the conditional branch instruction (see Figure 3.3). Are any of the five flag bits of the condition code register (CCR) unused? Are any useful combinations of these flags not included within the Bcc instruction?

2.3. The concept of program relocation is one of the very important and basic concepts that every "computer person" must fully understand. Using drawings, demonstrate what relocation consists of.

2.4. For each of the 14 addressing modes available on your model of the MC680XY (20 modes for the MC68020), give an annotated hypothetical numerical address calculation example.

2.5. Answer Exercise 2.4 using the microprogramming concepts of Figure 2.14. If the answer is materially different, explain why; if the answer is (almost) identical, explain why.

2.6. Consider Exercise 2.5 in the light of the nanoprogramming concepts of Figure 2.17. Does this additional concept change your answer? Why?

3

Program Flow
of Control

It must be heavily emphasized and fully understood that the normal default program flow of control is sequential statement-to-statement execution. The inherent power of a computational system to solve an involved problem stems from the ability of certain instructions to choose alternative processing strategies—to cause a branch or not to cause a branch—depending on the current state of some specified flag, register, or memory location. In higher-level languages, such as Pascal or PL/I, this is commonly expressed as follows:

```
IF A > B
    THEN DO;
        -
        -/* Execute these statements if A > B */
        -
        END;
    ELSE DO;
        -
        -/* Execute these statements if A <= B */
        -
        END;
NEXT:
```

This is the program structure shown diagrammatically in Figure 3.1. In MC680XY assembly language, the code section above could be written as follows (assuming that variable A is contained in register D3 and B in register D5):

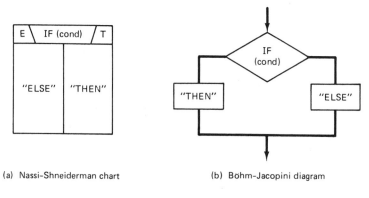

(a) Nassi-Shneiderman chart   (b) Böhm-Jacopini diagram

```
IF ⟨decision condition⟩
    THEN  begin 'true' action
            .
            .
            .
          end 'true' action;
    ELSE  begin 'false' action
            .
            .
            .
          end 'false' action;
       end if block;
```

Figure 3.1 ALTERNATION or IF-THEN-ELSE program flow-of-control structure. (From G. W. Gorsline, *16-Bit Modern Microcomputers: The Intel I8086 Family*, © 1985, p. 76. Reprinted by permission of Prentice-Hall, Inc., Englewood Cliffs, NJ.)

```
IF:       CMP.L    D3,D5
          BGE      ELSE
THEN:     -
          -        ;Execute these statements if [D3] > [D5]
          -
          BRA      NEXT
ELSE:     -
          -        ;Execute these statements if [D3] <= [D5]
          -
NEXT:     NOP
          -
          -
          -
```

UNCONDITIONAL BRANCHES

The formats of the MC680XY program unconditional flow-of-control instructions are given in Figure 3.2. These instructions correspond to the higher-level language construct.

Branch Always (offset from end of operation word = PC + 2)

BRA < label >   Condition = 0

15	14	13	12	11	10	9	8	7	6	5	4	3	2	1	0
0	1	1	0	0	0	0	0	8-bit Displacement								

16-bit displacement if 8-bit = 0

32-bit displacement (MC 68020 only)

Branch target effective address calculation:

    EA − PC + 2 + signed offset

Jump (indirect through address register or program counter; direct absolute)

JMP < EA >   Effective Address

15	14	13	12	11	10	9	8	7	6	5	4	3	2	1	0
0	1	0	0	1	1	1	0	1	1	mode			register			

16-(or 32-bit with MC 68020) Displacement or Absolute Address

32-bit Displacement for MC 68020 Memory Indirect only

Jump target effective address calculation:

    EA − any addressing mode allowed with processor model

Stop until Interrupt (16-bit = word immediate)

STOP value

15	14	13	12	11	10	9	8	7	6	5	4	3	2	1	0
0	1	0	0	1	1	1	0	0	1	1	1	0	0	1	0

16-bit immediate value for new SR

Action:
1. MOVE 16-bit immediate value to status register (SR)
2. Increment PC by 2 (as normal)
3. Halt until interrupt, trace, or reset
Privileged instruction (S bit = bit 13 of SR = 1; normally
reserved for use by operating system.

Figure 3.2 The Motorola MC680XY family has two unconditional branch instructions. The BRA instruction is really the B$_{cc}$ (branch on condition) instruction with a condition code of zero. The branch target is an offset in bytes from the end of the operation word (PC + 2). Although the JMP instruction allows an absolute address target, its main use is with targets whose address is derived indirectly; that is, they are register indirect with modifiers (and with the MC68020 are these and memory indirect from a register indirect).

GO TO THERE

Modern theories of programming strongly suggest that GO TO be avoided when programming in a higher-level language. The same prohibition is fully justified when coding in assembly language, although it is often impossible fully to avoid the assembly language unconditional jump. An example of the legitimate use of the unconditional branch is shown above in the assembly language version of the IF-THEN-ELSE construct. The use of the unconditional jump instruction is justified only in implementing the assembly language equivalents of the higher-level language structured programming constructs.

CONDITIONAL BRANCH INSTRUCTIONS

Conditional jump or branch instructions are of the *conditional offset* from the program counter (PC) type. Thus, they are only able to cause a jump to an instruction at a distance of +129 through −126 bytes for a byte-sized offset; +32769 through −32766 bytes for a word-sized offset; or +2 GB through −2 GB for a long-word-sized offset. In general, these instructions examine the setting of one or more bits in the CCR portion of the status register (SR) and either branch or not, accordingly. As an example, we give the following two branch on less than (BLT) instructions:

```
BLT    *+7        ;jump forward seven statements
BLT;   THERE      ;jump to label THERE
```

These examples will cause a branch iff (if and only if) the preceding arithmetic, compare, test, or move instruction has generated a condition code register (CCR) bit setting that allowed

$$N * \bar{V} + \bar{N} * V \longrightarrow 1$$

If the result of this logic is 0, the next sequential instruction will be executed; that is, a branch will not be taken. The action of these conditional branches is:

```
IF <condition true>
    THEN PC ← PC + signed displacement
    ELSE  PC ← PC + instruction SIZE (execute next instruction)
```

In the first example above, the amount (the distance) of the branch is expressed in terms of assembly language statements. We emphasize that the branch is to the seventh statement following the branch, not seven bytes. In the second example above, the branch is to a statement with the label THERE. This label must be within 129 bytes following the branch or 126 bytes preceding the branch if the displacement (offset) is a byte; within 32769 following the branch or 32766 preceding the branch; or, only with the MC68020, anywhere in the 4 GB memory. Note that the offset is +129 thru −126 bytes, as the program counter (PC) has already been incremented by 2 so as to point to the end of the operation word. The assembler calculates the offset during the assembly process. The bit format of the conditional branch instructions and a list of them are given in Figure 3.3.

The flag bits or certain specific flag bits are affected by the following groups of instructions:

Arithmetic instructions
Logic instructions
Compare/test instructions
Move instructions

Conditional Branch

Bcc < label > (where cc is one of the conditions below)

15 14 13 12	11 10 9 8	7 6 5 4 3 2 1 0
0 1 1 0	Condition	8-bit displacement
	16-bit displacement if 8-bit = 0	
	32-bit displacement (MC 68020 only)	

Branch target effective address ← (PC) + 2 + signed offset — exactly
the same as for BRA (which is Bcc with condition = 0000)

The CCR (condition code register) portion of the SR (status
register) is not affected.

Opcode	Meaning	Condition bits	CCR bit logic
Unsigned Arith./Logic/Move/Compare/Test			
BEQ	Equal	0 1 1 1	Z
BNE	Not Equal	0 1 1 0	$\overline{Z}$
BHI	High	0 0 1 0	$\overline{C} * \overline{Z}$
BLS	Low or Same	0 0 1 1	$C * Z$
BCC	No Carry	0 1 0 0	$\overline{C}$
BCS	Carry	0 1 0 1	C
Signed Arith./Logic/Move/Compare/Test			
BPL	Plus (Positive)	1 0 1 0	$\overline{N}$
BMI	Minus (Negative)	1 0 1 1	N
BEQ	Equal	0 1 1 1	Z
BNE	Not Equal	0 1 1 0	$\overline{Z}$
BGT	Greater Than	1 1 1 0	$(N * V * \overline{Z}) + (\overline{N} * \overline{V} * \overline{Z})$
BGE	Greater Than or Equal	1 1 0 0	$(N * V) + (\overline{N} * \overline{V})$
BLE	Less Than or Equal	1 1 1 1	$Z + (N * \overline{V}) + (\overline{N} * V)$
BLT	Less Than	1 1 0 1	$(N * \overline{V}) + (\overline{N} * V)$
BVC	No Overflow	1 0 0 0	$\overline{V}$
BVS	Overflow	1 0 0 1	V

Figure 3.3 The Motorola MC680XY conditional branch instruction is of the type
that branches direct to a label; however, note that the translation to machine code is
of the displacement from the program counter (PC) type.

Rotate/shift instructions
Load CCR or SR
Return from servicing an interrupt

Thus, results of instructions in these groups that precede a conditional jump instruction may result in a branch or may not result in a branch, depending on the result formed. The BRA, JMP, and Bcc instructions do not affect the bit settings in the
CCR.

COMPARISON INSTRUCTIONS

At this time we will examine the compare/test group of instructions because of their intimate relationship to the conditional branch instructions. The compare group of instructions causes the second operand to be subtracted from the first operand, with all appropriate flags being set and the result of the subtraction being discarded so that no memory locations or registers are affected (only the appropriate flags are affected). The test group of instructions causes the two operands to be combined using the logical AND operation, with the result being discarded (again, only the appropriate flags are affected). In effect, the comparison is to zero. Note in Figure 3.4 (1) that both instruction groups are available using byte, word, or long-word operands; and (2) that the register-to-register, memory-to-register, memory-to-memory, immediate-to-register, and immediate-to-memory versions are available with all memory addressing modes. Also note that the memory-to-memory compare using the address register indirect with postincrement addressing mode would allow loop construction to accomplish a form of a pseudoinstruction that might be termed SEARCH or FIND.

It is sometimes programmatically necessary to alter program flow of control depending on the setting of an individual bit in some datum. This type of decision is not uncommon within routines designed and implemented to accomplish input/output at the lowest physical level—the so-called device-driver routines. Although this testing of an individual bit could be accomplished by using the ANDI (and immediate) instruction, it is cleaner code to test the individual bit itself.

```
;    IF bit 3 of byte TEST_IT is 'ON'
;         THEN branch to THERE
;         ELSE continue sequentially
;
     LEA        TEST_IT,A1
     ANDI.B     #00001000b,(A1)        ;destroys contents of TEST-IT
     BNE        THERE
```

Note that the above code has the resulting side effect of destroying the contents of TEST-IT. The four bit-test instructions given in Figure 3.5 avoid this problem and, in addition, allow the postinstruction state of the tested bit to be controlled. Also note that the format that has the bit number to be tested (given as an immediate) implies that the programmer knows beforehand which bit is always involved. This is the usual and normal situation—called *static* by the Motorola designers. The above example could be programmed as follows without affecting the contents of TEST-IT:

```
;    IF bit 3 of byte TEST-IT is 'ON'
;         THEN branch to THERE
```

```
;          ELSE continue sequentially
;

           LEA     TEST_IT,A1
           BTST    #3,(A1)        ;contents of TEST-IT not changed
           BNE     THERE

           —       —
```

Test for positive, zero, negative

TST

00 — byte
01 — word
10 — long   mode   register

15	14	13	12	11	10	9	8	7	6	5	4	3	2	1	0
0	1	0	0	1	0	1	0	Size		Effective Address					

Value at EA not changed
CCR of Status Register
  bit 2 = Z = 0 if (EA) $\neq$ 0
            1 if (EA) = 0
  bit 3 = N = 0 if (EA) is positive
            1 if (EA) is negative

Compare Rn − (EA) → Discard after setting CCR bits

000 — byte ⎫
001 — word ⎬ data register
010 — long ⎭
011 — word ⎫ address register
111 — long ⎭

CMP < EA >, Dn
CMPA < EA>, An

mode   register

15	14	13	12	11	10	9	8	7	6	5	4	3	2	1	0
1	0	1	1	Register			Op-Mode			Effective Address					

Compare Immediate Value − (EA) → Discard after setting CCR bits

00 — byte
01 — word
10 — long   mode   register

CMPI I, < EA >

15	14	13	12	11	10	9	8	7	6	5	4	3	2	1	0
0	0	0	0	1	1	0	0	Size		Effective Address					

8-bit or 16-bit immediate value					

extension for 32-bit immediate value

Compare Memory to Memory (address register indirect post-increment only)
(A_{dest}) − (A_{source}) → Discard after setting CCR bits; Increment both Registers

00 — byte
01 — word
10 — long   Source

CMPM (An)+, (Am)+   Destination

15	14	13	12	11	10	9	8	7	6	5	4	3	2	1	0
1	0	1	1	Register			1	Size		0	0	1	Register		

Figure 3.4 The Motorola MC680XY compare instructions. The compare instruction acts as a "subtract," with the results discarded after the appropriate bits in the condition code register are set. The test against zero value affects only the Z (zero) bit and the N (negative/positive) bit of the CCR.

Bit Test (register — any of 32; memory — any of 8)

BTST $\begin{cases} \text{bit \#, EA} & \text{; bit number immediate = static in program} \\ \text{Dn, EA} & \text{; bit number in register = calculated in program} \end{cases}$

Action: IF bit = 0, Z bit of CCR = 1
              ELSE Z bit of CCR = 0

Bit Test and Clear (register — any of 32; memory — any of 8)

BCLR $\begin{cases} \text{bit \#, EA} & \text{; static as above} \\ \text{Dn, EA} & \text{; dynamic as above} \end{cases}$

Action: 1. set Z bit of CCR as above
             2. clear specified bit = 0

Bit Test and Set (register — any of 32; memory — any of 8)

BSET $\begin{cases} \text{bit \#, EA} & \text{; static as above} \\ \text{Dn, EA} & \text{; dynamic as above} \end{cases}$

Action: 1. set Z bit of CCR as above
             2. set specified bit = 1

Bit Test and Change (register — any of 32; memory — any of 8)

BCHG $\begin{cases} \text{bit \#, EA} & \text{; static as above} \\ \text{Dn, EA} & \text{; dynamic as above} \end{cases}$

Action: 1. set Z bit of CCR as above
             2. change specified bit (0 → 1 or 1 → 0)

Static Bit Instruction Format

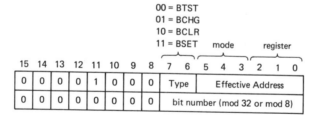

Dynamic Bit Instruction Format

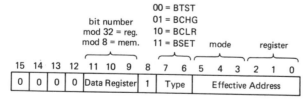

Figure 3.5 The four bit-test instructions set the Z (zero) bit in the CCR (condition code register). The variations include specifying the bit position as an immediate or as the contents of a data register as well as clearing, setting, changing, or doing nothing to the bit.

It is appropriate to direct your attention to the other bit-test instructions that allow the postinstruction control of the state of the tested bit (see Figure 3.5).

While attempting to solve certain logical situations that sometimes arise, it may be desirable to set the value of a byte variable to all zero bits or to all one bits, depending on the result of a just accomplished arithmetic, logic, move, compare, or test instruction. In other words, it often may be desirable to save the current logical result state of the condition code register (CCR) as tested by some condition. Although the CCR itself could be saved via the MOVE SR,EA instruction for later

Set Byte Conditionally (test CCR bit and set byte)

S$_{CC}$ label (where cc is one of the conditions below)

Action: IF < condition true >
      THEN set byte = 11111111b = FFh = −128 d
      ELSE set byte = 00000000b = 00h = 0 d

Opcode	Meaning	Condition Bits	CCR bit logic

Unconditional Action

Opcode	Meaning					CCR bit logic
ST	Set Always	0	0	0	0	—
SF	Clear Always	0	0	0	1	—

Unsigned Arith./Logic/Move/Compare/Test

Opcode	Meaning					CCR bit logic
SEQ	Equal	0	1	1	1	Z
SNE	Not Equal	0	1	1	0	$\overline{Z}$
SHI	High	0	0	1	0	$\overline{C} * \overline{Z}$
SLS	Low or Same	0	0	1	1	$C * Z$
SCC	No Carry	0	1	0	0	$\overline{C}$
SCS	Carry	0	1	0	1	C

Signed Arith./Logic/Move/Compare/Test

Opcode	Meaning					CCR bit logic
SPL	Plus (Positive)	1	0	1	0	$\overline{N}$
SMI	Minus (Negative)	1	0	1	1	N
SEQ	Equal	0	1	1	1	Z
SNE	Not Equal	0	1	1	0	$\overline{Z}$
SGT	Greater Than	1	1	1	0	$N * V * \overline{Z} + \overline{N} * \overline{V} * \overline{Z}$
SGE	Greater Than or Equal	1	1	0	0	$N * V + \overline{N} * \overline{V}$
SLE	Less Than or Equal	1	1	1	1	$Z + N * \overline{V} + \overline{N} * V$
SLT	Less Than	1	1	0	1	$N * \overline{V} + \overline{N} * V$
SVC	No Overflow	1	0	0	0	$\overline{V}$
SVS	Overflow	1	0	0	1	V

Figure 3.6 The set byte conditionally instruction allows the result of a prior compare, test, move, arithmetic, or logic instruction setting of a bit in the CCR (condition code register) to be saved for future program flow-of-control decisions.

restoration, using MOVE EA,SR with subsequent testing, for design reasons it is often desirable to test the CCR at this point in the problem solution and to save the result of this test for later use in the program logic. Note that this result condition could be extended to a word or to a long word through the use of the EXT.W or EXT.L (extend) instructions, which will be discussed in Chapter 4. As Figure 3.6 illustrates, the action of the set byte conditional (Scc) instruction is:

```
;    IF  <condition true>  THEN set byte to all one bits
;                          ELSE set byte to all zero bits
```

As shown, all 16 possible conditions are allowed, including always/never and prior unsigned data manipulation/signed data manipulation.

PROGRAM FLOW-OF-CONTROL STRUCTURES

In higher-level procedural-type languages, the three modern decision structures that allow program flow-of-control change are IF-THEN, IF-THEN-ELSE, and CASE. In an attempt to assist understanding, we will illustrate these control structures in MC680XY assembly language. In these examples, the procedural-level form will be given first, followed by the assembly-level form. In all cases involving numerical variables, we are assuming integer 32-bit data container declarations.

```
IF A >= B
     THEN DO;/* A >= B */
          -
          -
          END;
          -/* A < B */
          -
          -
          -

IF:            CMP.L     D2,D4
               BLT NEXT
THEN:          -            ;[D4] => [D2]
               -            ;
               -            ;
NEXT:          -            ;[D4] < [D2]
               -
               -
```

Note that the statements included in the THEN group (the true branch) are executed only if the condition is true. The IF-THEN construct might be characterized as a "do or skip" construct.

The IF-THEN-ELSE construct, illustrated in Figure 3.1, is a true alternation construct in that either the THEN group of statements or the ELSE group of statements is executed, with the other group being skipped.

```
IF A < B
    THEN DO;
        -                           /* A < B */
        -
        END;
    ELSE DO;
        -                           /* A >= B */
        -
        END;
    -                               /* collector node */
    -
    -
```

```
IF:                CMP.L  D3, D5
                   BGE    ELSE
THEN:              -                      ;[D5] < [D3]
                   -
                   BRA    NEXT
ELSE:              -                      ;[D5] >= [D3]
                   -
NEXT:              -                      ;collector node
                   -
                   -
```

The CASE construct is a generalization of the alternation scheme that allows a branch to one of N unique paths in the flow of control with a single collector node. Our example (see Figure 3.7) illustrates a CASE construct with three specified branches and an "otherwise" to encompass all conditions not specified.

```
    -
    -
CASE_OF_A;
        CASE A = 7 DO;
            -
            -
        END;
        CASE A = -2 DO;
            -
            -
        END;
```

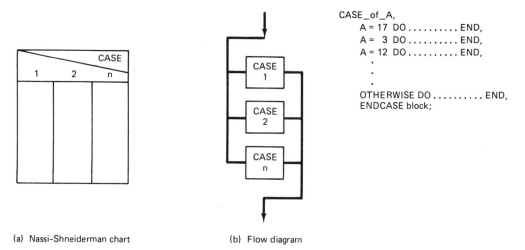

```
                                                    CASE_of_A,
                                                       A = 17  DO . . . . . . . . . END,
                                                       A =  3  DO . . . . . . . . . END,
                                                       A = 12  DO . . . . . . . . . END,
                                                       .
                                                       .
                                                       .
                                                    OTHERWISE DO . . . . . . . . . END,
                                                    ENDCASE block;
```

(a) Nassi–Shneiderman chart   (b) Flow diagram

Figure 3.7 CASE or multiway branch program flow-of-control structure. (From G. W. Gorsline, *16-Bit Modern Microcomputers: The Intel I8086 Family,* © 1985, p. 82. Reprinted by permission of Prentice-Hall, Inc., Englewood Cliffs, NJ.)

```
            CASE A = 1 DO;
               -
               -
            END;
         OTHERWISE DO;
               -
               -
            END;
         END_CASE;
            -
            -
      CASE_OF_A:
      ;
                        LEA           A,A1
                        MOVE.L        (A1),D6
      CASE_7:           CMPI.L        #7,D6
                        BNE           CASE_N2
                          -                            ;[D6] = 7
                          -
                        BRA           END_CASE_A
      CASE_N2:          CMPI.L        #−2,D6
                        BNE           CASE_1          ;[D6] = −2
                          -
                          -
                        BRA           END_CASE_A
```

```
CASE_1:              CMPI.L        #1,D6
                     BNE           OTHERWISE
                     -                                        ;[D6] = 1
                     -
                     BRA           END_CASE_A
OTHERWISE:           -             ;[D6] ≠ 7 ≠ −2 ≠ 1
                     -
                     -
END_CASE_A:          NOP           ;collector node
```

Looping

These same conditional branch instructions may be employed to implement program loops in order to accommodate iterative operations. We will illustrate possible approaches to seven modern and common loop constructs.

The first three illustrations of loop constructs are commonly known as DO COUNT. Because of the wide historical use of this loop construct in FORTRAN, we will follow the IBM practice of placing the test for termination at the loop end (thus, the loop is always executed at least once) and provide for the possible use of the loop counter index within the loop (thus, we employ the DO register for the counter index).

```
                -
                -
          DO I = 1 to 9 step 1;        /* loop 1 */
                -
                -
                END;
          -
          -            -
                       -
                     MOVE.B       #1,DO
LOOP1:               -
                     -
                     ADDQ.B       #1,DO
                     CMPI.B       #9,DO
                     BLE          LOOP1
                     -
                     -
          -
          -
          DO I = 1 to 9 step 2;        /* loop 2 */
                -
                -
          END;
```

```
                                  -
                                  -
                          -
                          -
                   MOVE.B          #1,DO
LOOP2:                    -          -

                   -                -
                   ADDQ.B          #2,DO
                   CMPI.B          #9,DO
                   BLE             LOOP2
                                   -

                          -        -
                   -
                   -
         DO I = 19 to −17 step −1;   /* loop 3 */
                   -
                   -
         END
                   -
                   -                      -
                                          -
                   MOVE.B          #19,DO
LOOP3:                    -

                   -                -
                   SUBQ.B          #1,DO
                   CMPI.B          #−17,DO
                   BGE             LOOP3
                                   -
                                   -
```

The DO_WHILE (Figure 3.8) and DO_UNTIL (Figure 3.9) constructs continue to loop until a specified condition is satisfied. The DO_UNTIL version tests the condition at the foot of the loop and thus requires that the loop body be executed at least once. The DO_WHILE version tests at the beginning of the loop and thus does not require any execution of the loop body.

```
                   -
                   -
         DO_UNTIL I <= J;                /* loop 4 */
                   -
                   -
         END;
                   -
                   -
```

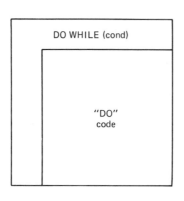

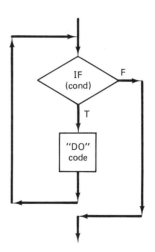

(a) Nassi-Shneiderman chart   (b) Bohm-Jacopini diagram

DO_WHILE ⟨decision condition⟩
        .
        .
        .   /* perform while condition true */
        .
        .
    END DO;   /* terminate through foot when false */

Figure 3.8 DO_WHILE looping or repeat program flow-of-control structure. (From G. W. Gorsline, *16-Bit Modern Microcomputers: The Intel I8086 Family,* © 1985, p. 86. Reprinted by permission of Prentice-Hall, Inc., Englewood Cliffs, NJ.)

```
                        -
                        -
            LEA         I,A1
            LEA         J,A2
            MOVE.L      (A1),DO
LOOP4:                  -
                        -
            CMP.L       (A2),DO
            BGT         LOOP4
                        -
                        -
    DO_WHILE I > J              /* loop 5 */
            -
            -
        END;
        -
        -                  -
                           -
```

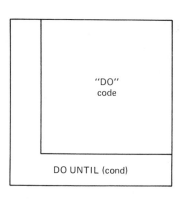

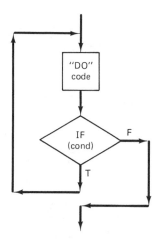

(a) Nassi-Shneiderman chart   (b) Bohm-Jacopini diagram

```
DO_UNTIL ⟨decision condition⟩
        •
        •
        •           /* perform until condition true;
        •              that is, while condition false */
        •
        •
     END DO;
        •
        •           /* terminate through foot when true */
        •
        •
```

Figure 3.9 DO_UNTIL looping or repeat program flow-of-control structure. (From G. W. Gorsline, *16-Bit Modern Microcomputers: The Intel I8086 Family,* © 1985, p. 87. Reprinted by permission of Prentice-Hall, Inc., Englewood Cliffs, NJ.)

```
                LEA        I,A1
                LEA        J,A2
                MOVE.L     (A1),DO
LOOP5:          CMP.L      (A2),DO
                BLE        LOOP_END
                 -
                 -
                BRA   LOOP5
LOOP_END:        -
                 -
```

Some procedural-level languages allow the DO_WHILE and DO_UNTIL to be combined.

```
         -
         -
DO_WHILE I > J UNTIL N >= 17;/* loop 6 */
            -
            -
         END;
      -
      -

            -
            -
         LEA          I,A1
         LEA          J,A2
         MOVE.L       (A1),D0
LOOP6:   CMP.L        (A2),D0
         BLE          LOOP_END
         -            -

         -            -
         CMP.L        #17,N
         BLT          LOOP6
LOOP_END:  -          -
```

A few modern procedural-level languages allow the exit of a loop from a place in the loop body other than the foot. The general form of this construct is known as the LEAVE statement. We will illustrate this construct using the DO_FOREVER form of the DO_WHILE.

```
            -
            -
DO_WHILE-TRUE.;        /* loop 7 - LEAVE */
         -
         -
         IF X < 1 LEAVE;
         -
         -
         END;
         -
         -

         -
         LEA      X,A1
LOOP7:   -        -

         -        -
         CMPI.L   #1,(A1)
         BGE      END_LOOP
         -        -
         -        -
```

```
                    BRA        LOOP7
        END_LOOP:
                     -

                     -
```

SPECIALIZED LOOP CONTROL INSTRUCTIONS

As illustrated in Figure 3.10, the MC680XY provides one loop control instruction that employs a register as the primary counter control. It must be emphasized that this loop control instruction was designed to implement the DO_COUNT loop and is almost useless in implementing the DO_UNTIL, the DO_WHILE, and the LEAVE constructs. Even in implementing the DO_COUNT loop, the assumption is made that the index will be stepped by a negative one. It must be concluded that the special loop control instruction of the MC680XY is of minimal utility in implementing the common loops of modern "structured" procedural languages.

The loop illustrated earlier as LOOP1 can be implemented as follows:

```
                -

                -
        DO I = to    step       /* loop 8 */

                -

                -
           END;

                -

                -

                -

                -
           MOVE    .W  #9,D0
   LOOP8:      -

                -
           DBF     LOOP8

                -

                -
```

The fact that the step must be minus one is an important limitation of the implementation of this instruction.

Although the DBcc instruction is not designed to accommodate the normal procedural-level language loop constructs, it does find utility in implementing specialized systems control routines. For example, it is often desired to move the contents of a character string from one place in memory to another place in memory, with the assumptions that the stream is at least one byte and not more than 133 bytes in length with a termination character of 0D hex (carriage return). A pseudolanguage version might be represented as follows, with two possible assembly language implementations.

Decrement and Branch or Condition or Count

Terminate loop on condition true *or* on decremented data register negative
Branch on condition not true and decrement register *or* branch not negative register
This is equivalent to:
IF < condition = true (CCR) >
  THEN continue with next sequential instruction
  ELSE decrement control register
    IF < control register = −1 >
      THEN continue with next sequential instruction
      ELSE branch to label
    END_IF
END_IF

DB$_{CC}$ Dn, label

word date register

15	14	13	12	11	10	9	8	7	6	5	4	3	2	1	0
0	1	0	1	Condition				1	1	0	0	1	Register		

16-bit Displacement

32-bit Displacement (MC 68020 only)

Branch Target Effective Address ← (PC) + 2 + signal offset
CCR not effected

Opcode	Meaning	Condition bits	CCP bit logic
Ignore CCP bits			
DBT	Do Not Branch	0 0 0 0	—
DBF DBRA }	Branch On Count	0 0 0 1	—
Unsigned Arith./Logic/Move/Compare/Test			
DBEQ	Equal	0 1 1 1	Z
DBNE	Not Equal	0 1 1 0	$\overline{Z}$
DBHI	High	0 0 1 0	$\overline{C} * \overline{Z}$
DBLS	Low or Same	0 0 1 1	C * Z
DBCC	No Carry	0 1 0 0	$\overline{C}$
DECS	Carry	0 1 0 1	C
Signed Arith./Logic/Move/Compare/Test			
DBPL	Plus (Positive)	1 0 1 0	$\overline{N}$
DBMI	Minus (Negative)	1 0 1 1	N
DBEQ	Equal	0 1 1 1	Z
DBNE	Not Equal	0 1 1 0	$\overline{Z}$
DBGT	Greater Than	1 1 1 0	$(N * V * \overline{Z}) + (\overline{N} * \overline{V} * \overline{Z})$
DBGE	Greater Than or Equal	1 1 0 0	$(N * V) + (\overline{N} * \overline{V})$
DBLE	Less Than or Equal	1 1 1 1	$Z + (N * \overline{V}) + (\overline{N} * V)$
DBLT	Less Than	1 1 0 1	$(N * \overline{V}) + (\overline{N} * V)$
DBVC	No Overflow	1 0 0 0	$\overline{V}$
DBVS	Overflow	1 0 0 1	V

Figure 3.10 The Motorola MC680XY specialized loop control instruction.

```
        DO I = 1 TO 133;/* loop 9 */
            CHAR = PLACE(I);
            IF CHAR = 0DH /* 29 base 10 */
                THEN LEAVE;
            BUFFER(I) = CHAR;
            END;
            -
            -

            -
            -
```

```
                  MOVE.W        #135,D0
                  LEA           PLACE,A0
                  LEA           BUFFER,A1
LOOP9A:           CMPI.B        #$0D,(A0)
                  BEQ           THATS_ALL
                  TST.W         D0
                  BEQ           THATS_ALL
                  MOVE.B        (A0)+,(A1)+
                  SUBQ.L        #1,D0
                  BRA           LOOP9A
THATS_ALL:        -             -
                  -             -
                  MOVE.W        #132,D0      ;Length −1 as DBcc test is −1
                  LEA           PLACE,A0
                  LEA           BUFFER,A1
LOOP9B:           CMPI.B        #$0D,(A0)
                  DBEQ          D0,THATS_ALL
                  MOVE.B        (A0)+,(A1)+
                  BRA           LOOP9B
THATS_ALL:        -             -
```

In processing strings of character data, a common need is to search for a character, to search for a group of characters, to determine that two strings are different, or to determine the position or address of a character. Our examples will employ a hypothetical higher-level language whose syntax and corresponding semantics are, it is hoped, self-explanatory. The strength of this code is two-fold: (1) the ability to determine if the loop was terminated because the ASCII period was found or because the search was unsuccessful; and (2) the avoidance of a special test to determine if the string was of length zero.

```
    FIND FIRST'.' IN STRG (LENGTH);          /* Find position of period */
```

```
              LEA      STR_LNGTH,A0    ;Address of String Length
              MOVE.W   (A0),D0
              LEA      STRING,A0       ;Address of String Start
              BRA      TEST
LOOP:         CMPI.B   #$2E,(A0)+      ;ASCII period
TEST:         DBEQ     D0, LOOP        ;fall-through means found or not in string
              CMPI.W   #-1,D0          ;was entire string searched without success?
              BNE      FOUND
NOT_FND:      -        -              ;A0 contains string-end address plus 1
              -        -              ;D0 contains -1
              BRA      NEXT
FOUND:        MOVE.W   STR_LNGTH,D1    ;A0 contains address plus one of period
              SUB.W    D0,D1           ;D0 contains number of characters to right of
                                       ;period
              -        -              ;D1 contains position of period
NEXT:         -        -
```

The code above obviously requires some explanation. The CMPI.B instruction (compare a byte of a string to an immediate) requires an extensive setup:

1. The address of the first byte of the string must be placed in an address register. The MOVEA.L (load effective address) instruction accomplishes this task.

2. The postincrement addressing mode specifies that the compare will continue employing the succeeding character as long as the compare is not equal. It forms a one-instruction loop.

3. The number of characters to be searched (the length of the string) minus one before declaring failure must be placed in a word data register.

The two-instruction loop at label LOOP compares the ASCII period with each character of the string, in turn, via the postincrement register indirect addressing mode. After each comparison, if equality is found (an ASCII period is encountered), the loop is terminated. If this is not true, the counter register (D0) is decremented and the loop is repeated. If an ASCII period is not found, the loop finally ends with register D0 having a value of −1. A test for this condition indicates whether the ASCII period was present (GO TO FOUND) or not (continue at NOT-FND). The position of the ASCII period is then calculated by subtracting the counter register contents (D0) from the length. Because the CMPI instruction allows word and long-word operands, this code is easily alterable to search for a numeric value in an array. As a second string example, consider the following

COMPARE STRNG_1 TO STRNG_2 (LENGTH, POSITION)   /*find position of non-match*/

```
              MOVE.W   LENGTH,D0
              SUBQ.W   #1,D0           ;DBcc tests for minus count
```

```
            LEA       STRNG_1,A1      ;setup address indirect
            LEA       STRNG_2,A2      ;setup address indirect
LOOP;       CMPM.B    (A1)+,(A2)+
            DBEQ      D0,LOOP         ;GO TO LOOP means same ;fall thru means
                                     ;not.
            CMPI.W    #-1,D0          ;Were entire strings a perfect match?
            BNE       DIFFER
SAME:       -         -               ;A1 and A2 contain string end addresses plus
            -         -               ;  one; D0 contains -1
            -         -
            BRA       NEXT
DIFFER:     MOVE.W    LENGTH,D1       ;A1 and A2 contain nonmatch addresses plus
                                     ;one
            SUB.W     D0,D1           ;D0 contains number of characters after
            -         -               ;  nonmatch; D1 contains position of
                                     ;nonmatch
            -         -
            -         -
NEXT:       -         -
```

Note the extremely close resemblance of this code to the code just preceding, which searched for a specific character within a string. Again, because the CMPM instruction allows word and long-word operands, this code is easily alterable to compare two numeric arrays for equality. Finally, consider the third example:

```
FIND STRNG_1 (LENGTH) EMBEDDED IN STRNG_2 (LENGTH,POSITION)
            LEA       LNG_1,A1
            LEA       LNG_2,A2
            MOVE.W    (A1),D1
            MOVE.W    (A2),D2
            LEA       STRNG_1,A1
            LEA       STRNG_2,A2
;
;   Find first character of string 1 within string 2
;
            SUBQ.W    #1,D2
            MOVE.B    STRNG_1,D0
TRY_FRST:   CMP.B     D0,(A2)+
            DBEQ      D2,TRY_FRST
            CMPI.W    #-1,D2
            BEQ       NOT_FND
FND_FRST:   CMP.W     D1,D2
            BGT       NOT_FND         ;not enough space for it is left
```

```
TRY_REST:  MOVE.W    D1,D3
           MOVEA.L   A1,A3
           MOVEA.L   A2,A4
TRY_INNR:  CMPM.B    (A3)+,(A4)+
           DBEQ      D3,TRY_INNR
           CMPI.W    #1,D3
           BEQ       FOUND
TRY_AGN:   BRA       TRY_FRST
NT_FND:      -          -
             -          -
             -          -
           BRA       NEXT
FOUND:     LEA       STRNG_2,A0
           SUBA.L    A2,A0          ;position of start of string 1 in string 2
             -          -
             -          -
             -          -
NEXT         -          -
```

The above algorithm illustrates first courses across the second string, searching for
an occurrence of the lead character of the first string that has been placed in register
D0. If this initial search is not successful in finding the first character, the entire algorithm is abandoned. If the first character is found, a check is made for sufficient
room for the first string to fit into the remainder of the second string. If there is insufficient space, the entire algorithm is abandoned. If space exists, the two strings
are compared. If there is no match, the entire search algorithm is restarted from this
position in the second string. If there is a match, the position of the start of string 1
within string 2 is calculated and placed in address register A0.

SUBPROCEDURES

Almost all computer languages allow a procedure to invoke and use a physically
separate block of code with eventual resumption of program flow just beyond the invocation point. Figure 3.11 illustrates the concept while emphasizing that a subprocedure can be invoked more than once from different calling procedures or from the
same one. Recall from Chapter 1 that there are three common methods of saving the
return address to allow resumption of processing just beyond the invocation point.
The most generalized of these employs a stack with the contents of the program
counter being PUSHed during the CALL and POPped back to the program counter
during the RETurn. The bottom of Figure 1.14 illustrates this concept, which is used
by the MC680XY in common with almost all microcomputers (the TI 99/X family
of micro- and minicomputers uses a variation of the method shown in Figure 1.17).
The call-return instructions of the MC680XY are shown in Figure 3.12.

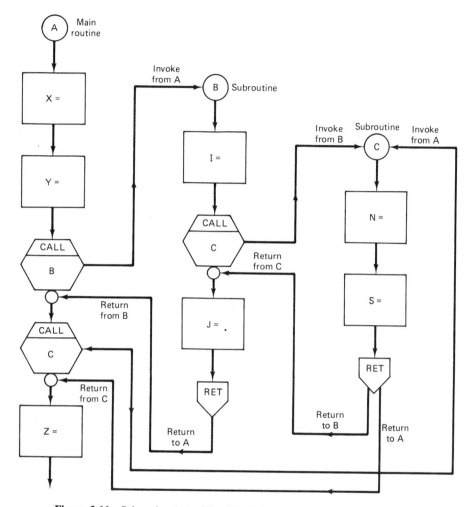

Figure 3.11 Subroutine (out-of-line block) invocation program flow of control. Control resumes in-line via a RETURN statement. (From G. W. Gorsline, *16-Bit Modern Microcomputers: The Intel 18086 Family*, © 1985, p. 94. Reprinted by permission of Prentice-Hall, Inc., Englewood Cliffs, NJ.)

When considering procedural-level languages, it is useful to distinguish between two types of subprocedure invocation:

1. CALL subroutines in which a keyword such as GOSUB or CALL conveys the order to branch or jump to the named out-of-line block of code, execute it, and eventually return to a point just beyond the invocation. Examples could be

GOSUB 127
CALL ANY

Branch to Subprocedure (usually an internal subprocedure)

BSR label

15	14	13	12	11	10	9	8	7 6 5 4 3 2 1 0
0	1	1	0	0	0	0	1	8-bit displacement

```
- - - - - - - 16/32-bit displacement (MC 68020 only) - - - - - - -
```

Action:
1. Save PC on stack (Push long address with decrement)
2. Add signed displacement to PC and place in PC

Jump to Subprocedure (usually an external subprocedure)

JSR <EA>   mode   register

15	14	13	12	11	10	9	8	7	6	5 4 3	2 1 0
0	1	0	0	1	1	1	0	1	0	Effective Address	

Action:
1. Save PC on stack (Push long address with decrement)
2. Move Physical Address [EA + RF] to PC

Return from Subprocedure and **Restore CCR** (condition code register)

RTR

15	14	13	12	11	10	9	8	7	6	5	4	3	2	1	0
0	1	0	0	1	1	1	0	0	1	1	1	0	1	1	1

Action:
1. Move stack-top to PC (Pop long address with increment)
2. Move stack-top to CCR (Pop word with decrement; use right byte only)

Return from Subprocedure (keep CCR as it was in subprocedure)

RTS

15	14	13	12	11	10	9	8	7	6	5	4	3	2	1	0
0	1	0	0	1	1	1	0	0	1	1	1	0	1	0	1

Action:
1. Move stack-top to PC (Pop long address with increment)

Figure 3.12 The Motorola MC68000 invoke a subprocedure and return to the invoking procedure instructions. Refer to Figure 3.15 for the LINK/UNLK instructions.

A CALL subprocedure may or may not have arguments to convey information between the caller and callee as well as to return any results. Refer to Figure 3.13.

2. Function subprocedures in which the use of the subprocedure name in a re-placement-assignment statement conveys the order to branch or jump to the named out-of-line block of code, execute it, place the single result in an ex-pected place, and eventually return to a point in the replacement-assignment statement just beyond the invocation. An argument is always required. FOR-TRAN and BASIC expect the result to be placed in the *default accumulator*

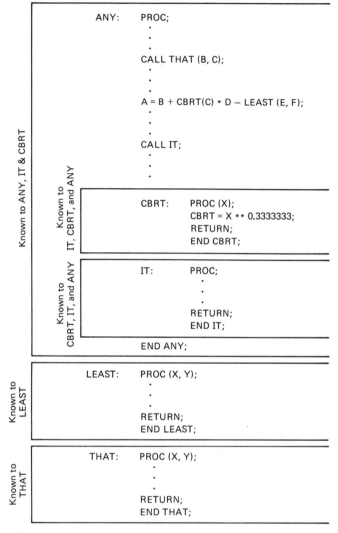

Figure 3.13 Internal versus external and CALL versus function subprocedure situations. (From G. W. Gorsline, *16-Bit Modern Microcomputers: The Intel 18086 Family,* © 1985, p. 96. Reprinted by permission of Prentice-Hall, Inc., Englewood Cliffs, NJ.)

(data register D0 of the MC680XY), whereas PL/I expects the result to be referred to as an implied extra argument. Again, refer to Figure 3.13.

When considering procedural-level languages, it is also useful to distinguish between two types of subprocedures viewed from a different logical dimension:

1. Internal subprocedures, in which the subprocedure block of code is physically

within the code of invoking procedure and is translated with it. Thus, the translator—the compiler or assembler—"knows" all about the variables and their addresses in both blocks of code. Figure 3.13 shows an example.

2. External subprocedures, in which the subprocedure block of code is physically separate and disjoint from the code of the invoking procedure and is translated separately and at a different time. Thus, the translator "does not know" anything about the variables or their addresses in the other block of code. Figure 3.13 also shows this situation.

Main procedures can be implemented in a procedural-level language or in assembly language; similarly, subprocedures can be implemented in a procedural-level language or in assembly language. Although it is easiest to implement a subprocedure in the same language as that used for the main procedure, it is possible to mix languages when external subprocedures are involved. It is particularly difficult to implement an assembly language main procedure correctly with a procedural language subprocedure. We will consider only four of the possible situations in two groups.

The Main Procedure: Assembly Language

As complex replacement/assignment procedures, particularly arithmetic, are not usual in programs implemented in assembly language, function subprocedures are not normal. Thus, we will consider only CALL subprocedures.

Internal call subprocedures: assembly language. Because both the invoking procedure and the subprocedure are assembled at the same time employing a common variable names dictionary (symbol table), each procedure "knows" about all of the data container names and addresses. For this reason, it is unnecessary, and not usual, to use arguments for communication between procedures. On the other hand, it is vital that the register values of the invoking procedure not be destroyed by the subprocedure. The contents of registers should be stored—"saved"—in a "save area in memory" at the start of the subprocedure and loaded—"restored"—from the save area just before the RETurn, using the MOVEM instruction. As values can be "returned" in a register, care must be taken not to destroy these values during the register restoration process.

```
;    Main Program  -   calls internal subprocedure with no arguments
;
START:        -            -
              -            -
              -            -
              BSR          SUBPROG
              -            -
              -            -
```

```
            STOP
;
;     Subprogram    -    internal subprocedure;thus assembled at the same time
;                        as the main program, with the assembler "knowing" all
;                        about everything in both the main and the subprocedure
;
SUBPROG    -                   -
           -                   -
           -                   -
           RTS                            ;return without restoring condition codes
           END
```

External call subprocedures: assembly language.   Because the invoking procedure is assembled separately from the subprocedure, neither has any knowledge of the other's variable names or their addresses. If communication of variable values or addresses is required, two methods are commonly employed: send/receive the value via an argument or send/receive the address via an argument. The MC680XY provides a stack and associated stack pointer register as a very handy place to pass arguments. Thus, the argument contents would occur in the stack just below the return address.

```
;     Main Program   -    call external subprocedure with two arguments
;
START         -                -
              -                -
              -                -
              -
           LEA       X,-(SP)      ;PUSH address of argument 1 onto stack
           LEA       Y,-(SP)      ;PUSH address of argument 2 onto stack
           JSR       SUBPROG
              -                -
              -                -
              -                -
           STOP
           END       START

;     Subprogram    -    external subprocedure;thus assembled at a different time
;                        from the main program, with any information passage
;                        between the two using arguments on the stack.
;
SUBPROG MOVEA.L    (SP)+,A2      ;POP address of argument 2 into A2
        MOVEA.L    (SP)+,A1      ;POP address of agrument 1 into A1
        MOVE.W     SR,-(SP)      ;PUSH status register to stack
```

                    -                    -
                    -                    -
                    -                    -
            RTR   ;return and restore condition codes.
            END

An alternative and perhaps preferable syntax involves the LINK and UNLK instructions (see Figure 3.14). In the scheme we are describing, any data private to the subroutine (in block-structured languages such as Pascal, the term *local data* would be appropriate) is allocated on the stack. Thus, the stack contains the following information for each subroutine in the form of a *stack frame*.

Local variables

Frame pointer for the stack frame of the calling routine

Return address

Parameters

Note that exactly the same information is present as the next deeper stack frame within the stack for the invoking routine; and, if that routine was a subroutine, the same information is in the next deeper stack frame for the calling routine, ad infinitum. Thus, a frame is created (PUSHed) for a routine as it is called and de-

Create a Data Frame on Stack

LINK An, #displacement

15	14	13	12	11	10	9	8	7	6	5	4	3	2	1	0
0	1	0	0	1	0	0	0	0	0	0	0	1	Register		

Word Displacement

Long Word Displacement

Action:
1. Current content of address register (old frame pointer) is pushed to stack [SP → 4 → SP; An → (SP)].
2. Updated SP loaded into address register (current frame pointer) [SP → An].
3. Displacement value (space for local variables) is added to SP [SP + displ. → SP].

Destroy a Data Frame on Stack

UNLK An

15	14	13	12	11	10	9	8	7	6	5	4	3	2	1	0
0	1	0	0	1	1	1	0	0	1	0	1	1	Register		

Action:
1. Load SP with contents of address register (current frame pointer) which points to old frame pointer [An → SP].
2. Load address register with contents of stack pointed to by SP (old frame pointer) [(SP) → An; SP + 4 → SP].

Figure 3.14 The LINK instruction creates a data frame on the stack for a subprocedure and then branches to the subprocedure; the UNLK destroys the data frame and returns to the invoking procedure.

stroyed (POPped) as it returns. As the frames are created/destroyed using a stack discipline, recursion is accommodated.

To firmly cement this concept into your mind, consider the following program fragment from Triebel and Singh (1986) in concert with Figure 3.15:

```
         MOVE.W    D0,-(SP)      ;parameter 1 passed to stack
         MOVE.W    D1,-(SP)      ;parameter 2 passed to stack
AA       JSR       SBRT          ;call subroutine SBRT
          .          .
          .          .
          .          .
          .          .
          .          .
          .          .
SBRT     LINK      A0.-#$8       ;FP and local storage established for called
                                 ;routine
```

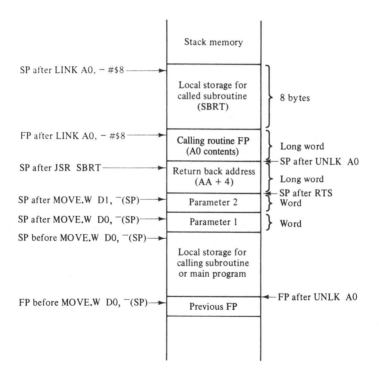

Figure 3.15   Stack for the example program. (From W. A. Triebel and A. Singh, *The 68000 Microprocessor: Architecture, Software, and Interfacing Techniques,* © 1986, p. 116. Reprinted by permission of Prentice-Hall, Inc., Englewood Cliffs, NJ.)

```
        .               .
        .               .
        .               .
        MOVE.W      10(A0),D5       ;parameter 1 accessed
        .               .
        .               .
        .               .
        UNLK        A0              ;FP for the calling routine established
        RTS                         ;return to main program
```

As we begin to execute the first instruction of the program segment, we will assume that the active SP points to the top of the data frame identified in Figure 3.15 as local storage area for the calling routine. Execution of the first two instructions

```
MOVE.W   D0,-(SP)
MOVE.W   D1,-(SP)
```

passes the contents of D0 and D1 as parameters onto the stack. Looking at Figure 3.15, we see that at the completion of these two instructions, SP points to the location where parameter 2 is stored.

The next instruction,

```
JSR  SBRT
```

which has the label AA, calls the subroutine starting at label SBRT. It causes the address of the instruction that follows it to be pushed onto the stack. This return address is AA + 4, since the JSR instruction takes up four bytes of program memory. Second, PC is loaded with the address of SBRT such that program control picks up execution from the first instruction of the subroutine.

The subroutine starts with the instruction

```
LINK   A0,-#$8
```

It causes the contents of A0 to be saved on the stack and then loads A0 from the active stack pointer register. This sets up a new frame pointer FP (A0 register). Then 8 is subtracted from the value in SP. Therefore, it points to the top of the data area identified in Figure 3.15 as *local storage* for the called subroutine.

As subroutine SBRT is being executed, we may need to access parameter 1. The frame pointer serves as a reference into the called routine's data frame. Parameter 1 is at a displacement of ten bytes from the frame pointer; therefore, the instruction

```
MOVE.W   10(A0),D5
```

can be used to access it. Execution of this instruction copies parameter 1 into D5.

The next instruction we see is

UNLK A0

It loads SP with the contents of A0 and then pops the contents at the top of the stack into A0. Now A0 once again contains the frame pointer for the calling routine and SP points to the location where the return address AA + 4 is stored.
    The last instruction

RTS

loads the return address into the program counter so that execution resumes in the calling routine.

The Main Procedure: Procedural-Level Language

As the subprocedures in assembly language must be assembled separately from the compilation of the invoking procedure, only external subprocedures are possible. This necessitates that arguments or global variables be used for interprocedural communication. Although information passage via global variables is possible, this method not only is more involved but is usually considered to be a questionable programming practice. We therefore suggest the use of arguments and discourage global variable communication, particularly in a mixed-language situation. In all cases, the exact methods (value, address, address of address) and location used for argument passage by the particular procedural language must be determined, understood, and meticulously followed, employing documentation that is usually less than ideal.

External call subprocedures: assembly language.   Happily, in most, if not all, MC680XY compiler implementations, argument values or addresses are pushed onto the stack just prior to the CALL and thus occur just prior to the return address in reverse order. It is easy for the subprocedure to acquire the arguments and to replace values before returning. Note that the eventual top of the stack must be the return address.

External function subprocedure: assembly language.   Again, MC680XY compilers generate code that places the arguments on the stack before the return address. As with CALL subprocedures, the function code can retrieve the arguments for use and eventually assure that the top of the stack contains the return address. Recall that the single result of a function is used directly in a procedural language replacement/assignment statement expression. This requires that the rules of the language implementation be followed carefully in order to place the returned function value exactly where it is expected to be. Often this place will be the accumulator (data register D0); sometimes this place will be an extra "dummy" argument. "Abnormal functions" change the value of one or more arguments or a global variable. The use of abnormal functions results in difficulties during procedure debugging and maintenance and should be avoided if not prohibited.

It must be emphasized that it is rapidly becoming accepted practice to limit the use of assembly language to short, fast, necessary support subprocedures to higher-level procedural languages. These ASM 68K subprocedures accomplish functions that are not easily coded or that execute slowly in the higher-level language of the main-line implementation. This is true of both systems and applications problem solutions.

MODULE SUPPORT (MC68020 ONLY)

The MC68020 includes support for modules with the call module (CALLM) and return from module (RTM) instructions. The CALLM instruction references a module descriptor. This descriptor contains control information for entry into the called module. The CALLM instruction creates a module stack frame, stores the current module state in that frame, and loads a new module state from the referenced descriptor. The RTM instruction recovers the previous module state from the stack frame and returns to the calling module. The module interface facilitates finer resolution of access control by external hardware.

Module Call/Module Return

The CALLM instruction is used to make the module call. For the type $00 module descriptor, the processor simply creates and fills the module stack frame at the top of the active system stack. The condition codes of the calling module are saved in the CCR field of the frame. If Opt is equal to 000 (arguments passed on the stack) in the module descriptor, the MC68020 does not save the stack pointer or load a new stack pointer value. The processor uses the module entry word to save and load the module data area pointer register and then begins execution of the called module.

The RTM instruction is used to return from a module. For the type $00 module stack frame, the processor reloads the condition codes, the program counter, and the module data area pointer register from the frame. The frame is removed from the top of the stack, the argument count is added to the stack pointer, and execution returns to the calling module.

The CALLM and RTM instructions are shown in Figure 3.16. We have chosen not to discuss the type $01 module descriptor and leave information on it to be acquired, if needed, from the MC68020 User's Manual.

Module Descriptor

Figure 3.17a illustrates the format of the module descriptor. The first long word contains control information used during the execution of the CALLM instruction. The remaining locations contain data that may be loaded into processor registers by the CALLM instruction.

Call a Module (MC 68020 only)

CALLM# bytes-of-args, < ea >

15	14	13	12	11	10	9	8	7	6	5	4	3	2	1	0
0	0	0	0	0	1	1	0	1	1	Effective Address					
										Mode			Register		
0	0	0	0	0	0	0	0	Argument Count							

Action:
  1. Effective address is location of external module descriptor.
  2. Create module frame on stack for old module state information save current module state on stack.
  3. Load new module state information from external module descriptor at < ea > load new module state.
  4. Number of bytes of arguments (0 to 255 bytes).

Return from Module (MC 68020 only)

RTM Rn

15	14	13	12	11	10	9	8	7	6	5	4	3	2	1	0
0	0	0	0	1	1	0	1	1	0	0	D/A		Register		

Action:
  1. Load previously saved old module state information from stack top.
  2. Increment caller's SP by argument count byte count in module state information.
  3. Rn is address or data register containing address of module descriptor that is be restored. If Rn = A7 = SP, then this pointer is lost.

Figure 3.16 The MC68020 call a module and return from a module instructions.

The Opt field specifies how arguments are to be passed to the called module. The MC68020 recognizes only the options of 000 and 100; all others cause a format exception. The 000 option indicates that the called module expects to find arguments from the calling module on the stack just below the module stack frame. In cases where there is a change of stack pointer during the call, the MC68020 will copy the arguments from the old stack to the new stack. The 100 option indicates that the called module will access the arguments from the calling module through an indirect pointer in the stack of the calling module. Hence, the arguments are not copied, but the MC68020 puts the value of the stack pointer from the calling module in the module stack frame.

The Type field specifies the type of the descriptor. The MC68020 only recognizes descriptors of type $00 and $01; all others cause a format exception. The $00 type descriptor defines a module for which there is no change in access rights, and the called module builds its stack frame on top of the stack used by the calling module. The $01 type descriptor defines a module for which there may be a change in access rights; such a called module may have a separate stack area from that of the calling module. The access level field is used only with the type $01 descriptor and is passed to external hardware to change the access control.

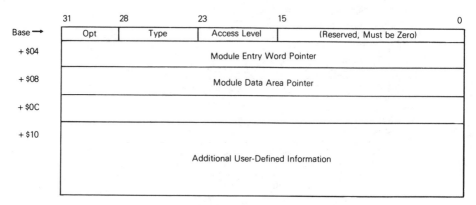

(a) Module Descriptor Format

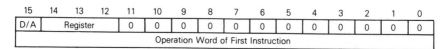

(b) Module Entry Word

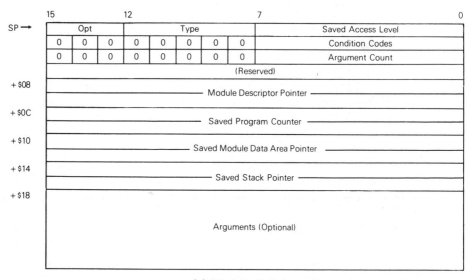

(c) Module Call Stack Frame

Figure 3.17   Data areas employed by the MC68020 CALLM instruction. (Courtesy of Motorola, Inc.)

The module entry word pointer specifies the entry address of the called module. The first word at the entry address (Figure 3.17b) specifies the register to be saved in the module stack frame and then loaded with the module descriptor data area pointer; the first instruction of the module starts with the next word. The module descriptor data area pointer field contains the address of the called module data area.

If the access change requires a change of stack pointer, the old value is saved in the module stack frame and the new value is taken from the module descriptor stack pointer field. Any further information in the module descriptor is user-defined.

All module descriptor types $10–$1F are reserved for user definition and cause a format error exception. This provides the user with a means of disabling any module by setting a single bit in its descriptor, without loss of any descriptor information.

Figure 3.17c illustrates the format of the module stack frame. This frame is constructed by the CALLM instruction and is removed by the RTM instruction. The first and second long words contain control information passed by the CALLM instruction to the RTM instruction. The module descriptor pointer contains the address of the descriptor used during the module call. All other locations contain information to be restored on return to the calling module.

The program counter is the saved address of the instruction following the CALLM instruction. The Opt and Type fields specify the argument options and type of module stack frame and are copied to the frame from the module descriptor by the CALLM instruction; the RTM instruction will cause a format error if the Opt and Type fields do not have recognizable values. The access level is the saved access control information, which is saved from external hardware by the CALLM instruction and restored by the RTM instruction. The argument count field is set by the CALLM instruction and is used by the RTM instruction to remove arguments from the stack of the calling module. The contents of the CCR are saved by the CALLM instruction and restored by the RTM instruction. The saved stack pointer field contains the value of the stack pointer when the CALLM instruction started execution, and that value is restored by RTM. The saved module data pointer field contains the saved value of the module data area pointer register from the calling module.

The MC68020 module mechanism supports a finer level of access control beyond the distinction between user and supervisor modes. The module mechanism allows a module with limited access rights to call a module with greater access rights. With the help of external hardware, the processor can verify that an increase in access rights is allowable or can detect attempts by a module to gain access rights to which it is not entitled.

Type $01 module descriptors and module stack frames indicate a request to change access levels. While processing a type $01 descriptor or frame, the CALLM and RTM instructions communicate with external access control hardware via accesses in the CPU space. Information relative to this ability can be obtained from the MC68020 User's Manual.

EXERCISES

3.1. The conditional branch instruction BLT (branch on less than) will jump to the label only if the flags of the CCR are

$$N * \overline{V} + \overline{N} * V = 1$$

Using symbolic logic (Boolean algebra), verify that these settings are correct for the desired action. Do the same for the BHI, BLS, BGT, BGE, and BLE versions of the Bcc instruction (see Figure 3.3).

3.2. An example was given early in this chapter:

```
BLT     *+7
```

whose semantics are: IF the condition was less than THEN jump forward seven statements. Test your assembler and report whether this form is allowed. Why is the use of this form of the conditional jump programmatically dangerous enough to be avoided in practice?

3.3. Name the 16 diadic Boolean algebra (symbolic logic) operations and show that they can all be accomplished using combinations of AND and OR or NAND and NOR.

3.4. The LEAVE a loop conditionally construct is a form of the GO TO construct. Nevertheless, some advocates of structured programming are not opposed to its use. Defend this thesis.

3.5. Example loop 9A and 9B in the text accomplish the same objective. Which is preferable, and why?

3.6. Design, implement, test, and document a program to search for a given word in an English text and to replace each instance with another given word. Print both the original and the resulting text, with explanatory notations.

3.7. Design, implement, test, and document a program to determine the frequency of each ASCII character in a text of unknown length. Print the text and the frequency data, with explanatory notations.

3.8. To the requirements of Exercise 3.7, add the frequency of words with different lengths. Be careful not to include punctuation marks as a portion of a word.

3.9. To the requirements of Exercise 3.8, add the necessity of using at least two assembly language subprocedures, with the main program written in a higher-level language such as Pascal.

4

Manipulating Data

From both a theoretical and pragmatic viewpoint, a digital computational system is an information-manipulating device. In a sense, it can be maintained that information must be stored before it can be manipulated and that the results must be stored after the manipulation. Thus, many workers also emphasize the information storage characteristics of a computer. The long-term and continuing growth and importance of data banks as permanent or semipermanent information repositories constitutes justification for this broader viewpoint.

In any case, only three general types of computer instructions are available to affect information directly:

1. *Data movement:* Instructions that cause the movement of data from one place in the computer to another without changing the information in any way.
2. *Transduction:* Instructions that change the physical encoding of the information without affecting the meaning; that is, the syntax is changed while the semantics are retained. (Example: The magnetic encoding of the character A on a magnetic tape is transformed via transduction to the settings of transistors in memory also encoding the character A.)
3. *Data operations:* Instructions that result in the manufacture of new information. (Example: Subtracting 7 from 11 gives the result 4; this result is new and has never existed before, even if many copies have existed.)

We are immediately faced with the philosophical and extremely practical question: Above the bit levels, *what is the fundamental unit of information?* Is the number 7 a fundamental unit? The number 78? The matrix A of order 17? The letter Z? The string ZEKE?

In dealing with digital computers, the answer is surprisingly definitive and simple: The fundamental unit of information is a portion of the language definition. It follows directly that the operations available to manipulate this fundamental information unit are also a portion of the language definition.

Some languages, such as BASIC or PL/I, provide for data aggregates such as a matrix or a string as one of their fundamental information units. On the other hand, assembly languages are a symbolic encoding of the hardware architectural design and are limited to manipulating those data types directly supported by the hardware, employing instructions provided by the design. This important point bears repeating: Assembly language data consist of simple nonaggregate elements, and assembly language instructions provide for manipulating a single simple datum, with no provision for aggregated data such as matrices. The MC680XY does allow indexing within arrays.

At the same time, it must be realized that some computers possess instructions that deal with multiple data elements. As an example of this, the IBM 360/370/ 308X/43X1 extended computer family implements a load multiple instruction:

LM   0,15,TEMP

that moves the contents of memory word location TEMP to register 0, TEMP + 1 to register 1, . . . , TEMP + 15 to register 15; and the reverse is true for the store multiple instruction:

STM   0,15,TEMP

In effect, load multiple is a single-instruction loop that moves the contents of successive memory word locations to consecutive registers starting with register I through register J. The MC680XY MOVEM instruction allows a specified set of the address/ control/status registers to be stored (saved) in memory or loaded (restored) from memory. Specific instructions in other computers could also be cited. Lest I be misunderstood, recall that the art and science of assembly language programming involves translating an algorithm into a series of correct, complete, and legal instructions to manipulate data—data that can be logically organized as simple single elements, as aggregates of simple single elements, or as aggregates of aggregates.

As computer designers react to justified pressures to support higher-level languages more efficiently and adequately, it should be expected that there will be an increased tendency to implement aggregate data types and corresponding manipulation instructions directly into the architectural design. Current technological developmental directions strongly suggest that this will be accomplished by employing microprogramming and/or programmed logic arrays. The relative costs of acquiring hardware versus producing software, as discussed in Chapter 1, are major economic incentives forcing this trend. On the other hand, one of the current arguments in computer architecture and organization involves complicated sets of instructions/addressing modes (complicated instruction set computers, or CISC) versus simplified instruction sets/addressing modes (reduced instruction set computers, or RISC).

DATA MOVEMENT INSTRUCTIONS

Address Movement

The basic design of the Motorola MC680XY family provides for memory access using one of two generalized addressing methods:

1. Through an absolute address, which is nonrelocatable (useful only under limited and specialized purposes, such as for certain modules of the operating system). It must be noted that at least one software system on the Apple Macintosh employs absolute addressing and then alters these addresses during execution by incorporating the contents of a base register while calculating the physical address from the effective address.
2. Indirectly, through an address register, which is relocatable.

Thus, to manipulate data—to input a datum, to move a datum, to manipulate a datum, to output a datum—it is necessary to calculate and load the effective address into an address register. The exception, of course, employs a displacement (offset) from the program counter (PC), perhaps with an index—those addressing modes that are known as program counter relative and that cannot be used to store a datum into memory. It follows that it is vital to consider and understand the usage of address registers as well as the movement and allowable manipulations of the addresses themselves.

From the above reasoning, it is obvious that the calculation of the effective address (EA) and its placement into an address register or in a known memory location is one of the basic necessary operations. It is also necessary to move addresses between address registers and memory and sometimes to use a data register as a fast but temporary address storage receptacle. In addition, when a user's application program calls a subprogram or requests service such as I/O from the operating system, the subordinate (called) routine must save at least some of the register contents of the calling program in memory in order to free them for its own use and then, just before returning, restore the values to the registers from memory. The available address movement instructions are shown in Figure 4.1 and are briefly discussed below. They provide a minimal but adequate operational set for the needed address manipulations.

The move data (MOVE) instruction also can be employed to move an address (word or long word), register to register, register to memory, memory to register,

Move to Address Register (word or long)

MOVEA EA, An

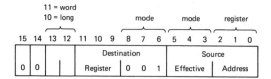

```
        11 = word
        10 = long                mode        mode      register
                                 ┌───┐      ┌───┐      ┌─────┐
 15  14  13  12  11  10   9   8   7   6   5   4   3   2   1   0
┌───┬───┬───────┬─────────────────┬─────────┬─────────────────┐
│   │   │       │   Destination   │         │     Source      │
│ 0 │ 0 │       │   Register      │ 0  0  1 │ Effective  Address│
└───┴───┴───────┴─────────────────┴─────────┴─────────────────┘
```

Exchange Address Register (32-bit = long only)

EXGA An, Am

```
 15  14  13  12  11  10   9   8   7   6   5   4   3   2   1   0
┌───┬───┬───┬───┬──────────┬───┬───┬───┬───┬───┬──────────────┐
│ 1 │ 1 │ 0 │ 0 │ Address  │ 1 │ 0 │ 1 │ 0 │ 0 │ 1 │ Address  │
│   │   │   │   │ Register │   │   │   │   │   │   │ Register │
└───┴───┴───┴───┴──────────┴───┴───┴───┴───┴───┴──────────────┘
                            └──── Operation Mode ────┘
```

EXGM { An, Dm
       { Dn, Am   Operation Mode

```
 15  14  13  12  11  10   9   8   7   6   5   4   3   2   1   0
┌───┬───┬───┬───┬──────────┬───┬───┬───┬───┬───┬──────────────┐
│ 1 │ 1 │ 0 │ 0 │ Data     │ 1 │ 1 │ 0 │ 0 │ 0 │ 1 │ Address  │
│   │   │   │   │ Register │   │   │   │   │   │   │ Register │
└───┴───┴───┴───┴──────────┴───┴───┴───┴───┴───┴──────────────┘
```

Move Multiple Registers (word or long)

MOVEM { Register List → EA
        { EA → Register List

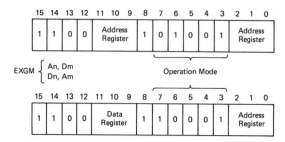

```
        0 = R → M        0 = word
        1 = M → R        1 = long    mode*      register
 15  14  13  12  11  10   9   8   7   6   5   4   3   2   1   0
┌───┬───┬───┬───┬───┬─────┬───┬───┬───┬─────────────────────────┐
│ 0 │ 1 │ 0 │ 0 │ 1 │dir. │ 0 │ 0 │ 1 │Sz │  Effective Address  │
├───┴───┴───┴───┴───┴─────┴───┴───┴───┴─────────────────────────┤
│     Register List Mask (A7, A6, ....., A0, D7, D6, ....., D0)**│
└───────────────────────────────────────────────────────────────┘
```

**Predecrement (M → R only) — register list in reserve order
*Postincrement (R → M only)
 Register direct and immediate not valid
 Program counter relative (M → R) only

Load Effective Address (32-bit = long only)

LEA label, An   mode   register

```
 15  14  13  12  11  10   9   8   7   6   5   4   3   2   1   0
┌───┬───┬───┬───┬──────────┬───┬───┬───┬─────────────────────────┐
│ 0 │ 1 │ 0 │ 0 │ Address  │ 1 │ 1 │ 1 │    Effective Address    │
│   │   │   │   │ Register │   │   │   │                         │
└───┴───┴───┴───┴──────────┴───┴───┴───┴─────────────────────────┘
```

Push Effective Address onto Stack (32-bit = long only)

PEA label   mode   register

```
 15  14  13  12  11  10   9   8   7   6   5   4   3   2   1   0
┌───┬───┬───┬───┬───┬───┬───┬───┬───┬─────────────────────────┐
│ 0 │ 1 │ 0 │ 0 │ 1 │ 0 │ 0 │ 0 │ 0 │ 1 │  Effective Address  │
└───┴───┴───┴───┴───┴───┴───┴───┴───┴─────────────────────────┘
```

Action:
  1. Decrement SP by 4 (USP or SSP).
  2. Calculate EA.
  3. MOVE to (SP).

Figure 4.1   The address movement instructions of the MC68000.

and memory to memory using any of the available addressing modes, with the usual restriction that the destination operand cannot be an immediate or a program counter relative address; that is, it cannot be in code space. Recall that the MC68020 also allows memory indirect from a register indirect addressing. The following constructs convey some of the freedoms allowed:

```
MOVE.W   D3,D4
MOVE.L   (A5),D1
MOVE.W   D3,-(A2)
```

The move (load) address register (MOVEA) instruction is limited to loading one of the seven address registers (word or long word) with the contents of any other register, an immediate value, or the contents of a location in memory whose address is derived by any of the addressing modes (including memory indirect with the MC68020). The following examples are typical:

```
MOVEA.W   A4,A3
MOVEA.L   (A4)+,A2
```

We remind you of the move (load/store) multiple registers (MOVEM) instruction for word or long-word data, which is normally involved with both data and address registers. MOVEM was very briefly discussed earlier in this chapter.

The load effective address (LEA) instruction first calculates the 32-bit effective address (EA) in memory of the source label (which may be indexed and/or may involve a displacement) and then moves this 32-bit long-word address value into the destination address register. Examples might be:

```
LEA   ANY,A1
LEA   (A2,D3),A1
```

The push effective address (PEA) instruction similarly first calculates the 32-bit effective address (EA) in memory of the source label (which, again, may be indexed and/or may involve an offset) and then decrements the stack pointer register (SP—either USP or SSP) and moves the derived address value to the top of the stack. This instruction is exactly equivalent to the illegal construct LEA ANY,-(A7). Examples of legal use are (note that the destination address at the top of the stack is implied):

```
PEA   ANY
PEA   (A2)(D3)
```

Long-Word, Word, and Byte Data Movement

We are defining data movement instructions as those instructions that cause a datum to be moved from one physical location to another physical location with no change in the bit pattern (syntax) and no implications regarding the meaning of the bit pattern (semantics). In the MC680XY, the generic data movement instruction is

MOVE   EAn,EAm   ;[EAn] $\longrightarrow$ [EAm]

where EAm can be any register or any address in writable memory accessible via any of the various addressing modes, as reviewed in Chapter 2, and where EAn can be any register or any address in memory accessible via any of the various addressing modes or an immediate datum. Appropriate status register bits are affected.

As discussed in Chapter 2, register-to-register, register-to-memory (store), memory-to-register (load), immediate-to-register, immediate-to-memory, and memory-to-memory datum moves are accommodated by the design. That is, complete freedom is allowed as to the datum container specified by EAn and by EAm, with only the following exceptions:

1. EAm must be an address in read/write memory or a register.
2. EAn cannot be an immediate datum.

The MC680XY provides a data movement instruction that exchanges the 32-bit contents of two registers without employing a temporary location:

EXG   Rn,Rm   ;[Rn] $\longleftrightarrow$ [Rm]

where Rn and Rm can be any data or address register. Note that this instruction always exchanges the full 32-bit contents of the two registers; that is, it is implied long.

The MC680XY provides two specialized and therefore fast move immediate instructions that are extremely useful, not only in specialized circumstances but in many more common programming situations. The clear any data or address register or any memory location instruction is a fast version of the generalized move immediate zero (see Figure 4.2):

CLR   EA   ;effective address of byte, word, or long word

In addition, a fast move immediate signed byte value instruction is available with two limitations: (1) the immediate value is a signed byte (+127 thru −128), which will be sign extended to 32 bits; and (2) the destination must be a data register.

MOVEQ   #byte_value,DRn   ;DRn is a long-word data register

Move Data

MOVE EA, EA

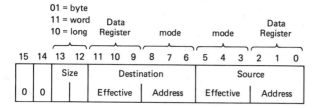

Exchange Data Registers (32-bit = long word only)

EXGD Dn, Dm

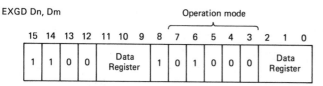

Move Quick Data (signed byte to data register long)

MOVEQ value, Dn

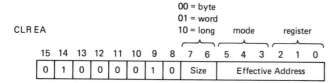

Clear Data Register or Memory

CLR EA

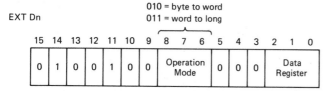

Extend Sign of Data Register (byte to word; word to long word)

EXT Dn

Figure 4.2 The data movement instructions of the MC68000. In addition, the bit set (BSET) and bit test (BTST) instructions can change a single bit, while the test and set (TAS) instruction can change a byte.

Move Multiple Registers

$$\text{MOVEM} \begin{cases} \text{Register List, EA} \\ \text{EA, Register List} \end{cases}$$

```
                    0 = R → M        0 = word
                    1 = M → R        1 = long   mode*        register
                                       ⌐‾⌐          ⌐‾‾‾‾⌐        ⌐‾‾‾‾‾‾‾‾⌐
  15  14  13  12  11  10   9   8   7   6   5   4   3   2   1   0
 ┌───┬───┬───┬───┬───┬────┬───┬───┬───┬────┬───────────────────┐
 │ 0 │ 1 │ 0 │ 0 │ 1 │Dir.│ 0 │ 0 │ 1 │ Sz │  Effective Address │
 ├───┴───┴───┴───┴───┴────┴───┴───┴───┴────┴───────────────────┤
 │        Register List Mask (A7, A6, . . . . ., A0, D7, D6, . . . . ., D0)** │
 └──────────────────────────────────────────────────────────┘
```

**Predecrement (M → R only) — Register List is in reverse order
*Postincrement only for R → M; Register Direct and Immediate not valid
Program Counter Relative only for M → R

Swap Halves of Data Register

SWAP Dn

```
  15  14  13  12  11  10   9   8   7   6   5   4   3   2   1   0
 ┌───┬───┬───┬───┬───┬───┬───┬───┬───┬───┬───┬───┬────────────┐
 │ 0 │ 1 │ 0 │ 0 │ 1 │ 0 │ 0 │ 0 │ 0 │ 1 │ 0 │ 0 │ 0 │  Data    │
 │   │   │   │   │   │   │   │   │   │   │   │   │   │ Register │
 └───┴───┴───┴───┴───┴───┴───┴───┴───┴───┴───┴───┴────────────┘
```

Figure 4.2 (*continued*).

As the MC680XY allows data to occupy one byte, two bytes, four bytes, or (in the MC68020) eight bytes, and for other reasons, the Motorola designers chose to generalize the more usual increment and decrement instructions of most computers into the more capable ADDQ, SUBQ, and MOVEQ instructions. Note that the MOVEQ instruction is available only for data or indexes resident in data registers and is not available for data resident in address registers or memory locations; that is, the destination must be a data register.

It is often true that a byte-sized datum must be employed in arithmetic or logic involving a word-sized datum and similarly a byte-sized or word-sized datum with a long-word-sized datum. The extend instruction is provided to solve this programmatic situation. Note that clearing (CLR) the upper (high bits) portion of the data container would not be a satisfactory solution if the content was a two's-complement negative number; in this case, the sign bit of the shorter value (bit 7 for byte or bit 15 for word) must be extended (copied) leftward. Only if the value is positive is the use of the CLR instruction a correct solution.

```
EXT.W   Dn    ;data register only, not allowed
EXT.L   Dn    ;  with an address register or memory
```

All arithmetic and logical data operations on the MC680XY must employ at least one of the eight available data registers. (Recall that arithmetic is allowed with address values and would involve at least one address register.) In addition, any index value may involve a data register. Thus, it is fairly obvious that data registers can easily become an extremely short-supply resource. When a data register is needed to solve a programming problem and all of the data registers are currently in use, the first solution that usually occurs to a programmer is to temporarily store the contents of a register somewhere, use the register as needed, and then restore the previous contents. We will examine this usual method for accomplishing this "save-restore" process momentarily. But first, there is a more subtle method of increasing the number of data registers available for byte-sized and for word-sized data, but not for long-word-sized data.

The swap register halves instruction will exchange the high-order 16-bit half of a data register with the low-order 16-bit half of the same data register:

SWAP   Dn $;Dn_{31\text{-}16} \longleftrightarrow Dn_{15\text{-}0}$

Recall that all operations on registers with byte-sized or word-sized operations involve only the low-order quarter or half register, with no effect on the other portion. This allows any one data register to be used as temporary storage for two byte-sized or word-sized data (including indexes). It is most important to realize that the datum that is to be used in an operation, including use as an index, must be in the low-order portion during such usage. Note that such simultaneous double use of a data register increases the probability of the program being both difficult to understand and difficult to modify correctly. It follows that this type of double register usage should always be adequately documented via comments.

The register save-restore process could be accomplished by using the MOVE or MOVEA instruction for each register store and later for each register restore. Alternately, iff an address register is currently free, then the exchange register instruction could be used for register store and later for register restore. Unfortunately, the normal situation usually involves the need to make several registers available. This commonly occurs at the beginning of execution of a subprocedure, with the implied necessity of also restoring the registers to their original state just before returning so that the invoking routine receives control back with the expected register values (the values present when it invoked the subroutine). The move multiple registers instruction (MOVEM), as discussed very briefly earlier, is an obvious solution to this very common save-restore registers need:

MOVEM.W   Dn,Dm, . . . ,D1,Dk,An,Am, . . . ,A1,Ak,EA
MOVEM.L   Dn,Dm, . . . ,D1,Dk,An,Am, . . . ,A1,Ak,EA
MOVEM.W   EA,Ak,A1, . . . ,Am,An,Dk,D1, . . . ,Dm,Dn
MOVEM.L   EA,Ak,A1, . . . ,Am,An,Dk,D1, . . . ,Dm,Dn

Note that the MOVEM instruction is available for the word-sized low-order register halves or for the entire 32-bit registers. From one to sixteen registers may be listed in any order, with the assurance that the order of restoration is opposite that of saving; that is, the proper values are restored to the proper registers with no effects of order of register notation within the assembly code. This is because the assembly instruction assembles with each register designation as a one bit in the proper position of the 16-bit operand word following the operation word of the instruction. It is necessary, of course, that the receiving area in memory be large enough to hold the contents of the *N*-word or long-word registers. If such is not the case, the instruction execution microprogrammed logic will assume that it is and will overwrite the needed memory and probably destroy necessary data.

In certain circumstances, it facilitates the construction of an algorithm to be able to employ an index into a table as a means of easily and quickly replacing a datum with another desired value. This process, which has become known as *translate*, is a fairly common instruction in computers. It is not implemented in the MC680XY family, but it can be easily simulated, as shown in Figure 4.3. The table in memory must have its address in an address register and must consist of appropriate and uniform-sized data elements. The index into the table must be an index register. Special programmatic provisions must be provided to prevent out-of-table addressing. Our illustration is for byte-sized data and thus implies a maximum translate table size of 256.

This simulation is more powerful than the usual translate instruction, as it allows the translation of a string of characters or word-sized or long-word-sized data

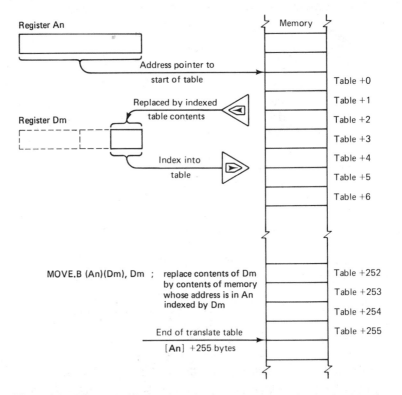

Figure 4.3 The translate instruction of many computers can be simulated on the MC680XY by the move indirect, indexed by the value to be replaced. (From G. W. Gorsline, *16-Bit Modern Microcomputers: The Intel I8086 Family,* © 1985, p. 103. Reprinted by permission of Prentice-Hall, Inc., Englewood Cliffs, NJ.)

in situ in memory instead of having to move each item to a register and then back to memory. Note that the simulation also allows the translation of word or long-word data, although the translate table would presumably become excessively large. A memory-to-memory character string translation program section could be:

```
;       string of length LNGTH = 64K starting at memory location STRNG
;       indexed by register D1.
;
;       translate table of length 256 bytes starting at location TABLE
;
        LEA       TABLE,A4
        LEA       STRNG,A5
        CLR.W     D1
NEXT:   MOVE.B    (A5)(D1),D2
        MOVE.B    (A4)(D2),D2
        MOVE.B    D2,(A5)(D1)
        ADDQ.W    #1,D1
        CMP.W     D1,LNGTH
        BLE       NEXT
          -         -
          -         -
```

As the final entry in these data movement instructions, we remind you of the set byte conditionally (Scc) instruction that we covered in Chapter 3. Figure 3.6 provides a summary. Recall:

IF <condition true>

THEN   set byte = FF_{hex} = $-128_{decimal}$

ELSE   set byte = 00_{hex} = $0_{decimal}$

A string is defined as an ordered set of data occupying a contiguous block of memory. Although most string processing will involve ASCII character (byte-sized) data, the MC680XY allows the same algorithmic construction involving word-sized data and long-word-sized data. The primary string data movement instructions are:

```
MOVE.B   (A1)+,(A2)+     ;movement is left to right in order
MOVE.B   -(A1),-(A2)     ;movement is right to left in order
```

where the datum at the effective address in the A1 register is moved to the effective address in the A2 register. Subsequently, the addresses in these registers are incremented (first example: with order of movement from left of string to right of string) or before each movement the registers are decremented (second example: with order

of data movement from right end of string toward the left beginning of string). To
repeat, a string can be processed from front to rear in the direction normally used to
read an English sentence; or a string can be processed from the rear end—that is, in
the reverse direction. It is normal, of course, for the move instruction to employ the
postincrement or predecrement indirect addressing mode in a loop and thus to employ a register as a counter for the loop, with this register being decremented by one
until it becomes zero, consequently forcing a loop fall-through (termination).

```
;     move character string STRNG_1 of length LNGTH to character string
;          STRNG_2 starting at left using the DBRA version of the decrement
;          and branch on condition or count instruction - see Figure 3.8
;
                    LEA       STRNG_1,A1
                    LEA       STRNG_2,A2
                    LEA       LNGTH,A3
                    MOVE.L    (A3),D1
                    SUBQ.L    #1,D1             ;DBRA tests for −1
DO_NEXT_LR:         MOVE.B    (A1)+,(A2)+       ;movement is in left-to-right order
                    DBRA      D1,DO_NEXT_LR
                      -         -
                      -         -


;     move character string STRNG_1 of length LNGTH to character string
;          STRNG_2 starting at right hand end
;
                    LEA       LNGTH,A1
                    MOVE.L    (A1),D1
                    ADDQ.L    #1,D1
                    LEA       STRNG_1,A1
                    ADD.L     D1,A1             ;address of right hand end
                    LEA       STRNG_2,A2
                    ADD.L     D1,A2             ;address of right hand end
                    SUBQ.L    #2,D1             ;DBRA test for −1
DO_NEXT_RL:         MOVE.B    −(A1),−(A2)       ;movement is in right-to-left order
                    DBRA      D1,DO_NEXT_RL
                      -         -
                      -         -
```

Array Data Movement

In considering the movement of string data and in simulating the translate instruction
of many computers—as well as in considering the pseudo-operation FIND, and the
like, in the specialized looping constructs of Chapter 3—we have been tacitly assuming (as is true) that a character string S of length N is in reality a single-dimensioned array S of N bytes. Although this viewpoint is perfectly natural and normal to

people who are used to Pascal and many dialects of FORTRAN, it is somewhat primitive, unnatural, and limiting to aficionados of SNOBOL, PL/I, BASIC, and other languages that provide direct support for string data. Accepting the mental discipline required to consider character string data as an array of single characters, it becomes somewhat obvious that data of any type (integer, floating-point, etc., as well as ASCII characters) and any length (byte, word, long word, quad word) that is grouped together into an ordered single-dimensioned array can be processed, as illustrated above, for strings using the postincrement or predecrement addressing mode and the DBRA (conditional branch on register count) instruction. (Note that if a more modern loop construct is used, a different branch instruction should be employed, as discussed in Chapter 3.) Thus, all single-dimensioned arrays may be processed as strings of contiguous elements of the specified data type, and all strings of contiguous elements may be processed as single-dimensioned arrays.

From previous experience in programming, you will recall that two-dimensional arrays are actually stored in memory as a single-dimensioned array consisting of the first group (either row 1 or column 1, depending on the language), followed by the second group, followed by the third group, and so on. FORTRAN is the example language that varies the first index the fastest; thus, the groups are ordered by the last index. Pascal and PL/I are example languages that vary the last index fastest; thus, the groups are ordered by the first index. Figure 4.4 will help illustrate this.

Address Offset	Memory (Element size = 4 bytes)				Array size = X(4, 3)	
					FORTRAN	Pascal or PL/I
Base address of array	Byte 1	Byte 2	Byte 3	Byte 4	Element	Element
0					1, 1	1, 1
4					2, 1	1, 2
8					3, 1	1, 3
12					4, 1	2, 1
16					1, 2	2, 2
20					2, 2	2, 3
24					3, 2	3, 1
28					4, 2	3, 2
32					1, 3	3, 3
36					2, 3	4, 1
					3, 3	4, 2
44					4, 3	4, 3
48					End of array	

Figure 4.4 The ordered storage arrangement of the elements of arrays in memory is different for different higher-level languages. In general, the languages that were defined and implemented very early (approximately 1957 or so), such as FORTRAN, have the first subscript (index) varying first and fastest. The later languages, such as Pascal, conform to the mathematical convention of varying the last subscript (index) first and fastest.

Using this knowledge, it is possible to calculate the displacement of any element from the beginning of the array for either situation—first subscript fastest or last subscript fastest. The appropriate calculations are [where size = maximum number in this dimension = (maximum dimension − minimum dimension + 1) and scale = number of bytes per element]:

- *One-Dimensional Arrays*

$$\text{Syntax} = X(I)$$

$$\text{Element} = I$$

$$\text{Address offset} = [(I - 1) * \text{scale}]$$

- *Two-Dimensional Arrays*
  FORTRAN style (first subscript varies fastest; stored by groups of second subscript)

$$\text{Syntax} = X(I,J)$$

$$\text{Element} = [(J - 1) * I\text{size}] + I$$

$$\text{Address offset} = \{[(J - 1) * I\text{size}] + (I - 1)\} * \text{scale}$$

  Pascal or PL/I style (last subscript varies fastest; stored by groups of first subscript)

$$\text{Syntax} = X(I,J)$$

$$\text{Element} = [(I - 1) * J\text{size}] + J$$

$$\text{Address offset} = \{[(I - 1) * J\text{size}] + (J - 1)\} * \text{scale}$$

- *Three-Dimensional Arrays*
  FORTRAN style (first subscript varies fastest; stored by groups of second subscript within groups of third subscript)

$$\text{Syntax} = X(I,J,K)$$

$$\text{Element} = \{[(K - 1) * J\text{size}] * (J * I\text{size})\} + [(J - 1) * I\text{size}] + I$$

$$\text{Address offset} = [\{[(K - 1) * J\text{size}] * (J * I\text{size})\}$$
$$+ [(J - 1) * I\text{size}] + (I - 1)] * \text{scale}$$

  Pascal or PL/I style (last subscript varies fastest; stored by groups of second subscript within groups of first subscript)

$$\text{Syntax} = X(I,J,K)$$

$$\text{Element} = \{[(I - 1) * J\text{size}] * (J * K\text{size})\} + [(J - 1) * K\text{size}] + K$$

$$\text{Address offset} = [\{[(I - 1) * J\text{size}] * (J * K\text{size})\}$$
$$+ [(J - 1) * K\text{size}] + (K - 1)] * \text{scale}$$

It should be noted that the foregoing calculations assume that the array subscripts start at positive one (+1). Some higher-level languages allow zero and negative subscripts, and a few also allow subscripts to progress negatively. For example, using PL/I syntax:

DCL X(0:9,−4:+5,4:−5) Fixed Binary(31)

declares the three-dimensional array named X, with each element consisting of a signed long-word integer (32 bits). The array has 1000 such elements (10 ∗ 10 ∗ 10), with ten master groups (subscript names = 0, 1, 2, 3, 4, 5, 6, 7, 8, 9), each with ten subgroups (subscript names = −4, −3, −2, −1, 0, 1, 2, 3, 4, 5), each with ten elements (subscript names = 4, 3, 2, 1, 0, −1, −2, −3, −4, −5). The beginning address of the array X is that of the element named

X(0,−4,+4)

and the address of the last element of the array X is that of the element named

X(9,+5,−6)

Calculating the memory address of an element for these situations requires transformations in the element-naming scheme of the source program to the scheme assumed by the above equations. As you might imagine, truly generalized versions of these indexing equations exist. At this stage in your education and experience, you should be able to derive the generalized indexing algorithms for an N-dimensional array, with each index having an arbitrary initial value, an arbitrary direction of change, and a specified stride (element size in bytes). The terminology "by row" and "by column" has been deliberately avoided in this discussion as suggesting a restriction to two-dimensional arrays—which is, of course, not true.

As only a single index register is allowed in an instruction of the MC680XY, it will often be necessary to employ one, two, or several data and/or address registers to calculate the appropriate offset into an array. It must be emphasized that the MC68020 indexing includes automatic scaling of the index for element size (1 for byte, 2 for word, 4 for long word, and 8 for quad-word).

Stack Data Movement

Similar to most microcomputers and some maxicomputers, the MC680XY provides a stack pointer (SP) register whose contents are the address of the stack top in memory. Two instructions are necessary to push data to the top of the stack and to pop data from the top of the stack:

PUSH
POP

where the specified datum can be any data register, any address register, or any location in memory via any of the addressing modes, and the implied other operand for the generic operation is a memory location addressed via the stack pointer indirect, −(SP). With the MC680XY, the equivalent operations are:

```
MOVE.L   A4,−(SP)     ;PUSH operation
MOVE.L   −(SP),A4     ;POP operation
```

Recall that, in microcomputers, the stack has its foot or base at high addresses and grows downward to lower addresses. Also recall that the stack has the primary design purpose of holding 32-bit addresses. Thus, the stack pointer (SP) register is most often decremented by 4 before the PUSH and incremented by 4 after the POP to accommodate addresses. Note that this pair of instructions also allows a memory-to-memory move and that at least one of the operands (the top of the stack) is a memory indirect through the stack pointer register, and the other would be a memory indirect through an address register. The MOVEA (move to, or load, address register) is actually the general MOVE instruction with the mode of the destination register being set as address register direct (001), as is shown in Figure 4.1.

At the beginning of executing a subprocedure, it is normal to save the contents of certain registers in memory so as to protect the information of the caller program with register restore just before returning. Often the memory area used as the *save area* is the stack; often it is not. In any case, the MOVEM (move multiple registers) instruction would most likely be used with predecrement (PUSH)/postincrement (POP) addressing mode, with either the stack pointer (SP or A7) or an alternate address register (An). Figures 4.1 and 4.2 give the particulars of this instruction.

In addition, it is sometimes desirable to calculate and PUSH the effective address (EA) of a datum to the top of the stack. The PEA (push effective address onto stack) instruction, also illustrated in Figure 4.1, is the logical choice to accomplish this action.

Control Register Contents Movement

In the section of Chapter 2 entitled "Two Stack Pointers—Why?" we introduced the idea of an operating system as the controlling entity of a computational system that chooses which applications program to work on next and performs services for the applications programs (such as I/O) that would be dangerous (from the standpoint of the system and other users) for them to perform for themselves. The idea of a user state in which certain operations are illegal and a system state in which all actions are allowed was briefly discussed. Among the actions that might prove dangerous for a user program to perform are changes to certain registers—particularly the status register (SR), but also the movement of the user stack of return addresses pointed to by the user stack register (USP). A user program often loses its use of the central processor for a period (say, the end of a time slice) with the expectation of again regaining control and continuing execution after another program has finished its time slice. In this case, the status register (SR) and the user stack register (USP) must be saved in memory by the operating system and then restored before resumption of the user program—that is, from time slice to time slice.

The move from/to user stack pointer register and move to status register are privileged instructions reserved to the operating system, executing with the S bit (bit 13) of the SR set ON = 1. The format and associated meanings (syntax and semantics) of these instructions are given in Figure 4.5.

On the other hand, it is often programmatically desirable for a user applications program to examine the state of the flags in the status register and thus be able

Move User Stack Pointer (32-bit = long only)

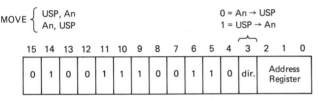

Note: Privileged instruction — that is, an operating system instruction (system mode only) not available to a user application program.

Move to Status Register (16-bit = word only)

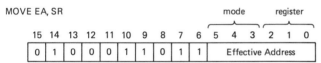

Note: Privileged instruction — that is, an operating system instruction (system mode only) not available to a user application program.

Move to Condition Code Register (source = 16-bit = word only; destination = right byte only)

Available to user application program. As only the CCR byte of the SR is changed, the user program cannot affect any other program.

Move from Status Register (16-bit = word only)

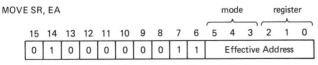

Available to user application program to allow examination of entire word. The CCR could be changed and reloaded with the move instruction just above [MOVE EA, CCR].

Figure 4.5 The control register movement instructions of the MC680XY. Note that the top two instructions are privileged.

to redirect program flow of control accordingly. In addition, in Chapter 3, you encountered two return from a subprogram instructions:

```
RTS     ;return with condition codes of subprocedure
RTR     ;return and restore condition codes of the
        ;  calling program from the stack
```

Thus, the RTR instruction assumes that the user program has moved the contents of the status register to the stack just before calling the subprocedure. The move from status register instruction (nonprivileged) allows this:

```
MOVE.L     SR,-(SP)
```

Incidentally, only the lower-order byte of the SR—the condition code register (CCR)—is restored by RTR. Note that the entire status register can be examined after it is moved to the stack and that the program can provide for appropriate actions—that is, it branches depending on the setting of any one or more of the bits.

As a last point, it is sometimes expedient for a user program to change bit setting in the condition code register (CCR). The move to condition code register instruction (nonprivileged) allows this:

```
MOVE.W     EA,CCR
```

This operation is peculiar in that a word (16 bits) must be moved to a byte register (8 bits). In actuality, the high-order byte (bits 8 thru 15) is destroyed and not used, and only the CCR portion of the SR is affected.

Bit Data Movement

The test-a-bit for ON or OFF and then set it, clear it, or change it instruction can be employed to affect the value of a bit within any data register, any address register (A0 through A6), and any location in data (read/write) memory. These instructions, which were discussed in Chapter 3 and detailed in Figures 3.5 and 3.6, are:

```
BCHG  #position,EA     ;change bit value
BCHG  Dn,EA

BCLR  #position,EA     ;clear bit to zero
BCLR  Dn,EA

BSET  #position,EA     ;set bit to one
BSET  Dn,EA
```

```
BTST   #position,EA      ;test bit and leave value unchanged
BTST   Dn,EA


Scc    EA                ;If <condition TRUE>
                         ;    THEN set byte at EA to hex FF
                         ;    ELSE set byte at EA to hex 00
```

Input/Output Data Movement

The input/output ports of the MC680XY are pseudomemory locations in the high address portion of main (primary) memory. That is, memory location FFFFFE is really the status register of a device (say, the CRT), and memory location FFFFFF is really the data register of the same device. In other words, although the status register and the data register of I/O devices in the MC680XY are physically within the I/O device control circuitry, they are attached to the computational system so as to be programmatically addressable as memory locations (almost always contiguous locations).

   As a result, any instruction (usually a MOVE, but not necessarily) that employs a destination operand addressing mode referring to read/write memory may be used as an output instruction. In addition, any instruction (also usually a MOVE, but not necessarily) that employs a source operand addressing mode referring to memory may be used as an input instruction.

   We will return to I/O in Chapter 5, where a fairly complete introduction will be given. In the meantime, it is expedient to mention that some I/O devices (particularly those designed for the predecessor 8-bit MC6800 microprocessor) expect data to be 8 bits = 1 byte in size and to occur in an even address byte, while the status information would have been in the preceding odd address byte. Restricting our attention to the MC68000, the MC68010, and the MC68012, which each have 16 data lines, it is necessary that the byte of data always be on lines 0 through 7 and that the status byte be on lines 8 through 15. With early versions of the MC68000, it was not uncommon for these older MC6800 peripherals to be used. To allow this degree of compatibility (which presumably could be an attractive sales pitch), the designers included a move peripheral data instruction (see Figure 4.6):

```
MOVEP.W    Dn,displ(Am)
```

which moves the contents of data register bits 15 through 8 to memory location displ(Am) and then moves data register bits 7 through 0 contents to memory location displ(Am)+2. Note the increment by 2, resulting in skipping bytes in memory—presumably the status register byte. The instruction

```
MOVEP.L    Dn,displ(Am)
```

Move Peripheral Data

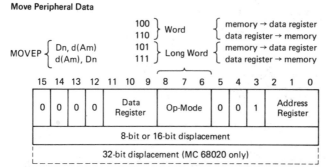

8-bit or 16-bit displacement

32-bit displacement (MC 68020 only)

Memory address <u>must</u> be address register indirect with
displacement [zero, 8-bit or 16-bit (32-bit in MC 68020 only)]

MOVEP.B — not legal
MOVEP.W ⎱ a byte obtained from, or sent to, every
MOVEP.L ⎰ other memory location to/from a data register.

Figure 4.6   The MC680XY instruction
that allows byte I/O using peripherals
designed for the predecessor 8-bit
MC6800 microcomputer.

acts similarly, with data register bits 31 through 24 going to location displ(Am); bits 23 through 16 going to location displ(Am)+2; bits 15 through 8 going to location displ(Am)+4; and finally, bits 7 through 0 going to location displ(Am)+6. In reality, the data would never be moved to actual real memory but would be removed (in the proper order) from the data bus lines 0 through 7 by the peripheral control logic and sent directly to the device data register. Chapter 5 will cover I/O in the necessary detail.

DATA TRANSDUCTION INSTRUCTIONS

By definition, data transduction produces a different data syntax without changing the semantics. The traditional example in computers is the transformation of the value of a datum on a punched card encoded as holes (whose position indicates the value) being transduced to the setting of the transistors in the data buffer register of the device controller whose interpretation (or meaning) is the same. This I/O type of data transduction is performed by the input/output devices of a computational system.

Our main interests at this time, however, are the data transductions (meaning-preserving encoding changes) that are sometimes algorithmically necessary within the computer after input or before output. These transductions are caused by specific instructions or by a series of instructions and essentially are changes in data type. The data types "designed into" the MC68000/MC68008/MC68010/MC68012/MC68020 are as follows:

> *Addresses*
> > Physical/Effective, 32-bit unsigned
> > Modifiers
> > > Long word, 32-bit signed

         Word, 16-bit signed
         Byte, 8-bit signed
         Quick, 3-bit unsigned
         Increment/decrement, 1-bit signed (MC68020 allows sizing)

Numerical data
         Integer, 32-, 16-, and 8-bit
         Unsigned
           Binary
           Decimal
             Binary-coded decimal, 4 bits per digit in pairs
         Signed (two's complement)
           Binary, 64-, 32-, 16-, and 8-bit
         Floating point (via software or the MC68881 processor), 32-, 64-, and 80-bit IEEE Standard format

Logical data
         Flags, 1 bit grouped in a long word, word, or byte
         Byte, 8-bit
         Word, 16-bit
         Long word, 32-bit

Character data
         Single character (ASCII), 8-bit byte
         Strings of characters, 0- to 4 G-byte aggregates

In addition, by combining instructions into special algorithms, it is possible to manipulate almost any kind of data with a well-defined syntax and associated semantics. Two examples will suffice as illustrations:

    1. *Rational numerical data.* The exact numerical value is expressed as a numerator/denominator pair in lowest form, expressed either as two signed binary- or decimal-coded integers of the necessary length. Software routines to manipulate this data type would allow exactly accurate computation, although the manipulation time and storage requirements are often excessively great. [Note: Other formats (syntaxes) for the rational data type are possible, do exist, and may be preferable.]

    2. *EBCDIC (Extended Binary-Coded Decimal Interchange Code).* An 8-bit code devised by and standard for the IBM 360/370/303X/43X1 extended family of computers. If it is necessary or desirable for an MC680XY computational system to communicate with an IBM computer employing the EBCDIC encoding, either the Motorola or the IBM system must transduce ASCII-encoded data to equivalent EBCDIC-encoded data, and the reverse. The translate (TR) instruction of the IBM system or the equivalent MOVE.B indirect MC680XY instruction discussed earlier in this chapter allows this transduction to be accomplished rapidly and economically.

    The MC680XY data transduction instructions cause the encoding of a value to be changed to a different encoding; that is, changing the data type of a value is a transduction. Certain instructions of the MC680XY allow such changes. In our present discussion, we are completely ignoring floating-point numerical data and any transduction requiring more than a single instruction.

The translate instruction was discussed earlier in this chapter, as it can also be considered a data movement instruction. Recall that a byte data register (Dn) contains an index into a table of byte data whose starting address is in the Am register. This instruction replaces the contents of the Dn register by the contents of the table location indexed by the Dn register.

MOVE.B   (Am)(Dn),Dn

where the index is an 8-bit unsigned quantity (usually an ASCII or EBCDIC character). As a philosophical comment, it is interesting that the existence of the indexed indirect through a register addressing mode allows a general-purpose instruction to replace one of several special-purpose instructions.

An instruction is provided to transform an 8-bit signed integer datum to a 16-bit signed integer datum:

EXT.W   Dn

where the source byte must be contained in a byte data register, and the destination is the same word data register. No flags are affected. Similarly, the

EXT.L   Dn

instruction has its source as a word data register, with the destination being the same long-word data register. Both instructions extend, or copy, the sign bit leftward; thus, if the source is positive, a 0 is extended leftward and the value is preserved; if the source is negative (i.e., two's complement), a 1 is extended leftward and the value is preserved. Admittedly, the identical net result could be achieved otherwise, but not as efficiently or with a single instruction. A principle is involved that is well worth mentioning. Many workers have established the theoretically possible existence of a single-instruction computational device with general abilities. It follows that additional instructions in a computer are not necessary but do facilitate the construction of algorithms that execute faster and occupy less space.

DATA OPERATION INSTRUCTIONS

Logical Instructions

The MC680XY provides one single-operand and three two-operand logical instructions, usable with byte, word, and long-word data resident in a register, in memory, or as an immediate value. The details of these instructions are shown in Figure 4.7.

Not (byte, word, long word)

NOT EA

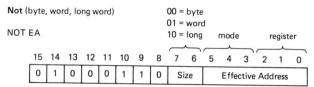

Action:
1. one's complement of operand (change state of each bit)
2. set CCR register to reflect result

And [logical Λ] (byte, word, long word)

AND { EA, Dn
       Dn, EA

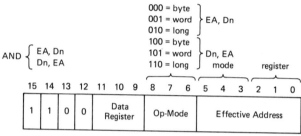

Action:
1. logical AND (Λ)
2. set CCR register appropriately

And Immediate (byte, word, long word)

ANDI value, EA

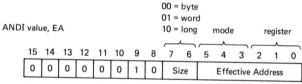

Action:
1. logical AND(Λ)
2. set CCR appropriately

Or [logical V] (byte, word, long word)

OR { EA, Dn
      Dn, EA

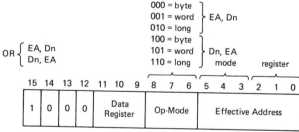

Action:
1. logical OR (V)
2. set CCR appropriately

Figure 4.7 The MC680XY logical instructions. The immediate data for the ANDI, ORI, and EORI instructions follow the operation word as 16 bits for byte/word operations or 32 bits for long-word operations.

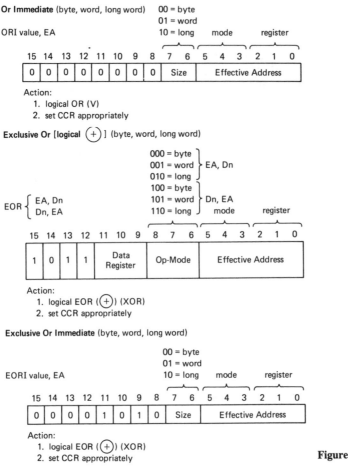

Or Immediate (byte, word, long word)

ORI value, EA

Action:
1. logical OR (V)
2. set CCR appropriately

Exclusive Or [logical (+)] (byte, word, long word)

Action:
1. logical EOR ((+)) (XOR)
2. set CCR appropriately

Exclusive Or Immediate (byte, word, long word)

EORI value, EA

Action:
1. logical EOR ((+)) (XOR)
2. set CCR appropriately

Figure 4.7 (*continued*).

```
NOT  Y       ;one's complement
AND  X,Y     ;and
OR   X,Y     ;inclusive or
XOR  X,Y     ;exclusive or
```

where Y can be register (data or address) or any location in read/write memory accessible via any addressing mode and X can be a data register or an immediate datum. In all cases, both X and Y must be equal length (byte, word, or long word). As before, memory-to-memory operations are not allowed.

Shift/Rotate Instructions

In computers, a shift instruction pushes bits in the direction of the shift within a data container, with bit contents being lost off the end of the data container in the direction of the shift and 0 bits introduced into the other end of the data container. A rotate, on the other hand, has the bits shifted out in the direction of the rotate introduced at the other end of the data container. In addition, a shift may include the leftmost bit (logical shift) and thus treat the data container as a logical or unsigned integer value cell, while the arithmetic shift treats the data container as a holder of a signed integer value and thus treats the sign bit as being sacrosanct (see Figure 4.8). The left shift arithmetic instruction shifts bits through the sign while introducing 0 bits on the right. As the sign bit is destroyed, the overflow bit (V) of the condition code register (CCR) is set $= 1$ if a sign change occurs. The right shift arithmetic instruction shifts bits out on the right end while reproducing the sign bit toward the right (thus preserving the legality of two's-complement negative and positive integer values). Rotates and shifts in the MC680XY are of length N bits and involve both the carry and extend flags (C and X) in one way or another. The amount of the shift or rotate is the first operand that is an immediate only if the shift amount is in the range 1 through 8 bits. This first operand (amount of shift) is a data register if the range is calculated in the program and has a value of 0 through 32 (the MC68020 allows a value of 0 through 63). Following are some examples:

1. Shift left logical/shift right logical:

```
LSL   #amount,X
LSR   #amount,X
```

where X can be a data register (byte, word, long word) or any word location in read/ write memory accessed via any of the addressing modes and the amount of the shift in bits (1 through 8 bits if an immediate, 0 through 63 bits if the amount is calculated and preloaded into a data register, or assumed 1 bit if X is in memory). In all cases, the last bit shifted out is placed in both the C and the X bits of CCR.

2. Shift right arithmetic:

```
ASL   #amount,X
ASR   #amount,X
```

where X can again be a byte, word, or long-word data register or a word memory location and amount is as indicated for the logical shift. Note, particularly, that the arithmetic left shift instruction is identical to the logical left shift except that the overflow bit (V) of the CCR is set iff the sign bit is changed. In these cases, the sign bit must be programmatically restored in order to assure that the expected action for an arithmetic left shift actually occurs. The shift right arithmetic instruction propagates the sign bit to the right and places the last bit shifted out of the right end of the data container into both the carry (C) and the extend (X) flags of the CCR.

3. Rotate left/rotate right:

```
ROL   #amount,X
ROR   #amount,X
```

Arithmetic Shift Left (register = byte, word, long word; memory = 1 bit — word only)

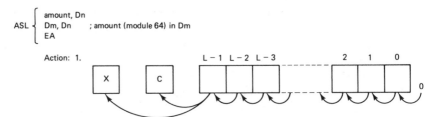

ASL { amount, Dn
Dm, Dn   ; amount (module 64) in Dm
EA

Action: 1.

2. Condition code register set appropriately.
3. V bit (overflow) of CCR set = 1 if sign change; = 0 if no sign change.

Arithmetic Shift Right (register = byte, word, long word; memory = 1 bit — word only)

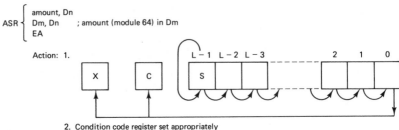

ASR { amount, Dn
Dm, Dn   ; amount (module 64) in Dm
EA

Action: 1.

2. Condition code register set appropriately
3. V bit (overflow) of CCR = 0

Logical Shift Left (register = byte, word, long word; memory = 1 bit — word only)

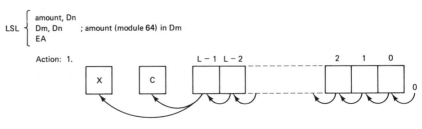

LSL { amount, Dn
Dm, Dn   ; amount (module 64) in Dm
EA

Action: 1.

2. CCR set appropriately (V = 0).

Logical Shift Right (register = byte, word, long word; memory = 1 bit — word only)

LSR { amount, Dn
Dm, Dn   ; amount (module 64) in Dm
EA

Action: 1.

2. CCR set appropriately (V = 0).

Figure 4.8 The shift instructions of the MC68000. The arithmetic left shift may destroy the sign but will signal such sign change via setting $V = 1$ in CCR. Memory shifts are limited to one bit in amount on word-length operands.

Data Register Shift Instruction Format

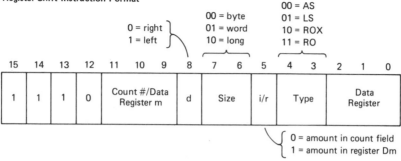

Memory Shift Instruction Format

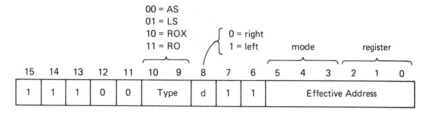

Figure 4.8 (*continued*)

where X is a byte, word, or long-word data register or a word memory data container and the amount of rotate in bits is given in the same manner as before. All rotates in the MC680XY family are logical in character and treat the sign bit in the same manner as any other bit (see Figure 4.9). These instructions rotate the "shifted-out" bit into the first bit position at the opposite end of the data container and copy that bit value into the carry flag (C) but do not affect the extend flag (X) of the CCR.

4. Rotate left through carry/rotate right through carry:

```
ROXL  #amount,X
ROXR  #amount,X
```

where X again is a byte, word, or long-word data register or a word memory data container and the amount of the rotate in bits is given in the same manner as before. These rotate instructions treat the extend flag (X) as an appended (or extra) bit on the left end of the data container to be rotated. Thus, a byte rotate with extend involves 9 bits, a word rotate with extend involves 17 bits, and a long-word rotate with extend involves 33 bits, formed by concatenating the extend flag with the datum. The extend bit (X) of the CCR is also copied into the carry bit (C).

Arithmetic Instructions

Instructions are provided in the MC680XY architectual design for byte-, word-, and long-word-length signed binary integer arithmetic; byte-, word-, long-word-length unsigned binary arithmetic; and result syntax corrections to accomplish BCD unsigned arithmetic (add, subtract, negate only). These are reviewed in Figure 4.10.

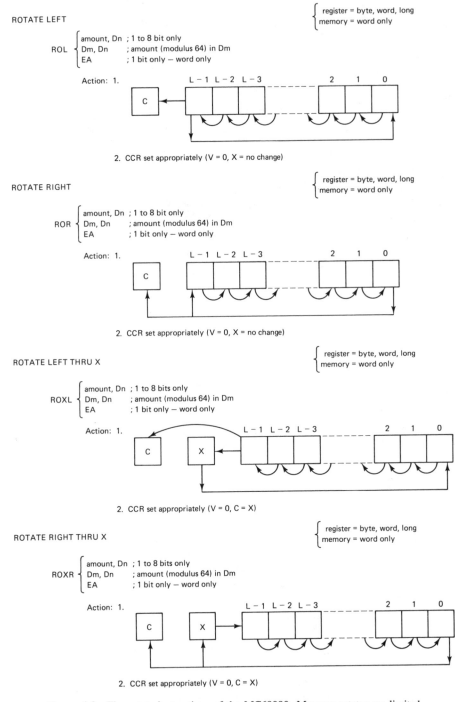

ROTATE LEFT

register = byte, word, long
memory = word only

ROL ⎰ amount, Dn ; 1 to 8 bit only
    ⎨ Dm, Dn   ; amount (modulus 64) in Dm
    ⎱ EA   ; 1 bit only — word only

Action: 1.

L − 1 L − 2 L − 3   2   1   0

C

2. CCR set appropriately (V = 0, X = no change)

ROTATE RIGHT

register = byte, word, long
memory = word only

ROR ⎰ amount, Dn ; 1 to 8 bit only
    ⎨ Dm, Dn   ; amount (modulus 64) in Dm
    ⎱ EA   ; 1 bit only — word only

Action: 1.

L − 1 L − 2 L − 3   2   1   0

C

2. CCR set appropriately (V = 0, X = no change)

ROTATE LEFT THRU X

register = byte, word, long
memory = word only

ROXL ⎰ amount, Dn ; 1 to 8 bits only
     ⎨ Dm, Dn   ; amount (modulus 64) in Dm
     ⎱ EA   ; 1 bit only — word only

Action: 1.

L − 1 L − 2 L − 3   2   1   0

C   X

2. CCR set appropriately (V = 0, C = X)

ROTATE RIGHT THRU X

register = byte, word, long
memory = word only

ROXR ⎰ amount, Dn ; 1 to 8 bits only
     ⎨ Dm, Dn   ; amount (modulus 64) in Dm
     ⎱ EA   ; 1 bit only — word only

Action: 1.

L − 1 L − 2 L − 3   2   1   0

C   X

2. CCR set appropriately (V = 0, C = X)

Figure 4.9 The rotate instructions of the MC68000. Memory rotates are limited to 1 bit in amount on word length operands. Rotate instructions employ the same general formats as the shift instructions shown in Figure 4.8.

178

Add Binary (byte, word, long word)

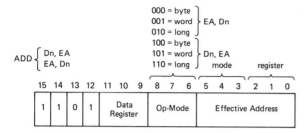

Add Immediate Binary (byte, word, long word)

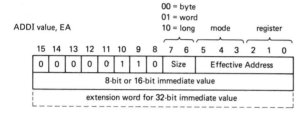

Add Quick Binary (value 1 through 8 immediate) (byte, word, long word)

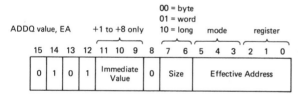

Subtract Binary (byte, word, long word)

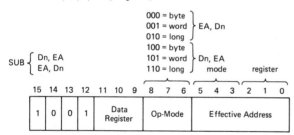

Subtract Immediate Binary (byte, word, long word)

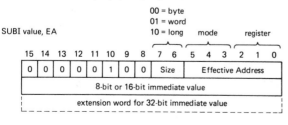

Figure 4.10 The signed binary arithmetic instructions of the MC68000. Three additional instructions (ADDX,SUBX, NEGX) are shown in Figure 4.13 in connection with multiprecision arithmetic.

Subtract Quick Binary (value 1 through 8 immediate) (byte, word, long word)

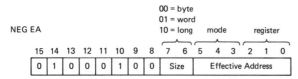

SUBQ value, EA   +1 to +8 only

15	14	13	12	11	10	9	8	7	6	5	4	3	2	1	0
0	1	0	1				1	Size		Effective Address					

00 = byte
01 = word
10 = long   mode   register

Negate (Two's Complement) Binary (byte, word, long word)

NEG EA

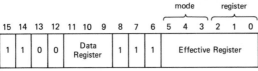

15	14	13	12	11	10	9	8	7	6	5	4	3	2	1	0
0	1	0	0	0	1	0	0	Size		Effective Address					

00 = byte
01 = word
10 = long   mode   register

Multiply Signed Binary (word only → long word; long → quad — MC 68020 only)

MULS EA, Dn ; destination must be data register

mode   register

15	14	13	12	11	10	9	8	7	6	5	4	3	2	1	0
1	1	0	0	Data Register			1	1	1	Effective Register					

Note: CCR set N and Z as expected
       C and V always 0
       X not changed

Divide Signed Binary $\left[\dfrac{Dn}{EA} \to Dn \right]$ (long/word → word-quotient;
                                                    quad/long → long-quotient — (MC 68020 only)

DIVS EA Dn ; destination must be data register

mode   register

15	14	13	12	11	10	9	8	7	6	5	4	3	2	1	0
1	0	0	0	Data Register			1	1	1	Effective Register					

Action:
1. quotient in least significant half of destination register
2. remainder in most significant half of destination register
3. divide by zero give trap
4. CCR bits N, C, V set by result; C = 0; not changed

Figure 4.10 (*continued*).

Signed binary arithmetic.

```
ADD    X,Y
SUB    X,Y
MULS   X,Y
DIVS   X,Y
ADDI   X,Y
SUBI   X,Y
NEG    X   ;two's complement
ADDQ   X,Y
SUBQ   X,Y
```

where Y can be a byte, word, or long-word data register or (with the exception of multiply and divide) a location in read/write memory accessible via any addressing mode, and X can be a register, a location in memory accessible via any addressing mode, or an immediate datum. All flags in the condition code register (CCR) are set; that is, the overflow, sign, zero, extend, and carry flags are set. Again, memory-to-memory operations are not allowed.

Although the ADD, SUB, ADDI, SUBI, and NEG instructions perform their data operations as expected, the other instructions demand further explanation. Thus, the extend (EXT and EXTB) instructions are often useful in converting byte data to word or long-word data before arithmetic and converting word to long-word data before word division.

The signed integer multiply instructions act as shown in Figure 4.11. Note that multiplying two 16-bit source data results in a 32-bit result datum and that, with the MC68020 only, multiplying two 32-bit source data results in either a 32-bit or a 64-bit results datum.

The signed integer divide instruction (Figure 4.12) acts as follows:

$$\frac{\text{32-bit register}}{\text{16-bit datum}} \longrightarrow \begin{array}{l} \text{16-bit quotient in low half of register} \\ \text{16-bit remainder in high half of register} \end{array}$$

Note that this implies that the signed word divide is really a long/word divide, whereas the signed long-word divide of the MC68020 (only) is really a quad/long divide.

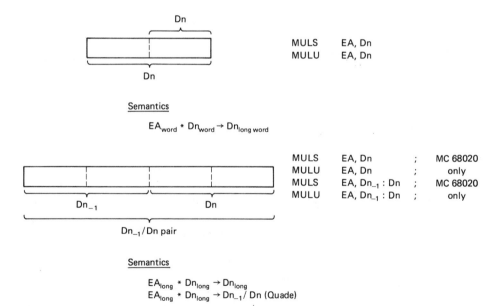

Semantics

$$EA_{word} * Dn_{word} \to Dn_{long\ word}$$

Semantics

$$EA_{long} * Dn_{long} \to Dn_{long}$$
$$EA_{long} * Dn_{long} \to Dn_{-1}/Dn\ (Quade)$$

Figure 4.11   The multiply signed integer and multiply unsigned integer instructions of the MC680XY give a double-length result. Only the MC68020 allows long-word source operands.

MC 68000, MC 68008, MC 68010, MC 68020

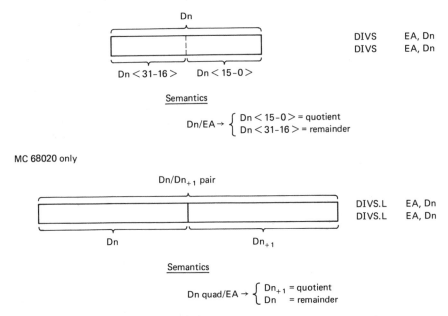

Figure 4.12 The divide signed integer and divide unsigned integer instructions require a double-length dividend and result in the quotient being placed in the low-order (rightmost) half of the destination and the remainder being placed in the high-order (leftmost) half of the destination location.

Unsigned binary arithmetic. Only two instructions are specifically provided by the MC680XY to perform unsigned binary integer arithmetic using unsigned source operands:

MULU   X,Y,
DIVU   X,Y

where the restrictions on Y and X are exactly those of the corresponding signed integer instructions, with the additional provision that both Y and X are considered unsigned positive integer values and the result (new Y) is also an unsigned positive integer value.

Addition and subtraction of unsigned (assumed positive) integer values involving or not involving the carry and extend flags are carried out using the instructions for signed integer data operations. Programmatic due care must always be taken to assure that subtraction does not inadvertently result in a "borrow," thus generating an incorrect result value.

Multiple-precision arithmetic. As you have seen, signed integer arithmetic is provided for with source and destination operand data contained in byte, word, and long-word register or memory containers. Thus, numeric values can be directly manipulated in the value range:

Byte: $+127$ through -128
Word: $+32,767$ through $-32,768$
Long word: $+2,147,483,647$ through $-2,147,483,648$

Although it is somewhat unusual to encounter a need to deal with numeric values with a greater magnitude than those allowed for with long words (approximately $\pm 2 * 10^{12}$), it nevertheless happens sometimes. Of course, one solution to this need is supplied by floating-point arithmetic, which we shall discuss in some detail in a later chapter. One of the major drawbacks of floating-point arithmetic is the necessary inclusion of inaccuracies in the values that can be represented. For most purposes, these representation errors can be at least partially controlled. However, there are applications where complete and total accuracy is required. The practical solution to such requirements is to employ integer arithmetic involving the necessary number of bits or digits.

The designers of the Motorola MC680XY family provided the five instructions (see Figure 4.13) to allow multiprecision arithmetic:

```
ADDX  X,Y      ;data register to data register or
SUBX  X,Y      ;  predecrement memory indirect to predecrement
               ;  memory indirect

NEGX  Y        ;all addressing modes available

MULU  X,Y      ;memory (all addressing modes) to
DIVU  X,Y      ;  data register only
```

The first three of the foregoing instructions assume that the extend bit (X) of the condition code register (CCR) contains the valid overflow bit from an addition/subtraction of the rightward quanta previously accomplished and that this X bit should, therefore, be a portion of the present arithmetic. Our first example will involve adding two quantities that each require five long words to contain their correct values.

	31 0	31 0	31 0	31 0	31 0
Addend	long word #4	long word #3	long word #2	long word #1	long word #0

	31 0	31 0	31 0	31 0	31 0
+ Augend	long word #4	long word #3	long word #2	long word #1	long word #0

	31 0	31 0	31 0	31 0	31 0
= Sum	long word #4	long word #3	long word #2	long word #1	long word #0

Add with Extend Binary Signed (byte, word, long word)

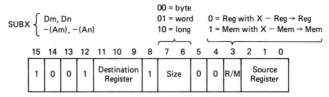

ADDX $\left\{\begin{array}{l}\text{Dm, Dn}\\-\text{(Am), }-\text{(An)}\end{array}\right.$

00 = byte
01 = word
10 = long

0 = Reg + Reg + X → Reg
1 = Mem + Mem + X → Mem

15	14	13	12	11 10 9 8	7	6 5	4	3	2	1 0
1	1	0	1	Destination Register	1	Size	0	0	R/M	Source Register

Note: Predecrement address register indirect if R/M = 1.

Subtract with Extend Binary Signed (byte, word long word)

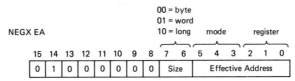

SUBX $\left\{\begin{array}{l}\text{Dm, Dn}\\-\text{(Am), }-\text{(An)}\end{array}\right.$

00 = byte
01 = word
10 = long

0 = Reg with X − Reg → Reg
1 = Mem with X − Mem → Mem

15	14	13	12	11 10 9 8	7	6 5	4	3	2	1 0
1	0	0	1	Destination Register	1	Size	0	0	R/M	Source Register

Note: If R/M = 1, predecrement address register indirect.

Negate with Extend Binary Signed (byte, word, long word)

NEGX EA

00 = byte
01 = word
10 = long   mode   register

15	14	13	12	11	10	9	8	7 6	5 4 3	2 1 0
0	1	0	0	0	0	0	0	Size	Effective Address	

Multiply Unsigned Binary Assumed Positive (word only for MC 68000; long also for MC 68020)

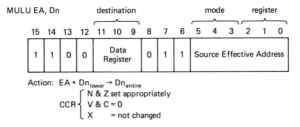

MULU EA, Dn   destination   mode   register

15	14	13	12	11 10 9	8 7 6	5 4 3	2 1 0
1	1	0	0	Data Register	0 1 1	Source Effective Address	

Action: EA ∗ Dn$_{lower}$ → Dn$_{entire}$

CCR $\left\{\begin{array}{ll}\text{N \& Z set appropriately}\\\text{V \& C = 0}\\\text{X}\quad\text{= not changed}\end{array}\right.$

Divide Insigned Binary Assumed Positive (word only for MC 68000; long also for MC 68020)

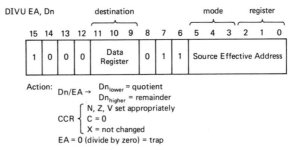

DIVU EA, Dn   destination   mode   register

15	14	13	12	11 10 9	8 7 6	5 4 3	2 1 0
1	0	0	0	Data Register	0 1 1	Source Effective Address	

Action: Dn/EA → $\begin{array}{l}\text{Dn}_{lower}\text{ = quotient}\\\text{Dn}_{higher}\text{ = remainder}\end{array}$

CCR $\left\{\begin{array}{ll}\text{N, Z, V set appropriately}\\\text{C = 0}\\\text{X = not changed}\end{array}\right.$

EA = 0 (divide by zero) = trap

Figure 4.13 The MC680XY arithmetic instructions that are most useful for multi-precision integer arithmetic.

Thus, the data containers are 160 bits in size and the possible values are $\pm 2^{159}$, which is a very large signed decimal value—approximately $5 * 10^{47}$ (5 followed by 47 zeros). As a matter of interest, if we had used six long words to contain our values, the possible magnitude would have far exceeded the best current estimate of the total number of elementary particles in the entire universe.

The traditional and correct plan of attack is to add, first, the rightmost portion (long word), then the next toward the left, incorporating any carry-out, then the next, and so on. As the input (source) values already exist in memory and as they are too large to fit into a register, it is most felicitous to employ the predecrement memory through an address register indirect addressing mode to access the data. Note that the two address-type arithmetic instructions of the MC680XY family would result in destroying the augend value by overwriting it with the sum; therefore, we preserve the value of the augend by copying it. Also note that the first addition (long word #0 plus long word #0) should not include a carry-out from a previous element (there was none); therefore, we will first clear the X bit of the CCR (in fact, we will clear the entire CCR).

```
;load effective addresses into address registers
;
        LEA       ADDEND,A1
        LEA       AUGEND,A2
        LEA       SUM,A3
;
;move augend value to sum so that two address instructions do not destroy value
;
           MOVE.W  #4,D0              ;counter = 5
SAVE_AUG:  MOVE.L  (A2)+,(A3)+
           DBRA    D0,SAVE_AUG
;
;A1 has address of long word #4 of addend—must point to long word #0
;A2 has address of long word #0 of addend—must point to long word #4
;A3 has address of long word #0 of sum—this is correct
;
        SUBQ.L   #4,A1
        SUB.L    #20,A2
        SUBQ.L   #4,A3
;
;accomplish memory-to-memory multiprecision addition
;
           MOVE.W  #4,D0              ;counter = 5
           MOVE.W  #$0000,CCP         ;extend bit (X) = 0
ADD_THEM:  ADDX.L   -(A1),-(A3)
           DBRA    D0,ADD_THEM
;
;A1, A2, A3 have the address of the left end of each number, as expected
;
```

If you will recall your early primary school arithmetic, it will be clear that multi-precision subtraction would employ the same algorithm [the extend bit (X) of the CCR would represent a borrow].

Also recall that multiplication is essentially a series of additions, even though this is not the most efficient method of implementation. Think about how you accomplish multiplication by hand with decimal numbers on a piece of paper. In essence, you use the rightmost digit of the multiplier to multiply all the digits of the multiplicand; then you use the next leftward digit of the multiplier, with this partial answer shifted leftward one digit in respect to the first partial answer, and so on. As an elementary example in base 10:

193	(multiplicand)
× 241	(multiplier)
193	(partial product)
772	(shifted partial product)
386	(doubly shifted partial product)
46513	(product)

You will remember that if the signs of two input (source) operands are alike, the product will be positive; but if the signs are different, the product will be negative.

We will not present a multiprecision shift-and-add multiplication program section for the MC680XY; rather, we will leave this as practice problem. However, a few suggestions are in order:

1. Using two's-complement arithmetic, the multiplier should be positive. If this requires that you negate a negative value, be sure to presave the original value for possible use later in your program. In fact, with two-address instructions, it is always a good idea to presave the multiplier, as it will be overlain by the product.

2. Although, with two's-complement arithmetic, the multiplicand could be negative if your algorithm always extends the sign bit of each partial product leftward, this process is so tedious in multiprecision software that I highly recommend that the multiplicand also be made positive (after saving the original value).

3. Therefore, I strongly recommend that the sign bit of both source operands be tested [BTST #31,(An)] and that each negative source operand be converted to positive.

4. The shift-and-add algorithm illustrated above for decimal number multiplication is suggested as the basis for multiprecision binary multiplication of positive numbers (or of numbers you have converted to be positive).

5. If the input operands had identical signs (both positive or both negative), the positive product is correct; if the signs were different, the product must be two's-complement converted to negative form.

As you can imagine, multiprecision division can be accomplished using a series of subtractions and stopping one step before the temporary dividend would change sign—that is, when the remainder is smaller than the divisor. Algorithms commonly exist that execute faster than the subtract-and-test method; that is, they are equivalent to the shift-and-add multiply algorithm discussed above. These division algorithms are fairly complicated and are not very fast in execution speed. The relatively slow speed of division algorithms in digital computers can be emphasized by noting that the very fast supercomputers of CRAY Research, Inc., do not contain a divide operation. Rather, they provide a reciprocal instruction that uses Newton's iteration followed by a multiply. It is very possible that you might find this avoidance of division via a reciprocal and multiply a viable suggestion for multiprecision arithmetic.

Binary-coded decimal arithmetic.   The data format of BCD (binary-coded decimal) unsigned decimal numeric values uses a nibble for each decimal digit and thus provides two digits per byte, as illustrated on the top of Figure 4.14. All values are assumed positive by the MC680XY instructions shown in Figure 4.15. These instructions employ the algorithms shown in Figure 4.14 to derive the correct base 10 arithmetic result. Particularly note that subtracting a larger value from a smaller value results in the ten's complement of the expected result (or results in the nine's complement if the extend bit was set ON by the operation).

The process of converting a two-digit ASCII number to BCD can be illustrated as follows:

```
LEA       VALUE,A1       ;contents of VALUE = 3731 hex
SUB.W     #$3030,(A1)    ;contents of VALUE = 0701 hex
MOVE.B    (A1),D0        ;contents of D0 = 07 hex
LSL.B     #4,D0          ;contents of D0 = 70 hex
ADD.B     D0,1(A1)       ;contents of VALUE = 0771 hex
CLR.L     D0
MOVE.B    1(A1),D0       ;contents of D0 = 0071 decimal
MOVE.W    D0,(A1)        ;contents of VALUE = 0071 decimal
```

On the other hand, the normal binary-coded decimal value will consist of a signed string of 4-bit nibbles grouped in contiguous two-nibble pairs per byte, with a separate byte on the left end encoding the sign and possibly the length in digits. Addition and subtraction would be accomplished from right to left in the strings with the operation (add/sub) and the sign of the result both being a function of the desired operation, the magnitude of the BCD strings, and their respective signs. The rules of ordinary base 10 arithmetic, as learned in elementary school, would apply. As a simple example, we will add the two equal-length BCD strings below, giving a third string as the result. The first byte of the strings will contain the length and sign in signed-magnitude form, ranging from $+127$ through -127.

byte = plus
length = 22 digits in 11 bytes = 16 hexadecimal

16	01	23	45	67	89	98	76	54	32	10	01

+

16	09	87	65	45	21	00	12	34	56	78	90

sum

16	11	11	11	11	10	98	77	77	77	77	91

```
;set-up for indirect addressing
;
            LEA        ADDEND,A1
            LEA        AUGEND,A2
            LEA        SUM,A3
;
;move augend to sum because two-address instruction (i.e.; save augend value)
;
            MOVE.B     (A1),D0          ;contains sign and length
            BCLR       #7,D0            ;make sign plus
            EXT.W      D0               ;now contains length
SAVE_AUG:   MOVE.B     (A2)+,(A3)+
            DBRA       D0,SAVE_AUG
;
;get the original addresses
;
            LEA        AUGEND,A2
            LEA        SUM,A3
;
;are the signs and the lengths the same?
;
            CMP.B      (A1),(A3)
            BNE        DO_DIFFERENT
;
;initialize extend bit (X) of CCP = 0
;
            MOVE.W     SR,D0
            BCLR       #4,D0
            MOVE.W     D0,CCP
```

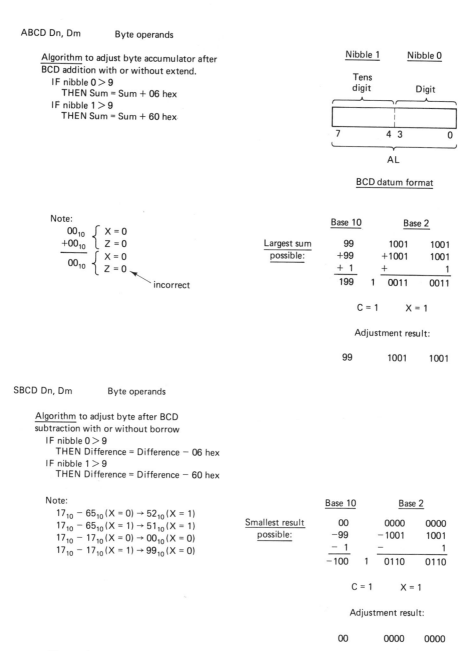

Figure 4.14 The BCD adjustment algorithms used by MC680XY instructions ABCD and SBCD.

Add Decimal with Extend (two digits = byte only)

ABCD $\begin{cases} \text{Dm, Dn} \\ -(\text{Am}), -(\text{An}) \end{cases}$ 0 = Reg-to-Reg
                                                        1 = Mem-to-Mem

15	14	13	12	11 10 9	8	7	6	5	4	3	2 1 0
1	1	0	0	Destination Register	1	0	0	0	0	R/M	Source Register

Notes:
 1. Memory address <u>must</u> be predecrement address register indirect.
 2. CCR bits N and V not defined.

Subtract Decimal with Extend (two digits = byte only)

SBCD $\begin{cases} \text{Dm, Dn} \\ -(\text{Am}), -(\text{An}) \end{cases}$ 0 = Reg-to-Reg
                                                        1 = Mem-to-Mem

15	14	13	12	11 10 9	8	7	6	5	4	3	2 1 0
1	0	0	0	Destination Register	1	0	0	0	0	R/M	Source Register

Notes:
 1. Memory address <u>must</u> be predecrement address register indirect.
 2. CCR bits N and V not defined.

Negate Decimal with Extend (two digits = byte only)

NBCD EA   mode   register

15	14	13	12	11	10	9	8	7	6	5 4 3	2 1 0
0	1	0	0	1	0	0	0	0	0	Effective Address	

Notes:
 1. If extend = 0
    THEN result = ten's complement of source
    ELSE result = nine's complement of source
 2. $Result_{10} \leftarrow 0_{10} - source_{10} - X_{10}$
 3. CCR bits N and V not defined.

Figure 4.15 The base 10 [decimal or binary-coded decimal (BCD)] instructions of the MC680XY.

```
;
;set up loop counter and indirect addresses to be from left end
;
        MOVE.B   (A3),D0          ;sign and length
        BCLR     #7,D0            ;make length plus
        EXT.W    D0
        EXT.L    D0
        ADDA.L   D0,A1            ;left byte address
        ADDA.L   D0,A3            ;left byte address
        SUBQ.L   #1,D0            ;correct counter for DBRA using -1
;
;the actual addition—finally
```

```
;
DO_NEXT:    ABCD      -(A1),-(A3)
            DBRA      D0,DO_NEXT
            BRA       ALL_DONE
;
;EXCEPTIONAL CONDITIONS
;              1. SUM could be digit longer than sources = C bit of CCP would be set
;              2. If signs or lengths are different, special cases are needed—
;                 they are not shown
;
ALL_DONE:      -          -
               -          -
```

FIVE SMALL EXAMPLE PROGRAMS

We end this chapter by presenting five short example programs in Figure 4.16 through 4.20, adapted from Triebel and Singh (1986).

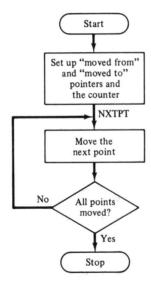

```
        LEA       BLK1,A1
        LEA       BLK2,A2
        MOVE.L    N,D0
NXTPT   MOVE.W    (A1)+,(A2)+
        SUBQ.L    #1,D0
        BNZ       NXTPT
```

Figure 4.16 Block transfer flowchart and program. (From W. A. Triebel and A. Singh, *The 68000 Microprocessor: Architecture, Software, and Interfacing Techniques,* © 1986, p. 100. Reprinted by permission of Prentice-Hall, Inc., Englewood Cliffs, NJ.)

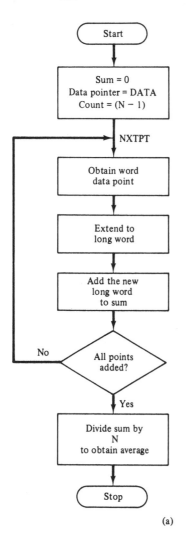

D_0 = counter
D_7 = sum
A_1 = pointer to data points
D_1 = temporary register for
        holding data point

(a)

	LEA	AVERAGE,AL
	CLR.L	D7
	LEA	DATA,A1
	MOVE.L	#(N−1),D0
NXTPT	MOVE.W	(A1)$^+$,D1
	EXT.L	D1
	ADD.L	D1,D7
	DBF	D0,NXTPT
	DIVS	#N,D7
	MOV.W	D7,(A2)

(b)

Figure 4.17 Flowchart and program for finding the average of N signed numbers. (From W. A. Triebel and A. Singh, *The 68000 Microprocessor: Architecture, Software, and Interfacing Techniques,* © 1986, p. 103. Reprinted by permission of Prentice-Hall, Inc., Englewood Cliffs, NJ.)

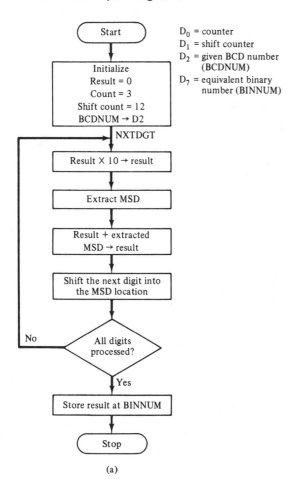

D_0 = counter
D_1 = shift counter
D_2 = given BCD number
      (BCDNUM)
D_7 = equivalent binary
      number (BINNUM)

(a)

```
            LEA        BCDNUM,A1
            LEA        BINNUM,A2
            CLR.L      D7
            MOVE.L     #3,D0
            MOVE.L     #12,D1
            MOVE.W     (A1),B2
NXTDGT      MULI       #10,D7
            MOVE.W     D2,D3
            LSR.W      D1,D3
            ADD.W      D3,D7
            LSL.W      #4,D2
            DBF        D0,NXTDGT
            MOVE.W     D7,(A2)
```

(b)

Figure 4.18 Flowchart and program for BCD-to-binary conversion routine. (From W. A. Triebel and A. Singh, *The 68000 Microprocessor: Architecture, Software, and Interfacing Techniques,* © 1986, p. 105. Reprinted by permission of Prentice-Hall, Inc., Englewood Cliffs, NJ.)

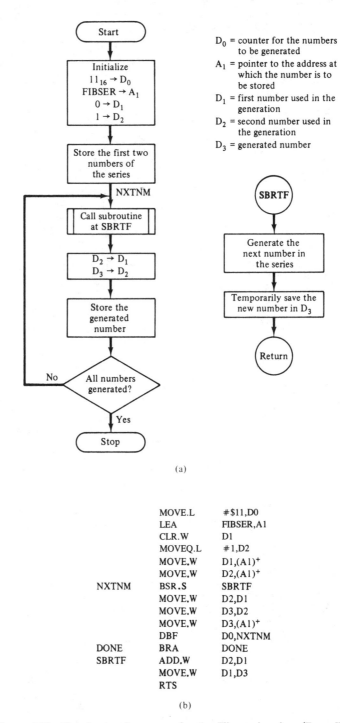

D_0 = counter for the numbers to be generated

A_1 = pointer to the address at which the number is to be stored

D_1 = first number used in the generation

D_2 = second number used in the generation

D_3 = generated number

(a)

	MOVE.L	#$11,D0
	LEA	FIBSER,A1
	CLR.W	D1
	MOVEQ.L	#1,D2
	MOVE.W	D1,(A1)$^+$
	MOVE.W	D2,(A1)$^+$
NXTNM	BSR.S	SBRTF
	MOVE.W	D2,D1
	MOVE.W	D3,D2
	MOVE.W	D3,(A1)$^+$
	DBF	D0,NXTNM
DONE	BRA	DONE
SBRTF	ADD.W	D2,D1
	MOVE.W	D1,D3
	RTS	

(b)

Figure 4.19 Flowchart and program for the Fibonacci series. (From W. A. Triebel and A. Singh, *The 68000 Microprocessor: Architecture, Software, and Interfacing Techniques,* © 1986, p. 112. Reprinted by permission of Prentice-Hall, Inc., Englewood Cliffs, NJ.)

A_1 = $PNTR_1$ = pointer to first element
A_2 = $PNTR_2$ = pointer to next element
A_3 = $PNTR_3$ = pointer to last element

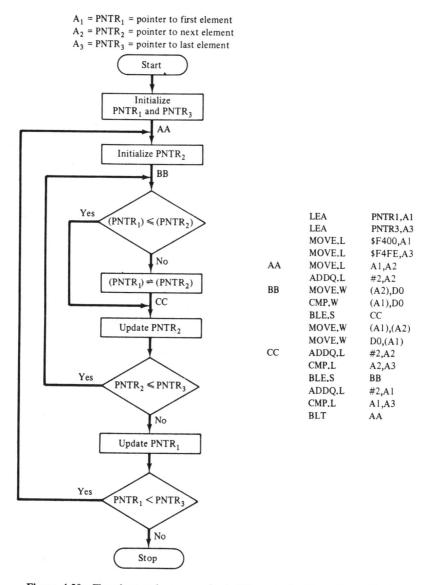

	LEA	PNTR1,A1
	LEA	PNTR3,A3
	MOVE.L	$F400,A1
	MOVE.L	$F4FE,A3
AA	MOVE.L	A1,A2
	ADDQ.L	#2,A2
BB	MOVE.W	(A2),D0
	CMP.W	(A1),D0
	BLE.S	CC
	MOVE.W	(A1),(A2)
	MOVE.W	D0,(A1)
CC	ADDQ.L	#2,A2
	CMP.L	A2,A3
	BLE.S	BB
	ADDQ.L	#2,A1
	CMP.L	A1,A3
	BLT	AA

Figure 4.20 Flowchart and program for bubble sort algorithm. (From W. A. Triebel and A. Singh, *The 68000 Microprocessor: Architecture, Software, and Interfacing Techniques,* © 1986, p. 107. Reprinted by permission of Prentice-Hall, Inc., Englewood Cliffs, NJ.)

EXERCISES

4.1. Give example instructions that accomplish the following:
   (a) Data operation.
   (b) Data transduction.
   (c) Data movement.

4.2. When considering computer memory, it is absolutely vital that you always distinguish between the address of a location in memory and the contents of that location. We commonly refer to the contents as data. In almost all programs, it is necessary to move addresses into address registers (and memory locations) and often to perform calculations with addresses. During this process, the addresses are the contents of registers (and memory locations). Therefore, the addresses are data. Carefully distinguish between address data and program data.

4.3. Distinguish between a string and a one-dimensional array.

4.4. Generalize the within-array address offset formulas in the text so as to allow zero and negative subscripts as well as subscripts that progress negatively.

4.5. Design, implement, test, and document a program to accomplish multiprecision multiplication of signed integer values in the range $\pm1 \times 2^{127}$ using the shift-and-add algorithm.

4.6. Design, implement, test, and document a program to accomplish multiprecision division of signed integer values in the range $\pm1 \times 2^{127}$ using three methods:
   (a) The reciprocal (Newton's iteration) and multiply.
   (b) The division algorithm you learned in primary school.
   (c) The subtract until sign change.
   Compare and report execution times, program sizes, and accuracies.

5

Macros
and Conditional
Assembly

MACROS

A programmer implementing an algorithm in assembly language is often forced to
use the same fragment of code in several places within a procedure; that is, some
blocks of code are repeated many times in the program. This code block may save
register contents in the memory stack, perform a particular set of operations such as
string reversal, invoke an operating system's I/O operation, and so on. The task of
entering these repeated code fragments into the source version of a program is often
facilitated by a good editor system, although excellent editors are somewhat rare.
One viewpoint of a macro holds that it is a method whereby a programmer can
define and use instructions that the computer designer did not include in the instruction set because of economic considerations, technical limitations, lack of programming experience, oversight, ignorance, or stupidity. In addition, the purpose of the
code block may not be self-evident; the mnemonics of the instructions may not read-
ily reveal the algorithmic-level task. For example, the use of the instruction

```
TRAP    n
```

invokes an interrupt that causes the interrupt server routine to perform some desirable action, as indicated by the interrupt number. For this discussion, let us imagine
that n is 47 and that the action will be the transfer of a line (with EOL) of ASCII

characters from the keyboard to the input buffer in the program. Program clarity would be vastly improved by using one of the action mnemonics.

```
GET_LINE    TERMINAL
READ        TERMINAL
```

A MACRO facility is an adjunct to a basic assembler that allows the programmer to order the macro processor to substitute predefined code blocks in the place of the macro name. Thus, the use of the macro name GET_LINE or READ would cause the macro processor to substitute TRAP n into the code of the assembly procedure at that place before the assembler is invoked. This process is termed *expansion* because (usually) a block of code is substituted for a macro name, with the result that the assembly procedure is expanded and enlarged.

A macro consists of a *macro definition* and at least one reference to or *invocation of* the macro. In general, the macro definition consists of several portions: a *named beginning,* the *body,* and the *end.* Different assemblers may require slightly different syntaxes, as illustrated by two examples:

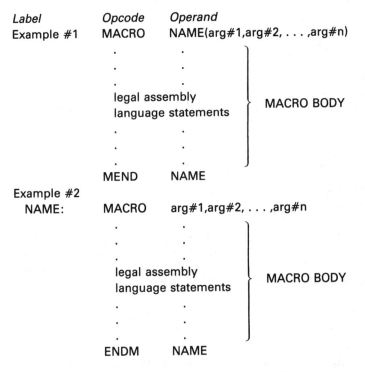

```
Label          Opcode      Operand
Example #1     MACRO       NAME(arg#1,arg#2, . . . ,arg#n)
                  .            .
                  .            .
                  .            .
               legal assembly           ⎫
               language statements      ⎬  MACRO BODY
                  .            .         ⎭
                  .            .
                  .            .
               MEND         NAME
Example #2
  NAME:        MACRO       arg#1,arg#2, . . . ,arg#n
                  .            .
                  .            .
                  .            .
               legal assembly           ⎫
               language statements      ⎬  MACRO BODY
                  .            .         ⎭
                  .            .
                  .            .
               ENDM         NAME
```

Almost all, if not all, macro assemblers require that macro definitions physically precede the macro reference statements in which they are invoked within an assembly module. A reference to the above macro could be

NAME   arg#1,arg#2, ... ,arg#n

This macro reference or invocation would result in the macro reference line being replaced by the body of the macro. It is most important to be very clear about the macro assembler completely accomplishing this replacement before the assembler starts the normal assembly process. Therefore, the body of the macro must form syntactically legal and logically correct assembly code within the context of the larger assembly code module.

The Pros and Cons of Macros

We have already seen that one of the advantages of programming with macros occurs if a piece of code is to be repeated in several places within the program. In this case, the use of a macro not only can save typing time but can also reduce the number of errors due to careless typing by allowing us to enter the macro definition once and then subsequently refer to it many times. Placing the macro definition in a macro library and including it in the code of other programs is a viable way of allowing other workers to share in your expertise. Note how the use of arguments would allow us to change the data used within each different macro reference. In addition, arguments can be used to change the macro itself—as we shall see somewhat later.

Allow me to remind you that the above reasons for using macros are also among the reasons for using subprocedures within the programming process. Thus, we must consider when a macro should be employed and when a subprocedure should be used. Recall, from your experience with a procedural-level language such as Pascal and from your study of Chapter 3, that a subprocedure is defined once and translated once, occurs a single time in the linked object code, and is invoked (called) as needed during program execution. The implications for subprocedures are as follows:

1. They occur once in the object code; therefore, the object code use of memory space is relatively small.
2. The translation process (assembling) requires relatively less time, as the subprocedure code is translated only once.
3. The linking process, at least for external subprocedures, is relatively complicated and time-consuming, as addresses in both the calling and in the called module must be adjusted.
4. The process of invoking (calling) the subprocedure and returning from it during execution at each invocation is relatively time-consuming, as the PC and the other registers must be saved in memory (usually on the stack), the arguments acquired, and, finally, the registers restored just before returning.

The conclusion is correct that subprocedures are somewhat parsimonious of memory space and translation time but are not parsimonious of link time and of execution time.

The corresponding implications for macros are as follows:

1. The full body of the macro occurs in the object code each and every time the macro is referenced; therefore, the object code is relatively large.
2. As the full body of the macro is translated (assembled) for each reference, the assembly process consumes relatively more time.
3. As the addresses within the macro body are determined during assembly, the linking process is simplified and speeded up, or even eliminated, if no subprocedures are used.
4. As there is no transfer of control during execution but merely sequential instruction fetch-execution, and as no registers need saving/restoring or arguments acquired, execution tends to be faster.

This comparison of macros to subprocedures is another example of the almost universal trade-off that programmers have been plagued with since the beginning—say, since the very late 1940s or very early 1950s. This trade-off has been known by various names (including a number of short Anglo-Saxon expletives), the most common being *the time-space trade-off*. Thus, we note that, with all else being equal, a program using macros will execute faster but will use more memory than the same program using subprocedures, which will tend to execute more slowly but use less memory. In addition, although not generally as important, a macro-based program will assemble more slowly but will link faster than the equivalent subprocedure-based program.

Although the foregoing treatment is true and must be the basis for all comparative costs analyses, it is almost too direct and simple. There are other extenuating factors that must also be considered. Although I am sure you can imagine most of them, allow me to lead your thinking a trifle. Our somewhat shallow analysis is predicated on the almost universal truism that the proper choice between using a macro or using a subprocedure should depend on economic considerations unless a system limitation is of overriding importance.

As an example at one extreme, consider the various microcomputers that are almost universally used to control carburetion in present-day automobiles. Although the computational task is by no means trivial, it is not particularly complicated, and the time of reaction constraints are fairly liberal (milliseconds) in terms of computer cycles. This carburetion control system must operate reliably in a fairly computer-hostile environment of extremes in temperature, in shaking, and in shock, in addition to being turned on and turned off continually. Read-only memory (ROM) seems necessary for program and constant storage, while work area storage could employ volatile random access memory (RAM). In addition, because the physical system will be duplicated well over a million times, any saving of memory space will presumably be economically important. Thus, serious consideration of the use of sub-procedures is indicated for all sections of code that are used repeatedly.

As an example at the other extreme of the space-time trade-off, consider the fairly common situations where reaction time in microseconds is essential and where the consequences of even very short delays are so extreme or so costly as to negate any consideration of unduly limiting memory size. The trite and usual example is the control of missiles. Under these circumstances, the call register, save argument, acquisition, work, register restore, return sequence necessary for subprocedure usage may literally slow execution to the extent that the use of macros, with their attendant additional memory needs for storage of repeated code blocks, is absolutely necessary. In fact, in some cases, the need for speed is so rigorous that program loops are "unwound"; that is, the loop conditional test and repeat or go-on is too time-consuming and the loop-body code is physically repeated the requisite number of times. Although this loop unwinding technique is not possible for those loops that calculate or input the termination condition, it is possible for certain loops (example: Newton's iteration). Note the clear-cut space-time trade-off.

As you would imagine, not many real-world space-time trade-off decisions are as clear-cut as the above examples. So how do you arrive at a defendable decision? Realistically, you should depend on your team leader (or his or her team leader) for directions and/or guidance. In addition, the specifications and requirements document for the system being implemented should clearly include any memory size constraints, execution speed requirements, reaction time necessities, and so forth. And as a last, very true (but perhaps asinine-sounding) remark: over time you will gain experience that will allow more realistic judgments in this space-time trade-off business.

It remains to be emphasized that some programming niceties and tasks that are almost trivial to accomplish by using macros are much more difficult to accomplish via subprocedures. Although the opposite is undoubtedly true, it has been my experience that macros can be somewhat easily designed and implemented to accomplish almost any task that subprocedures could accomplish, with the probable exception of recursion. Nevertheless, in our enthusiasm for macros, let us not forget that subroutines have the advantage of memory space conservation and, as normally used, of residence in a library of useful and well-tested routines as well as the large advantage of separate assembly/compilation (at least in the more usual case of external subprocedures).

Substitution Macro Programming

We will approach the problem of communicating an understanding of the power of macro-assembly programming via examples. In its very simplest form, the use of a macro name in an assembly procedure is the use of an alias for a block of code and thus is an order to replace the macro name with the block of code. Suppose that we wish to use the following exact sequence of instructions at several points in our procedure:

```
LEA        WORDS,A1
MOVEM.W    (A1)+,D1,D2,D3,D4
```

where the data container is defined via the pseudoinstruction

```
DATUM:    WORDS    4
```

If we defined a macro as follows:

```
MACRO      LOAD_4              ;start of macro definition

LEA        WORDS,A1            ;⎫
MOVEM.W    (A1)+,D1,D2,D3,D4   ;⎬body of macro
MEND       LOAD_4              ;end of macro definition
```

we could employ the macro name as follows:

```
LOAD_4
```

as the operations code at any point in the code segment of our procedure, with the result that this macro reference (or macro call) will be expanded into and replaced by the two instructions constituting the body of the macro.

One of my personal habits in programming is to associate the use of a stack with the operations PUSH and POP. The MC680XY does not furnish these mnemonics but requires that I use the fully equivalent forms:

```
MOVE.L    D0,-(SP)       ;PUSH
MOVE.L    (SP)+,D0       ;POP
```

Not only do my ingrained habits almost require that I use the terminology of PUSH and POP, but I also maintain that this more universal usage makes my programs somewhat clearer and easier to understand. Thus, I prefer to define the following two macros in my programs:

```
MACRO      PUSH(&DATUM)
MOVE.L     &DATUM,-(SP)        ;PUSH
MEND       PUSH


MACRO      POP(&DATUM)
MOVE.L     (SP)+,&DATUM        ;POP
MEND       POP
```

I know that I have not saved myself any keyboard entry work—in fact, I have increased it—but it does make my program syntax more closely agree with the semantics burned into the circuits of my mind. I can also argue that such practices tend to reduce errors in programming.

Macro arguments.   Further suppose that when our LOAD_4 macro is expanded the first time, we wish it to refer to the data container named DATUM and that we require that the second use refer to THAT. This can be accomplished by employing an argument:

```
MACRO        LOAD_4(&THIS)
LEA          &THIS,A1
MOVEM.W      (A1)+,D1,D2,D3,D4
MEND         LOAD_4
```

To expand this macro with the memory operand referring to DATUM, we would use

```
LOAD_4    DATUM
```

and reference to the data container THAT would be

```
LOAD_4    THAT
```

resulting in the substitution of code in the two references placed as follows:

First Reference

```
LEA        DATUM,A1
MOVEM.W    (A1)+,D1,D2,D3,D4
```

Second Reference

```
LEA        THAT,A1
MOVEN.W    (A1)+,D1,D2,D3,D4
```

Multiple arguments are sometimes useful:

```
MACRO    LOAD_4(&HERE,&THERE,&HOME,&AWAY)
MOVE.L   &HERE,D1
MOVE.L   &THERE,D2
MOVE.L   &HOME,D3
MOVE.L   &AWAY,D4
MEND     LOAD_4
```

In this case, also note that the addressing-mode portion of the memory resident operand data container may be specified in the macro reference:

LOAD_4   #17,(A3),4(A3),#231

In addition, note that a register reference may be specified in an argument.
       Labels may be specified in an argument as follows:

```
           MACRO      STORE_4 (&LABEL,&SAVE)
&LABEL:    MOVEM.L    D1,D2,D3,D4,&SAVE
           MEND       STORE_4
```

The expansion reference in the program could be

STORE_4   LOOP,-(A1)

       Label arguments are often necessary to overcome the problem of duplicate labels. Also note that arguments may occur in either or both operand positions, the first (the from) operand or the second (the to) operand. The problem of duplicate labels within the several expanded versions of a multiply referenced macro with internal labels is often very bothersome. Some macro processors provide a facility for *generating unique labels*. This can be illustrated as

```
           MACRO      STORE_6(&LABEL#,&SAVE)
&LABEL#:   LEA        &SAVE,A1
           MOVEM.L    D0,D1,D2,D3,D5,D7,-(A1)
           MEND       STORE_6
```

where the # character appended to the label argument causes a system-incremented number to be inserted during each expansion of the macro. Thus, the first reference,

STORE_6   LOOP#,DATA_AREA

will expand with the label LOOP1; the next call,

STORE_6   LOOP#,THERE

will have the label LOOP2; and so on.

       Macro references within macros.   In some programming situations, it is highly desirable to allow one macro to refer to another macro within its body. As an example, it may often be desirable to save the contents of certain registers to allow their alternative use for other purposes. Later, it may be desirable to restore or load the initial contents back while saving the (then) current contents. A macro to exchange register contents can be constructed using the previously defined two macros: LOAD_4 and STORE_4.

```
MACRO       EXCH_4(&NEW_SAVE,&OLD_SAVE)
STORE_4     &NEW_SAVE
LOAD_4      &OLD_SAVE
MEND        EXCH_4
```

This macro would be referenced in the assembly language source code as

```
EXCH_4      OLD_REG_AREA,NEW_REG_AREA
```

and would generate eight instructions and substitute them into the source code for input into Pass 1 of the assembler.

Instruction variation with macros. It is usually possible to control the length specifier of the instructions within a macro so as to have byte, word, or longword instructions generated into the expanded version:

```
        MACRO       SAVE_ALL(&LABEL,&LNG,&AREA)
&LABEL: LEA         &AREA,A1
        MOVEM.&LNG  D0,D1,D2,D3,D4,D5,D6,D7,A0,A1,A2,A3,A4,A5,A6,A7,−(A1)
        MEND        SAVE_ALL
```

If this macro is referenced using

```
SAVE_ALL        'SAVE_1','L',SAVEAREA
```

the expanded version substituted into the assembly code would be

```
SAVE_1: LEA         SAVEAREA,A1
        MOVEM.L   D0,D1,D2,D3,D4,D5,D6,D7,A0,A1,A2,A3,A4,A5,A6,A7,−(A1)
```

Alternatively, if this macro is referenced as follows:

```
SAVE_ALL        'THERE','W',SPOT
```

the expanded version substituted into the assembly code would be

```
THERE:  LEA         SPOT,A1
        MOVEM.W   D0,D1,D2,D3,D4,D5,D6,D7,A0,A1,A2,A3,A4,A5,A6,A7,−(a1)
```

Thus, it is true that a macro assembler could allow any and all portions of a macro to be varied during expansion through the use of appropriate arguments. This could include the whole operations code or only the length specifier of any or all instructions. Similarly, this expansion variation via arguments could include the entire symbolic operand reference, only the addressing mode portion, or the necessary portions of any or all instructions. Although most macro processors do not provide for this extreme argument substitution freedom during expansion, the usual limitations are not normally onerous or particularly limiting for program composition.

CONDITIONAL ASSEMBLY PROGRAMMING

Conditional macro expansion provides a powerful tool to control which instructions are generated by the macro processor into the expanded code that is input to the assembler. Although there is no processing reason why conditional assembly could not be allowed within non-macro-assembly source code, it often has been limited to macro generation. The macro assembler for the IBM/360, the IBM/370, the IBM 434X, and IBM 308X extended computer family allows many aspects of conditional assembly in nonmacro contexts. The usual limitation of conditional assembly to the macro processor does provide a convenient but not necessary location for the translation process and does prevent the "cluttering up" of the assembler with the conditional assembly processing algorithms. In addition, no real program composition limitation results, as any portion of an assembly program can be presented by the programmer to the macro assembler as a macro. Indeed, the entire procedure may be defined as a macro.

Conditional Directives

With your attention focused on the fact that conditional assembly occurs during the generation of code that will later be processed by the assembler, we emphasize that the two basic conditional directives are AIF and AGO. By using these two directives, it is possible to construct loops that repeat blocks of code (identical repeats or repeats with variations), that skip blocks of code, that choose between alternate blocks of code, and so on. That is, the conditional branch and the absolute branch provide the means to build an arbitrarily complex flow of statement expansion during macro processing. The latter generalization is not unexpected, as it is also true of all algorithmic processes. Note that we are pointing out that although such conditional assembly directives as ACASE, ALOOP, AREPEAT, ASTOP, and so on, may exist in some macro-assembler systems, they are unnecessary—but nice. As the usage of such additional directives is somewhat obvious from their mnemonic name, we will restrict our discussion to AGO and AIF as well as the associated syntax for specifying expansion-time labels (which will not appear in the generated code), the expansion-time conditional operations, and the creation/use of expansion-time constants and variables. Although the AGO expansion-time directive is simpler, its use is easier to comprehend after an understanding of AIF. Therefore, we treat AIF first.

The AIF conditional assembly directive.   The generalized format of this conditional branch expansion-time directive is

Label: AIF(condition)action

where

1. The label starts in column 1, and may consist of a "permanent" label that will occur in the code passed to the assembler or may be an expansion-time label of the form .LABEL (starting with a period and alphabetic character).
2. AIF occupies the operations code field.
3. The condition is enclosed in parentheses and always explicitly specifies a comparison: EQ, NE, LT, GT, LE, or GE, with the usual meaning. The operands of this expansion-time conditional can involve the macro arguments, expansion-time variables, or expansion-time constants. Depending on the type of the conditional operands, the operations +, −, *, /, & (and), | (or), and | | (concatenate or join end to end) may be employed within an operand to be evaluated at expansion time.
4. The action is performed if, and only if, the conditional expression evaluates to true. Only one action is allowed; thus, AIF resembles the FORTRAN logical IF and *does not resemble* the more powerful IF-THEN-ELSE. In effect, AIF specifies a "do the action if true" or "skip the action if false" expansion-time operation. Two general actions are possible:
   a. Conditional branch to a label within the macro of the permanent or expansion-time type. In this case AIF becomes an AIF (true) go-to or AIF (false) continue.
   b. Perform the single action specified, such as increment a variable. The action would be of the form

      &Variable = expression

      and can only involve an expansion-time variable on the left-hand side. The right-hand-side expression can include the operation/operand complications allowed within a conditional expression operand (see rule 3).

The AGO conditional assembly directive.   The generalized format of this unconditional branch expansion-time directive is

Label: AGO   Label of branch target

where the label and AGO follow rules 1 and 2 of AIF, while the branch target label follows rule 4a of AIF for labels.

Expansion-Time Conditional Assembly Labels

Expansion-time labels are signified by the first character being a period and the second character being a letter—that is, a normal label preceded by a period. The entire purpose of expansion-time labels is to serve as branch targets for the AIF and AGO conditional assembly directives. In some programming situations, algorithm construction is facilitated by branching to an expansion-time label of a dummy statement. This could be accomplished by the use of the operation code NOP (no operation), but this solution would result in two bytes of useless code appearing in the final binary object machine code. For this reason, some macro processors furnish the conditional assembly directive ANOP for use in these circumstances:

```
.Label:     ANOP
```

The ANOP conditional assembly directive fully corresponds to the CONTINUE statement in FORTRAN.

Algorithm construction also is sometimes facilitated by the ability to branch (AIF or AGO) directly to the MEND statement and thus terminate expansion of the macro immediately. The use of a labeled ANOP immediately preceding the MEND statement will allow this. Alternatively, some macro processors make available the conditional assembly directive MEXIT. It can be used with either the AIF or AGO:

```
AGO         MEXIT
AIF         (condition)MEXIT
```

and results in the immediate termination of the expansion of the macro.

Expansion-Time Conditional Assembly Data

Constant values for use only at expansion time are specified by the occurrence of the constant value. In other words, as in almost all computer languages, constants are self-naming. The coding of the value is assumed to be decimal (base 10) unless the value is preceded by a $, indicating hexadecimal (base 16); or it is enclosed in quotes with an appended B for bit; or, in the case of ASCII, by enclosing the character string in single or double quotation marks. The following are examples of legal macro expansion-time constant values:

```
987       = 987 decimal numeric
7.3       = 7.3 floating-point numeric
$7A       = 122 decimal numeric
'O'B      = logical false
'GEORGE' = ASCII string
```

Variable data containers are usually, but not always, restricted to scalar-size areas; thus, the use of arrays or structures is not commonly provided for. All variable data containers are declared by setting them equal to an appropriate constant, using an expansion-time directive, as in the following three examples:

```
&Variable:      SET     9
&FALSE:         SET     'O'B
&NAME:          SET     'GEORGE'
```

Changes to the contents of a variable data container are also accomplished by the SET assembly-time directive:

```
&COUNTER:       SET     &COUNTER+1
&ALPHA:         SET     &NAME| |'b'| |'GORSLINE'
```

All of the operations allowed within the AIF condition operand evaluation (see rule 3 in that section) are normally allowed. Thus, we would expect the operations $+$, $-$, $*$, $/$, &, |, and | |, as well as parentheses, to be valid. The right-hand-side expression of a SET directive statement can contain expansion-time constants, expansion-time variables, and/or macro arguments.

Example

```
                MACRO   LOAD_REGS(&NUM,&SAV)
                AIF     (&NUM LT 0) ERROR
                AIF     (&NUM GT 16) ERROR
                AIF     (&NUM EQ 0) MEXIT
&COUNT:         SET     0
&REGS:          SET     'D0','D1','D2','D3','D4','D5','D6','D7',
                        'A0','A1','A2','A3','A4','A5','A6','A7'

.LOOP:          MOVE.L  (&COUNT*4)&SAV,&REGS(&COUNT)

&COUNT:         SET     &COUNT+1
                AIF     (&COUNT GE &NUM)MEXIT
                AGO     .LOOP
.ERROR:         ANOTE   '*****'
                ANOTE   'MACRO ARGUMENT WRONG'
                ANOTE   '*****'
&SYSERROR:      SET     '1'
                MEND    LOAD_REGS
```

This example contains two new constructs available in many macro processors: (1) the use of the conditional assembly directive ANOTE to cause a single line consisting of the alphanumeric constant in the operand field to be placed in the assembly listing, and (2) the use of a systems variable to communicate a condition to the macro-assembler system. (In this case, we choose &SYSERROR as the vehicle to inform the assembly system that the object file should not be stored, so that loading and execution would not be attempted.)

This example conditional assembly macro could be called using

```
LOAD_REGS    NUMBER,SAVE_AREA
```

provided that the data container NUMBER had previously been given a value between zero and 16, indicating the number of registers to be loaded from the data container SAVE_AREA consisting of the same number of long words.

For all the power and fanciness that it is possible to obtain using the full facilities of a good macro assembler with excellent conditional assembly features, it is often true that the simpler method is best. Thus, although it is true that a macro to generate the generalized version of the structured programming construct IF-THEN-ELSE is possible, it may not be the best approach to programming in assembly language. Presumably, we wish to have code somewhat like the following to be substituted into our code at those places where the macro is referenced:

```
            CMP.L   (A1),D3             ;line 1
            BEQ     THEN_CLAUSE         ;line 2
            BRA     ELSE_CLAUSE         ;line 3
THEN_CLAUSE:    .       .
                .       .               text for then portion
                .       .
            BRA     END_IF              ;line 8
ELSE_CLAUSE:    .       .               ;line 9
                .       .               test for else portion
                .       .
END_IF:         .       .               ;line 13
                .       .
```

Several problems become apparent with only a little thoughtful consideration. Although each of these problems is fully solvable, the solution may not be worth it. First, it seems a shame that we must have two consecutive branches in lines 2 and 3. The cure, of course, would be to negate the condition of the test in line 2 to give something like

```
            CMP.L   (A1),D3             ;line 1
            BNE     ELSE_CLAUSE         ;lines 2 & 3 replacement
THEN_CLAUSE:    .       .
                .       .
                .       .
```

Although this conditional negation can be accomplished algorithmically in a macro context, the conditional macro-assembly code to do so becomes a little complicated and opaque.

Second, we have no idea at the time we construct the macro definition of how many statements long the THEN clause will be or how many statements long the ELSE clause will be. I know you could place the code for the THEN clause and for the ELSE clause in the macro definition itself, but I hasten to suggest that this practice would not result in a generalized macro for the branch on condition situation but would require a new and different definition for each reference. This effectively destroys one of the main reasons for using macros in the first place. In addition, your program would end up with the macro reference

```
IF_THEN_ELSE     (A1),'EQ',D3
```

and the actions (the THEN clause and the ELSE clause) would be elsewhere in the definition. This physical separation of associated code results in difficulties in following and understanding program logic. It is akin to undisciplined use of the GO TO. Alternatively, we could solve this clause length/code separation problem by referencing appropriate macros within the IF_THEN_ELSE macro:

```
               MACRO    IF_THEN_ELSE(&VAR1,&COND,&VAR2)   ;line 0
               CMP.L    &VAR1,&VAR2                       ;line 1
               B&COND   THEN_CLAUSE                       ;line 2
               BRA      ELSE_CLAUSE                       ;line 3
THEN_CLAUSE:   THEN                                       ;MACRO REFERENCE
               BRA      END_IF                            ;line 8
ELSE_CLAUSE:   ELSE                                       ;MACRO REFERENCE
END_IF:        ANOP                                       ;line 13
               MEND     IF_THEN_ELSE                      ;line 14
```

But, of course, this pseudosolution raises the question of the possible need for arguments to allow the THEN and/or ELSE macros to accomplish their purpose with the ability to reference and to use the appropriate data while doing so. Note how the generalized macro solution to the relatively simple IF-THEN-ELSE situation becomes less and less tractable and causes more and more problems and complications as we consider it.

As a third difficulty, I call your attention to the duplicate labels problem; that is, if we used the above IF_THEN_ELSE macro in more than one place (referenced it more than once) in our program, we would have forced the assembler to generate duplicate labels and, as a result, a syntactically incorrect program. This duplicate label problem is extremely easy to solve, of course. Depending on the syntax specified for your assembler, invoke the append system number to the label facility. Each time the macro is expanded, the label will be concatenated with a system-incremented number, so that no duplicated labels will result. One possible syntax would be

```
                MACRO   IF_THEN_ELSE(&VAR1,&COND,&VAR2)   ; line 0
                CMP.L   &VAR1,&VAR2                       ; line 1
                B&COND  THEN_CLAUSE#                      ; line 2
                BRA     ELSE_CLAUSE#                      ; line 3
THEN_CLAUSE#:   THEN                                      ; MACRO REFERENCE
                BRA     END_IF#                           ; line 8
ELSE_CLAUSE#:   ELSE                                      ; MACRO REFERENCE
END_IF#:        ANOP                                      ; line 13
                MEND    IF_THEN_ELSE                      ; line 14
```

But a serious problem still remains if this macro is used (referenced) more than once and, as is almost certain to happen, the THEN clause and the ELSE clause of the second usage must be different from those of the first usage. Although I suspect that this problem could be solved by a guru using some fancy conditional macro assemblers, I do not think that I would want this task in ordinary real-life assembly language programming. Even then, I suspect that the contents of the THEN and ELSE clauses should be fairly uniform from reference to reference so that arguments and conditional assembly facilities can be used to accommodate the necessary differences from reference to reference.

After all this thought and consideration, we finally arrive with the conclusion that although generalized macros that correspond to the IF-THEN-ELSE, the DO-WHILE, or the DO-UNTIL are possible to construct, their design, implementation, and use tends to become so complicated as not to result in reductions in programming time and may very well make programs more difficult to compose, to debug, to understand, and to maintain (change). Perhaps the correct conclusion involves constructing such structured program flow-of-control constructs from scratch each time one is needed. The techniques presented in Chapter 3 are suggested as justified approaches.

This discussion brings us again to the point of repeating the cardinal rule of program design—a rule that has somewhat universal application in many fields: *Simplicity contributes to reliability*. This maxim should not be interpreted to mean that complicated problems should not be attempted; rather, it means that *unnecessary* complications should be avoided. Some of us doddering old-time computer types may internalize this rule as the "KISS" rule—*Keep It Simple Stupid*. In using this rule, we are not implying that we are stupid; we are merely admitting to our personal limitations. No one is perfect—not I, not you, not anyone! I dare say that, over the years, you will probably make almost as many inexcusable (stupid) errors as I have. I wish I could honestly claim that I don't make the same error twice, but I cannot claim this. In any case—as you have already discovered—programming requires thought, practice, study, and perseverance. In my mind, the last is as important as the others.

One of the most common situations in programming involves CALLing an external subprocedure with the use of parameter-argument pairs. Is it possible to generalize this process without introducing unwanted complexity into the program design and implementation process? I invite you to draw your own conclusions from the following:

```
            MACRO     CALL(&SUB,&ARG1,ARG2, . . . . ,ARGn)
&ARG_NO:    SET       1
.LOOP:      SET       &ARG_NO + 1
            AIF       ARGUMENTS(&ARG_NO) NOT_BLANK
            PEA       ARGUMENTS(&ARG_NO)
            AGO       .LOOP
            AEND_IF
            SET       &ARG_NO − 1
            MOVE.L    &ARG_NO,−(SP)      ;pass number of args as an arg
            JSR       &SUB
            MEND      CALL

            MACRO     ARG_PTR
            MOVEM.L   A0,A1,A2,A3,A4,A5,A6,A7,D0,D1,D2,D3,D4,D5,D6,D7,−(SP)
            MOVEA.L   SP,A0              ;SP points to top of register save space
            ADDA.L    #64,A0             ;get pointer around space for registers
            MOVE.L    −(A0),D7           ;RETURN address
            MOVE.L    #4,D6              ;long word factor = 4 bytes
            MULT.L    D7,D6              ;storage space for arguments
            SUBA.L    D7,D6              ;pointer to argument # 1
            MOVE.W    SR,−(SP)           ;save status register
            MEND      ARG_PTR
            MACRO     REST_RET
            MOVEM.L   (SP)+,A0,A1,A2,A3,A4,A5,A6,A7,D0,D1,D2,D3,D4,D5,D6,D7
            MOVEA.L   D7,SP
            RTR
            MEND      REST_RET
```

SOME ADVANCED TOPICS

Macros Referencing Macros

We have already discussed the situation where it is programmatically advantageous for the definition of a macro to invoke (reference) another macro. As a reminder:

```
MACRO          ALSO_USE
   .              .
   .              .
   .              .
MEND           ALSO_USE

MACRO          REFER_TO
   .              .
   .              .
   .              .
ALSO_USE
   .              .
   .              .
   .              .
MEND           REFER_TO

MACRO          ANY_MAC
   .              .
   .              .
   .              .
REFER_TO
   .              .
   .              .
   .              .
MEND           ANY_MAC
```

This technique is valuable in the sense that its use allows us, as programmers, to make use of simple code sections (i.e., simple tools that may already exist) to construct more complicated sections of code (i.e., more complicated tools). That is, it allows us to use one of the basic precepts of programming: to modularize a problem into separate, isolated, individual, small problems and then, intelligently and somewhat automatically, to combine them into a viable problem solution. The example above illustrates two levels of macro reference nesting. The depth of nesting allowed depends on the design of the assembler being used; however, because almost all assemblers can temporarily suspend the expansion of a macro to allow the expansion of a referenced macro and then resume the previous expansion, there normally is no limit to the depth of nesting. The only normal requirement is that the definition of a macro physically precede any reference to it.

Macro Definitions Within Macro Definitions

Some macro assemblers allow a macro definition to physically occur within the definition of a macro. The implication is that during the expansion of the "outer" macro, the definition of the "inner" macro will be encountered, causing the inner definition to be expanded at that place within the outer macro. For example:

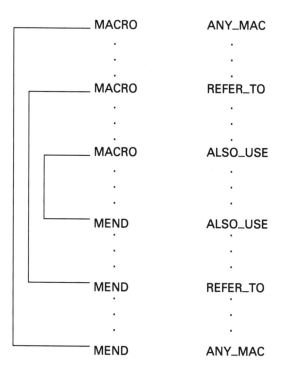

Note that the macro name operand in the MEND statement allows the assembler logic to keep the macros separate and distinct during expansion. As an additional safety-in-programming rule: Connect each macro start and end by lines, and assure yourself that no such lines cross. This rule, of course, is the same safety rule that is so useful for nested loop checking. In general, the expanded assembly code will be identical to that expanded using the technique described in the previous section on macros referencing macros.

Recursive Macro References

If a macro definition can reference (invoke) another macro, it is natural to imagine that it could reference (invoke) itself and thus end up with a situation analagous to recursion. A few very fancy macro assemblers employ a stack during their expansion process and thereby allow recursive macro references. It must be emphasized that many macro assemblers do not allow recursive macro references. In addition, the macro definition that allows correct expansion of a recursive macro reference must always allow for termination of the self-reference portion, in the same sense that the construction of a recursive subprocedure does. If this termination condition is not provided, the expansion will continue *ad infinitum* and will cause a macro expansion stack overflow, with disastrous and unwanted consequences during the as-

sembly process. A simple example of a recursive macro reference should aid your
understanding:

```
;recursive MACRO that does the work of generating sequential numbers into
;   consecutive long words
;
            MACRO           NEXT(&LNGTH,&NUM)
            AIF             (LESSEQUAL,&NUM,&LNGTH)MEXIT
            DEFLONG         &NUM
            SET             &NUM = &NUM + 1
            NEXT            &LNGTH,&NUM
            ENDIF
            MEND            NEXT
;
;MACRO for generating sequential numbers into consecutive long words
;
;recursively references MACRO NEXT
;
            MACRO           TABLE&(LNGTH)
            SET             &NUM = 1
            NEXT            &LNGTH,&NUM
            MEND            TABLE
```

It is correct for us to ask if this recursive macro reference solution is better than, or
even as good as, the equivalent iterative conditional assembly macro:

```
            MACRO           TABLE(LNGTH)
            SET             &NUM = 1
.DOAGAIN:   SET             &NUM = &NUM + 1
            DEFLONG         &NUM
            AIF             (LESSEQUAL,&NUM − &LNGTH)MEXIT
            AGO             .DOAGAIN
            ENDIF
            MEND            TABLE
```

   It is my opinion that recursion is a very powerful and valuable tool that should
be applied to those cases that either defy transformation to iteration or in which the
iterative solution is unnecessarily opaque or complicated. If these criteria are accepted, the recursive macro reference solution in this section is not as "good" a solution as the iterative solution. Nevertheless, it is important that we never forget that
recursive solutions are sometimes necessary and also that they are sometimes preferable. On the other hand, it is worth noting that an iterative solution is usually preferable if it is possible.

Default Parameter (Argument) Substitution

Consider the following macro definition, which will provide a three-address memory-to-memory add instruction. (This action is equivalent to the FORTRAN statement C = A + B.)

```
MACRO          ADDMML3(&A,&B,&C)
LEA            &B,A2
LEA            &C,A3
MOVE.L         (A2),(A3)
LEA            &A,A2
MOVE.L         (A2),D1
ADD.L          D1,(A3)
MEND           ADDMML3
```

The reference (invocation) statement could be

```
ADDMML3        I,J,K
```

Now let us suppose that, for some unknown reason, we wish to use this macro for the equivalent of the FORTRAN statement C = B + C, using the reference (invocation)

```
ADDMML3        ,B,C
```

The assembler using the macro definition above would not behave correctly; it would get into trouble. To accomplish what we wish, we could change our definition of the macro to

```
MACRO          ADDMML3(&A,&B,&C)
AIF            (BLANK,&A)MEXIT
LEA            &B,A2
LEA            &C,A3
MOVE.L         (A2),D1
ADD.L          D1,(A3)
MEXIT                            ; code complete for C = B + C
ENDIF
LEA            &A,A1
LEA            &B,A2
LEA            &C,A3
MOVE.L         (A2),(A3)
MOVE.L         (A1),D1
ADD.L          D1,(A3)
MEND           ADDMML3
```

The utility of default parameters in macros is of great programmatic importance in some circumstances. They are most common in the context of operating systems, particularly in connection with complicated I/O routines, which very often have two or three parameters that must always be used and a relatively large number of default options that can be replaced when necessary through the use of additional arguments. These macro references (invocations) can look extremely awkward. For example:

```
DO_INPUT           ,,,7,,,A,,
```

gives directions to use the value of 7 for argument number 4 and the value of A for argument 7 but to use the default values already defined within the macro for arguments 1, 2, 3, 5, 6, 8, and 9. In such cases, the syntax invites mistakes, which are extremely easy and common in practice (many programmers get the count of commas wrong), resulting in unexpected and wrong results. This type of parameter-argument substitution depends on position within the argument list and therefore is called *positional argument passing*.

Keyword Parameters-Arguments

When a macro reference (invocation) requires many positional arguments, some of which may be omitted in favor of default values, the probability of errors in the reference statement becomes excessively high. Some macro assemblers allow the use of self-defining or *keyword argument passing* as a tool in partially alleviating this type of error difficulty. We will instruct by example:

```
    MACRO      ANY(A,B,C,D,E,F,G)
;
; arguments A, B, D, F, and/or G may be omitted. In each case a defined
;   default value will be used for the omitted argument
;
    MEND       ANY
```

A positional argument style reference could be

```
ANY                ,,X,,Y,,
```

and the corresponding keyword style reference could be

```
ANY                E=Y,C=X
```

Note that in the keyword reference style example, we have deliberately reversed the order of the two specified arguments to emphasize that position has no meaning within the keyword reference style.

EXERCISES

5.1. Design, implement, test, and document a macro that will accept a person's name in the form

George W. Gorsline, Jr.

and replace it with the form

Gorsline, George W. Jr.

5.2. Design, implement, test, and document a macro that will accept a byte, word, or long-word integer and replace it with its absolute value.

5.3. Design, implement, test, and document a macro that will correctly convert a signed numerical ASCII string to a signed numerical BCD string. All incorrect ASCII coding should be detected and converted to ASCII zero.

5.4. Design, implement, test, and document a macro that will correctly convert a signed numerical BCD string to binary long-word integer form. Incorrect BCD coding should be detected and converted to BCD zero.

5.5. Design, implement, test, and document a macro that will correctly convert a signed byte, word, or long-word integer into a signed ASCII string of length N, where N is an argument. If N provides insufficient space, the ASCII string should be made all asterisks.

5.6. Test the assembler available on your computational system and report the exact syntax and semantics of each available conditional assembly directive.

5.7. Test the assembler available on your computational system and report whether it allows:
(a) Macro references within a macro definition.
(b) Macro definitions within a macro definition.
(c) Recursive macro references.
(d) Keyword macro arguments.

6

Input/Output

An explosion of computer applications has caused, or is the result of, the availability of the scores of new and different I/O devices that are now a part of computer systems. Despite this proliferation of devices, the techniques employed to connect I/O devices into a computer system are fairly standard. On the other hand, the characteristics of I/O devices vary widely. Nevertheless, a programmer who understands the basic principles of I/O interfacing and programming can rapidly learn the characteristics of any new device and can somewhat easily design and code programs to interact correctly with the device.

I/O ORGANIZATION

Figure 6.1 shows a computer consisting of a processor (arithmetic-logic unit and control), with memory connected to the processor by a memory bus and input/output connected to the processor by an I/O bus. In this scheme, provisions exist for identifying the peripheral device (via an I/O address); for initiating, terminating, and otherwise controlling the device action (via the I/O control path); and for transferring the data (via the I/O data path). No possibility for interference with memory usage exists, as one bus is provided for memory accesses and a physically separate bus is provided for I/O accesses.

The I/O subsystem in Figure 6.1 contains several sets of I/O devices and interfaces. Whereas the data and control lines between each peripheral device and its specialized interface are unique to that device, the connections between the interface and the I/O bus are generalized and usually exactly alike. Thus, the I/O interface

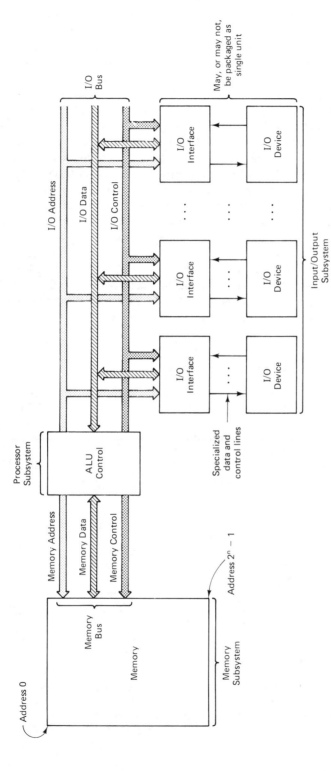

Figure 6.1 Conceptual diagram of a computer with a bus serving the memory subsystem and a separate bus serving the input/output subsystem. (From G. W. Gorsline, *16-Bit Modern Microcomputers: The Intel 18086 Family*, © 1985, p. 127. Reprinted by permission of Prentice-Hall, Inc., Englewood Cliffs, NJ.)

221

(i.e., the device interface) provides uniform control, uniform timing, a uniform address, and a uniform data connection between the I/O bus and the peripheral device. It controls the operation of the device according to commands from the processor subsystem and converts data from the bus format to that required by the device, and vice versa, as well as being the physical I/O address (or port).

Additional detail is shown in Figure 6.2 for a keyboard input device (read-only by design) and for a light-emitting diode seven-segment digit display device (write-only by design). In both cases, the bus interface–I/O bus connection is general, while the circuits of the interface itself provide specialized services to the specific device. In the case of the keyboard, the depression of a key causes an electrical pulse to be transmitted to the circuits of the encoder, which generate a key-specific 7-bit ASCII code that is transmitted to the I/O register (or I/O port) of the bus interface. In most cases a high-order 0 bit is appended to make an 8-bit data "package," although some devices may employ this high-order bit for other specific purposes. For this reason, programmers must never assume that bit 7 of ASCII data received from a device is zero. It should always be "masked" out. Thus, the I/O register of a keyboard interface will contain the 7-bit ASCII code corresponding to the key being depressed or 00000000 if no key is currently depressed.

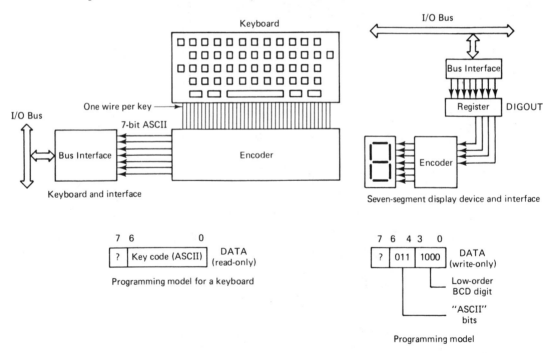

Figure 6.2 Diagram of a keyboard device and associated bus interface as well as a light-emitting diode seven-segment display device and associated bus interface. In both cases the programming model consists of the I/O register (or I/O port). (From G. W. Gorsline, *16-Bit Modern Microcomputers: The Intel 18086 Family,* © 1985, p. 128. Reprinted by permission of Prentice-Hall, Inc., Englewood Cliffs, NJ.)

To read data from the keyboard, a program executes an instruction that transfers the contents of the I/O register in the bus interface into a register in the processor, where it can be manipulated as ordinary data. Any attempt of a program to write data from a processor register to the keyboard interface I/O register will be unsuccessful (and may result in an error condition); therefore, this keyboard device employs an "input port." Also note that the input ASCII character must be transferred from the interface I/O register while the key is depressed, or it will be replaced by 00000000 and lost.

In the case of the diode display, the transmission from a processor register of an ASCII numeric character with control and device address via the I/O bus will be recognized by the display interface and accepted into the I/O register of the interface. The interface will transmit the low-order 4 bits to the diode display encoder, which will interpret them into the correct electrical pulses to energize the appropriate light-emitting diodes of the seven-segment display to represent the value as an arabic numeral. As the I/O register of the display device interface is an output port, it is a true storage register whose value does not change until the next output operation. Thus, the light-emitting seven-segment display remains lighted with the correct arabic numeral configuration until it is purposely changed. Any attempt of a program to input data from this output port will be unsuccessful and may result in an error condition or may simply be ignored.

INPUT/OUTPUT TYPES

The design of many computers allows input/output through the accumulator, in which case overlap of the I/O function with the compute function is virtually impossible. I/O is also allowed via pseudomemory locations through a scheme that has become known as *memory-mapped* I/O, which will be described and discussed very shortly. The Motorola MC680XY family of computers uses this scheme, as do the Digital Equipment Corporation PDP 11 and VAX families. Again, overlap of the I/O function with the compute function can be difficult, although it can be, and often is, implemented using an additional processor for I/O. In general, I/O direct to or from memory is possible through the use of a second processor (sometimes specialized) that can access memory independent of the central processor. This scheme, often termed *direct memory access* (DMA), can be implemented via an I/O DMA processor.

Accumulator-Based I/O

The Motorola MC680XY family does not have instructions available for I/O to or from the registers. However, many computers, including many microcomputers, do possess special I/O instructions. These instructions move a byte, a word, or a long word of data from or to a register to or from the I/O register in the interface permanently associated with the port number used as the immediate operand in the I/O instruction.

Memory-Mapped I/O

In this I/O scheme, certain specific memory locations do not exist but are physically wired to the interface of a peripheral device. Figure 6.3 illustrates the scheme. Thus, the I/O register of a device exists as a pseudomemory location, and an access of that memory location via a MOVE instruction results in device action. Consequently, an input port responds to any processor instruction that moves data from the "memory" location with that address, and an output port responds to any processor instruction that moves data to the "memory" location with that address. The control aspects of the device interface must correspond to the control aspects of memory.

Any processor can employ memory-mapped I/O if the system fabricator attaches device interface I/O registers (ports) to the bus in such a way that they respond to memory control signals and thus become pseudomemory addresses. The Digital Equipment Corporation pioneered the concept of memory-mapped I/O in small computers with their PDP 11, on which no special I/O instructions exist. The Motorola MC680XY family employs memory-mapped I/O.

Direct Memory Access I/O

Although we will present a fuller explanation of DMA later, when discussing the MC68450 DMA processor, a brief introduction is justified at this point.

A direct memory access channel is an arrangement of hardware that allows a device interface to transfer data rapidly directly to or from main memory without processor intervention. A DMA channel allows the processor to issue a single high-level command, such as

READ PORTNO,MEM_ADRS,NO_BYTES

to indicate a sequence of low-level I/O events, such as transferring individual bytes of data. This is accomplished by transferring data directly between an I/O device interface and memory without any central processor work beyond initiating the transfer and noting its completion.

Ordinarily, the processor is master of the bus. The CPU provides the address and control signals for each transfer that takes place. However, a DMA channel has the logic temporarily to become master of the bus to control the transfer of I/O data directly between the I/O port register in the peripheral device interface and a series of locations in main memory.

Because a DMA channel transfers data between the device and memory with no processor intervention after initiation, the transfer has no effect on the processor state (assuming that DMA data do not overwrite code or data being used by the executing program). The only effect of DMA operations on program execution is that instructions occasionally take a trifle longer because they must wait for a memory access. For example, suppose that a disk is able to transfer one byte of data every 8 microseconds and that main memory has a cycle time of 1 microsecond. The DMA

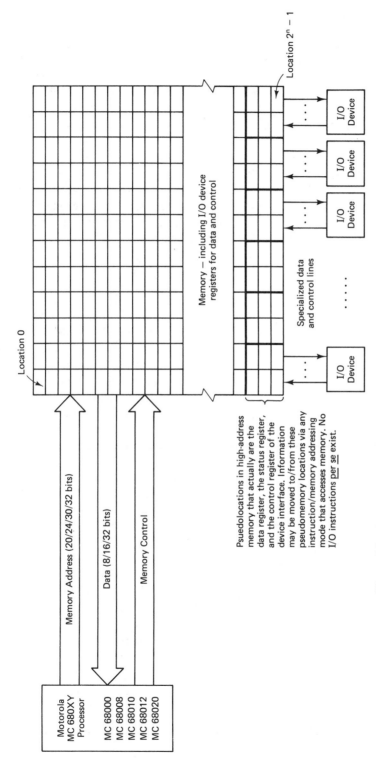

Location 0

Location $2^n - 1$

Memory — including I/O device registers for data and control

Specialized data and control lines

Psuedolocations in high-address memory that actually are the data register, the status register, and the control register of the device interface. Information may be moved to/from these pseudomemory locations via any instruction/memory addressing mode that accesses memory. No I/O instructions per se exist.

I/O Device

Memory Address (20/24/30/32 bits)

Data (8/16/32 bits)

Memory Control

Motorola MC 680XY Processor

MC 68000
MC 68008
MC 68010
MC 68012
MC 68020

Figure 6.3 Conceptual diagram of a computer with memory-mapped I/O. The Motorola MC680XY and Digital Equipment Corporation PDP-11 and VAX are computers with memory-mapped I/O.

channel could "steal" one memory cycle out of every eight to transfer disk data when and if the disk needed servicing. Seven memory cycles out of every eight would remain available for the processor to use in the worst of circumstances, when the disk–memory data transfer is taking place at its maximum rate. In this example, the processor is slowed down by a maximum of 12.5 per cent. The actual slowdown will probably be much less because of two very likely circumstances:

1. The DMA transfer of data between memory and disk will not occur continuously but will be intermittent.
2. The DMA channel may steal memory cycles that the processor had no use for—it did not need memory at that instant. For example, the processor may have been occupied in executing an instruction not requiring a memory access, such as a register-to-register multiply or divide.

BUS ORGANIZATION

The system bus is used by both the memory subsystem and the I/O subsystem as needed to transfer data to and from the processor and memory or memory-mapped I/O ports. A bus is a physically contiguous group or bundle of "wires," with each simultaneously carrying one bit of information, followed by another bit, and another bit, and so on, from the port at one place on the bus to another port on the bus under the detailed control of the processor that is the current bus master.

The system bus of the Motorola MC680XY family of processor chips is usually electrically and physically connected to a "bus extender" that allows the information signals to be transferred from or to greater distances—say, to another chip mounting board. Although specially designed buses exist and are used, the Motorola Corporation markets the VMX bus to physically extend the system bus from board to board within a uniprocessor system. If more than one processor is involved—and in other somewhat complicated situations—the more expensive Motorola VME bus may be necessary or advantageous. Again, specially designed and competing buses exist and are used.

The bus of the Motorola MC680XY logically consists of three subbuses: the address lines, the data lines, and the control lines. Ignoring the control lines for a moment and concentrating on the address and data lines, it is necessary to emphasize that the processors available at this time are different:

	Address Lines(#)	Maximum Memory	Data Lines(#)
MC68008	20	$2^{20} =$ 1 MB	8
MC68000	23	$2^{24} =$ 16 MB	16
MC68010	23	$2^{24} =$ 16 MB	16
MC68012	29	$2^{30} = 1024$ MB $= 1$ TB	16
MC68020	32	$2^{32} = 4096$ MB $= 4$ TB	32

A few conclusions can and should be derived from the above data. First, an 8-bit (single data byte bus) processor is available that can support up to 1 megabyte of primary (main) memory. The instructions, registers, and addressing modes are identical to those of the other processors (the MC68020 is a superset). Note that a memory data access quantum of one byte requires that every byte in memory be addressable and that 20 address lines are needed to allow this with a 1 megabyte memory. This allows data and/or instructions to be placed into memory without regard to even or odd addresses. (If full program compatability is desired, so that a given program written for the MC68008 will also execute correctly on the other processors of the family, then the even-address-only directly addressable restrictions must be observed.) As all instructions are at least two bytes in length—and many are four bytes, some are six bytes, and a few are eight bytes in length—an instruction fetch can require significant time to accomplish the required multiple memory accesses. Multiple memory accesses are also required for word and long-word data. I strongly suspect that this processor was designed and offered for sale as a direct competitor for the Intel I8088 that was used in the original IBM PC and clones. The Intel I8088 had the same memory size and data bus width restrictions as the MC68008. Although I have not actually searched for a system based on the MC68008, I have not run across one, and I suspect that this processor has not exactly been a best-seller.

The standard or "type" Motorola MC68000 has a 16-bit data bus and can access up to 16 megabytes of memory, using only 23 address lines to specify the location. This addressing trick is accomplished by having the memory interface "manufacture" and append a twenty-fourth low-order 0 bit to the transmitted address. As a result, only even-address bytes can be directly addressed in memory; but as the data bus (path) is 16-bits = 2 bytes wide, the odd-address bytes are also available. This even-address-only directly addressable situation results in the rigid requirement that all instructions start on an even address. In addition, the placement of data on an even address versus an odd address can materially affect the execution speed of a program. Assemblers, compilers, linkers, and loaders must be designed and implemented with this addressing restriction in mind. Assembly language programmers should be particularly aware of this restriction when manipulating byte-length and ASCII (character) data.

The MC68010 and MC68012 processors both fully support the instructions, data path widths, and memory addressing modes of the standard MC68000 and, in addition, allow *virtual memory*. (If this is a new term to you, ignore it for the present. We will study virtual memory in the chapter on program relocation, and an understanding of it is not necessary at this time.) Note that the MC68010 provides 23 address lines to address 2^{24} bytes of memory and that the MC68012 provides 29 address lines to address 2^{30} bytes of memory. From this fact you can correctly conclude that the even-address-only directly addressable situation of the MC68000 also applies to the computers based on these more advanced processors.

The MC68020 processor fully supports the same instructions (plus a few additional) and the same memory addressing modes (plus memory indirect), while also supporting virtual memory, an address bus of 32 lines, and a data bus of 32 lines.

Note that this scheme directly allows the access of any byte in memory without regard to even versus odd addresses (word alignment). Nevertheless, because all instructions are in word (16-bit) increments (2 bytes, 4 bytes, 6 bytes, or 8 bytes long), assemblers, compilers, and linkers should always produce code that conforms to the even-address-only (word alignment) restriction. Loaders should probably conform to the long-word alignment rule (the beginning address of a procedure should end in two binary zeros). On the other hand, data to be manipulated—whether byte, word, or long word—can start at any address. Nevertheless, I strongly recommend that assembly language programmers and compiler writers observe the rule that all word data be word-aligned and that all long-word data be long-word-aligned. In addition, 64-bit and 96-bit floating-point data should be long-word-aligned for the same reasons.

At the beginning of this section, we used the term *bus master*. To be a bus master, an electrical device must have the intelligence to issue timing and other control signals onto the control lines, to put an address on the address lines, and to send or receive data on the data lines at exactly the correct instant. In other words, only a processor can be a bus master. In general, only two types of processors occur in a Motorola MC680XY-based system: (1) one, two, or many MC680XY processors; and (2) two, four, or more DMA (direct memory access) processors. For simplicity in the following discussion, we will assume that our system has one MC68000 processor and more than one DMA processor or that it has one MC68020 processor and more than one DMA processor.

In this very common and not very complicated case, it is correct to assume that the central processor (the MC68000 or MC68020) normally and usually is the bus master and therefore controls and has use of the bus for memory information transfers (and thus also controls the memory-mapped I/O). Consider a case that probably will occur fairly often: One of the DMA processors has a "chunk" of data that it needs to store into memory. (Logically, this is a memory-to-memory data MOVE; but physically, it requires sending data over the bus from the physical device interface data register to the physical memory of the system.) To accomplish this, the DMA processor must ask the current bus master (in this case, the central processor) to give up bus control and allow it (the DMA) temporarily to have bus control so that it can transmit its input data to memory and then return bus control to the central processor. Because humans designed these processors to be "nice" to each other, we expect the central processor to relinquish control of the bus as requested when it has completed its own current work. Similarly, we expect the DMA processor to return bus control after it has used the bus. This is very good, and it actually happens in this manner. But recall that we specified more than one DMA, which means that two or more processors could request bus control at the exact same instant. Which gets control? As a human programmer, you do not want this decision left to pure chance or even to the machine itself. You wish to control your own destiny! So let us add some logic (actually, a very simple-minded processor) to our system that allows you to give a certain processor (DMA or CPU) highest bus priority, another second highest priority, and so on. Please understand that this is not a preemptive priority—

it doesn't stop bus usage in the middle of a transfer; rather, it is a priority that allows a processor to claim bus control when the bus next becomes idle.

When a processor desiring to transfer information over the bus becomes bus master, the sequence of events shown in Figure 6.4 occurs if a read is specified and the sequence shown in Figure 6.5 occurs if a write is specified for the Motorola MC68000. Let us examine the read cycle for word-sized data as performed by the MC68000.

Referring to Figure 6.4, note that we are assumming that the processor wishing to read (obtain) data from memory or from a memory-mapped device is currently the bus master. (A bit later we will detail the process of obtaining mastery of the bus.) Perhaps the most fundamental fact to be fully understood is that the two devices must cooperate in the data transferral over the bus. First, the bus master (which must be a processor) must send certain information over the bus to the slave—information such as whether it is a read or a write; what the function is, such as user/supervisor and data/program; which device is involved, as specified by a memory address; and whether a word or low-order/high-order byte is desired.

Second, as the slave device will be continually monitoring the bus, it will recognize its own address and acquire the above information from the bus. It will then place electrical pulses on the proper bus lines representing the data—in the example, a full word that is either the contents of the memory word addressed or the contents of the word data register in the device interface that had the pseudo-memory address. It will also send a signal that this is the requested data transfer.

Third, the bus master will acquire the data from the bus and change the setting of the signals specifying data word or upper/lower byte as well as the address signal. Note that the electrical charges representing the datum remain on the bus.

Fourth, and last, the slave will remove the data from the bus and signal that the read bus cycle is completed. At this time, and only at this time, the bus can be captured for another cycle by the highest-priority processor (MC68000 or DMA processor).

To facilitate the exactness necessary to describe the input process accurately, in Figure 6.4 I have used the names of particular bus lines and the corresponding processor chip signal connectors or pins. Figure 6.6 gives explanatory details that should be helpful for full understanding. Included are the semantics of the settings of the FC0, FC1, FC2 lines; the UDS and LDS lines; and a timing diagram. The student is urged to integrate the signal timing information in Figure 6.6 with the action information in Figure 6.4.

It is important to be aware of the fact that it is possible to use memory in an MC680XY processor-based system that is not physically fast enough to keep up with the clock signals of the processor. It is also possible and fairly common to use memory-mapped I/O devices that are slower than desirable. When either of these situations occurs, wait states—wait for slow memory or wait for the device—are automatically inserted between clock strobes S4 and S5, as shown on the right side of the timing diagram in Figure 6.6.

The corresponding process to transfer a datum over the 32-bit data bus of the

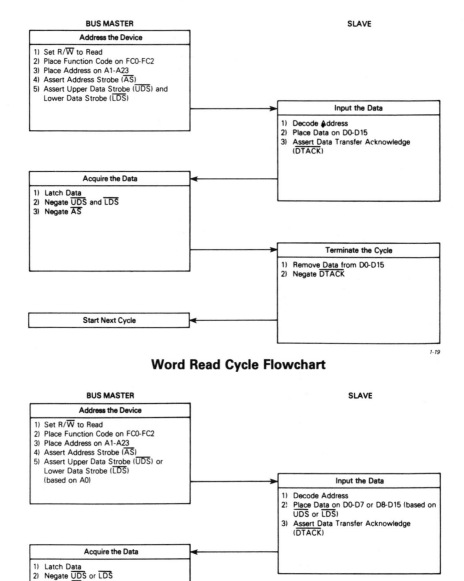

BUS MASTER

Address the Device

1) Set R/$\overline{W}$ to Read
2) Place Function Code on FC0-FC2
3) Place Address on A1-A23
4) Assert Address Strobe ($\overline{AS}$)
5) Assert Upper Data Strobe ($\overline{UDS}$) and
   Lower Data Strobe ($\overline{LDS}$)

SLAVE

Input the Data

1) Decode Address
2) Place Data on D0-D15
3) Assert Data Transfer Acknowledge
   ($\overline{DTACK}$)

Acquire the Data

1) Latch Data
2) Negate $\overline{UDS}$ and $\overline{LDS}$
3) Negate $\overline{AS}$

Terminate the Cycle

1) Remove Data from D0-D15
2) Negate $\overline{DTACK}$

Start Next Cycle

1-19

Word Read Cycle Flowchart

BUS MASTER

Address the Device

1) Set R/$\overline{W}$ to Read
2) Place Function Code on FC0-FC2
3) Place Address on A1-A23
4) Assert Address Strobe ($\overline{AS}$)
5) Assert Upper Data Strobe ($\overline{UDS}$) or
   Lower Data Strobe ($\overline{LDS}$)
   (based on A0)

SLAVE

Input the Data

1) Decode Address
2) Place Data on D0-D7 or D8-D15 (based on
   $\overline{UDS}$ or $\overline{LDS}$)
3) Assert Data Transfer Acknowledge
   ($\overline{DTACK}$)

Acquire the Data

1) Latch Data
2) Negate $\overline{UDS}$ or $\overline{LDS}$
3) Negate $\overline{AS}$

Terminate the Cycle

1) Remove Data from D0-D7 or D8-D15
2) Negate $\overline{DTACK}$

Start Next Cycle

1-20

Byte Read Cycle Flowchart

Figure 6.4 The actions of the bus master and the slave memory-mapped device for a Motorola MC68000-based system performing a word or byte read. (Courtesy of Motorola, Inc.)

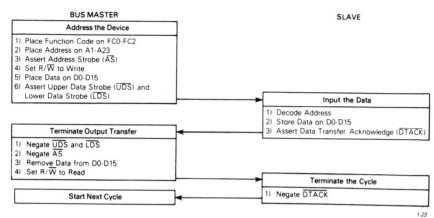

Word Write Cycle Flowchart

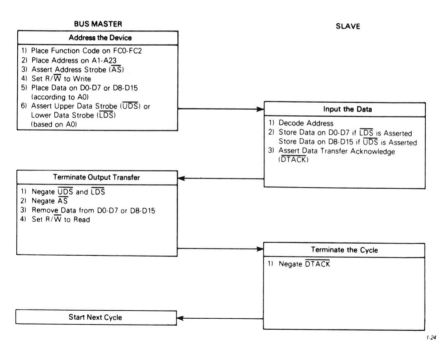

Byte Write Cycle Flowchart

Figure 6.5 The actions of the bus master and the slave memory-mapped device for a Motorola MC68000-based system performing a word or byte write. (Courtesy of Motorola, Inc.)

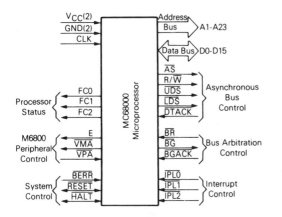

Input and Output Signals

Data Strobe Control of Data Bus

$\overline{UDS}$	$\overline{LDS}$	$R/\overline{W}$	D8-D15	D0-D7
High	High	—	No Valid Data	No Valid Data
Low	Low	High	Valid Data Bits 8-15	Valid Data Bits 0-7
High	Low	High	No Valid Data	Valid Data Bits 0-7
Low	High	High	Valid Data Bits 8-15	No Valid Data
Low	Low	Low	Valid Data Bits 8-15	Valid Data Bits 0-7
High	Low	Low	Valid Data Bits 0-7*	Valid Data Bits 0-7
Low	High	Low	Valid Data Bits 8-15	Valid Data Bits 8-15*

*These conditions are a result of current implementation and may not appear on future devices.

Function Code Outputs

Function Code Output			Cycle Type
FC2	FC1	FC0	
Low	Low	Low	(Undefined, Reserved)
Low	Low	High	User Data
Low	High	Low	User Program
Low	High	High	(Undefined, Reserved)

Function Code Output			Cycle Type
FC2	FC1	FC0	
High	Low	Low	(Undefined, Reserved)
High	Low	High	Supervisor Data
High	High	Low	Supervisor Program
High	High	High	Interrupt Acknowledge

Signal Summary

Signal Name	Mnemonic	Input/Output	Active State	Hi-Z On HALT	Hi-Z On BGACK
Address Bus	A1-A23	Output	High	Yes	Yes
Data Bus	D0-D15	Input/Output	High	Yes	Yes
Address Strobe	$\overline{AS}$	Output	Low	No	Yes
Read/Write	$R/\overline{W}$	Output	Read-High Write-Low	No	Yes
Upper and Lower Data Stobes	$\overline{UDS}$, $\overline{LDS}$	Output	Low	No	Yes
Data Transfer Acknowledge	$\overline{DTACK}$	Input	Low	No	No
Bus Request	$\overline{BR}$	Input	Low	No	No
Bus Grant	$\overline{BG}$	Output	Low	No	No
Bus Grant Acknowledge	$\overline{BGACK}$	Input	Low	No	No
Interrupt Priority Level	$\overline{IPL0}$, $\overline{IPL1}$, $\overline{IPL2}$	Input	Low	No	No
Bus Error	$\overline{BERR}$	Input	Low	No	No
Reset	$\overline{RESET}$	Input/Output	Low	No[1]	No[1]
Halt	$\overline{HALT}$	Input/Output	Low	No[1]	No[1]
Enable	E	Output	High	No	No
Valid Memory Address	$\overline{VMA}$	Output	Low	No	Yes
Valid Peripheral Address	$\overline{VPA}$	Input	Low	No	No
Function Code Output	FC0, FC1, FC2	Output	High	No[2]	Yes
Clock	CLK	Input	High	No	No
Power Input	V_{CC}	Input	—	—	—
Ground	GND	Input	—	—	—

NOTES:
1. Open drain
2. Function codes are placed in high-impedance state during HALT for R9M, T6E, and BF4 mask sets

Signal Summary

Figure 6.6 Details of the pins and the corresponding bus lines of the Motorola MC68000 as well as the bus cycle signal timings. (Courtesy of Motorola, Inc.)

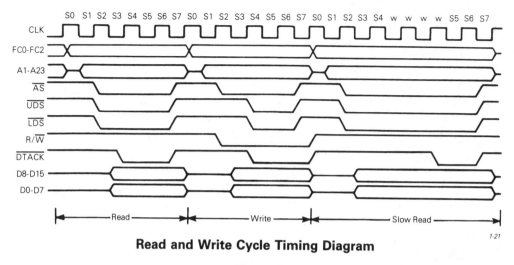

Read and Write Cycle Timing Diagram

1-21

Figure 6.6 *(continued)*

Motorola MC68020 is shown in Figure 6.7, and the semantics of the various signals (pins and lines) are given in Figure 6.8. Example transfer timings are shown in Figure 6.9. Again, the student is urged to integrate the signal timing information in Figure 6.9 with the actions in the corresponding bus cycle action flowcharts of Figure 6.7.

I/O PROTOCOLS

The keyboard and light-emitting seven-segment diode display discussed previously are very simple devices to control. Most peripheral devices require a more complicated control sequence, including some type of "handshake" protocol—as was discussed in the previous section and illustrated in Figures 6.4, 6.5, and 6.7.

Device interfaces contain three types of information that are typically held in three registers.

1. A *data register* containing the data to be input to the bus master processor or a receptacle for the data to be output by the bus master processor
2. A *status register* containing an indication of when data are available to input or when the data register can receive data, whether or not errors have occurred, and other information about the device
3. A *control register* containing information used to initialize the mode of operation and to control the logical and physical characteristics of the channel data.

All three registers are not always required or present. In some cases, only the data register is present; in some cases, the interface is automatically initialized when

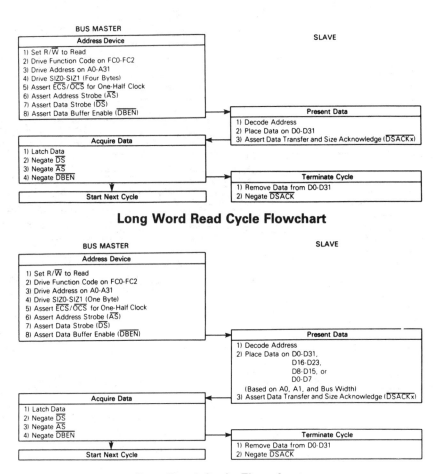

Long Word Read Cycle Flowchart

Byte Read Cycle Flowchart

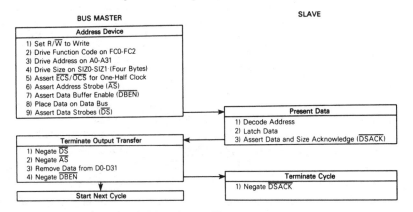

Write Cycle Flowchart

Figure 6.7 The actions of the bus master and the slave memory-mapped device for a Motorola MC68020-based system performing a read and performing a write. (Courtesy of Motorola, Inc.)

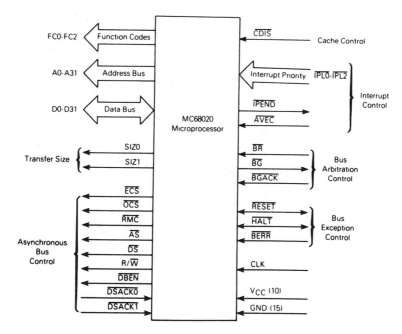

Functional Signal Groups

SIZ1	SIZ0	Size
0	1	Byte
1	0	Word
1	1	3 Byte
0	0	Long Word

SIZE Output Encodings

A1	A0	Offset
0	0	+ 0 Bytes
0	1	+ 1 Byte
1	0	+ 2 Bytes
1	1	+ 3 Bytes

Address Offset Encodings

DSACK1	DSACK0	Result	
H	H	Insert Wait States in Current Bus Cycle	
H	L	Complete Cycle	Data Bus Port Size is 8 Bits
L	H	Complete Cycle	Data Bus Port Size is 16 Bits
L	L	Complete Cycle	Data Bus Port Size is 32 Bits

DSACK Codes and Results

Figure 6.8   Details of the pins and the corresponding bus lines of the Motorola MC68020. (Courtesy of Motorola, Inc.)

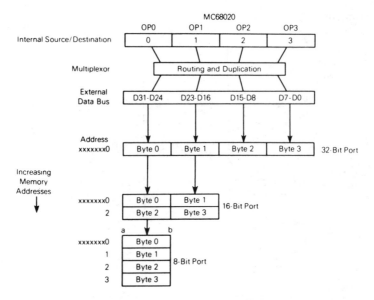

MC68020 Interface to Various Port Sizes

Transfer Size	Size		Address		Source/Destination External Data Bus Connection			
	SIZ1	SIZ0	A1	A0	D31:D24	D23:D16	D15:D8	D7:D0
Byte	0	1	x	x	OP3	OP3	OP3	OP3
Word	1	0	x	0	OP2	OP3	OP2	OP3
	1	0	x	1	OP2	OP2	OP3	OP2
3 Byte	1	1	0	0	OP1	OP2	OP3	OP0
	1	1	0	1	OP1	OP1	OP2	OP3
	1	1	1	0	OP1	OP2	OP1	OP2
	1	1	1	1	OP1	OP1	OP2	OP1
Long Word	0	0	0	0	OP0	OP1	OP2	OP3
	0	0	0	1	OP0	OP0	OP1	OP2
	0	0	1	0	OP0	OP1	OP0	OP1
	0	0	1	1	OP0	OP0	OP1*	OP0

*On write cycles this byte is output, on read cycles this byte is ignored.

x = don't care

NOTE: The OP labels on the external data bus refer to a particular byte of the operand that will be read or written on that section of the data bus (see Figure 5-4).

MC68020 Internal to External Data Bus Multiplexor

Figure 6.8 (*continued*).

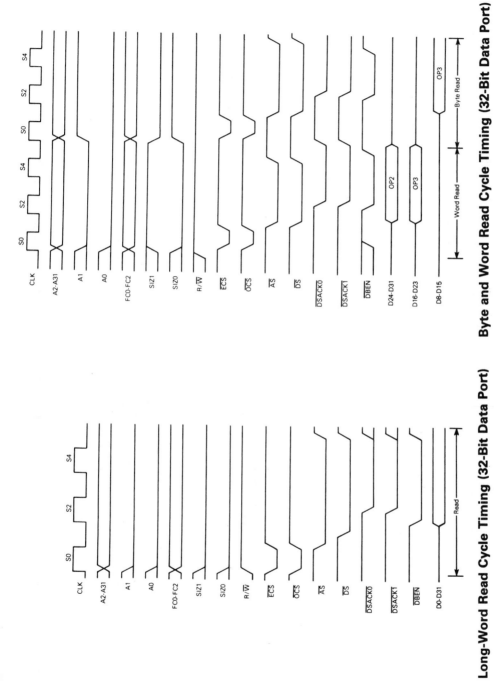

Long-Word Read Cycle Timing (32-Bit Data Port)   **Byte and Word Read Cycle Timing (32-Bit Data Port)**

Figure 6.9   Example bus cycle timings of the Motorola MC68020. (Courtesy of Motorola, Inc.)

237

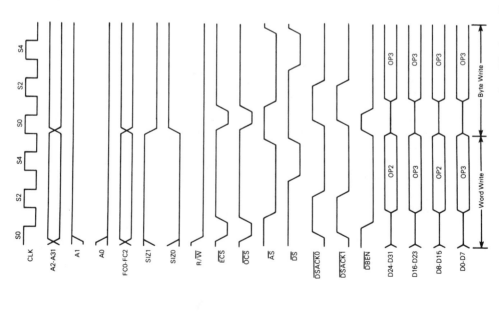

Byte and Word Write Cycle Timing (32-Bit Data Port)   **Long Word Operand Write Timing (16-Bit Data Port)**

Figure 6.9 (*continued*).

power is applied, thus rendering the control register unnecessary. A schematic of a typical interface is shown in Figure 6.10.

As an example of a simple I/O process, we will employ a common communications terminal consisting of a keyboard and a cathode ray tube (CRT) display or visual display unit (VDU) as well as a printer. The combination input/output device and printer will employ a MC68681 dual universal asynchronous receiver-transmitter (DUART) and an RS-232 interface driver chip set as its transducer to the MC680XY system bus (Figure 6.11). Data will be transmitted independently, one character at a time, and will not be buffered at the keyboard/CRT terminal or at the printer.

This type of data transmission is often referred to as serial input/output (SIO). Note that we must be very specific in our example. This specificity is typical, as each device and interface has very specific and often unique transmission characteristics.

The MC68681 DUART chip requires that I/O commands and data be presented to it by the processor. The processor can use a register for this purpose, or the stack may be used, or an area in memory pointed to by an address in a register or on the stack may be used. The last method, often termed a *task block,* is the common method employed by operating systems. We will keep our example very simple by using a register to contain the datum and the system stack to contain the command information.

The MC68681 DUART requires three different input/output control specifications:

1. *Data path width:* 7-bit or 8-bit characters are allowed. Our example will use 7-bit characters with 2 stop bits and even parity.
2. *Data transfer speed:* We will specify 9600 bits per second as the maximum rate for the terminal and 300 bits per second for the printer.
3. *Handshake protocol:* We will have the interface determine whether data can be transmitted; that is, we will program the MC68681 DUART to perform the handshake protocol.

Thus, we are implying that a program has certain functions to execute to accomplish the transfer of a character. It is usual to centralize the functions necessary to communicate with a device/interface pair into an I/O driver routine that can be used as needed by an applications program. Our example, therefore, will be directed toward designing and implementing an I/O driver routine for a keyboard CRT terminal and printer interface pair. This process is shown in Figure 6.12. Our example terminal driver must first transmit control information to the interface (MC68681) and receive status information from it before data can be transmitted (either input or output).

The MC68681 DUART is a communications device that provides two independent full-duplex asynchronous receiver/transmitter channels, a 6-bit parallel input port, an 8-bit parallel output port, and a 16-bit counter/timer in a single package.

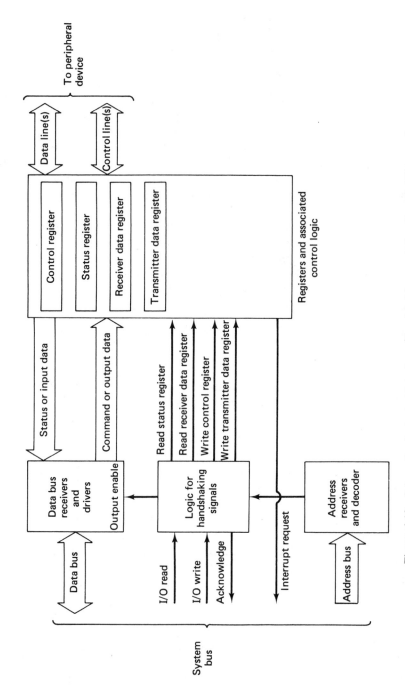

Figure 6.10 Schematic of a typical interface. (Reprinted by permission from G. Gibson and Y. Liu, *Microcomputers for Engineers and Scientists*, Prentice-Hall, Englewood Cliffs, NJ, 1980) From G. A. Gibson and Y. Liu, *Microcomputers for Engineers and Scientists*, © 1980, p. 288. Reprinted by permission of Prentice-Hall, Inc., Englewood Cliffs, NJ.)

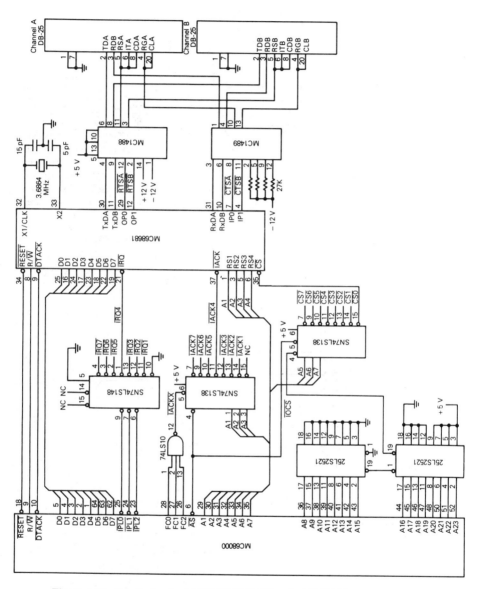

Figure 6.11 Interfacing the MC68681 DUART to the MC68000 central processor requires relatively few additional chips. (Courtesy of Motorola, Inc.)

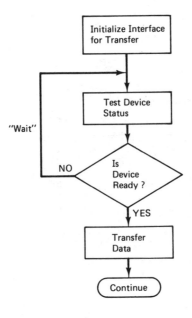

Figure 6.12 The generalized structure of a simple I/O device driver routine. The CPU (central processing unit = MC680XY) directly requests device action. (From T. L. Harman and B. Lawson, *The Motorola MC68000 Microprocessor Family: Assembly Language, Interface Design, and System Design.* © 1985, p. 333. Reprinted by permission of Prentice-Hall, Inc., Englewood Cliffs, NJ.)

Also, the MC68681 can be programmed to generate interrupts under any of the following conditions:

Channel A transmitter ready
Channel A receiver ready
Channel A change-in-break
Channel B transmitter ready
Channel B receiver ready
Channel B change-in-break
Counter/timer ready
Input port change-of-state

Channels A and B of the MC68681 can operate in four different modes: normal, automatic echo, local loopback, and remote loopback. A channel operating in normal mode allows full-duplex communication. A channel operating in automatic-echo mode operates exactly as in normal mode but automatically retransmits any received data. The local-loopback and remote-loopback modes are diagnostic modes that can be used to verify correct operation of a channel.

The MC68681 has a 6-bit parallel input port and an 8-bit parallel output port. Each of the inputs and outputs can be used as general-purpose inputs and outputs. However, each has programmable alternate functions. Finally, the MC68681 has a

16-bit programmable counter/timer that can be used to measure elapsed time between events or to generate periodic interrupts. It can be programmed to operate as a free-running timer (cannot be stopped and started) or as a counter (can be stopped and started).

Very efficient terminal and printer I/O can be achieved in an MC68000-based system using only the MC68681 DUART and an RS-232 interface driver chip set. As an extra bonus, a dual-tasking scheme can be implemented easily using the counter/timer chip on the MC68681 to generate periodic time-slice interrupts to the MC68000. This allows the MC68000 to appear to be executing two tasks simultaneously. Typically, one of the tasks would be a printing task so that printing can be done as a "background" task to something else being executed by the MC68000.

An Example of an I/O Driver

Considerations that must be taken into account when designing and programming an I/O driver include the following:

1. *Initialize the channel.* When power is applied to the system, the MC68681 DUART powers up in an unknown state. The I/O driver will put the channel into a known state.
2. *Input a single character.* When this function is requested, the driver reads the status port and waits until data are available; then the driver reads the data port and passes the information back to the system.
3. *Output a single character.* When this function is requested, the system must pass the character to be output, or a pointer to that character, to the driver. The driver reads the status port and waits until the transmitter is available. When the transmitter is available, the driver will transfer the specified character to the data port.
4. *Check the channel's status.* Perhaps the system does not need to read a character; rather, it needs to know if a character is available. Under such circumstances, the system will read the status port contents.
5. *Send control information to the channel.* The system may need to alter the state of the channel, for example, to allow the channel to check for parity errors.
6. *Input a series of characters from the channel.* You may wish to input characters until some terminating condition is detected. For example, a carriage return may constitute a terminating condition, or a fixed number of characters may have to be input. Five numeric characters constitute a ZIP code, for example. The I/O driver will read data from the channel. This involves waiting for

data to be available, then reading the information present at the data port while saving the data in a designated place in memory, then testing to determine if the terminating condition has been reached.

7. *Output a series of characters to the channel.* The system may wish to output a series of characters until a terminating condition is detected. Possible termination conditions might include either the detection of a predetermined end-of-string character or the output of a specific number of characters. The I/O driver will test for the termination condition; if the terminating condition is not detected, the I/O driver will load data from a specified memory location and send the data to the channel.

This example is derived from Harper (1984). The flowcharts in Figures 6.13 and 6.17 and the routines in Figures 6.14, 6.15, 6.16, and 6.18 are copyrighted by Motorola, Inc., and are used with permission.

We will consider the initialization routine first. In our example—shown in Figures 6.13, 6.14, 6.15, and 6.16—the parameters are made available (are passed) to the initialization routine via the system stack. The DUART initialization routines consist of DINIT, CHCHK, and CTRCHK. DINIT is the DUART initialization routine and is called at system initialization time. After DINIT initializes the DUART channels and counter, it checks channel A, channel B, and the counter for operational errors. Before DINIT is called, the calling routine must allocate three words on the system stack. Upon return to the calling routine, DINIT will pass back three status words on the system stack that reflect the operation of channel A, channel B, and the counter. If DINIT finds no errors in channel A, it will enable the channel A receiver and transmitter. Likewise, if DINIT finds no errors in channel B, it will enable the channel B transmitter. CHCHK and CTRCHK are routines that are called by DINIT to perform the actual checks. CHCHK checks a channel for proper operation. DINIT calls CHCHK twice—the first time to check channel A and the second time to check channel B. After placing the channel in local-loopback mode, CHCHK checks the channel for the following errors: transmitter never ready, receiver never ready, framing error, parity error, and incorrect character received. CTRCHK checks the counter for proper operation by verifying that the counter interrupts the MC68000 properly after reaching terminal count.

We will next consider the three actual I/O device driver routines shown in Figures 6.17 and 6.18: INCH, OUTCH, and POUTCH. INCH is the terminal input character routine. INCH gets a character from the channel A receiver and places it in the lower byte of register D0. OUTCH is the terminal output character routine. OUTCH sends the character in the lower byte of register D0 to the channel A transmitter. POUTCH is the printer output character routine. POUTCH sends the character in the lower byte of register D0 to the channel B transmitter.

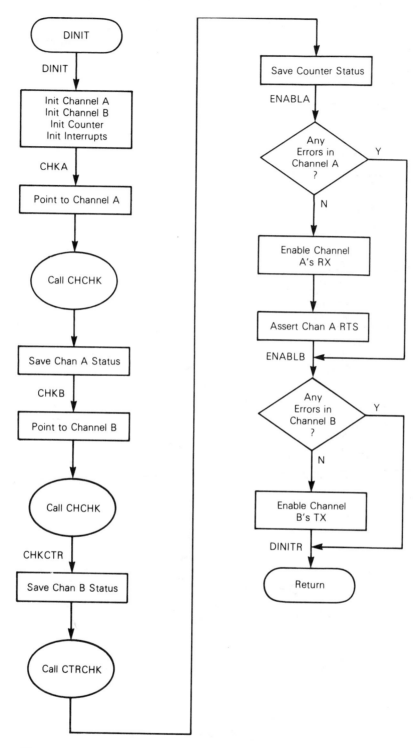

Figure 6.13 The logic for the I/O routines DINT, CHCHK and CTRCHK. (Courtesy of Motorola, Inc.)

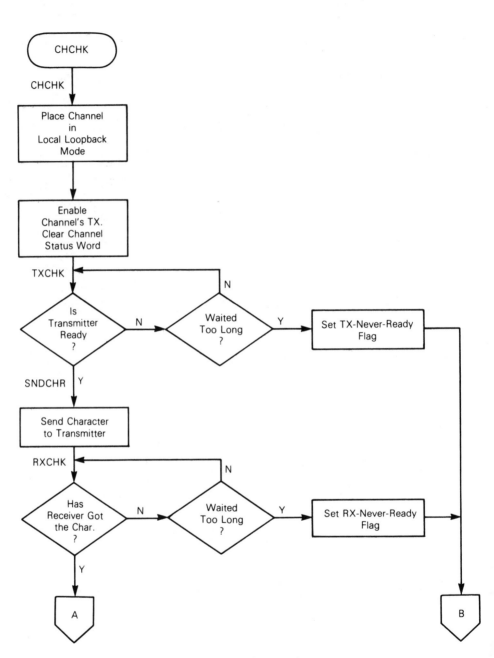

Figure 6.13 *(continued)*.

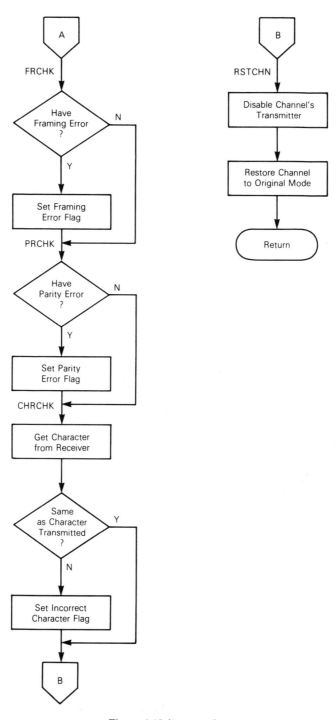

Figure 6.13 (*continued*).

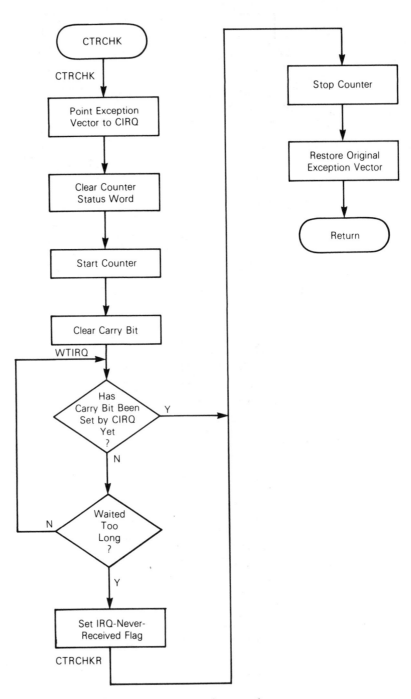

Figure 6.13 (*continued*).

```
* DINIT - DUART INITIALIZATION ROUTINE.
*         AFTER INITIALIZING THE DUART'S CHANNELS & COUNTER FOR
*         OPERATION, DINIT CHECKS CHANNEL A, CHANNEL B, & THE
*         COUNTER FOR OPERATIONAL ERRORS.
*
*   ENTRY CONDITIONS:
*
*       ALLOCATE THREE WORDS ON SYSTEM STACK BEFORE CALLING.
*
*   EXIT CONDITIONS:
*
*       THREE STATUS WORDS ARE PLACED ON THE SYSTEM STACK.
*
*       THE STATUS WORDS' FORMATS ARE AS FOLLOWS:
*
*           WORD        BIT      STATUS (1=ERROR, 0=NO ERROR)
*           ----        ---      ----------------------------
*           (A7)+0       0      CHAN A TRANSMITTER NEVER READY
*             "          1        ":: RECEIVER NEVER READY
*             "          2        "  FRAMING ERROR
*             "          3        "  PARITY ERROR
*             "          4        "  INCORRECT CHARACTER RECEIVED
*             "          5-15    (NOT USED)
*
*           (A7)+2       0      CHAN B TRANSMITTER NEVER READY
*             "          1        "  RECEIVER NEVER READY
*             "          2        "  FRAMING ERROR
*             "          3        "  PARITY ERROR
*             "          4        "  INCORRECT CHARACTER RECEIVED
*             "          5-15    (NOT USED)
*
*           (A7)+4       0      COUNTER IRQ NEVER RECEIVED
*             "          1-15    (NOT USED)
*
*       IF NO ERRORS ARE FOUND IN CHAN A, DINIT WILL ENABLE A'S RX.
*       IF NO ERRORS ARE FOUND IN CHAN B, DINIT WILL ENABLE B'S TX.
*       THE COUNTER WILL NOT BE RUNNING.
*       ALL REGISTER CONTENTS ARE UNALTERED.
*
* CONSTANTS
*
CHASTS  EQU     12              STACK OFFSET TO CHAN A STATUS WORD
CHBSTS  EQU     14              STACK OFFSET TO CHAN B STATUS WORD
CTRSTS  EQU     16              STACK OFFSET TO COUNTER STATUS WORD
*
DINIT   MOVEM.L A0/D0,-(A7)     SUBROUTINE USES REGS A0-A4 & D0
* INITIALIZE DUART CHANNELS & COUNTER
*
        MOVE.B  #$30,ACR        BRG SET 1, CNTR MODE, CLK SRCE: x1/16
        MOVE.B  #$BB,CSPA       A: RX & TX AT 9600 BAUD
        MOVE.B  #$84,MP1A       * RX-RTS, CHAR ERR, FRCE PAR, 7 CHAR
        MOVE.B  #$4F,MR2A       * A-ECHO, NO TX-RTS, NO CTS-TX, 2 STOPS
        MOVE.B  #$44,CSRB       B: RX & TX AT 300 BAUD
        MOVE.B  #$0A,MR1B       * NO RX-RTS, CHAR ERR, FRCE PAR, 7 CHAR
        MOVE.B  #$17,MR2B       * NORMAL, NO TX-RTS, CTS-TX, 1 STOP
        MOVE.B  #255,IVR        INIT IVR WITH IRQ VECTOR NUMBER
        MOVE.B  #$00,CTUR       INIT COUNTER/TIMER REGISTERS
        MOVE.B  #$73,CTLR
        MOVE.B  #IRQMSK,IMR     INIT IRQ MASK REGISTER
*
* CHECK CHANNEL A FOR OPERATIONAL ERRORS
*
CHKA    LEA.L   CHANA,A0        LOAD CHANNEL A ADDRESS FOR CHECK
        BSR     CHCMK           CHECK CHANNEL A
        MOVE.W  D0,CHASTS(A7)   PLACE CHAN A STATUS WORD IN STACK
*
* CHECK CHANNEL B FOR OPERATIONAL ERRORS
*
CHKB    LEA.L   CHANB,A0        LOAD CHANNEL B ADDRESS FOR CHECK
        BSR     CHCMK           CHECK CHANNEL B
        MOVE.W  D0,CHBSTS(A7)   PLACE CHAN B STATUS WORD IN STACK
*
* CHECK COUNTER FOR OPERATIONAL ERRORS
*
CHKCTR  BSR.L   CTRCMK          CHECK COUNTER
        MOVE.W  D0,CTRSTS(A7)   PLACE COUNTER STATUS WORD IN STACK
*
* DUART CHECK COMPLETE, ENABLE CHANNELS UNLESS ERRORS WERE FOUND,
* THEN RETURN TO CALLING ROUTINE.
*
ENABLA  TST.W   CHASTS(A7)      ARE THERE ERRORS IN CHANNEL A?
        BNE     ENABLB          YES, SKIP NEXT PART
        MOVE.B  #$01,CRA        NO, ENABLE A'S RX,
        MOVE.B  #$01,BTST       ASSERT A'S RTS OUTPUT
ENABLB  TST.W   CHBSTS(A7)      ARE THERE ERRORS IN CHANNEL B?
        BNE     DINITR          YES, SKIP NEXT PART
        MOVE.B  #$04,CRB        NO, ENABLE B'S TX
DINITR  MOVEM.L (A7)+,D0/A0     RESTORE REGISTER CONTENTS
        RTS
*
* CHCMK - CHANNEL CHECK ROUTINE.
*         CHECKS A 68681 DUART CHANNEL FOR OPERATIONAL ERRORS.
*         AFTER PLACING CHANNEL IN LOCAL LOOPBACK MODE, CHCMK
*         CHECKS FOR THE FOLLOWING CHANNEL ERRORS:
```

Figure 6.14 The code for the I/O routine DINIT, which initializes the MC68681 DUART. (Courtesy of Motorola, Inc.)

```
CHCHK - CHANNEL CHECK ROUTINE.
          CHECKS A 68681 DUART CHANNEL FOR OPERATIONAL ERRORS.
          AFTER PLACING CHANNEL IN LOCAL LOOPBACK MODE, CHCHK
          CHECKS FOR THE FOLLOWING CHANNEL ERRORS:

*                    TRANSMITTER NEVER READY
*                    RECEIVER NEVER READY
*                    FRAMING ERROR
*                    PARITY ERROR
*                    INCORRECT CHARACTER RECEIVED
*
*       ENTRY CONDITIONS:
*
*                    CHANNEL IS ALREADY CONFIGURED FOR OPERATION, BUT NOT ENABLED
*                    AO CONTAINS BASE ADDRESS OF DUART CHANNEL.
*
*       EXIT CONDITIONS:
*
*                    CHANNEL IS RESTORED TO ORIGINAL OPERATING MODE.
*                    A CHANNEL STATUS WORD IS PLACED IN REGISTER DO.
*
*                    THE CHANNEL STATUS WORD FORMAT IS AS FOLLOWS:
*
*                        BIT        STATUS (1=ERROR, 0=NO ERROR)
*                        ---        ----------------------------
*
*                         0         TRANSMITTER NEVER READY
*                         1         RECEIVER NEVER READY
*                         2         FRAMING ERROR
*                         3         PARITY ERROR
*                         4         INCORRECT CHARACTER RECEIVED
*                        5-15       (NOT USED)
*
*                    ALL OTHER REGISTERS ARE UNALTERED.
*
*

CHCHK    MOVEM.L  D1-D3,-(A7)          SUBROUTINE USES REGS D1-D3

* CHANGE ORIGINAL CHANNEL MODE TO LOCAL LOOPBACK MODE & CLEAR STATUS WORD

         MOVE.B   (AO),D3             SAVE ORIGINAL MR2x REGISTER CONTENTS
         ORI.B    #$80,(AO)           PUT CHANNEL IN LOCAL LOOPBACK MODE &
         ANDI.B   #$AF,(AO)           MAKE SURE CTS-TX IS DISABLED FOR CHECK
         MOVE.B   #$05,4(AO)          ENABLE CHANNEL'S TX
         CLR.W    DO                  CLEAR CHANNEL STATUS WORD

* CHECK CHANNEL'S TRANSMITTER

         MOVE.W   #TXCNT,D1           INIT TX WAIT LOOP COUNT
TXCHK    BTST.B   #2,2(AO)            WAIT FOR TX TO BECOME READY
         DBNE     D1,TXCHK            WAITED TOO LONG?
         BNE      SNDCHR              NO, SKIP NEXT PART
         ORI.W    #$0001,DO           YES, SET TX-NEVER-READY FLAG BIT
         BRA      RSTCHN              & SKIP REST OF CHECK
SNDCHR   MOVE.B   #$55,6(AO)          TX IS READY, SEND TEST CHARACTER

* CHECK CHANNEL'S RECEIVER

         MOVE.W   #RXCNT,D1           INIT RX WAIT LOOP COUNT
RXCHK    BTST.B   #0,2(AO)            WAIT FOR RX TO RECEIVE CHARACTER
         DBNE     D1,RXCHK            WAITED TOO LONG?
         BNE      FRCHK               NO, SKIP NEXT PART
         ORI.W    #$0002,DO           YES, SET RX-NEVER-READY FLAG BIT
         BRA      RSTCHN              & SKIP REST OF CHECK
FRCHK    BTST.B   #6,2(AO)            RX HAS CHAR, HAVE FRAMING ERROR?
         BEQ      PRCHK               NO, SKIP NEXT PART
         ORI.W    #$0004,DC           YES, SET FRAMING ERROR FLAG BIT
PRCHK    BTST.B   #5,2(AO)            HAVE PARITY PARITY ERROR?
         BEQ      CHRCHK              NO, SKIP NEXT PART
         ORI.W    #$0008,DO           YES, SET PARITY ERROR FLAG BIT
CHRCHK   MOVE.B   6(AO),D2            NO STATUS ERRORS, GET CHAR FROM RX
         CMP.B    #$55,D2             IS IT THE SAME CHAR TX'D?
         BEQ      RSTCHN              YES, SKIP NEXT PART
         ORI.W    #$0010,DC           NO, SET INCORRECT-CHAR-RX'D FLAG BIT

* CHANNEL CHECK COMPLETE, STACK STATUS WORD & RESTORE
* CHANNEL TO ORIGINAL MODE OF OPERATION.

RSTCHN   MOVE.B   #$0A,4(AO)          DISABLE CHANNEL'S TX
         MOVE.B   D3,(AO)             RESTORE CHANNEL TO ORIGINAL MODE

         MOVEM.L  (A7)+,D1-D3         RESTORE REGISTER CONTENTS
         RTS
```

Figure 6.15 The code for the channel-checking routine CHCHK for the MC68681 DUART. (Courtesy of Motorola, Inc.)

```
*
* CTRCHK - COUNTER CHECK ROUTINE.
*           CHECKS DUART COUNTER FOR OPERATIONAL ERRORS.
*           AFTER RE-POINTING THE DUART'S EXCEPTION VECTOR
*           TO ITS OWN INTERRUPT HANDLER, CTRCHK STARTS THE
*           COUNTER & WAITS FOR THE COUNTER TO GENERATE AN IRQ.
*
*           ENTRY CONDITIONS:
*
*                     DUART CONFIGURED FOR A COUNTER IRQ (IMR[3]=1).
*                     IRQ VECTOR REGISTER IS ALREADY INITIALIZED.
*                     COUNTER UPPER & LOWER REGISTERS ARE ALREADY INITIALIZED.
*                     COUNTER IS NOT RUNNING.
*
*           EXIT CONDITIONS:
*
*                     ORIGINAL DUART EXCEPTION VECTOR IS RESTORED.
*                     A COUNTER STATUS WORD IS PLACED IN REGISTER DO.
*
*                     THE ERROR STATUS WORD FORMAT IS AS FOLLOWS:
*
*                             BIT        STATUS (1=ERROR, 0=NO ERROR)
*                             ---        ----------------------------
*
*                             0          COUNTER IRQ NEVER RECEIVED
*                             1-15       (NOT USED)
*
*                     ALL OTHER REGISTERS ARE UNALTERED.
*
*

CTRCHK    MOVEM.L   D1,-(A7)           SUBROUTINE USES REG D1

          MOVE.L    DIRQVEC,-(A7)      SAVE ORIGINAL EXCEPTION VECTOR

          MOVE.L    #CIRQ,DIRQVEC      RE-POINT EXCEPTION VECTOR


          CLR.W     DO                 CLEAR COUNTER STATUS WORD
          TST.B     STRC               START COUNTER

          MOVE.W    #IRQCNT,D1         INIT IRQ WAIT LOOP COUNT
          ANDI.B    #$FE,CCR           CLEAR CARRY BIT
WTIRQ     DBCS      D1,WTIRQ           WAIT FOR COUNTER IRQ: WAITED TOO LONG?

          BCS       CTRCHKR            NO, SKIP NEXT PART
          ORI.W     #$01,DO            YES, SET IRQ-NEVER-REC'D FLAG BIT

* COUNTER CHECK COMPLETE, STOP COUNTER, RESTORE ORIGINAL EXCEPTION VECTOR,
* & STACK ERROR STATUS WORD.

CTRCHKR   TST.B     STPC               STOP COUNTER
          MOVE.L    (A7)+,DIRQVEC      RESTORE ORIGINAL EXCEPTION VECTOR

          MOVEM.L   (A7)+,D1           RESTORE REGISTER CONTENTS
          RTS
```

Figure 6.16 The code for the counter-checking routine CTRCHK for the MC68681 DUART. (Courtesy of Motorola, Inc.)

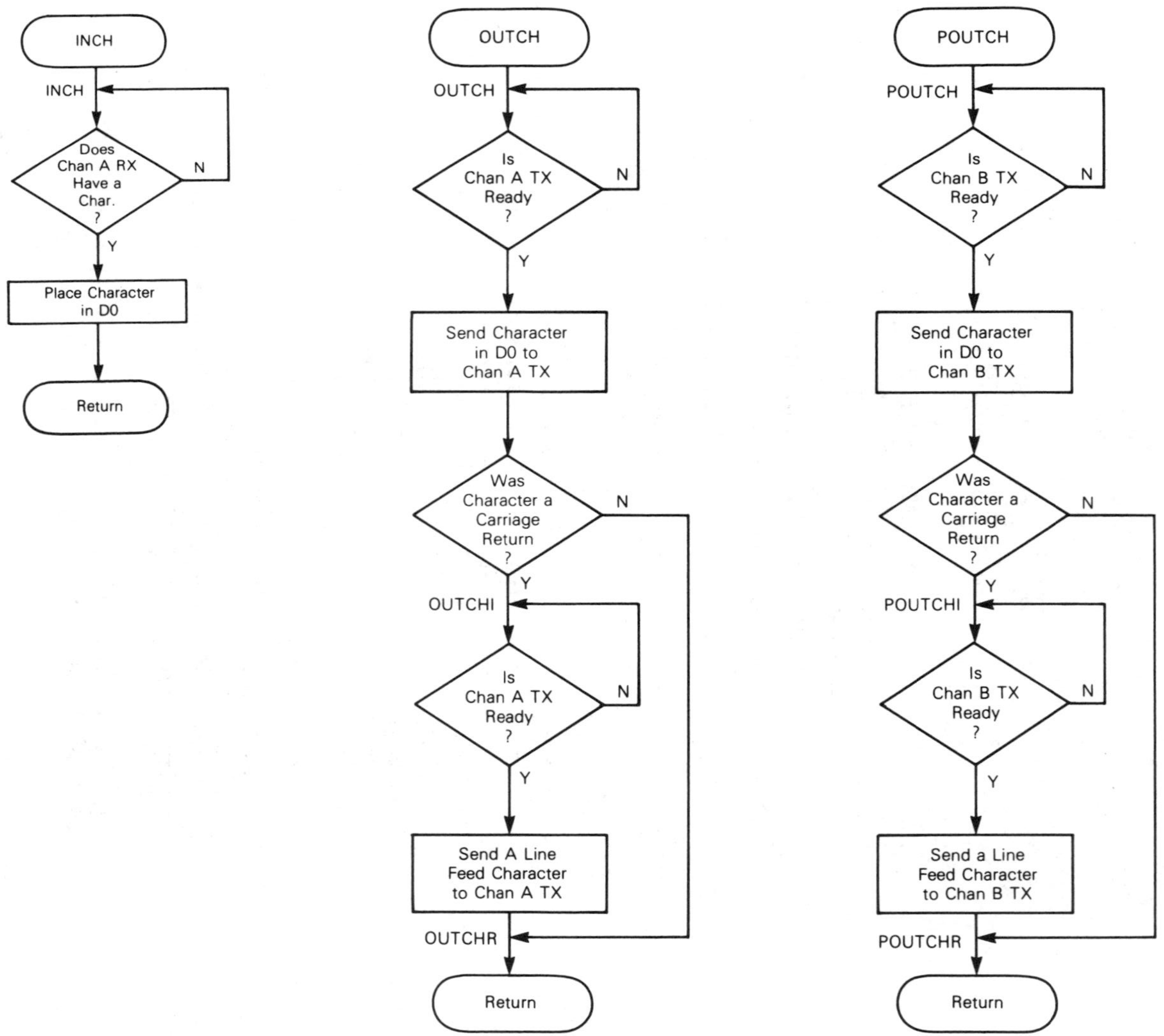

Figure 6.17 The logic for the terminal input routine INCH, the terminal output routine

```
*
* INCH - TERMINAL INPUT CHARACTER ROUTINE.
*          GETS CHARACTER FROM TERMINAL VIA DUART CHANNEL A,
*          THEN PLACES IT IN D0.
*          (BECAUSE CHAN A IS IN AUTO-ECHO MODE, CHARACTER DOES NOT NEED TO
*          BE RE-TRANSMITTED BACK TO TERMINAL BY SOFTWARE.)
*
*          ENTRY CONDITIONS:
*
*                    DUART CHANNEL A RX & TX ENABLED.
*
*          EXIT CONDITIONS:
*
*                    RECEIVED CHARACTER PLACED IN D0.
*                    ALL OTHER REGISTERS UNALTERED.
*
*
INCH      BTST.B    #0,SRA                   WAIT FOR CHAN A'S RX TO GET A CHAR

          BEQ       INCH
          MOVE.B    RBA,D0                   GET CHARACTER FROM RECEIVER
          RTS


* OUTCH - TERMINAL OUTPUT CHARACTER ROUTINE.
*          OUTPUTS CHARACTER IN D0 TO TERMINAL VIA CHAN A'S TX.
*          IF CHARACTER IN D0 IS A CARRIAGE RETURN, OUTCH WILL
*          OUTPUT BOTH A CARRIAGE RETURN & LINE FEED CHARACTER.
*
*          ENTRY CONDITIONS:
*
*                    DUART CHANNEL A TX ENABLED.
*                    CHARACTER TO BE TRANSMITTED IN D0.
*
*          EXIT CONDITIONS:
*
*                    ALL REGISTERS UNALTERED.
*                    CHARACTER SENT TO CHANNEL A TX.
*
*
OUTCH     BTST.B    #2,SRA                   WAIT FOR CHAN A'S TX TO BECOME READY

          BEQ       OUTCH
          MOVE.B    D0,TBA                   SEND CHAR TO TRANSMITTER
          CMP.B     #CR,D0                   WAS IT A CARRIAGE RETURN?
          BNE       OUTCHR                   NO, SKIP NEXT PART
OUTCH1    BTST.B    #2,SRA                   YES, WAIT FOR TX TO BECOME READY AGAIN

          BEQ       OUTCH1
          MOVE.B    #LF,TBA                  SEND A LINE FEED

OUTCHR    RTS

* POUTCH - PRINTER OUTPUT CHARACTER ROUTINE.
*          OUTPUTS CHARACTER IN D0 TO PRINTER VIA CHAN B'S TX.
*          IF CHARACTER IN D0 IS A CARRIAGE RETURN, POUTCH WILL
*          OUTPUT BOTH A CARRIAGE RETURN & LINE FEED CHARACTER.
*
*          ENTRY CONDITIONS:
*
*                    DUART CHANNEL B TX ENABLED.
*                    CHARACTER TO BE TRANSMITTED IN D0.
*
*          EXIT CONDITIONS:
*
*                    ALL REGISTERS UNALTERED.
*                    CHARACTER SENT TO CHANNEL B TX.
*
*
POUTCH    BTST.B    #2,SRB                   WAIT FOR CHAN B'S TX TO BECOME READY

          BEQ       POUTCH
          MOVE.B    D0,TBB                   SEND CHAR TO TRANSMITTER
          CMP.B     #CR,D0                   WAS IT A CARRIAGE RETURN?
          BNE       POUTCHR                  NO, SKIP NEXT PART
POUTCH1   BTST.B    #2,SRB                   YES, WAIT FOR TX TO BECOME READY AGAIN

          BEQ       POUTCH1
          MOVE.B    #LF,TBB                  SEND LINE FEED TO TRANSMITTER
```

Figure 6.18 The code for the low-level I/O routine INCH, OUTCH, and POUTCH. (Courtesy of Motorola, Inc.)

DIRECT MEMORY ACCESS

As discussed briefly earlier in this chapter, a DMA channel allows the processor to request an I/O sequence to be accomplished while the processor continues execution of the program. Because the I/O transfer is directly between the device and memory, bypassing the processor, the processor must relinquish control of the bus to the DMA channel controller intermittently as each byte or word is transferred. In addition, logic is required to count the number of bytes/words transferred and to increment the memory address appropriately. Finally, the finish of the block transfer must be recognized and the processor notified via an interrupt.

The general arrangement of this DMA control logic within a computational system is illustrated in Figure 6.19. Note that the controller accepts I/O action parameters from the executing program, which then continues normal processing. The controller interprets these parameters (device identification, which may include track/sector information, main memory starting address, block length, and word/ byte mode) and accomplishes the data transfer by capturing the systems bus for each byte/word movement, after which it relinquishes the bus, increments the main memory address, and decrements the count. At the completion of the block transfer, the processor is notified via an interrupt.

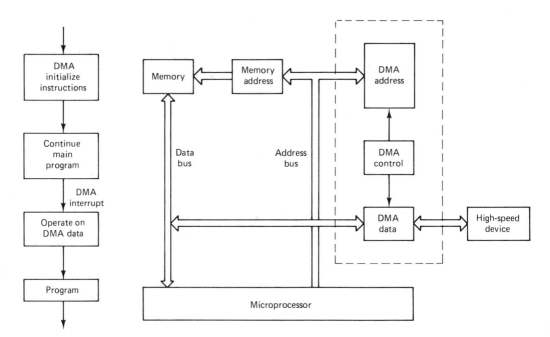

Figure 6.19 Interconnection logic of direct memory access controller (DMA). A short pseudolanguage section of a program employing DMA for input is also shown. (From G. W. Gorsline, *16-Bit Modern Microcomputers: The Intel I8086 Family*, © 1985, p. 167. Reprinted by permission of Prentice-Hall, Inc., Englewood Cliffs, NJ.)

It is necessary to emphasize that the program employing a DMA channel data transfer is proceeding with the execution of its instructions independently of the transfer. Referring to the program schematic on the left of Figure 6.19, it would be disastrous if the program used "data" in calculations before such data had been delivered to memory via the independently executing DMA. Thus, the program designer must be aware of such a possibility and insert a "wait for DMA completion interrupt" at appropriate places in the program. Note that the analogous situation can occur during a DMA output operation. The generic name for this situation of two (or more) independent but interdependent procedures executing simultaneously is *coroutines*. We will examine this fairly common concept when we discuss the MC68450 DMA input/output processor in Chapter 7.

Data Transmission

Up to this point, we have considered transferring data in a parallel mode—that is, one line for each bit to be transmitted, as illustrated on the bottom of Figure 6.20. Notice that an entire datum can be transmitted in one time unit but that 4 signal lines are required to transfer a hexadecimal digit, 7 lines for an ASCII character, 8 lines for a byte, 16 lines for a word, and 32 lines for a long word.

On the other hand, some I/O devices require that they receive/transmit data in the bit-serial transmission mode. Thus, a system of logic must be employed to transform data to/from the parallel transmission mode of the system bus from/to the bit-serial mode often required.

Let us consider a device transmitting a stream of bits to another device that must receive them one bit at a time. Each time the clock of the sending device "beats," a bit is sent; each time the clock of the receiving device beats, a bit is received. If the two clocks "drift" too far out of time synchronization, a bit will be lost. In some cases, the receiving device can adjust its clock to the rate of the sending device clock; in other cases, this is not attempted.

If the transmitting and receiving device clocks are not synchronized, the rate of drift makes it impossible to transfer more than 10 or 15 bits correctly before a bit is "missed." For this reason, asynchronous transmission is one character at a time, with a start bit, a stop bit (often two stop bits), and sometimes an error-detecting parity bit. This asynchronous mode of data transmission is illustrated in Figure 6.20. Double-bit errors cannot be detected and error correction is impossible. For this reason, many asynchronous transmission schemes transmit each character back to the sender for comparison and retransmission if the comparison fails—indicating an error.

If the transmitting and receiving device clocks are synchronized, it is possible to transmit correctly a fairly long stream of characters in bit-serial mode. Thus, a message or packet can contain many characters, including error-correcting codes. Such messages are preceded by clock synchronizing characters (usually two). Thus, synchronous transmission allows multicharacter messages and can allow fairly sophisticated error-correcting techniques.

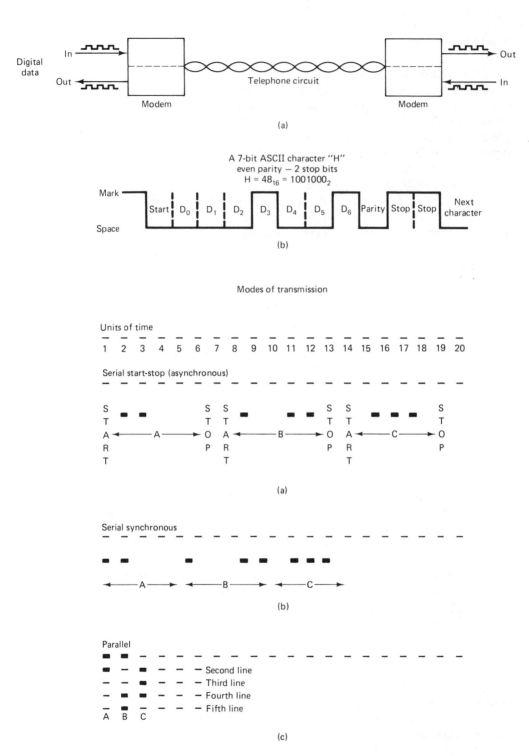

Figure 6.20 Asynchronous bit-serial, synchronous bit-serial, and parallel modes of data transmission. (From G. W. Gorsline, *16-Bit Modern Microcomputers: The Intel I8086 Family,* © 1985, p. 170. Reprinted by permission of Prentice-Hall, Inc., Englewood Cliffs, NJ.)

As would be expected, many corporations market chips to accomplish parallel-to-serial data transduction and bit-serial data receive/transmit in either the asynchronous or the synchronous modes. These are termed the *UART* (universal asynchronous receiver/transmitter), illustrated in Figure 6.21, and *USART* (universal synchronous/asynchronous receiver/transmitter).

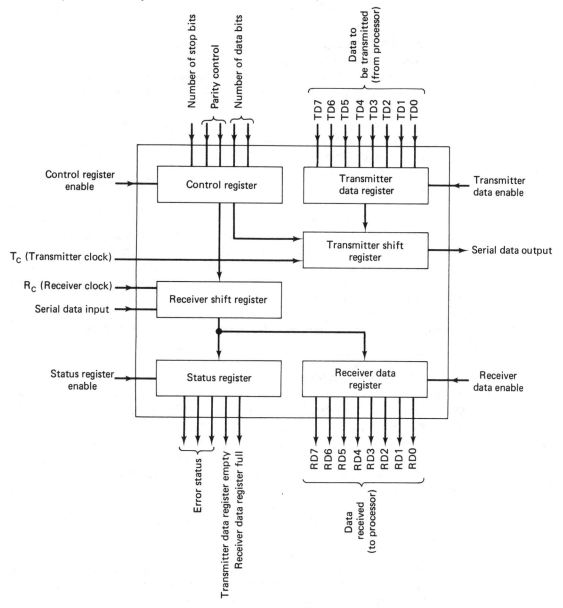

Figure 6.21 Block diagram of a UART (universal asynchronous receiver/transmitter). (Reprinted with permission from G. Gibson and Y. Liu, *Microcomputers for Engineers and Scientists,* Prentice Hall, Englewood Cliffs, NJ, 1980.) (From G. A Gibson and Y. Liu, *Microcomputers for Engineers and Scientists,* © 1980, p. 295. Reprinted by permission of Prentice-Hall, Inc., Englewood Cliffs, NJ.)

Although telephone lines are able to transmit data coded digitally, it is more usual to transform them to audible tones, where one tone could signify a binary 1 and another tone a binary 0. More complicated schemes are possible and are commonly employed. The device employed to transform a bit stream from digital to sound form (analog), and vice versa, is called a *modulator-demodulator* (MODEM). The logical placement of MODEMs in a system is shown in Figures 6.20 and 6.22.

The production and detection of changes in tone encoding a bit stream of information has a physical speed termed BAUD. Technically, BAUD specifies the number of changes per second and normally is 100, 150, 300, or 1200. As shown in Figure 6.23, the normal character in asynchronous transmission is usually coded as 11 bits or as 10 bits. Thus, a 100-BAUD transmission line can transfer approximately 10 characters per second.

As a last point, transmission lines can be *simplex* (transmission in one direction only), *half-duplex* (transmission in both directions but in only one direction at a time), and *full duplex* (transmission in both directions simultaneously).

Slow Devices

Although the types of devices that can accept data from or send data to the processor are currently extensive and constantly proliferating, we shall treat briefly only a few of the more common ones. Figure 6.24 illustrates a fairly typical interactive stand-alone small business system eminently suited to scientific and engineering problem solution, to education, and to the storage and manipulation of inventory, sales, and other records in addition to its fairly nice abilities for word processing. This particular system, marketed by Apple Computer, Incorporated, is built around a MC68000 processor and includes a keyboard/CRT terminal, a floppy disk drive, a hard disk drive, and a printer.

Keyboard/CRT–keyboard/hardcopy devices.   It is necessary that a microcomputer possess a keyboard for data, program, and command input. Sometimes these ASCII character keyboards are physically boxed separately, although it probably is more common for them to be associated physically with a CRT output screen or typewriterlike hardcopy output device. Some keyboards involve significant physical key movement to cause a circuit to close, whereas others react to the slightest pressure. The printing mechanism to produce hardcopy may involve a ball-like element or a matrix of wires, or may actually "throw" ink at the paper in an ink jet, as shown in Figure 6.25. The choice of an input/output terminal will involve such factors as original cost, reliability, cost and availability of repair, clearness of the final copy, and so on.

The integrated keyboard/CRT terminal concept is illustrated in Figure 6.26. Some of the more economical, less capable screens are only capable of one-color character generation. Other, more expensive screens have true graphics, with line-segment-producing ability as well as multiple colors.

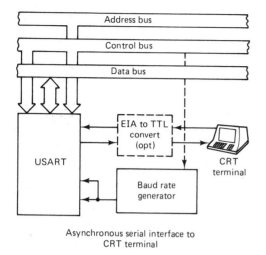

Asynchronous serial interface to
CRT terminal

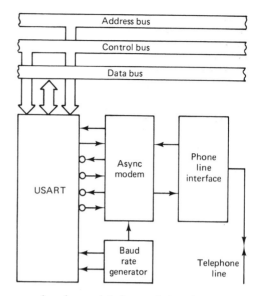

Asynchronous interface to telephone lines

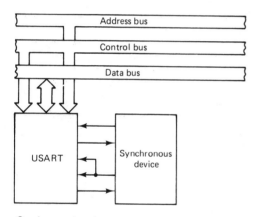

Synchronous interface to terminal or peripheral device

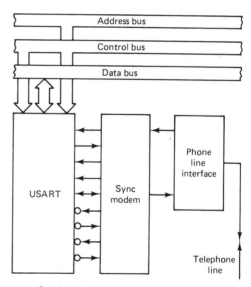

Synchronous interface to telephone lines

Figure 6.22 Input/output arrangements for common devices. A commonly available integrated-circuit chip to facilitate such communication is a universal synchronous/asynchronous receiver/transmitter (USART). Asynchronous transmission is limited to a single character and requires that the communication line be established before starting transmission. Synchronous transmission allows messages of more than one character and may include device addresses and line-switching information. (Reprinted with permission from S. E. Greenfield, *The Architecture of Microcomputers*, Winthrop, Cambridge, Mass., 1980.)

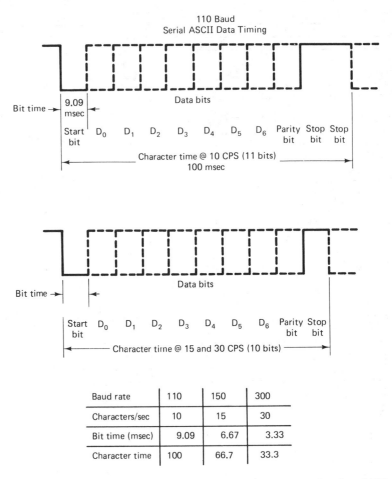

Figure 6.23 ASCII character transmission timing. (From G. W. Gorsline, *16-Bit Modern Microcomputers: The Intel I8086 Family,* © 1985, p. 174. Reprinted by permission of Prentice-Hall, Inc., Englewood Cliffs, NJ.)

Printers. The difference between the hardcopy output device with an associated keyboard and the separate hardcopy printer is often small or nonexistent. Alternatively, for microcomputers possessing fairly extensive data storage and manipulating abilities that service a small business or that are employed for extensive word processing, a higher-quality, more durable line printer may be required. One rapidly emerging technology employs a controlled jet of ink, as illustrated in Figure 6.25. The cost, durability, maintainability, print appearance, speed, and overall suitability of hardcopy printers vary immensely.

Small business systems for record storage and word processing. The small business or the branch office of a large firm needs a system to record

Figure 6.24 Motorola MC68000-based Apple Macintosh microcomputer system. (Photo courtesy of Apple Computer, Inc.)

transactions, trace inventory, maintain personnel and accounting information, as well as to automate myriad other "clerk-based" tasks. Not the least of the prospective office-type candidate tasks for microcomputer-based assistance is word processing, where a system allows the entry of text and assists in its editing and final production.

Usually, a keyboard/CRT, printer, floppy-disk-based system, such as that illustrated in Figure 6.24, is adequate for the relatively small beginning office operation. Care should be exercised in choosing this starter installation so that provisions for growth exist, such as specifying a 16/32-bit processor and an operating system that allows growth.

MC680XY-based systems not only are commonly available but usually include software that is designed particularly for office automation. Although many of the 8-bit processor-based systems commonly available have excellent software, it must be noted that the potential for the expansion of their abilities is severely limited. That is, they are almost at the point of being the "top of the line." A 16/32-bit processor-based system avoids this restriction. Current pricing trends (1986) indicate that MC680XY-based systems with comparable or superior software are becoming available at fully competitive prices. If office systems expansion in the future is a possibility, as it usually is, the acquisition of an 8-bit or 16-bit processor-based system is very questionable.

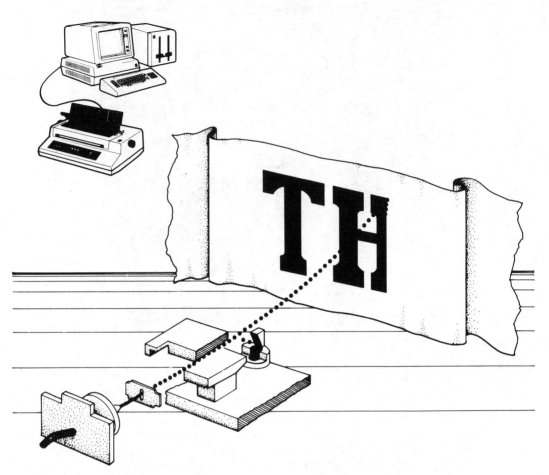

Figure 6.25 Ink-jet printer concept. (Reprinted with the permission of International Business Machines Corporation.)

Process control.   We will not attempt to explore this vitally important and rapidly growing applications area beyond noting two points. For many process control situations, such as the automobile carburetor or the microwave oven, a 4-bit or 8-bit processor is eminently capable and suitable. For other situations, additional ability and/or speed requires the use of a 16-bit or 32-bit processor. The examples of process control shown in Figure 6.27 are typical. It is also probably true that a fairly capable home control microcomputer will become an economically justified feature of many homes almost immediately. The control of lighting, heating, security, and so on, would be involved, as well as family financial records, Christmas lists, bills, and entertainment.

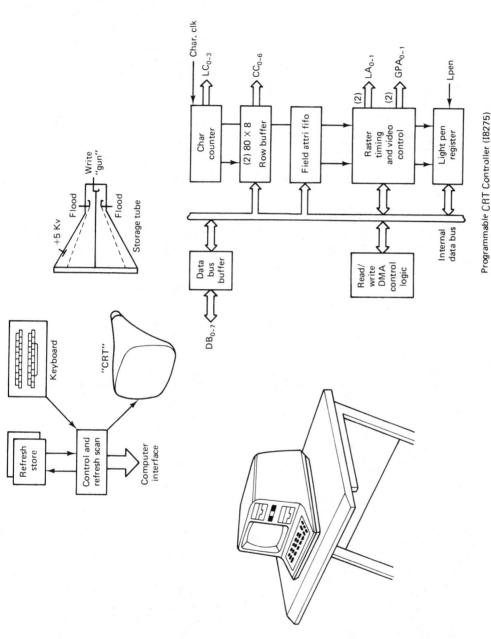

Programmable CRT Controller (I8275)

Figure 6.26 Keyboard/CRT computer terminal. (From G. W. Gorsline, *16-Bit Modern Microcomputers: The Intel I8086 Family*, © 1985, p. 177. Reprinted by permission of Prentice-Hall, Inc., Englewood Cliffs, NJ.)

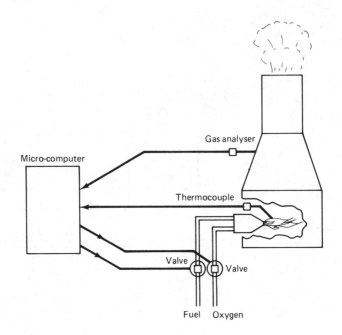

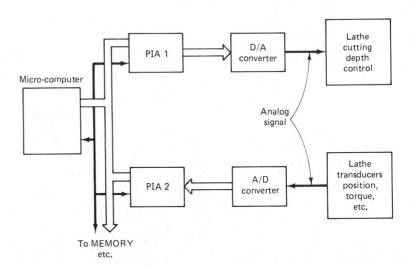

Figure 6.27   The microcomputer is being widely applied in process control situations. (From G. W. Gorsline, *16-Bit Modern Microcomputers: The Intel I8086 Family*, © 1985, p. 179. Reprinted by permission of Prentice-Hall, Inc., Englewood Cliffs, NJ.)

Fast Devices

In general, the devices in this group provide mass storage for data beyond the capacity of main memory. These devices are often termed *secondary memory* and are accessed via I/O commands. Usually, a DMA channel is employed. We will examine three types of devices: disk, magnetic tape, and magnetic bubble memory.

Rotating memory devices. The rotating portion of the disk is named for its geometric shape. Information is recorded as magnetic spots in concentric circles, known as tracks, on the flat surface (Figure 6.28). Often both the top and bottom surfaces are used. In the case of an early-model floppy disk, one read/write head for the single surface is located on an extendable-retractable arm whose placement is under programmatic control. A disk is an example of a direct access memory in which the time to access a storage cell is a nonlinear function of the address distance between the present read/write position and the position of the desired datum:

$$\text{Access time} = \left\{ \left[\text{modulus} \left(\begin{matrix} \text{number of blocks} & \text{number of} \\ \text{to desired datum,} & \text{blocks/track} \end{matrix} \right) * \begin{matrix} \text{time to} \\ \text{read one} \\ \text{block} \end{matrix} \right] + \begin{matrix} \text{time to move head} \\ \text{to needed track} \end{matrix} \right\}$$

Floppies were introduced in June 1970 as a storage device for the microprograms to control the IBM 3330 disk storage system. They were also used to contain the microcode for the reloadable control storage of the IBM/370 models 115, 125, 135, 145, and 155. A sales possibility has stimulated the development of the floppy disk and its associated drive as an economical direct-access device for microcomputers. A system has from one to eight drives, a controller, a power supply, an interface, interconnecting cables, diagnostics, and software to control the device (a driver).

The IBM 3740 diskette is a magnetic-oxide-coated Mylar computer tape cut as a 7.8-inch disk, packaged in an 8-inch-square plastic envelope with apertures for drive-hub mounting, index-mark sensing, and read/write head access. Because the inside of the envelope has a soft surface, the disk can rotate while the envelope is held stationary. As shown in Figures 6.29, 6.30, and 6.31, the floppy cartridge is slipped into the drive, positioned by the drive hub, and then held against the rotating drive spindle by a hub clamp. Pressure pads hold the read/write head in physical contact with the disk recording medium. A servomotor and feedback mechanism controls track-to-track head movement and track-head positioning. This device has 77 tracks, 3200 bits per inch (bpi), 26 sectors, storage of 242K bytes per track, 360 rpm, 250 kHz transfer rate, and a total capacity of 3.1M bits.

Although standards have not been published, the industry has largely concentrated on 8-, 5.25-, and 3-inch floppy disks. Figure 6.32 gives current data. The in-contact read/write head causes diskette wear, although most vendors guarantee 2 million passes per track. All schemes of sectoring have an index hole in the diskette, detectable by a photoelectric cell, to mark the beginning of the tracks to the drive

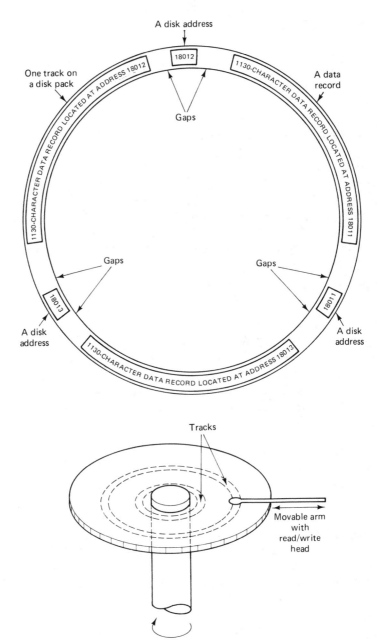

A disk address

One track on
a disk pack

1130-CHARACTER DATA RECORD LOCATED AT ADDRESS 18012

18012

1130-CHARACTER DATA RECORD LOCATED AT ADDRESS 18011

A data
record

Gaps

Gaps

Gaps

18013

18011

A disk
address

A disk
address

1130-CHARACTER DATA RECORD LOCATED AT ADDRESS 18013

Tracks

Movable arm
with
read/write
head

Disk organization showing the single-movable-head arrangement

Figure 6.28   Disk organization showing the single movable head and the arrangement of addresses and data on a single track. (From G. W. Gorsline, *16-Bit Modern
Microcomputers: The Intel I8086 Family,* © 1985, p. 181. Reprinted by permission
of Prentice-Hall, Inc., Englewood Cliffs, NJ.)

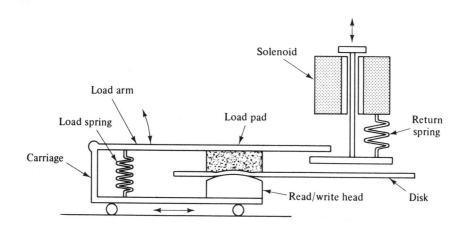

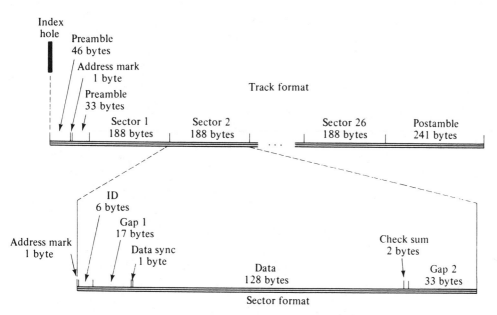

Figure 6.29 IBM 3740-compatible floppy disk drive and diskette soft-sectoring scheme. (From G. W. Gorsline, *16-Bit Modern Microcomputers: The Intel I8086 Family*, © 1985, p. 182. Reprinted by permission of Prentice-Hall, Inc., Englewood Cliffs, NJ.)

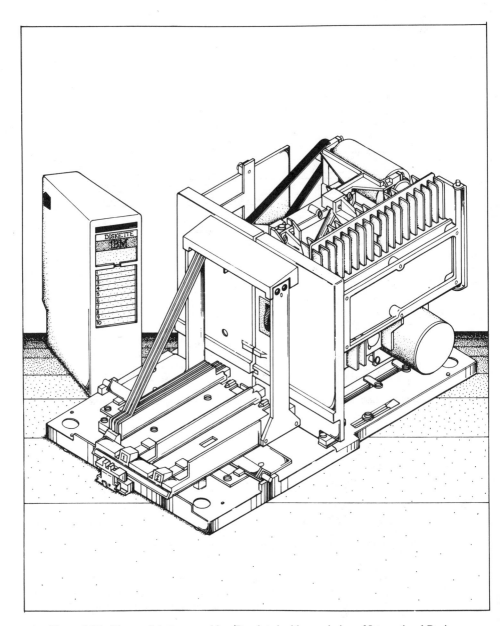

Figure 6.30 Floppy diskette assembly. (Reprinted with permission of International Business Machines Corporation.)

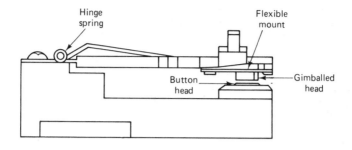

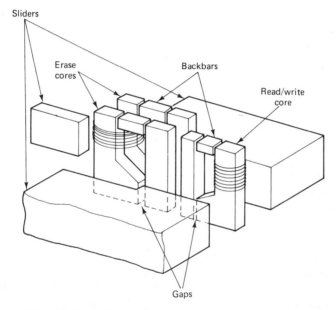

Figure 6.31   Read/write floppy disk head arrangement employed by one vendor of double-sided double-recording-density 5.25-inch minifloppy disks. (From G. W. Gorsline, *16-Bit Modern Microcomputers: The Intel I8086 Family,* © 1985, p. 184. Reprinted by permission of Prentice-Hall, Inc., Englewood Cliffs, NJ.)

controller. Sectoring divides the diskette into equal-size pie-shaped slices. Thus, each track is sectored to form a matrix of track-sector units that are addressable in mailbox fashion—track:sector. After moving the head to the proper track of a soft-sectored disk, the controller, on being informed that the index hole has been found by the photoelectric cell, instructs the read/write head to read the track until it finds the desired sector. *Hard sectoring* identifies each sector with a hole in the diskette that is sensed by a photoelectric cell in the same fashion as the track index hole. The sector hole is sensed and the controller signals the head to read the magnetically encoded sector ID. After the controller receives the sector ID, it counts the number of sector holes that it must pass to find the desired sector.

8-Inch disk	1974	1978	1983
Sides	1	2	2
tpi	48	48	48
bpi	3000	68000	68000
Capacity (bytes)	256 K	1600 K	1600 K
Cartridge design	PVC open jacket	PVC open jacket	PVC open jacket
End-user price/megabyte	$40	$5	$4
5-Inch disk			
Sides		1	2
tpi		48	96
bpi		3000	6000
Capacity (bytes)		125K	1000K
Cartridge design		PVC open jacket	PVC open jacket
End-user price/megabyte		$40	$5
3-Inch disk			
Sides			2
tpi			135
bpi			7600
Capacity (bytes)			900 K
Cartridge design			Plastic sealed jacket
End-user price/megabyte			$7

Figure 6.32 Floppy disk characteristics. (From G. W. Gorsline, *Computer Organization*: *Hardware/Software, Second Edition*, © 1986, p. 294. Reprinted by permission of Prentice-Hall, Inc., Englewood Cliffs, NJ.)

Floppy disks are presently used as direct-access devices for microcomputers, for keyboard microprocessor-based data-entry devices, and as auxiliary memory for various microprocessor-based keyboard terminals. Standards do not currently exist for floppy disks, so various sizes and configurations are available.

Floppy disks are an example of direct-access memory (DAM). The term *direct-access memory* means that any address may be next but that the time to access a particular datum is a nonlinear function of the addressing distance. Thus, access time for a movable-head disk is composed of three portions:

$$\text{Access time} \longleftarrow \begin{array}{c} \text{time to move} \\ \text{head to desired} \\ \text{track} \end{array} + \begin{array}{c} \text{time for desired} \\ \text{sector to rotate} \\ \text{under head} \end{array} + \begin{array}{c} \text{time to} \\ \text{read} \\ \text{sector} \end{array}$$

When using disks with movable heads, the arrangement of data on the device can have gross effects on the speed of access. For example, if block 1 is on track 7, block 2 is on track 77, and block 3 is on track 50, a large amount of time will be consumed in head movement. In fact, it would be best to place these three blocks in sectors of the same track. Some devices cannot access a sector without a preceding minimum time that prevents accessing of contiguous sectors. This characteristic would result in large access-time savings if contiguous blocks were placed on the device in every other sector. You can imagine the effects with large files. In many cases, a job will use more than one file; in almost all cases, these files should be placed on separate devices to minimize head movement.

The *Winchester disk,* as employed with microcomputers, is marketed in both a permanently mounted (fixed) version and a removable/mountable cartridge version. In at least one case, as illustrated in Figure 6.33, both types are assembled into a single package. The advantages of the Winchester disk include larger capacity, a lower error rate, faster data transfer, and quicker head movement. The initial cost of the drive and of the cartridges is relatively high, although the cost per unit of information storage is usually low.

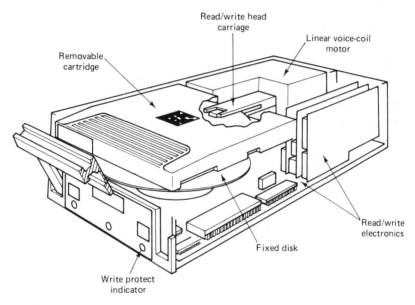

Figure 6.33   Example of Winchester disk technology. (From G. W. Gorsline, *16-Bit Modern Microcomputers: The Intel I8086 Family,* © 1985, p. 185. Reprinted by permission of Prentice-Hall, Inc., Englewood Cliffs, NJ.)

In terms of commercial marketing, there has been a continuing intense development effort to produce a more economical product from three standpoints: (1) lower original total cost, (2) lower cost per byte of storage, and (3) higher storage capacity. Figure 6.32 is instructive in revealing the results of these efforts in the floppy disk arena. Fully as dramatic advances have been made in the Winchester arena. One currently emerging technique is *vertical recording* (Figure 6.34), which allows the tracks to be crowded closer together. Very recently, the so called *hard card* appeared in which a complete Winchester disk with controller and all associated electronics is packaged on a thicker than normal circuit board that occupies the

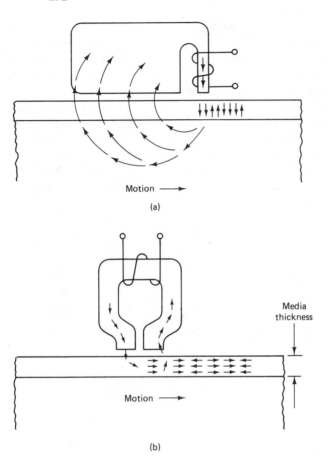

(a)

(b)

Motion ⟶

Motion ⟶

Media
thickness

Figure 6.34 Vertical versus longitudinal recording. To squeeze more data into
a linear inch, vertically oriented media
stand magnetic particles on end (a),
whereas longitudinal methods lay them
on the substrate's surface (b). (From
G. W. Gorsline, *Computer Organization: Hardware/Software, Second Edition,* © 1986, p. 292. Reprinted by permission of Prentice-Hall, Inc., Englewood Cliffs, NJ.)

space of two or three normal circuit boards. You may also see advertisements for the
Bernoulli disk, incorporating the physical effect named for Bernoulli and resulting in
a device that is reputed to better withstand lateral and vertical shocks without the
read/write head inadvertently coming into contact with the recording surface and
thereby ruining both. These so-called head crashes can be catastrophic, not only to
the equipment but also to the information contained in the files on the disk.

Optical Data Storage Systems.   An optical disk is a device in which the data
are written when a laser beam of high-energy coherent light burns holes in the metallic film on a transparent substrate, as shown in Figure 6.35. If the laser beam is focused to a small spot on the thin metallic film, it will melt a small area of the film,
which will curl back, because of surface tension, forming a toroidal rim. When the
laser is employed for reading at a lower power, each hole through the metallic film
allows light transmission through the transparent substrate. Thus, a binary 0 can be
distinguished from a binary 1. Figure 6.36 illustrates a possible read/write system. It
must be emphasized that optical disk technology is extremely new and presently is
not widely marketed. The write-once characteristic can be viewed as a major short-

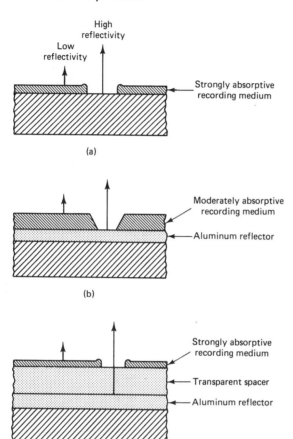

High
reflectivity

Low
reflectivity

Strongly absorptive
recording medium

(a)

Moderately absorptive
recording medium

Aluminum reflector

(b)

Strongly absorptive
recording medium

Transparent spacer

Aluminum reflector

(c)

Figure 6.35 Configurations for optical data storage medium. Single layer (a) offers simplicity; antireflection bilayer (b) and trilayer (c) structures broaden range of useful materials and recording mechanisms. (From G. W. Gorsline, *Computer Organization: Hardware/Software, Second Edition,* © 1986, p. 297. Reprinted by permission of Prentice-Hall, Inc., Englewood Cliffs, NJ.)

coming, although the size of storage available, coupled with its low cost per quantum of storage, has resulted in a proposal to rewrite the updated data area completely. There are reasons to believe that the audit process for business records will be facilitated by the write-once/read-many (WORM) characteristics, as it effectively prevents electronic tampering with records. Of course, the physical destruction of recording surfaces is still possible. Research is being carried out on rewritable optical disks, so far with some promise but without great practical success. Several corporations introduced write-once optical storage systems in the 1983–1985 period. The optical disk configuration for microcomputer-based systems will probably consist of a removable 5.25-inch disk capable of storing one-fifth gigabyte (200MB).

Magnetic tape. A *serial-access memory* is one in which the time to access a storage cell is a linear function of the address distance between the present position and the desired datum. The cells of serial-access memories, such as a cassette tape, do not have a physically designated address; the programmer must keep track of his

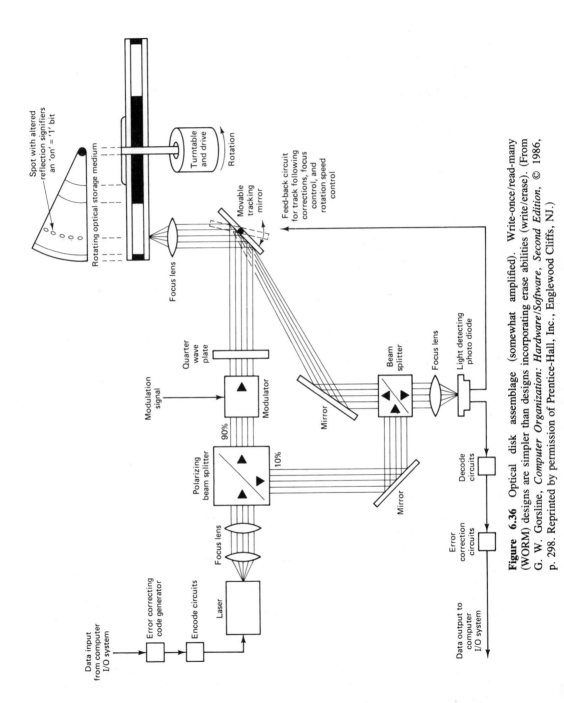

Figure 6.36 Optical disk assemblage (somewhat amplified). Write-once/read-many (WORM) designs are simpler than designs incorporating erase abilities (write/erase). (From G. W. Gorsline, *Computer Organization: Hardware/Software, Second Edition,* © 1986, p. 298. Reprinted by permission of Prentice-Hall, Inc., Englewood Cliffs, NJ.)

or her position within the memory by count. In general, if the start of the desired block is N blocks in distance and the time of access for each block is t, the time required to access that block is $t * N$.

$$\text{Access time} \longleftarrow \frac{\text{number of blocks to}}{\text{desired datum}} \times \frac{\text{time to read}}{\text{one block}}$$

A magnetic tape system includes not only the tape and suitable cassette or cartridges but also a magnetic read/write head, a transport, and electronic circuitry to control tape motion and data transduction. The tape transport (often called a *tape drive*) is linked to the data path of the computer through a DMA channel control unit. This tape control unit provides a data buffer for synchronizing data transfer, executing the tape imperatives (e.g., REWIND, BACKSPACE, etc.), and reporting the status of the transport.

The tape itself is typically Mylar plastic with a thin coating of ferromagnetic material on one side. Information recording is accomplished by applying electromagnetic signals to the tape by a write head. This creates small, very local, magnetically saturated regions in the ferric oxide coating on the tape. During a read operation, this magnetized spot creates a field in the gap between the tape and the read head, inducing a voltage in the output coil as a result of the tape motion. Figure 6.37 illustrates magnetic tape principles.

The inertia involved in mechanically starting and stopping the tape absolutely prevents starting or stopping the tape between characters. Contiguous characters are grouped into blocks, separated by blank tape segments called *interblock gaps*. These gaps serve both as a delimiter and as a coasting area for mechanically starting and stopping the tape motion. Programmers will recognize that the buffer in memory and the block on tape are the same size. Logical records are a programming device and are normally a portion of a buffer (and a block). The mechanical accuracy of starting and stopping a tape is not great enough to replace a block *in situ*. For this work, all record update work employing tapes is performed tape to tape and involves copying/correcting the entire tape.

The magnetic tape cartridge (Figure 6.38) is similar in structure to the familiar audio cassette, with two take-up hubs and a self-contained drive mechanism, although the data cartridge is somewhat larger and much more sturdily constructed. It is built on a half-inch aluminum base plate to give it the dimensional stability to allow up to 11 tracks on the $\frac{1}{4}$-inch tape, with about 100,000 bytes per foot = approximately 6,000 bits per inch per track. Common tape lengths are 150, 300, 450, and 600 feet, giving capacities from about 15 million to 60 million bytes. The entire package is 6 by 4 by $\frac{1}{2}$ inch, enclosed in a transparent shell with a spring-loaded cover that opens to expose the tape to the read/write head when loaded into the drive unit. At least some cartridges have a write-protect switch to help alleviate the common problem of careless overwrite of data.

The primary uses of a tape cartridge in a microcomputer system are (1) disk backup and (2) the transfer of massive amounts of data between systems. Without doubt, the main use is disk backup. Two methods are in common use: disk image

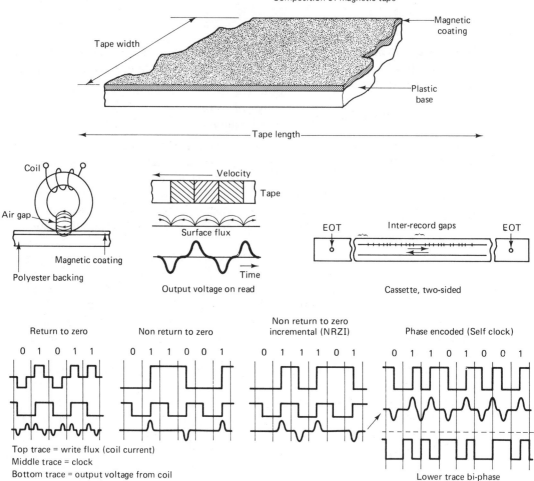

Composition of magnetic tape

Tape width

Magnetic coating

Plastic base

Tape length

Coil

Air gap

Magnetic coating

Polyester backing

Velocity

Tape

Surface flux

Output voltage on read

Time

EOT

Inter-record gaps

EOT

Cassette, two-sided

Return to zero

0 1 0 1 1

Non return to zero

0 1 1 0 0 1

Non return to zero incremental (NRZI)

0 1 1 1 0 1

Phase encoded (Self clock)

0 1 1 0 1 0 0 1

Top trace = write flux (coil current)
Middle trace = clock
Bottom trace = output voltage from coil

Lower trace bi-phase

Figure 6.37 Magnetic tape recording principles. (From G. W. Gorsline, *16-Bit Modern Microcomputers: The Intel I8086 Family,* © 1985, p. 187. Reprinted by permission of Prentice-Hall, Inc., Englewood Cliffs, NJ.)

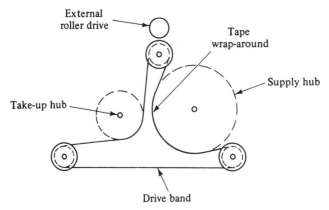

External roller drive

Tape wrap-around

Supply hub

Take-up hub

Drive band

Figure 6.38 The 3M magnetic tape cartridge. (From G. W. Gorsline, *Computer Organization: Hardware/Software, Second Edition,* © 1986, p. 274. Reprinted by permission of Prentice-Hall, Inc., Englewood Cliffs, NJ.)

backup and per-file backup. Image backup writes a track-by-track mirror image of the contents of the disk onto the cartridge. This is often called *streaming* backup, since a pure image backup system can operate so fast that the tape winds through the cartridge without stopping.

Per-file backup works in conjunction with the operating system file structure to copy each file from the hard disk onto the backup cartridge. A per-file tape is structured into a discrete set of files one after another on the tape, whereas an image backup tape generally mixes parts of different files together, just the way they are located on the disk. To recover individual files off an image tape, the backup program has to know the operating system's file allocation scheme.

The primary advantage of an image backup system is speed; a per-file system's strength is flexibility. An image backup system can copy data very quickly because it copies an entire track at a time, thus avoiding the extra time needed to go through the operating system file directory to locate the data for each separate file—often stored in widely separated parts of the disk.

In addition, a pure image backup method suffers from several substantial defects that severely limit its usefulness. First, since it is an exact copy of a particular disk, a backup image can be restored only to the same type and size disk drive as that from which it was backed up. This means that you cannot use an image backup system to move a set of files from one computer to another computer that has a different type of hard disk. Second, because a pure image system has no knowledge of the file structure, you cannot selectively restore files but, rather, must restore everything that was backed up.

It follows that imaging is satisfactory if you must recover from a disk catastrophe, such as a head crash, but imaging has drawbacks if you need to recover a single file that may have been accidentally destroyed.

Worst of all, a pure image system cannot cope with the fact that a very small fraction of every hard disk's capacity is not usable because of flaws in the recording surface. These bad sectors are automatically located and set aside by the operating system so that they will never be incorporated into files. However, a pure image backup system copies the entire disk, bad sectors included. This eventuality is not a problem if you restore onto the same physical disk, since the bad sectors in the image will be copied back to the same bad sectors on the disk, which are not used by the file system anyway. But if you have had an actual disk head crash and are restoring the image to a new and different hard disk, the new disk will have a different set of bad sectors. When the backup image is restored, certain sector images that contain data will be restored to bad sectors of the new disk, and certain sector images from bad sectors will be restored to good sectors of the new disk. Thus, some of the restored files may be corrupted and large parts of the file system may be inaccessible.

The per-file backup method does not have any of these problems and does not need any complicated tinkering to make it work. Since it operates in conjunction with the operating system to locate and copy each file on the disk, it will work with any drive. A backup tape can be restored to a different type or size of disk drive, individual files can be restored from the backup tape, and the problems associated with bad disk sectors are avoided. However, the time for backup and restoration is materially longer.

Magnetic bubble memories.   Information is stored in the form of magnetized regions or bubbles in cylindrical domains within a thin layer of magnetic material with magnetization opposite to that of the surrounding area. Figures 6.39 and 6.40 illustrate some of the details and Figure 6.41 illustrates one implementation of a magnetic bubble memory (MBM) controller. The presence or absence of a magnetized bubble at a specific location corresponds to a binary digit (on or off) at that location. Bits are made available by moving the bubbles within the solid layer to an access device. The storage material can be either a magnetic garnet grown epitaxially on a nonmagnetic garnet substrate or an amorphous metallic magnetic layer sputtered onto a substrate such as glass.

Four basic functions are required to operate a magnetic bubble memory organized as a single loop of bubbles: propagation, generation, detection, and annihilation. Such an organization possesses serial-access characteristics, with a single bit being followed by a single bit, and so forth. The more usual block organization shown in Figure 6.40 would need the replication and transfer functions in addition to the four basic functions. An important characteristic of MBM systems is that they can be stopped or turned off (no bubble movement) without information loss. Thus, they are nonvolatile and static. The four basic functions operate as follows:

1. *Bubble propagation* is required to move the bubbles within the substrate and thus for access to the information on the MBM chip. The usual method at present is to magnetize Permalloy patterns with an in-plane rotating field. These patterns can have any one of several shapes.

2. *Bubble generation* is the process of writing information into the memory, usually with a nucleate generator (a horseshoe-shaped conductor loop that produces a magnetic bubble inside the horseshoe when energized by a current pulse).

3. *Bubble detection* for reading is generally accomplished in a section of the propagation circuit. The magnetic bubbles are stretched into wide strips that cause a distinct change in the magnetoresistance of the Permalloy equivalent to preamplification. This assures a sense signal of several millivolts when the detector pattern and three bubbleless dummy patterns are interconnected as a bridge.

4. *Bubble annihilation* clears the memory data and is usually combined with a replicator to allow a nondestructive read operation. By duplicating information, one copy of the bubble can be read (and thus destroyed) while a copy of the original bubble is retained. Most replicators stretch the bubble, cut it in half, and send the pieces to different destinations.

The organization of the magnetic bubble memory chips currently (and originally) marketed have the major/minor loop arrangement shown in Figure 6.40. To

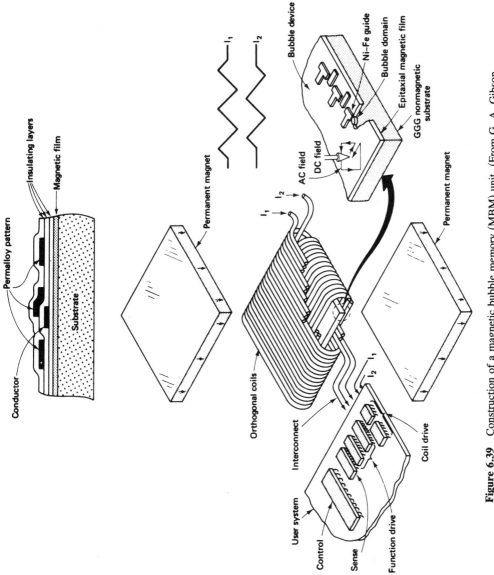

Figure 6.39 Construction of a magnetic bubble memory (MBM) unit. (From G. A. Gibson and Y. Liu, *Microcomputers for Engineers and Scientists*, © 1980, p. 342. Reprinted by permission of Prentice-Hall, Inc., Englewood Cliffs, NJ.)

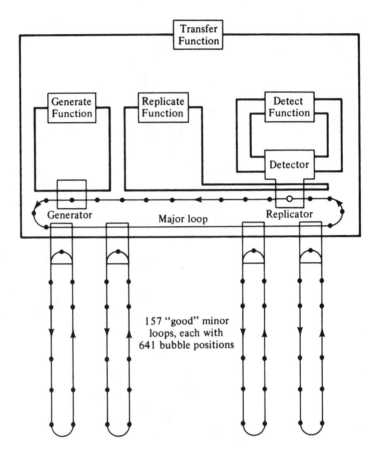

Figure 6.40 Magnetic bubble memory, illustrating the usual major and minor loop organizaiton of the 92K LSI chip. (From G. W. Gorsline, *Computer Organization: Hardware/Software, Second Edition,* © 1986, p. 277. Reprinted by permission of Prentice-Hall, Inc., Englewood Cliffs, NJ.)

access data, corresponding bubbles (or the absence of bubbles) in each minor loop are first shifted (rotated) to the position closest to the major loop. Then a bubble or its absence is transferred from all minor loops simultaneously to the major loop. The major loop is then shifted (rotated) to be read, annihilated, or replicated, as required, and finally transferred back to the minor loops in the original positions.

A recent development in MBM technology is the Intel iPAB (Plug-a-Bubble) memory system, which is a 128K-byte (1 megabit) removable bubble memory cassette. This particular product furnishes automatic error correction, write protection, an average access time of 48 milliseconds, and a burst transfer rate of 12.5K bytes per second (100 kilobits/sec).

Mass storage economics.   As illustrated in Figure 6.42, there is a general relationship between the cost of storing a quantum of information and the time re-

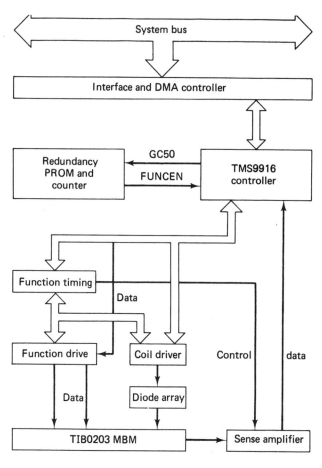

Figure 6.41 Block diagram of a magnetic bubble memory and its control circuiting. (From G. A. Gibson and Y. Liu, *Microcomputers for Engineers and Scientists,* © 1980, p. 344. Reprinted by permission of Prentice-Hall, Inc., Englewood Cliffs, NJ.)

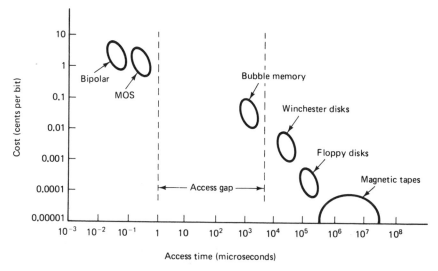

Figure 6.42 Cost versus access time for representative types of memory, illustrating the economics of the speed/cost relationship. (From G. W. Gorsline, *Computer Organization: Hardware/Software, Second Edition,* © 1986, p. 275. Reprinted by permission of Prentice-Hall, Inc., Englewood Cliffs, NJ.)

quired to access that information. An examination of this relationship strongly suggests that MBM fills an "access gap" as illustrated. On the other hand, the rapidly diminishing cost of VLSI RAM chips may shortly remove this cost/speed gap in storage technologies.

EXERCISES

6.1. Determine and report whether your computational system includes a DMA. If so, how many channels are supported?

6.2. The documentation furnished with many computational systems includes the assembly source code for the I/O driver routines necessary for the correct operation of each peripheral device. If such documentation is available to you, compare the algorithms and coding with those in Figures 6.13 through 6.18. Report and explain any discrepancies. Note that some systems may have implemented the I/O driver routines in the system language C. If this is the case with your system, you should be able to at least compare the algorithms employed.

6.3. If you are fully convinced that you can improve on the code of an I/O driver routine that is a portion of your computational system, then you should attempt to do so. *Important note:* Because the replacement of an I/O driver routine with an unsatisfactory version can cause strange and uncorrectable troubles—including the destruction of files—extreme caution should be employed. In addition, the generation of unexpected voltages or timings could "burn" circuits. Thus, this process should be approached only with extreme care. I firmly suggest that backup copies of the system and of all files be made before any testing of a new I/O driver.

7

Interrupts, Direct Memory Access, and Channel-Oriented Input/Output

Employing FORTRAN, we are used to I/O statements such as

```
READ(5,99) A,B,C
WRITE(6,91) X,Y
```

In programming with procedural-level languages, we are depending on the compiler (the language translator) to transform such I/O statements into parameterized calls to the input/output control system (IOCS) of the operating system. In effect, the FORTRAN READ and WRITE statements request that the control software system perform a service. Usually, the programmer is not particularly concerned about the method employed.

Similarly, employing an assembly language, it would be extremely nice if we could parameterize our I/O needs in an analogous manner and use statements something like

```
INPUT       A,B,C,TTY,LABEL99
OUTPUT      X,Y,CRT,LABEL91
```

Again, we would be depending on the assembler (the language translator) to transform these fairly high level I/O orders to parameterized sections of code that accomplish the I/O. This code either could be inserted into the assembly procedure at each appropriate place, macro style, or it could be referenced as a call-style out-of-line subroutine with only one copy existing.

As noted in Chapter 5, when programming the MC680XY, all of the methods noted above would eventually result in a

TRAP   n

software interrupt (supervisory call) through the interrupt vector table to an appropriate routine to accomplish the actual physical data transfer. With a modern operating system, much of the noninteractive input would have been prefetched from the device into a memory-resident input buffer, from which the program would "read" data via MOVE instructions. Similarly, the program would "output" data via MOVE instructions to a memory-resident output buffer, the contents of which would finally be written to the appropriate device by the operating system IOCS (input/output control system).

A TECHNOLOGICAL PERSPECTIVE

At the most elementary level, a microprocessor is forced to deal directly with the individual bits one at a time. First-generation microprocessors in the early 1970s and first-generation computers in the 1940s were stuck with this albatross-like performance limitation of very primitive input and output of each bit, requiring action by the computer.

Almost immediately after their introduction, provisions were provided in microprocessors that allowed the input or output of a nibble or byte in parallel. Unfortunately, this early nibble- or byte-oriented I/O required the detailed control and attention of the microprocessor in controlling the individual actions of the external device. Input and output were tedious to program and extremely slow during execution. Detailed knowledge of the device timings and line voltages was required. The I4004 and the I8008 were typical microprocessors of this era.

One important advance associated with second-generation microprocessors such as the MC6800 was the availability of single-chip interface controllers such as those discussed in Chapter 6. Figures 6.10 to 6.12 will remind you of the functionality of the MC68681 DUART as an example of a single-chip device interface controller. These devices removed the lowest-level device control from the microprocessor and allowed the transfer of an entire byte to and from a device in parallel under microprocessor control.

A second important advance, also associated with second-generation microprocessors such as the MC6800 and almost necessary with third-generation microcomputers such as the MC680XY, was the introduction and availability of direct memory access (DMA) controllers such as those discussed briefly in Chapter 6. DMA allowed a whole block of data to be input or output without microprocessor intervention beyond initiating and noting the termination of the transfer. In addition, if register resident data were available, the microprocessor could continue data manipulation in parallel with the DMA transfer. A primitive form of compute-I/O multiprocessing became available using microcomputers. The twin availability of I/O device controllers and DMA allowed the application of microcomputers to problems that required moderate amounts and speeds of I/O.

The third generation of microcomputers, characterized by the MC680XY, has also seen the development and introduction of the semiautonomous input/output processor into the world of the small. Originally conceived and implemented in the mid-1950s for "supercomputers" with the aid of federal development funds, the microcomputer version of interest to us employs a second special-purpose microprocessor to accomplish all I/O. The microprocessor used as an I/O processor continues the trend of removing yet another level of control from the microprocessor by assuming all device controller overhead, "soft-error" recovery, and block I/O data transfers. A further separation of processing responsibilities is achieved, resulting in a cleaner implementation of the compute function in the processor with I/O in a separate processor. This constitutes a viable form of multiprocessing with simultaneously executing specialized processors communicating via messages in a common system memory (mailbox fashion). The interrupt structure of the host MC680XY microprocessor is utilized to force attention to the message-in-system-memory mailbox.

When utilizing the DMA facility, the MC680XY processor performs an I/O operation by building a message in system memory that defines the I/O function. The I/O processor reads the message, configures itself appropriately, carries out the I/O function, and notifies the MC680XY processor via a software interrupt when it is finished with an indication of any errors. All I/O devices appear to be transmitting or receiving entire blocks (buffers) of data to or from system memory. High-level logical input/output is facilitated using a separate modularized function in a manner that allows an intelligently and independently designed and maintained IOCS portion of an operating system.

NOTICING EVENTS WITHIN THE COMPUTER SYSTEM

In general, three types of events can occur in a computational system:

1. Those events whose occurrence is not only expected but whose timing with respect to the sequence of program instructions is known. We refer to these as *synchronous events* or as *time-expected events*. An example would be the input of a character using the example I/O driver shown in Figures 6.17 and 6.18.

2. Those events whose occurrence is expected at some time but the exact time in respect to the sequence of program instruction is unknown. We refer to these as *asynchronous events* or as *time-unexpected events*. An example would be the completion of an I/O via DMA.

3. Those events whose occurrence is not expected and, therefore, are a surprise both in terms of the event and in terms of its time in respect to the sequence of program instructions. We also refer to these as *asynchronous events* or as *time-unexpected events*. An example would be a power failure or a divide by zero.

These three types of events are of two kinds: (1) those events that the program itself purposely creates at a known and specific point in the program code and (2) those events that the program or the software system must react to that occur at an unplanned point in the program code.

Events of the first kind are equivalent to type 1 and will be disregarded for the rest of this chapter. Events of the second kind are equivalent to types 2 and 3 and will be the subject of our attention for the next several pages.

Two methods of detecting time-unexpected events are implemented in computers in two general ways:

1. *Software polling:* In this scheme, the program is responsible for examining each possible interesting condition so that a reactive routine may be invoked if necessary. This implementation technique places the entire responsibility for tracking events on the applications programmer and usually results in excessive overhead. It essentially prevents overlap of I/O and processing except in those cases where device timing is exactly known and the programmer calculates instruction timings and thus can interface the I/O-compute process intelligently. Although programmers were expected to know, be proud of, and use such techniques in the early days, current programmers have no desire, normally do not care about, and rarely program in this fashion. Figure 7.1 illustrates the device polling concept.

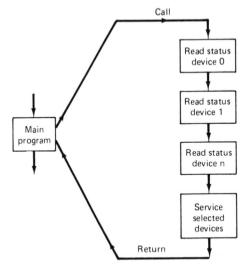

Figure 7.1   General schema for software polling of peripheral devices to determine the need for I/O service. (From G. W. Gorsline, *Computer Organization: Hardware/Software, Second Edition,* © 1986, p. 227. Reprinted by permission of Prentice-Hall, Inc., Englewood Cliffs, NJ.)

2. *Interrupt system:* An interrupt is a time-asynchronous hardware notation that an event has happened. This is usually accomplished by the setting of a flag (a flip-flop) by the event itself and the subsequent recognition of the flag ON condition by the control subsystem of the processor. The instruction cycle becomes a three-step loop:

a. Fetch the instruction and update the program counter.
b. Execute the instruction.
c. Check for interrupt indicator.

Figure 7.2 may be helpful.

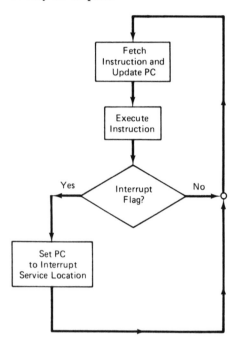

Figure 7.2 Instruction cycle of a processor with an interrupt system. Note that essentially no time is expended checking for an event but that the occurrence of an event forces, through hardware, a "subroutine" branch to a routine to react to the event with an eventual "return" to normal program processing. (From G. W. Gorsline, *Computer Organization: Hardware/Software, Second Edition,* © 1986, p. 228. Reprinted by permission of Prentice-Hall, Inc., Englewood Cliffs, NJ.)

It should be obvious that an interrupt system simplifies programming, allows more efficient use of computational system resources, and speeds program execution. Interrupts may be serviced from any point in the program, as illustrated in Figure 7.3.

A Sample Dual-Tasking Application

Now that we have examined an example device driver (in Chapter 6) and have briefly approached interrupts, we can combine our newly acquired understanding of these concepts into a sample dual-tasking application. Our example, which will employ two tasks that cooperate with each other to accept characters from a keyboard/ CRT terminal and then print them on a line printer, is derived from Harper (1984). The flowcharts in Figures 7.5, 7.7, 7.10, 7.12 and the routines in Figures 7.6, 7.8, 7.9, 7.11, 7.13 are copyrighted by Motorola, Inc., and are used with permission.

The two sample tasks are INPTTSK and PRNTTSK. The tasks work together to perform two typical I/O operations: character string input from a terminal and character string output to a printer. Because I/O hardware is character-oriented, not

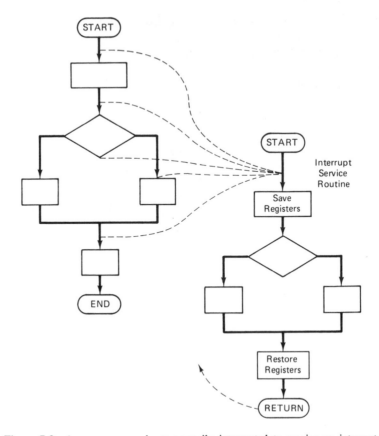

Figure 7.3 A program may be temporarily interrupted to service an interrupt event at many locations. (From G. W. Gorsline, *Computer Organization: Hardware/Software, Second Edition,* © 1986, p. 229. Reprinted by permission of Prentice-Hall, Inc., Englewood Cliffs, NJ.)

string-oriented, character string I/O must be transformed into character I/O by using buffers and queues. Character string input is accomplished through the use of an input buffer. Characters are placed in this buffer as they come in from the terminal. When the carriage return character is received and placed in the buffer, the string has been completely assembled and is moved elsewhere so that another one can be assembled.

Character string printing is accomplished through the use of a print buffer and a print queue. For efficient character string printing, the print buffer should be capable of holding more than one character string. This is because the MC68000 can supply strings to be printed much faster than the printer can print them. A multiple-string print buffer allows the MC68000 to queue character strings bound for the printer and then go on to more important things, rather than acting as a slave to the printer. The print queue is required to determine where the next string arriving at the buffer will go and where the next string departing from the buffer can be found.

Print "tags," indicating that there are character strings in the print buffer, are placed in this queue. The queue has an input and output pointer and acts in a first-in/first-out (FIFO) manner. Thus, strings in the print buffer will be sent to the printer in the order that their print tags arrived at the print queue. In other words, one task continually monitors a terminal (attached to DUART channel A) for incoming characters, assembles them into a character string in an input buffer, then places the string in a print queue; the other task continually monitors the print queue for character strings destined to be printed and sends them to the printer (attached to DUART channel B).

The terminal is attached to DUART channel A and will be programmed to transmit and receive at 9600 BAUD, with 7 bits/character, even parity, and two stop bits. The channel will be programmed to operate in automatic-echo mode so that the character typed at the terminal keyboard will appear on the CRT screen. So that the channel receiver FIFO is not overrun, channel A will be programmed to use the receiver RTS/CTS (request to send/clear to send) handshake protocol. This protocol works as follows: The receiver RTS output is connected to the CTS input of the terminal. So long as the receiver has room in its FIFO for another character, the receiver will assert RTS. If the FIFO becomes full, the receiver will negate RTS. When the FIFO once again has room for another character, it will automatically reassert RTS. Assuming that the terminal will not transmit a character unless it sees CTS asserted, receiver overrun will not occur. Finally, the BREAK key will be used as an abort button, so that the user can exit to the monitor (or operating system) at any time. Channel A will therefore be programmed to generate an interrupt to the MC68000 when it receives a BREAK character from the terminal.

The printer is attached to DUART channel B, and the channel will be programmed to operate in normal mode, transmitting at 300 BAUD, with 7 bits/character, even parity, and one stop bit. So that the channel does not send characters to the printer faster than the printer can handle them, channel B will be programmed to use the transmitter RTS/CTS handshake protocol. This protocol works as follows: When channel B needs to send a character to the printer, it will assert RTS and then wait for the printer to assert CTS before transmitting the character.

The MC68681 counter/timer will be programmed to generate the time-slice interrupts to the MC68000 required for dual-tasking. The counter/timer must be able to be stopped and restarted; therefore, it is programmed to operate in counter mode. After initializing the counter registers with the count value, the counter will be started. When the counter reaches terminal count, it will generate an interrupt to the MC68000. The MC68000 will then stop the counter, clear the interrupt, swap tasks being executed, and start the counter again. When the counter is started again, it will be reinitialized using the value found in the counter registers.

The interrupt servicing routines (often termed *interrupt handlers*) necessary for the above-described I/O processing can be viewed as the ordered invocation of different routines—each invocation being caused by an interrupt. The overall concept of interrupt-controlled I/O is shown in Figure 7.4, and the specifics of the interrupt service routines (DIRQ and CIRQ) are given in Figures 7.5 and 7.6.

DIRQ is the DUART interrupt handling routine. After the DUART generates an interrupt, the MC68000 begins executing DIRQ. DIRQ determines whether the

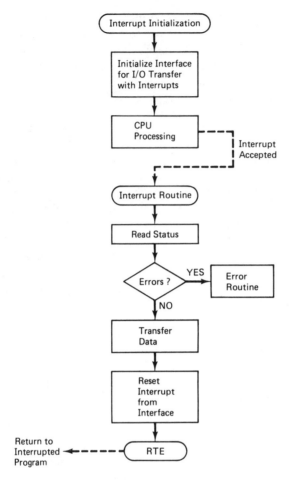

Figure 7.4 The generalized structure of interrupt-controlled I/O, where device action is the result of setting an interrupt bit within the interface device. (From T. L. Harman and B. Lawson, *The Motorola MC68000 Microprocessor Family: Assembly Language, Interface Design, and System Design,* © 1985, p. 334. Reprinted by permission of Prentice-Hall, Inc., Englewood Cliffs, N.J.)

interrupt was caused by the counter or by a channel A change-in-break. If the interrupt was caused by the counter, DIRQ causes the MC68000 to swap tasks being executed. (This process is discussed later.) If the interrupt was caused by a channel A change-in-break interrupt (beginning of break), DIRQ clears the interrupt source, waits for the next change-in-break condition interrupt (end of break), clears the interrupt source again, and then returns from exception processing to the system monitor. CIRQ is used instead of DIRQ as the DUART interrupt handling routine when CTRCHK is executing. When the counter generates an interrupt during execution of CTRCHK, CIRQ sets the carry bit in the status register, thus informing CTRCHK that the counter interrupt was generated correctly.

The dual-tasking software required for this application is flowcharted in Figure 7.7, and the assembly language code is shown in Figures 7.8 and 7.9. The routines

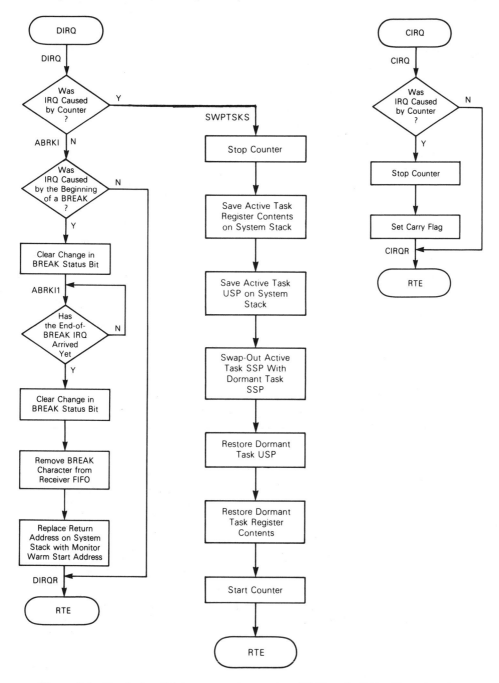

Figure 7.5 The logic of interrupt service routines DIRQ and CIRQ. Note that the SWPTSKS module logic is included. (Courtesy of Motorola, Inc.)

```
*
* DIRQ - DUART IRQ HANDLING ROUTINE.
*           AFTER THE DUART GENERATES AN IRQ, DIRQ DETERMINES THE CAUSE OF
*           INTERRUPT. DIRQ CHECKS FOR THESE POSSIBLE CAUSES:
*
*                       COUNTER READY
*                       CHANGE IN CHANNEL A BREAK
*
*           ENTRY CONDITIONS:
*
*                       DUART'S INTERRUPT MASK HAS BEEN INITIALIZED.
*                       DUART HAS GENERATED AN INTERRUPT.
*
*           EXIT CONDITIONS:
*
*                       IF IRQ SOURCE IS:       THEN:
*                       ------------------      --------------------------------
*                       COUNTER                 SWAP TASKS BEING EXECUTED BY 68000
*                       CHANGE IN CH A BRK       EXIT TO MONITOR
*
*                       OTHERWISE, DIRQ RETURNS TO INTERRUPTED ROUTINE WITH
*                       ALL REGISTER CONTENTS UNALTERED.
*
*
DIRQ      BTST.B    #3,ISR              WAS IRQ CAUSED BY THE COUNTER?

          BEQ       ABRKI               NO, SKIP NEXT PART
          BRA       SWPTSKS             YES, SWAP TASKS

ABRKI     BTST.B    #2,ISR              WAS IT A CHAN A BEGINNING-OF-BREAK IRQ?

          BEQ       DIRQR               NO, SKIP NEXT PART
          MOVE.B    #$50,CRA            YES, CLEAR CHN A BRK IRQ BIT IN ISR

ABRKI1    BTST.B    #2,ISR              WAIT FOR END-OF-BREAK IRQ

          BEQ       ABRKI1
          MOVE.B    #$50,CRA            CLEAR CHN A BRK IRQ BIT IN ISR AGAIN

          TST.B     RBA                 PULL BREAK CHARACTER FROM CHN A RX FIFO
          LEA.L     BRKMSG,A5           PRINT MESSAGE TO SCREEN
          LEA.L     LBRKMSG(A5),A6
          MOVE.B    #243,D7
          TRAP      #14
          MOVE.L    #MONITOR,2(A7)      NO, EXIT TO MONITOR
*
* CIRQ - COUNTER CHECK IRQ HANDLING ROUTINE.
*           DUART IRQ HANDLING ROUTINE USED DURING CTRCHK ONLY.
*
*           ENTRY CONDITIONS:
*
*                       DUART IRQ.
*
*           EXIT CONDITIONS:
*
*                       IF COUNTER WAS CAUSE OF DUART IRQ:
*                               COUNTER/TIMER READY BIT CLEARED IN DUART'S ISR,
*                               & CARRY BIT SET.
*                       OTHERWISE:
*                               CARRY BIT REMAINS CLEARED.
*
*
CIRQ      BTST.B    #3,ISR              WAS IRQ CAUSED BY COUNTER?

          BEQ       CIRQR               NO, SKIP NEXT PART
          TST.B     STPC                YES, STOP COUNTER
          ORI       #$0001,(A7)         & SET CARRY BIT OF SR ON STACK
CIRQR     RTE
```

Figure 7.6   The code for the interrupt service routines DIRQ and CIRQ. (Courtesy of Motorola, Inc.)

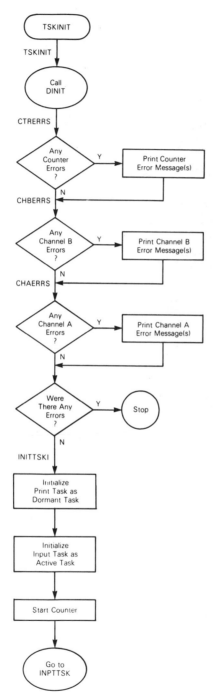

Figure 7.7 Logic of the routine TSKINIT that initializes the two tasks. (Courtesy of Motorola, Inc.)

```
*
* TSKINIT - ROUTINE TO INITIALIZE THE TWO TASKS TO BE EXECUTED BY THE 68000.
*           TSKINIT INITIALIZES & CHECKS THE DUART CHANNELS & COUNTER, ENABLES
*           THE CHANNELS, INITIALIZES THE PRINT TASK AS THE DORMANT TASK,
*           STARTS THE COUNTER, THEN BEGINS EXECUTION OF THE INPUT TASK.
*
*

TSKINIT  LEA.L   -6(A7),A7          ALLOCATE STACK SPACE FOR STATUS WORDS
         BSR.L   DINIT              INITIALIZE & CHECK DUART
         MOVEM.W (A7)+,D0-D2        PULL STATUS WORDS OFF STACK

CTRERRS  TST.W   D0                 COUNTER ERROR(S)?
         BEQ     CHBERRS            NO, SKIP NEXT PART
         LEA     CTRERR,A5          YES, PRINT COUNTER ERROR MESSAGE
         LEA     LCTRERR(A5),A6
         BSR.L   PRTMSG

CHBERRS  TST.W   D1                 CHANNEL B ERROR(S)?
         BEQ     CHAERRS            NO, SKIP NEXT PART

CHBERR1  BTST    #0,D1              YES, IS IT TX NEVER READY?
         BEQ     CHBERR2            NO, SKIP NEXT PART
         LEA     CHBMSG1,A5         YES, PRINT TX-NEVER-READY MESSAGE
         LEA     LCHBMSG1(A5),A6
         BSR.L   PRTMSG

CHBERR2  BTST    #1,D1              IS IT RX NEVER READY?
         BEQ     CHBERR3            NO, SKIP NEXT PART
         LEA     CHBMSG2,A5         YES, PRINT RX-NEVER-READY MESSAGE
         LEA     LCHBMSG2(A5),A6
         BSR.L   PRTMSG

CHBERR3  BTST    #2,D1              IS IT A FRAMING ERROR?
         BEQ     CHBERR4            NO, SKIP NEXT PART
         LEA     CHBMSG3,A5         YES, PRINT FRAMING-ERROR MESSAGE
         LEA     LCHBMSG3(A5),A6
         BSR     PRTMSG

CHBERR4  BTST    #3,D1              IS IT A PARITY ERROR?
         BEQ     CHBERR5            NO, SKIP NEXT PART
         LEA     CHBMSG4,A5         YES, PRINT PARITY-ERROR MESSAGE
         LEA     LCHBMSG4(A5),A6
         BSR     PRTMSG

CHBERR5  BTST    #4,D1              IS IT A BAD CHARACTER?
         BEQ     CHAERRS            NO, SKIP NEXT PART
         LEA     CHBMSG5,A5         YES, PRINT BAD-CHARACTER MESSAGE
         LEA     LCHBMSG5(A5),A6
         BSR     PRTMSG

CHAERRS  TST.W   D2                 CHANNEL A ERROR(S)?
         BEQ     ERRCHK             NO, SKIP NEXT PART

CHAERR1  BTST    #0,D2              YES, IS IT TX NEVER READY?
         BEQ     CHAERR2            NO, SKIP NEXT PART
         LEA     CHAMSG1,A5         YES, PRINT TX-NEVER-READY MESSAGE
         LEA     LCHAMSG1(A5),A6
         BSR     PRTMSG

CHAERR2  BTST    #1,D2              IS IT RX NEVER READY?
         BEQ     CHAERR3            NO, SKIP NEXT PART
         LEA     CHAMSG2,A5         YES, PRINT RX-NEVER-READY MESSAGE
         LEA     LCHAMSG2(A5),A6
         BSR     PRTMSG

CHAERR3  BTST    #2,D2              IS IT A FRAMING ERROR?
         BEQ     CHAERR4            NO, SKIP NEXT PART
         LEA     CHAMSG3,A5         YES, PRINT FRAMING-ERROR MESSAGE
         LEA     LCHAMSG3(A5),A6
         BSR     PRTMSG

CHAERR4  BTST    #3,D2              IS IT A PARITY ERROR?
         BEQ     CHAERR5            NO, SKIP NEXT PART
         LEA     CHAMSG4,A5         YES, PRINT PARITY-ERROR MESSAGE
         LEA     LCHAMSG4(A5),A6
         BSR     PRTMSG

CHAERR5  BTST    #4,D2              IS IT A BAD CHARACTER?
         BEQ     INPTTSK            NO, SKIP NEXT PART
         LEA     CHAMSG5,A5         YES, PRINT BAD-CHARACTER MESSAGE
         LEA     LCHAMSG5(A5),A6
         BSR     PRTMSG
```

Figure 7.8 Code for the task initialization routine TSKINIT. (Courtesy of Motorola, Inc.)

```
ERRCHK    OR.W     D1,D0               WERE THERE ANY ERRORS?
          OR.W     D2,D0
          BEQ      INITTSK1            NO, CONTINUE WITH DEMO
          BRA      *                   YES, STOP.

PRTMSG    MOVE.B   #243,D7             PRINT MESSAGE TO SCREEN
          TRAP     #14
          RTS

*
* INITIALIZE PRINT TASK (PRNTTSK) AS DORMANT TASK, INITIALIZE
* PRINT QUEUE, START COUNTER, THEN BEGIN EXECUTION OF THE INPTTSK.
* 68000 WILL EXECUTE INPTTSK UNTIL THE COUNTER GENERATES AN IRQ.
* THE 68000 WILL THEN BEGIN EXECUTING PRNTTSK AND INPTTSK WILL
* BECOME THE DORMANT TASK.
*

INITTSK1  MOVE.L   #PSSP,A7            INIT PRINT TASK'S SYSTEM STACK POINTER
          MOVE.L   #PRNTTSK,-(A7)      INIT PRINT TASK'S PROGRAM COUNTER
          MOVE.W   #$2300,-(A7)        INIT PRINT TASK'S STATUS REGISTER:IPL4-7
          MOVEQ.L  #14,D0              INIT PRINT TASK'S REGISTERS
INITTSK2  CLR.L    -(A7)
          DBRA     D0,INITTSK2
          MOVE.L   #PUSP,-(A7)         INIT PRINT TASK'S USER STACK POINTER
          MOVE.L   A7,DTSKSSP          SAVE PRINT TASK'S SYSTEM STACK POINTER

          CLR.B    PQIN                INIT PRINT QUEUE INPUT POINTER
          CLR.B    PQOUT               INIT PRINT QUEUE OUTPUT POINTER

          MOVE.L   #IUSP,A7            INIT INPUT TASK'S USER STACK POINTER
          MOVE.L   A7,USP
          MOVE.L   #ISSP,A7            INIT INPUT TASK'S SYSTEM STACK POINTER
          MOVE.W   #$2300,SR           INIT INPUT TASK'S STATUS REGISTER:IPL4-7

          TST.B    STRC                START COUNTER
```

Figure 7.8   (*continued*).

```
*
* SWPTSKS - ROUTINE TO SWAP TASKS BEING EXECUTED BY THE 68000.
*           SWPTSKS SWAPS BETWEEN TWO TASKS BY EXCHANGING THE
*           SYSTEM STACK POINTER, REGISTER CONTENTS, USER STACK POINTER,
*           STATUS REGISTER, & PROGRAM COUNTER OF ONE TASK TO THAT OF THE OTHER
*
*           ENTRY CONDITIONS:
*
*                    DRMNT TASK'S SSP IN DTSKSSP.
*                    ACTIVE TASK'S SSP IN A7.
*                    SSP+0 - ACTIVE TASK'S STATUS REGISTER CONTENTS.
*                    SSP+2 - ACTIVE TASK'S PROGRAM COUNTER CONTENTS.
*
*           EXIT CONDITIONS:
*
*                    NEW DRMNT TASK'S SSP IN DTSKSSP.
*                    NEW ACTIVE TASK'S SSP IN A7.
*                    SSP+0 - NEW ACTIVE TASK'S STATUS REGISTER CONTENTS
*                    SSP+2 - NEW ACTIVE TASK'S PROGRAM COUNTER CONTENTS
*

SWPTSKS   TST.B    STPC                STOP COUNTER

          MOVEM.L  A0-A6/D0-D7,-(A7)   SAVE ACTIVE TASK'S REGISTER CONTENTS
          MOVE.L   USP,A6              SAVE ACTIVE TASK'S USER STACK POINTER
          MOVE.L   A6,-(A7)

          LEA.L    (A7),A6             SAVE TEMP COPY OF ACTIVE TASK'S SSP
          MOVE.L   DTSKSSP,A7          GET DRMNT TASK'S SYSTEM STACK POINTER
          MOVE.L   A6,DTSKSSP          SAVE ACTIVE TASK'S SYSTEM STACK POINTER

          MOVE.L   (A7)+,A6            GET DRMNT TASK'S USER STACK POINTER
          MOVE.L   A6,USP
          MOVEM.L  (A7)+,D0-D7/A0-A6   GET DRMNT TASK'S REGISTER CONTENTS

          TST.B    STRC                START COUNTER
          RTE                          RETURN FROM EXCEPTION TO NEW ACTIVE TASK
```

Figure 7.9 Code for the task swapping routine, SWPTSKS. (Courtesy of Motorola, Inc.)

can be broken down into two categories: the routines that facilitate dual-tasking and the two sample tasks themselves. The routines that facilitate dual-tasking consist of SWPTSKS and TSKINIT.

SWPTSKS is the task swapping routine executed when DIRQ determines that the counter has generated an interrupt. SWPTSKS swaps the task currently being executed with the task that is currently dormant. The swap process works as follows: The counter interrupt causes the MC68000 to begin exception processing. During exception processing, the MC68000 stacks the active task program counter and status register on the active task system stack and then executes DIRQ. DIRQ determines that the interrupt was caused by the counter and branches to SWPTSKS. SWPTSKS stops the counter, then saves the active task register contents and user stack pointer on the active task system stack. After saving this information on the active task system stack, SWPTSKS swaps the active task system stack pointer with the dormant task system stack pointer (stored in a reserved memory location). SWPTSKS then pulls the dormant task user stack pointer and register contents off the dormant task system stack (this information was placed on the dormant system stack by a previous task swap operation) and restarts the counter. Finally, because the dormant task status register contents and program counter are now at the top of the dormant task system stack, the MC68000 will return from exception, where the dormant task had been interrupted, thereby reactivating it.

TSKINIT is the task initialization routine. It initializes the DUART by calling DINIT, then checks for operational errors in the two channels and the counter. If errors are found in either of the channels or the counter, TSKINIT prints the appropriate error messages to a "command console" and then stops. If no errors are found, TSKINIT then initializes the print task as the initial dormant task. The initialization procedure works as follows: The dormant task system stack pointer is initialized, the start address of the print task is stacked on the system stack, and then an initial status register content is stacked. This is the order in which the MC68000 requires information to be stacked when returning from exception. Next, the print task initial register contents and user stack pointer are stacked on the system stack. This is the order in which SWPTSKS requires information to be stacked to perform its task swap operation. After initializing the print task as the dormant task, TSKINIT initializes the input task user and system stack pointers, starts the counter, then begins execution of the input task.

The frequency at which the MC68000 swaps between tasks is directly determined by the frequency at which the DUART counter generates interrupts. This is determined by the count value placed in the upper and lower counter registers. The main concern in determining the count value is making sure that the task swapping is transparent to the user sitting at the terminal. That is, the user must not be aware that he or she does not have the attention of the system all the time.

The system on which this application was developed performed well with the count value set at $0073. With the counter clock source programmed to be the 3.6864 MHz crystal divided by 16, this count value causes an interrupt to occur approximately every 500 microseconds.

Let us not forget that our objective over the last few pages has been to present the interface required for efficient poll-driven serial I/O using the MC68681 DUART. Recall, also, that it uses the normal, automatic-echo, and local-loopback modes. It also utilizes two of the MC68681 DUART interrupt sources: the channel A change-in-break IRQ and the counter/timer IRQ. In addition, one of the output port pins and one of the input port pins will necessarily be used as RTS/CTS handshake lines.

A character string is terminated by a carriage return, and maximum string length is set by the constant CSLNTH. CSLNTH is used to define the width of the input buffer and the width of the print buffer. The print queue length is set by the constant PQLNTH. PQLNTH is used to define the length of the print queue and the length of the print buffer. Both CSLNTH and PQLNTH must be assigned values that are powers of 2 and can have a maximum value of 256. Because maximum string length is 256 bytes, the print tag need only be a byte value. When a character string is to be sent to the print buffer, it must be moved into the print buffer and an associated print tag placed in the print queue. When a character string is to be sent to the printer, it must be taken from the print buffer and its associated print tag removed from the print queue.

As shown in Figures 7.10 and 7.11, INPTTSK continually monitors the terminal attached to DUART channel A for incoming characters, assembles them into a character string in the input buffer, then queues the string into the print buffer. INPTTSK consists of two routines: ISTRG and QSTRG. ISTRG is the routine that assembles characters received from the terminal (via the INCH routine) into a character string in the input buffer. QSTRG is the routine that queues the character string into the print buffer. QSTRG first checks the status of the print queue. If the queue is full, QSTRG will wait until there is room in the queue for a print tag. If the queue is not full, QSTRG will move the character string into the print buffer and place a print tag in the print queue.

At the same time, as shown in Figures 7.12 and 7.13, PRNTTSK continually monitors the print queue for print tags. If it finds a print tag in the queue, PRNTTSK prints the string and removes the tag from the queue. PRNTTSK consists of two routines: RSTRG and PSTRG. RSTRG is the routine that releases a character string from the print buffer and sends it to the printer via the PSTRG routine. RSTRG checks the status of the print queue. If it is empty, RSTRG will wait until a print tag appears in the queue. If the queue is not empty, RSTRG will call routine PSTRG, then remove the print tag from the print queue. PSTRG is the routine that sends a character string to the printer character by character (via the POUTCH routine).

The Interrupt Structure of the Motorola MC680XY

The interrupt structure of the MC680XY computational system is based on a table of service routine addresses (the interrupt vector table) stored by software in 1024 bytes of main memory. The purpose of the interrupt vector table is to contain the entry addresses of the various interrupt service routines. As each address must contain the 32

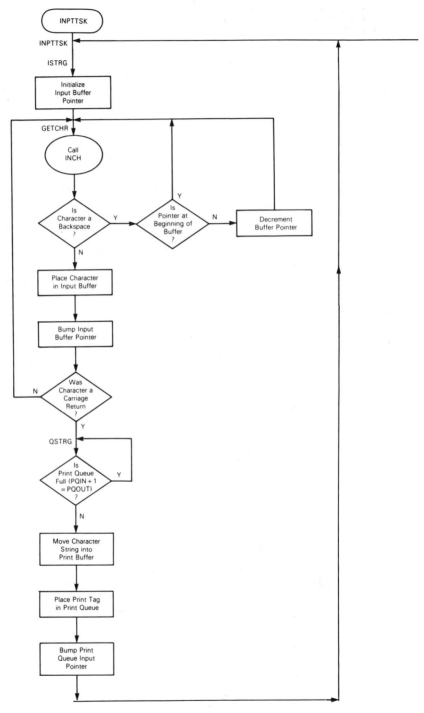

Figure 7.10 Logic of the input-a-character routine, INPTTSK. (Courtesy of Motorola, Inc.)

```
*
* INPTTSK - TASK THAT CONTINUALLY CHECKS TERMINAL FOR INCOMING CHARACTER
*           STRINGS. WHEN THE COMPLETE CHARACTER STRING HAS BEEN RECEIVED,
*           INPTTSK SUBMITS THE STRING TO THE PRINT QUEUE.
*

INPTTSK   BSR.L     ISTRG                 INPUT STRING FROM CHANNEL A
          BSR       QSTRG                 SUBMIT STRING TO PRINT QUEUE
          BRA       INPTTSK

*
* ISTRG   - ROUTINE TO INPUT A CHARACTER STRING FROM THE TERMINAL & PLACE
*           IT IN INPUT BUFFER.
*           A CHARACTER STRING CAN BE A MAXIMUM OF 256 CHARACTERS LONG
*           (AS DEFINED BY THE CSLNTH), & ENDS WITH CARRIAGE RETURN CHARACTER.
*           IF A BACKSPACE IS RECEIVED, ISTRG WILL DECREMENT THE INPUT
*           BUFFER POINTER UNLESS POINTER IS AT FIRST POSITION IN BUFFER.
*
*           ENTRY CONDITIONS:
*
*                     (NONE)
*
*           EXIT CONDITIONS:
*
*                     CHARACTER STRING IS IN INPUT BUFFER.
*                     A0 CONTAINS START ADDRESS OF INPUT BUFFER.
*                     D1 CONTAINS LENGTH OF STRING.
*                     ALL OTHER REGISTERS ARE RESTORED.
*

ISTRG     MOVEM.L   D0,-(A7)              SUBROUTINE USES REGISTERS D0

          LEA.L     INBUF,A0              GET BASE ADDRESS OF INPUT BUFFER
          CLR.W     D1                    INIT INPUT BUFFER POINTER
GETCHAR   BSR.L     INCH                  GET CHARACTER FROM CHANNEL A

BSCHK     CMP.B     #BS,D0                IS IT A BACKSPACE CHARACTER?
          BNE       PUTCHAR               NO, SKIP NEXT PART
          TST.B     D1                    YES, ARE WE AT BEGINNING OF BUFFER?
          BEQ       GETCHAR               YES, DO NOT DECREMENT POINTER
          SUBQ.B    #1,D1                 NO, DECREMENT BUFFER POINTER
          BRA       GETCHAR               THEN GET NEXT CHARACTER

PUTCHAR   MOVE.B    D0,0(A0,D1.W)         PUT CHARACTER IN INPUT BUFFER,
          ADDQ.B    #1,D1                 BUMP BUFFER POINTER
          ANDI.B    #CSLMSK,D1            (KEEP IT WITHIN STRING LENGTH BOUNDS)
          CMP.B     #CR,D0                WAS IT A CARRIAGE RETURN?
          BNE       GETCHAR               NO, GET NEXT CHAR

          MOVEM.L   (A7)+,D0              YES, RESTORE REGISTER CONTENTS & RETURN
          RTS

*
* QSTRG   - SUBROUTINE TO SUBMIT A CHARACTER STRING TO PRINT QUEUE.
*           QSTRG CHECKS THE STATUS OF THE PRINT QUEUE. IF IT IS
*           FULL, QSTRG WILL WAIT UNTIL THERE IS ROOM IN THE QUEUE FOR
*           A TAG. IF THE QUEUE IS NOT FULL, QSTRG WILL MOVE THE CHARACTER
*           STRING INTO THE PRINT BUFFER, & PLACE A PRINT TAG IN THE PRINT
*           QUEUE.
*           A PRINT TAG IS A BYTE CONTAINING THE LENGTH OF THE STRING TO BE
*           PRINTED.
*
*           ENTRY CONDITIONS:
*
*                     A0 CONTAINS STRING'S START ADDRESS.
*                     D1 CONTAINS STRING'S LENGTH (MAX = 256 CHARACTERS).
*
*           EXIT CONDITIONS:
*
*                     CHARACTER STRING MOVED INTO PRINT BUFFER.
*                     PRINT TAG PLACED IN PRINT QUEUE.
*                     ALL REGISTERS UNALTERED.
*
*

QSTRG     MOVEM.L   A0-A1/D0-D3,-(A7)     SUBROUTINE USES REGS A0,A1,D2-D4

          CLR.W     D2                    GET PRINT QUEUE INPUT POINTER
          MOVE.B    PQIN,D2
          ADDQ.B    #1,D2                 BUMP INPUT POINTER
          ANDI.B    #PQLMSK,D2            (KEEP POINTER WITHIN QUEUE BOUNDS)
QSTRG1    CMP.B     PQOUT,D2              IS PRINT QUEUE FULL (PQIN+1=PQOUT)?
          BEQ       QSTRG1                YES, WAIT UNTIL HAVE ROOM FOR TAG

          LEA.L     PRTBUF,A1             NO, MOVE STRING INTO PRINT BUFFER:
          CLR.L     D3                    GET STRING DESTINATION ADDRESS BY
          MOVE.W    D2,D3                 ADDING INPUT OFFSET (PQIN * CSLNTH)
          MULU.W    #CSLNTH,D3            TO
          LEA       0(A1,D3.L),A1         PRINT BUFFER BASE ADDRESS
```

Figure 7.11 Assembly language code for the INPTTSK routine. (Courtesy of Motorola, Inc.)

```
           CLR.W    D0                        GET STRING LENGTH
           MOVE.B   D1,D0
           SUBQ.B   #1,D0                     DECREMENT IT BY 1
           ANDI.B   #CSLMSK,D0                (KEEP IT WITHIN STRING LENGTH BOUNDS)

 QSTRG2    MOVE.B   (A0)+,(A1)+               MOVE STRING
           DBRA     D0,QSTRG2

           LEA.L    PQUE,A1                   PLACE PRINT TAG IN PRINT QUEUE
           MOVE.B   D1,0(A1,D2.W)

           MOVE.B   D2,PQIN                   UPDATE PRINT QUEUE INPUT POINTER

           MOVEM.L  (A7)+,A0-A1/D0-D3         RESTORE REGISTER CONTENTS
           RTS
```

Figure 7.11 (*continued*).

bits used to define the entry address of the service routine that was previously loaded
somewhere else in memory, the interrupt vector is four bytes long. Thus, the interrupt vector table allows for 256 distinct interrupts. Figure 7.14 details the structure
of this table. It should be noted that the Motorola documentation employs the term
exception and reserves the term *interrupt* for exceptions caused by peripheral devices
requesting (demanding) central processor action. Thus, exceptions can be classified
as follows:

Processor-generated exceptions (internal exceptions)
- Instructions
  —TRAP instructions
  —CHK instructions
  —CALLM, RTM, TRE instructions
  —DIV instruction (divide by 0)
- Address errors, including privilege violations
- Trace
- Breakpoints
- Coprocessor protocol violations

Externally generated exceptions
- Interrupts (peripheral device requests for service)
- Bus errors
- RESET [requires vector numbers 0 and 1 (2 long words = 8 bytes)]
- Coprocessor-detected errors

As we are currently discussing interrupts from peripheral (I/O) devices [vector
numbers 64_{10} through 255_{10} (with table offsets of 100_{16} through $3FC_{16}$)], it is important to note that the device controller provides its system-unique exception vector 8-
bit number on data bus lines D0–D7 during the interrupt acknowledge bus cycle.
The MC680XY processor translates this vector number into a 32-bit offset, as shown
in Figure 7.15. Note that this offset is an absolute address in low-address memory
for the MC68008 and MC68000, implying that the exception vector table must occupy memory locations 0000_{16} through $03FF_{16}$. On the other hand, the exception

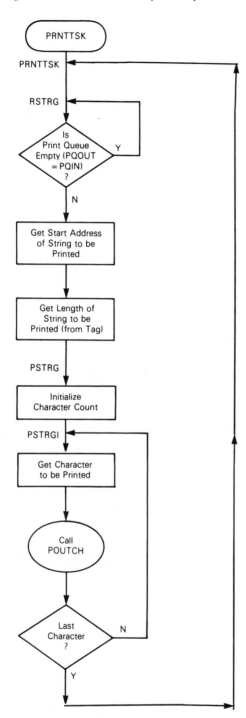

Figure 7.12 Logic of the routine PRNTTSK used to print a line of characters. (Courtesy of Motorola, Inc.)

```
*
* PRNTTSK - TASK THAT CONTINUALLY CHECKS PRINTER QUEUE FOR STRINGS TO BE
*           PRINTED. WHEN A STRING IS TO BE PRINTED, PRNTTSK WILL SEND THE
*           STRING FROM THE PRINT BUFFER TO THE PRINTER. IF NO STRINGS NEED
*           TO BE PRINTED, PRNTTSK WILL CONTINUE CHECKING QUEUE FOR STRINGS
*           TO BE PRINTED.
*

PRNTTSK  BSR      RSTRG                  RELEASE STRING FROM PRINT QUEUE
         BRA      PRNTTSK                CHECK QUEUE FOR ANOTHER PRINT TAG


* RSTRG - SUBROUTINE TO RELEASE A CHARACTER STRING FROM PRINT QUEUE.
*         RSTRG CHECKS THE STATUS OF THE PRINT QUEUE. IF THE QUEUE IS
*         EMPTY, RSTRG WILL WAIT UNTIL A PRINT TAG APPEARS IN THE QUEUE.
*         A PRINT TAG IS A BYTE CONTAINING THE LENGTH OF THE STRING TO
*         BE PRINTED.
*         IF THE PRINT QUEUE IS NOT EMPTY, RSTRG WILL SEND THE STRING
*         FROM THE PRINT BUFFER TO THE PRINTER, THEN PULL THE TAG FROM THE
*         PRINT QUEUE.
*
*         ENTRY CONDITIONS:
*
*                 (NONE)
*
*         EXIT CONDITIONS:
*
*                 CHARACTER STRING IS SENT FROM THE PRINT BUFFER
*                 TO CHANNEL B.
*                 PRINT TAG IS REMOVED FROM PRINT QUEUE.
*                 ALL REGISTERS UNALTERED.
*

RSTRG    MOVEM.L  D0-D1/A0-A1,-(A7)      SUBROUTINE USES REGS D0, D1, A0, & A1

         CLR.W    D0                     GET PRINT QUEUE OUTPUT POINTER
         MOVE.B   PQOUT,D0
RSTRG1   CMP.B    PQIN,D0                IS PRINT QUEUE EMPTY (PQOUT=PQIN)?
         BEQ      RSTRG1                 YES, WAIT FOR A TAG TO APPEAR IN QUEUE

         LEA.L    PRTBUF,A0              NO, RELEASE STRING:
         CLR.L    D1                     GET STRING SOURCE ADDRESS BY
         MOVE.W   D0,D1                  ADDING OUTPUT OFFSET (PQOUT * CSLNTH)
         MULU.W   #CSLNTH,D1             TO
         LEA.L    0(A0,D1.L),A0          PRINT BUFFER BASE ADDRESS

         LEA.L    PQUE,A1                GET STRING LENGTH
         CLR.W    D1                     FROM
         MOVE.B   0(A1,D0.W),D1          PRINT TAG

         BSR      PSTRG                  SEND STRING TO CHANNEL B

         ADDQ.B   #1,D0                  BUMP PRINT QUEUE OUTPUT POINTER
         ANDI.B   #PQLMSK,D0             (KEEP POINTER WITHIN QUEUE BOUNDS)
         MOVE.B   D0,PQOUT               UPDATE PRINT QUEUE OUTPUT POINTER

         MOVEM.L  (A7)+,D0-D1/A0-A1      RESTORE REGISTER CONTENTS
         RTS

*
* PSTRG - ROUTINE TO SEND A CHARACTER STRING TO THE PRINTER.
*
*         ENTRY CONDITIONS:
*
*                 A0 CONTAINS STRING'S START ADDRESS.
*                 D1 CONTAINS STRING'S LENGTH (MAX = 256 CHARACTERS).
*
*         EXIT CONDITIONS:
*
*                 CHARACTER STRING IS SENT TO PRINTER VIA CHANNEL B.
*                 ALL REGISTERS ARE UNALTERED.
*

PSTRG    MOVEM.L  A0/D0-D1,-(A7)         SUBROUTINE USES REGS A0,D0,D1

         SUBQ.B   #1,D1                  INIT CHARACTER COUNT FROM STRING LENGTH
         ANDI.B   #CSLMSK,D1             (KEEP IT WITHIN STRING LENGTH BOUNDS)
PSTRG1   MOVE.B   (A0)+,D0               GET CHAR OF STRING TO BE PRINTED
         BSR.L    POUTCH                 PRINT CHARACTER
         DBRA     D1,PSTRG1              WAS IT THE LAST CHARACTER OF STRING?

         MOVEM.L  (A7)+,A0/D0-D1         YES, RESTORE REGISTER CONTENTS
         RTS
```

Figure 7.13 Assembly language code for the PRNTTSK routine. (Courtesy of Motorola, Inc.)

Vector number(s)	Vector offset		Assignment
	Hex	Space	
0	000	SP	Reset: Initial Interrupt Stack Pointer
1	004	SP	Reset: Initial Program Counter
2	008	SD	Bus Error
3	00C	SD	Address Error
4	010	SD	Illegal Instruction
5	014	SD	Zero Divide
6	018	SD	CHK, CHK2 Instruction
7	01C	SD	cpTRAPcc, TRAPcc, TRAPV Instructions
8	020	SD	Privilege Violation
9	024	SD	Trace
10	028	SD	Line 1010 Emulator
11	02C	SD	Line 1111 Emulator
12	030	SD	(Unassigned, Reserved)
13	034	SD	Coprocessor Protocol Violation
14	038	SD	Format Error
15	03C	SD	Uninitialized Interrupt
16 Through 23	040 05C	SD SD	(Unassigned, Reserved)
24	060	SD	Spurious Interrupt
25	064	SD	Level 1 Interrupt Auto Vector
26	068	SD	Level 2 Interrupt Auto Vector
27	06C	SD	Level 3 Interrupt Auto Vector
28	070	SD	Level 4 Interrupt Auto Vector
29	074	SD	Level 5 Interrupt Auto Vector
30	078	SD	Level 6 Interrupt Auto Vector
31	07C	SD	Level 7 Interrupt Auto Vector
32 Through 47	080 0BC	SD SD	TRAP #0–15 Instruction Vectors
48	0C0	SD	FPCP Branch or Set on Unordered Condition
49	0C4	SD	FPCP Inexact Result
50	0C8	SD	FPCP Divide by Zero
51	0CC	SD	FPCP Underflow
52	0D0	SD	FPCP Operand Error
53	0D4	SD	FPCP Overflow
54	0DB	SD	FPCP Signaling NAN
55	0DC	SD	Unassigned, Reserved
56	0E0	SD	PMMU Configuration
57	0E4	SD	PMMU Illegal Operation
58	0E8	SD	PMMU Access Level Violation
59 Through 63	0EC 0FC	SD SD	Unassigned, Reserved
64 Through 255	100 3FC	SD SD	User Defined Vectors (192)

SP = Supervisor Program Space
SD = Supervisor Data Dpace

Figure 7.14 The syntax and semantics of the MC680XY exception vector table. (Courtesy of Motorola, Inc.)

Exception Vector Format

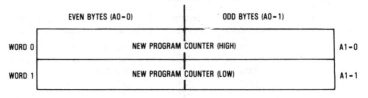

EVEN BYTES (AO‑0) ODD BYTES (AO‑1)

| WORD 0 | NEW PROGRAM COUNTER (HIGH) | A1‑0 |
| WORD 1 | NEW PROGRAM COUNTER (LOW) | A1‑1 |

Figure 7.14 *(continued)*

Peripheral Vector Number Format

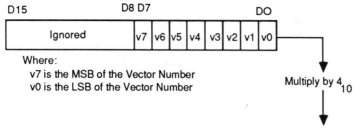

D15   D8 D7   DO

| Ignored | v7 | v6 | v5 | v4 | v3 | v2 | v1 | v0 |

Where:
  v7 is the MSB of the Vector Number
  v0 is the LSB of the Vector Number

Multiply by 4_{10}

Address Translated from 8-bit Vector Number (MC68000, MB68008)

A31   A10 A9 A8 A7 A6 A5 A4 A3 A2 A1 A0

| All Zeroes | v7 | v6 | v5 | v4 | v3 | v2 | v1 | v0 | 0 | 0 |

Exception Vector
Address

Exception Vector Address Calculation (MC68010, MC68012, MC68020)

31   0

| Contents of Vector Base Register |

31   10   0

| All Zeroes | v7 | v6 | v5 | v4 | v3 | v2 | v1 | v0 | 0 | 0 |

(+)

Exception Vector
Address

Branch to Exception Service Routine

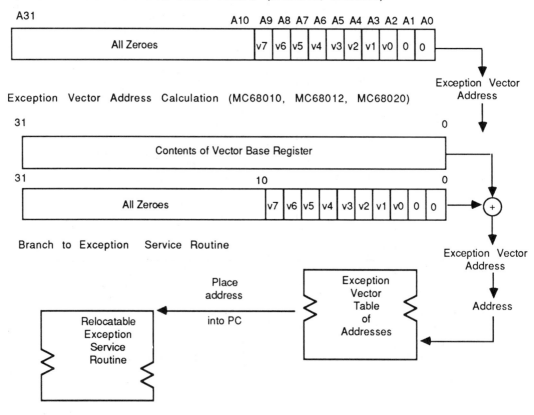

Place address into PC

Exception
Vector
Table
of
Addresses

Address

Relocatable
Exception
Service
Routine

Figure 7.15 The physical address of a relocatable exception service routine is derived indirectly. (Courtesy of Motorola, Inc.)

vector address table is relocatable in the MC68010, MC68012, and MC68020. As shown in Figure 7.15, these more advanced processors provide a *vector base address register* (VBR) that is automatically added into the address calculation. It is vital to recall that the processor is deriving the address within a table of addresses of the specific interrupt service routine to handle the request from a specific peripheral I/O device. In other words, the interrupt service routines in memory are addressed indirectly through a memory-resident table of addresses. Note that the MC68010, MC68012, and MC68020 will act like the MC68008 and MC68000 in respect to exceptions if the vector base address register (VBR) is set to 0. As the VBR is initialized to 0 on a RESET, the more advanced processors will assume that the exception vector table starts at address 0000_{16} until the address in the VBR is deliberately changed via the MOVEC instruction.

The exceptions shown in Figure 7.14 are classified into five priority groups, as shown in Figure 7.16 for the MC68020. In the earlier processors (MC68008, MC68000, MC68010, and MC68012), groups 3 and 4 were not required and therefore were not implemented. The relative priority of two exceptions determines which of the two will be serviced first. The servicing of one exception can be suspended to allow servicing of a higher-priority exception; thus, preemptive exception priorities are allowed. This priority scheme is very important in determining the order in which exception handlers are executed in those commonly occurring situations in which multiple exceptions occur. As a general rule, the lower the priority of an exception, the more quickly the handler routine for that exception will be executed. For example, if simultaneous trap, trace, and peripheral device interrupt exceptions are all pending, the trap exception is processed first, followed immediately by exception processing for the trace and then the peripheral device interrupt. Thus, when the processor finally resumes normal instruction execution, it is in the peripheral device interrupt handler, which returns to the trace handler, which returns to the trap handler. The sole exception to this rule is the RESET exception, which is the highest priority and is also the first exception serviced, since all other exceptions are cleared by the RESET condition.

Figure 7.17, showing the instruction cycle of the MC680XY, emphasizes the distinction that Motorola makes between *processing an exception* and *executing the service routine*. This semantic distinction corresponds to the necessity of fielding multiple exceptions in priority order. In the X cycle portion of the normal instruction cycle of Figure 7.17, note that a check is made for the existence of an exception request. If no such request is pending, the next instruction will be fetched using the current contents of the program counter (PC) of the applications program, of the operating system module, or of the exception service routine—whichever currently controls the PC. If an exception is pending, its priority level is checked using bits in the status register (SR). If the priority is the same or lower (group level is higher) than the currently executing exception, the next instruction will be fetched using the current contents of the PC. If the priority is higher (group level is lower), then the four steps shown in Figure 7.17 as "process interrupt" will be accomplished. Thus, exception processing occurs in four identifiable steps. In the first step, an internal

Group/ Priority	Exception and Relative Priority	Characteristics
0	0.0 – Reset	Aborts all processing (instruction or exception) and does not save old context.
1	1.0 – Address Error 1.1 – Bus Error	Suspends processing (instruction or exception) and saves internal context.
2	2.0 – BKPT #n, CALLM, CHK, CHK2, cp Mid-Instruction, Cp Protocol Violation, cpTRAPcc, Divide-by-Zero, RTE, RTM, TRAP #n, TRAPV	Exception processing is part of instruction execution.
3	3.0 – Illegal Instruction, Line A, Unimplemented Line F, Privilege Violation, cp Pre-Instruction	Exception processing begins before instruction is executed.
4	4.0 – cp Post-Instruction 4.1 – Trace 4.2 – Interrupt	Exception processing begins when current instruction or previous exception processing is completed.

0.0 is the highest priority, 4.2 is the lowest.

Exception Groups

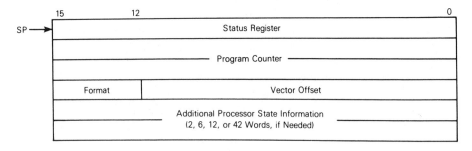

Exception Stack Frame

Format	Frame Type
0000	Short Format (4 Words)
0001	Throwaway (4 Words)
0010	Instruction Exception (6 Words)
0011-0111	(Undefined, Reserved)
1000	MC68010 Bus Fault (29 Words)
1001	Coprocessor Mid-Instruction (10 Words)
1010	MC68020 Short Bus Fault (16 Words)
1011	MC68020 Long Bus Fault (46 Words)
1100-1111	(Undefined, Reserved)

Stack Frame Format Definitions

Figure 7.16 Exception priorities (groups 3 and 4 are implemented only in the MC68020). The concept of an exception stack frame is discussed in the text. (Courtesy of Motorola, Inc.)

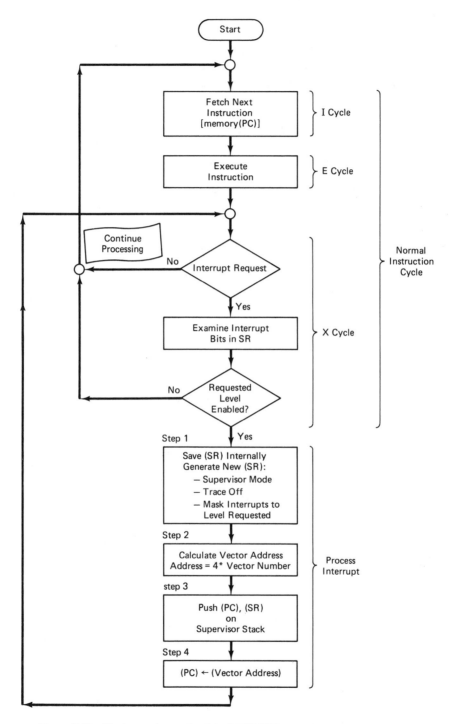

Figure 7.17 The instruction cycle of the MC680XY expanded to illustrate the details of exception determination and initiation of exception processing.

copy is made of the status register. After the copy is made, the S bit is asserted, putting the processor into the supervisor privilege state. Also, the T bit is negated, which will allow the exception handler to execute unhindered by tracing. For the reset and interrupt exceptions, the interrupt priority mask is also updated.

In the second step, the vector number of the exception is determined. For interrupts, the vector number is obtained by a processor fetch and classified as an interrupt acknowledge. For all other exceptions, internal logic provides the vector number. This vector number is then used to generate the address of the exception vector.

The third step is to save the current processor status, except for the reset exception. The current program counter value and the saved copy of the status register are stacked using the supervisor stack pointers, as shown in Figure 7.16. The stacked program counter value usually points to the next unexecuted instruction; however, for bus error and address error, the value stacked for the program counter is unpredictable and may be incremented from the address of the instruction that caused the error. Additional information defining the current context is stacked for the bus error and address error exceptions. This context is organized in a format called the *exception stack frame*. This information always includes the status register, the program counter, and the vector offset used to fetch the vector. The processor also marks the frame with a frame format. The format field allows the RTE instruction to identify what information is on the stack so that it may be properly restored and the stack space deallocated. The various formats are shown in Figure 7.18.

The last step is the same for all exceptions. The new program counter value is fetched from the exception vector. The processor then resumes instruction execution. The instruction at the address given in the exception vector is fetched, and normal instruction decoding and execution is started.

We will briefly treat the actions that transpire for the various exceptions, starting with highest priority/lowest group (RESET) and progressing to the lowest priority/highest group (peripheral device interrupt).

RESET (priority 0.0). The $\overline{\text{RESET}}$ signal provides for system initialization and recovery from catastrophic failure. Any and all processing in progress at the time of a RESET is aborted and cannot be recovered. The status register is initialized; tracing is disabled (both trace bits are cleared); supervisor interrupt state is entered (the supervisor bit is set and the master bit is cleared); and the processor interrupt priority mask is set to the highest-priority level (level 7). The RESET instruction does not affect any internal registers, but it does reset all external devices, allowing recovery software to initialize the entire system to the desired and known state preparatory to processing the next instruction.

Address error (priority 1.0). An address error exception will occur if the processor attempts to fetch an instruction from an odd-numbered address. After exception processing begins, the sequence of actions is the same as for a bus error and thus will be different for the MC68008/MC68000 than for the MC68010/MC68012

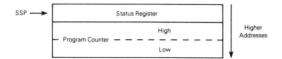

Exception Stack Order (Groups 1 and 2)

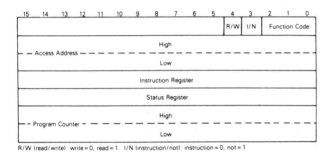

R/W (read/write): write = 0, read = 1. I/N (instruction/not): instruction = 0, not = 1

Exception Stack Order (Group 0)

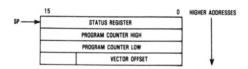

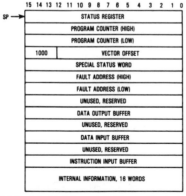

NOTE: The stack pointer is decremented by 29 words, although only 26 words of information are actually written to memory. The three additional words are reserved for future use by Motorola.

Exception Stack Order (Bus and Address Error)

Figure 7.18 The format for the various exception stack frames of the MC680XY family of processors. (Courtesy of Motorola, Inc.)

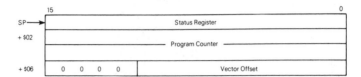

Format $0 — Four Word Stack Frame

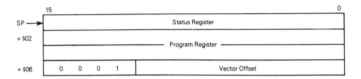

Format $1 — Throwaway Four Word Stack Frame

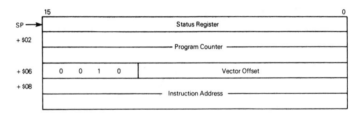

Format $2 — Six Word Stack Frame

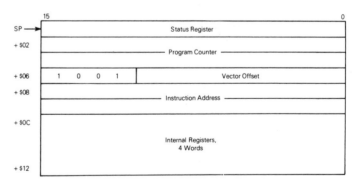

Format $9 — Coprocessor Mid-Instruction Exception Stack Frame (10 Words)

Figure 7.18   (*continued*)

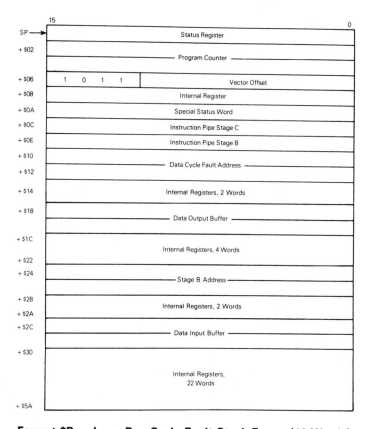

Format $A — Short Bus Cycle Fault Stack Frame (16 Words)

Format $B — Long Bus Cycle Fault Stack Frame (46 Words)

Figure 7.18 (*continued*)

and different yet for the MC68020. If an address error is posted during exception processing for a RESET, a bus error, or an address error, the processor will be halted.

Bus error (priority 1.1).   We must treat three cases—one for each of the three different subfamilies of processors.

MC68000/MC68008.   Exception processing follows the usual action sequence, but because the processor is in the midst of executing an instruction, additional information must be pushed onto the supervisory stack for eventual restoration. Figure 7.18 details this information. The PC has a value at least two bytes and as much as ten bytes beyond the start of the executing instruction—that is, within or at the end of it.

MC68010/MC68012.   Again, because the processor is in the midst of executing an instruction, additional information (22 words) must be saved [pushed onto the supervisory stack for eventual restoration by a return from an interrupt (RTE) instruction]. Because these processors prefetch instructions sometime before they are needed, the PC may be advanced beyond the current instruction by any value up to 10 bytes = 5 words. Even so, correct recovery is accomplished. The format of the special status word necessary for correct recovery is

15	14	13	12	11	10	9	8	7 – 3	2	1	0
RR	*	IF	DF	RM	HB	BY	RW	*		FC2-FC0	

RR — Re-run flag; 0 = processor re-run (default), 1 = software re-run.
IF — Instruction fetch to the Instruction Input Buffer.
DF — Data fetch to the Data Input Buffer.
RM — Read-Modify-Write cycle.
HB — High byte transfer from the Data Output Buffer or to the Data Input Buffer.
BY — Byte transfer flag; HB selects the high or low byte of the transfer register. If BY is clear, the transfer is word.
RW — Read/Write flag; 0 = write, 1 = read.
FC — The function code used during the faulted access.
* — These bits are reserved for future use by Motorola and will be zero when written by the MC68010/MC68012.

MC68020.   Similar to the predecessor processors, a bus error may occur in the midst of executing an instruction, necessitating the saving (via pushing) on the supervisory stack of the internal information necessary for restoring the processor to its correct state after the RTE instruction is executed. For efficiency, the designers implemented two different stack frame formats (shown in Figure 7.18): an abbreviated stack frame (16 words) for that case when the bus error occurs just as an instruction is beginning execution and a full stack frame (46 words) for the more usual case of a bus error occurring during the execution of an instruction. The format of the special status word (SSW) necessary for correct recovery contains more information than the SSW of the MC68010/MC68012:

15	14	13	12	11	10	9	8	7	6	5	4	3	2	1	0
FC	FB	RC	RB	0	0	0	DF	RM	RW	SIZ		0	FC2-FC0		

FC	— Fault on Stage C of the Instruction Pipe
FB	— Fault on Stage B of the Instruction Pipe
RC	— Rerun Flag for Stage C of the Instruction Pipe*
RB	— Rerun Flag for Stage B of the Instruction Pipe*
DF	— Fault/Rerun Flag for Data Cycle*
RM	— Read-Modify-Write on Data Cycle
RW	— Read/Write for Data Cycle – 1 = Read, 0 = Write
SIZ	— Size Code for Data Cycle
FC0-FC2	— Address Space for Data Cycle
*1 = Rerun Faulted Bus Cycle, or Run Pending Prefetch	
0 = Do Not Rerun Bus Cycle	

The SSW indicates whether the bus error fault—or address fault—was caused by the instruction stream, by the data stream, or by both. In general, for all MC680XY processors, if a bus error occurs during exception processing for a bus error, address error, or RESET, or while internal state information is being loaded (restored/popped) from the supervisory stack, the processor will halt.

Instruction traps (priority 2.0). As used by Motorola, the term *trap* refers to three different conditions, which we will treat separately. Note that the trap exception is posted during instruction execution.

Illegal Operand Value. The DIVS and DIVU instructions will force an exception if a divide by 0 is attempted. Similarly, the CALLM and RTM instructions (module call and return—see Chapter 3) will cause a format exception if an illegal privilege level is requested or if invalid parameters are used in the type or option fields.

Software Traps, Software Interrupts, Supervisory Calls. A programmer may generate an interrupt by executing the instruction

TRAP   n

where n is the entry in the interrupt vector table containing the address of the software interrupt service routine that will perform some desired or necessary action for the program. Software interrupts may be numbered from 0 base 10 through 16 base 10.

Software interrupts are extremely useful (almost vital) in constructing an operating system. As the prime example, most operating systems and procedural-level languages prevent the applications programmer from directly using I/O instructions and require that the program request such I/O services from the operating system. Thus, the FORTRAN statement "READ (5,10) Variable" would be translated to TRAP #, where # is the vector entry of the software interrupt service routine that will actually input the value of the variable from the peripheral device interface corresponding to unit 5 according to the format specifications in statement 10. In actuality, the value will probably be transferred from an operating system prefilled buffer corresponding to the device.

Note that in the TRAP, $n+32_{10}$ is the interrupt vector number in the instruction stream (acquired from the instruction queue). Thus, the processor does not have to acquire this information from an interface via the bus. Also note that software interrupts are specifically requested by the program, are maskable, and are invoked by the software at a time known in respect to the program code.

Conditional Software Traps (Interrupts).   The TRAPV, TRAPcc, cpTRAPcc, CHK, and CHK2 instructions force an exception if the condition is true. Such events, often termed *run-time errors,* include such universally undesirable events as arithmetic overflow and subscript out-of-bounds as well as events that are specific to the situation, such as arithmetic carry, T/F, $+/-$, $=/\neq/>/=>/</<=$.

Illegal instruction/operand (priority 3).   Motorola employs this terminology and exception priority to encompass four situations in which exception servicing is appropriate before instruction execution begins.

Operand Format Error.   The processor routinely checks for the validity of control operation values of specific instructions. These include the type and option fields of the module descriptor of CALLM, the type and option fields of the module stack frame of RTM, the validity of the supervisory stack format code for RTE, and the coprocessor save area format for cpRESTORE.

Privilege Violations.   To provide a modicum of system security, certain instructions can be executed only when the processor is in the supervisory state—that is, in the operating system. An attempt to execute a privileged instruction while in the user state—that is, from an applications program—will cause a privilege violation exception. The privileged instructions are

$$\left.\begin{array}{l} \text{ANDI} \\ \text{EORI} \\ \text{ORI} \\ \text{MOVE to} \end{array}\right\} \text{STATUS REGISTER}$$

MOVE—USP (user stack pointer)

$$\left.\begin{array}{l} \text{MOVEC} \\ \text{MOVES} \end{array}\right\} \text{MC68010, MC68012, MC68020 only}$$

RESET
RTE
STOP

$$\left.\begin{array}{l} \text{cpSAVE} \\ \text{cpRESTORE} \end{array}\right\} \text{MC68020 coprocessor only}$$

Illegal (Unimplemented) Instructions.   An illegal instruction is any bit pattern that does not exactly correspond to the legal bit pattern of the first word of a defined MC680XY instruction. Four subsets are provided:

- *Currently unused bit patterns.* System implementors must be aware that any illegal bit pattern not among those given here are fair game for future processor design augmentation. To allow assured software system augmentation, the two patterns 4AFA and 4AFB are reserved for customer use. All other illegal bit patterns may be used without notice by Motorola in implementing future improved (augmented) MC680XY processors.
- *A-line opcodes* have the bit pattern AXYZ, cause an exception to vector number 10, and are intended to allow software emulation of operations implemented on a more advanced processor in the MC680XY family but not implemented on the specific processor being used.
- *F-line opcodes* have the bit pattern FXYZ, cause an exception to vector number 11, and are used to specify an instruction for a coprocessor such as the MC68881 floating-point coprocessor. Note that these instructions could be, and often are, emulated in software.
- *Eight breakpoint instructions* are provided by the MC68010, MC68012, and MC68020 to allow these processors to be used in a hardware emulator for detailed in-line program testing. These eight breakpoint instructions, with the bit patterns 4848 through 484F cause the processor to enter the illegal instruction exception processing as usual but also force a breakpoint bus cycle before the stacking operation. If the bus cycle terminates with $\overline{\text{DSACKx}}$, the data returned are used as the next instruction. If this bus cycle terminates with a $\overline{\text{BERR}}$, the usual illegal instruction exception processing occurs.

TRACE (priority 4.1).   To aid in program development, the MC680XY processors include a trace facility to allow instruction-by-instruction tracing through the use of the T bit in the supervisor portion of the status register (SR). The MC68020 extends this ability to allow either instruction-by-instruction tracing or tracing for branch instructions only (change in control flow, such as BRA, JMP, etc.).

In general terms, a trace exception can be viewed as an extension to the function of any instruction. Thus, if a trace exception is generated by an instruction, the execution of that instruction is not complete until the trace exception processing associated with it is completed. If the instruction does not complete execution because of a bus error or address error exception, trace exception processing is deferred until after the execution of the suspended instruction is resumed (by the associated RTE), and the instruction execution is completed normally. If the instruction is executed and an interrupt is pending on completion, the trace exception processing is completed before the interrupt exception processing starts. If, during the execution of the instruction, an exception is forced by that instruction, the forced exception is processed before the trace exception is processed.

If the processor is in the trace mode when an attempt is made to execute an illegal or unimplemented instruction, that instruction will not cause a trace, since it is not executed. This is of particular importance to an instruction emulation routine that performs the instruction function, adjusts the stacked program counter to beyond the unimplemented instruction, and then returns. Before the return is executed, the status register on the stack should be checked to determine if tracing is on; if so, then the trace exception processing should also be emulated so that the trace exception handler can account for the emulated instruction.

Device interrupts (priority 4.2).   External peripheral devices or other processors may request service by setting the three interrupt lines to an appropriate value. Note that these device interrupts have the lowest priority of all exceptions. Peripheral device interrupt requests do not force immediate exception processing but may be made pending. Higher-priority pending exceptions are preemptive and are serviced at the conclusion of the current instruction.

To service a device interrupt, an internal copy of the status register (SR) is made, the processor state is set to supervisory, tracing is suppressed, and the processor interrupt level is appropriately set. Next, the processor fetches an interrupt vector number (64_{10} through 255_{10}), sets the bus cycle to interrupt acknowledge, and sends the interrupt level number out on lines A1, A2, and A3. Once the interrupt vector number is obtained, usual exception processing proceeds with saving the vector offset, the PC, and the SR on the supervisor stack. Almost all MC680XY family peripherals provide for programmable interrupt vector numbers. If this vector number is not initialized after a RESET, the uninitialized interrupt vector number 0 will result.

After exception stacking operations have been accomplished for all pending exceptions, normal instruction execution resumes at the address in the interrupt vector of the last exception to be processed. This exception service (handler) routine is terminated by the return-from-exception (RTE) instruction. The RTE instruction checks the top stack frame for validity and then restores the appropriate execution context. Note in Figure 7.18 that sufficient information is included in all stack frames to allow correct restoration of the status register, the program counter, and the supervisory stack pointer, as well as any necessary internal registers if appropriate.

Every interrupt service routine should protect the program that was interrupted by saving the contents of any registers that it will use before such contents are destroyed and restoring these register contents before returning via the RTE instruction to the interrupted program. This protection scheme is shown in generalized flow diagram form in Figure 7.19.

Interrupt priorities in the MC680XY family of microprocessors for multiple external peripheral devices that require interrupt capabilities are available with the MC68153 bus interrupt module (BIM). Through its ability to be programmed, it allows full control of four independent interrupt request sources to be routed to any of the seven MC680XY exception levels.

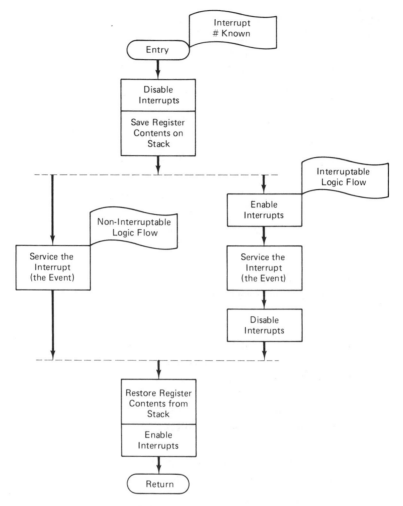

Figure 7.19 Interrupt service routine logic diagram. (Adapted from G. W. Gorsline, *16-Bit Modern Microcomputers: The Intel 18086 Family,* © 1985, p. 164. Reprinted by permission of Prentice-Hall, Inc., Englewood Cliffs, NJ.)

DIRECT MEMORY ACCESS

Direct memory access is a special hardware data transfer path and control logic that allows a block of data to be rapidly transferred directly from a device interface to system memory, or vice versa, without intervention by the microprocessor during the transfer. The microprocessor must define, set up, and initiate the transfer as well as note its completion.

The transfer path for DMA is almost always via the system bus, including the data, the address, and the control lines. The control logic for DMA is usually a

VLSI programmable DMA controller chip. The appropriate device to use with an MC680XY microcomputer is an MC68440, MC68442, or MC68450. The MC68450 DMA controller is illustrated in Figure 7.20.

The MC68450 direct memory access controller (DMAC) performs memory-to-memory, memory-to-device, and device-to-memory data transfers by utilizing the following features:

1. Four independent DMA channels with programmable priority
2. Asynchronous MC68000 bus structure with a 24-bit address and a 16-bit data bus
3. Fast transfer rates: up to 5 megabytes per second at 10 MHz, no wait states
4. Fully supports all M68000 bus options, such as halt, bus error, and retry
5. FIFO locked step support with device transfer complete signal
6. Flexible request generation:
   • Internal, maximum rate
   • Internal, limited rate
   • External, cycle steal (with or without hold)
   • External, burst
   • Mixed internal and external
7. Programmable 8-bit or 16-bit peripheral device types:
   • Explicitly addressed, M68000 type
   • Explicitly addressed, M6800 type
   • Implicitly addressed:
     —Device with request and acknowledge
     —Device with request, acknowledge, and ready

The DMAC will move blocks of data between the peripheral controllers and memory at rates approaching the limits of the memory bus, since the simple function of data movement is implemented in high-speed hardware. A block of data consists of a sequence of byte, word, or long-word operands starting at a specific address in memory, with the length of the block determined by a transfer count. A single-channel operation may involve the transfer of several blocks of data between the memory and a device.

Any operation involving the DMAC will follow the same basic steps:

1. Channel initialization by the system processor: The host processor loads the registers of the DMAC with control information, address pointers, and transfer counts and then starts the channel.
2. Data transfer: The DMA accepts requests for operand transfers and provides addressing and bus control for the transfers.
3. Block termination: This occurs after the operation is complete, when the DMAC indicates the status of the operation in the status register.

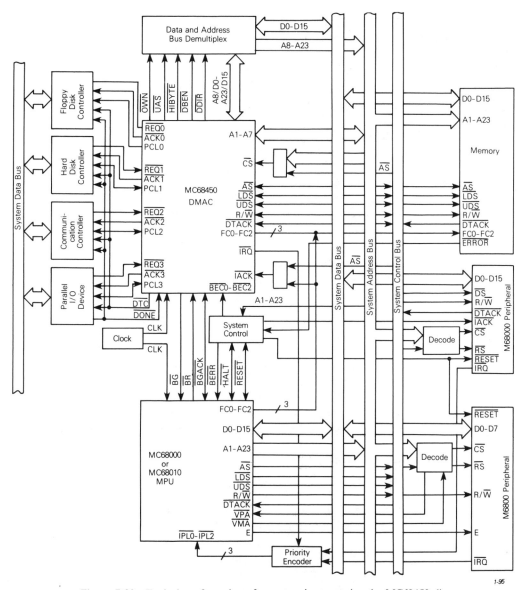

Figure 7.20 Typical configuration of a system incorporating the MC68450 direct memory access controller (DMAC). (Courtesy of Motorola, Inc.)

During all phases of a data transfer operation, the DMAC will be in one of three operating modes:

1. IDLE is the state that the DMAC assumes when it is reset by an external device and is waiting for initialization by the system processor or an operand transfer request from a peripheral.

2. MPU is the state that the DMAC enters when it is chip-selected by another bus master in the system (usually the main system processor). In this mode, the DMAC internal registers are written or read to control channel operation or to check the status of a block transfer.

3. DMA is the state that the DMAC enters when it is acting as a bus master to perform an operand transfer.

Besides fully supporting the MC68000 family bus, the DMAC also supports transfers to or from MC6800 family peripheral devices.

Operand Transfer Modes

The DMAC can perform implicit address or explicit address data transfers using any of the following protocols:

1. Explicitly addressed MC68000-compatible device.
2. Explicitly addressed MC6800-compatible device.
3. Implicitly addressed device with acknowledge.
4. Implicitly addressed device with acknowledge and ready.

In the first two protocols, data are transferred from the source to an internal DMAC holding register and then, on the next bus cycle, moved from the holding register to the destination.

Explicitly addressed devices require that a data register within the peripheral device be addressed. No signals other than the MC68000 asynchronous bus control signals are needed to interface with such a device, although any of the five device control signals may also be used. Because the address bus is used to access the peripheral, the data cannot be directly transferred to/from memory, since memory also requires addressing. Therefore, data are transferred from the source to an internal holding register in the DMAC and then transferred to the destination during a second bus transfer, as shown in Figure 7.21a. Since both memory and the device are addressed during such a data transfer, this method is called the *dual-address method*.

Besides providing data transfers from a device interface direct to memory (WRITE) and direct from memory to a device interface (READ), the MC68450 DMAC allows memory-to-memory block data moves, using one channel as the source and another channel as the destination. This programmatic style can facilitate the movement of blocks of data and programs from one area of memory to another with minimal programming effort and with a minimum expenditure of microprocessor time. Its employment with operating systems is of obvious utility.

Protocols 3 and 4 require only one bus cycle for data transfer, since only one device needs to be addressed. With these protocols, communication is performed using a two-signal and three-signal handshake, respectively.

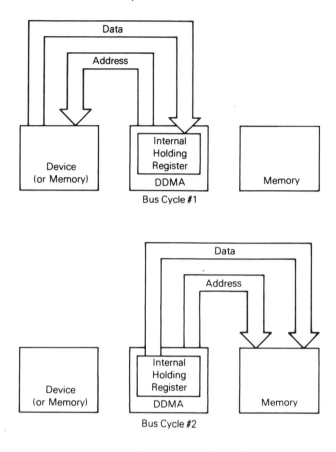

(a) DUAL-ADDRESS TRANSFER SEQUENCE

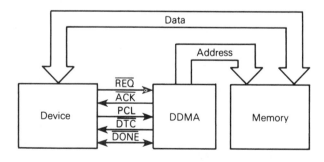

(b) IMPLICIT ADDRESS DEVICE INTERFACE

Figure 7.21 The MC68450 direct memory access controller (DMAC) allows two data transfer modes: (a) a two-bus-cycle mode, which allows memory-to-memory transfers as well as device ↔ memory, and (b) a single-bus-cycle mode for device ↔ memory transfers. (Courtesy of Motorola, Inc.)

Implicitly addressed devices do not require the generation of a device data register address for a data transfer. Such a device is controlled by a five-signal device control interface on the DMAC during implicit address transfers, as shown in Figure 7.21b. Since only memory is addressed during such a data transfer, this method is called the *single-address method*.

Channel Operating Modes

There are three types of channel operations:

1. Single block transfers.
2. Continued operation.
3. Chained operations.

The first two modes utilize on-chip registers; the last mode uses an on-chip address register to point to address and count parameters stored in system memory.

When transferring single blocks of data, the memory address and device address registers are initialized by the user to specify the source and destination of the transfer. The memory transfer count register is also initialized to count the number of operands transferred in a block. Repeated transfers are possible with the continue mode of operation, in which the memory address and transfer count registers are automatically loaded from internal registers upon completion of a block transfer. See Figure 7.22.

The two chaining modes are array chaining and linked array chaining. The *array chaining mode* operates from a contiguous array in memory, consisting of memory addresses and transfer counts. The base address register and base transfer count register are initialized to point to the beginning address of the array and the number of array entries, respectively. As each block transfer is completed, the next entry is fetched from the array, the base transfer count is decremented, and the base address is incremented to point to the next array entry. When the base transfer count reaches zero, the entry just fetched is the last block transfer defined in the array. See Figure 7.23a.

The *linked array chaining mode* is similar to the array chaining mode, except that each entry in the memory array also contains a link address, which points to the next entry in the array. This allows a noncontiguous memory array. The last entry contains a link address set to 0. No base transfer count register is needed in this mode. The base address register is initialized to the address of the first entry in the array. The link address is used to update the base address register at the beginning of each block transfer. This chaining mode allows array entries to be moved or inserted easily without having to reorganize the array into sequential order. Also, the number of entries in the array need not be specified to the DMAC. See Figure 7.23b.

The DMAC will interrupt the MPU for occurrences such as the completion of a DMA operation or at the request of a peripheral device. The user must write inter-

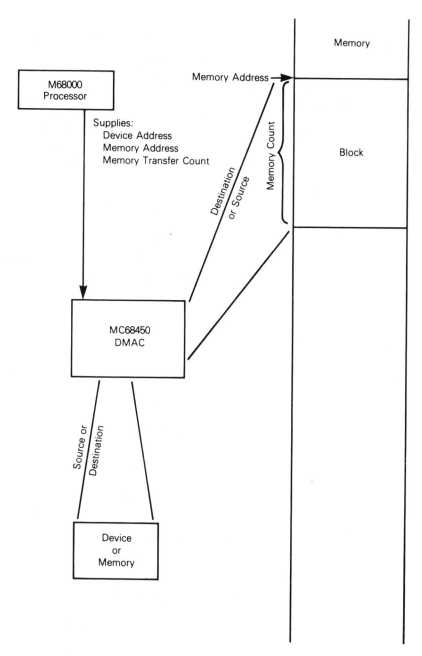

Figure 7.22 MC68450 DMAC single data block transfer operation. (Courtesy of Motorola, Inc.)

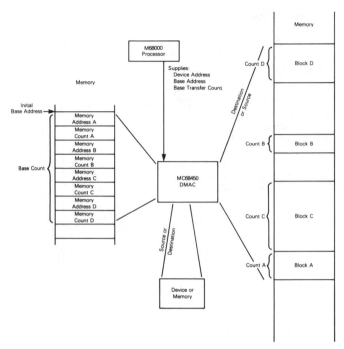

ARRAY CHAIN TRANSFER

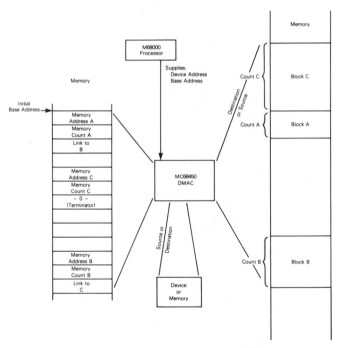

LINKED ARRAY CHAIN TRANSFER

Figure 7.23 MC68450 DMAC chain of data blocks transfer operations. (Courtesy of Motorola, Inc.)

rupt vectors into an on-chip vector register for use on the MC68000 vectored interrupt structure. Two vector registers are available for each channel.

Each channel may be given a priority level of 0, 1, 2 or 3. If several channel requests occur at the same priority level, a round-robin arbitration scheme is used to select the first channel to be serviced.

Requests may be externally generated by a device or internally generated by the auto-request mechanism of the DMAC. Auto-requests may be generated either at the maximum rate, where the channel always has a request pending, or at a limited rate determined by selecting a portion of the bus bandwidth to be available for DMA activity. External requests can be either burst requests or cycle-steal requests that are generated by the request signal associated with each channel.

Register Description

The register description given here is for a single channel, but it applies to all channels since they are identical. When the operation of a register affects the four channels differently or is common to all channels, that fact will be included in the description. Figure 7.24 shows the register complement both as a programmers model and as the memory-mapped locations of the registers for each channel. Figure 7.25 shows the register summary and may be used for a quick reference to the bit definitions within each register.

All registers within the DMAC are always accessible as bytes or words by the MC68000 (assuming that the MPU can gain control of the DMA bus); however, some registers may not or should not be modified while a channel is actively transferring data. If a register may not be modified during operation and an attempt is made to write to it, an operation timing error will be signaled and the channel operation aborted.

The three 32-bit address registers (MAR, DAR, and BAR) contain addresses that are used by the DMAC to access memory while it is a bus master. Since the DMAC has only 24 address lines available externally, the upper 8 of these registers are truncated; however, the upper byte is supported for reads and writes for compatibility with future expanded address capabilities. The upper 8 bits will also be incremented if necessary.

The memory address register (MAR) contents are used whenever the DMAC is executing a bus cycle to fetch or store an operand part in memory. Likewise, the device address register (DAR) contents are used when the DMAC is executing a bus cycle to transfer an operand part to or from a peripheral device during a dual-address transfer. The base address register (BAR) contents are used when the DMAC is performing table accesses in the chained modes of operation. The BAR is used by the DMAC in the continue mode of operation to hold the address to be transferred to the MAR in response to a continue operation.

The 4-bit function code registers (MFCR, DFCR, and BFCR) contain function code values that are used by the DMAC in conjunction with the three address registers during a DMA bus cycle. The address space value on the function code lines

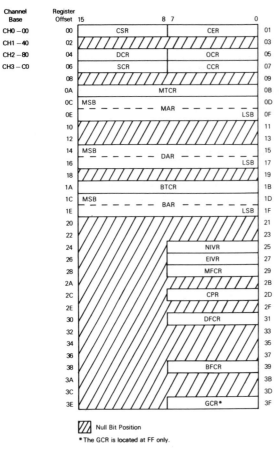

Channel Base
CH0 — 00
CH1 — 40
CH2 — 80
CH3 — C0

Null Bit Position

* The GCR is located at FF only.

REGISTER MEMORY MAP

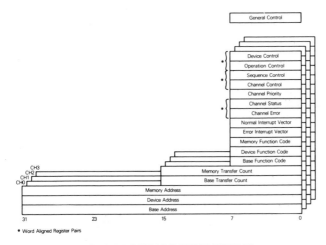

* Word Aligned Register Pairs

DMAC PROGRAMMER'S MODEL

Figure 7.24 The MC68450 DMAC memory-mapped pseudoregisters and the programming register model. (Courtesy of Motorola, Inc.)

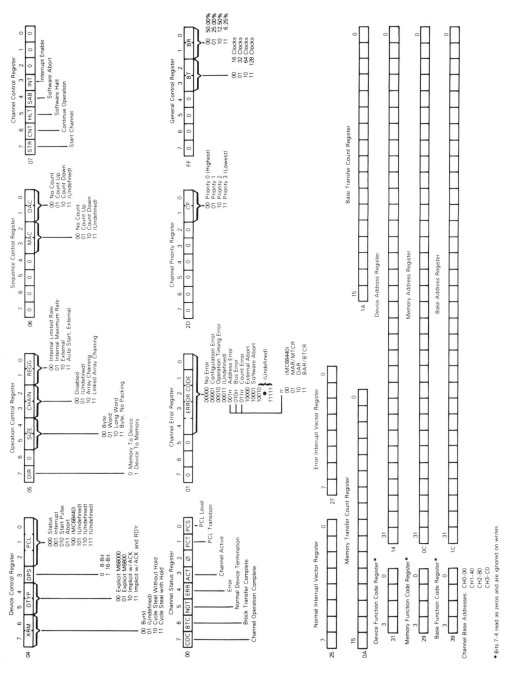

Figure 7.25 MC68450 direct memory access controller (DMAC) register specifics. (Courtesy of Motorola, Inc.)

may be used by an external memory management unit (MMU) or other memory protection device to translate the DMAC logical addresses into the proper physical addresses. The value programmed into the memory function code register (MFCR), the device function code register (DFCR), or the base function code register (BFCR) is placed on pins FC2–FC0 during a bus cycle to further qualify the address bus value, which will be the contents of the MAR, DAR, or BAR, respectively. The BFCR is used by the DMAC in the continue mode of operation to hold the function code to be transferred to the MFCR in response to a continue operation request. Note that these are 4-bit registers, with bit 3 readable and writable for future compatibility; however, it is not available as an external signal. Bits 4–7 of the function code registers will always read as zeros and are not affected by writes.

The 16-bit transfer count registers (MTCR and BTCR) are programmed with the operand count for a block transfer. The memory transfer count register (MTCR) is decremented each time the DMAC successfully transfers an operand between memory and a device until it is zero, at which time the channel will terminate the operation. The base transfer count register (BTCR) is used in the sequential array chained mode to count the number of block transfers to perform during a channel operation. The BTCR is used in the continue mode of operation to hold the operand count to be transferred to the MTCR in response to a continue operation request.

The two 8-bit interrupt vector registers (NIVR and EIVR) are used by the DMAC during interrupt acknowledge bus cycles. When the IACK signal is asserted to the DMAC, the contents of the normal interrupt vector register (NIVR) or the error interrupt vector register (EIVR) for the highest-priority channel with an interrupt pending will be placed on A8/D0–A15/D7. If the ERR bit in the corresponding channel status register is clear when IACK is asserted, the contents of the NIVR will be used; otherwise, the contents of the EIVR will be used. Both of these registers are set to the uninitialized vector number ($OF) by a reset operation.

The channel priority register (CPR) determines the priority level of a channel. When simultaneous operand transfer requests are pending in two or more channels, the highest-priority channel will be serviced first. When two or more channels are at the same priority level, a round-robin service order is used to resolve simultaneous requests. The same priority scheme is used to resolve simultaneous pending interrupts during an interrupt acknowledge cycle; however, two independent circuits within the DMAC perform the priority arbitration for operand transfer requests and interrupt requests.

The four control registers control the operation of the DMA channels by selecting various options for operand size, device characteristics, and address sequencing. The device control register (DCR) defines the characteristics of the device interface, including the device transfer request type, bus interface, port size, and the function of the PCL line. The XRM field determines the method used by the device to request operand transfers: burst, cycle-steal, or cycle-steal with hold. In the latter mode, the DMAC will retain ownership of the bus for a programmable period after an operand transfer waiting for the next request. This will usually reduce bus arbitration overhead and should result in faster device response time.

The operation control register (OCR) defines the type of operation that will be performed by a channel. The parameters programmed into this register are the direction of the transfer, the operand size to be used, whether the operation is chained, and the type of request generation to be used.

The sequence control register (SCR) controls the manner in which the memory and device address registers are incremented during transfer operations. Each address register may be programmed to remain unchanged during an operand transfer or to be incremented or decremented after each operand is successfully transferred. The value by which a register is incremented or decremented after each DMA bus cycle depends on the operand size and the device port size.

The channel control register (CCR) is used to control the operation of the channel. By writing to this register, a channel operation may be started, set to be continued, halted, and aborted. Also, the channel can be enabled to issue interrupts when an operation is completed. The STR and CNT bits are used to start the channel and to program it for continued operation. These bits can be set only by writing to them and are cleared internally by the DMAC. The HLT bit may be used to suspend the channel operation at any time by writing a 1 to it, and the operation may then be continued by clearing HLT. If it is desired to stop the channel and not continue at a later time, the SAB bit may be set at any time to abort a channel operation. The INT bit controls the generation of interrupts by the DMAC. If the INT bit is set and the COC, BTC, or PCT (with PCL programmed as a status with interrupt input) bits are set in the CSR, then the IRQ signal will be asserted. If the PCL line is not programmed as an interrupt input, the PCT bit will be set by a high-to-low transition but will not generate an interrupt. If a 1 is written to the STR bit position, the 1 will not be stored, but the CSR will reflect the status of the channel after the start operation is executed; the ACT bit in the CSR will be set if no error occurs. The STR bit always reads as 0, and writing a 0 to this position will have no effect on the channel operation.

The channel status register (CSR) reflects the status of a channel operation. The status information supplied indicates whether the channel is active or complete, whether an error has occurred, and whether or not the PCL signal has been asserted during the operation.

The channel error register (CER) indicates the cause of the first error that has occurred since the ERR bit in the channel status register was last cleared. When the ERR bit in the CSR is set, bits 0–4 indicate the type of error that occurred.

The general control register (GCR) is a global register that may affect the operation of both channels. If a channel is programmed for internal limited-rate request generation, the GCR is used to determine the time constants for the limited-rate timing. If a channel is programmed for cycle-steal with hold-request generation, the DMAC will retain ownership of the bus until the end of the next full sample period after an operand transfer is completed.

The instruction execution portions of the MC68450 DMAC can service either of two "independent" DMA channels but only one at any one instant. Each channel has the ability to execute channel programs (task blocks). In addition, a channel may be idle. As shown in Figures 7.24 and 7.25 each channel has its own private set of registers and associated control logic that govern channel operation during DMA block data transfers. Peripheral device transfer timing control (synchronized transfer) allows the channel to wait for a signal on the DMA request line before performing the next fetch-and-store sequence of the data block transfer. Between DMA data fetch and data store, the data will be within the MC68450 DMAC.

Both channels can be active concurrently, but only one can actually transmit a datum at a time. In technical terminology, each channel can be

> *Active awake:* executing an instruction or transmitting a datum.
> *Active asleep:* waiting for access to the channel control unit or to a data bus.
> *Inactive asleep:* idle and available for assignment.

Only one channel at a time may be *active awake*. During this period, the other channels may be *active asleep* or *inactive asleep*. A little thought could convince you that if one channel is active asleep, one other should be active awake, but this may not be true, as the needed bus may be currently in use by the MC680XY CPU. On the other hand, both channels may be inactive asleep; that is, all channels may be idle and available for work assignment.

At the finish of each IOP internal cycle, the channel control unit assigns the next internal cycle on the following basis:

1. An inactive asleep channel does not receive a cycle. If all channels are inactive asleep, the next internal cycle does nothing except consume time.
2. If only one channel is active and it is awake, it will be assigned the internal cycle.
3. If all channels are active asleep, the next internal cycle does nothing but consume time. This can happen if all channels need the system bus and it is in use by the MC680XY CPU or by another processor.
4. If one channel is active awake and the other channels are active asleep and not blocked by nonavailability of the system bus due to use by the MC680XY CPU, the next internal cycle will be assigned to another channel if it is involved in an activity of equal or higher priority. Otherwise, the active awake channel will be given the next internal cycle. Note that this rule can result in a flip-flop of cycles between channels executing activities of equal priority with no resource blocking conditions.

When a DMA block data transfer terminates for any reason, the channel will execute an internal program to terminate the channel in an orderly manner, allowing correct channel resumption.

DMA/PROGRAM SYNCHRONIZATION

As was mentioned in Chapter 6, a program employing a DMA channel to input or output data (or perhaps to move data within memory) can continue the execution of its non-I/O instructions quite independently of the DMA transfer. It is thus possible for program execution in the MC680XY to get "ahead" of the DMA transfer and use the contents of a memory location as "data" before the DMA controller has delivered the data to that memory location—or, in the case of a DMA output, to change the contents of a memory location to a new value before the DMA controller has output the "data" from that memory location. Either situation would result in incorrect program action and would be disastrous. The program designer must be aware of these possibilities and must insert "wait for DMA completion signal" instructions at appropriate places in the program. Compilers for languages such as FORTRAN must generate these synchronization "waits" where needed. You will recall that the generic name for this situation of independently executing interdependent procedures is *co-routines*. We will examine this concept in some depth, as synchronization of cooperating co-routines is vital to DMA input/output and fundamental to operating systems.

A Process

It is constructive to consider the concept of a process when discussing co-routines. *A process is a program in execution.* The current state of a process is a "snapshot" of all of the contents of its memory locations and registers. The state of a process changes over time as each instruction is executed. In an environment involving co-routines—and this involves any program in an interrupt environment—a program can be viewed as a nonempty set of processes that are activated, suspended, resumed, and terminated during the execution of the program.

An *active process* has one or more of its instructions executed and has one or more of its instructions yet to be executed. An active process is *awake* if its instructions are currently being executed; otherwise, an active process is *asleep*. An *inactive process* is *asleep* or *terminated*. An *asleep inactive process* may be activated only by an awake active process explicitly *awakening* it. An *asleep active process* may be awakened by an event or interrupt. The possible conditions of the process P can be summarized as a process that has started execution:

1. Active
   a. Awake: P's instructions are currently being executed.
   b. Asleep: Instructions of some other process are currently being executed and P is awaiting wakeup via an interrupt or event.
2. Inactive
   a. Asleep: Instructions of some other process are currently being executed and P cannot be awakened by an interrupt. P can be activated only by another process, such as the operating system, explicitly awakening it.
   b. Terminated: P is completely finished.

Figure 7.26 should be helpful in conceptualizing this scheme.

Concurrency

To achieve efficient use of computational system resources, computation and input/output should be overlapped and should occur simultaneously via co-routines whenever feasible. The program roughly diagrammed in Figure 7.26 does this. The typical program is often of the general form:

1. Initialize
2. Read
3. Calculate
4. Print
5. If more data, then repeat from 2; else, stop.

If these steps must all be accomplished in strict sequential order, an unnecessarily inefficient use of available resources will result. The situation illustrated in Figure 7.26 is much better. However, in many cases involving interactive computing with a one-user (uniprogramming) microcomputer, the efficient use of the time available to the computational system is of minor importance compared to the psychologically satisfying use of the human user's time. In this common situation with single-user microcomputers, the strictly sequential order of execution illustrated above may be the most satisfactory plan for terminal I/O with DMA overlap execution for disk data being utilized for preexisting input data and for SPOOLing summary data to the printer after execution is complete (SPOOL = simultaneous process/output on line).

   In some realistic situations with multiuser high-ability microprocessor systems, such as are easily possible with the MC680XY, all of the data will be systems-resident before the program is initiated. One possible situation will illustrate this not-so-rare situation: Consider a microcomputer system accepting inventory changes (materials bought and sold) from several stores after closing each day. After all the data from each store are transferred, the microcomputer will load and execute an inventory file update and materials-ordering program. Input will consist of the old inventory file, the transaction files from each store, and the file of materials already ordered. Output will consist of a new (updated) inventory file, a stack of materials orders, and a new (updated) materials-ordered file. We would expect, and therefore will assume, that this microcomputer system would be under the control of an operating system with an adequate concurrent process (co-routine) facility to allow fairly adequate simultaneous use of computational resources. It should also be noted that this example is very similar to the traditional "batch programming mode" of punched card/line printer maxi- and minicomputers.

   During the period when output for the previous program is being SPOOLed to the printer from disk, we would expect the operating system also to be loading our example program and filling double-input buffers from the input sources. Thus,

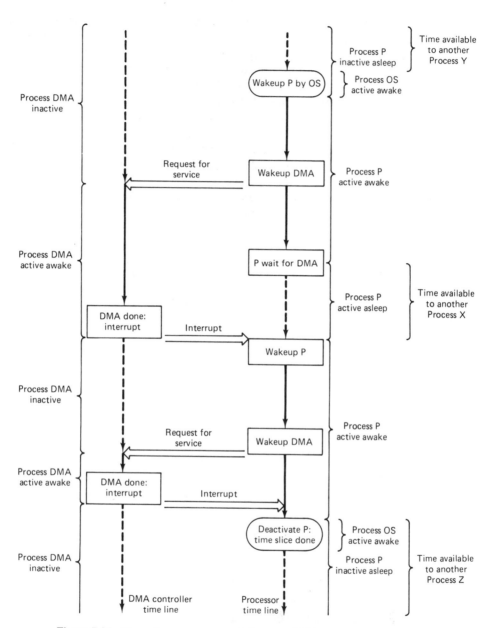

Figure 7.26 Co-routine process control diagram of DMA processor cooperation. (From G. W. Gorsline, *16-Bit Modern Microcomputers: The Intel 18086 Family,* © 1985, p. 264. Reprinted by permission of Prentice-Hall, Inc., Englewood Cliffs, NJ.)

when our program starts execution, its initial input is already in buffers in systems memory and no input time is expended. Anytime one of the input buffers is exhausted via MOVEs by our program (pseudoinputs from buffers), the program will switch to the other buffer of the double-buffer pair for each device and the operating system will simultaneously invoke DMA to refill the empty buffer. The program never performs physical input but only MOVEs input data from buffers kept full by the operating system. Any output is similarly MOVEd to one of the double output buffers for each file. When one output buffer becomes full, the program will switch to the other buffer of the double-buffer pair for each device and the operating system will simultaneously invoke DMA to empty the full buffer to the disk output files—one of which is the printer SPOOL file, which will be time-overlap-printed during the loading/execution of the subsequent program. Figure 7.27 and 7.28 may be helpful in understanding this concept.

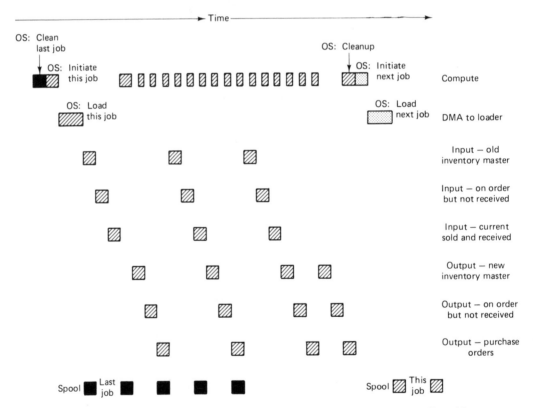

Figure 7.27   Resource utilization of an I/O-bound program using three input files with cooperating processes for DMA I/O with double-buffered prefetch/postput. (From G. W. Gorsline, *16-Bit Modern Microcomputers: The Intel 18086 Family,* © 1985, p. 266. Reprinted by permission of Prentice-Hall, Inc., Englewood Cliffs, NJ.)

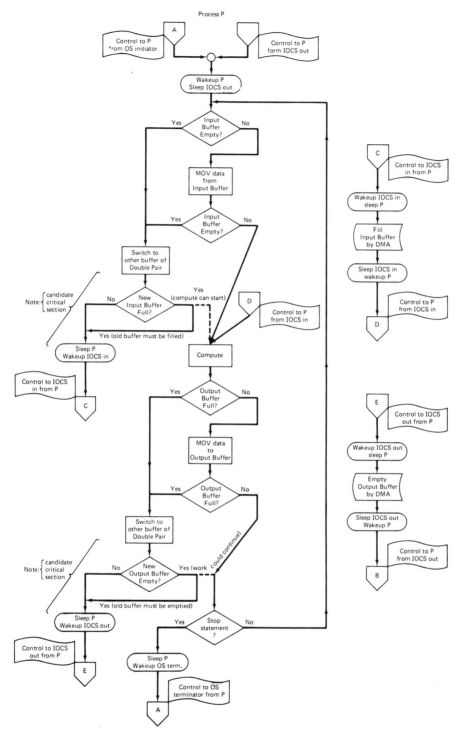

Figure 7.28 Logic control diagram of cooperating processes to accomplish the program execution timing shown in Figure 7.27. Some minor simplification is included; for example, I/O error interrupts effects are ignored. One assumption is that one DMA block will fill/empty a complete buffer. Also, one "shot" of compute uses/fills an entire buffer. (From G. W. Gorsline, *16-Bit Modern Microcomputers: The Intel 18086 Family,* © 1985, p. 267. Reprinted by permission of Prentice-Hall, Inc., Englewood Cliffs, NJ.)

335

Critical sections.   The scheme shown in Figure 7.28 for suspending process P contains several important timing-dependent sequences of instructions. Examining Figure 7.28, note the labeled critical section on the left associated with input. Suppose that the new input buffer is not full; therefore, process P should immediately invoke process "IOCS in" and put itself to sleep. If this sequence of instructions is interrupted in any manner that does not allow return to that exact point with none of the control variables changed, there will be a real danger (a nonzero probability) that process P and process "IOCS in" will both be in the sleep state, with each waiting for the other to awaken it—and because each is asleep, it cannot do anything, including awakening the other. Thus, a *deadlock* might exist. Two processes are deadlocked if neither can continue until the other continues. A critical section encompasses that contiguous sequential group of instructions that cannot be separated in execution lest a deadlock result. To avoid timing-dependent errors, including deadlocks, a critical section must be allowed to execute to completion with no intervening instructions from the other process. The student is asked to determine under which conditions the two candidate critical sections noted in Figure 7.28 are really critical sections and when they are not critical sections. Implementation details and conditions can determine if a candidate critical code section is a truly critical section and must be individually executed without interruption. Thus, general rules for detecting critical sections are not particularly helpful.

Semaphore manipulation.   The TAS (test and set) instruction is used primarily with a semaphore variable to control access to a memory data area shared between two or more co-routines that may be executing simultaneously in one or more processors. The universally accepted assumption is made that if a shared data area is currently being used by one processor, then an area access control variable—a *semaphore*—will have a nonzero value; if the shared data area is not currently being used, then the semaphore will have a zero value. It is absoutely essential that the process of testing the semaphore and setting it to a nonzero value be accomplished as a single nondivisible action, lest a false indication of the semaphore value be given. Consider what could happen if this nondivisibility were not true: Process A wishes to access the commonly held (shared) data, so it tests the semaphore and finds that it is zero. Before it can set the semaphore to nonzero, Process B (also wishing to access the shared data) tests the semaphore and finds that it is zero. They both set the semaphore to nonzero and both blithely use the shared data at the same time—resulting in all sorts of unexpected and extremely undesirable happenings, such as using "data" before they were input, and the like. For this reason, instructions that are designed to examine and manipulate semaphores are designed to be *indivisible*. In the MC680XY processor family, this implies the use of a read-modify-write memory cycle during the execution of the TAS instruction:

```
TAS  EA    ; byte-sized operand in data alterable area.
```

Two actions always result:

1.   IF <bit-7 = 0>

> THEN SET Z (zero) bit of status register = 1
> SET N (negative) bit of status register = 0

> ELSE SET Z (zero) bit of status register = 0
> SET N (negative) bit of status register = 1

2.   SET bit-7 of operand = 1

(The instruction format is shown later, in Figure 7.30.) A routine wishing to access a shared data area whose access is controlled by the semaphore named SEMFR could employ the following code:

```
TRY_SEM:    TAS     SEMFR
            BNE     TRY_SEM
GOT_AREA:    .          .
             .          .
             .          .
```

Note that it is not necessary to test both the Z and N bits of the status register, as their setting as a result of the TAS instruction is mutually exclusive.

Our example will emphasize the timing of a data buffer usage situation where channel 1 of the MC68450 is reading data from a device and filling the input buffer; an applications program of the MC680XY CPU is obtaining these data from the input buffer, manipulating the data, and placing the results in an output buffer, whereupon channel 2 of the MC68450 will write the contents of the output buffer to a device. The entire process will be repeated many times. It is important that the filling of a buffer be completed before the use of that buffer starts.

In other words, the input process, the calculation process, and the output process are executing on independent processors but accessing common data areas in a predetermined order. If the input buffer is accessed for data to use in calculation before it is input, the results will be wrong; if the output buffer is output before calculation is complete and placed in the output buffer, the results will be wrong. Therefore, the three processes executing in the three independent processors must be interleaved in a very specific order and not allowed to proceed prematurely. Note that our example requires time-synchronized access to shared data. Thus, it is somewhat natural to provide a variable that controls such access. By accepted convention, such a variable is termed a *semaphore*. In terms of the TAS instruction, the first operand—a byte location in common memory—is the shared-data-area access-control semaphore. When the semaphore has a value of zero, access is allowed; when the semaphore has a nonzero value, access is prohibited. Figure 7.29 illustrates the program schema.

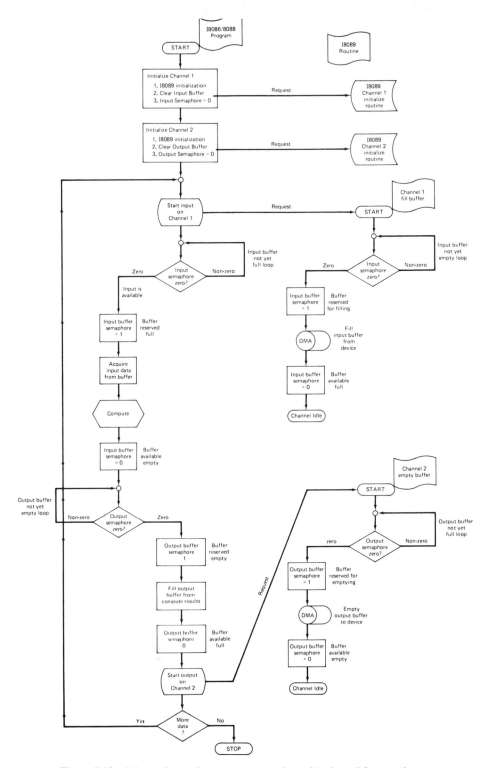

Figure 7.29 Schema for applications program/channel 1/channel 2 co-routines to use shared input buffer and shared output buffer using (From G. W. Gorsline, *16-Bit Modern Microcomputers: The Intel 18086 Family*, © 1985, p. 289. Reprinted by permission of Prentice-Hall, Inc., Englewood Cliffs, NJ.)

Although the test-and-set (TAS) instruction that is available on the entire MC680XY family of processors is adequate for all situations, it sometimes requires somewhat convoluted program code to solve some complicated data area access control problems when several physical processors are involved. This is because the semaphore is, in effect, a binary semaphore—it is either ON or OFF. The MC68020 processor also furnishes two additional semaphore instructions—the compare-and-swap instructions CAS and CAS2. For CAS:

```
        B
CAS.W        CMPR,UPDTR,EA        ; CMPR = data register to be compared;
    L                             ; UPDTR = data register with update value;
                                  ; EA = effective address of semaphore
```

the action is

compare <[EA] − [CMPR]> and SET status register (SR) bits:

>   IF <Z set>

>>   THEN [UPDTR] ⟶ [EA]

>>   ELSE [EA] ⟶ [CMPR]

The instruction format is shown in Figure 7.30. The other more complicated instruction is

```
CAS2.W      CMPR1:CMPR2,UPDTR1:UPDTR2,RN1:RN2
    L
```

where RN = address or data register containing the address of the semaphore. Again, the action is

compare <[RN1] − [CMPR1]> and SET status register (SR) bits:

>   IF <Z set>

>>   THEN compare <[RN2] − [CMPR2]> and SET SR bits:

>>>   IF <Z set>

>>>>   THEN   [UPDTR1] ⟶ [RN1]
>>>>   [UPDTR2] ⟶ [RN2]

>>>>   ELSE NULL

>>>   ELSE   [RN1] ⟶ [CMPR1]
>>>   [RN2] ⟶ [CMPR2]

Test and Set Semaphore (byte only)

TAS < ea >

										mode			register		
15	14	13	12	11	10	9	8	7	6	5	4	3	2	1	0
0	1	0	0	1	0	1	0	1	1	Effective Address					

Action:
1. Test byte operand and set status register bits:
   N   Set if the most significant bit of of the operand was set. Cleared otherwise
   Z   Set if the operand was zero. Cleared otherwise
   V   Always cleared
   C   Always cleared
   X   Not affected
2. Set operand value = 10,000,000 = 80 hex.

Compare and Swap Semaphore (MC 68020 only)

CAS Dc, Du, < ea > (byte, word, long word)

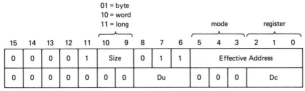

01 = byte
10 = word
11 = long

										mode			register		
15	14	13	12	11	10	9	8	7	6	5	4	3	2	1	0
0	0	0	0	1	Size		0	1	1	Effective Address					
0	0	0	0	0	0	0	Du			0	0	0	Dc		

Action:
Compare [EA] − [Dc] and set status register bits:
N   Set if the result is negative; cleared otherwise
Z   Set if the result is zero; cleared otherwise
V   Set if an overflow is generated; cleared otherwise
C   Set if a carry is generated; cleared otherwise
X   Not affected
IF   Z = 1
    THEN [Du] → [EA]
    ELSE [EA] → [Dc]

CAS2 Dc1 : Dc2, Du1 : Du2, (Rn1) : (Rn2) (word, long word)

10 = word
11 = long

15	14	13	12	11	10	9	8	7		5	4	3	2	1	0
0	0	0	0	1	Size		0	1	1	1	1	1	1	0	0
D/A1	Rn1			0	0	0	Du1			0	0	0	Dc1		
D/A2	Rn2			0	0	0	Du2			0	0	0	Dc2		

Action:
Compare [Memory Indirect Through Rn1] − [Dc1] and set SR bits
IF Z = 1
    THEN Compare [Memory Indirect Through Rn2] − [Dc2]
        and set SR bits
        IF Z = 1
            THEN Du1 → Memory (Rn1)
                 Du2 → Memory (Rn2)
            ELSE Null
    ELSE Memory (Rn1) → Dc1
         Memory (Rn2) → Dc2
D/A1, D/A2 fields — Specify whether Rn1 and Rn2 reference data or address registers, respectively.
    0 — The corresponding register is a data register.
    1 — The corresponding register is an address register.
Rn1, Rn2 fields — Specify the numbers of the registers which contain the address of the first and second tested operands, respectively. If the operands overlap in memory, the results of any memory update are undefined.
Du1, Du2 fields — Specify the data registers which hold the update values to be written to the first and second memory operand locations if the comparison is successful.
Dc1, Dc2 fields — Specify the data registers which contain the test values to be compared against the first and second memory operands, respectively. If Dc1 and Dc2 specify the same data register and the comparison fails, the data register is loaded from the first memory operand.

Figure 7.30   Instruction formats for semaphore manipulation instructions.

The CAS instruction allows secure updating of system counters, history information, and globally shared pointers. Security is provided in single-processor systems, multitasking environments, and in multiprocessor environments. In a single-processor system, the noninterruptable update operation provides security in an interrupt-driven environment; in a multiprocessor environment, the indivisible bus cycle operation provides the security mechanism. For example, suppose that location SYS_CNTR contains a count of the number of times a particular operation has been done and that this operation may be done by any process or any processor in the system. Then the following sequence guarantees that SYS_CNTR is correctly incremented:

```
              MOVE.W   SYS_CNTR,D0      ; get the old value of the counter
INC_LOOP:     MOVE.W   D0,D1            ; make a copy of it
              ADDQ.W   #1,D1            ; and increment it
              CAS.W    D0,D1,SYS_CNTR   ; if counter value is still the same,
                                        ;   update it
              BNE      INC_LOOP         ; if not, try again
```

The CAS and CAS2 instructions together allow safe operations in manipulation of system stacks and system queues. A stack can be managed last-in/first-out; thus, only a single location HEAD need be controlled. If the stack is empty, HEAD contains the NULL pointer (0). The following sequence illustrates the code for insertion and deletion from such a stack. Figure 7.31a and b illustrates the insertion and deletion, respectively.

```
SINSERT:                               ; allocate new entry, addr in A1
              MOVE.L   HEAD,D0          ; move head pointer value to D0
SILOOP:       MOVE.L   D0,(NEXT,A1)     ; establish fwd link in new entry
              MOVE.L   A1,D1            ; move new entry ptr value to D1
              CAS.L    D0,D1,HEAD       ; if we still point to top of stack,
                                        ;   update the head ptr
              BNE      SILOOP           ; if not, try again


SDELETE:                               ; load addr of head ptr into A0
              LEA      HEAD,A0          ; load addr of head ptr into A0
              MOVE.L   (A0),D0          ; move value of head ptr into D0
SDLOOP:       TST.L    D0               ; check for null head ptr
              BEQ      SDEMPTY          ; if empty, nothing to delete
              LEA      (NEXT,D0),A1     ; load addr of fwd link into A1
              MOVE.L   (A1),D1          ; put fwd link value in D1
              CAS2.L   D0:D1,D1:D1,(A0):(A1)  ; if still point to entry to be deleted,
                                        ;    then update head and fwd ptrs
              BNE      SDLOOP           ; if not, try again
SDEMPTY:                               ; successful deletion, addr of de-
                                        ;    leted entry in D0 (may be null)
```

A. Linked List Insertion

Before Inserting an Element:

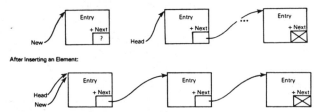

After Inserting an Element:

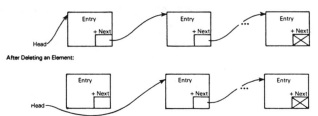

B. Linked List Deletion

Before Deleting an Element:

After Deleting an Element:

C. Doubly Linked List Insertion

Before Inserting New Entry:

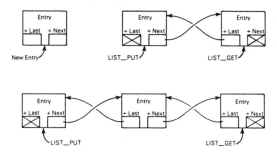

D. Doubly Linked List Deletion

Before Deleting Entry:

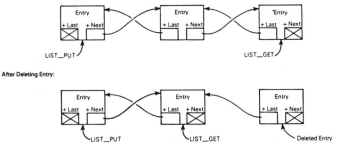

After Deleting Entry:

Figure 7.31 The process of linked list data manipulation. (Courtesy of Motorola, Inc.)

The CAS2 instruction may be used to maintain a first-in/first-out doubly linked list safely. Such a linked list needs two controlled locations, LIST_PUT and LIST_GET, which point to the last element inserted in the list and the next to be removed, respectively. If the list is empty, both pointers are NULL (0). The following sequence illustrates the insertion and deletion operations in such a linked list. Figure 7.31c and d illustrates the insertion and deletion from a doubly linked list.

```
DINSERT:                                    ; (allocate new list entry, load
                                            ;    addr into A2)
          LEA      LIST_PUT,A0              ; load addr of head ptr into A0
          LEA      LIST_GET,A1              ; load addr of tail ptr into A1
          MOVE.L   A2,D2                    ; load new entry ptr into D2
          MOVE.L   (A0),D0                  ; load ptr to head entry into D0
DILOOP:   TST.L    D0                       ; is head ptr null (0 entries in list)?
          BEQ      DIEMPTY                  ; if so, we need only to establish
                                            ;    ptrs
          MOVE.L   D0,(NEXT,A2)             ; put head ptr into fwd ptr of new
                                            ;    entry
          CLR.L    D1                       ; put null ptr value in D1
          MOVE.L   D1,(LAST,A2)             ; put null ptr in bkwd ptr of new
                                            ;    entry
          LEA      (LAST,D0),A1             ; load bkwd ptr of old head entry
                                            ;    into A1
          CAS2.L   D0:D1,D2:D0,(A0):(A1)    ; if we still point to old head entry,
                                            ;    update pointers
          BNE      DILOOP                   ; if not, try again
          BRA      DIDONE
DIEMPTY:  MOVE.L   D0,(NEXT,A2)             ; put null ptr in fwd ptr of new entry
          MOVE.L   D0,(LAST,A2)             ; put null ptr in bkwd ptr of new
                                            ;    entry
          CASE2.L  D0:D0,D2:D2,(A0):(A1)    ; if we still have no entries, set both
                                            ;    pointers to this entry
          BNE      DILOOP                   ; if not, try again
DIDONE:                                     ; successful list entry insertion

DDELETE:
          LEA      LIST_PUT,A0              ; get addr of head ptr in A0
          LEA      LIST_GET,A1              ; get addr of tail ptr in A1
DDLOOP:   MOVE.L   (A1),D1                  ; move tail ptr into D1
          BEQ      DDDONE                   ; if no list, quit
          MOVE.L   (LAST,D1),D2             ; put bkwd ptr in D2
          BEQ      DDEMPTY                  ; if only one element, update ptrs
          LEA      (NEXT,D2),A2             ; put addr of fwd ptr in A2
          CLR.L    D0                       ; put null ptr value in D0
```

```
                 CAS2.L   D1:D1,D2:D0,(A1):(A2)   ; if both ptrs still point to this entry,
                                                  ;   update them
                 BNE      DDLOOP                  ; if not, try again
                 BRA      DDDONE
     DDEMPTY:    CAS2.L   D1:D1,D2:D2:(A1):(A0)   ; if still first entry, set head and tail
                                                  ;   ptrs to null
                 BNE      DDLOOP                  ; if not, try again
     DDDONE:                                      ; successful entry deletion, addr of
                                                  ;   deleted entry in D1 (may be null)
```

INTELLIGENT PERIPHERAL CONTROLLER

The MC68120 (Figure 7.32) is an intelligent peripheral controller (IPC) that provides an interface between an MC680XY processor and the final peripheral device through the system bus and control lines. In the context of computational devices, the term *intelligent* almost always means programmable—that is, able to react to service requests in a preplanned (programmed) manner. Thus, all programmable processors, including the MC680XY family, are intelligent. It must be noted that the term *artificial intelligence* (AI) implies a particular approach to problem solving using a programmable processor. An intelligent peripheral controller is definitely not in the realm of AI, although most AI applications would make use of an IPC.

The MC68120 is an 8-bit IPC that can be configured to function in a wide variety of applications. This flexibility is provided by its ability to be hardware-programmed into eight different operating modes. These operating modes allow the IPC to operate on its local bus and communicate with an external system bus through the internal dual-ported RAM.

The standard MC68120 comes preprogrammed with a monitor in the ROM. Custom programs are placed in ROM by special order. Note that the IPC is not user-programmable but that programs for the IPC are permanently encoded into read-only memory (ROM) during chip fabrication. This means that system implementors must specify the programs when they order the IPC.

The IPC contains an enhanced MC6800 MPU, with additional capabilities and greater throughput. It is upward-source and object-code compatible with the MC6800 and directly compatible with the MC6801. The programming model is depicted in Figure 7.33, where accumulator D is a concatenation of accumulators A and B. The following is a summary of the features:

2048 bytes of ROM

128 bytes of dual-ported RAM

Multiple operation modes, ranging from single-chip to expanded, with 64K-byte address space

Six shared semaphore registers

21 parallel I/O lines and 2 handshake lines

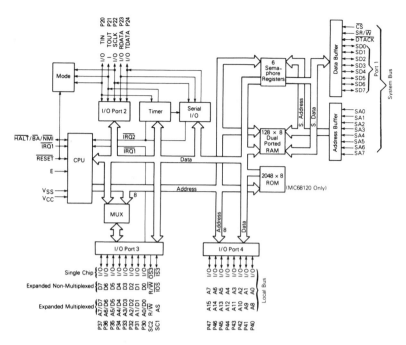

INTELLIGENT PERIPHERAL CONTROLLER

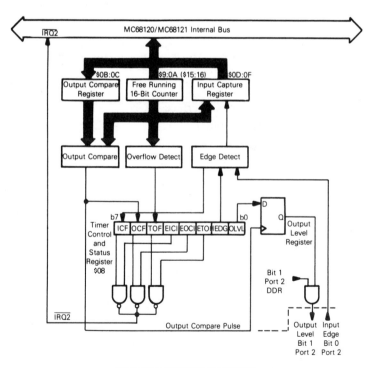

PROGRAMMABLE TIMER

Figure 7.32 The MC68120 intelligent peripheral controller (IPC). (Courtesy of Motorola, Inc.)

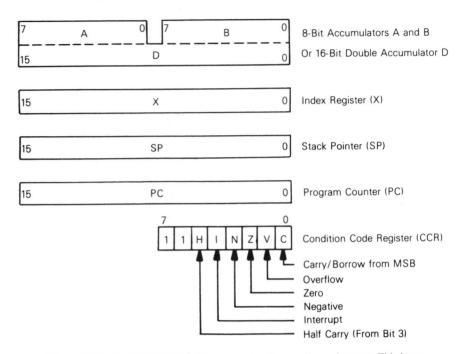

Figure 7.33   The MC68120 intelligent peripheral controller register set. This is an exact duplicate of the 8-bit MC6801 microprocessor register set and has the same instruction set. (Courtesy of Motorola, Inc.)

Serial communications interface (SCI)

16-bit three-function timer

8-bit CPU and internal bus

Halt/bus available capability control

The dual-ported RAM provides a vehicle for devices on two separate buses to exchange data without directly affecting the devices on the other bus. The dual-ported RAM is accessible from the MC68120 CPU and is accessible synchronously or asynchronously to the system bus through Port 1. Semaphore registers are provided as a software tool to arbitrate shared resources, such as the dual-ported RAM. The semaphore registers are accessible from both buses in the same way each bus accesses the dual-ported RAM.

The remaining ports (2, 3, and 4) are I/O ports, each controlled by its own data direction register. The CPU has direct access to each port through its data register. Port 2 is a 5-bit port, which may be configured for I/O or for the use of the on-chip timer and serial communications interface (SCI). Ports 3 and 4 may be used as 16 bits of I/O or may form a local address and data bus, with control lines allowing communications with external memory and peripherals.

The IPC provides eight different operating modes, which are selectable by hardware programming. As shown in Figure 7.34, the eight modes of the IPC can be grouped into three fundamental modes, which refer to the type of bus each mode supports: single-chip, expanded nonmultiplexed, and expanded multiplexed.

In the single-chip modes (modes 4 and 7), three of the four IPC ports are configured as parallel input/output data ports. The IPC functions as a complete mi-

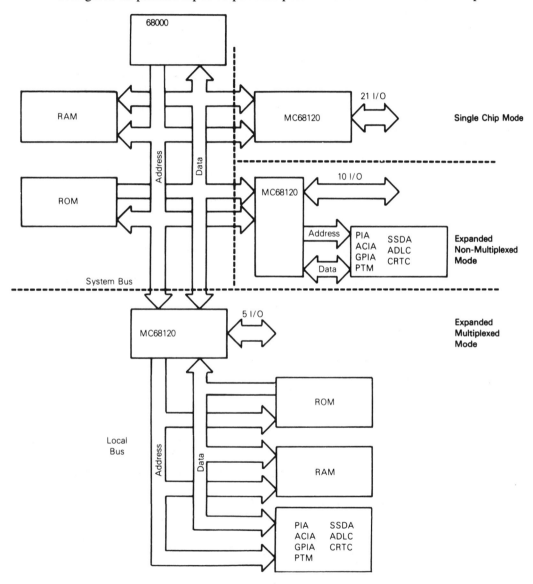

Figure 7.34 The eight operating modes of the MC68120 IPC are grouped into three fundamental modes. (Courtesy of Motorola, Inc.)

crocomputer in these two modes without external address or data buses. A maximum of 21 I/O lines and two Port 3 control lines are provided. Port 4 functions as an 8-bit I/O port, where each line is configured by the Port 4 data direction register.

A modest amount of external memory space is provided in the expanded non-multiplexed mode (mode 5) while retaining significant on-chip resources. Port 3 functions as an 8-bit bidirectional data bus, and Port 4 is configured as an input data port. Any combination of address lines A0–A7 may be provided while retaining the remainder as input data lines. Any combination of the eight least-significant address lines may be obtained by writing to the Port 4 data direction register. The IPC interfaces directly with MC68000 family parts and can access 256 bytes of external address space at addresses $100 through $1FF. This provides an address decode of external memory ($100–$1FF) and may be used as an address or chip select line. In this mode, Port 4 is configured from RESET as an 8-bit input port, where the data direction register can be written, to provide any or all of address lines A0–A7. Internal pullup resistors are intended to pull the lines high until the data direction register is configured.

In the expanded multiplexed modes (modes 0, 1, 2, 3, 6), the IPC has the ability to access a 64K-byte memory space. Port 3 functions as a time-multiplexed address/data bus, with the address valid on the negative edge of address strobe (AS) and the data bus valid while E is high. In modes 0–3, Port 4 provides address lines A8–A15. However, in mode 6, Port 4 can provide any subset of A8–A15 while retaining the remainder as input lines. Writing 1's to the desired bits in the data direction register (DDR) will output the corresponding address lines, while the remaining bits will remain inputs (as configured from RESET or from 0's written to the DDR). Internal pullup resistors are provided to pull Port 4 lines high until software configures the port. Initialization of Port 4 to mode 6 must be done to obtain any upper address lines externally.

The dual-ported RAM may be accessed from both the MC68120 CPU and the external system bus. The six semaphore registers are tools provided for the programmer's use in arbitrating simultaneous access of the same resource. For the internal CPU, the dual-ported RAM is located at addresses from $0080 through $00FF in all modes except 3 and 4. In mode 3, the dual-ported RAM has been relocated in high memory from $C080 through $C0FF, thus allowing use of direct addressing mode on external memory/peripherals. Note that no direct addressing of internal RAM is possible in mode 3. In mode 4, the internal RAM is not fully decoded and appears in locations $XX80 through $XXFF. From the external system bus, the dual-ported RAM is found in locations % 10000000–11111111.

The semaphore registers allow arbitration between shared resources, which may be part or all of the dual-port RAM or a peripheral. The semaphore registers may also be used to indicate that nonreentrant code is in use or that a task is in process or is complete. To prevent the writing or reading of erroneous data from the dual-ported RAM, all simultaneous accesses involving a write to the dual-ported RAM should be avoided. The responsibility for mutual exclusion resides in software. The semaphore registers are a convenient means for the software to control simultaneous accesses involving a write to the dual-ported RAM. Each of the six semaphore registers consist of a semaphore bit (SEM, bit 7) and an ownership bit (OWN, bit 6). The remaining 6 bits (b0–b5) will read all zeros. Basically, the semaphore bit is cleared when written and set when read, during a single processor access. The data written is disregarded and the information obtained from the read may be interpreted as 0 = resource available, 1 = resource not available. Thus, any write to a semaphore clears the semaphore bit and makes the associated resource "available."

An access in which both the IPC and the system processor attempt to read or write the same semaphore register simultaneously is a contested access. During a contested access, the hardware decides which processor reads a clear semaphore bit and which reads a set semaphore bit. The IPC always reads the actual semaphore bit; the system processor reads the semaphore bit in all cases except the simultaneous read of a clear semaphore bit. This arbitration during a simultaneous read ensures that only one processor reads a clear bit and therefore controls the resource; that processor is arbitrarily the IPC.

The ownership bit is a read-only bit that indicates which processor sets the semaphore bit. If the semaphore bit is set, the ownership bit indicates which processor set it. If the semaphore bit is not set, the ownership bit indicates which processor last set the semaphore bit: OWN = 0, the other processor set SEM; OWN = 1, this processor set SEM.

Port 1 is a mode-independent 8-bit data port that permits the external system bus to access the dual-ported RAM and semaphore registers either asynchronously or synchronously with respect to the E clock. In addition to the eight data lines (SD0–SD7); eight address lines (SA0–SA7) and three control lines (SR/W, CS, DTACK) are used to access the dual-ported RAM and semaphore registers.

Port 2 is a mode-independent 5-bit I/O port in which each line is configured by its data direction register. During reset, all lines are configured as inputs. Inputs on the least-significant three bits (P20, P21, and P22) determine the operating mode, which is latched into the program control register. Port 2 also provides an interface for the serial communications interface and timer. Bit 1, if configured as an output, is dedicated to the timer output compare function and cannot be used to provide output from the Port 2 data register.

Port 3 can be configured as an I/O port, a bidirectional 8-bit data bus, or a multiplexed address/data bus, depending upon the operating mode.

Port 4 is configured as an 8-bit I/O port, as an address output port, or as a data input port, depending on the operating mode.

Interrupts

The IPC supports two types of interrupt requests: maskable and nonmaskable. A nonmaskable interrupt (NMI) is always recognized and acted upon at the completion of the current instruction. Maskable interrupts are controlled by the condition code register I bit and by individual enable bits. The I bit controls all maskable interrupts.

There are two types of maskable interrupts: IRQ1 and IRQ2. The programmable timer and the serial communications interface use an internal IRQ2 interrupt line, as shown in the block diagram of the IPC. External devices (and IS3) use IRQ1. An IRQ1 interrupt is serviced before an IRQ2 interrupt if both are pending.

All IRQ2 interrupts use hardware-prioritized vectors. The single SCI interrupt and three timer interrupts are serviced in a prioritized order in which each is vectored to a separate location. The program counter, index register, accumulator A, accumulator B, and condition code register are pushed to the stack. The I bit is set to inhibit maskable interrupts, and a vector is fetched corresponding to the current highest priority interrupt. The vector is transferred to the program counter and instruction execution is resumed.

The programmable timer can be used to perform input waveform measurements while independently generating an output waveform. Pulse widths can vary from several microseconds to many seconds.

The timer control and status register (TCSR) is an 8-bit register of which all bits are readable and bits 0–4 can be written. The three most-significant bits provide the timer status, indicating that

1. A proper level transition has been detected, or
2. A match has been found between the free-running counter and the output compare register, or
3. The free-running counter has overflowed.

Each of the three events can generate an IRQ2 interrupt and is controlled by an individual enable bit in the TCSR.

A full-duplex asynchronous serial communications interface (SCI) is provided with two data formats and a choice of BAUD rates. The SCI transmitter and receiver are functionally independent but use the same data format and bit rate. Serial data formats include standard mark/space (NRZ) and biphase. Both formats provide one start bit, eight data bits, and one stop bit.

A programming model for the MC68120 was shown in Figure 7.33. Accumulator A can be concatenated with accumulator B and jointly are referred to as accumulator D, where A is the most significant byte. Any operation that modifies the double accumulator will also modify accumulator A and/or accumulator B. Other registers are defined as follows:

The *program counter* is a 6-bit register that always points to the next instruction.

The *stack pointer* is a 16-bit register that contains the address of the next available location in a pushdown/pullup (LIFO) queue. The stack resides in random access memory at a location specified by the software.

The *index register* is a 16-bit register that can be used to store data or to provide an address for the indexed mode of addressing.

The IPC contains two 8-bit *accumulators,* A and B, which are used to store operands and results from the arithmetic-logic unit (ALU). They can also be concatenated and then are referred to as the D (double) accumulator.

The *condition code register* records the condition of the results of an instruction and includes the following five condition bits: negative (N), zero (Z), overflow (V), carry/borrow from MSB (C), and half-carry from bit 3 (H). These bits are testable by the conditional branch instructions. Bit 4 is the interrupt mask (I bit) and inhibits all maskable interrupts when set. The two unused bits, b6 and b7, are read as ones.

Instructions

The MC68120 IPC has an instruction set that is somewhat typical for 8-bit microprocessors—after all, it is compatible with the MC6801 second generation microprocessor. As shown in Figure 7.35, the instructions can be logically partitioned into four groups:

1. Accumulator/memory operations.
2. Condition code operations.
3. Pointer operations.
4. Flow-of-control operations.

Addressing Modes

The MC68120 provides six addressing modes that can be used to reference memory:

Immediate addressing: The operand is contained in the following byte(s) of the instruction, where the number of bytes matches the size of the register. These are 2- or 3-byte instructions.

Direct addressing: The least significant byte of the operand address is contained in the second byte of the instruction, and the most significant byte is assumed to be $00. Direct addressing allows the user to access $00 through $FF using 2-byte instructions, and execution time is reduced by eliminating the additional memory access. In most applications, this 256-byte area is reserved for frequently referenced data. Note that no direct addressing of internal control registers is possible in mode 3.

Extended addressing: The second and third bytes of the instruction contain the absolute address of the operand. These are 3-byte instructions.

Indexed addressing: The unsigned offset contained in the second byte of the instructions is added with carry to the index register and used to reference memory without changing the index register. These are 2-byte instructions.

Inherent addressing: The operand(s) are registers, and no memory reference is required. These are single-byte instructions.

Accumulator and Memory Operations	MNE	Boolean Expression
Add Acmltrs	ABA	A + B → A
Add B to X	ABX	00:B + X → X
Add with Carry	ADCA	A + M + C → A
	ADCB	B + M + C → B
Add	ADDA	A + M → A
	ADDB	B + M → A
Add Double	ADDD	D + M:M + 1 → D
And	ANDA	A · M → A
	ANDB	B · M → B
Shift Left, Arithmetic	ASL	
	ASLA	
	ASLB	
Shift Left Dbl	ASLD	
Shift Right, Arithmetic	ASR	
	ASRA	
	ASRB	
Bit Test	BITA	A · M
	BITB	B · M
Compare Acmltrs	CBA	A - B
Clear	CLR	00 → M
	CLRA	00 → A
	CLRB	00 → B
Compare	CMPA	A - M
	CMPB	B - M
1's Complement	COM	$\bar{M}$ → M
	COMA	$\bar{A}$ → A
	COMB	$\bar{B}$ → B
Decimal Adj, A	DAA	Adj binary sum to BCD
Decrement	DEC	M - 1 → M
	DECA	A - 1 → A
	DECB	B - 1 → B
Exclusive OR	EORA	A ⊕ M → A
	EORB	B ⊕ M → B
Increment	INC	M + 1 → M
	INCA	A + 1 → A
	INCB	B + 1 → B
Load Acmltrs	LDAA	M → A
	LDAB	M → B
Load Double	LDD	M:M + 1 → D
Logical Shift, Left	LSL	
	LSLA	
	LSLB	
	LSLD	

Accumulator and Memory Operations	MNE	Boolean Expression
Shift Right, Logical	LSR	
	LSRA	
	LSRB	
	LSRD	
Multiply	MUL	A X B → D
2's Complement (Negate)	NEG	00 - M → M
	NEGA	00 - A → A
	NEGB	00 - B → B
No Operation	NOP	PC + 1 → PC
Inclusive OR	ORAA	A + M → A
	ORAB	B + M → B
Push Data	PSHA	A → Stack
	PSHB	B → Stack
Pull Data	PULA	Stack → A
	PULB	Stack → B
Rotate Left	ROL	
	ROLA	
	ROLB	
Rotate Right	ROR	
	RORA	
	RORB	
Subtract Acmltr	SBA	A - B → A
Subtract with Carry	SBCA	A - M - C → A
	SBCB	B - M - C → B
Store Acmltrs	STAA	A → M
	STAB	B → M
	STD	D → M:M + 1
Subtract	SUBA	A - M → A
	SUBB	B - M → B
Subtract Double	SUBD	D - M:M + 1 → D
Transfer Acmltr	TAB	A → B
	TBA	B → A
Test, Zero or Minus	TST	M - 00
	TSTA	A - 00
	TSTB	B - 00

CONDITION CODE REGISTER

Operations	Mnemonic	Boolean Operation
Clear Carry	CLC	0 → C
Clear Interrupt Mask	CLI	0 → I
Clear Overflow	CLV	0 → V
Set Carry	SEC	1 → C
Set Interrupt Mask	SEI	1 → I
Set Overflow	SEV	1 → V
Accumulator A → CCR	TAP	A → CCR
CCR → Accumulator A	TPA	CCR → A

Pointer Operations	Mnemonic	Boolean/Arithmetic Operation
Compare Index Reg	CPX	X - M : M + 1
Decrement Index Reg	DEX	X - 1 → X
Decrement Stack Pntr	DES	SP - 1 → SP
Increment Index Reg	INX	X + 1 → X
Increment Stack Pntr	INS	1 SP + 1 → SP
Load Index Reg	LDX	M → X_H, (M + 1) → X_L
Load Stack Pntr	LDS	M → SP_H, (M + 1) → SP_L
Store Index Reg	STX	X_H → M, X_L → (M + 1)
Store Stack Pntr	STS	SP_H → M, SP_L → (M + 1)
Index Reg → Stack Pntr	TXS	X - 1 → SP
Stack Pntr → Index Reg	TSX	SP + 1 → X
Add	ABX	B + X → X
Push Data	PSHX	X_L → M_{SP}, SP - 1 → SP; X_H → M_{SP}, SP - 1 → SP
Pull Data	PULX	SP + 1 → SP, M_{SP} → X_H; SP + 1 → SP, M_{SP} → X_L

Figure 7.35 The instruction set of the MC68120 IPC is identical to that of the second-generation MC6801 microprocessor. It can be partitioned into four groups: arithmetic/logic group, condition code group, pointer group, and branch group. (Courtesy of Motorola, Inc.)

Relative addressing: Relative addressing is used only for branch instructions. If the branch condition is true, the program counter is overwritten with the sum of a signed single-byte displacement in the second byte of the instruction and the current program counter. This provides a branch range of −126 to +129 bytes from the first byte of the instruction. These are 2-byte instructions.

JUMP AND BRANCH Operations	Mnemonic	Branch Test
Branch Always	BRA	None
Branch Never	BRN	None
Branch If Carry Clear	BCC	C = 0
Branch If Carry Set	BCS	C = 1
Branch If = Zero	BEQ	Z = 1
Branch If ≥ Zero	BGE	N⊕V = 0
Branch If > Zero	BGT	Z + (N⊕V) = 0
Branch If Higher	BHI	C + Z = 0
Branch If Higher or Same	BHS	C = 0
Branch If ≤ Zero	BLE	Z + (N⊕V) = 1
Branch If Carry Set	BLO	C = 1
Branch If Lower Or Same	BLS	C + Z = 1
Branch If < Zero	BLT	N⊕V = 1
Branch If Minus	BMI	N = 1
Branch If Not Equal Zero	BNE	Z = 0
Branch If Overflow Clear	BVC	V = 0
Branch If Overflow Set	BVS	V = 1
Branch If Plus	BPL	N = 0
Branch To Subroutine	BSR	See Special Operations — Figure 38
Jump	JMP	
Jump To Subroutine	JSR	
No Operation	NOP	
Return From Interrupt	RTI	See Special Operations — Figure 38
Return From Subroutine	RTS	
Software Interrupt	SWI	
Wait For Interrupt	WAI	

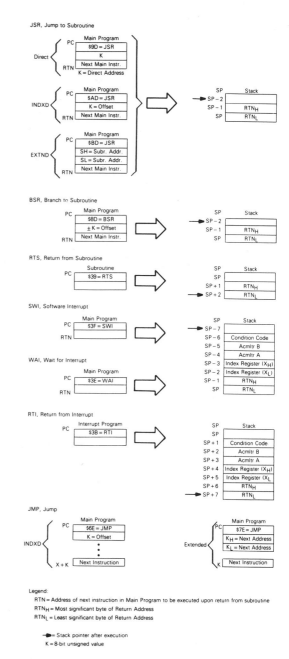

Figure 7.35 *(continued).*

EXERCISES

7.1. Design, implement, test, and document a software interrupt (TRAP n) routine that will eject a page on your printer, print your name (centered) on the first line of the new page, and then skip two lines.

7.2. Combine the concepts of the MC680XY instruction cycle given in Figure 7.17 with the two-level microprogramming/nanoprogramming instruction cycle implementation technique of Figure 2.17 by diagramming the instruction cycle for the DIV instruction:

DIV   D2,(A3)+

when a divide-by-zero condition arises and when it does not.

7.3. Design, implement, test, and document a program to simulate (act like) a jukebox. The jukebox shall have a common memory accessible by two cooperating processors: one to accept and queue record requests and the other to dequeue the requests and play them. The semaphore concept must be used and the critical sections identified. This program can be implemented in Concurrent Pascal, C, assembly language, or a combination.

8

Assemblers

In Chapter 3 we gave the following code fragment for an IF-THEN-ELSE construct in both procedural-level language code and MC680XY assembly language:

```
IF A > B                        IF:        CMP.L    D3,D5
    THEN DO;                               BGE      ELSE

                                THEN:
        -/* Some things */
        -                                  -; some things
    END;                                   -
ELSE DO;
                                           BRA      NEXT
        -                       ELSE:      -
        -/* Other things */                -
        -                                  - ; other things
    END;                                   -
NEXT:                           NEXT:
```

Although we noted in Chapter 3 that the MC680XY does not actually execute either of the foregoing versions of the program fragment, at this point it is again necessary to emphasize that all conventional computers (including the MC680XY) can execute only programs presented to them as binary machine code entities. That is, the circuits of the computer are designed and implemented to recognize, interpret, and execute operations codes expressed as bit patterns as well as operand addresses expressed as binary numbers. Thus, the code segment above would be executed in the following form:

Program/Data Location (Hex)	16-Bit Operation Code/ Operand Address in Hexadecimal	Notes
30	C685	CMP.L instruction (register-to-register)
32	6C0A	BGE instruction with displacement to 3E
34	.	
36	.	Instructions in the THEN clause
38	.	
3A	.	
3C	6006	BRA instruction with displacement to 46
3E	.	
40	.	Instructions in the ELSE clause
42	.	
44	.	
46	.	Instructions following the IF-THEN-ELSE
48	.	
4A	.	

Note that there is a one-to-many relationship between the statements of a procedural-level language (such as Pascal or PL/I) and assembly language and that the statements in a procedural-level language do not directly correspond on a one-to-one basis with the statements in the assembly language equivalent. On the other hand, there is a direct one-to-one correspondence between the statements of assembly language and the equivalent binary machine code.

It is perfectly possible to compose programs in binary machine language, even though it is tedious, error-prone, time-consuming, and an unnecessary waste of intellectual powers. Very early in this age of the computer (1950 or before), someone (probably several geniuses in many places) made the now obvious inference: Why not write a program to convert mnemonic operation code–symbolic operand name combinations to binary operations code–binary numeric operand address combinations? It was tried; it worked; and the symbolic assembler process was born. At the present point in the development of computers, an assembler seems obvious; when the idea was new, it was not obvious and was not universally accepted. Many journeymen programmers resisted the idea and employed myriad "reasons" to continue coding in binary. Such reasoning seems archaic at present. Happily, it resulted in essentially no slowdown of progress. Nevertheless, it should be noted that the Vanguard rocket (America's answer to the Sputnik in 1957) was controlled by a program coded in binary machine language and contained a single simple mistake that resulted in a spectacular and explosive fiasco.

The "automatic programming systems" provided by an assembly language translator for each computer naturally led to the idea of also converting more mathematically oriented and business English-like syntax to binary machine code. Thus, by the mid-1950s the compiler was born, and by 1957 the first popular procedural-level language—FORTRAN—existed. Again, many journeymen programmers resisted for a variety of reasons. Happily, this intellectual tempest is almost dead. Lest I be completely misunderstood, at this time and probably for some time to come, several somewhat special situations exist for which assembly language coding is justified. In some cases, a higher-level language is not available for the processor or the needed operations are not defined in the available language. The number and diversity of these situations is rather rapidly diminishing, however. The justification for employing assembly language must be an economic justification; that is, the savings in memory space and execution time must more than offset the increased programming effort and cost. Thus, the usual case would involve a situation where several hundred thousand uses of the program would be expected. An obvious example involves the microcomputers currently employed to control carburetion and timing in automobiles, where millions of copies are involved.

It is extremely important to realize that the foregoing reasoning depends entirely on the assumption that a good assembly language programmer can code a specific algorithm so that it is smaller and/or executes faster than the code output by the compiler of an available procedural-oriented language. For most situations in the past, this was true; for many situations at present, this is true; for a few situations in the future, this will continue to be true. However, it is also true that newer languages and their associated compilers are getting better and better, so that the use of assembly language is diminishing and presently is relatively minor. At the same time, serious programmers and all educated people should have an understanding and appreciation of what goes on behind the obvious. One method of guaranteeing this knowledge relative to computers is to learn and use an assembly language for at least a few programs.

Perhaps the most important reason for computer science students to practice and learn the design principles and implementation methods for an assembler is that the process of transliterating symbolic assembly source code to binary object code involves somewhat simplified versions of many of the more involved techniques employed in compilers. As all program designers and implementors should thoroughly understand what a compiler does and how it does it, it behooves us to start our process of learning about translators at the simplest level—the assembler.

THE COMPUTATIONAL PROCESS

Each and every time a new computer is designed and produced, it presents the same problem to the producing company and through it to the intended user. Imagine, if you will, that one of your brilliant computer architects working with several designers has just informed you that they have evolved a breakthrough in chip design that will allow the capture of a significant portion of the word processing/office automation market. This could mean millions of dollars of profit for your company and thousands of dollars in your personal paycheck.

Attractive—you bet. But wait; they propose to design, implement, and deliver an excellent computer that will interpret and execute binary machine language! Binary machine language! Nobody, but nobody, programs in binary machine language. For this new computer to be useful and to sell, you must design, implement, and deliver with the hardware such things as an operating system, compilers, editors, and in this specific case, a "turnkey" applications system for word processing/office automation. Without these, and probably more, the product will not sell, the profits will not materialize, and your personal paycheck and future are doomed. In addition, you cannot wait until the new computer is designed and a prototype implemented before you start work on the software. If you do, your competition will beat you to the market. You must develop the hardware and its software in parallel. Both must be ready at about the same time.

Is this an impossible technical management task? No! Recall that computers are really somewhat general-purpose information-manipulating machines. You can use one of your present computers to produce the software for your new computer. The critical requirement is that you know exactly and precisely what the binary machine code of the new computer will be. Is this requirement realistic? Can your architect and designer define the binary machine code well enough? Probably not exactly, but probably well enough.

You decide to go ahead. Among the software you need is an assembler and among your resources is an existing computer that has a procedural-level language available. Unfortunately, the textbook coverage and professional literature regarding the design and implementation of an assembler are somewhat sparse. This is in contrast to the copious literature available regarding compilers and operating systems. At this time, I am able to cite only four texts on assemblers that might be helpful: Barron (1972), Beck (1985), Calingaert (1979), and Donovan (1972).

Almost invariably, the process of preparing a program for execution consists of a series of steps somewhat like those illustrated in Figure 8.1 and reviewed in the following list:

1. *Algorithm design:* After a problem is defined, it is usual to break it into logical and independent subproblems (modules) each of whose solutions is somewhat easy and constitutes an independent function with well-specified inputs, a defined manipulation, and the desired output. This is a human intellectual task of high order.

2. *Code into computer language:* Each of the modules defined above is translated into the correct and legal syntax of the chosen computer languages. It is impor-

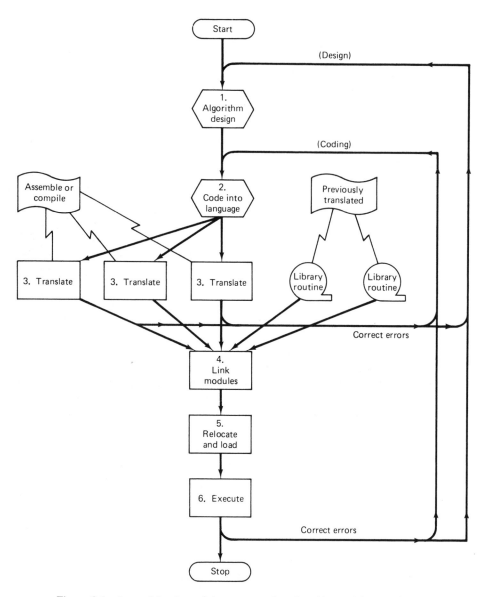

Figure 8.1 A possible view of the computer-based problem-solving process. In this chapter, we concentrate on the translation step with emphasis on assembly, on the module-linking step, and on the relocation/load step. (From G. W. Gorsline, *16-Bit Modern Microcomputers: The Intel 18086 Family,* © 1985, p. 344. Reprinted by permission of Prentice-Hall, Inc., Englewood Cliffs, NJ.)

tant to identify and correct any coding errors at this point. It is also important to test each module by itself in order to find and correct any logic errors in the problem solution strategy.

3. *Translate (assemble or compile):* The translation system of programs transforms (transliterates in the case of assembly language, translates in the case of a procedural-level language) the source code statements from step 2 to binary machine code for the target computer (usually termed *object code*). If the translation system is correct (the assembler and/or compiler is correct), the syntax of the module will be transformed but the semantics will not be altered. Syntax errors are often identified during compilation or assembly. An overall design for the assembly process will be detailed shortly.

4. *Link modules:* If the design and coding of the problem solution strategy involves any subordinate modules (subroutines and/or functions), as is usual, it is necessary to combine the separately translated modules into a single coordinated whole. It is usual for each module to be translated into binary machine code, with the addresses beginning at zero. Linking is the concatenation of the code from the different modules into a single "load module" whose beginning address is zero and involves the resolution of intermodule address references caused by such instructions as JSR. All code addresses will be byte offsets within the code segment. Object code (translated) modules may be derived directly from the compiler/assembler or may be obtained from libraries of previously translated modules.

5. *Relocate and load into main memory:* The movement of each byte of the code into main memory is termed *loading* and is usually accomplished via disk-to-memory I/O instructions. In addition, the address of the beginning of the code must be loaded into the PC. In the MC680XY, this constitutes relocation and allows the program to be loaded into main memory at any address divisible by 2. Note that code/data relocation precludes the use of absolute addresses (non-relocatable addresses) except in special circumstances such as the interrupt vector situation. It is somewhat common for the linking step and the relocating loader step to be combined into a single operating system functional module known as a *linking loader*.

6. *Execute:* After loading is completed, execution of the linked/relocated/main-memory-resident program is started by the operating system initializing the program counter to the offset of the initial executable instruction of the main program. The setting of the PC is usually accomplished by the operating system executing a CALL instruction (or equivalent) to the user program, so that it is, in effect, a subprogram of the operating system. The user program is terminated, in the normal nonerror case, via a RTS instruction (or equivalent) to the operating system. Alternatively, this program initiation/termination process may be implemented as "software interrupts" employing specific interrupt vector numbers.

THE ASSEMBLY PROBLEM

From our foregoing discussion, we can define an *assembler* as a program that *transliterates* a program module expressed in the assembly language of a specific computer model (the *source code*) into the binary machine language of a specific computer model (the *object code*). The complications caused by macros will be covered later in this chapter. Several terms warrant emphasis:

> *Transliterate:* a form of translation in which the correspondence between items is one-to-one; a one-to-one mapping of each source code statement to a corresponding object code instruction with the same semantics.
>
> *Source code:* the particular source module with the defined syntax and associated semantics of the assembly language that is to be transliterated statement by statement to form the object module with the exact same semantics; the source for translation.
>
> *Object code:* the particular binary machine language object module resulting from the translation; the object of the translation.
>
> *Assembler:* a program that transliterates (assembles) assembly language source code to binary machine language object code for one specific computer model.
>
> *Cross-assembler:* an assembler that executes on a computer model and assembles source code to object code for a different computer model. The two computers may be architecturally closely related or they may be very different.

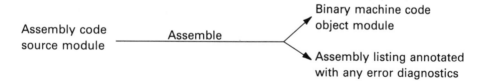

The *object module* (with extremely rare exceptions) is a file containing the ordered binary machine code instructions: that is, it consists of an ordered series of diads (pairs) of

[relative address : binary machine instruction]

It is common, but not universal, for the relative addresses to be implied to start at zero and to be consecutive. Thus, the object file would consist only of the string of binary machine code (often recorded in hexadecimal). Additional information necessary to the process of linking (binding) separately translated (assembled and/or compiled) modules together is usually included at the beginning of the object module file.

The *assembly listing* is a file in a format suitable for printing on paper or displaying on a CRT. It contains

- The assembly source statements (usually in the exact form submitted).
- Generated line numbers.
- The generated binary machine code equivalent of each source statement, usually expressed in hexadecimal.
- Error messages and warnings. Preferably, these physically follow the offending statement and are meaningful in context. Certain error conditions cannot be associated with a particular statement and therefore must be noted physically at the end of the listing. The use of error numbers, which must be looked up in a manual, interrupts and interferes with the mental debugging process. It possibly was justified when disk storage space was very small, but currently, such poor design indicates an assembler that should be replaced immediately, and the vendor should be placed on a "technically suspect" list.
- Appropriate headings generated by the assembler and/or supplied by the user (such as module name).
- A sorted cross-reference table of symbols = labels = variable names, each with an ordered list of the source code line numbers in which they appear. A cross-reference table in alphabetical sort order allows the fast and easy detection of mistyped variable names. Unfortunately, many assemblers neglect to produce and make available a cross-reference table.
- A summary of the assembler actions, containing such information as number of statements in the module, number or errors, length of object module, and so on.

The transliteration (mapping) from source code to object code must assign object code values to all symbols in the source code. The types of symbols that can occur in assembly source code are

- System symbols
  —Operation code mnemonics (opcodes)
  —Assembly directives (pseudo-ops)
  —Register names
- Programmer-defined symbols
  —Labels
  —Address expressions
  —Constants
  —Macro names

The process of mapping symbolic assembly source code to binary machine object code is greatly facilitated and vastly simplified by the very regular and limited syntax rules of almost all assembly languages. Recall—from Chapter 2 and from your practice—that a source code assembly statement follows the plan:

```
label:   Opcode field   Operand(s) field        ; comment
```

with a limited number of well-defined exceptions. That is, the label is optional; any statement beginning with a certain character (common examples: semicolon, asterisk) is entirely a comment; the opcode field may contain the mnemonic name of an operations code, a pseudo-operation (assembly directive) often starting with a certain character (common example: period), or the name of a previously defined macro; the operand(s) field may be absent for certain instructions or may contain a single operand reference, two operand references, three operand references and so on; and the trailing comment field is optional and must be preceded by a certain character (common examples: blank, semicolon, comma). Operand references are symbolic aliases for addresses within the module (offsets from the beginning) being assembled (relocatable addresses) or within the main memory of the computer (absolute addresses), the names of registers, the names or aliases of peripheral devices, constants (immediates), the names or aliases of global entities, and so forth. These operand addresses may involve variations that may necessitate the evaluation of relatively simple arithmetic expressions that often are incorporated into the object code instruction as an offset or displacement.

Substituting values for the system symbols is generally simple and straightforward. A table of symbolic operation code mnemonics (opcodes) is easily searched and the associated equivalent binary opcode value found and placed into the binary machine instruction in the proper position. If the opcode is not found, the assumption is made that the content of the opcode field was a pseudo-op (assembly directive), and the table of symbolic pseudo-ops is similarly searched. If the symbol is still not found (is neither an opcode nor a pseudo-op), either it must be the name of a macro or it is an error (mistyping is the common error). If the opcode table and the pseudo-op table are searched first, the mnemonics within them constitute reserved words; that is, they cannot be used for macro names. On the other hand, if the (previously defined) macro name table is searched before the opcode and pseudo-op tables, the opcode and pseudo-op mnemonics are not reserved words. My point is that the design of the assembler has effects on the allowed assembly language syntax.

Similarly, substituting values for the programmer-defined symbols that are constants—that is, immediate values—consists of converting the numerical value to base 2 or expressing the character value as binary and inserting these bits into the proper position of the binary machine code object instruction.

Substituting values for the programmer-defined symbols that are labels consists of determining their addressing distance in bytes from the start of the assembly language module and then using this value in place of the label. This process is easiest to accomplish by initializing an addressing offset variable (traditionally called a *location counter*) at the beginning of the assembly process and appropriately incrementing it for the length of each instruction or data area. Recall that labels can occur not only in the label area of an instruction but also in the operand area and that a label may designate—that is, name or identify—(1) a point in the code to which a branch is made or (2) a data area. In addition, recall that a label is really a programmer-defined name (alias) for (1) an offset address (relocatable) from the start of the module, (2) an absolute address (nonrelocatable offset from the start of main memory), or (3) a currently unknown address of a subprocedure entry point or data area that will be furnished at a later time (after assembly is completed) by the link routine (discussed in Chapter 9). One complication found with operand field occurrences of labels—particularly with code that employs the technique of using address registers (as the MC680XY does)—is that the address reference often includes an address adjustment arithmetic expression that must be evaluated by the assembler and expressed in base 2 notation, and the resulting bits must be inserted into the proper position (usually an offset byte/word/longword) of the binary machine object code instruction.

Note that the derivation of an offset address for a label is relatively straightforward if and only if the label has been previously encountered in the label field of an instruction. That is, when a label is first encountered in the label field, it and the current value of the location counter are both entered into a *symbol table*. All occurrences of the label symbol in the operand field are looked up in this symbol table and replaced by the relative address (the distance in bytes from the assembly module start). Now, everything is fine so long as all labels are defined (occur in the label field of an instruction) before they are used (occur in the operand field of an instruction). Unfortunately, programmers do not—and cannot—always compose programs that way. All too often, we must branch to a label on a statement further down (further along) in our program. Thus, the address—the value—of many labels is not yet known when they occur in the operand field of an instruction. This complicating situation, known as the *forward-reference problem,* occurs in both assemblers and compilers.

It is important to realize that the forward-reference problem is not limited to forward branching of branch (or jump) instructions. Some assemblers allow the declaration of data areas to follow the code (or even to occur within the code). In these assemblers, all memory direct references to data within the code will involve the forward-reference problem. In the MC680XY, these references would normally be limited to the LEA (load effective address) and PEA (push effective address) instructions, as this architecture is essentially a memory indirect through address register architecture. On the other hand, many other computer architectures and their assemblers allow (some require) direct memory addressing, so that the data forward-reference problem is even more ubiquitous. Of course, the straightforward and simple solution to the data forward-reference problem is to require that all data declarations occur at the start of the assembly language module, before any code. The DEC PDP 11 and VAX assemblers have adopted this nonbothersome programmatic requirement—as has the Motorola MC680XY assembler.

Knowing that the forward-reference problem will occur—if not for data, then at least for the target of some branches (including subprocedures)—what is the cure?

The use of a symbol table (in reality, a programmer-defined symbol table) is not, in itself, a cure, although it will greatly facilitate keeping track of label values (the relative address = location counter content). Unfortunately, a symbol table cannot contain the relative address of a label not yet encountered in the label field. The only practical cure is to have the assembler go through the program once to derive all the label relative addresses from the label field using the location counter value, thus building the complete symbol table, and only then, later, go through the program a second time to use these label addresses as needed in the operand field processing. Thus, most assemblers involve *two passes:*

> *Pass 1:* Build symbol table; that is, evaluate (derive the relative address for) all labels = programmer-defined symbols.
>
> *Pass 2:* Generate binary machine object code; that is, evaluate (substitute values for) all symbolic opcodes, all assembly directives (pseudo-ops), all labels, and so on, and generate a listing/cross-reference/statistics file with annotated error messages.

Note that this division of tasks between Pass 1 and Pass 2 of an assembler, though somewhat traditional, has the result of minimizing the amount of work accomplished in Pass 1 and maximizing the amount of work left to be accomplished in Pass 2. A valid alternative approach would accomplish all possible work in Pass 1 and minimize the work left for Pass 2.

> *Pass 1:* Build symbol table, generate all possible machine code, and generate as complete a listing file as possible. The extreme approach would accomplish all work except for the forward references in the operand field, which would be noted for "back-patching" during Pass 2.
>
> *Pass 2:* Fill in (back-patch) the forward-reference operand fields in the object code and in the listing file, as noted during Pass 1.

In fact, Pass 2 may become so abbreviated as to constitute a kind of afterthought. Some assemblers of this nature are even termed *one-pass assemblers.*

Which of these two strategic design approaches is best? As usual, it depends! Because the approach that abbreviates Pass 2 usually requires more main (primary) memory or a much larger number of disk accesses, in the past—say, 1965 or before for maxicomputers, 1975 or before for minicomputers, and 1980 or before for microcomputers—the tendency was to use the approach that minimized Pass 1 or at least did not maximize Pass 1. At present, when main (primary) memory size is no longer a prime programming consideration, the choice between the two strategic design approaches is not extremely vital and becomes almost a matter of program designer preference. Nevertheless, some marketing groups may claim advantages for one approach or the other—without much data to justify the claims. Thus, you may see advertising extolling the virtues (usually speed) of a one-pass assembler or the small memory requirements of a particular two-pass assembler. *Caveat emptor!*

To cement the concepts of an assembler and the work it performs in transliterating an assembly language source code module into a binary machine object code
module, we present almost identical algorithms for a two-pass assembler: one in
structured English (Figure 8.2) and the other as flowcharts (Figure 8.3).

Pass 1:
1. Initialize LC.
2. Read a line of source code.
3. Decode from free format to fixed format.
4. What type of statement is it?
   a. *.end?* Go to Pass 2.
   b. An assignment statement? Evaluate the expression and either enter
      the symbol and its value into the symbol table or adjust LC. Go to 2.
   c. Label present? If so, set it equal to LC and enter its value into the sym-
      bol table.
   d. Macro CALL? If so, expand macro substituting arguments and per-
      forming conditionals. Go to 2.
   e. Machine instruction? Compute needed size in bytes (using default
      conventions if necessary) and adjust LC. Go to 2.
   f. Assembler directive? Compute needed size in bytes and adjust LC. Go
      to 2.
   g. Comment? Go to 2.
   h. If we make it here, there is an error. Process the error. Go to 2.

Pass 2:
1. Initialize LC.
2. Read a line of source code. Insert into proper field of listing line.
3. Using decoded form of statement from Pass 1, what type of statement
   is it?
   a. *.end?* Go to *exit.*
   b. Assignment statement? Evaluate the expression and adjust LC. Go
      to 4.
   c. Machine instruction? Evaluate operation code and all operands using
      addressing modes, symbol table searches, expression evaluation, and
      permanent symbol values. Place machine code into proper field of
      listing line, and into object file. Adjust LC. Go to 4.
   d. Assembler directive? Perform required function (data generation if
      needed). Output such data, if created, to object file with LC value.
      Place into listing line. Adjust LC. Go to 4.
   e. Comment? Go to 4.
   f. If we make it here, there is an error. Process it. Go to 4.
4. Based upon listing control parameters, output listing line. Go to 2.

Figure 8.2 Algorithm for a two-pass assembler expressed in structured English. (Compare
to Figure 8.3.) Adapted with permission from K. A. Lemone and M. E. Kaliski, *Assembly
Language Programming for the VAX-11*. Boston: Little, Brown and Co., 1983.

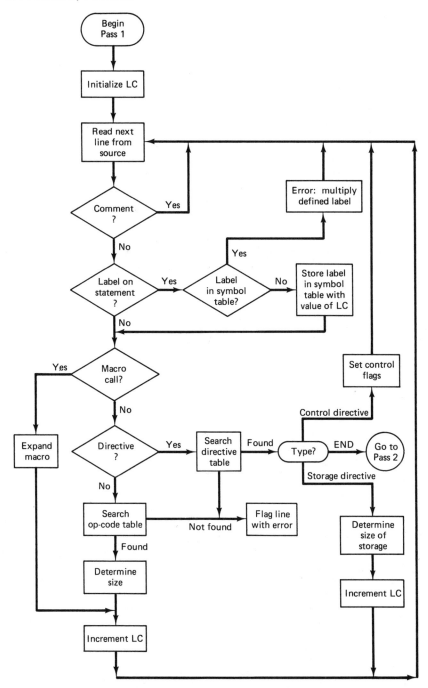

Figure 8.3 Algorithm for a two-pass assembler expressed as two flowcharts. (Compare to Figure 8.2.) Adapted with permission from S. El-Asfouri, O. Johnson, and W. K. King, *Computer Organization and Programming: VAX-11*. Reading, Mass.: Addison-Wesley, 1984.

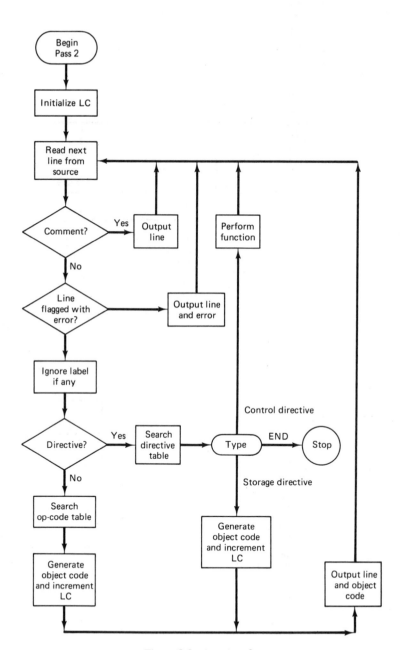

Figure 8.3   (*continued*).

DESIGNING AN ASSEMBLER

It is almost certain that several hundred production/commercial assembly systems have been designed, implemented, and marketed over the past 35 years or so (at least one for each different computer). In addition, it is probable that many thousand additional assemblers for simplified versions of real and imaginary computers have been designed and implemented as class projects by as many long-suffering computer science sophomore/junior-level students in scores of academic institutions around the world. My point is that the problem of designing and implementing a symbolic assembly system has been accomplished so often by so many people for so many computers using so many languages that the design is well defined and the choices available during implementation are clear.

We will consider the design of an assembler from three viewpoints:

1. The source syntax and associated semantics of the assembly language.
2. The data containers necessary or convenient to accomplish the assembler actions.
3. The abstraction of the assembler actions into convenient and independent modules that can be correctly combined to form a viable and robust assembler system.

The Language

It is necessary for us to define the syntax and other characteristics of our example assembly language. In the interest of helping comprehension of the underlying process of translation (for assembly code, it is really transliteration), we keep the syntax fairly simple and uniform but somewhat realistic and useful.

1. An assembly language statement shall consist of one instruction that shall occupy one record that is terminated by an end-of-line (EOL) ASCII character.
2. Each statement shall be "free-format," except that if a label occurs, it shall start in column 1 and be terminated by a colon (:). The operations code shall be surrounded by one or more blanks and shall precede the operand(s), which shall be separated by commas and contain no blanks. An EOL or semicolon (;) character shall delimit (end) a statement.
3. A comment shall begin with a semicolon (;) and be terminated by an EOL character. Thus, a semicolon in column 1 of a record defines the entire record (line) as a comment. In addition, a statement may be followed by a comment.
4. An assembly language module shall start with the pseudo-operation operand diad

    PROCEDURE   ANY_NAME

and shall be terminated by the pseudo-operation operand diad

END   ANY_NAME

5. An assembly language module shall consist of two main portions:
   (a) The first portion shall define the container areas of the data segment as well as record external references.
   (b) The second portion shall contain the code segment.
6. The first portion shall have as its first statement the pseudo-operation/operand diad

DATA AREAS

followed by the appropriate data area definitions. The end of the data definition section and the start of the code area will be signified by the pseudo-operation

CODE AREA

The physical end of the module shall be signified by the pseudo-operation

END PROCEDURE

7. References to other modules and references to external data areas shall be specified in the first portion by the pseudo-operation

EXTERNAL

Data areas that will be available as externals to other modules will be declared as

GLOBAL

8. Identifiers or labels (and thus code branch destinations, data, stacks, and strings) must start with an alphabetic ASCII character, must be ten characters or less in length, and may not include any embedded blanks.
9. To simplify the generation of the actual binary instructions, only the following addressing modes will be supported:
   a. Data register direct
   b. Address register direct
   c. Address register indirect to memory
   d. Address register indirect to memory with postincrement
   e. Address register indirect to memory with predecrement
   f. Address register indirect to memory with displacement
   g. Program counter indirect to memory with displacement

10. Similarly, to simplify the generation of the actual binary instructions, only the following instructions will be supported:

ADD	AND	CMP	LEA	JSR	B_{cc}
ADDA	OR	CMPA	PEA	RTS	BRA
SUB	EOR	TST	MOVE	RTR	DB_{cc}
SUBA	NEG			RTR	JMP
MULS	NOT			TRAP	
DIVS					

The limitations of points 8 and 9 greatly simplify Pass 2 of the assembler while still allowing the full principles of designing and implementing a realistic assembler as a class project. The inclusion of the additional instructions and addressing modes available with the MC68000/MC68008/MC68010/MC68012/MC68020 processors would be straightforward (but messy). The overall format of a source module for entry into the MC680XY assembler whose design we are discussing is given in Figure 8.4.

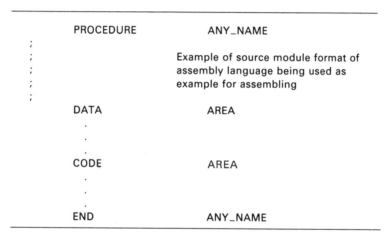

Figure 8.4 Overall format of the source assembly language module for input into the assembler described in the text. (From G. W. Gorsline, *16-Bit Modern Micro-computers: The Intel 18086 Family*, © 1985, p. 349. Reprinted by permission of Prentice-Hall, Inc., Englewood Cliffs, NJ.)

Data Containers

Remembering that the vital task of Pass 1 is the determination of addresses (the forward-reference problem) and that Pass 2 will generate the memory addresses (at least of foward-branch code), we have chosen to accomplish as much of the assembly task as convenient in Pass 1. As we choose to allow access to data defined and addressed in other modules (external data), it is convenient to require that all data symbols (names) be defined at the beginning of the program. Thus, all noncode labels (data labels) could be assigned an address in their segment before the code segment is encountered. This would allow the generation during Pass 1 of the binary machine code for all instructions except forward-reference branch instructions. We have chosen not to generate binary machine code operand addresses until Pass 2, even though we do move the binary version of the operations code to the machine code area during Pass 1. It is worth noting that all of the assembly processing for a syntax that requires all data definitions to precede the code could be accomplished in Pass 1 except for the addresses of forward-reference branches and that these could be resolved in a very brief type of Pass 2, almost an afterthought. On the other hand, it is as justifiable to minimize the work of Pass 1 and delay as much processing as possible for Pass 2. The usual approach is a compromise.

Our example assembler will have two inputs:

1. The source assembly module to be translated.
2. A table of legal operations codes and pseudo-operations in source language form and in machine language form and their associated instruction lengths.

This assembler will output two files:

1. An annotated listing of the module, giving the source version, the binary machine code version (in hexadecimal), the associated relative addresses, and any error messages.
2. A file of 80-character records, containing the relocatable binary machine code version of the module with sufficient note information to allow linking, relocation, and loading. The format of this file will be that given in Figure 8.5.

Note that the start and end of the binary machine code file are indicated by a unique record and that the body of the file consists of four types of records: EXTRN—one record for each external data container or procedure referenced, with the reference location in the code segment given to allow the link routine to insert addresses during the linking process; GLOBL—one record for each global data container, with the segment number and reference location within the segment to allow the link routine to resolve external references of other modules; DATA—one record for each defined container, with the value and starting location in the appropriate segment (a constant longer than 30 bytes will require extra records); and CODE—one record for every 30 bytes (locations to have external addresses supplied by the link routine should be set to zero). The requirement is to supply all information that will be needed by the link routine for it to function correctly.

In our assembler, we have chosen to combine many of the traditional internal working data areas into a single fairly large combined table. Thus, we require three internal data areas (Figure 8.6):

1. A symbol table that has a large enough capacity to contain the identification (name) of each unique label occurring in the module as well as its relative lo-

Record 1

Columns		
	1–4	'PROC'
	7–16	Module name
	20–29	'CODE' size (in four hexadecimal digits)
	30–39	'DATA' size (in four hexadecimal digits)
	40–49	'Stack' size
	50–59	'EXTRA' size
	76–80	'00001' (record sequence number)

Records 2 to N

Columns		
	1–5	'EXTRN' or 'GLOBL'
	7–16	Symbolic name
	18–22 24–28 30–34 36–40 42–46 48–52 54–58 60–64 66–70	Segment number and location in segment one plus four hexadecimal digits (up to nine references per card)
	76–80	Sequence number

Records N+ 1 to M

Columns		
	1–5	'DATA' or 'STACK' or 'EXTRA'
	7–10	Location in segment of constant
	11–70	Hexadecimal digit pairs giving value of constant (30 hexadecimal pairs per record allowed)
	76–80	Sequence number

Record M+ 1 to K

Columns		
	1–4	'CODE'
	7–8	Location in segment of start
	12–13	Number of bytes in this record (30 allowed)
	11–70	Binary machine code in hexadecimal pairs
	76–80	Sequence number

Record K+ 1

Columns		
	1–3	'END'
	7–16	Module name
	76–80	Sequence number

Figure 8.5 Object code syntax and associated semantics for the assembler and linker discussed in the text. (Adapted from G. W. Gorsline, *16-Bit Modern Microcomputers: The Intel 18086 Family,* © 1985, p. 350. Reprinted by permission of Prentice-Hall, Inc., Englewood Cliffs, NJ.)

cation. As each symbol is encountered during Pass 1, it is placed in the symbol table together with its relative location. External symbols are also entered with a location of zero. As all languages prohibit duplicate labels (all languages that I know of, anyway), it is necessary to search the table for the possible existence of a label before it is entered. This search occurs during a period (Pass 1) when the table is being added to. In addition, during Pass 2, the symbol table

```
DECLARE
  SOURCE_FILE(500) CHAR(80),
  OP_CODE_TABLE 1(25),                        /* This table is initialized to the */
    2 NAME CHAR(10),                          /* correct values via an */
    2 TYPE FIXED DEC(1),                      /* INITIAL clause */
    2 LENGTH FIXED DEC(1),
    2 BINARY_CODE BIT(6);
DECLARE
  SYMBOL_TABLE 1(250),
    2 NAME CHAR(10),
    2 TYPE FIXED DEC(1)                       /* Segment */
    2 LOCATION CHAR(10);                      /* Hexadecimal digits */
DECLARE
  MASTER_TABLE 1(999),
    2 LINE_NO FIXED DEC(3),
    2 STMNT_NO FIXED DEC(3),
    2 KEY FIXED DEC(1),                       /* Segment */
    2 LOCATION CHAR(10),                      /* Hexadecimal digits */
    2 BINARY_CODE CHAR(10),                   /* Hexadecimal digits */
    2 SOURCE_STMNT CHAR(80),
    2 LABEL CHAR(10),
    2 OP_CODE CHAR(10),
    2 LENGTH CHAR(1),                         /* B, W, L */
    2 FIRST_OPERAND CHAR(10),
    2 SECOND_OPERAND CHAR(10),
    2 REPEAT_CODE CHAR(10);
DECLARE
  OBJECT_FILE(400) CHAR(80);
DECLARE
  LINE_COUNTER FIXED DEC(3),
  STMNT_COUNTER FIXED DEC(3),
  LOCATION_COUNTER FIXED DEC(5);
```

Figure 8.6 Necessary data areas for the assembler discussed in the text. (Adapted from G. W. Gorsline, *16-Bit Modern Microcomputers: The Intel I8086 Family*, © 1985, p. 352. Reprinted by permission of Prentice-Hall, Inc., Englewood Cliffs, NJ.)

must be searched to determine the location within which segment of each operand. As a search of the symbol table must be accomplished repeatedly, it is important that the search operation be fast.

2. A master table in which to store almost all of the information about the module being assembled, such as the source statement, the line number, the statement number, the binary machine code, and the relative location, as well as the extracted symbolic label, operation code, and operands.

3. A small group of miscellaneous variables, such as a container for the line counter, the statement counter, the relative location counter, and so on.

We have chosen to combine many data containers usually encountered in an assembler into one comprehensive table called the *master table*. If the implementation language supports relatively complicated data structures, they can somewhat simplify the logical design of an assembler. We assume an implementation language with this facility in our design and thus are contemplating a language for implementation such as PL/G. If the implementation language is lacking this ability, it would be necessary to break the master table of this design into several data areas. A little thought should allow the student to incorporate this complication into the design of an assembler.

Modularization

We can identify the need for the following modules in our assembler design:

I/O module
Decoder from free-format module
Table entry/search module
Location counter adjustment module
Error handler module
Assembler directive processor module (contains submodules)
Machine code generator module
Expression evaluation module
Listing module
Coordination (executive) module

The algorithms for these modules are adapted from the presentation in Lemone and Kaliski (1983).

I/O module.   This module clearly interfaces the assembler with the outside world, performing all input/output functions.

Input: A record to read in from or write out to some device.
Output: In the case of reading, a "core image" of the record, accessible via a pointer; in the case of writing, the "core image" is output to the device.
General procedure: We leave this open here. For the purposes of initial assembler operation, simple Pascal-like read/write statements will suffice.
Exceptional conditions, technical notes: Those usually associated with I/O.

Free-format decode module.   This module takes the assembler source code, written according to free-format rules, and decodes it—that is, formats it into *label* (if present), *operation, operand,* and *remark* fields. It may save the free-format form of the line of code for listing purposes, but all other modules, for reasons of efficiency, use the decoded statement form.

Input: A unformatted (free-format) source code line.

Output: A formatted source line containing the standard statement fields in fixed positions easily accessible by pointers.

General procedure: Basically, this procedure involves a search of the character strings comprising the line, looking for such characters as ":" or ";". We leave the detailed design of the module as an exercise for the reader.

Exceptional conditions: Typical of the types of errors to be encountered are "label field has too many symbols" or "illegal character found."

Technical notes: (1) This module might be termed a "lexical scanner" in compiler design. (2) In all probability, the input is a pointer and the output four pointers, one for each type of statement field (possibly, some are null). These output pointers will be used to reference this decoded statement in all subsequent processing operations in Pass 1 and Pass 2, saving unnecessary reformatting. Only in the listing generation process will the original form of the statement possibly by used.

Table entry/search module.   This module handles all table operations: searching, sorting (if needed), and entry.

Inputs: A table name, a keyword, a flag, and possibly a value.

Output: Possibly a value.

General procedure: There are two modes of operation of this module—entry (flag = 0) and search (flag = 1). In search mode, this operates as a search routine, looking for the keyword in the appropriate table and returning its found value. In entry mode, then, it is a table "builder," entering the keyword and its value into the specified table. The question of how keywords are stored (lexicographically, hashed, etc.) and how tables are searched (linear, binary, hashed, etc.) is discussed briefly below in the paragraph on technical notes.

Exceptional conditions: Any table operation that cannot be properly processed generates an error—for example, a request to search for a keyword that is not present or to enter a (keyword, value) pair when the keyword has already been entered (multiply defined symbol).

Technical notes: Many good references exist on searching/entry/sorting techniques. The general rule of thumb is that if tables are small (say, 50 elements or so), then the linear search on an unordered table is more than adequate. For larger tables, particularly if they are *static* (like the machine operation table), by ordering the table so that the most commonly used entries are first, a linear search can often be used without serious penalty. What kinds of tables are needed in an assembler? There are *read-only* (static) tables, which are always searched and never modified during assembly time, and there are *read/write* (dynamic) tables. The two general types of organization are *fixed entry size* and *variable entry size*. The former is less efficient in the use of space [as the maximum (keyword, value) space must be allocated for each entry, irrespective of its actual size]. However, tables so organized are easy to sort and search. The latter is more efficient in its use of space, but some space must be allowed for linkage between successive, variable-size entries. "Pointer chasing," however, is quite time-consuming. Read-only tables include the *machine operation table* (machine instruction mnemonics, operation codes, etc.), the *assembler directive table* (assembler directive mnemonics and their "action pointers"), and the *error message table*. The *user-defined symbol table* is a read/write table.

Let us further consider the proposition of searching a table. In general, there are three types of table search: linear (sometimes known as *sequential*), binary (sometimes known as *logarithmic*), and hash coding.

Linear (Sequential) Table Insertion and Search.   The table is searched sequentially from its start to its finish. New items are added at the end; thus, the table is ordered in the order that labels are encountered in the module. This method is suitable for tables that change size (grow) between searches. The average search time is the time required to search one-half the table. For a very large table, the sequential search method is usually considered too slow. As a general rule of thumb, this method should be employed only on tables of 50 to 100 entries or less.

Binary (Logarithmic) Insertion and Search.   The table must be in sorted order before search; thus, the binary search method is not considered suitable for tables that change size (grow) between searches because of the difficulty and time required to add new labels in their lexicographical sort position. A sorted table may be probed at its midpoint to see if the desired item is in the fore half or the back half. The indicated half is then treated similarly until the item is found or a "not found" is indicated. The average search time is the log base 2 of the table size, which is the power-of-2 number above the table size. As a general rule, this method is not suitable for symbol table searches, although a linked-list method may alleviate the objection noted above.

Hash Table Search and Insertion.   Hash table techniques are eminently suited to symbol table use, as they are fast and work for tables that change in size. The idea is to use a function to transform the symbol (the label) into an index or position in the table; that is,

table_index ← hash (symbol_ID)

As a rule of thumb, the table should be about one-half larger than the size expected to be needed. The major difficulty with hash table techniques is finding a function that will distribute the symbols (the labels) evenly over the table, with a minimum number of them being indexed to the same position, called a *collision*.

Collisions are often "solved" by placing or searching for "symbol" (the label) in the next available sequential table location. Collisions are a real problem because of the traditional habit of programmers to use such data names as I, X, STACK1, and so on, thus limiting their variable names' vocabulary. In the absence of collisions, the search time (the "probe" time) for a hash table consists of the calculation time for the hash function plus the indexing time. Various more advanced schemes for designing hash tables have been developed (such as two-level hashing); the literature on searching is very large, sometimes interesting, and often reveals valuable programming techniques that are useful in other contexts.

Cook and Oldehoeft (1982) give a heuristic for the Cichelli (1980) method of constructing a minimal perfect hash table—minimal space with minimal collisions—for small static sets of words such as an opcode table. Cichelli used the function:

index ← length of word + value of first letter + value of last letter

Under many conditions, a solution requires much time. We give the algorithm of Cook and Oldehoeft as a useful tool.

1. Compute the frequency of letters occurring at either end of words in the set. If a letter appears as both the first and last letter of the same word, assign it a large value.
2. Order the letters by decreasing frequency, resolving ties arbitrarily.
3. Let each word be represented by a triple: (letter 1, letter 2, length), where letter 1 is the first letter and letter 2 is the last letter. For each triple (word), interchange letter 1 and letter 2 if letter 2 precedes letter 1 in the letter ordering.
4. Using letter 2 as the key, sort the list of triples in descending order.
5. Assign letter values. Begin with the first triple. For each group of triples with the same letter 2, attempt to find a letter value assignment for letter 2. Note that for this group of triples, either letter 2 = letter 1 or letter 1 precedes letter 2 in the letter ordering and letter 1 has previously been assigned a value. Thus, only letter 2 needs to be assigned a value to place the group of triples (words) in the hash table. Beginning with 0, search for a value for letter 2 that maps the group of triples to distinct empty table slots. If it finds a value, it assigns the value to letter 2 and places the group of triples (words) in the table. If it does not find a value, it backs up, depending on the reason for its failure. One reason for failure is that two triples in the group have the same value of letter 1 and length sums. Hence, the two triples will have identical hash values for any value assignment to letter 2. In this case, the algorithm backs up to the nearest group that computes a value assignment for a letter 1 of one of the two triples. For all other failures, the algorithm backs up to the previous group of triples. Note that when the algorithm backs up, it unassigns letter values and removes the associated hash table entries along the way.

Location counter adjuster module.   This module keeps track of the location counter during the assembly process. Based upon addressing modes used, instruction mnemonics, assembler directive types, default conventions, and so on, it adjusts the location counter to correctly allocate virtual memory and to properly define symbol values.

Inputs: The operation and operand fields of a source language statement and the old value of the location counter plus special information in the case of assembler directives.

Output: The new value of the location counter.

General procedure: The location counter adjuster must allocate the required amount of space for the instructions/assembler directives. In the case of instructions, the mnemonic provides information on the data types of the operands; the addressing modes complement this to give an accounting of space required for the instruction. Default conventions must be employed, for example, in the case of relative mode addressing involving forward references. In the case of assembler directives, directive-specific interpretations must be provided to the location counter adjuster by the assembler directive module.

Exceptional conditions: Any situation that prevents unambiguous adjustment is an error.

Technical notes: How much does the executive module do before calling the location counter adjuster? Does the executive module count the required number of bytes, reducing this module to a routine that essentially "increments" the LC, or is most of the work done within this module? For assembler directives, the allocation of responsibility between this module and the assembler directive processor presents even more subtle problems. This assignment of tasks is one of the key issues in assembler design. We must make sure that every necessary function is performed once and only once. Since "addressing modes" are critical to the proper operation of this module, and since these modes are indicated by distinct strings of characters, there could be an advantage to designing a somewhat more sophisticated free-format decoder that, during its scan, first checked to see if it had found an instruction mnemonic (by invoking the table entry/search module) and, finding this to be the case, continued its scan to pull off addressing modes. We would gain efficiency in the location counter adjustment problem but add complexity and loss of "independence" to the free-format decoder. This type of trade-off is typical in modular software design.

Error handler module.   This module is the source of diagnostic messages and the coordinator of all error conditions. It is called whenever an error is detected and, depending on the nature of the error, produces a message for the listing module and takes other appropriate actions.

Inputs: A module "code" and an error code.

Outputs: An error message and an "action" code (pointer).

General procedure: The error handler module basically performs a table lookup function, involving the table entry/search module. It produces a line of message for insertion into the listing file and sends back an action code (pointer) to the executive module, which can then take appropriate action.

Exceptional conditions: These occur only if an illegal message error code is encountered.

Technical note: There is no real logical need for this module, in that it could be part of the table entry/search module. But from the point of view of modular design, it is useful to view the error handler as a distinct module and the table entry/search module as a kind of utility.

Assembler directive processor module.   This module is multifaceted and is, in reality, a collection of submodules, one for each assembler directive. Based upon the specific assembler directive encountered, the appropriate submodule is called to perform the required function. Different functions are required for an assembler directive, depending on the pass the assembler is in.

Inputs: The operation and operand fields of an assembler directive and a *pass* flag (1 or 2).

Output: For Pass 1, there is no direct output, just a location counter adjustment. For Pass 2, depending on the directive, object code may be generated and placed into the object file.

General procedure: There are really several "modules" contained with this single module, based upon the pass we are in and the type of assembler directive. Some directives allocate and possibly initialize portions of virtual memory; others merely affect the listing, for example. Associated with each directive in the assembler directive table is an "action pointer" to a procedure to process it. There may be two such pointers, one for each pass. The pointers are followed and modules such as the location counter adjuster may be called. A special part of the assembler directive processor will be the object code generator, which processes directives such as *.word* or *.ascii*.

Exceptional conditions: Again, there are too many to enumerate, but typical ones would be a value too large for a *.byte* directive or a missing delimiter in an *.ascii* directive.

Technical notes: This module may logically be viewed as consisting of two parts—a Pass 1 processor and a Pass 2 processor. The only "Pass 1" directives are those that affect the location counter value; the action pointers for all of the other assembler directives may be viewed as being *"null"* for the Pass 1 part. All directives must be processed in Pass 2. As indicated in the "Technical notes" portion of the "Location counter adjuster module," there is a delicate allocation of responsibilities to be performed among the various modules. For example, if the line

.byte 50[30]

appears, does the executive module, the location counter adjuster, or the assembler directive processor do the multiplication by 30?

Machine code generator module.   This module generates the "traditional" object code of the assembler—that is, pairs of the form (virtual memory location, word contents). To do this, it uses the output of the expression evaluation and table search modules, along with the addressing modes and permanent symbol values.

Inputs: The operation and operand fields of a machine code instruction.

Output: Object code—that is, pairs of the form (location, byte contents) corresponding to the machine code for the instruction.

General procedure: The operation of the module is fairly clear in general terms. Using the table entry/search module, the operation code for the mnemonic can be obtained, as well as default information about the instruction operands. For each operand, using calls to the expression evaluation module or table entry/search module where needed, the appropriate machine code can be generated. It can also be placed in the listing file.

Exceptional conditions: Typical of conditions here are inappropriate addressing modes for the instruction type or operands that, as forward references, were allocated default space and turn out to have values that are too large to "fit" into the allocated space.

Technical notes: Some thought has to be given to the role, if any, that instruction operand access and data types play in the machine code generation process. Some subtle interplay issues arise here between this module and the expression evaluation and table entry/search modules. How is a single user-defined symbol to be evaluated? Should all operands be directly passed to the expression evaluator, even if the "expression" is just a symbol? This module will probably contain some base conversion utility procedures for going from the default notation of decimal into hexadecimal or binary.

Expression evaluation module.   This module evaluates expressions found in the assembler source program, using symbol table searches if necessary. The exact rules concerning the legal forms of expressions and their evaluation are part of the syntax of the assembly language.

Input: An expression made up of operands and operations.

Output: The value of the expression.

General procedure: In many systems, this would be considered a *utility* module. The concept of an expression is well defined; so is the concept of the value of an expression. This module, through calls to the table entry/search module (for obtaining the values of user-defined symbols), performs such evaluation following the precedence and syntax rules of common procedural languages, such as Pascal, FORTRAN, PL/I, and the like.

Exceptional conditions: There are generally two types of exceptional conditions: "syntactic" and "semantic." In the former category, the form of the expression is illegal—for example, unmatched angle brackets or an illegal character. In the latter case, either a symbol is undefined or the obtained value is too large (overflow).

Technical notes: Some of the syntax checking could be done in the free-format decoder module—for example, illegal operators or unbalanced brackets. We come back again to the issue of the "division of labor"—this can be done at the price of a more complex, less independent free-format decoder.

Listing module.   This module, under the guidance of various listing control parameters, produces a listing of the source program and the object code, along with any error messages generated by the error handler module. Optionally, symbol tables and so on may be listed, based upon these parameters.

Input: The listing file and a table of control parameters.

Output: A modified listing file.

General procedure: We will say little about this module, which is principally controlled by parameter values set by assembler directives (or by default values). A "master" listing file is kept during the assembly process, containing the complete object code in ASCII and tables of symbols, cross-references, and so on. The modified listing file is an abridged version of this file, based upon user requests through the use of the assembler directives. Directives such as *.title* may actually add to this file.

Exceptional conditions: It is hard to imagine any errors that would explicitly be detected by this module—errors in listing specifications would be caught by the assembler directive processor module, errors in characters and so on by the I/O module.

Technical notes: The master file has a default size and is reserved in a working storage area of the listing module. The listing probably contains the free-format version of the source code or, optionally, the decoded, formatted version. The module will add line numbers, and the listing file, as modified, will contain appropriate error messages. It is reasonable to assume that the line numbers are attached to statements during the free-format decoding phase of Pass 1 and thereafter carried around with all processing of the statement. The error handler, when it creates an error message, can attach this line number, and the listing module will do the final synthesis to make sure that the line numbers of the error message and the listing coincide.

Coordination (executive) module.   This module directs all Pass 1 and Pass 2 activity of the assembler, calling the other modules in accordance with the plan above. It coordinates all such calls as well as error handling. It does a minimal amount of "computation" itself. We give an informal calling net—that is, a graphical structure of "who" calls "whom"—in Figure 8.7.

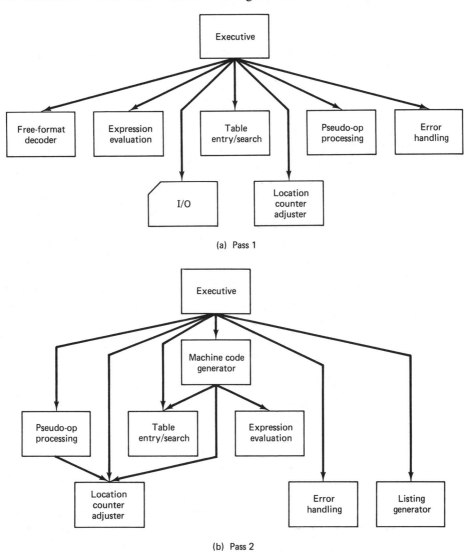

(a) Pass 1

(b) Pass 2

Figure 8.7   The assembler module "call graph."

A POSSIBLE IMPLEMENTATION

Pass 1

Pass 1 must process the source module one input record at a time after first initializing the data areas discussed above. All input records, including comments, are stored without change in the master table with the appropriate line and statement count. The statement is then subjected to lexical analysis, as shown in the flowchart in Figure 8.8a.

Lexical analysis is the process of assembling and extracting lexical elements from the character string constituting the statement. *Syntactical analysis* is the process of identifying the extracted elements. If a higher-level language, such as PL/G—which offers suitable character string primitives for finding the next blank— is employed for implementation, lexical analysis becomes trivial. The restricted syntax of an assembly language also trivializes syntactical analysis. If the first element starts in column 1, it is a label; if column 1 is blank, the label does not exist. The first nonlabel element will be the operations/pseudo-operations code followed by one or two operand addresses, register designations, or immediate value. As these syntactical elements are extracted and identified by the subprocedure shown at the bottom right of the flowchart in Figure 8.8a, they are moved to the master table for later use. The symbolic operations code is immediately used as the search key into the operations code table.

As we have previously discussed the three methods of table search, it will suffice to note that the opcode table is completely initialized and does not grow during the assembly process; thus,it could be stored in sorted order and a binary (logarithmic) search employed. Alternatively, it is often possible to identify a function that allows hash searching of the opcode table with almost no collisions and with a minimum of extra space consumed, as discussed earlier. When the opcode is identified as either a pseudo-operation code (the key is moved to the master table) or an operations code (the key of 4 and the binary machine version is moved to the master table), the length is found (from the opcode table for operations codes, from the operand field for pseudo-operations). Finally, the relative location counter is incremented accordingly.

The key, just identified, is used in a decision block to direct further processing, as shown near the top of the flowchart in Figure 8.8b. If available in the implementation language, a CASE statement would be suitable for this multiway branch; if not, a series of nested conditional branches will suffice. Referring back to our definition of the source language syntax of an input module to our assembler, recall that the first record encountered must be a PROCEDURE name (kind = 0) record. This record will generate the initial record of the output binary machine code file.

The next input source code record will identify that the following records, until a CODE record is encountered, will specify an external module name or data areas (external or internal). The specific pseudo-operation found in the record will indicate the segment involved. The appropriate key will be used to control which relative lo-

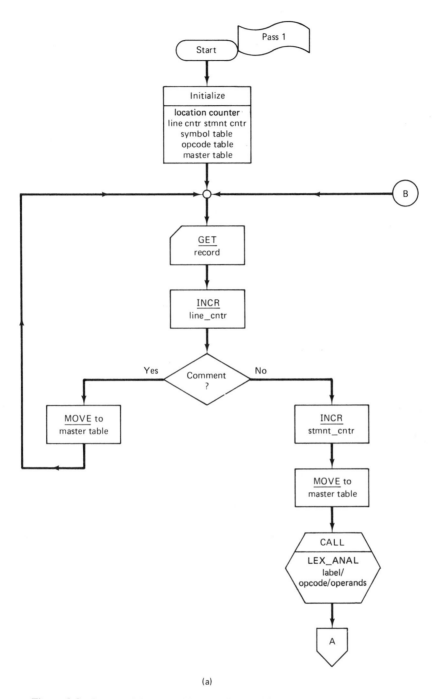

(a)

Figure 8.8 Pass 1 of the assembler, as discussed in the text. (Adapted from G. W. Gorsline, *16-Bit Modern Microcomputers: The Intel I8086 Family,* © 1985, pp. 355, 357, and 358. Reprinted by permission of Prentice-Hall, Inc., Englewood Cliffs, NJ.)

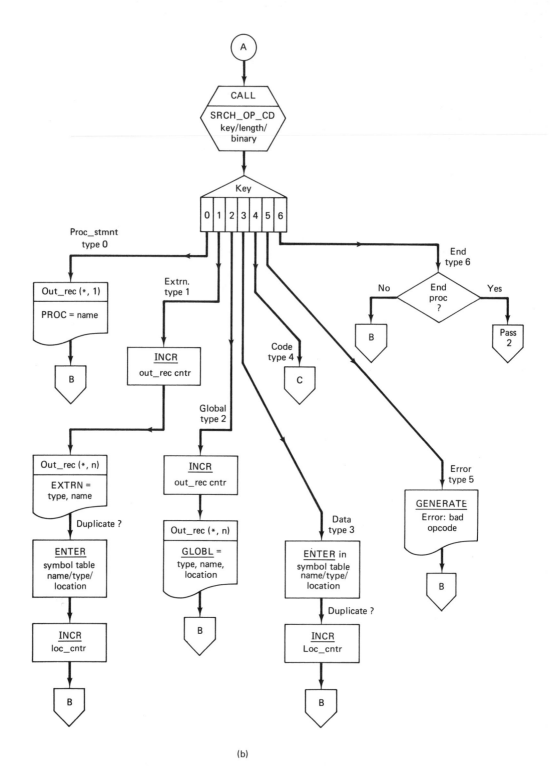

(b)

Figure 8.8 (continued).

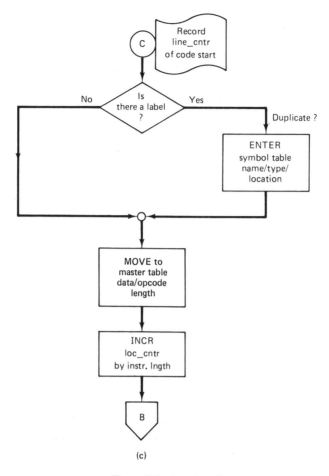

Figure 8.8 (*continued*).

cation counter is incremented (which segment is currently involved). If a reference to an external module (subprocedure) is involved in the code segment, the specifications of our example assembly language syntax require that the programmer furnish an EXT pseudo-operation for each such unique procedure referenced. Similarly, references to external data areas also require that an EXT pseudo-operation be the references to external data, stack, or extra segment data containers for variable or constant data. Each external reference input record will cause an entry in the symbol table, with key = 1 and a relative location of zero. In addition, each external reference input record will cause an EXTRN output record to be generated. Note that references to external data areas and procedures must have the relative location in the appropriate segment recorded in the EXTRN output record during the symbol table search of Pass 2. The programmer can allow data areas in the module to be accessed via EXT references in other modules by specifying them using the GLOBAL pseudo-operation.

References, via labels, to data containers for variables and for constants can be defined via pseudo-operations. In our example assembly language, we specify that a data container must have a label, one of the following pseudo-operation mnemonics, and a length in the case of a variable or a value in the case of a constant. The pseudo-operation available to specify data segment containers are

label:	LNGWRDS	number of long words
label:	WORDS	number of words
label:	BYTES	number of bytes
label:	CONSTANT	value followed by the letter B for bit, D for decimal, H for hexadecimal, or C for ASCII

Stack data containers are limited to long-word-size variable data containers whose addresses always start at the high-address end of the area and progress downward.

label:	STACK	size in long words

Good coding practice might suggest that data containers be specified in some particular order—say, external, global, data. Nevertheless, our assembler should possess the ability to interpret correctly data container definitions that occur in any order. The end of the data container definitions and the start of the code segment is signaled by the pseudo-operation CODE, as shown in Figure 8.4.

Each source language input record in the CODE section consists of an optional label, an operations code, and one or two operands (with an intervening comma). The main task of Pass 1 is to assign a relative location to each label. This task requires that the length of each instruction be determined by looking up the operation code in the opcode table and then incrementing the location counter appropriately. As this process makes the binary machine code version of the operations code available, it is moved to the master table at this time. Any labels are recorded in the symbol table with their relative location and a type = 4. This process continues, statement by statement, until the pseudo-operation END is found, which will cause a branch to Pass 2.

Pass 2

At the conclusion of Pass 1, all processing is completed relative to label addresses and operation codes. The main tasks remaining to be accomplished in Pass 2 are the resolution of operand addresses, the output of a suitable listing, and the output of the binary machine code object file in the format expected by the link routine.

When examining the flowchart of Pass 2 shown in Figure 8.9, it should be realized that we are examining assembly language in which the syntax

Operation A,B

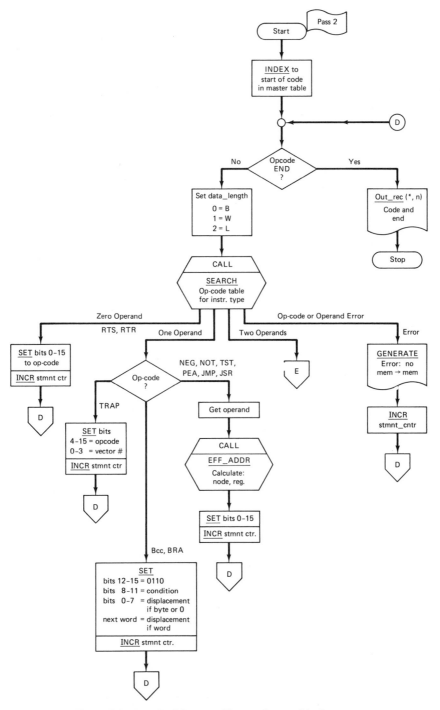

Figure 8.9 Pass 2 of the assembler, as discussed in the text.

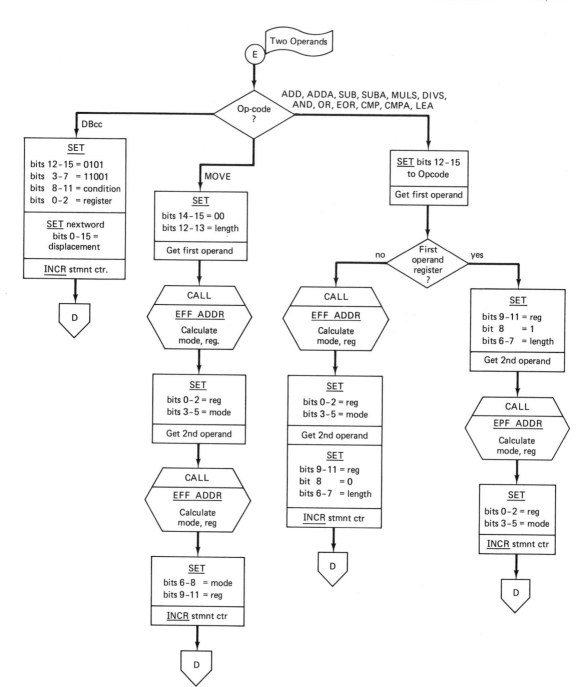

Figure 8.9 (*continued*).

has the semantics

$$A + B \rightarrow B$$

The final value of the second operand is determined by the initial value of the second operand plus the value of the first operand, with no change to the first operand occurring. The source-level format must be transformed to the binary machine code format.

When an external symbol is encountered while resolving memory addresses in Pass 2, it is necessary to record the relative location of the reference in the appropriate EXTRN record of the binary machine code file for use by the link routine.

When the END symbolic pseudo-operation is encountered, it is still necessary to write the binary machine object code file to an appropriate device—probably a floppy or Winchester disk—while recording the file name (procedure ID), file type (object file), physical address, and length in the library directory.

In addition, it is also necessary to display a listing of the assembly source code with its associated relative locations and binary machine code in hexadecimal notation. Any error notations should be interspersed in this listing so that they immediately follow the statement in question. Presumably, the existence of an error would preclude the writing of the binary machine object code file to a disk-based library. On the other hand, it is often desirable to store the assembly source language version of a procedure on a disk-based library for later use and possible change.

MACRO EXPANSION

In Chapter 5, we discussed the utility of macros in the composition of assembly language programs. From that discussion and from your programming practice, you will recall that a macro is a programmer-named definition (possibly with parameters) that is to be substituted in line into the assembly source code at each place where the macro name occurs (is invoked or is called) in the opcode field. During the substitution process, the parameters in the definition (if any) are replaced by the arguments in the invocation (call), and any conditional assembly directives are carried out. During our discussion of a processor to expand macro references during the assembly process, we will assume that you have read, have studied, have understood, and have practiced the use of macros and the use of conditional assembly.

Recall that we have referred to the assembling of an assembly source module to a binary machine code object module as a one-statement-for-one-statement transliteration. In contrast, the normal and common macro invocation (call) results in from one to many instructions being placed into the assembly source code. Thus, it is an expansion of the source code and resembles a translation more than a transliteration. This macro expansion process can occur during Pass 1 of the assembler—as shown in Figures 8.2 and 8.3. If this design strategy is chosen, the macro processor would constitute an additional module of the assembler. The assembly call graph, shown in Figure 8.7, would be amended to include this independent and complicated "macro expansion module." Many commercially available assemblers adopt this design strategy. Alternatively, the macro expansion process can be accomplished as a sort of preprocessing before Pass 1. In this case, it would be proper to term the macro expansion section *Pass 0*. The advantages and disadvantages of one design strategy relative to the other are not great. For instance, although the Pass 0 strategy results in a cleaner, less cluttered Pass 1, it does require an additional examination of the source code, with a resultant time penalty.

A more difficult design choice is involved in the treatment of conditional assembly. It is possible to treat the conditional assembly directives—such as AIF, AGO, and so on—as assembly directives and to process them in the context of that module of the assembler. As you can imagine, the use of temporary assembly time labels may be somewhat convoluted and difficult, while such directives as MEXIT are almost meaningless outside the bounds of a macro. Therefore, the use and processing of conditional assembly directives (orders) is usually, but not universally, restricted to be within macros.

As a very abbreviated review, we present the chief features of macro definitions. The usual syntax for a macro definition is

Label field   *Opcode field*   *Operand field*

Sample style # 1

              MACRO   NAME,param1,param2, ... ,paramN
                .
                .   body of macro
                .
              MEND   NAME

Sample style # 2

    NAME   MACRO   param1,param2, . . . ,paramN
                .
                .   body of macro
                .
              ENDM   NAME

Sample style # 3

              MACRO   NAME,param1 = default,param2 = default,
                                . . . ,paramN = default
    NAME   .
                .   body of macro
                .
              MEND   NAME

Similarly, the usual syntax for a macro invocation (call) is

Label field	*Opcode field*	*Operand field*

Sample style # 1

	NAME	arg1,arg2, . . . ,argN

Sample style # 2

	NAME	arg1 = value,arg2 = value, . . . ,argN = value

It is important to note that the character strings MACRO and MEND (or ENDM), as well as all the conditional assembly directives, such as AIF, AGO, MEXIT, and so on, constitute reserved words with the assembly language. It is also important to recall that a macro must be defined before it is invoked (called), that a macro definition can occur nested within a macro definition, and that a macro definition may invoke (call) a previously defined macro.

THE MACRO EXPANSION PROBLEM

From our discussion above, we can now define a *macro processor* as a portion of the assembler that expands in place a macro invocation (call) into corresponding assembly source code statements using the macro definition previously encountered in the source code module. The object statements emanating from a macro processor are assembly language source code.

If the macro expansion is performed as a portion of Pass 1 of the assembler (as shown in Figure 8.2 and 8.3), the resulting assembly statements can and will be immediately assembled. If the macro expansion is performed as a Pass 0 preprocessor, then the macro definitions and the macro invocations (calls) must be marked in some manner so that they will be ignored by Pass 1 and Pass 2 while the generated statements are being assembled. The definitions and the invocation (call) statements should appear in the listing to allow the programmer to examine the actual input.

In general, the overall task of the macro processor constitutes a kind of character string processing. Certain predefined character strings must be recognized; if the string is a parameter, a substitution of a different character string (the corresponding argument) must be made or, if the string is a conditional assembly directive, a specific action must be taken (usually involving the search for a label). Notice that these two main tasks reduce to two lower-level, more generalized tasks:

SEARCH   for a character string
MOVE   (replace) a character string

Some procedural-level languages support the character string data type, allowing the declaration of a string of length N. In PL/I, the declaration could be

DCL   STRNG1,STRNG2,STRNG3 CHAR(10);

and then it is possible to specify

```
IF (STRNG1 = STRNG2)
    THEN DO;
        STRNG3 = STRNG1:
        END;
    ELSE DO;
        .
        .
        END;
```

In Pascal, the equivalent declaration could be

```
type
    NameString = packed array 1 . . . 10 of char;
Var
    Strng1:NameString
    Strng2:NameString
    Strng3:NameString
```

and then it is possible to specify:

```
if Strng1 = Strng2   then
    Strng3 := Strng3
else
    begin
        .
        .
    end;
```

In languages that do not support the character string data type, strings must be processed as one-dimensional arrays of single characters. In many older FORTRAN dialects, the problem would be tedious:

```
CHARACTER   STRNG1(10),STRNG2(10),STRNG3(10)
```

with the comparison being performed character by character:

```
        DO 7  I = 1,10
            IF (STRNG1(I) .NE. STRNG2(I)) GO TO 10
    7           CONTINUE
C
C   if we get to this point, the strings were identical
C
```

```
      DO 8   I = 1,10
            STRNG3(I) = STRNG1(I)
  8         CONTINUE
C
C  if we get this point, the strings were different
C
  10              .

                 .

                 .
      GO TO 999
```

The instruction sets of some computers include assembly language construct equivalents of actual machine instructions to support character string comparisons and character string movements. The Intel I8086 family (I8088/I8086/I188/I186/I286/I386) and the DEC VAX family designs include such instructions. Compilers for procedural-level languages for such computers can employ these instructions to generate efficient code to manipulate character strings. Alternatively, if extreme speed of processing is required, the character string portions of the program could be implemented as assembly-level subprodcedures. The instruction set of the Motorola MC680XY family of computers does not support character string manipulations, forcing compilers to employ character-by-character tactics somewhat similar to the FORTRAN example above to accomplish the comparison and movement of character strings.

If and only if the syntactical rules of the macro facility of the assembly language require that the macro definitions occur before they are used (invoked or called), the equivalent of the forward-reference problem does not occur in the macro processor. This programmatic restriction is not onerous and constitutes no limitation on the ability of programmers to express desirable algorithms using macros. In addition, this restriction—requiring a macro to be defined before it is used—is an almost universally accepted convention. Therefore, we will adopt it in our consideration of macro processor design and implementation techniques.

Thus, we are requiring that a macro processor (Pass 0 or a module of Pass 1) recognize and save all macro definitions before any macro invocation (call) statements are encountered and acted upon. The general plan of a macro processor employing this strategy is twofold:

Part 1: While scanning the assembly language source code, build a table of macro definitions and a directory into this table by name.

Part 2: While still scanning the assembly language source code, recognize macro invocations (calls) and expand them *in situ,* including any and all conditional assembly directives.

To firmly cement the concepts of a macro processor and the work it accomplishes while expanding macros into the equivalent assembly language statements *in situ,* we present almost identical algorithms for a one-pass macro processor in two forms: in structured English (Figure 8.10) and as a flowchart (Figure 8.11). To stress

Part 1: Find and record macro definitions.
1. Initialize table counters/indexes.
2. Read next line of source code and output to Pass 1 input file.
   IF not MACRO pseudo-op
       THEN IF CODEAREA pseudo-op
           THEN go to Part 2
           ELSE go to 2
3. Read next line of source code and output to Pass 1 input file.
   a. Enter parameters into parameter table with index number and incre-
      ment.
   b. Enter macro name in macro definition table directory with pointer into
      macro definition table. Increment directory index.
   c. Enter macro name into macro definition table and increment pointer.
4. Read next line of source code and output to Pass 1 input file.
   a. Substitute an index number for each actual parameter.
   b. Enter line into macro definition table and increment pointer.
   c. IF MEND pseudo-op
       THEN go to 2
       ELSE go to 4

Part 2: Find macro invocations and expand each.
1. Read next line of source code and output to Pass 1 input file.
   IF opcode field is not a macro name (is not an invocation)
       THEN IF opcode field is END pseudo-op
           THEN go to Pass 1
           ELSE go to 1
2. Get next line from macro definition table and increment pointer.
   IF opcode field is MEND pseudo-op
       THEN go to 1
       ELSE substitute invocation arguments for parameter indexes
3. IF line contains conditional assembly directive
   a. THEN
      (1) Evaluate any condition.
      (2) Find line in macro definition with needed label.
          IF label is not found
              THEN generate error code and go to 1
      (3) Adjust macro definition pointer and get line with needed label.
      (4) Go to 2.
   b. ELSE go to 2

Figure 8.10 Algorithm for one-pass macro processor expressed in structured
English. (Compare to Figure 8.11.)

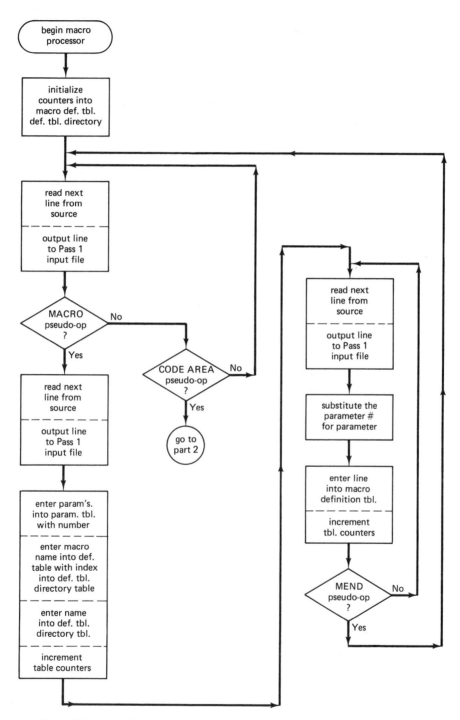

Figure 8.11 Algorithm for a one-pass macro processor expressed as a flowchart. (Compare to Figure 8.10.)

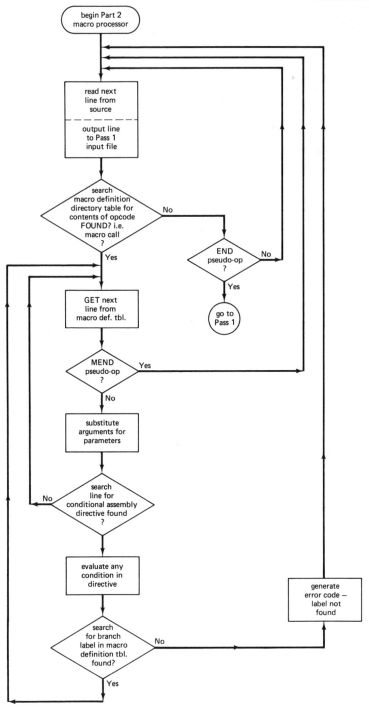

Figure 8.11 *(continued)*.

principles, these algorithms do not allow for the possibility of a macro invocation (call) within a macro definition and do not allow for the possibility of a macro definition being nested within a macro definition. We will approach solutions to these difficulties later.

DESIGNING A MACRO PROCESSOR

We will consider the design and implementation of a macro processor from three viewpoints:

1. The source language syntax and the associated semantics of the macro definitions and conditional assembly directives that our example macro processor will accommodate.
2. The data containers necessary or convenient to accomplish the macro processing task.
3. The abstraction of the macro processor actions into convenient and independent modules that can be correctly combined to form a viable and robust system.

Our first design decision is to implement our macro processor as a Pass 0 preprocessor.

The Language

The overall format of the input for our example assembler, as given in Figure 8.4, must be changed to include a section for macro definitions, as shown in Figure 8.12. If the definition of a referenced macro is not found in this area, the systems library file catalog should be searched for the name and the definition added. The contents of the macro definition area will be ignored (but copied into the master table) during Pass 1 of the assembler. It may facilitate macro processing to remove this task to the macro processor. Our example macro assembler will follow this plan. We will insert the character "%" into column 1 of these source statements to signal Pass 1 to copy and ignore them—to treat them similarly to comments. If a label occurs in the macro definition, as is possible, the label will be moved one column to the right so that the label has the format % LABEL: . Thus, the decision block in the middle of the Pass 1 flowchart of Figure 8.8a must also recognize the "%" character as well as the ";" character. This is the only change necessary to the assembler, although it will sometimes facilitate processing to have the master table constructed by the macro processor (Pass 0), as we will illustrate in our example processor.

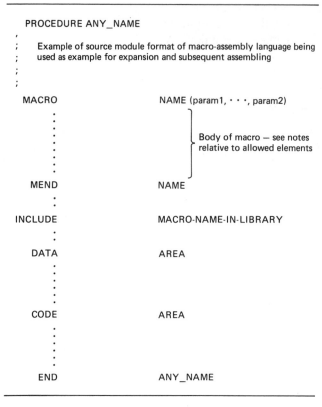

PROCEDURE ANY_NAME

'
;   Example of source module format of macro-assembly language being
;   used as example for expansion and subsequent assembling
;
;

    MACRO   NAME (param1, · · ·, param2)
      .
      .
      .   ⎫
      .   ⎬ Body of macro — see notes
      .   ⎭ relative to allowed elements
      .
    MEND   NAME
      .
  INCLUDE   MACRO-NAME-IN-LIBRARY
      .
    DATA   AREA
      .
      .
      .
      .
    CODE   AREA
      .
      .
      .
      .
    END   ANY_NAME

Note 1: Any element in body of macro of the form
         and param# will be replaced by the
         corresponding argument during expansion
Note 2: Supported conditional assembly directives are
              AGO   ANOTE   MEXIT
              AIF   SET
Note 3: A label can be generated by appending an #:
              LABEL#

Figure 8.12   Overall format of the source macro-assembly language module for input into the macro assembler described in the text.

The definition of our example macro will have the format

&label:MACRO   NAME(param1,param2, . . . ,param N)
        -                                  ; body of macro
        -                                  ; to be expanded
        -                                  ; and substituted
       MEND   NAME

where the items in lowercase letters are optional. Note that labels and/or parameters may or may not occur. A reference to a macro and thus an order to expand the definition and substitute the results at this place in the assembly source code will consist of the use of the macro name in the assembly operation code field with the arguments (if any) occurring in the operand address field (separated by commas and with no blanks; the arguments must correspond to the definition parameters in type, precision, and position):

label: NAME (arg1,arg2, . . . ,argn)

again, where the items in lowercase letters are optional.

The four tasks that a macro processor must accomplish are

1. *Recognize the macro definition* by the word delimiters MACRO and MEND. In our example, this task is simplified by the requirement that all macro definitions immediately follow the PROCEDURE statement and precede the DATA areas. Intervening comments are allowed, as shown in Figure 8.12. Note that our example processor will not correctly process nested macro definitions, although it will allow macro references (calls) within macro definitions to an arbitrary depth.

2. *Save the definition* for use during the expansion process. In our example, the definitions will be placed in the master table together with all of the source program statements, comments, and expanded references. Thus, this task is being removed from Pass 1 of the assembler and accomplished by the macro processor—Pass 0. The assembler flowchart in Figure 8.8a will be affected. A table of macro names must also be constructed. We will allow macro definitions to occur in the systems library and be incorporated into the macro source code by defining a macro pseudo-operation,

   INCLUDE NAME

   that will cause the system program library to be searched and the referenced macro definition to be inserted into the procedures.

3. *Recognize macro references* (calls) within the DATA areas and within the CODE segment. This will require that the symbolic contents of the operations code field of every statement be searched for in the macro names table constructed in task 2. As our example macro processor allows macro references within macro definitions, this search will also be required for each expanded statement generated in task 4.

4. *Expand macro references* (calls) while following the conditional assembly directives and substituting symbolic values for dummy macro arguments found within the body of the definition. As each expanded statement is generated, it must be entered into the master table as a sequential portion of the source code that will be assembled by Pass 1.

A careful examination of the tasks of the macro processer (Pass 0) and of the assembler Pass 1 of our example should reveal that no incompatible tasks exist. Thus, it would be possible to combine the macro processer (Pass 0) into the assembler Pass 1 and perhaps shorten total assembly time at the expense of clarity. We will not follow this approach but will keep the macro processor functionally separated from our basic assembler.

Data Containers

Recalling that the vital task of Pass 0—the macro processor—is to substitute the conditionally expanded macro definitions into the assembly source program at the macro reference (call) points, we will require input data containers, temporary work data areas, and output data containers. Our example macro processor will need two inputs:

1. The assembly language source code module.
2. If any library-resident macros are referenced, these macro definitions are required to be in the program library.

Our assembler will produce as output:

1. An augmented version of the source code in the master table with the IN-CLUDEd library-resident macro definitions, the conditionally expanded macro references, and any notes encountered via ANOTE directives. The definition and reference (call) statements will be marked with a "%" in column 1.
2. A bit variable indicating success or failure of the macro processor.

Our example Pass 0 (macro processor) will use two data containers as work areas during processing:

1. A macro name table that will be dynamically built as macro definitions and INCLUDE directives are encountered. This table of macro names will be used in task 3 to allow recognition of macro references (calls).
2. A parameter list table that will be built from the macro reference (call) and used to facilitate substitution of actual for dummy arguments during macro expansion. If nested macro references (a call within a definition) are encountered, this table will be augmented using a special character to separate the different argument groups. These groups will be created and destroyed using a stack discipline.

Modularization

We will approach the specification of the modules in much the same way that we did for the assembler Pass 1 and Pass 2. The modules are as follows:

I/O module
Definition entry module

Call recognition module
Argument list preparer module
Text generation module—arguments and conditionals
Error handler module
Coordination (executive) module

The algorithms are adapted from the presentation of Lemone and Kaliski (1983).

I/O module. There is little difference in the I/O module in macro processor design and that in assembler design. Recall that the macro processor is a preprocessor to the assembler. Its input is a macroassembly program with macro definitions and calls. Its output is a "pure" assembly language program, devoid of both definitions and calls, the calls having been marked "%" and replaced with expanded text. It is the role of the input/output module, in part, to create these various I/O files and to interface properly with the user and assembler.

Definition entry module. This module enters into a directory of macro definitions the body of the macro.

Inputs: The source statements comprising the definition of a macro, including the MACRO and the MEND statements.

Outputs: An updated macro definitions directory and source file.

General procedure: This module updates the master directory of macro definitions. The macro name, parameter list, and macro body are recorded in the directory.

Exceptional conditions: Typical of the types of errors that this module may detect are "multiply defined" macros (if we wish to regard this as an error—some systems permit the redefinition of a macro), excessive length of body, illegal syntax in the MACRO statement, and the like.

Technical notes: Accompanying this table will be a "directory" that is of fixed block size and that allows rapid linear searching of macro definitions. Macro parameters can be specially marked during entry to avoid repetitive searches for them during call expansion. Usually a non-user-allowed character, delimiting the parameter on both sides, will suffice here. This module is called when a MACRO statement is seen in the source by the executive module. This statement and all ensuing source statements up to and including the statement are copied into a special file and then passed to the definition entry module for entry.

Call recognition module. This module performs a search of the macro definitions table to see whether or not the operation field of a statement is indeed a macro call.

Input: The operation field of a source statement in the macroassembly language.

Output: A flag (*yes* if it is a macro call; *no* if it is not) and a pointer to the body of the macro if it is a call.

General procedure: The macro definitions table is searched for the name in the operand field. If it is found, then a macro call has occurred. The "directory" points to the stored body of the macro. This pointer is returned.

Exceptional conditions: None.

Technical notes: Usually a linear search will suffice, as most macro libraries are limited in size. Sometime this module is merged with the argument list preparer.

Argument list preparer module. This module "prepares" the list of macro call arguments, whether they be user-specified or default values and whether the specification be positional or keyword.

Input: The operand field of a macro call.

Output: The argument list to be used in expanding the macro.

General procedure: Using the form of the operand field (keyword or positional), the default values that appear in the definition, and the nondefault values that appear in the call, a list is produced containing the strings to be substituted for each parameter in the macro definition.

Exceptional conditions: Illegal syntax in the argument specifications, using a name in keyword specification that is not that of a parameter, and using illegal characters for arguments are typical of the types of errors that can occur here.

Technical notes: Many macro processors restrict parameters and arguments to having only certain characters. Basically, the output of the module is a sequence of pairs of the form (parameter name, argument string).

Text generation module. During the processing of a macro call, the macro processor goes through the body of the macro definition line by line, replacing macro parameters with their "call values" as prepared by the argument list preparer. This module performs a specialized form of text editing.

Input: The body of a macro and a prepared argument list.

Output: The "expanded" body, obtained by substituting for each parameter in the body the corresponding argument string.

General procedure: Each line of the body is searched for the specially marked parameters, as prepared by the definition entry module. The parameters in the line, along with their special markers, are removed and are replaced by the entries appearing in the argument list.

Exceptional conditions: The primary type of error that can occur here is one of a "text editing" flavor—for example, the expanded line is too long.

Technical notes: The problems of text substitution are well known. Certain parameters become shorter and others longer when substitutions are done. In certain macro processors, there are special characters, called *concatenation characters,* that serve to "fuse together" pieces of text and then disappear.

Error handler module.   As in the assembler, this module is the "clearinghouse" for all error message and related actions.

Coordination (executive) module.   The basic sequence of module calls controlled by the executive module is as follows: Check each statement to see if it is a MACRO statement. If it is a MACRO statement, pass it and all statements up to the matching *.endm* to the definition entry module. If it is not a MACRO statement, invoke the call recognition module to see if it is a call. If it is a call, invoke the argument list preparer and then the text generation module to expand the call.

The executive module produces, in conjunction with the I/O module, an output file formed as follows: All noncalls or nondefinitions are passed to this output file in the order they occur in the source program. All expansions of calls are also passed to it, replacing the call statements.

A POSSIBLE IMPLEMENTATION: PASS 0 MACRO PROCESSING

Although it is usual to divide a macro processor into Pass 1 and Pass 2, our source language requirement that all macro definitions occur before the data areas and the code segment, together with our use of the master table for storing the bulk of the information, have allowed us to consider the macro processor as a single processor—Pass 0. This design also allows us to relax completely the usual restriction that macro definitions that are referenced within a macro definition must physically precede the referencing macro definition. In essence, the traditional Pass 1 is contained in Figure 8.13a and the traditional Pass 2 (the expansion phase) occupies Figure 8.13b and 8.13c.

Figure 8.13a gives the logic of Pass 0A of our example macro processor. The main task of this portion is to identify macro definitions, whether they be library resident (INCLUDE) or occur in the source file. All macro definitions are transferred *in toto* to the master table for later use during the expansion phase, with column 1 being made a "%" character as a signal for the assembler routine (Pass 1 and Pass 2) to ignore them. In addition, the macro name is entered into the macro name table together with the line number of the definition in the master table to aid the expansion phase in locating the definition when needed. The end-of-procedure statement is also found (presumably after the expansion phase) and serves as the signal that macro processing is complete. A transfer to Pass 1 of the assembler then occurs.

An important element of the traditional two-pass macro processor will occur after all macro definitions have been found and copied to the master table as deter-

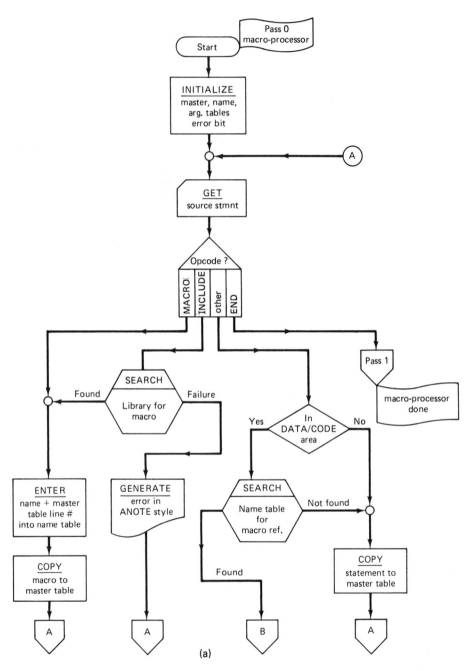

Figure 8.13 Flow diagram of the macro processor (Pass 0) discussed in the text. (Adapted from G. W. Gorsline, *16-Bit Modern Microcomputers: The Intel I8086 Family,* © 1985, pp. 381, 382, and 383. Reprinted by permission of Prentice-Hall, Inc., Englewood Cliffs, NJ.)

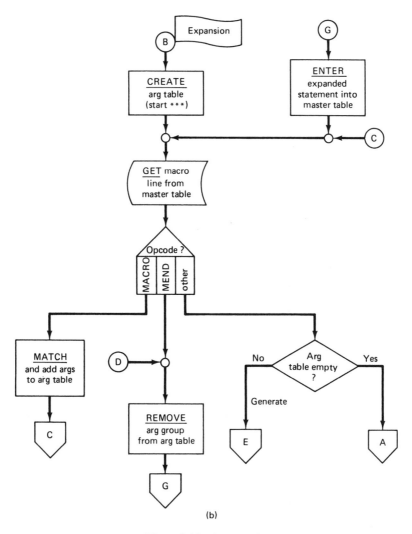

(b)

Figure 8.13   (*continued*).

mined by encountering a DATA AREA or CODE AREA statement. Each operations code must be identified as a macro reference (call) or as a symbolic assembly opcode of a normal instruction for the MC680XY. Our design searches the (now complete) macro name table for this purpose. A failure of this search is assumed to indicate a normal assembly statement, which is then copied *in toto* to the master table for later assembly by Pass 1 and Pass 2. A search success indicates a macro reference (call) and therefore invokes the expansion phase, as shown in Figure 8.13b and 8.13c.

The first task of the expansion phase is the construction of an argument table, with one entry for each argument of the macro reference in occurrence order and indexed by position. As our design allows macro references within macro definitions,

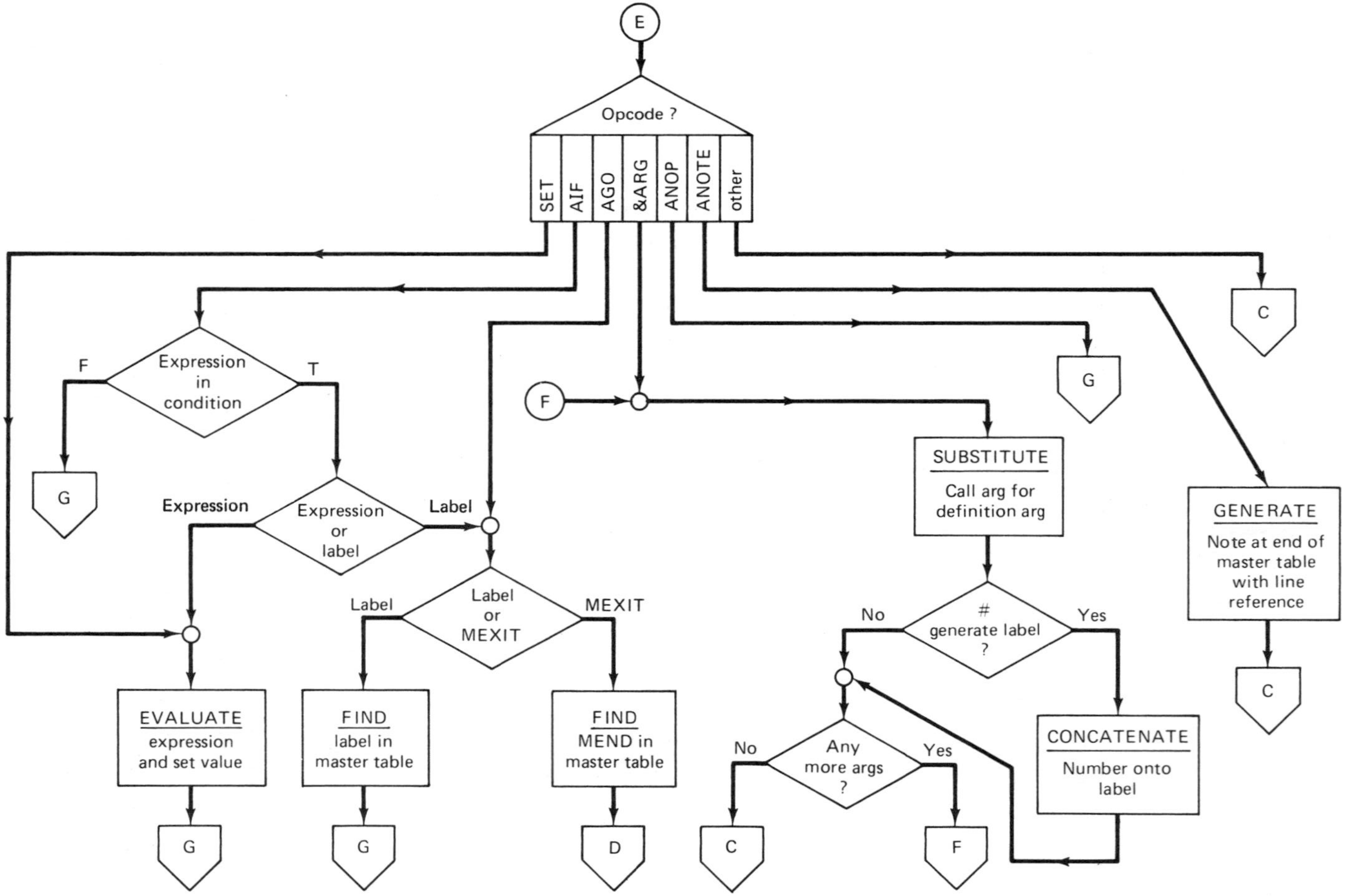

Figure 8.13 (*continued*).

this table may contain, at any instant, arguments from more than one macro. There-fore, the end of argument group for a macro is marked by a series of asterisks for identification purposes. Note that these argument names are those employed by the programmer in the reference (call) and are different from the dummy argument names used in the macro definition. These dummy names are also entered into the argument table in their respective positions during expansion processing of the MACRO statement of the definition (left-hand side of Figure 8.13b).

The argument groups in the argument table with embedded macro references form a sort of stack. Therefore, when a MEND (end of macro definition) statement is found, an argument group is removed from the table (up to an asterisk line), as shown in the center bottom of Figure 8.13b. The occurrence of an asterisk group as the last entry in the argument table is used as the test (right-hand side of Figure 8.13b) to determine if another macro definition statement should be obtained from the master table (transfer to point E in Figure 8.13c) or if another statement should be input from the programmer-furnished assembly source code (transfer to point A in Figure 8.13a).

The actual macro expansion is illustrated in Figure 8.13c. Each expanded statement is entered into the master table at point C in Figure 8.13b just before the next line of the current macro definition is obtained for expansion. The actions that are processed by the different macro definition directives are given from left to right in Figure 8.13c.

The SET directive invokes a routine to evaluate the expression in the operand field. This interpretive routine must recognize parentheses and initiate evaluation at the point of deepest nesting. Arithmetic expression evaluation in our example will follow the rules of FORTRAN, BASIC, Pascal, and PL/I arithmetic expressions, with the limitations that macro references are not allowed and that all constants and variables must be of the same type (all integer or all floating-point and all of the same precision). The operations allowed are $+$, $-$, $*$, $/$, and (). The storage recepta-cle in the label position must also agree in type and precision. Logical expression evaluation also follows the same rules, with the operators allowed being &, |, XOR, NOT, and (). ASCII character string expressions may contain the concatenate opera-tor "| |." It is important to note that we are allowing one-dimensional data contain-ers, as defined earlier. A reference to a specific array element is accomplished as

&ARRAY(subscript)

where the subscript can be constant or an &variable derived from a SET statement or from an argument. For processing simplicity—to disallow the evaluate routine from invoking the evaluate routine (a recursive routine invocation)—we are not allowing expression subscripts.

The AIF directive first invokes the expression evaluation routine to evaluate a TRUE (do the right-hand-side operand) or a FALSE (proceed to the next macro definition line) condition. If the AIF condition expression is true, the operand can be either an expression (equivalent and treated exactly like a SET directive) or a label.

In the case of a label, an expansion-time go-to is implied that results in a search within the macro definition in the master table for the label and subsequent expansion of that statement. Note that the branch target may be MEXIT, signifying a branch to the MEND statement.

The AGO directive results in a search for the label and subsequent expansion of the target macro definition statement. Again, the branch may be to the MEND statement.

The &ARG directive directs the expansion phase to search the argument table for the dummy macro definition argument and replace it with the reference (call) actual argument. In addition, any LABEL# generation situations will result in appending an incremented systems number in the place of the # directive. Note that the &ARG directive may be invoked repeatedly for any one macro definition statement (point F in Figure 8.13c).

The ANOTE directive causes this macro definition line to be appended at the end of the master table with a reference to the line number involved. As the position of the end of the master table is not known at this time (expansion is not completed), temporary storage with subsequent appending is necessary.

All other macro definition statements are copied *in toto* directly into the master table.

EXERCISES

8.1. Design, implement, test, and document the two-pass minimal assembler described in the text.

8.2. Design, implement, test as a portion of the assembler produced in Exercise 8.1, and document the macro expansion facility described in the text.

9

Relocation: Linking and Loading

In Chapter 3, when we first discussed subprocedures, we suggested that the compilers for many procedural-level languages (FORTRAN, COBOL, Pascal, C, etc.) presently produce binary machine language object code that requires not much more memory space and executes almost as fast as if the algorithm had been implemented in assembly language by a competent programmer. We were very careful, though, to enunciate the *caveat* that certain exotic data and/or address manipulations required in some algorithms are not easily expressed in the allowable syntax of the procedural language being used and that, more important, the binary machine language produced by the compiler for these usually small sections of source code is very unsatisfactory and often constitutes a time-of-execution bottleneck. We suggested that these bottlenecks be implemented as assembly language subprocedures. Note that this implementation strategy necessitates at least two separate object modules and that it therefore is necessary to use a *link* program to join them into a single integrated whole that can be loaded into main (primary) memory and subsequently executed.

In addition, even if we decide to implement the solution to some problem entirely in one single language, it is usually extremely advantageous to work on one relatively small, preferably independent module at a time. In fact, the process of program (system) design is largely a process of identifying, defining, and specifying such independent problem solution portions. Whether a single person implements each of the portions one after the other or whether the portions are allocated to different members of a team, at some point each portion must be translated (compiled or assembled) and tested. After adequate testing of each portion (involving corrections, etc.), this implementation strategy also necessitates that the several separate object modules be combined—linked—into a single integrated whole that can be loaded into main (primary) memory and subsequently executed. Linking is the process of correctly joining (fusing) independently translated (complied and/or assembled) object modules together to form a single complete entity (a load module) that is fully prepared for loading into main (primary) memory preparatory to execution.

THE LINKAGE PROBLEM

Because the linking process is so intuitively obvious and straightforward, we often neglect to consider exactly what is required to accomplish it and why. Consider a main procedure (program) that references no subprocedures, uses only data that are internally declared, and uses no absolute addresses. In essence, this main procedure is complete unto itself. It can be loaded (placed) into main (primary) memory at any desired location, and (because all addresses are relative to the program counter or are offsets from the procedure start) the program counter (PC) can be loaded with the entry point and execution successfully initiated. Note that during loading, we accomplished *relocation*. If this main procedure contains a subprocedure *entirely within itself*, the situation would be identical. Note that we are considering the case of an internal subprocedure and indirectly specifying that the main procedure and subprocedure were translated (compiled or assembled) as a single source code entity, resulting in a single binary machine code object module. These situations do not require the process of linking because independent compilation and/or assembly was not involved. However, both loading and relocation were necessary. (A few "user nonfriendly" systems may require the use of the linker merely to reformat the object module into a loadable load module. Such a requirement raises serious questions concerning the technical ability and foresight of the system designers.)

The necessity of linking occurs only when two or more independently translated (compiled and/or assembled) binary machine language object modules exist that must be combined into a single, integrated, and complete binary machine language load module. Although it is not absolutely necessary we will assume, for simplicity, that each object module has been translated with all addresses made relative to zero (the start of the module) and that the combined load module will also have all addresses made relative to zero (the start of the main procedure within the load module). Now imagine a main procedure that calls one or more subprocedures that were translated at different times. Each procedure has all addresses relative to its own start. In addition, at least some of these procedures have one or more references to one or more data areas defined in another procedure; in the terminology of Chapter 8, some procedures have declared external data and some have declared global data. The task of the linker is to combine these procedures into a single load module, with all addresses relative to the start of the load module—that is, relative to zero.

Note that we have two different kinds of address references to map from multiple relative address spaces into a single integrated address space:

1. Entry points of subprocedures.
2. Global = external data areas.

The task of the linker is to accomplish this address mapping from the multiple object modules into the single load module. The linking task will be greatly facilitated if the compiler or assembler furnishes the following information:

1. The name of each subprocedure called and the relative address(es) within the object module of the call(s).
2. The name of each referenced external data area and the relative address(es) within the object module of the usage(s).
3. The name of each global data area being made available to other procedures and the relative address within the object module of the data area declaration.

Note, in Figure 8.5, that the example assembler we considered in Chapter 8 combined 1 and 2 above into a single category. Almost all assembly languages and most compiler languages provide equivalent syntax with similar semantics. Also from Figure 8.5, note that each object module that will be input to the linker has a separate record for each external subprocedure reference, for each external data reference, and for each global data area being made available to other procedures. Thus, the linker will not be forced to perform the onerous task of finding these in the binary machine code—a task that would be almost akin to executing the procedure. Almost all object modules furnish these types of information via well-defined syntax rules. Step 4 in Figure 8.1 diagrammatically places the linking process into the problem-solving context, following translation (compilation and/or assembling) and preceding relocation and loading.

The input to the linker consists of the binary machine language object modules for a single main procedure and from zero to many independently translated subprocedures that satisfy all external call references to subprocedures and all external data references to global data areas. The format of the object modules will vary from system to system, although the example format shown in Figure 8.5 is somewhat typical. Note that the example object module file contains:

1. An object module identifier—typically, the main procedure name.
2. An object module length—often the code area length and the data area length are given separately to facilitate linking code areas separately from data areas so as to allow *pure code*.
3. An external symbol table—the external references and global data information.

Note that the linker has no access to and no reason to have access to any local programmer-defined symbols—that is, labels—or to any of the original source module statements. This last rule is necessarily violated by linkers that are a portion of *trace* and/or *debug* packages that report errors and execution flow information in terms of the original source module statements.

The output from a linker consists of:

1. A named single binary machine language load module, with all external symbol references (subprocedure calls and external data references) resolved into addresses.
2. A linkage map, specifying the relative address of the start of each subprocedure and global data area.

In addition, appropriate error and diagnostic messages may be included in the output. The total length of the load module is almost universally reported along wth the linkage map.

The process of linking is most easily accomplished in two passes, for the same general reason that two passes were necessary for the assembly process—the forward-reference problem. That is, the linker will almost always encounter an external symbol before it knows the relative address of that symbol in the final load module. Therefore, the linker will be required to build a global external symbol table using each object module's local external symbol table (records 2 through N of Figure 8.5). Included in the global symbol table will be the names of each called external module and its relative address from the beginning of the load module and each referenced global (external) data area and its relative address from the beginning of the load module. This global external symbol table will be built during Pass 1.

During Pass 2, all references to external symbols within each object module will be replaced by the relative load module addresses obtained from the global external symbol table built during Pass 1. Recall that each object module has a record for each external symbol, including the offset(s) within the module of the operand reference(s) that need amending within the load module relative address.

We present an algorithm for a relatively simple link routine in two forms: in structured English (Figure 9.1) and as flowcharts (Figure 9.2).

DESIGNING A LINKER

A link routine must have the ability to form a single loadable object file from one or more binary machine object code files of separately assembled and/or compiled procedures. It must

1. Transform all addresses of subprocedure reference instructions to the offset location within the concatenated load module.
2. Transform all operand address references (includng external references) to the offset location within the load modules, as assigned during concatenation of the object modules.
3. Copy the binary machine instructions and constant data into the correct locations within the load module binary machine code file that is ready for loading and then execution.

Pass 1: Build the global external symbol table.
1. Initialize the symbol table, the symbol table pointer, and the location counter.
2. Get name of main procedure and enter it into symbol table.
3. Search for object file. If not found, write error message and stop.
4. Input record and determine type.
   a. Procedure name record:
      (1) Save module size.
      (2) Mark procedure as found in global symbol table.
      (3) Increment symbol table pointer.
      (4) Go to 4.
   b. Global data area record:
      (1) Enter global data area name into symbol table and mark as found.
      (2) Add offset into object module to location counter and put into symbol table as relative load module address.
      (3) Increment symbol table pointer.
      (4) Go to 4.
   c. External reference record (subprocedure or data reference):
      (1) IF not in symbol table
          THEN enter into symbol table.
      (2) Go to 4.
   d. End of module record:
      (1) Add size of module to location counter.
      (2) IF all entries in symbol table have an address
          THEN go to Pass 2
          ELSE set symbol table pointer to next entry with no address and go to 3.

Pass 2: Generate load module.
1. Initialize symbol table pointer and location counter.
2. Fetch object module pointed to in symbol table from file storage to a memory buffer.
3. Update all external references using:
   a. Object module address offsets in its external records.
   b. Load module relative addresses from global symbol table.
4. Move all code and all data records to load module and then update symbol table pointer and location counter.
5. IF no more symbol table entries
       THEN stop
       ELSE go to 2.

Figure 9.1 Algorithm for two-pass link routine expressed in structured English. (Compare to Figure 9.2.)

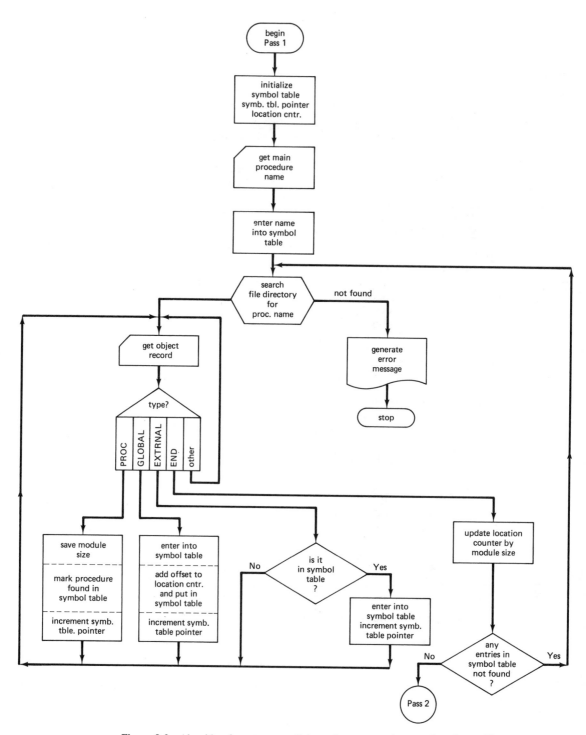

Figure 9.2 Algorithm for a two-pass link routine expressed as two flowcharts. (Compare to Figure 9.1.)

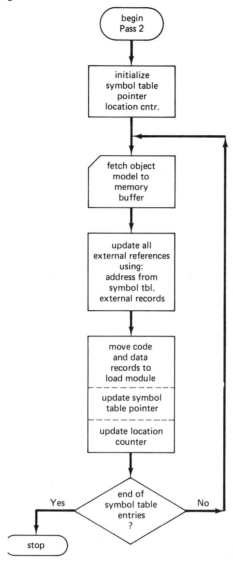

```
        ┌─────────┐
        │  begin  │
        │ Pass 2  │
        └─────────┘
             │
    ┌──────────────────┐
    │    initialize    │
    │  symbol table    │
    │     pointer      │
    │  location cntr.  │
    └──────────────────┘
             │
             ▼
    ┌──────────────────┐
    │  fetch object    │
    │    model to      │
    │    memory        │
    │    buffer        │
    └──────────────────┘
             │
             ▼
    ┌──────────────────┐
    │   update all     │
    │external references│
    │     using:       │
    │  address from    │
    │   symbol tbl.    │
    │ external records │
    └──────────────────┘
             │
             ▼
    ┌──────────────────┐
    │   move code      │
    │    and data      │
    │   records to     │
    │   load module    │
    │- - - - - - - - - │
    │  update symbol   │
    │  table pointer   │
    │- - - - - - - - - │
    │  update location │
    │    counter       │
    └──────────────────┘
             │
             ▼
           end of
  Yes   symbol table   No
          entries
             ?
    │
    ▼
  ┌────────┐
  │  stop  │
  └────────┘
```

Figure 9.2 (*continued*)

Recall that the assembler produces as output an object file for a each procedure that consists of up to five different kinds of records (refer to Figure 8.5 to refresh your memory). One or more of these single-procedure binary machine code object files will constitute the input to the link routine. The user of the link routine will name the main program, and the system will follow the external subprocedure references in finding and incorporating the additional object files needed. The output of the link routine will be a single binary machine code load module file.

The general design of our example link routine consists of two first-level modules: Pass 1 and Pass 2 (following traditional terminology). Pass 1 will assign ad-

dresses to the start of each procedure and copy the object code with new offsets from
the load module start addresses. Similarly, it will assign addresses to the constants,
if any, and copy the values into these locations. In addition, it will construct and
maintain a symbol table containing the names of all needed procedure and external
data container references, with notes as to the locations needing address information
amendment later. As procedures are found (the binary machine code file is located)
and as global data references within these procedures occur, the symbol table entry
will be marked (global data containers will correspond to external references).

When all external references are satisfied, Pass 2 will amend the address information of the load module with the relative location of the external references, as
calculated in Pass 1. The linked binary machine object code file will then be cataloged and written to a floppy or Winchester disk for later loading and then execution.

Data Containers

Again, as with the assembler, the main task of Pass 1 of the linker is to resolve the
addresses of data areas and of instructions, while the main task of Pass 2 is to enter
these addresses into the concatenated load module. Our link routine will have one or
more binary machine object code files with identical formats as input, each with
multiple records, as defined in Figure 8.5. The first of these files—the main program—is identified by the user when invoking the link routine. The link routine will
output one binary machine code load module and an indication of successful completion or error messages as output. The format of the load module is specified in
Figure 9.3. Several internal work data area containers are also necessary, including a
symbol table, a location counter, and containers to save references to external references. These are specified in Figure 9.4.

Columns 1–5	'DATA' or 'CODE' or 'END'
Columns 7–11	Starting address within segment of object bytes or constant data in hexadecimal digit notation
Columns 13 and 14	Number of bytes (hexadecimal pairs) noted on this record
Columns 17–76	Hexadecimal digit pairs represent-ing bytes of object code or con-stant data — 30 bytes (hexadecimal pairs) allowed
Columns 78–80	Sequence number (0 to n) of record within file

Figure 9.3   Format of record within the load module file output by the link routine
discussed in the text as an example. (Adapted from G. W. Gorsline, *16-Bit Modern
Microcomputers: The Intel I8086 Family,* © 1985, p. 364. Reprinted by permission
of Prentice-Hall, Inc., Englewood Cliffs, NJ.)

```
Declare
  SYMBOL_TABLE(999) 1,
    2 NAME CHAR(10),                    /* Procedure or external/global */
    2 TYPE FIXED DEC(1),
    2 LOCATION CHAR(4),                 /* Hexadecimal */
    2 FOUND BIT(1),
    2 REFERENCES CHAR(2,18);            /* Hexadecimal within */
                                        /* procedure */

Declare
  SYM_TAB_LINE_CNTR FIXED DEC(3),       /* Hexadecimal */
  LOCATION_CNTR(2),|CHAR(4),
  INPUT_RECORD CHAR(80),
  OUTPUT_RECORD CHAR(999,80);
```

Figure 9.4 Necessary data areas for the link routine discussed in the text. (From
G. W. Gorsline, *16-Bit Modern Microcomputers: The Intel I8086 Family,* © 1985,
p. 364. Reprinted by permission of Prentice-Hall, Inc., Englewood Cliffs, NJ.)

Modularization

Because the task of the link routine is fairly simple, the number of modules necessary are few:

> I/O module (Passes 1 and 2)
> Global symbol directory creator module (Pass 1)
> Relocation/linking module (Pass 2)
> Load module creator module (Pass 2)
> Coordination (executive) module

The algorithms are adapted from the presentation of Lemone and Kaliski (1983).

I/O module.   This module is invoked in Pass 1 to read in the object files to
be linked together and in Pass 2 to write the load module into the appropriate file
(and possibly the global symbol directory as well, if a trace or debug load module is
desired).

> *Input:* An object file cataloged in the file system.
> *Output:* A load file to the file system.
> *General procedure:* Use available I/O of implementation language.
> *Exceptional conditions:* Those usually associated with I/O.

Global symbol directory creator module.   This module, invoked in Pass
1, calculates the "true values" for all external global symbols and creates a master
directory of global data areas, their entry points and their values, called the global

symbol table. It does this by using the external symbol table of each module and the "segment lengths" of the modules.

Inputs: The external symbol table of a module, its segment length, and a starting address (relative address in the load module).

Outputs: An entry into the global symbol table for each external record in the external symbol table. The form of the entry is (symbol name, address), where the relative address of the symbol appearing in the external symbol table is the updated starting address of the subprocedure or global data area.

General procedure: The procedure is straightforward. The external symbol table for module X is searched. For each symbol found, calculate the relative address. This value, along with the symbol name, is entered into the global symbol table. A simple table entry/search procedure is assumed to be available. After all symbols in the external symbol table have been processed, proceed to next object code module.

Exceptional conditions: Multiply defined symbols (i.e., symbols defined in two different segments) would be detectable by this module during its global symbol table entry phase.

Relocation/linking module.   This module, invoked in Pass 2, modifies all relocatable address or external address references found in the object file of the segment by consulting the relocation and linkage directory of the segment.

Inputs: The relocation and linkage directory of the module, its "conventional object code," and the global symbol table.

Output: An object file with all relocatable address and external address references correctly linked/relocated.

General procedure: Each entry in the relocation and linkage directory is examined in turn. Recall that it is of the form (*address, symbol name*). The *symbol name* is searched for in the global symbol table. Its value is added to the appropriate field of the machine code in m_j assembled at relative address *address,* so as to relocate/link the machine code. This new machine code (so modified) replaces the "old" machine code at *address.*

Exceptional conditions: It will not always find an entry in the global symbol table for the symbol.

Technical note: The format of the relocation and linkage directory can be chosen so as to maximize linker efficiency, as it is not primarily a user-visible file.

Load module creator module.   This module, also invoked in Pass 2, moves the relocated/linked code of the object file (and all the remaining code as well) into the load module.

Inputs: An object module suitably linked by the linking module; a starting address a.

Outputs: None.

General procedure: This is basically a block move routine, which moves the modified machine code of module X to "location" a in memory. This value, a, is most likely an offset (relative address) from a base address that is to be determined at the time the "load module" is loaded by the system.

Technical notes: With no relocation and linkage directory or external symbol table of its own, it cannot be linked with other load modules and any further relocation must be "virtual" (i.e., done by loader routine).

Coordination (executive) module. We can summarize the action of the executive module as follows:

Pass 1. Select a_1. For $J = 1, \ldots, k$ (k = number of segments), do the following: Call the global symbol table creator for module m_j with starting address a_j.

Pass 2. For $j = 1, \ldots, k$, do the following: Call the linking module. Afterward, call the load module creator. Store the complete load module; optionally print out the global symbol table. Note that a_1 must be selected by the executive module to initiate the global symbol directory creator call "loop." In a virtual memory system, choosing a_1 to be 0 is a reasonable choice.

A POSSIBLE IMPLEMENTATION

Referring to the flowchart of the link routine in Figure 9.5, after initializing the data areas to character blanks, numeric zeros, or bit zero, depending on the data type, the first processing task is initiated by the programmer via a request to execute the link routine while furnishing the name of the main program. This name is then entered into line 1 of the symbol table, and a search is initiated for the binary machine code object file in the catalog. Later, this search point will be returned to for each subprocedure specified by an external reference record. If the needed object file is not found, an error message is written and processing is immediately terminated.

Records from each binary machine code object file are input one by one and examined for type—one of PROC, EXTRN, GLOBL, DATA, CODE, or END. The first record of each object file will be a PROC record, while the last record will be an END record. The CODE records will follow the other records and immediately precede the END record. The first record (type 1 = PROC) contains the size of the procedure, which is placed in the location counter. When the procedure END (type 6) record is encountered, the size will be added to the current starting address for the procedure in the location counter to give the start of the next procedure to be linked. The next record of the current procedure is then obtained. We will briefly discuss the actions taken for each of the record types.

An EXTRN (external = type 2) record indicates that a subprocedure or a data area in another procedure is referenced as an operand by one or more instructions

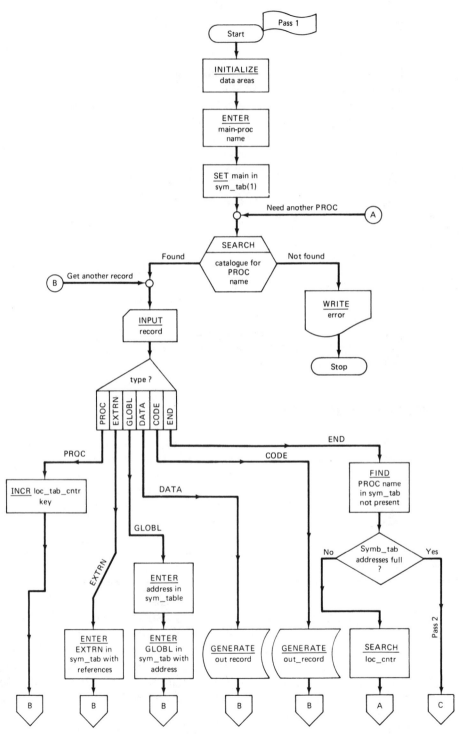

Figure 9.5 Logic of the link routine described in the text. (Adapted from G. W. Gorsline, *16-Bit Modern Microcomputers: The Intel I8086 Family,* © 1985, pp. 365 and 366. Reprinted by permission of Prentice-Hall, Inc., Englewood Cliffs, NJ.)

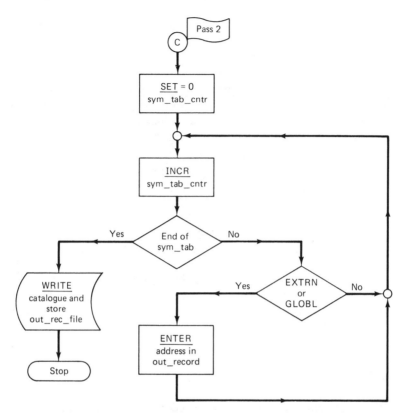

Figure 9.5 (*continued*).

(and therefore locations) of this procedure. The referenced external name must be entered in the symbol table (if a reference to a data container, it may be present as a GLOBL in the symbol table), and the relative locations within the procedure of the references must be changed to locations within the linked load module and recorded in the symbol table for use in Pass 2.

A GLOBL (global = type 3) record indicates that a data container in this procedure is being made available for reference by another procedure via an EXTRN record in another procedure. The referenced global data container name must be found in the symbol table (or entered into it, if the external reference has not yet been encountered). The relative location within the procedure is changed to the location within the load module and also recorded as the location in the symbol table for use in Pass 2.

A DATA (type 4) record will contain the hexadecimal coding of a constant at a procedure segment location. This within-procedure load address must be changed to the correct location within the load module segment, and the information must be placed in the output record format and thence into the load module file. Similarly, a CODE (type 5) record will have its within-procedure start location transformed to a load module location, and the code information must be placed in the load module file.

An END (type 6) record signifies the end of the current-procedure binary machine code object file and causes the symbol table to be searched for an external procedure name not yet linked into the load module. If such a not-yet-linked reference is found, the address of the start within the load module is calculated and then a transfer is made to the search-the-file catalog routine for the needed procedure binary machine code object file (point A in Figure 9.5). If all external procedure references have been satisfied, a branch to Pass 2 of the link routine is made.

The entire task of Pass 2 (shown in the continuation of Figure 9.5) is to insert linked load module locations of external references into the operand address locations of instructions referencing subprocedures or global/external data areas. This is accomplished by sequencing through the symbol table and using the load module reference addresses for each external reference (as recorded in the symbol table) as repositories for the load module addresses of the external symbol (as recorded in the symbol table).

When the entire symbol table has been processed—all external reference addresses resolved—the completely linked load module object file is ready for loading and execution. It is cataloged and stored in the file system of the MC680XY on a floppy or Winchester device.

LOADING

For execution to commence, the linked binary machine language load module (with all external references satisfied and with all addresses sequential and relative to the start of the module) that is cataloged and stored in the file system must be *loaded* (placed) into main (primary) memory, and the physical address of the first instruction of the main program must be moved into the program counter (PC). In concept, this process is a fairly straightforward and simple block input movement from disk to memory. In reality, we must consider several different aspects that cause the loading process to be more than a simple block data input. In outline form, the different situations are as follows:

1. Nonrelocatable code with absolute memory addresses—that is, with physical memory addresses (i.e., the physical memory addresses and the effective memory addresses are identical). The load module can be block input moved (loaded) into main (primary) memory, starting at the required physical address, the program counter loaded with this physical address, and execution allowed to commence.

2. Relocatable code with direct-to-memory addresses relative to the start of the load module. In some way, the direct-to-memory addresses have to be mapped (transformed) into physical memory addresses. Among the various possible solutions, two are common enough to merit explanation:

    a. The *relocating loader* alters all relocatable effective memory addresses in the load module by a *relocation constant* during movement to memory. The relocation constant is the physical address of the start of the load module in memory after loading. Note that the loader must alter each and every address in the load module—a somewhat lengthy task. Although not absolutely necessary, in practice the load module will occupy a single contiguous set of physical memory locations throughout its execution, and if it is temporarily removed from memory for some valid system or error condition reason, it must be reloaded back into the exact same locations. Example systems that use (or used) this method include many of the present-day MDOS and CP/M-based microcomputer systems and most of the mainframe computers of the 1950s–1960s era.

    b. The load module is block input moved (loaded) into the desired area in main (primary) memory and a *relocation register* is loaded with the physical memory address of the start of this area. All addresses are required to be relocatable (absolute addressing is not allowed). During the execution of each instruction, the necessary physical address in memory of each operand is derived by hardware as

PA $\longrightarrow$ EA + [relocation register]

In practice, the load module may be divided into sections, each with its own relocation register (temporary or permanent). Note that a program can be removed from memory and later be reloaded into a different physical memory area merely by changing the contents of the relocation register(s) appropriately. The Control Data Corporation CDC 6600 family of large, numerically oriented computers employed this tactic to advantage. As you will see shortly, this general method is used in *virtual memory* systems (the relocation register is then termed a *page register* or a *segmentation register*). During execution, the physical memory addresses are calculated with hardware assistance as:

PA $\longrightarrow$ EA + [page register]

3. Relocatable code with no direct-to-memory addresses—that is, all memory addressing is relative to the program counter or is indirect through an address register. Absolute addresses can be allowed. Just before execution commences, the relocating loader loads the program counter with the physical address of the first instruction of the already loaded load module. The specialized instructions necessary to load the address registers with physical memory addresses must be designed and implemented in such a way as to allow them to calculate the appropriate physical memory addresses. Because the label definition has been translated as its relative address within the module, at least two methods are possible to accomplish this task: the use of an offset from the

program counter or the use of an offset from the start of the loaded load module. Your understanding may be helped by realizing that many (most?) assemblers and compilers translate a label as its address. In general, a physical address is the contents of an address register (with possible variations, such as indexing, etc.):

PA $\longrightarrow$ [address register]

If this general method (register indirect to memory addressing) is employed with virtual memory (as it is with the MC68010, the MC68012, and the MC68020), the page register or segmentation register would also be involved:

PA $\longrightarrow$ [address register] + [page register]

At this point, it seems appropriate to discuss the different types of systems that we have mentioned in somewhat more detail, starting with a historical perspective.

A HISTORICAL PERSPECTIVE

Although many authors maintain that the ENIAC machine of J. Presper Eckert and John Mauchly of the University of Pennsylvania was the first electronic digital computer, numerous other developmental efforts are serious contenders for the honor, such as those of Konrad Zuse in Germany, the Turing group in Great Britain, and John V. Atanosoff of Iowa State College (now University) at Ames. Perhaps we are too close to the events and to the people themselves to truly sort it all out; or perhaps the records will indicate almost true simultaneity, because the concepts were so elegant and self-evident that many people found them without intellectual cross-fertilization.

Similarly, it is almost impossible to assign definitive credit for the organization of the vital computer control ideas and their implementation into complete operating systems. Among these developments were assemblers, compilers, relocation, I/O subsystems, libraries of both programs and data, and so on. Without any intent to precipitate an argument regarding specific credit, I hasten to mention Admiral (Dr.) Grace Murray Hopper, USNR, and Professor Maurice Wilkes of Great Britain as two of the truly inventive and influential pioneers.

For our purposes, it is not necessary to give credit and accolades to the people; rather, a brief account of the trends is appropriate. In the beginning, as we should all recall once in a while, there were a few physically large, very expensive, relatively slow, logically small, almost unique computers without software that were programmed in absolute binary. In effect, the computer was the personal property of the designer guru, who ungraciously allowed a privileged few acolytes to test the circuits while calculating exotic but useful results.

   In 1951, the first commercially available computer, the UNIVAC I, became available, followed by the IBM 701, the IBM 650, and a host of other entries into the promising but infant entrepreneurial information-processing world. In these early systems, each programmer personally operated the computer—loading paper tape or decks of cards, punching buttons, examining the contents of storage via banks of lights, and so on—that is, actually spending more time getting the computer ready for a job than was spent in the useful execution of the job. In addition, those early systems constituted a scarce resource. There was not nearly enough time to satisfy the demand; people waited in line in the dark of night to "get time on the computer." The computer guru and the lesser priests become salespeople extolling the use of the system. Wilkes (and others) "invented" the system of subprograms, which grew into program libraries; Hopper (and others) "invented" the assembler and the compiler. Job-by-job processing came into vogue and persisted until the mid-1950s.

   Then someone (actually, quite a few people in many places) automated the process of cleaning up from one job and starting the next job. With the availability of both ingenuity and hardware, the batch-processing executive came into being and was widely adopted. From our present standpoint, it is important to remember that the batch-processing executive systems of the latter half of the 1950s and the early 1960s were implemented on the "giant" computers of that era and were aimed primarily at "scientific" applications. In the context of processing ability, I would guess that the earlier batch systems (implemented on pretransistor vacuum-tube-based machines) had about the power of the present-day MC68008 system. Of course, the later transistor-based systems [such as the CDC 1604, the IBM 7090, the UNIVAC (ERA) 1103] possessed significantly more processing power—say, about that of an MC68020. In addition, with the use of transistors in implementing computers becoming fairly standard in about 1959, a class of relatively small and slow character-oriented machines for business data processing became available.

   Some genius someplace (more likely, quite a few semigeniuses at many places) dreamed of combining the available hardware into a "distributed system" for fast sequential processing of jobs one at a time. Using the more common IBM line of products, these early batch systems could be distributed as shown in Figure 9.6. Essentially, the IBM 1401 was a dedicated input/output computer under the control of a fairly simple "executive" program that read cards from the card reader and built an input tape, as well as reading an output tape and printing/punching it as directed. Although to the user it appeared to be accomplishing two tasks, in reality the resident single program was executing straightforward input/output. The IBM 7090 was under the control of an adequate but fairly straightforward sequentially scheduled uniprogramming executive or operating system. This operating system (the IBM version was called IBSYS; the SHARE version was called SOS) would execute one program from the input tape, producing results on the output tape, then proceed to the next program on the input tape, and so forth. Note that only one program was in memory and executing at any one time—hence the term *uniprogramming*—and that programs were executed strictly sequentially in the order of their occurrence on the

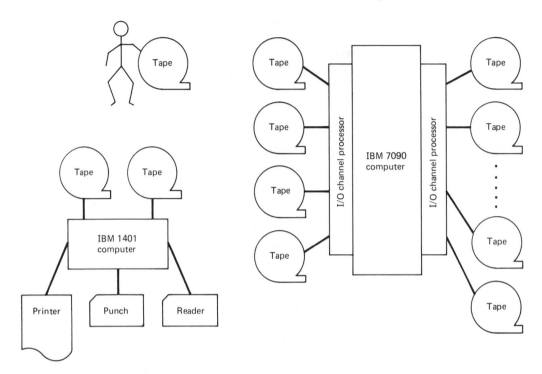

Figure 9.6 Example of "batch processing" circa 1960. An operator would build a "batch" of jobs sequentially on a tape, using the card reader of the 1401; dismount, carry, and mount the tape on the 7090 as input; and dismount, carry, and mount another output from the preceding batch from the 7090 to the 1401, where it was printed/punched while the current batch was processing and building another output tape. (From G. W. Gorsline, *16-Bit Modern Micro-computers: The Intel 18086 Family,* © 1985, p. 306. Reprinted by permission of Prentice-Hall, Inc., Englewood Cliffs, NJ.)

input tape. In many ways, the modern microcomputer operating systems, CP/M and MDOS, are equivalent to these early batch uniprogrammed executives.

As we shall consider in some detail momentarily, uniprogramming a comparatively large, very expensive, fairly rare system still resulted in less than optimum performance, both from the user standpoint and from the standpoint of the utilization of available resources. For example, the single program most often did not fully occupy memory—thus, it was maintained that the memory resource was being wasted; the single program very often had to wait for an input or an output to be completed before proceeding—thus, it was maintained that the arithmetic-logic resource was being wasted. Of course, it was possible to maintain that this waste was a necessary penalty while using the computer, but the computer was a scarce, very valuable, and necessary piece of equipment, and work was available and waiting. In addition, at times, a very long running job "captured" the machine for hours while literally hordes of users awaited their turn—and they did not wait patiently or quietly. They complained, they screamed, they got people fired.

Because the tautology that "necessity is the mother of invention" is at least partially valid, the idea of multiprogramming was implemented at a number of universities and by a number of commercial computer vendors. Just who had the idea first will probably never be known; just who had a system implemented and successfully operating is still a matter of interesting argument. Be that as it may, the consequences have been manifold. Now we could "fill" memory with programs and, when one program was waiting for I/O, "give" the ALU to another program. Thus, in one brilliant stroke, the problem of wasted memory and wasted time was solved. But was it?

In a very real sense, multiprogramming did solve many of the resource utilization problems while causing other problems. As one example, there was a particularly brilliant user (who shall remain unidentified) at one installation (which shall also be unidentified) who immediately rearranged a massive arithmetic-oriented program to do all input at the beginning, calculate for long periods, and only then do all output—thus capturing the computer for hours and effectively shutting out and alienating other users. Of course, the solution was simple: If the computer has a time-out clock interrupt, give one person the ALU for a few seconds, and then give it to the next person for a few seconds, and then the next, and so on, in a round-robin sort of arrangement. Did this strategy solve the "user wait" situation? Well, partially, at least. Note that this time-out (time slicing, really) allowed a priority scheme, so that preferential service could be given to certain important (*affluent* is a more correct term) users. Also note that the complexity of the operating system increased—dramatically—in both memory needs and running time. Some users complained that the operating system used much too much memory and hogged up to half the time (or more). At about this time (1963–1964), the minicomputer became available and underwent, over the years, the same software trend of development—job-by-job processing through uniprogramming to multiprogramming. That is, the minicomputer vendors and users did not seem to profit from the previous experience of the maxi-computer area; rather, they had to undergo the same path of learning all over again. Unfortunately, the advent of the microcomputer in the 1970s has shown the same intellectual development trends.

Returning to the multiprogrammed systems, note that the ALU could now be busy almost all the time and that memory would be full. But this "perfect" situation in fact did not occur. What we found was that computer memory was too small to hold enough programs to keep the ALU busy during the I/O. The solution—obviously, larger memories; but memories of the required size just did not exist, and if they were to be developed and become available in the then current technology, they would have been too expensive. Again, human ingenuity came to the rescue. So there were 3 or 7 or 15 or even 127 programs in memory, each taking its turn with a short time slice of the ALU to execute a few hundred or even several thousand instructions and then relinquish control for a while before getting another time slice. But recall that each of these many programs is executing only a relatively small portion of its total instructions during any one time slice and that only the executing instructions and associated data must be in memory at that time. The rest of each program could be elsewhere—say, on a disk.

Thus, the concept of paging, segmentation, and virtual memory was derived for the Atlas machine in Great Britain in 1959 and introduced to America in 1963 with the Burroughs B5000. In this scheme, the system divides a program up into "chunks," sometimes called pages (equal-sized chunks) and sometimes called segments (unequal module-sized chunks). Only those pages (or segments, as the case may be) that are currently necessary for program execution are placed in memory at any one time; the rest are kept on disk. Pages/segments are shuffled into and out of memory from disk as needed during program execution. In this manner, the memory needs for each program are minimized and more programs can be serviced in these *virtual memory* multiprogrammed operating systems. Note that this process involves a cost—sometimes a large cost—in facilities and time overhead. First, logic must be available to recognize when a new page or segment is needed, which one is needed, and which one can be removed from memory (replaced) to make room for the new one. This logic often involves additional hardware, which costs money and usually involves additional operating system modules that occupy memory space. In addition, the data paths (buses) to and from the necessary additional disks will be kept fairly busy and often may become overloaded. The trite comment that "nothing is really free" is true.

TYPES OF OPERATING SYSTEMS

Uniprogramming Operating Systems

Uniprogramming operating systems tend to be smaller in size, simpler in design, materially easier to understand, and easier to maintain correctly, as well as cheaper to purchase. Implied is a need for less memory and less disk space. As the previous discussion has indicated, the chief disadvantage is the sequential nature of executing one program to completion before starting the next.

It must be pointed out that a uniprogramming environment is eminently suited for many applications of microcomputers, such as MC680XY systems. Most personal computers, almost by definition, are used by one person at a time. This one-user environment is naturally and most satisfactorily serviced by a relatively clean and simple uniprogrammed operated system. If there is no need for servicing two (or more) users at once, there is no advantage to having the ability to do so. In some cases, it may be truly economical to purchase and use a second system rather than purchasing a second terminal and multiprogramming the microcomputer. In other cases, the reverse may be true.

Figure 9.7 illustrates the normal and traditional assignment of memory areas when employing a uniprogrammed operating system. Almost invariably, some memory space is not utilized. Although this seems wasteful, it must be remembered that sufficient memory must be available to accommodate the largest program that will be executed. If only one program at a time is required to be executed, this "waste" of memory may be the most satisfactory and economical compromise.

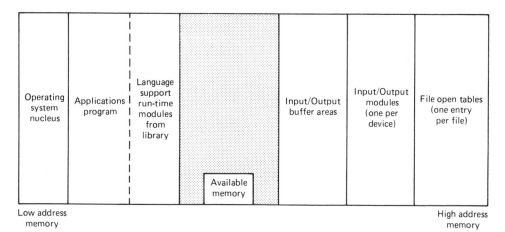

Figure 9.7 When using a uniprogramming operating system, memory is traditionally allocated with the applications program and any unused area in the middle addresses. The operating system resident nucleus and interrupt vector table are placed in low-address memory, while the I/O modules, tables, and buffers are placed in high-address memory. (From G. W. Gorsline, *16-Bit Modern Microcomputers: The Intel I8086 Family,* © 1985, p. 310. Reprinted by permission of Prentice-Hall, Inc., Englewood Cliffs, NJ.)

Figure 9.8 illustrates two of the infinitely possible resource utilization situations employing a uniprogrammed operating system. Although it is possible to have DMA input/output time exactly match and mesh (interplay on a wall clock basis), it is almost certain that this perfect match will never occur and that computer resources will be wasted. Again, note that "wasting" resources is of absolutely no importance and should be completely ignored if those resources are not needed at that time for other purposes. As an example in another context, most people own three or four ensembles of clothing, of which only one set is used at a time and none at all during sleep. We do not usually consider hanging a jacket in the closet as "wasting" that jacket. If you will, an idle resource is wasteful only if some useful purpose exists for it and the resource is not usable—is not currently capturable.

Multiprogramming Operating Systems

Multiprogramming operating systems tend to be larger in size, more complicated in design, often difficult to understand and maintain, as well as more expensive to purchase. A need for more memory and more disk space is implied. The chief advantages are the possibility of more efficient CPU and DMA channel usage; the possibility of priority processing of certain jobs, resulting in the possibility of nonsequential job processing; and the possibility of two or more interactive terminal users thinking that they have the entire system for their private use.

A multiprogramming environment is practical employing the MC68010/68012/68020 microcomputer, particularly if the CPU is augmented by a DMA and

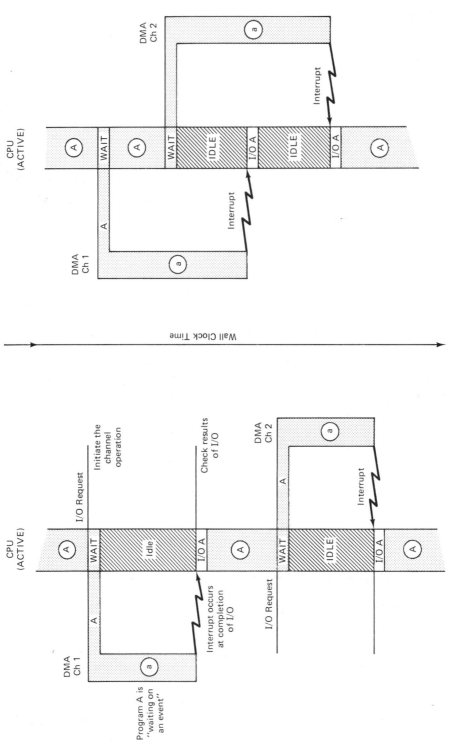

Figure 9.8 System hardware resource utilization under a uniprogramming operating system. (*Left*) The situation when the CPU, DMA channel 1, and DMA channel 2 all must access the same identical memory area for data. (*Right*) The situation when there is some but not complete independence of data area access in memory. (From G. W. Gorsline, *16-Bit Modern Microcomputers: The Intel 18086 Family*, © 1985, p. 311. Reprinted by permission of Prentice-Hall, Inc., Englewood Cliffs, NJ.)

sufficient memory is available. With the Bell Laboratory UNIX operating system, such a system should have at least the throughput capacity of many of the minicomputer systems currently available. If this memory-rich system also had the MC68881 floating-point processor and sufficient "hard" Winchester-type disks, it is probable that it would have about one-fifth the production ability of the DEC VAX 11/780 midicomputer.

Such an augmented MC68020/MC68881/DMA memory-rich Winchester-disk-supported system could be employed to provide up to an eight-terminal system for office automation, medium-size to small business accounting/inventory applications, medical-dental professional records applications, instructional systems, small engineering calculations, building security–environment control, and so on. The hardware for such systems could retail for $4000 to $15,000 (1986 prices), with the software (systems and applications) probably costing anywhere from $5000 to $25,000 or much more, depending on its availability and the necessity to customize it.

Figure 9.9 illustrates two of the many possible resource utilization situations employing a multiprogramming operating system. It would be most unlikely that the needs of several programs for the CPU and for the DMA channels would ever time-match as perfectly as is indicated in the right-hand diagram of Figure 9.9. Rather, it is very probable (almost certain) that at least one of the resources will constitute a bottleneck and that the other resources, and consequently the programs, would have to wait for service. If the critical resource bottleneck is always memory, more memory is indicated as a possible "cure"; if it is CPU cycles, an additional CPU is implicated as a possible cure; if it is I/O channels, another DMA channel is indicated. The performance analysis for bottlenecks of even a small multiprogrammed computer system can be difficult, and the true situation is often counterintuitive and nonobvious.

Virtual Memory Operating Systems

We must also consider a historically real and increasingly common class of cases where the management of program and data movement between primary and secondary memory is handled in such a way that the address space available to programmers as non-I/O operands is larger than the actual address space of primary memory. It is currently accepted to refer to the available address space of primary memory as *real memory* and the address space available to the programmer as *logical memory*. Historically, the common situation has had logical memory equivalent to, and during execution physically synonymous with, real memory. When logical memory is not real memory, a mapping function and movement algorithm(s) must be implemented to move logical address locations from secondary memory to primary memory. This mapping function may be based on sectioning the program and data, as determined by the programmer during the problem analysis and coding process, or it may be based on automatically sectioning the program and data, as determined by the programming system (assembler/compiler/linkage-editor/loader).

MULTIPROGRAMMING

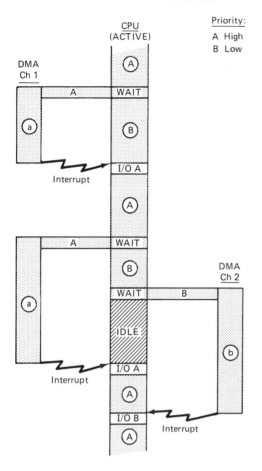

Figure 9.9 System hardware utilization under a multiprogramming operating system. (*Left*) A low degree of multiprogramming may result in "wasted" CPU cycles. (*Right*) Higher degrees of multiprogramming may result in a better balance of system resources, although normally one or more resources will be in short supply and will constitute a bottleneck. (From G. W. Gorsline, *16-Bit Modern Microcomputers: The Intel 18086 Family*, © 1985, p. 313. Reprinted by permission of Prentice-Hall, Inc., Englewood Cliffs, NJ.)

In the largely historical case where program segmentation is determined by the programmer, two schemes are worthy of mention:

1. The program is broken into a root segment (or overlay) and two or more transient segments (or overlays) that are invoked by a call to that portion of the operating system designed to control the overlay process (including some type of a relocating loader). This invocation is often accomplished by a call to a subprogram in the language being used (e.g., in FORTRAN, CALL LINK or CALL OVERLAY, with at least one parameter specifying which segment is needed).

2. Certain subprograms are declared at program load time to be nonresident except during time periods when actually needed. The FORTRAN II disk-based system of the IBM 1620 accomplished this scheme by allowing certain subprograms to be declared *local*. The invocation of any one of these local subprograms resulted in a pause in execution while the operating system located and moved the code from the disk to a known primary memory area. Execution could then resume at the first executable instruction of the subprogram: argument values would be accessed, the data manipulations accomplished, the specified arguments given new values, and finally a return made to the invoking program. The use of data held in COMMON was also allowed.

In the currently common case where program segmentation is automatically determined by the programming system, the resulting program (instructions and data) is divided into equal-sized pages (and perhaps groups of pages = segments) or the program is divided into unequal-sized segments, usually consisting of individual routines. Movement of pages or segments between secondary memory (program logical address space = virtual memory space) and primary memory (real or physical memory space) is controlled and accomplished by the operating system (often aided by special hardware). In addition to the discussions of virtual memory systems by Denning (1970, 1971), you may wish to refer to the Burroughs implementation, discussed by Organick (1973), or the Intel implementation, as discussed by Gorsline (1985). Most operating system texts contain excellent coverage of this subject. Two current references are Peterson and Silberschatz (1983), and Deitel (1982). The discussion of Coffman and Denning (1973) is excellent, though somewhat advanced and with a statistical flavor.

Because the program counter (PC) contains a pointer to the instruction in physical primary (real) memory to be fetched and because the operand addresses of non-input/output instructions must be primary (real) memory addresses, it is necessary that at least these items be resident in primary (real) memory. It is somewhat irrelevant just where the rest of the program is. It is usual that program instructions tend (albeit imperfectly) to be executed somewhat sequentially. Similarly, it is also somewhat irrelevant where the rest of the data are, although it is also somewhat common that the next reference to data will be to an operand with an address fairly close to the previous reference. This tendency of instruction references to cluster and of operand references to cluster allows us to generalize to some extent the first sentence of this paragraph: It is necessary for the currently referenced section of the program instructions and for the currently referenced section(s) of the data (operands) to be resident in primary (real) memory. This generalization allows us to consider groups of instructions and groups of data. Those groups currently being referenced must be in primary (real) memory; those groups not currently being referenced can be stored anyplace—perhaps on a disk, perhaps in primary memory.

This insight allows us to consider the possibility of dividing a program and its data areas into chunks or sections and arranging our system so that only those sections of program and data currently being referenced are in primary memory, with the rest of the chunks being stored on larger, slower, less expensive memory—say, a disk. When a new section is needed, it can be brought into primary (real) memory, replacing a section not currently being used. Because a smaller-sized primary memory would be needed, savings would ensue, but at a cost of determining which section (chunk) of program instructions and/or data is needed and of moving it to primary memory, where it will replace an already used section.

Although it really makes no difference, let us restrict ourselves, for simplicity, to a program with data areas declared within the addresses of the completely linked program and assume no use (reference to) external files or I/O buffers. This restriction allows us to specify that all addresses of instructions and of data in the fully compiled/assembled and linked program are relative to the start of that program; that is, addresses of subprocedure instructions and data have been adjusted. The addresses in this load module (size $= N$) start at 0 and progress to 1, to 2, . . . , to $N - 1$ (the last and largest address). These addresses are *program* or *logical addresses*. If the entire load module is loaded into contiguous addresses of primary memory starting at location M through $M + N$, the primary memory or *real* or *physical address* of the Kth logical address would be $M + K$. The relocation amount, M, becomes a portion of the real memory address either by (1) keeping it in a relocation register and adjusting each address as it is used or (2) adjusting each operand and branch address in the linked load module as it is loaded into contiguous addresses of primary memory. Note how important it is always to distinguish between logical (program) addresses and physical (real) addresses.

Let us now be a little more specific and consider the case of a fairly large program/data diad executing on a computer without enough available primary memory for it all to be simultaneously resident. From earlier discussion in this section, we know that the load module with logical addresses can be sectioned into chunks. Let us allow the link routine (or, alternatively, the load routine) to accomplish this for us; further, let us specify that the chunks be of a uniform size, for which we will now start using the proper term, *logical pages*. Our linked program will now consist of L uniform-sized logical pages with the numeric names 0, 1, 2, . . . , $N - 1$. If, as is the case with the IBM 43X1 system, each logical page is of size 4K bytes, then logical page 0 would contain the logical addresses 0 through 4095, logical page 1 would contain logical addresses 4096 through 8191, and so on. Note that the logical address becomes a diad, page number/offset within page, and that the mapping functions are

logical page number = floor (logical address/page size)
offset within page   = modulus (logical address, page size)

    During execution, the operating system, usually with hardware/microprogram assistance for efficiency, can be designed with algorithms that allow a program to be partially resident (have only one or a few pages) in real memory, with the rest being kept on disk in virtual memory. Each logical page in real memory has a known starting real address; thus, each logical address in the program will have an address in real memory:

real address = start of page real address + offset within page

when resident in real memory. Alternatively, the page will be on disk (in virtual memory) and must be "paged in" before its constituent contents can be accessed. It is normal for the starting addresses of pages to be kept in a *page table* available to and maintained by the operating system. The address of the page table is normally kept in a systems register; thus, access to the page table is restricted to the operating system.
    During execution, a program is normally allocated a given number of pages in real memory—that is, R real pages—which often are contiguous but not necessarily. In fact, a few systems allow programs to acquire pages as needed from the "pool" of entire memory, with some limitations depending on charge schemes. We must be careful to distinguish between real pages and logical (program) pages. For convenience, and because it is often done that way, let us divide the physical (real) primary memory into real pages of the same uniform size as the logical pages and name them numerically: $0, 1, 2, \ldots, R - 1$. As an example, let us (actually, it is the operating system that does this) allocate our small, hypothetical, $44,938_{10}$-byte program of 11 logical pages the use of 4 real (physical) pages during execution, with these being pages R17, R18, R19, and R20. Before execution, the operating system would construct a page table with 11 entries for our program and enter its real memory address into a known systems place for loading into the systems register when execution starts. The current disk addresses of each of the 11 logical pages would be entered into their respective places in the page table and a note made (a flag set) for each to indicate that it was a virtual address on disk.
    Just before execution, the operating system would load the address of the page table into the systems register and then move the first logical page from virtual memory (address from page table) and change its virtual address in the page table to be the real address in primary memory, as well as setting the flag to indicate available for access. Some operating systems would fill the allocated space completely at this time. The program counter would be set to point to the first executable statement and execution would begin. When an off-page instruction or data item is needed, an addressing fault will occur, which will result in a search of the page table to determine if the needed page is already in real memory. If its available flag is marked *yes,* the PC would be appropriately changed to the correct real address if an instruction was needed, or the appropriate real operand address would be used (page start real ad-

dress plus offset) and execution would continue. If the available flag is marked *no*, then the needed page would have to be moved to real memory, after which the real address would be resolved as above and execution would continue. Presumably, no room would be available in the allocated space in which to place the needed page; consequently, a page would have to be removed to make room.

Over the years, many different algorithms that choose which page to replace have been investigated, with the objective of minimizing total page replacement and, hence, speed execution. Although the theoretically best algorithm would involve a look-ahead to see what would happen in the future if this page or that page were replaced, in practice such an approach is not practical. In effect, it would necessitate executing the program with the specific data under all possible replacement orders to determine the best replacement strategy—not a particularly practical approach.

Of the three commonly considered strategies—pick at random (RAND), pick page longest in real memory (FIFO), and pick page not referenced for longest period (LRU)—the LRU strategy is the usual choice because it most closely approaches the look-ahead ideal. (References to the theoretical and empirical research supporting this conclusion can be found in any of the excellent texts on operating systems referenced earlier in this section.) Thus, it will be necessary for the operating system to record page usage to allow LRU replacement. Often this is implemented in the page table as a flag. Every so often (every few milliseconds), these *use flags* are cleared, with subsequent setting if and upon the use of each page. In some cases, it may be advantageous to employ counting flags or to record the last usage, although the implementation of seemingly attractive nonsimple schemes involves a time penalty that may not be offset by the seeming advantages.

The following is also clear:

1. A page to be replaced might have been changed (written to) while in real memory; therefore, it must be copied back to virtual memory, replacing the out-of-date virtual memory resident predecessor copy.
2. A page to be replaced might not have been changed (read from but not written to) since it was last loaded into real memory, in which case the copy in virtual memory on disk is an exact duplicate, and it will not be necessary to copy the page back to disk, thus saving time.

Many, if not all, operating systems keep a record in the page table relative to page changes—the *change flag*—that allows a decision regarding the need to write out pages during the replacement process. Copying a page from real to virtual memory requires time and should be avoided when possible. Note that *pure code* (containing only non-self-altering instructions and constants) is read-only and that pages of pure code will not necessitate write-back during replacement.

An important as well as interesting characteristic of programs during execution is their paging rate—the ratio of the number of pages replaced to the number of logical pages in the program. A minimal paging rate is associated with a minimization of branches in the program and with data arrangements in the order of their access during execution. Experience seems to support the thesis that the set of precepts known as structured programming almost always results in an approach toward minimizing the paging rate. It should be noted, though, that certain dynamic data structures involving address pointers (e.g., linked lists) involve address sequences in practice that are almost certain to result in fairly high paging rates, even to the point of thrashing.

With complete programs and data resident in a multiprogramming system, it is usual to have more than one program completely resident in real (physical) memory at any one time. The CPU is given to one program for a while (for a *time slice*) or until it cannot use the arithmetic/logic unit (often because of I/O requirements); then the CPU is given to another program and then another in some priority scheme. Virtual memory with multiprogramming uses time slices and priority scheduling of the CPU in the same manner. The difference is that only those portions (segments or pages) of programs and data currently or almost currently being accessed are kept in real memory; the rest reside on disk in virtual memory until needed. They are then shuffled into real memory as needed (*demand paging*), replacing those not currently being used. If the portions of programs and data that are moved back and forth between real and virtual memory as needed are all of the same size, they are called pages; if they are of unequal size, they are called segments. The DEC VAX 11 family and the IBM 43X1 family use pages of equal size. The IBM 370/303X/308X family uses pages of equal size grouped together into segments that allow very large programs without excessively sized page tables. The Burroughs B5000/B6000/B7000 family and the Intel iAPX 286 employ segments, with each procedure and independent data area being a segment. Figure 9.10 covers these ideas generally.

An address of an instruction or of a datum in the memory mode consists of two portions—a segment identifier and an offset within the segment—in a manner reminiscent of addressing in a base address-offset design. The segment identifier (the segment selector) is a pointer to the appropriate entry of a memory-resident segment table that contains, among other information, the real memory beginning address of the segment. The real memory address of the desired datum is then derived as the sum of the segment start and the offset within the segment.

It must be emphasized, first, that the MC68010/MC68012/MC68020 virtual memory system with sufficient main (primary) memory (probably at least 1 MB), with an MC68881 floating-point processor, and with one or more DMA I/O processors is not in the same performance class as the usual 8-bit or 16-bit microcomputer. It definitely is well beyond the class of personal computers and most present-day business-oriented microcomputer-based small systems. The "loaded" MC68020 virtual memory system is fully as capable as most minicomputers, and with the MC68881 floating-point processor, it is probably in the performance class of the lower-end 32-bit midicomputers. In addition, the numerical characteristics of the floating-point processor may result in such superior iteration convergence characteristics compared to many midicomputer processors that faster-than-expected execution may be obtained for numerous numerical algorithms.

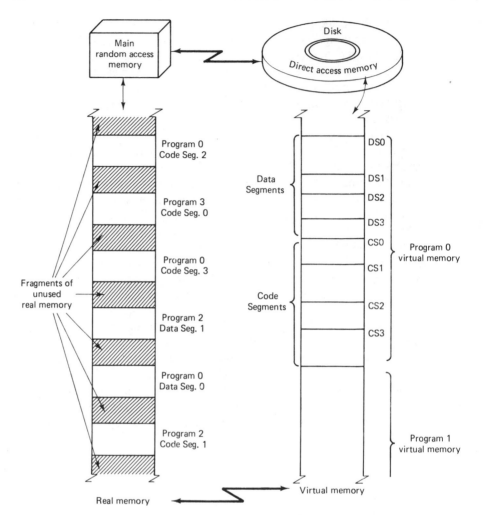

Figure 9.10 The general concept of virtual memory involves movement of code and data portions from the disk to the main memory as they are needed. Other portions of the same or other program may need to be moved to the disk to create space as new portions are needed. As the segments are of unequal sizes, main memory fragments may be unused. (From G. W. Gorsline, *16-Bit Modern Microcomputers: The Intel I8086 Family,* © 1985, p. 423. Reprinted by permission of Prentice-Hall, Inc., Englewood Cliffs, NJ.)

Second, the very characteristics mentioned above result in a virtual memory system normally operating as a multiprogrammed time-sliced system, with the modern mode being interactive time sharing. Although special circumstances rarely may necessitate a single very high priority critical program "capturing" all of the cycles, this eventuality can be accommodated by manipulating job priorities within the capabilities of available multiprogramming and/or time-sharing operating systems.

Third, the cost of acquiring a computational system in this performance class is dominated by the cost of disk storage, terminals, communications lines, printers, and other I/O equipment, with the cost of memory being relatively cheap and the cost of the central processor being almost insignificant.

Fourth, the cost of designing, coding, documenting, debugging, and maintaining programs far exceeds the cost of the computational system itself. These original and continuing software expenses probably consume well over three-fourths of the total computing budget. Various reports place them at about 80 percent, with a range from over 50 percent to nearly 90 percent, with the central tendency on the high side.

Managing System Resources

The most fundamental and important viewpoint of a computational system views it as a *tool* being used by a human as an aid in problem solving. This conceptual view is so important that it bears repeating in different words: A computer with auxiliary memory, an input/output terminal, and software is a device that may be used by a human being as a tool to assist in solving a problem. This philosophy places the person at center stage and relegates the computational system to its proper role—the same role as that occupied by an automobile, a hammer and nails, a stove, or any other tool—as a vital aid to a person in accomplishing a desirable task. It is important that human beings never forget that they—individual persons, that is—are the centrally necessary portion of the extended computational system. You—the person sitting at the terminal—are the only reason that the system exists. The ultimate measure of the usefulness of the system is fundamentally the measure of how well (or badly) the system assists you in solving your very specific problems without unnecessary effort or undue travail. The computational system should serve you—you should not serve the system. (At the same time, a good worker understands the use of, and maintains, his or her tools.)

The *memory management* modules of an operating system are concerned with the management of main (primary) memory. Four functions are important:

1. Keeping track of the current status of each location of primary memory. A location is either allocated to a specific use or "free" and available for allocation. Allocation is usually made in blocks.
2. Deciding which memory requester will be assigned how much memory. In multiprogramming systems, this decision process may necessitate conflict resolution and attention to priority. An allocation policy is thus implemented.
3. Deciding exactly which group of locations will be assigned to which requester. In virtual memory systems, this decision process may necessitate reclaiming a page/segment from another requester.
4. Deciding when to deallocate and reclaim which memory block.

In all cases, the bookkeeping implied above must be kept current. The policies implemented by the memory management modules may reflect a desire to keep the modules small and simple, to increase system flexibility, to maximize system efficiency, or (usually) some combination of these and other factors.

The *processor management* modules of an operating system are concerned with the assignment of processors to processes. It is usual to identify the following three divisions in processor management:

1. Job scheduling, which creates the processes and decides, in multiprogrammed systems, which of the ready processes will receive the processor or, in a multiprocessor, which ready process will be assigned which processor.
2. Processor scheduling, which, in multiprogramming/multiprocessing, decides which process gets which processor now and for how long. Often, this decision involves a priority policy.
3. Traffic control, or the recording of the status of each process and processor.

From this viewpoint, the computer user considers his or her job as a collection of tasks that he or she wishes the system to perform. The operating system creates processes to accomplish the tasks. Job scheduling is concerned with the management of jobs and thus is a macro scheduler—choosing which jobs to run when. Processor scheduling is concerned with the management of processes and thus is a micro scheduler—assigning processors to the processes of already scheduled jobs. In a uniprogrammed operating system, job scheduling is usually very simple (often sequential) and processor scheduling follows directly as a simple sequential expansion of the job—compile, link, load, and execute.

The *device management* modules of an operating system are concerned with the management of input/output devices, such as terminals, printers, disks, and so on, as well as the supporting logic, such as control units and DMA channel controllers. Although many designs choose to include the management of files with the management of the repository devices, we choose to separate the two in our present discussion. It is usual to identify four divisions in device management that parallel those treated in memory management (in fact, memory is often treated as a device by hardware and sometimes by software):

1. Keeping track of the current status of all I/O devices and their control units. In general, a device can either be allocated to a specific use or be "free" for allocation.
2. Deciding which device requester will be assigned the device, when the assignment will take place, and for how long. Devices can be *dedicated* to a single process while that process is active, *shared* by two or more processes, or be a *virtual device*, whereby one physical device is simulated using another physical device (usually a disk).

3. Allocating or physically assigning a device/control unit/DMA channel to a process.

4. Deallocating or reclaiming a device/control unit/DMA channel from a process.

A satisfactorily mnemonic name for the module that keeps track of the allocation states of I/O devices could be "I/O traffic controller." Recall that the modules that are associated with the operation of the device itself are called "I/O device handlers."

The *information management* modules of an operating system are concerned with the storage and retrieval of information within the computational system. By common tradition, information is held as a file—that is, a named collection of records. The contents of each file can be either data or program (and a program is data to another program, such as a compiler or loader). Thus, it is common to speak of program libraries, of data collections, and of directories or indexes. Note that the IBM term *data set* is completely synonymous with our use of the term *file*. Again, in small uniprogrammed systems, device management and information management are often enclosed in one common set of modules. Such simplification in design is often justified because information must be stored on devices. It follows that the same four somewhat parallel functional decisions are involved in information management as were involved in device management:

1. Keeping track of all the information (all the files) in the system via various tables, such as a file directory that contains the name, location, and accessing rights of each and every file. Note that every user who can write, and thus change, the file directory can allow himself or herself the power to read, change, and/or destroy any and all files in the system, including the modules of the operating system itself.

2. Deciding which file access requester process (and thus which user) will be allowed to store/retrieve information in what form and location on/from which devices. The policy governing these decisions should reflect efficient disk space utilization, efficient access time (minimal head movement and interdisk interference), file protection, information security, and flexibility of use.

3. The allocation modules must locate the desired information and allow access within the appropriate access rules.

4. When the information is no longer needed by the process, the file must be deallocated. Any temporary table entries and pointers must be destroyed. If the file was changed (updated), the original may or may not exist and may or may not be preserved as the backup version (the father file).

Note that we are not considering a data base management system (DBMS) at this time.

Specialized MC680XY Support for Virtual Memory

Recall that a virtual memory system keeps a copy of the program and its data on a secondary direct access memory (DAM) storage device, copies pieces of that memory image into relatively small random access memory (RAM) main (primary) storage only when they are needed, and returns such pieces (only if they have been changed) to the DAM storage device when they are not needed and when space is needed in primary (real) memory. Also recall that program addresses are relative to the start of the load module (program); they are termed *logical addresses* or *virtual addresses,* and they consist of two portions:

Logical Address = Segment# : Offset-within-segment

if the pieces that are moved are unequal in size (usually determined by the size of the individual object modules) or, if the program pieces are of equal size:

Logical Address = Page# : Offset-within-page

On the other hand, the execution of the program requires that each instruction be fetched from primary (real) memory using the address in the program counter (PC) that is relative to the start of the RAM physical real memory, not to the start of the program addresses = logical addresses = virtual addresses. Similarly, the data used as an operand by each instruction is referenced using logical/virtual addresses that are offsets from the start of the program's load module. Nevertheless, such data must be fetched from or stored into primary (real) memory using addresses that refer to physical (real) memory. Thus, there is a need for an address-mapping algorithm and for algorithms to determine if a "chunk" (page/segment) of program needs moving from/to virtual space on a DAM storage device to/from real space in the RAM physical (real) storage. These algorithms can be implemented entirely in software— indeed, in early systems, they were—or they can be implemented almost entirely in hardware. If software is employed as the implementation method, the speed of the resultant system would seriously suffer and almost certainly would not be commercially viable. Therefore, it is no surprise to find that Motorola, Inc., has designed and implemented integrated circuit devices to carry out the virtual memory functions necessary to implement an efficient system.

The MC68008 and MC68000 processors are not designed to support virtual memory. The 16-bit bus-oriented MC68010 and MC68012 are designed to support virtual memory with the virtual-to-real address mappings and segment/page movements supported via the MC68451 memory management unit (MMU). The 32-bit bus-oriented MC68020 is also designed to support virtual memory using the MC68851 MMU. The main differences between the two MMUs are as follows:

	MC68451	MC68851
Processors supported	MC68010/12	MC68020
Bus width supported	16-bit	32-bit
Maximum logical address space	2^{20} = 16 MB	2^{32} = 4 GB
Maximum real address space	2^{20} = 16 MB	2^{32} = 4 GB
Minimum segment/page size	256 bytes	256 bytes
Maximum segment/page size	2^{20} = 16 MB	2^{32} = 4 GB
Addressing restrictions	No odd addresses	None

We have chosen to discuss the MC68451 while also noting the differences incorporated into the MC68851. The MC68451 memory management unit (MMU) is the basic element of a memory management mechanism in an MC680XY family system. The operating system is responsible for ensuring the proper execution of user tasks in the system environment, and memory management is basic to this responsibility. The MC68451 provides the operating system with the capability to allocate, control, and protect the system memory. A block diagram of a single-MMU system is shown in Figure 9.11.

A memory management mechanism, implemented with one or more MC68451 MMUs, can provide address translation, separation, and write protection for the system memory. The MC68451 can be programmed to cause an interrupt when a chosen section of memory is accessed and can directly translate a logical address into a physical address, making it available to the MPU for use by the operating system. Using these features, the memory management mechanism can provide separation and security for user programs and allow the operating system to manage the memory efficiently for multitasking.

The MC68451 MMU provides address translation and protection for the 16-MB addressing range of the MC680XY MPU. Each bus master (or processor) in the MC680XY family provides a function code and an address during each bus cycle. The function code specifies an address space, and the address specifies a location within that address space. The function codes distinguish between user and supervisor spaces and, within these, between data and program spaces. This separation of address spaces provides the basis for memory management and protection by the operating system. Provision is also made for other bus masters, such as the MC68450 DMAC, to have separate address spaces for logical DMA. Features of the MC68451 include:

Provides fast translation times

Is compatible with the MC68000 and MC68008

Provides virtual memory support for the MC68010 and MC68012

Provides efficient memory allocation

Separates address spaces of system and user resources

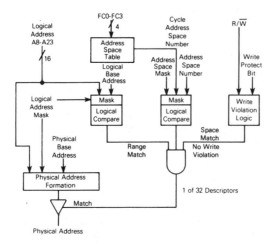

Functional Block Diagram

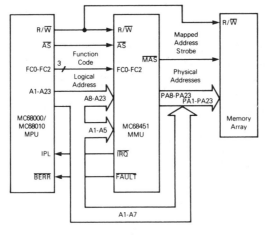

Simplified Block Diagram of Single-MMU System

Figure 9.11 Motorola MC68451 memory management unit (MMU) functional block diagram and its possible placement within a system. (Courtesy of Motorola, Inc.)

Provides write protection

Supports paging and segmentation

Provides 32 segments of variable size with each MMU

Has multiple MMU capability to expand to any number of segments

Allows intertask communication through shared segments

The memory management mechanism partitions the logical address space into contiguous pieces called *segments*. Each segment is a section of the logical address space of a task, which is mapped into the physical address space. Each task may have any number of segments. Segments may be defined as user or supervisor, data-only or program-only, or program and data. They may be accessed by only one task or shared between two or more tasks. In addition, any segment can be write-protected to ensure system integrity. A fault (MC68000 bus error) is generated if an undefined segment is accessed.

Each bus master in the MC680XY family (including the MC68550 DMA controllers) provides a function code during each bus cycle to indicate the address space to be used for the cycle. The address bus then specifies a location within this address space for the operation taking place during that bus cycle.

The function codes appear on the FC0–FC2 lines of the MC680XY and divide the memory references into two logical address spaces—the supervisor and the user spaces. Each of these is further divided into program and data spaces. A separate address space is also provided for internal CPU-related activities, such as interrupt acknowledge, giving a total of five defined function codes. The address space of the MC68000 is shown in Figure 9.12a.

Address space, descriptors, and translation using the MC68451 MMU.
Each task in a system has an address space that comprises all the segments defined for that task. This address space is assigned a number by giving all the address space number (ASN) fields in its descriptors the same value. This value can be considered a task number. The currently active task's number is kept in the appropriate entrys in the address space table (AST).

The AST is a set of MMU registers that define which task's segments are to be used in address translation for each cycle type (supervisor program, supervisor data, etc.). The AST contains an 8-bit entry for each possible function code. Each entry is assigned an ASN (task number), and this is used to select which descriptors may be used for translation. The logical address is then translated by one of these to produce the physical address. Figure 9.12b is a typical memory map of a task's address space.

Address translation is done using descriptors. A descriptor is a set of six registers (nine bytes) that describe a memory segment and how that segment is to be mapped to the physical addresses. Each descriptor contains the base addresses for the logical and physical spaces of each segment. These base addresses are then masked with the logical address masks. The size of the segment is then defined by "don't cares" in the masks. This method allows segment sizes from a minimum of 256 bytes to a maximum of 16 MB in binary increments (i.e., powers of 2). This also forces both logical and physical addresses of segment boundaries to lie on a segment size boundary. That is, a segment can start only on an address that is a multiple of 2K. The segments can be defined in such a way to allow them to be logically or physically shared between tasks. Descriptor mapping is shown schematically in Figure 9.12c.

During normal translation, the MMU translates the logical address provided by the MC680XY to produce a physical address, which is then presented to the memory

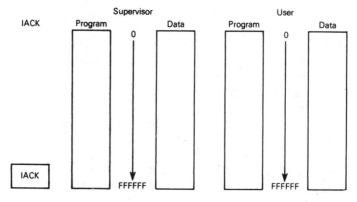

Address Space of MC68000

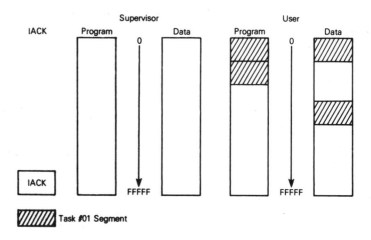

Task #01 Segment

Memory Map of Typical Task Address Space

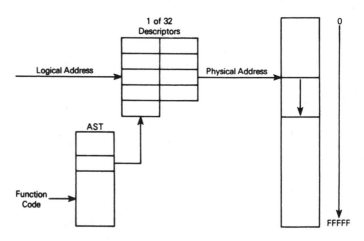

Schematic Diagram of Descriptor Mapping

Figure 9.12 Memory addressing of the MC680XY system, employing the MC68451 memory management unit (MMU), (Courtesy of Motorola, Inc.)

array. This is accomplished by matching the logical address with the information in the descriptors and then mapping it into the physical address space. (A block diagram of the MC68451 MMU is shown in Figure 9.11.)

The logical address is composed of address lines A1–A23. The upper 16 bits of this address (A8–A23) are translated by the MMU and mapped into a physical address (PA8–PA23). The lower 7 bits of the logical address (A1–A7) bypass the MMU and become the low-order physical address bits (PA1–PA7). In addition, the data strobes (UDS and LDS) remain unmapped and become the physical data strobes, for a total of eight unmapped address lines.

Programmer's model of the MC68451 MMU.   Figure 9.13 shows a programmer's model of the MC68451 MMU. The MMU registers consist of two groups: the descriptors and the system registers. Each of the 32 descriptors is nine bytes long and defines one memory segment.

The system registers contain both information local to the MMU and information global to the memory management mechanism. Each bit in the system registers and the segment status registers, except the address space table, is one of four types:

Control bits can be set or cleared by the MC68010/12 MPU to select MMU options. These are read/write bits.

Status alterable (SA) bits are set or cleared by the MMU to indicate status information. These are also read/write bits.

Status unalterable (SU) bits are set or cleared by the MMU to reflect status information. These bits cannot be written by the MPU.

Reserved bits are reserved for future expansion. They cannot be written and are zero when read.

The system registers are all directly addressable from the physical address space. Accessing registers causes certain operations to be performed. The descriptors are not directly addressable but are accessed using the descriptor pointer and the accumulator.

Each MMU contains 32 descriptors (0–31), each of which can define one memory segment. A descriptor is loaded by the MPU using the accumulator and descriptor pointer with a load descriptor operation. The segment status register (SSR) can be written to by the MPU indirectly using the descriptor pointer. Each descriptor consists of the following registers.

The *logical base address (LBA)* is a 16-bit register that, with the logical address mask (LAM), defines the logical addressing range of a segment. This is typically the first address in the segment, although it can be any address within the range defined by the LAM. The LAM is a 16-bit mask that defines the bit positions in the LBA that are to be used for range matching. In the mask, 1's mark significant bit positions and 0's indicate "don't care" positions. A range match occurs if, in each bit position in the LAM that is set to 1, the LBA matches the incoming logical address.

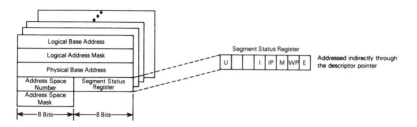

U   U (used) is set by the MMU if the segment was accessed since it was defined. This bit
           is status alterable.
           Set: a)   By a segment access (successful translation using the segment)
                       b)   By an MPU write of "1"
           Cleared: a)   Reset (in segment #0 of master)
                       b)   MPU write of "0"

I   If the I (interrupt) control bit is set, an interrupt is generated upon accessing the seg-
           ment.
           Set: a)   MPU writes a "1"
           Cleared: a)   MPU writes a "0"
                       b)   Reset (segment #0 of master)

IP   IP (interrupt pending) is set if the I bit is set when the segment is accessed. IRQout is
           asserted if an IP bit, in one or more SSRs, is set and IE in the global status register
           (GSR) is set. IRQout is negated when all the IP bits in all SSRs are clear or IE is cleared.
           IP is status alterable and should be cleared by the interrupt service routine.
           Set: a)   Segment access and I is set
                       b)   MPU writes a "1"
           Cleared: a)   MPU writes a "0"
                       b)   Reset (in segment #0 of master)
                       c)   E bit is a "0"

M   The M (modified) bit is set by the MMU if the segment has been written to since it was
           defined. The M bit is status alterable.
           Set: a)   Successful write to the segment
                       b)   MPU writes a "1"
           Cleared: a)   MPU writes a "0"
                       b)   Reset (segment #0 in master)

WP   If the WP (write protect) control bit is set, the segment is write protected. A write ac-
           cess to the segment with WP set will cause a write violation.
           Set: a)   MPU writes a "1"
           Cleared: a)   MPU writes a "0"
                       b)   Reset (segment #0 in master)

E   E (enable) is a control bit which, when set, enables the segment to participate in the
           matching process. E can be cleared (the segment disabled) by a write to the SSR, but a
           load descriptor operation must be performed to set it.
           Set: a)   Load descriptor operation with AC7, bit #0 set
                       b)   Reset (segment #0 in master)
           Cleared: a)   MPU writes a "0"
                       b)   Unsuccessful load descriptor operation on this descriptor
                       c)   Load descriptor operation with AC7, bit #0 cleared

(a) Descriptors (32)

Figure 9.13 The programmer's model of the MC68451 memory management unit
(MMU). (Courtesy of Motorola, Inc.)

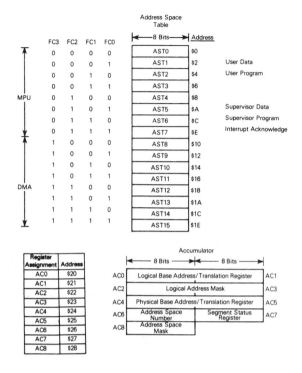

Address Space Table

FC3	FC2	FC1	FC0	Name	Address	
0	0	0	0	AST0	$0	
0	0	0	1	AST1	$2	User Data
0	0	1	0	AST2	$4	User Program
0	0	1	1	AST3	$6	
0	1	0	0	AST4	$8	
0	1	0	1	AST5	$A	Supervisor Data
0	1	1	0	AST6	$C	Supervisor Program
0	1	1	1	AST7	$E	Interrupt Acknowledge
1	0	0	0	AST8	$10	
1	0	0	1	AST9	$12	
1	0	1	0	AST10	$14	
1	0	1	1	AST11	$16	
1	1	0	0	AST12	$18	
1	1	0	1	AST13	$1A	
1	1	1	0	AST14	$1C	
1	1	1	1	AST15	$1E	

(MPU: 0000–0111; DMA: 1000–1111)

Register Assignment:

Register Assignment	Address
AC0	$20
AC1	$21
AC2	$22
AC3	$23
AC4	$24
AC5	$25
AC6	$26
AC7	$27
AC8	$28

Accumulator

	← 8 Bits →	← 8 Bits →	
AC0	Logical Base Address/Translation Register		AC1
AC2	Logical Address Mask		AC3
AC4	Physical Base Address/Translation Register		AC5
AC6	Address Space Number	Segment Status Register	AC7
AC8	Address Space Mask		

Miscellaneous Registers

	7	6	5	4	3	2	1	0	Address
Descriptor Pointer				DP4	DP3	DP2	DP1	DP0	$29
Interrupt Vector Register	IV7	IV6	IV5	IV4	IV3	IV2	IV1	IV0	$2B
Global Status Register	F	DF						IE	$2D
Local Status Register	L7	L6	L5	L4	RW	GAT	GAL	LIP	$2F
Interrupt Descriptor Pointer	NVI			I4	I3	I2	I1	I0	$39
Result Descriptor Pointer	NVR			R4	R3	R2	R1	R0	$3B

(b) System Registers   **Figure 9.13** (*continued*).

The *physical base address (PBA)* is a 16-bit address that, with the LAM and the incoming logical address, is used to form the physical address. The logical address is passed through to the physical address in those bit positions in the LAM that contain 0's (the "don't cares") and the PBA is gated out in those positions that contain 1's.

The *address space number (ASN)* is an 8-bit number that, with the address space mask (ASM), is used in detecting a match with the cycle address space number. The ASM is an 8-bit mask that defines the significant bit positions in the ASN that are to be used in descriptor matching. As in the LAM, the bit positions that are set are used for matching and the bit positions that are clear are "don't cares." A space match occurs if, in the significant bit positions, the cycle address space number matches the ASN.

Each descriptor has an 8-bit *segment status register (SSR)*. The SSR can be written to in two ways: using the load descriptor operation or indirectly, using the descriptor pointer in a write status register operation. Each bit is labeled as control or status alterable. Bits 5 and 6 are reserved for future use.

The *system registers* consist of the address space table, accumulator, and miscellaneous registers, which include the global status register, local status register, descriptor pointer, result descriptor pointer, interrupt descriptor pointer, and interrupt vector register. Each MMU has a local copy of the address space table (AST). This table is organized as 16 8-bit read/write registers located at even byte addresses starting at address $00. Each entry is programmed by the operating system with a unique address space number, which is associated with a task. During a memory access, the MMU receives a 4-bit function code (FC0–FC3), which is used to index into the AST to select the cycle address space number. This number is then used to check for a match with the ASN in each of the 32 descriptors within the MMU.

The MC680XY MPU and the MC6450 DMAC provide only a 3-bit function code, FC0–FC2. In a system with more than one bus master, the BGACK signal from the MPU could be inverted and used as FC3. This would result in the AST organization shown in Figure 9.13. The accumulator (shown in Figure 9.13) is used to access the descriptors, perform direct translation, and latch information during a fault. The accumulator consists of nine 8-bit registers located at byte addresses from $20 to $28. The register assignments for each operation in which it participates are also shown in Figure 9.13, as are six other miscellaneous registers. In general, they are involved in and reflect faults and interrupts. If more detailed information is necessary, the documentation for the MC68451 MMU should be obtained from Motorola, Inc.

FUNCTIONAL DESCRIPTION OF VIRTUAL MEMORY

The basic mechanism used in a virtual memory system consists of keeping an image of a large "virtual memory" on a secondary storage device (such as a high-speed disk drive) and bringing pieces of that image into a small physical memory only when they are needed. Reims (undated) gives an understandable summary of the implementation of virtual memory on the MC68020 processor using the MC68451 memory management unit.

When the processor presents an address to the system, the MMU checks to see if that address corresponds to data that are currently in the physical memory or present only in the virtual memory image. If the data are not in physical memory, the MMU directs the processor to stop what it is doing and bring the needed virtual memory data into the physical memory. It is at this point that previous microprocessors (MPUs) could not fully support virtual memory. When the MMU indicates that an address is not in physical memory, the MPU must abort the current bus cycle, perform some functions to bring the data into physical memory, and then continue the previously aborted bus cycle. To recover from the bus cycle abortion and continue execution, enough state information must be saved by the MPU to return to a known state; the MC68010 contains enhancements to the original MC6800 MPU that allow it to do exactly that. Basically, this approach involves starting an instruction, flagging a fault to the CPU before the instruction ends, and suspending the instruction in an order fashion (Figure 9.14a). It then provides a mechanism to allow the instruction to pick up where it left off, once the fault is corrected, and continue through completion. To do this, when a page fault occurs, the processor stores its internal state; after the page fault is repaired, it restores that internal state and continues to execute the instruction.

To implement instruction continuation, the MC68010 uses a bus-error (BERR) signal—which can cause any and all instructions to abort before even a bus cycle is completed—to warn the processor that there is a problem with the bus cycle in progress. When the MC68010 receives a BERR signal, it aborts the bus cycle and begins a special internal procedure to suspend the instruction (as opposed to forgetting it, as in instruction restart). The MPU does this by saving its internal state on the supervisor stack and resuming execution at a location determined by the exception vector number 2. It loads that address into the program counter and resumes normal execution. The routine at the vector address is then responsible for determining why the fault occurred, updating descriptors and pages in memory, and so forth. Once the fault handler routine has completed its required operations, it then executes a return from exception (RTE) instruction to reload the previously saved internal information and return control to the routine that caused the fault.

As shown in Figure 9.14b, when the CPU returns from the correction routine, the RTE instruction reloads the MC68010 with the internal state stored on the stack, reruns the faulted bus cycle, and then continues the suspended instruction.

In a worst-case example, neither the operating code nor its source or destination operand is in primary memory when an instruction begins. First, an opcode fetch shows that the instruction is not in primary memory. One bus fault and fault correction routine later, however, the processor re-executes and finds the opcode. Trying to fetch the source operand results in a second bus error. After another bus-error routine, the source operand becomes available. A write attempt to the destination location results in yet another bus fault. Again, fault correction can get the destination operand into primary memory and, after recovery, the processor completes the instruction.

The MC68451 MMU provides the checking function that determines whether or not a given address is currently in physical memory or in virtual memory. As shown in the system diagram, the MC68010/12 CPU presents logical address information to the MMU, which is checked and translated into physical address information used by the rest of the system. The term *logical address* refers to the address at which a program expects instructions or data to reside within the virtual address space. The MC68010 presents a 24-bit logical address to the MMU; thus, the virtual address space is 16 MB. However, the virtual address space is mapped, in small pieces, into the physical memory at addresses that do not necessarily correspond to the virtual addresses. Thus, the MMU performs a translation function in addition to

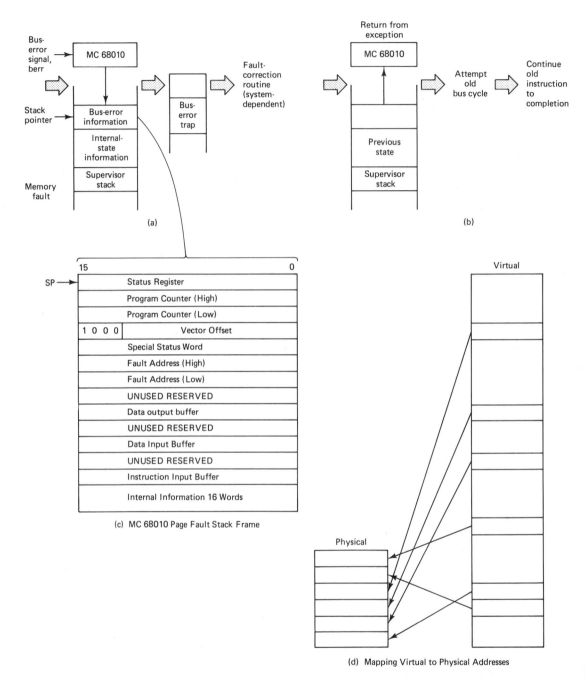

Bus-error signal, berr

MC 68010

Stack pointer

Bus-error information

Internal-state information

Supervisor stack

Memory fault

Bus-error trap

Fault-correction routine (system-dependent)

(a)

Return from exception

MC 68010

Previous state

Supervisor stack

Attempt old bus cycle

Continue old instruction to completion

(b)

15   0

SP →

| Status Register |
| Program Counter (High) |
| Program Counter (Low) |
| 1 0 0 0 | Vector Offset |
| Special Status Word |
| Fault Address (High) |
| Fault Address (Low) |
| UNUSED RESERVED |
| Data output buffer |
| UNUSED RESERVED |
| Data Input Buffer |
| UNUSED RESERVED |
| Instruction Input Buffer |
| Internal Information 16 Words |

(c) MC 68010 Page Fault Stack Frame

Virtual

Physical

(d) Mapping Virtual to Physical Addresses

Figure 9.14 Using an instruction-continuation technique, Motorola's MC68010 receives a bus-error signal (BERR) when a page fault—page not in physical memory—occurs and then aborts the instruction. It saves all the information on the supervisor stack so that when the CPU returns from the correction routine, the return from exception (RTE) instruction reruns the faulted bus cycle and the instruction continues to execute.

the checking function so that the MPU will receive the correct data that resides at a given virtual address. A diagrammatic representation of this mapping function, employing equal-sized pages, is shown in Figure 9.14d.

For the MMU to perform the translation and checking functions depicted in Figure 9.14, it must be told (by the MPU's operating system) about each piece of the virtual memory image that is currently in the physical memory array. This information is kept in what is called a *descriptor*. In the MC68451, there are 32 descriptors, so that it can map 32 pieces of the virtual image at any one time, and multiple MMUs can be placed in parallel to increase this number by increments of 32 (i.e., 64, 96, 128, etc.) to improve system performance. Each descriptor in the MMU determines how large a piece (normally called a memory segment) of the virtual image is, what its virtual address is, and where it is within the physical memory. Figure 9.14a shows the format of each segment descriptor in the MMU. The logical base address determines where in the virtual address space the page mapped by this descriptor is located. The logical address mask determines the size of the page by indicating if a logical address bit is to be passed through the MMU or translated into the value in the physical base address, which determines where this page is located within the physical memory array. The size of a segment may be from 256 bytes up to 16 MB; however it is a common practice to make all segments in a system the same size, such as 1 KB.

The basic flow of operations in translating a logical address to a physical address is as follows: First, the logical address from the MPU is compared with each of the logical addresses programmed into the MMU's 32 segment descriptors. If a match is found (only one descriptor will match), the physical address information contained in the matching descriptor replaces the logical address and the resulting address is sent to the physical memory array. In most systems, only the upper-order address bits are checked and translated. For example, in a system using 1 KB pages, the lower 10 address bits are simply passed through the MMU from the logical to the physical address bus and the upper 14 are translated. If a logical address is sent from the MPU to the MMU and it does not match any of the logical addresses in the MMU descriptor array, the MMU signals an error to the MC68010/12 MPU in order to abort the bus cycle. The MPU responds to the error signal by saving its current state and determining why the error occurred.

If a matching descriptor is not found in the descriptor table (in very simple systems, the descriptors in the MMU may be the only descriptors used), then the MPU must fetch the required page from the virtual storage medium, place it in physical memory, and update the required descriptors so as to properly map the new page. Once these procedures have been completed, the processor continues with the next step. Very often, to allow for acceptable sized programs along with their data, the number of segments/pages in the system must be far greater than the 32 allowed with a single MC68451 MMU. Although multiple MMUs are allowed and are often configured within a single system, a large number is not usually cost-effective. Rather than keeping the descriptor for every page in physical memory within an MMU, most systems use a few (64, for example) descriptors in hardware and maintain any "extra" descriptors in a special table in physical memory (which requires the use of one or more pages, depending on the size of the tables). When a page fault occurs in such a system, the first thing the MPU must do is to check the descriptor tables in memory to see if the desired virtual address is mapped into physical memory but its descriptor is not currently active. If a match is found in the descriptor table, the matching descriptor is made active by placing it into the MMU. (Another descriptor must be made inactive by removing it from the MMU and putting it into the table.) Then the processor can go on to the next step.

Once the physical memory and the MMU have been updated for the new descriptor and page, the MPU can complete the operation that previously caused a page fault. The MC68010 does this by executing a return from exception (RTE) instruction that reloads the processor internal state information that was saved in response to the BERR signal assertion when the MMU detected a page fault. Once this internal state information has been restored, the MPU reruns the bus cycle that caused the page fault (which will complete normally if the descriptors were properly updated) and thus continues with the execution of the suspended instruction. In this manner, the processor returns to the normal state of execution, and the fact that the page fault occurred is transparent to the application program that caused it.

In multiuser, multitasking, or real-time systems, the amount of time that the MPU must wait while the disk interface is reading the new page may degrade system performance more than is desirable. To achieve better performance, a DMA disk interface is used to allow concurrent disk I/O while the MPU performs other tasks. In the example system, the MPU instructs the disk controller (through the PI/T interface) to read a certain page from the disk and tells the DMA controller where to put that page in memory. The DDMA and PI/T will then perform the disk-to-memory transfer without further assistance from the MPU. While the disk operation is taking place, the MPU switches contexts and begins executing another task concurrently with the disk read. When the disk I/O is complete, the DMA controller will interrupt the MPU.

Besides supporting virtual memory, instruction continuation and a secure supervisor mode allow the MC68010 to support *virtual processing* concepts. As described above, a virtual processor system allows the user applications programs to "see" a hardware device that is not actually present in the system; thus, the term *virtual machine* is often given to such a system. With a virtual machine system, user programs written to execute on a system that has a line printer and a tape drive could be run on a system that has only CRT display units and disk drives, for example. Also, a hierarchical operating system structure can be supported to allow several different users each to run under a different operating system because of the secure supervisor mode of operation on the MC68010. Such a multilevel operating system concept is shown in Figure 9.15.

In the virtual machine environment shown in Figure 9.15, the main control program (CP) performs the virtual memory support and hardware emulation functions described above and any I/O operations required by the underlying operating systems. The hardware interface seen by the operating systems may not be the actual

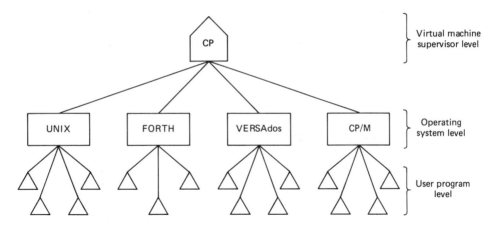

Figure 9.15   Virtual processing heirarchy.

configuration of the system but the configuration that each operating system is written to execute on. Whenever one of the underlying operating systems, which run in the user mode, attempts to execute a supervisory function, such as an I/O operation or a privileged instruction an exception will occur and control will be turned over to the control program. The CP will then perform the required function for the operating system, either by emulating the function or executing it directly, after which control is returned to the operating system.

Software Considerations

In constructing segments, the size of a given segment is determined by the logical address mask. Although there are no constraints on which bits are significant, one approach is to allow only contiguous, low-order 0's ("don't cares"). With this constraint, if there are N 0's, the size of the segment is 2 bytes. Since the seven low-order address lines bypass the MMU, the smallest possible segment is 128 words (256 bytes).

In the logical address space, a segment defined this way extends from the address formed by the LBA, with 0's in the "don't care" positions in the LAM, to the address formed by the LBA, with 1's in the "don't care" bit positions. In the physical address space, the segment extends from the address formed by the PBA, with 0's in the "don't care" bit positions in the LAM, to the address formed with 1's in the "don't care" positions.

Since segment sizes must be multiples of 2, multiple descriptors can be used to map a segment of nonbinary size. For example, a segment of 70K bytes could be constructed using two descriptors: one of 645K bytes and one of 8K bytes, losing 2K bytes to internal fragmentation. A purely binary system would allocate 128K bytes while wasting 58K bytes. For this reason, a modified binary "buddy" allocation algorithm should be used.

The MC68451 MMU supports virtual memory systems as well. In a virtual memory system, the virtual address is larger than the physical RAM available, and a combination of memory management hardware and software maintains a portion of the address space on a fast-backing store such as a disk.

Virtual memory systems are usually implemented with a paging type of memory management system. In paging systems, the logical (virtual) address space is divided into equal-length pages. A task is then allocated a certain number of these pages at initial load time, and the memory management hardware is programmed to map these virtual pages to physical pages. This is equivalent to setting all descriptors to the same length. Thus, the MMU serves as a content-addressable translation buffer of 32 pages. In such a system, a page fault is caused when an access is attempted to a page that is not currently mapped by the MMU. This is an error in a nonvirtual system but signals a page fault in a virtual system.

The other ingredient in a virtual memory system is a processor that is capable of aborting any instruction and finishing it at a later time. This is necessary because any memory access could potentially be the cause of a page fault. When this occurs, the faulting bus cycle is suspended and the operating system takes corrective action. The bus cycle is then rerun and the instruction is continued.

The MC68000 does not save enough information when processing a bus error to return and finish the instruction that was being executed. Therefore, a true virtual memory system is not possible using a single MC68000 MPU. The MC68010 virtual microprocessor (VMPU) will allow a faulted bus cycle to be rerun and the instruction to be continued. This processor can be used, in conjunction with the MC68451 MMU, to implement a virtual memory system.

The MMU also provides hardware assistance for virtual paging systems. The logical address, the cycle address space number, and the read/write line are latched in the accumulator on a fault. This information is used by the page fault handler to fix the page fault. In addition, the used and modified bits in the segment status register allow the implementation of a variety of page replacement algorithms.

After a reset (power-on or processor-initiated), the master MMU (the MMU for which CS was asserted during reset) will map the logical address unchanged into the physical address space using descriptor 0 (see Figure 9.16). This will allow the processor to fetch its supervisor stack and program counter (if it was a power-on reset) and begin executing the operating system initialization routine.

The operating system would then set up descriptors for itself and system resources (such as the MMU). To load a descriptor, the operating system loads the descriptor number in the descriptor pointer register and the LBA, LAM, PBA, ASN, and ASM into the accumulator. The processor then reads from the appropriate physical address to begin the loading operation. The memory management mechanism globally checks for conflicts. It loads and enables the descriptor if none are found. As a result of the read, the processor gets a status byte in the low byte of the word. The status will read $00 if the load was successful and $FF if there was a conflict. If a conflict occurred, the result descriptor pointer can be used to find the highest-priority conflicting descriptor. A descriptor can be quickly disabled by writing to its seg-

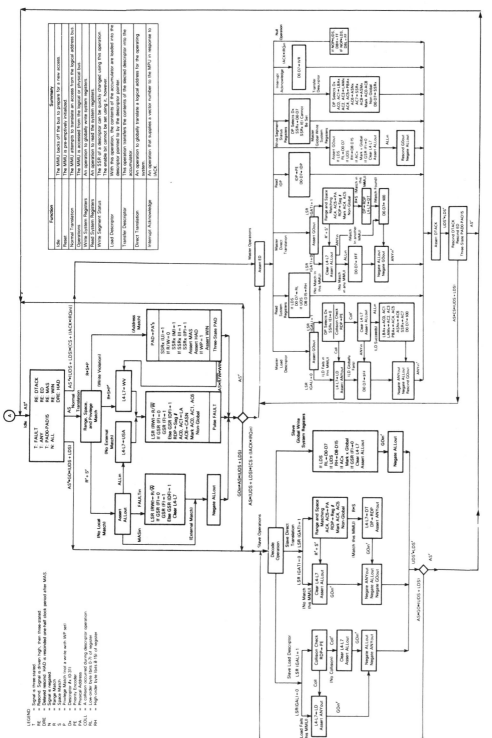

Figure 9.16 Flow diagram of the MC68451 memory management unit's actions. (Courtesy of Motorola, Inc.)

459

ment status register. The I and WP bits can be programmed and the U and M bits can be cleared, but the E bit can be set only by a load descriptor operation.

Descriptors would then be set up for the user tasks and a task would be selected to execute. Address space table entries AST1 and AST2 would then be loaded with the address space number of the task to be run. These are the address spaces of user data and user program in the MC6800. The program counter and status register to be used by the task are then pushed onto the system stack. The processor then executes an RTE instruction, which fetches the status register and program counter off the stack. The status register should have had the supervisor bit cleared so that the processor will enter the user state and its accesses are then mapped through AST1 and AST2 to start the user task.

To return to the operating system from a user task, a watchdog timer could be used to interrupt the processor. The exception processing caused by this would switch the processor to the supervisor state and the supervisor address spaces would be mapped by the operating systems descriptors.

Switching the MMU from one user task to the other is very efficient. Suppose two user tasks were present in memory and the processor had returned to the operating system as described above. To switch tasks, the operating system would change AST1 and AST2 to the ASN of the user task which it wished to execute. It would then push the new status register and program counter on the stack and execute an RTE.

Switching between two supervisor tasks is more complex. If AST5 and AST6 are changed while the processor is in the supervisor state, subsequent accesses are immediately mapped through the new address space. A move multiple (MOVEM), using the predecrement mode, followed by an illegal instruction can be executed to perform the switch. The processor prefetch pipeline fetches the MOVEM and the illegal instruction, alters AST6 and AST5 (data entry last), and then traps through the illegal instruction routine to the new supervisor task. A flag (possibly the illegal instruction opcode) is used to distinguish between normal illegal instructions and attempts to switch tasks in this manner. Another method is to have a task in the user space perform the switch. The supervisor stack pointer is set up, the processor alters the status register to put itself in the user state, AST5 and AST6 are changed, and the processor traps to the supervisor task.

EXERCISES

9.1. Design, implement, test, and document the linker described in the text in such a way that it will successfully accept multiple object modules produced by the assembler specified in Exercise 8.1.

9.2. Design, implement, test, and document a loader for a "real memory" computational system where the user specifies the physical memory location in which loading will commence. The loader must initiate execution of the just loaded program and accept control from it after it terminates. This can be accomplished by treating the just loaded program as a subprocedure called by the loader.

10

The MC68881
Floating-Point
Coprocessor

Very often, while solving an applications problem, it is necessary to deal with numeric quantities involving fractional values. At times it is also necessary to manipulate numbers whose values exceed the range that is provided for with the integer representation of the computer being used. As might be expected, methods have already been developed for dealing with both of these situations.

THE PROBLEM OF VERY LARGE NUMBERS

Very large numbers are often represented using multiple words in memory and software multiple-precision program packages to accomplish the manipulation. In this manner, complete accuracy is maintained. Multiple-precision addition and subtraction present few problems and are easily programmed using the external flag (XF) of the MX680XY. On the other hand, multiplication and division are somewhat difficult and involve rather esoteric solutions in the general case. Nevertheless, multiple-precision arithmetic packages are necessary for those cases where complete accuracy is necessary. As an indication of the methodology, we give a possible implementation of an algorithm of double-precision integer addition (64-bit):

```
     -
     -
     -
; 64-BIT INTEGER ADDITION EXAMPLE
;    (MEMORY TO MEMORY - THREE ADDRESS)
```

```
;
;    C ← A + B
;
     LEA         A,A1            ; Address of high-order half
     LEA         B,A2
     LEA         C,A3
     MOVE.L      (A1)+,D1        ; Increment address to low-half
     MOVE.L      (A1),D2
     ADD.L       (A2+4),D2       ; Add low-order half first
     ADDX.L      (A2),D1         ; Use any overflow
     MOVE.L      D1,(A3)+
     MOVE.L      D2,(A3)
     BCS         OVFLW_ERR
```

If and only if complete accuracy is not required, it is possible to scale the numeric quantities by some consistent value and thus perform the calculations using single-precision arithmetic. Thus, in dealing with 64-bit values where the least-significant 32 bits are not required (e.g., they are only rough estimations of the true values), it is sometimes possible to disregard them by scaling. In our example, this method would require the use of only the high-order 32-bit word of each variable. Expressed in a different way, the approximate value of $A = A' \times 2^{32}$; $B = B' \times 2^{32}$; and $C = C' \times 2^{32}$. The scaled arithmetic becomes

$$C' \longleftarrow A' + B'$$

The notation $A' \times 2^{32}$ is often termed scientific notation and is closely related to logarithms.

Fractional numbers may be exactly represented as numerator/denominator pairs and can be manipulated employing the algebraic rules for operating on fractions. In computer terminology, such manipulations and data representations are known as *rational arithmetic*. In designing algorithms to accomplish symbolic algebra on computers, important operations involve the coefficients of the term (perhaps cancellation) and thus require complete accuracy in their representation. Rational number arithmetic is commonly employed in these applications.

It is important to realize that certain fairly common values are not exactly representable as fractions. Pi (π) and e (the base of natural logarithms) are among these values. As these values are usually "carried along" in symbolic form during algebraic manipulations, they do not constitute a major problem in rational arithmetic. On the other hand, fractional values developed during rational arithmetic manipulations often involve an excessively long numerator or denominator, even when reduced to lowest form. Thus, complicated algorithms for storage will most likely be involved.

Two forms of rational arithmetic and data storage have been, and are, the subject of research and use. The *pure rational* method expresses numeric values as a numerator/denominator diad, with either the numerator or the denominator being signed. A report by Thacker (1978) strongly suggests that the length of the two component portions often becomes excessively long. Nevertheless, the pure rational number data format is employed by some algebraic manipulation packages. The *fixed-slash rational* method expresses numeric values as an integral portion/numerator portion/denominator portion triad, where the fractional part is always between zero and one and the integral portion is a signed integer. Kornerup and Matula (1978) have reported research on this data representation that demonstrates its superiority to the pure rational form in most circumstances.

In some applications where a determined accuracy is required, *scaling* of the quantity is perfectly satisfactory. In operations with dollars and cents, it is often perfectly legitimate and extremely easy to accomplish all manipulations in terms of mills (1/10 cent) by scaling all values by 1000 and utilizing integer arithmetic on the mill-scaled equivalents. Thus,

$$\$100.93 + \$7.14 = \$108.07$$

becomes

$$100930 + 7140 = 108070$$

A data diad is employed in the *fixed-point* format to express numbers involving a fraction where the integral portion is expressed as one integer value and the fractional portion as a second integer value (scaled to become an integer). Thus, 100.93 could be expressed and manipulated as

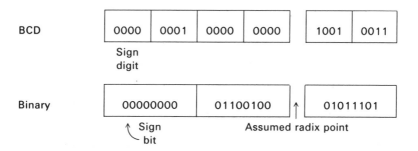

Care must be taken to allow a carry-out from the fractional portion to the integral portion during addition and a borrow from the integral portion to the fractional portion during subtraction. With the BCD format, the sign-magnitude style is suggested, whereas the two's-complement style is satisfactory for the binary format. It must also be realized that multiprecision arithmetic may be required.

FLOATING-POINT NUMBERS

The Floating-Point Data Format

An adaptation of scientific notation that was developed for very early computers used for numerical mathematics is known as *floating point*. Various styles of this format are used and manipulated by appropriately implemented hardware or software packages on super-, maxi-, midi-, mini-, and microcomputers. In all cases, an adaptation of the two-part scientific notation is used:

$$+0.731 \times 10^1$$

whose interpretation is +7.31. This value is obtained by taking the significand (+0.731) and multiplying it by the base raised to power of the exrad (+1); in this case, $+0.731 \times +10 = +7.31$.

The two portions of a floating-point number *each* must specify four pieces of information, for a total of eight pieces of information:

1. The number base
2. The sign
3. The position of the radix point
4. The magnitude

The internal representations (the syntax) of the two portions are known as *significand* and *exrad,* and their interpretations (the semantics) are known respectively as *mantissa* and *exponent.*

With microcomputers, it is usual to specify explicitly only a portion of the eight items of information necessary for a valid interpretation while implicitly specifying the rest. In a commonly employed syntax,

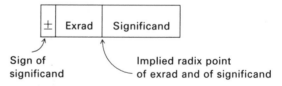

The syntax of the exrad is interpreted as follows:

1. The number base is assumed to be 2; thus, the value is binary.
2. The radix point is assumed on the extreme right; thus, the value is integral.
3. The sign is interpreted as negative if the value is below the midpoint of the possible magnitude and positive if it is above the value; thus, if the leftmost exrad bit is zero, the exponent is negative, and if the leftmost bit of the exrad is one, the exponent is positive.
4. The magnitude of the exponent is derived as the *deviation* from the midpoint value of the exrad.

The syntax of the significand is interpreted as follows:

1. The number base is assumed to be 2; thus, the value is binary.
2. The sign is the leftmost bit of the floating-point format and occupies the same position as the sign of an integer number.
3. The radix point is assumed on the extreme left; thus, the value is always fractional.
4. The magnitude of the mantissa is derived as the signed-magnitude binary fraction, as specified by the significand bit pattern.

It is usual for the fractional significand to have no leading zero bits. If such leading zero bits are generated, the significand is shifted left until they are lost, while the exrad is adjusted appropriately to preserve the value. This process is termed *normalization* and may involve shifting in zeros from the right.

It should be noted that the *magnitude* or *range* of a floating-point number is determined largely by the exponent, as the value of a floating-point number is the product of the fractional mantissa and the number base raised to the power of the exponent:

$$\text{value} = \text{mantissa} \times 2^{\text{exponent}}$$

It follows that the values that can be exactly represented are more dense (occur closer together) when the exponent is small (as the interpreted values approach zero as a limit) than when the exponent is large (as the interpreted values diverge from zero); or oppositely, the values that can be exactly represented are less dense (occur farther apart) when the interpreted value is large than when it is small. Thus, the average absolute error necessarily is greater for a large number than it is for a small number.

It must also be emphasized that the conversion of an external base 10 fractional quantity to an internal base 2 fractional mantissa, and vice versa, generally contains some error. This base conversion error will exist for all fractional mantissas not exactly representable in both cases (.25, .5, .75, etc.). In addition, the significand contains a finite number of bits (23, 52, or 64 bits with the MC68881 floating-point coprocessor). Therefore, the large majority of the desired base 10 mantissa values cannot be exactly represented by the finite fractional binary significand.

Overflow occurs when a floating-point value becomes so large in magnitude that the exrad cannot represent the value of the exponent. *Underflow* occurs when a floating-point value becomes so close to zero magnitude that the exrad is zero and the significand cannot be normalized. In some schemes that allow denormalized floating-point values, absolute underflow occurs when the exrad is zero and the significand is zero. This condition can be termed *gradual underflow*.

Finite Representation and Errors

The syntax and associated semantics of binary floating-point arithmetic specified in the IEEE Standard (Coonen et al., 1979; Stevenson, 1981) as implemented by the

MC68881 floating-point coprocessor use a fixed number of bits to represent the different portions of numbers in each data format. In the internal extended real format, the biased binary exrad occupies 15 bits, the binary significand, which has a value between 1.0 and 2.0, occupies 64 bits, and its sign occupies 1 bit. The value is

$$\pm 1.\text{significand} \times 2^{\text{exrad}-16383}$$

The close affinity of this notation to scientific notation and to logarithms was discussed earlier.

The representable numbers group naturally into intervals of the form

$$2^n,\ 2^{n+1},\ 2^{n+2},\ \ldots$$

called *binades* (from the analogous term *decades*). Within each binade, representable numbers are uniformly spaced with a separation of 1 bit in their least significant place. As the numbers increase in magnitude via an increase in the magnitude of the exponent, this absolute spacing of exactly representable numbers increases by a value of 2 from binade to binade, and the average accuracy of the number becomes correspondingly less. Similarly, as the numbers approach zero, this absolute spacing of exactly representable numbers decreases by a value of 2 from binade to binade and covers half the remaining distance to zero with the average accuracy of the number becoming correspondingly greater. This relationship is shown in Figures 10.1 and 10.2.

Earlier in this chapter, we defined a normalized floating-point number as one in which the most significant bit of the mantissa is a 1 bit. If normalization is mandatory, all numbers of less value than allowed would be made zero, and an exception flag would be set indicating underflow. If nonnormalization is allowed, numbers of smaller value (closer to zero) are allowed, although an exception flag should be set. This is termed *gradual underflow*. Figure 10.2 illustrates these concepts (Coonen, 1981).

A value whose floating-point representation cannot be contained by the largest exrad/significand diad has a magnitude too large for the available format. The development of such a value should set the overflow exception flag. The appropriate subsequent action is usually problem-dependent and cannot be completely generalized.

Assuming no overflow for mathematically well-defined results, a satisfactory model for floating-point arithmetic is: Compute the results with infinite precision and range and then, if necessary, round to the appropriate representable number (nearest, next higher, next lower). This concept can be represented as

$$\text{Finite stored result} = \text{true infinite result} \pm \text{roundoff}$$

where roundoff is no more than $\frac{1}{2}$ ulp (unit in the last place) for nearest rounding or no more than 1 ulp for rounding up or rounding down (truncation).

Roundoff errors, then, result from using a finite set of binary fractions to represent an infinitely fine graduation over a range of real numbers. Quantization errors due to format size limitations result from the inexact binary representation for almost all of the numbers. Since two consecutive significand values span an infinity of real

Floating-point quantities

Sign	Exponent	Significand	Quantity
0	MAX	> 0	+ NaN
0	MAX	0	+ Infinity
0	0 < E < MAX	> 0	+ Real
0	0	> 0	+ Denormalized
0	0	0	+ 0
1	0	0	− 0
1	0	> 0	− Denormalized
1	0 < E < MAX	> 0	− Real
1	MAX	0	− Infinity
1	MAX	> 0	− NaN

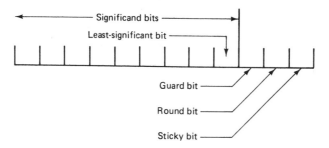

Guard, round and sticky bits ensure accurate unbiased rounding of computed results to within half a unit in the least-significant bit. Two bits are required for perfect rounding; the guard bit is the first bit beyond rounding precision, and the sticky bit is the logical OR of all bits thereafter. To accommodate post-normalization in some operations, the round bit is kept, beyond the guard bit, and the stickly bit is a logical OR of all bits beyond round.

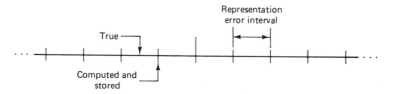

Figure 10.1 The error effects of employing finite representations for infinitely precise quantities necessarily includes roundoff. (Adapted from *SIGNUM (ACM) Newsletter*, October 1979.) (From G. W. Gorsline, *16-Bit Modern Microcomputers: The Intel 18086 Family*, © 1985, p. 216. Reprinted by permission of Prentice-Hall, Inc., Englewood Cliffs, NJ.)

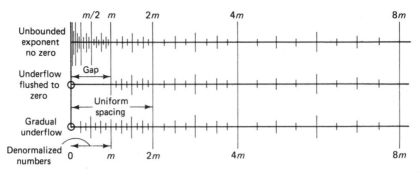

Each vertical tick stands for a 4-bit significand binary floating-point number. The underflow threshold m is a power of ½ depending upon the allowed range of exponents; every floating-point number bigger than m, but none smaller, is representable as a normalized floating-point number. Flushing underflows to zero introduces a gap between m and 0 much wider than between m and the next larger number. Gradual underflow fills that gap with denormalized numbers as densely packed between m and 0 as are normalized numbers between m and $2m$. Doing so relegates underflow in most computations to a status comparable with roundoff among the normalized numbers.

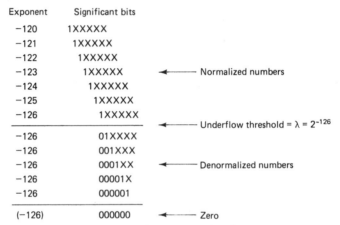

Exponent	Significant bits	
−120	1XXXXX	
−121	1XXXXX	
−122	1XXXXX	
−123	1XXXXX	← Normalized numbers
−124	1XXXXX	
−125	1XXXXX	
−126	1XXXXX	
−126	01XXXX	← Underflow threshold = $\lambda = 2^{-126}$
−126	001XXX	
−126	0001XX	← Denormalized numbers
−126	00001X	
−126	000001	
(−126)	000000	← Zero

A six-bit analog of the proposed single format, showing representative "numbers" beside their unbiased exponents.

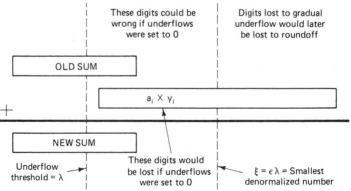

The effect of gradual underflow and store 0 on small sums

Figure 10.2 The gradual underflow effect necessarily increases computational accuracy. (Adapted from *SIGNUM (ACM) Newsletter*, October 1979.)

numbers, of which only the largest and smallest are represented precisely, roundoff error can be assumed in the floating-point representations of all (or very nearly all) numbers.

Using the term *ex* for the roundoff error in the floating-point representation of the true infinite value of X and *xx* for the finite stored result, we can see that

$$X + Y = (xx + ex) + (yy + ey) = (xx + yy) + (ex + ey)$$

$$X - Y = (xx + ex) - (yy + ey) = (xx - yy) + (ex - ey)$$

$$X \times Y = (xx + ex) * (yy \times ey) = (xx \times yy) + (xx \times ey)$$
$$+ yy \times ex) + (ex \times ey)$$

$$\frac{X}{Y} = \frac{(xx + ex)}{(yy + ey)} \cong \frac{xx + ex - (X \times ey)}{yy + ey - (Y \times eY)} \qquad \text{(where} \cong \text{means approxi-}$$
$$\text{mately equal)}$$

An examination of the absolute error formulas above requires that particular attention be directed to three commonly encountered sources of unnecessary programmatic errors:

1. When two numbers of nearly identical magnitude are subtracted, the magnitude of the absolute error term may approach or exceed the magnitude of the difference. This cancellation effect can result in erroneous results that differ from the correct result by orders of magnitude.

2. When the denominator is small in relation to the numerator in a division, the magnitude of the absolute error term may render the quotient useless.

3. When comparing two floating-point quantities whose true infinite values are equal or near equal, the results of the comparison $(=, >, <, =>, <=)$ will usually be determined solely by the absolute error term and will not reflect the true infinite values. Any program branch logic based on such a comparison will often be erroneous.

Unfortunately, absolute error expressions are not really appropriate for floating-point roundoff error analysis. Instead, it is the relative error that is really important. The relative error of any term X is

$$\frac{ex}{xx}$$

The relative errors for the four basic arithmetic operations above are

$$RE(X + Y) = \frac{xx}{xx + yy} \times \frac{ex}{xx} + \frac{yy}{xx + yy} \times \frac{ey}{yy}$$

$$RE(X - Y) = \frac{xx}{xx + yy} \times \frac{ex}{xx} - \frac{yy}{xx - yy} \times \frac{ey}{yy}$$

$$\mathrm{RE}(X \times Y) = \frac{ex}{xx} + \frac{ey}{yy}$$

$$\mathrm{RE}\!\left(\frac{X}{Y}\right) = \frac{ex}{xx} - \frac{ey}{yy}$$

We close this discussion of roundoff errors by quoting John Palmer (1980):

> Mathematical software is easy for the uninitiated to write but notoriously hard for the expert. This paradox exists because the beginner is satisfied if his code usually works in his own machine while the expert attempts, against overwhelming obstacles, to produce programs that always work on a large number of computers. The problem is that while standard formulas of mathematics are fairly easy to translate into FORTRAN they often are subject to instabilities due to roundoff error.

At least some of the generalized numerical solutions to common mathematical procedures have coding that is so involved and tricky—to take care of all possible roundoff contingencies—that they have been termed "pornographic algorithms."

Fortunately, the internal extended (temporary) real format implemented in the MC68881 version of the IEEE Floating-Point Standard, as well as the control of rounding and other features, means that code written by programmers who are unfamiliar with analyzing their programs for roundoff errors and other problems will have a much greater chance of working correctly.

Characteristics of MC68881 Floating-Point Arithmetic

Rounding.   A major contribution of the IEEE Standard and the MC68881 to accurate numerical computation is the ability to control the rounding mode after computation and before storage of the result. Thus, the programmer can specify how infinitely precise results are to be rounded to fit the designated storage format.

It is important to note that if the correct infinitely precise result is exactly representable in the designated storage format, the exact result is stored regardless of any programmatic rounding orders. If storage of the exact result is impossible—that is, if roundoff must be employed—four modes are available under program control:

1. *Round to nearest* (in case of a tie, round to the one with a zero in the least significant bit): As noted earlier, this rounding mode will generally result in the smallest roundoff error and is the recommended mode for almost all cases.
2. *Truncation:* Round toward zero. Truncation is commonly implemented on floating-point processors in mini-, midi-, maxi-, and supercomputers. In general, truncation introduces a roundoff bias toward results with a smaller magnitude.
3. *Round to next smaller* (less than or equal to true result).
4. *Round to next larger* (greater than or equal to true result).

The last two directed rounding modes are vital in implementing interval arithmetic, which we will describe shortly.

Recall that all data types (single real, double real, extended real, word integer, long-word integer, packed decimal real) are first converted to extended real when loaded into a MC68881 register, with *no* roundoff error relative to their storage representation in system memory. In addition, all arithmetic within the MC68881 employs extended real and stores the result in internal registers as extended real. If storage of an infinitely precise result is not possible, the indicated rounding mode is employed and the inexact flag is set (INEX2 for imprecise, not INEX2 for precise). The imprecise flag is also set when rounding occurs during a push or store to system memory. Thus, *exact arithmetic* may be implemented via software.

Interval arithmetic.   Interval arithmetic is practical to implement using the round-to-next-smaller and round-to-next-larger rounding modes, so that calculations within an algorithm can be programmed to include all possible roundoff error in both directions. This will ensure that the two answers delineate or bound the area where the infinitely precise answer lies. In addition, interval arithmetic can be used to estimate the effects of noisy data (in a measurement sense). Thus, if the yield of maize is recorded as 100 bushels per acre, with a probable measurement error of $2\frac{1}{2}$ bushels, the calculations involving this datum would proceed with both $97\frac{1}{2}$ and $102\frac{1}{2}$ bushels per acre.

In effect, the interval data type employs an ordered pair for each datum:

X = [X low : X high]

and uses the round down and round up modes as well as the signed zeros and signed infinities of the MC68881, as specified in the IEEE Standard. In the usual case where X low is equal to or less than X high, the interval X includes all numbers within the interval. The other possible case where X low is greater than X high implies that the interval X includes all numbers not within the interval. The signs on zero and infinity permit open intervals (X low is greater than X high) or closed intervals (X low $<\pm$ X high) when zero or infinity is an endpoint, with the sign signifying which case pertains. If an interval endpoint is neither zero nor infinity, the interval is closed (X low > X high). A more complete discussion of interval arithmetic is not appropriate in this text. Students with a need for more complete information are referred to an article by R. E. Moore (1979).

Infinity.   Infinity has a format with the exrad all 1 bits and the significand all 0 bits. Infinity is the default response to overflow and to divide by zero. Infinity using the MC68881 has a sign and thus allows minus infinity, less than all other numbers, and plus infinity, greater than all other numbers. The affine infinity mode requires a minus zero and plus zero, which are equal in comparison and in all arithmetic except division, where

$$\frac{+1}{+0} = +\text{infinity} \qquad \frac{+1}{-0} = -\text{infinity}$$

Signed zeros and signed infinities often represent underflowed or overflowed quantities. The rules of affine mode arithmetic preserve many of the relationships that would hold among underflowed or overflowed quantities. Note that the programmer accepts full responsibility for determining that such arithmetic is valid for both the algorithm and the data.

Not-a-number.   Not-a-number (NAN) has a format with the exrad all 1 bits and the significand nonzero. Arithmetic operations involving NAN result in a NAN and the setting of the invalid operation flag. One obvious use of NAN is to start all floating-point data receptacles as NAN and thus cause a fault during any computation with an uninitialized datum. In addition, if the significand field of array element NAN starting values contains the array element index, a reference to an uninitialized array element would indicate not only that it was uninitialized but also which element it was. This technique would be a powerful and very economical debugging aid, particularly for novice programmers.

Packed decimal real arithmetic.   Many applications involving monetary quantities, such as those commonly encountered in business data processing, are stored and manipulated as binary-coded decimal (BCD) entities. The commonly employed procedural-level language for these applications, COBOL, employs BCD storage and manipulation for many data entities. Referring to the examples of BCD arithmetic employing these algorithms in Chapter 4, it is obvious that the programming is tedious and the operations slow. Multiplication and division present further difficulties.

If a processor is available, the use of the extended floating-point internal format can be used to manipulate one-digit BCD floating-point numbers. Converted floating-point BCD numbers can be manipulated in a manner analogous to other extended real quantities. For business data processing purposes, exact mode arithmetic is strongly suggested.

The IEEE Floating-Point Standard and the MC68881

The MC68881 floating-point coprocessor shown in Figure 10.3 implements the IEEE Standard for Binary Floating-Point Arithmetic (Task P754) as well as additional data types and their associated operations, as shown in Figure 10.4. As is also shown in Figure 10.3, the connection between the MC68881 and the MC680XY is a simple extension to the bus interface. The selection of the MC68881 coprocessor as the execution vehicle for an instruction is determined during the decoding of the opcode and results in a chip select. It should be immediately noted that the MC68881 can be used with the 8-bit data bus of the MC68008 and with the 16-bit data bus of

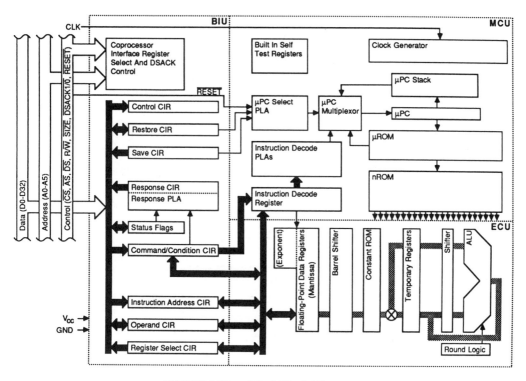

MC68881 Simplified Block Diagram

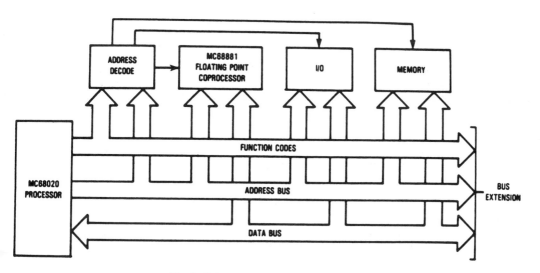

Typical Coprocessor Configuration

Figure 10.3   The MC68881 floating-point coprocessor, (Courtesy of Motorola, Inc.)

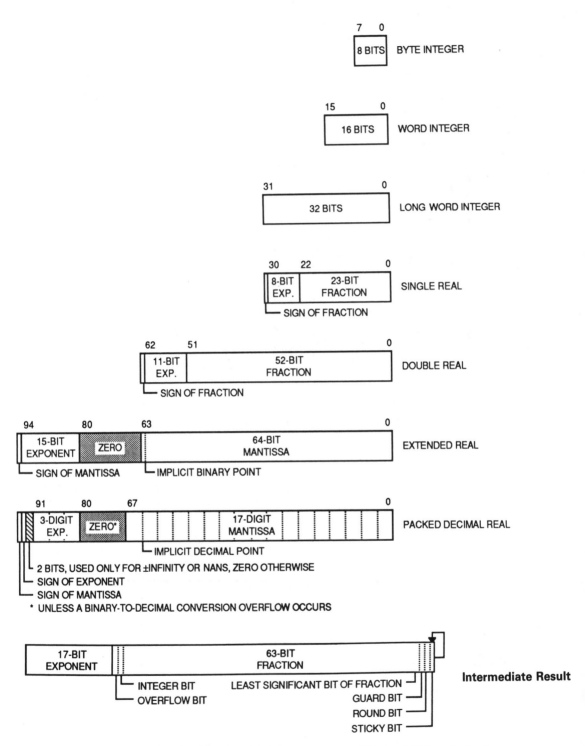

Figure 10.4 MC68881 data format summary. (Courtesy of Motorola, Inc.)

FORMAT OF NORMALIZED NUMBERS

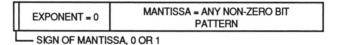

FORMAT OF DENORMALIZED NUMBERS

EXPONENT = 0	MANTISSA = 0

SIGN OF MANTISSA, 0 OR 1

FORMAT OF ZERO

EXPONENT = MAXIMUM	MANTISSA = 0*

SIGN OF MANTISSA, 0 OR 1

FORMAT OF INFINITY

EXPONENT = MAXIMUM	MANTISSA = ANY NON-ZERO BIT PATTERN*

SIGN OF MANTISSA, 0 OR 1

FORMAT OF NOT-A-NUMBERS

*For the extended precision format, the most significant bit of the mantissa
(the integer bit) is a don't care.

Figure 10.4 (*continued*).

the MC68000/MC68010/MC68012, although in these cases it acts as a peripheral device. It acts as a coprocessor when used with the 32-bit data bus of the MC68020. No differences will be noticed in applications programming, but execution is materially slower with the narrower buses, as additional bus cycles will be necessary for data transfers.

Note that the MC68881 is internally divided into three processing elements: the bus interface unit (BIU), the execution control unit (ECU), and the microcode control unit (MCU). The BIU communicates with the MC68020, and the ECU and MCU execute all MC68881 instructions. The BIU contains the coprocessor interface registers and the 32-bit control, status, and instruction address registers. In addition to these registers, the register select and DSACK timing control logic is contained in the BIU. Finally, the status flags used to monitor the status of communications with the main processor are contained in the BIU. These registers are shown in Figure 10.3. All communications between the MC68020 and the MC68881 occur via standard MC680XY family bus transfers. The MC68881 is designed to operate on 8-, 16-, or 32-bit data buses. The MC68881 contains a number of coprocessor interface registers (CIRs), which are addressed in the same manner as memory by the main processor. The MC680XY family coprocessor interface is implemented via a protocol of reading and writing to these registers by the main processor. The MC68020 implements this general-purpose coprocessor interface protocol in hardware and microcode.

When the MC68020 detects a typical MC68881 instruction, the MC68020 writes the instruction to the memory-mapped command CIR and reads the response CIR. In this response, the BIU encodes requests for any additional action required of the MC68020 on behalf of the MC68881. For example, the response may request that the MC68020 fetch an operand from the evaluated effective address and transfer the operand to the operand CIR. Once the MC68020 fulfills the coprocessor request(s), the MC68020 is free to fetch and execute subsequent instructions.

The eight 80-bit (physically, 96-bit) floating-point registers (FP0–FP7) are located in the ECU. In addition to these registers, the ECU contains a high-speed 67-bit arithmetic unit (as implied by the intermediate result format in Figure 10.4), used for both significand and exrad calculations, a barrel shifter that can shift from 1 bit to 67 bits in one machine cycle, and ROM constants for use by the internal algorithms or by user programs. All calculations are performed using the extended real data format for source operands, with the result being temporarily expressed in the intermediate result format before being rounded to the programmer-directed precision and subsequent storage in the specified floating-point data register.

The MCU contains the clock generator, a two-level microcoded sequencer that controls the ECU, the microcode ROM, the nanocode ROM, and self-test circuitry. The built-in self-test capabilities of the MC68881 enhance reliability and ease manufacturing requirements; however, these diagnostic functions are not available to the user.

Floating-point numbers may be encoded in three different data formats: single precision (32 bits), double precision (64 bits), and double extended precision (96 bits, 80 of which are used). All three of these formats fully comply with the IEEE Standard for Binary Floating-Point Arithmetic. The single extended precison data format defined in the IEEE Standard is redundant when the double extended precision format is included. Since all MC68881 internal operations are performed in extended precision, single and double precision operands are converted to extended precision values before the specified operation is performed. Thus, mixed-mode arithmetic is implicity supported.

The exponent in all three binary formats is an unsigned binary integer with an implied bias added to it. The bias values for single, double, and extended precision are 127, 1023, and 16383, respectively. When the bias is subtracted from the value of the exponent, the result represents a signed, two's-complement power of 2, which, when multiplied by the mantissa, yields the magnitude of a normalized floating-point number. Note that the use of biased exponents allows floating-point numbers in memory to be compared using the MC680XY family integer compare (CMP) instruction, regardless of the absolute magnitude of the exponents.

Data formats for single and double precision numbers differ slightly from the data format for extended precision numbers in the representation of the mantissa. A normalized mantissa, for all three precisions, is always in the range <1.0 . . . 2.0>. The extended precision data format explicitly represents the entire mantissa, including the explicit integer part bit. However, for single and double precision data formats, only the fractional portion of the mantissa is explicitly represented and the integer part is always 1. Thus, the integer part bit is implicit—hidden—for single and double precision formats.

The IEEE Standard has created the term *significand* to bridge this difference and to avoid the historical implications of the term *mantissa*. The IEEE Standard defines a significand as that component of a binary floating-point number that consists of an explicit or implicit leading bit to the left of the implied binary point and a fraction field to the right of the implied binary point:

Single precision mantissa	= single precision significand
	= 1.<23-bit fraction field>
Double precision mantissa	= double precision significand
	= 1.<52-bit fraction field>
Extended precision mantissa	= extended precision significand
	= 1.fraction
	= <64-bit mantissa field>

Each of the three floating-point data formats can represent five unique floating-point data types:

- Normalized numbers
- Denormalized numbers
- Zeros
- Infinities
- Not-a-numbers (NANs)

The normalized data type never uses the maximum or minimum exponent value for a given format (except for the extended precision format, as noted below). These exponent values in each precision are reserved for representing the special data types: zero, infinities, denormalized numbers, and NANs. Figure 10.4 illustrates the five data formats.

1. *Normalized numbers* encompass all representable real values between the overflow and underflow thresholds—that is, those numbers whose exponents lie between the maximum and minimum values. Normalized numbers may be positive or negative. For normalized numbers, the implied integer part bit in single and double precision is a 1. In extended precision, the integer bit is explicitly a 1.

2. *Denormalized numbers* represent real values near the underflow threshold (underflow is detected for a given data format and operation when the result exponent is less than or equal to the minimum exponent value). Denormalized numbers may be positive or negative. For denormalized numbers, the implied integer part bit in single and double precision is 0. In extended precision, the integer bit is explicitly a 0. Traditionally, floating-point number systems perform a "flush-to-zero" when underflow is detected. This leaves a large gap in the number line between the smallest magnitude normalized number and zero. The IEEE Standard implements gradual underflow, where the result mantissa is shifted right (denormalized) while incrementing the result exponent until the result exponent reaches the minimum value. If all mantissa bits of the result are shifted off to the right during this denormalization, then the result becomes zero. In many instances, gradual underflow reduces the potential underflow damage to no more than a roundoff error. (This underflow and denormalization description ignores the effects of rounding and the user-selectable rounding modes.) Thus, the large gap in the number line created by "flush-to-zero" floating-point number systems is filled with representable (denormalized) numbers in the IEEE "gradual underflow" floating-point number system. Since the extended precision data format has an explicit integer part bit, a number can be formatted with a nonzero exponent (that is, not equal to the maximum value), and a zero integer bit, which is not defined by the IEEE standard. Such a number is called an *unnormalized number*. The MC68881 never generates an unnormalized number as the result of any operation, and unnormalized inputs are always converted to normalized or denormalized numbers or zero before being used.

3. *Zeros* are signed (positive or negative) and represent the real values $+0.0$ and -0.0.

4. *Infinities* are signed (positive or negative) and represent real values that exceed the overflow threshold. Overflow is detected for a given data format and operation when the result exponent is greater than or equal to the maximum exponent value. (This overflow description ignores the effects of rounding and the user-selectable rounding modes.) For extended precision infinities, the most significant bit of the mantissa (the integer bit) is a "don't care."

5. When created by the MC68881, *not-a-numbers* (NANs) represent the results of operations that have no mathematical interpretation, such as infinity divided by infinity. All operations involving a NAN operand as an input will return a NAN result. Two different types of NANs—differentiated by the most significant bit (MSB) of the fraction (the MSB of the mantissa for single and double precision, the MSB minus one of the mantissa for extended precision)—are implemented. NANs with a leading fraction bit equal to 1 are nonsignaling NANs; NANs with a leading fraction bit equal to 0 are signaling NANs (SNANs). SNANs can be used as escape mecha-

nisms for user-defined non-IEEE data types. The MC68881 never creates a SNAN as a result of an operation. When NANs are created by the MC68881, the NANs always contain the same bit pattern in the mantissa; for any precision, all bits of the mantissa are 1's. When created by the user, any nonzero bit pattern can be stored in the mantissa. For extended precision NANs, the most significant bit of the mantissa (the integer bit) is a "don't care." The IEEE specification defines the manner in which NANs are handled when used as inputs to an operation. Particularly if a SNAN is used as an input and the SNAN trap is not enabled, it is required that a nonsignaling NAN be returned as the result. The MC68881 does this by using the source SNAN, setting the most significant bit of the fraction, and storing the resultant nonsignaling NAN in the destination. Because of the IEEE formats for NANs, the result of setting the most significant fraction bit of a SNAN will always produce a nonsignaling NAN. When created by the user, NANs can protect against uninitialized variables and arrays or can represent user-defined special number types.

The packed decimal floating-point data format consists of a 24-digit packed decimal string, as shown in Figure 10.4. Decimal floating-point source operands are converted to extended precision values before the specified operation is performed. Thus, mixed-mode arithmetic is implicitly supported. All MC68881 internal operations are performed in extended precision. All external operands, regardless of the data format, are converted to extended precision values before the specified operation is performed. The format of an intermediate result is shown in Figure 10.4. The intermediate result exponent for some dyadic operations (multiply and divide) can easily overflow or underflow the 15-bit exponent. To simplify overflow and underflow detection, intermediate results in the MC68881 maintain a 17-bit two's-complement integer exponent. Subsequent detection of an overflow or underflow intermediate result always converts the intermediate 17-bit exponent back into a 15-bit biased exponent before storing in a floating-point data register. In addition, mantissas are maintained internally as 67 bits for rounding purposes but are always rounded to 64 bits (or less, depending on the selected rounding precision) before storing into a floating-point data register.

Conversions between data formats are of two types:

1. Convert an operand in any memory data format to the extended precision data format and store it in a floating-point data register or use it as the source operand for an arithmetic operation.
2. Convert the extended precision value in a floating-point data register to any data format and store it in a memory destination.

The basic architecture of the MC68881 is that of a floating-point multiple register processor with a floating-point arithmetic-logic unit, including automatic data type conversion during register loads and stores as well as for memory-resident source operands. The generic arithmetic instruction is two-address:

$$\text{Source1} + \frac{\text{Source2}}{\text{(destination)}} \xrightarrow{\text{operation}} \text{Destination}$$

Note that the source 2 and the destination operand is the same identical floating-point register and that the original contents of this register are lost—that is, replaced by the result. In this regard, it is vital always to recall that all applications-oriented procedural-level languages—such as Pascal, FORTRAN, BASIC, COBOL, and the like—not only are based on a memory-to-memory plan but also implicitly assume that no value is changed unless it is explicitly directed to be changed. That is, the statement:

C := A + B

will only change the value of C and will not effect the value of A or of B. To accomplish this action on a two-address instruction-style machine like the MC68881 (or the MC680XY) would require code of the following type:

```
MOVE      A,C
ADD       B,C
```

Two types of arithmetic instructions are supported—which we illustrate using the floating-point add (FADD) instruction:

FADD.fmt   <EA>,FR$_n$

which means: Convert the value at the MC680XY effective address (either a register or memory) to internal extended real format and add it to the value in floating-point register n, storing the result in floating-point register n while setting any and all appropriate flags. The "fmt" suffix designates that the source1 operand is a byte integer, word integer, long-word integer, packed decimal real, single precision real, double precision real, or extended precision real.

FADD.x   'FR' sub 'm'   'FR' sub 'n'

means: Convert the values in floating-point registers m and n to the internal extended precision real format and add them, storing the rounded result in floating-point register n while setting any and all appropriate flags. The "x" suffix designates that the operands are single precision real, double precision real, or extended precision real.
    Returning to the procedural language statement cited earlier:

C := A + B

and assuming that the variables in memory are all double precision real, the necessary MC680XY/MC68881 combined code could be

```
LEA        A,A1
LEA        B,A2
LEA        C,A3
FMOVE.D    (A1),FR1
FADD.D     (A2),FR1
FMOVE.D    FR1,(A3)
```

The Programming Model

Figure 10.5 shows a pictorial representation of the registers in the MC68881 programming model. The eight 80-bit floating-point data registers (FP0–FP7) are
analogous to the integer data registers (D0–D7) of all MC680XY family processors.
Floating-point data registers always contain extended precision numbers. The data
format used is the extended precision data format, except that the reserved (unused
16 of 96) bits are deleted. All external operands, regardless of the data format, are
converted to extended precision values before any calculations or storage in a
floating-point data register are performed.

The control register can be read or written to by the user. Bits 16 through 31
are reserved for future definition by Motorola, will always read as 0, and are ignored
during write operations (but should be zero for future compatibility). When cleared,
this register provides the IEEE Standard defaults. The 32-bit *floating-point control
register (FPCR)* contains an exception enable byte, which enables/disables traps for
each class of floating-point exceptions, and a mode byte, which sets the user-
selectable modes. The exception enable byte (see Figure 10.5) contains one bit for
each floating-point exception class. The user may separately enable traps for each
class of floating-point exceptions. If a bit in the floating-point status register (FPSR)
exception byte is set by the MC68881 and the corresponding bit in the control register enable byte is also set, an exception will be taken to a specific vector address corresponding to the exception. Note that the bits in the FPSR exception byte and the
FPCR enable byte are in the same positions within each byte. A user write of the
control register enable byte that enables a class of floating-point exceptions will not
cause a trap to be taken because of previously generated floating-point exceptions,
regardless of the value in the status register exception byte.

Dual and triple exceptions can be generated by a single instruction execution in
a few cases. When multiple exceptions occur with traps enabled for more than one
exception class, the highest-priority exception will be taken; the lower-priority exceptions will never be reported or taken. It is the responsibility of the exception handler routine to check for multiple exceptions. The bits of the enable byte are organized in decreasing priority, left to right; that is, BSUN is the highest-priority bit and
INEX1 is the lowest-priority bit. The only multiple exception possibilities are

SNAN and INEX1
OPERR and INEX2

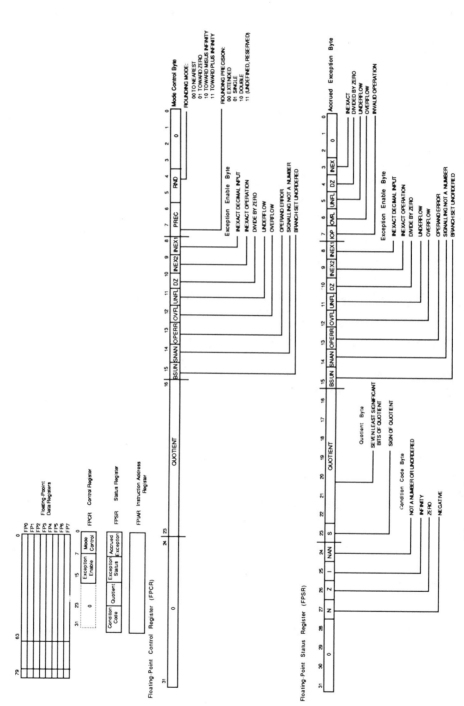

Figure 10.5 MC68881 programming model. (Courtesy of Motorola, Inc.)

    OPERR and INEX1
    OVFL and INEX2 and/or INEX1
    UNFL and INEX2 and/or INEX1

In general, floating-point exceptions are treated exactly like main processor exceptions, with each exception having a unique exception vector number assigned to it. The exact meaning of each exception, as well as possible recovery actions, will be discussed later.

The mode byte (see Figure 10.5) controls user-selectable rounding modes and rounding precisions. A 0 in this byte selects the IEEE defaults. The rounding mode is used to determine how inexact results should be rounded. *Round to nearest* specifies that the nearest number to the infinitely precise result should be selected as the rounded value. In case of a tie, the even result is selected. *Round toward zero* chops the result. *Round toward plus infinity* always rounds numbers toward plus infinity. *Round toward minus infinity* always rounds numbers toward minus infinity. The rounding precision selects where the rounding will occur in the mantissa. For extended precision, the result is rounded to a 64-bit boundary. A single precision result is rounded to a 24-bit boundary, and a double precision result is rounded to a 53-bit boundary. The rounding algorithm is as follows:

```
BEGIN
    IF GUARD, ROUND AND STICKY = 0
        THEN (RESULT IS EXACT)
            DON'T SET INEX1 OR INEX2
            DON'T CHANGE THE INTERMEDIATE RESULT

        ELSE (RESULT IN INEXACT)
            SET INEX1 OR INEX2 IN THE FPSR EXC BYTE

            SELECT THE ROUNDING MODE
                RM: IF INTERMEDIATE RESULT IS POSITIVE THEN ADD 1 TO LSB
                RN: IF GUARD = 1 AND ROUND AND STICKY = 0 (TIE CASE)
                        THEN IF LSB = 1 ADD 1 LSB
                        ELSE ADD 1 TO LSB
                    END IF
                RP: IF INTERMEDIATE RESULT IS NEGATIVE THEN ADD 1 TO LSB
                RZ: (FALL THROUGH; GUARD, ROUND AND STICKY ARE
                    CHOPPED)
            END SELECT

            IF OVERFLOW = 1
                THEN
                    SHIFT MANTISSA RIGHT BY ONE BIT
                    ADD 1 TO THE EXPONENT
                END IF
```

```
          SET GUARD, ROUND AND STICKY TO 0
      END IF
END
```

Note that the rounding precisions of single and double are provided for emulation of machines that support only those precisions. When the MC68881 performs any operation, the calculation is carried out using extended precision inputs and the intermediate result is calculated as if to produce infinite precision. After the calculation is complete, this intermediate result is rounded to the selected precision and stored in the destination. The execution speed of all instructions is degraded significantly when these modes are used. Note that the result obtained by performing a series of operations with the rounding mode set to single or double precision may not be the same as the result of performing the same operations in the extended precision mode and storing the final result in the single or double precision format. If the destination is a floating-point data register, the stored value will be in the extended precision format rounded to the precision specified by the PREC bits. This means that all mantissa bits beyond the selected precision are 0 after the rounding operation. Also, the exponent value will be in the correct range for the single or double precision format, although it is stored in extended precision format. If the destination is a memory location, the PREC bits are ignored. In this case, a number in the extended precision format is taken from the source floating-point data register, rounded to the destination format precision, and written to memory.

The *floating-point status register (FPSR)*, shown in Figure 10.5, contains a floating-point condition code byte, a floating-point exception status byte, quotient bits, and a floating-point accrued exception byte. All bits in the FPSR can be read or written to by the user. Execution of most floating-point instructions will modify parts of this register. The floating-point condition code (FPCC) byte contains four condition code bits:

N—negative
Z—zero
I—infinity
NAN—not-a-number

which are set at the end of all arithmetic instructions involving the floating-point data registers, except for the FMOVE FP, <ea> (move multiple floating-point data register and move system control register) instruction. The operation result data type determines how the four condition code bits are set. Loading the FPCC byte with one of the other condition code bit combinations and performing a conditional instruction may produce an unexpected branch condition. The IEEE Standard defines the following four conditions and requires the generation of the condition codes only as a result of a floating-point compare operation. In addition to this requirement, the MC68881 can test these conditions at the end of any operation that affects the condition codes.

EQ	(equal to)	= Z
GT	(greater than)	= N & NAN & Z
LT	(less than)	= N & NAN & Z
UN	(unordered)	= NAN

An unordered condition occurs when one or both of the operands in a floating-point compare operation is a NAN.

The quotient byte is set at the completion of the module (FMOD) or IEEE remainder (FREM) instructions. This byte contains the seven least significant bits of the quotient (unsigned) and the sign of the entire quotient. The quotient bits can be used in argument reduction for transcendentals and other functions. For example, seven bits are more than enough to determine in which quadrant of a circle an operand resides. The quotient bits remain set until they are cleared by the user or until another FMOD or FREM instruction is executed.

The exception status (EXC) byte contains a bit for each floating-point exception that may have occurred during the last arithmetic instruction or move operation. This byte is cleared by the MC68881 at the start of most operations; operations that cannot generate any floating-point exceptions (the FMOVEM and FMOVE control register instructions) do not clear this byte. This byte can be used by an exception handler to determine which floating-point exception(s) caused a trap. If a bit is set by the MC68881 in the EXC byte and the corresponding bit in the control enable byte is also set, an exception will be signaled to the main processor. When a floating-point exception is detected by the MC68881, the corresponding bit in the EXC byte will be set even if the trap for that exception class is disabled. (A user write operation to the status register, which sets a bit in the EXC byte, will not cause a trap to be taken, regardless of the value in the enable byte). Note that the bits in the status EXC byte and control enable byte are in the same bit positions within each byte. The eight floating-point exception classes will be described in greater detail later in this chapter.

The accrued exception (AEXC) byte contains the five exception bits required by the IEEE Standard for trap-disabled operation. These exceptions are logical combinations of the bits in the EXC byte. The AEXC byte contains the history of all floating-point exceptions that have occurred since the user last cleared the AEXC byte. In normal operations, only the user will clear this byte by writing to the status register. The AEXC byte is cleared by the MC68881 only by a reset or a null state size restore operation. Many users will elect to disable traps for all or part of the floating-point exception classes. To allow these users to avoid polling the EXC byte after each floating-point instruction, the AEXC byte is provided. At the end of most operations (all but the FMOVEM and FMOVE control register instructions), the bits in the EXC byte are logically combined to form an AEXC value, which is logically ORed into the existing AEXC byte. This creates "sticky" floating-point exception bits in the AEXC byte, which the user need poll only once (at the end of a series of floating-point operations, for example).

The setting or clearing of bits in the AEXC byte has no effect on whether or not the MC68881 will take an exception. The relationship between the bits in the

EXC byte and the bits in the AEXC byte is given below. At the end of each operation that can affect the AEXC byte, the following equations are used to generate the the new AEXC bits:

```
AEXC(IOP)   = AEXC(IOP) ∨ EXC(BSUN ∨ SNAN ∨ OPERR)
AEXC(OVFL) = AEXC(OVFL) ∨ EXC(OVFL)
AEXC(UNFL) = AEXC(UNFL) ∨ EXC(UNFL ∧ INEX2)
AEXC(DZ)    = AEXC(DZ) ∨ EXC(DZ)
AEXC(INEX) = AEXC(INEX) ∨ EXC(INEX1 ∨ INEX2 ∨ OVFL)
```

where:

"∨" = logical OR
"∧" = logical AND

A majority of the MC68881 instructions operate concurrently with the MC68020, such that the MC68020 can be executing instructions while the MC68881 is executing a floating-point instruction. As a result of this nonsequential instruction execution, the program counter value stacked by the MC68020 in response to an enabled floating-point exception trap may not point to the offending instruction.

For the subset of the MC68881 instructions that can generate floating-point exception traps, the 32-bit *floating-point instruction address register (FPIAR)* is loaded with the logical address of an instruction before the instruction is executed (unless all arithmetic exceptions are disabled). This address can then be used by a floating-point exception handler to locate a floating-point instruction that causes an exception. Since the MC68881 FMOVE (to/from the FPCR, FPSR, or FPIAR) and FMOVEM instructions cannot generate floating-point exceptions, they do not modify the FPIAR; thus, these instructions can be used to read the FPIAR in the trap handler without changing the previous value.

MC68881 Instructions

Data movement operations. This group of instructions provides the means to load or store the user-visible registers (see Figure 10.5) of the MC68881 and to move operands into, between, or out of the floating-point registers. All external data formats are converted to extended precision real for internal storage and are converted to the data type and precision specified for storage in the MC680XY system using the rounding specified by the user in the mode control byte of the floating-point control register (FPCR).

As would be expected, operations are provided to store or to load the control registers (FPCR and/or FPSR) into or from system memory or registers. The bit set operations of the MC680XY main processor may be used to alter the settings of the individual bits as desired when they are within the MC680XY registers or memory and before loading to the MC68881 control registers. Operations to move the system control registers into and out of the MC68881 are also provided. The move constant

ROM (FMOVECR) instruction allows floating-point data registers to be loaded quickly with commonly used constants such as π, e, 0.0, 1.0, and so forth. Figure 10.6 gives a summary of the data movement instructions that are available and the operand data formats that are supported.

Arithmetic operations.   The dyadic floating-point instructions provide several arithmetic functions that require two input operands, such as add, subtract, multiply, and divide. For these operations, the first operand may be located in memory, in an integer data register, or in a floating-point data register and the second operand must always be contained in a floating-point data register. The results of the operation are stored in this register. All operations support any data format and are performed to extended precision, with the exception of the single precision multiply and divide (FSGLMUL and FSGLDIV), which support any precision inputs but return results accurate only to single precision. These two instructions provide very high speed operations by sacrificing accuracy.

The monadic floating-point instructions provide several arithmetic functions that require only one input operand. Unlike the integer counterparts to these functions (e.g., NEG <ea>), a source and a destination may be specified. The operation is performed on the source operand, and the result is stored in the destination, which is always a floating-point data register. When the source is not a floating-point data register, all data formats are supported; the data format is always extended precision for register-to-register operations. The general format of these instructions is shown in Figure 10.7.

Program control operations.   The program instructions provide a means of affecting program flow on the basis of conditions present in the floating-point status register after any operation that sets the condition codes. Besides allowing direct control of program flow with the branch conditionally (FBcc) and the decrement and branch conditionally (FDBcc) instructions, the set conditionally (FScc) instruction allows the user to set a Boolean variable based on the floating-point condition codes as an intermediate result in the evaluation of a complex Boolean equation. Also included is a test operand (FTST) instruction that sets the floating-point condition codes for use by the the other program and system control instructions and a no operation (FNOP) instruction that may be used to force synchronization of the MC68881 with the main processor. Figure 10.8 gives a summary of the program control instructions that are available.

The MC68881 supports 32 conditional tests, which are separated into two groups—16 that will cause an exception if an unordered condition is present when the conditional test is attempted and 16 that will not cause an exception if an unordered condition is present. (An unordered condition occurs when an input to an arithmetic operation is a NAN.) Figure 10.8 lists the 32 condition code mnemonics along with the conditional test function. One important consideration of which programmers must be cognizant is that the inclusion of the NAN data type in the IEEE floating-point number system means that each conditional test must include the NAN condition code bit in the Boolean equation for that test. Because a comparison of a

Instruction	Operand Syntax	Operand Format	Operation
FMOVE	FPm,FPn <ea>,FPn FPm,<ea> FPm,<ea>{#k} FPm,<ea>{Dn} <ea>,FPcr FPcr,<ea>	X B,W,L,S,D,X,P B,W,L,S,D,X P P L L	source → destination
FMOVECR	#ccc,FPn	X	ROM constant → FPn
FMOVEM	<ea>,<list>¹ <ea>,Dn <list>¹,<ea> Dn,<ea>	L,X X L,X X	listed registers → destination source → listed registers

NOTE:
The register list may include any combination of the eight floating-point registers, or it may contain any combination of the three control registers FPCR, FPSR, and FPIAR. If the register list mask resides in a main processor data register, only floating-point data registers may be specified.

In the FMOVECR instruction, # 000 employs the following ROM offsets:

Offset	Constant
$00	π
$0B	$Log_{10}(2)$
$0C	e
$0D	$Log_2(e)$
$0E	$Log_{10}(e)$
$0F	0.0
$30	$ln(2)$
$31	$ln(10)$
$32	10^0
$33	10^1
$34	10^2
$35	10^4
$36	10^8
$37	10^{16}
$38	10^{32}
$39	10^{64}
$3A	10^{128}
$3B	10^{256}
$3C	10^{512}
$3D	10^{1024}
$3E	10^{2048}
$3F	10^{4096}

Figure 10.6 Data movement operations. (Courtesy of Motorola, Inc.)

488

Instruction	Operand Syntax	Operand Format	Operation
F<dop>	<ea>,FPn FPm,FPn	B,W,L,S,D,X,P X	FPn <function> source → FPn

NOTE: <dop> is any one of the dyadic operation specifiers.

FADD	add
FCMP	compare
FDIV	divide
FMOD	modulo remainder
FMUL	multiply
FREM	IEEE remainder
FSCALE	scale exponent
FSGLDIV	single precision divide
FSGLMUL	single precision multiply
FSUB	subtract

Dyadic Operation

Instruction	Operand Syntax	Operand Format	Operation
F<mop>	<ea>,FPn FPm,FPn FPn	B,W,L,S,D,X,P X X	source → function → FPn FPn → function → FPn

NOTE: <mop> is any one of the monadic operations specifiers.

FABS	absolute value
FACOS	arc cosine
FASIN	arc sine
FATAN	arc tangent
FATANH	hyperbolic arc tangent
FCOS	cosine
FCOSH	hyperbolic cosine
FETOX	e^x
FETOXM1	e^x-1
FGETEXP	extract exponent
FGETMAN	extract mantissa
FINT	extract integer part
FINTRZ	extract integer part, rounded-to-zero
FLOGN	$\ln(x)$
FLOGNP1	$\ln(x+1)$
FLOG10	$\log_{10}(x)$
FLOG2	$\log_2(x)$
FNEG	negate
FSIN	sine
FSINH	hyperbolic sine
FSQRT	square root
FTAN	tangent
FTANH	hyperbolic tangent
FTENTOX	10^x
FTWOTOX	2^x

Monadic Operation

Instruction	Operand Syntax	Operand Format	Operation
FSINCOS	<ea>,FPc:FPs FPm,FPc:FPs	B,W,L,S,D,X,P X	SIN(source) → FPs; COS(source) → FPc

Dual Monadic Operation

Figure 10.7   Arithmetic operations. (Courtesy of Motorola, Inc.)

Program Control Operations

Instruction	Operand Syntax	Operand Size or Format	Operation
FBcc	\<label\>	W,L	if condition true, then PC + d → PC
FDBcc	Dn,\<label\>	W	if condition true, then no operation; else Dn – 1 → Dn; if Dn ≠ –1 then PC + d → PC
FNOP	none	none	no operation
FScc	\<ea\>	B	if condition true, then 1's → destination else 0's → destination
FTST	\<ea\> FPn	B,W,L,S,D,X,P X	set FPSR condition codes

IEEE Nonaware Tests

All of the conditional tests below set the BSUN bit in the status register exception byte if the NAN condition code bit is set when a conditional instruction is executed.

No Exception on Unordered

OGE	ordered greater than or equal
OGL	ordered greater than or less than
OR	ordered
OGT	ordered greater than
OLE	ordered less than or equal
OLT	ordered less than
UGE	unordered or greater than or equal
UEQ	unordered or equal
UN	unordered
UGT	unordered or greater than
ULE	unordered or less than or equal
ULT	unordered or less than
EQ	equal
NE	not equal
F	always false
T	always true

IEEE Aware Tests

Do not set the BSUN bit in the status register exception byte.

Exception on Unordered

GE	greater than or equal
GL	greater than or less than
GLE	greater than or less than or equal
GT	greater than
LE	less than or equal
LT	less than
NGE	not (greater than or equal)
NGL	not (greater than or less than)
NGLE	not (greater than or less than or equal)
NGT	not greater than
NLE	not (less than or equal)
NLT	not less than
SEQ	signalling equal
SNE	signalling not equal
SF	signalling always false
ST	signalling always true

Figure 10.8 Program control operations. (Courtesy of Motorola, Inc.)

NAN with anything is unordered (i.e., it is impossible to determine whether a NAN is bigger or smaller than an in-range number), the compare instruction sets the NAN condition code bit when an unordered compare is attempted. All arithmetic instructions also set the NAN bit if the result of an operation is a NAN. The conditional instructions interpret the NAN condition code being set as the unordered condition.

The inclusion of the unordered condition in floating-point branches destroys the familiar trichotomy relationship (greater than, equal, less than) that exists for integers. For example, the opposite of floating-point branch greater than (FBGT) is not floating-point branch less than or equal (FBLE). Rather, it is floating-point branch not greater than (FBNGT). If the result of the previous instruction was unordered, FBNGT is true, whereas both FBGT and FBLE would be false, since unordered fails both of these tests (and sets BSUN). Compiler programmers should be particularly careful of the lack of trichotomy in the floating-point branches, since it is common for compilers to invert the sense of conditions. The conditional tests are broken into three main categories: (1) IEEE nonaware tests, (2) IEEE aware tests, and (3) miscellaneous.

The IEEE nonaware test set is best used when porting a program from a system that does not support the IEEE Standard to one that does, or when generating high-level language code that does not support IEEE floating-point concepts (i.e., the unordered condition). When using the IEEE nonaware test set, the user receives a BSUN exception whenever a branch is attempted and the NAN condition code bit is set, unless the branch is an FBEQ or an FBNE. If the BSUN trap is enabled in the FPCR register, the exception causes a trap. Therefore, the IEEE nonaware program is interrupted if something unexpected occurs. The IEEE aware test set should be used by compilers and programmers who are knowledgeable about the IEEE Standard and wish to deal with ordered and unordered conditions. Since the ordered or unordered attribute is explicitly included in the conditional test, the BSUN bit is not set in the status register EXC byte when the unordered condition occurs.

System control operations.   The system control instructions are utilized for communications with the operating system via a conditional trap (FTRAPcc) instruction and for saving or restoring (FSAVE or FRESTORE) the non-user-visible portion of the MC68881 during context switches in a virtual memory or other type of multitasking system. The conditional trap instruction uses the same conditional tests as the program control instructions and allows as optional 16- or 32-bit immediate operand to be included as part of the instruction for passing parameters to the operating system. Figure 10.9 gives a summary of the system control instructions that are available.

MC68020/MC68881 Addressing Modes

Because of the nature of the MC68020/MC68881 coprocessor interface, the MC68881 supports all MC68020 addressing modes. The MC68020 effective address modes are categorized by the manner in which the modes are used:

Instruction	Operand Syntax	Operand Size	Operation
FRESTORE	<ea>	none	state frame → internal registers
FSAVE	<ea>	none	internal registers → state frame
FTRAPcc	none #xxx	none W,L	if condition true, then take exception

Figure 10.9 System control operations. (Courtesy of Motorola, Inc.)

Address Modes	Mode	Register	Data	Memory	Control	Alterable	Assembler Syntax
Data Register Direct	000	reg. no.	X	–	–	X	Dn
Address Register Direct	001	reg. no.	–	–	–	X	An
Address Register Indirect	010	reg. no.	X	X	X	X	(An)
Address Register Indirect with Postincrement	011	reg. no.	X	X	–	X	(An)+
Address Register Indirect with Predecrement	100	reg. no.	X	X	–	X	–(An)
Address Register Indirect with Displacement	101	reg. no.	X	X	X	X	(d16,An)
Address Register Indirect with Index (8-Bit Displacement)	110	reg. no.	X	X	X	X	(d8,An,Xn)
Address Register Indirect with Index (Base Displacement)	110	reg. no.	X	X	X	X	(bd,An,Xn)
Memory Indirect Post-Indexed	110	reg. no.	X	X	X	X	([bd,An],Xn,od)
Memory Indirect Pre-Indexed	110	reg. no.	X	X	X	X	([bd,An,Xn],od)
Absolute Short	111	000	X	X	X	X	(xxx).W
Absolute Long	111	001	X	X	X	X	(xxx).L
Program Counter Indirect with Displacement	111	010	X	X	X	–	(d16,PC)
Program Counter Indirect with Index (8-Bit Displacement)	111	011	X	X	X	–	(d8,PC,Xn)
Program Counter Indirect with Index (Base Displacement)	111	011	X	X	X	–	(bd,PC,Xn)
PC Memory Indirect Post-Indexed	111	011	X	X	X	–	([bd,PC],Xn,od)
PC Memory Indirect Pre-Indexed	111	011	X	X	X	–	([bd,PC,Xn],od)
Immediate	111	100	X	X	–	–	#<data>

Figure 10.10 Effective addressing mode categories. (Courtesy of Motorola, Inc.)

Data: If an effective address is used to refer to data operands, it is considered a data addressing mode.

Memory: If an effective address is used to refer to memory operands, it is considered a memory addressing mode.

Alterable: If an effective address is used to refer to alterable (writable) operands, it is considered an alterable addressing mode.

Control: If an effective address is used to refer to memory operands that do not have an associated size, it is considered a control addressing mode.

Figure 10.10 summarizes the effective addressing mode categories.

THE COPROCESSOR CONCEPT

Instructions for the MC68881 and for the MC680XY are combined into a single program that carries out the desired data manipulations, as defined by the programmer, to solve the problem at hand. The program is a single, unified, and ordered sequence of instructions for manipulating data in a single systems memory, regardless of whether the instructions are to be executed by the MC680XY central processor or by the MC68881 floating-point coprocessor. It is obvious that the command processor (the MC680XY) must be able to recognize its own instructions and act only on them while also recognizing instructions for the other processor (the MC68881) and sending them to it for execution. It is also obvious that some method must exist to prevent one of the processors from attempting to use data produced by the other processor before it has been delivered; that is, the processors must be kept in phase—they must be synchronized. In the scheme employed by the Motorola designers, the MC680XY and the MC68881 are allowed to execute different instructions of the same program simultaneously but under the overall control of the MC680XY central processor.

In many ways, the MC68881 floating-point coprocessor appears as an extension of the instruction set of the MC680XY central processor that allows particular data manipulations to be accomplished. As a matter of fact, all of the instructions to manipulate floating-point data could be accomplished employing subprocedures or macros executing on the MC680XY. From this viewpoint, the MC68881 is a hardware implementation of an extensive floating-point program library; such a software library exists and can be obtained. However, the implementation of the floating-point data manipulation functions in hardware (the MC68881) not only allows increased processing speed but results in smaller programs (as the software routines do not exist) and allows a modicum of concurrent instruction processing. This concurrency of processing is also true for DMA I/O as introduced in Chapters 5 and 6.

Instruction execution of the combined MC680XY/MC68881 fully ordered instructions (the program) is always initiated by the control portions of the MC680XY obtaining an instruction from memory (or from its prefetched queue of instructions).

All instructions for the MC68881 have the leftmost 4 bits set ON (bits 15, 14, 13, and 12 of the operation word are 1's). Thus, these instructions are termed *F-line operation* instructions. Note that it is possible to attach up to eight coprocessors, including more than one floating-point coprocessor, to a single central processor.

When the MC68020 central processor encounters an F-line operation instruction, it executes bus cycles with the addresses specified as being within CPU space and sends certain command information to the CPU space memory-mapped coprocessor interface registers (CIRs) (Figure 10.11). These registers are used solely as communication ports—each with a specific function—and are not a portion of the programming model. On the other hand, if the MC68881 is used as a peripheral processor with the MC68008, MC68000, MC68010, or MC68012, software must transmit correct values to these CIRs. This would be accomplished in the exception handler routine for the F-line operation instruction exceptions. Thus, to applications programmer and compiler writers, no differences in programming exists between a MC68020-based system with a MC68881 and such a system based on the older and less capable processors. All CIR transfers of information to the MC68881 are initiated by the MC680XY. The logical uses of the different CIRs are as follows:

Response CIR (16-bit read-only): used by the MC68881 to request service from the MC680XY.

Control CIR (16-bit write-only): used by the MC680XY CPU to issue an exception acknowledge or instruction abort to the MC68881.

Save CIR (16-bit read-only): used by the MC680XY to issue a context save command to the MC68881 and to return the format word of the save state frame.

Restore CIR (16-bit read/write): used by the MC680XY CPU to issue a context restore command to the MC68881, which immediately aborts any current action; also used to validate the format word of a state frame.

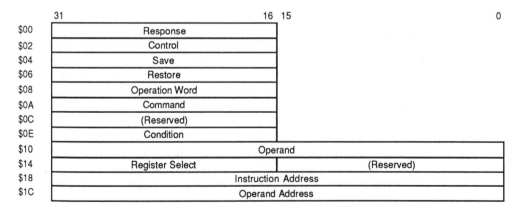

Figure 10.11   MC68881 coprocessor interface register (CIR) map. (Courtesy of Motorola, Inc.)

Operation word CIR (16-bit write-only): not implemented in the MC68881 floating-point coprocessor but defined for possible use in future coprocessor designs.

Command CIR (16-bit write-only): used by the MC680XY CPU to initiate a coprocessor general type instruction. If the MC68881 is busy, the response CIR is set to the null primitive; because the main CPU cannot proceed—that is, cannot fetch another instruction—it is forced into a synchronization wait.

Condition CIR (16-bit write-only): used by the MC680XY CPU to initiate a coprocessor conditional type instruction. Again, if the MC68881 is busy, the response CIR is set to the null primitive.

Operand CIT (32-bit read/write): used to transfer data to/from the CPU from/ to the coprocessor.

Register select CIR (16-bit read-only): used by the MC680XY CPU to transfer the register mask during a move multiple foating-point registers operation.

Instruction address CIR (32-bit write-only): used by the MC680XY CPU to transfer the address of the MC68881 instruction if and when necessary.

Operand address CIR (32-bit read/write): not used by or implemented in the MC68881.

Consider the following program fragment (which accomplishes no logically useful work):

```
       .              .
       .              .
       .              .
ADDA.L        (A1),(A2)              ; line 1
FMOVE.L       (A2),FPRO              ; line 2
FMUL.D        FPRO,FPRO              ; line 3
FMOVE.L       FPRO,(A2)             ; line 4
MOVE.L        (A2),(A1)              ; line 5
       .              .
       .              .
       .              .
```

In this code fragment, the instruction in line 1 is fetched and executed by the MC680XY CPU. The instruction in line 2 is fetched by the MC680XY CPU, then transferred via the CIRs to and executed by the MC68881 FPCP. Note that the memory-to-memory register indirect ADDA instruction of line 1 must be completed and the result available in CPU register A2 before the floating-point instruction in line 2 can be executed, although it could be prefetched in parallel with (at the same time as) the execution of the ADDA instruction. If the source operand in line 2 at the memory location indirect through address register A2 is obtained by the MC680XY CPU and sent to the MC68881 FPCP via the operand CIR before the address was stored in A2 by the MC680XY instruction in line 1, the value sent to the MC68881 FPCP would be incorrect. The *sequential semantics* of the program fragment would be violated. Is this mix-up possible? In this particular MC680XY/MC68881 situation, the answer is *no!* The design reason is that the MC680XY CPU is fetching instructions, performing address calculations, and fetching operands for both processors and, therefore, can easily keep track of and naturally enforce the correct sequence of instruction steps to conform to the sequential semantics implicitly required. On the theory that later releases of the MC680XY CPU may contain more parallelism, which could conceivably allow the instruction in line 2 above to commence before the instruction in line 1 was finished—that is, to violate the sequential semantics—we note two things:

1. The Motorola Corporation has assured its customers that all future enhanced processors will correctly execute "correct" programs of presently delivered processors.
2. If you, as a programmer, are not completely assured by the Motorola corporate statement, a programmatic means is already available to avoid possible synchronization troubles of this kind. We suggest:

```
        .              .
        .              .
        .              .
ADDA.L      (A1),(A2)              ; line 1
NOP                                ; line 1a = synchronization
FMOVE.L     (A2),FPRO             ; line 2
        .              .
        .              .
        .              .
```

The action of the MC680XY CPU NOP instruction is to prevent all instruction overlap (parallelism) by forcing a CPU wait until all pending bus cycles are completed.

Now let us consider lines 4 and 5 of the earlier program fragment. Recall that the MC680XY CPU will fetch the FMOVE.L instruction of line 4, send it to the MC68881 via CIRs, and then commence fetching the MOVE.L instruction of line 5. Sometime during this period, the coprocessor will deliver the converted contents of FPRO via a CIR to the CPU for storage in memory at A2. Will this storage be completed before the CPU instruction in line 5 accesses the value in memory at location A2? Probably not! Why? Because the data type conversion of the coprocessor is relatively time-consuming. Thus, there is a nonzero probability that the instruction in line 5 will use an incorrect source datum, and this *must* be prevented (a program must give the same results with the same inputs each and every time). That is, a computational system must be deterministic, and the main reason for sequential semantics is to assure this deterministic characteristic.

To solve this synchronization problem, the Motorola designers have chosen to require programmer intervention. Recall that the MC680XY CPU fetches all instructions and sends those for the MC68881 FPCP to it via the CIRs. If the FPCP is busy, then the CPU is informed of such via the response CIR, and the CPU simply waits—without fetching the next instruction. Note that this wait happens with two consecutive FPCP instructions and that it does not happen for an MC680XY instruction following an MC68881 instruction. The synchronization solution, therefore, is to insert a "wait for the MC68881 to finish" instruction into the program. We suggest:

```
        .                    .
        .                    .
        .                    .
FMOVE.L         FPRO,(A2)            ; line 4
FNOP                                 ; line 4a = synchronization
MOVE.L          (A2),(A1)            ; line 5
        .                    .
        .                    .
        .                    .
```

We rewrite the entire code fragment to emphasize the synchronization aspects, although I have yet to find a specific situation where line 1a is necessary. On the other hand, line 4a is most definitely necessary.

```
        .                    .
        .                    .
        .                    .
ADDA.L          (A1),(A2)            ; line 1
NOP                                  ; line 1a = synchronization (necessity ?)
FMOVE.L         (A2),FPRO            ; line 2
FMUL.D          FPRO,FPRO            ; line 3
FMOVE.L         FPRO,(A2)            ; line 4
FNOP                                 ; line 4a = synchronization
MOVE.L          (A2),(A1)            ; line 5
        .                    .
        .                    .
        .                    .
```

When the MC680XY CPU fetches a FNOP instruction, one of two actions will result:

1. If the MC68881 FPCP is busy executing an instruction, the MC680XY CPU will wait and do nothing until the MC68881 FPCP is finished.
2. If the MC68881 FPCP is not busy, the MC680XY treats the FNOP instruction as a NOP.

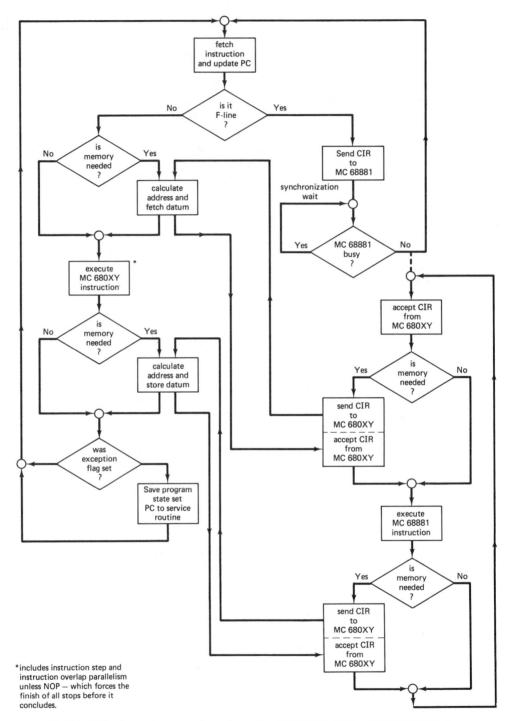

*includes instruction step and
instruction overlap parallelism
unless NOP — which forces the
finish of all stops before it
concludes.

Figure 10.12 Instruction execution scheme for MC680XY CPU and MC68881 floating-point coprocessor. The MC680XY performs all instruction fetches, calculates all memory addresses, performs all memory accesses, and thus is the command processor.

Thus, the FNOP instruction is the programmatic mechanism whereby the programmer can force coprocessor synchronization and assure that the MC680XY and MC68881 do not get out of phase. The instruction execution scheme shown in Figure 10.12 for the coprocessor situation should be helpful in fully understanding this limited but effective implementation of the more general semaphore control of the co-routine synchronization problem. It must be noted that no mechanism, beyond programmer care, exists to prevent the MC680XY from inadvertently overwriting MC68881 data, or vice versa.

MC68881 INSTRUCTIONS

The generalized instruction format for the MC68881 floating-point coprocessor is given in Figure 10.13. If a datum in a MC680XY CPU register or memory is involved, the right-most six bits (bite 5 through 0) of the operation word gives the address mode and register designation information necessary for the MC680XY CPU

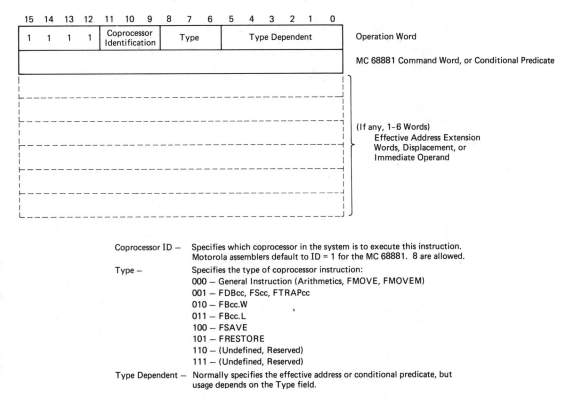

```
15  14  13  12  11  10  9   8   7   6   5   4   3   2   1   0
+---+---+---+---+-----------+-----------+-------------------+
| 1 | 1 | 1 | 1 |Coprocessor|   Type    |  Type Dependent   |   Operation Word
|   |   |   |   |Identification|        |                   |
+---+---+---+---+-----------+-----------+-------------------+
|                                                           |   MC 68881 Command Word, or Conditional Predicate
+-----------------------------------------------------------+
```

(If any, 1–6 Words)
Effective Address Extension
Words, Displacement, or
Immediate Operand

Coprocessor ID —   Specifies which coprocessor in the system is to execute this instruction.
                   Motorola assemblers default to ID = 1 for the MC 68881. 8 are allowed.

Type —   Specifies the type of coprocessor instruction:
                   000 — General Instruction (Arithmetics, FMOVE, FMOVEM)
                   001 — FDBcc, FScc, FTRAPcc
                   010 — FBcc.W
                   011 — FBcc.L
                   100 — FSAVE
                   101 — FRESTORE
                   110 — (Undefined, Reserved)
                   111 — (Undefined, Reserved)

Type Dependent —   Normally specifies the effective address or conditional predicate, but
                   usage depends on the Type field.

Figure 10.13   The generalized MC68881 instruction format, known as an F-line operation because of the 4 ON bits in positions 12–15 [1111b = Fh]. Although up to eight coprocessors are allowed, of the same or different design, the text discusses only the situation where one exists.

to calculate the effective address. A summary of the effective address modes is given in Table 10.5. Note from Figure 10.8 that six types of instructions are implemented in the MC68881 Floating-Point Coprocessor.

General Type (Type = 000) Coprocessor Instructions

This large group of instructions is divided into six subgroups (opclasses). A summary can be gleaned from Figure 10.14.

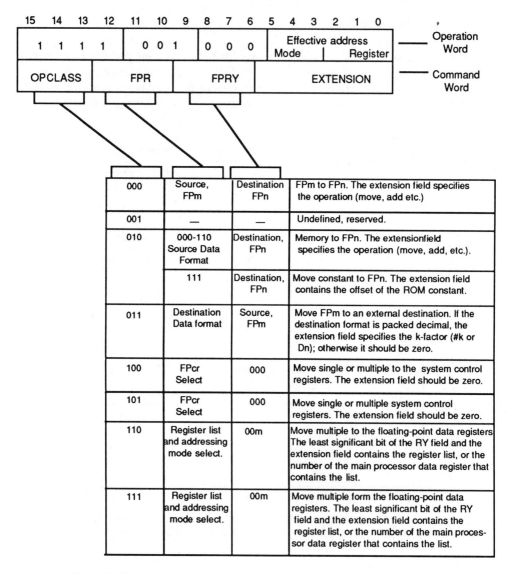

Figure 10.14   General type coprocessor instruction format. (Courtesy of Motorola, Inc.)

Register-to-register instructions (opclass = 000). This class of instructions within the general instruction type includes:

FPRm $\xrightarrow{\text{move}}$ FPRn

FPRm <operation> FPRn $\xrightarrow{\text{store}}$ FPRn

FPRm <operation> $\xrightarrow{\text{store}}$ FPRm

The 38 instructions include:

Instruction	Extension Field	Instruction	Extension Field
FMOVE to FPn	$00	FABS	$18
FINT	$01	FCOSH	$19
FSINH	$02	FNEG	$1A
FINTRZ	$03	FACOS	$1C
FSQRT	$04	FCOS	$1D
FLOGNP1	$06	FGETEXP	$1E
FETOXM1	$08	FGETMAN	$1F
FTANH	$09	FDIV	$20
FATAN	$0A	FMOD	$21
FASIN	$0C	FADD	$22
FATANH	$0D	FMUL	$23
FSIN	$0E	FSGLDIV	$24
FTAN	$0F	FREM	$25
FETOX	$10	FSCALE	$26
FTWOTOX	$11	FSGLMUL	$27
FTENTOX	$12	FSUB	$28
FLOGN	$14	FSINCOS	$30-$37
FLOG10	$15	FCMP	$38
FLOG2	$16	FTST	$3A

CPU-to-register and constant-to-register instructions (opclass = 010).
This class of instructions within the general instruction type includes:

CPURm <operation> FPRn $\xrightarrow{\text{store}}$ FPRn

Memory <operation> FPRn $\xrightarrow{\text{store}}$ FPRn

CPURm <operation> $\xrightarrow{\text{store}}$ FPRn

Memory <operation> $\xrightarrow{\text{store}}$ FPRn

FPCP$_{\text{ROM}}$ $\xrightarrow{\text{move}}$ FPRn

The 38 instructions are those given for opclass 000. The source field of the command word (FPRn = bits 10–12 in Figure 10.14) is coded to indicate the format of the MC680XY CPU datum or the MC68881 FPCP ROM. In the former case, only data effective addressing modes are allowed, and in the case of data requiring more than 32 bits for storage, they must be in memory (data types 010, 011, 101 below).

In the last case (111), the extension field contains the FPCP ROM offset address of the desired floating-point constant. (The available constants and their ROM offset addresses are given in Figure 10.6.)

Source Format Encoding	CPU Operand Data Format	Length (in Bytes)
000	Long-word integer	4
001	Single precision real	4
010	Extended precision real	12
011	Packed decimal real	12
100	Word integer	2
101	Double precision real	8
110	Byte integer	1
111	ROM constant	—

Move register-to-CPU instructions (opclass = 011). This class of instructions within the general instruction type includes:

FPRn $\xrightarrow[\text{round}]{\text{convert}}$ CPURm

FPRn $\xrightarrow[\text{round}]{\text{convert}}$ Memory

The single instruction FMOVE.X constitutes this group in which the source FPRn is coded into bits 7–9 of the command word and the destination data type (X) is coded into bits 10–12 of the command word, using the encoding given above for CPU to FPR, with the exception that encoding 111 signifies packed decimal real with a dynamic k-factor and requires 12 bytes of memory for storage. The last encoding (111) allows the MC68881 to convert a floating-point number to a packed BCD string of digits with k digits to the right of the implied decimal point specified as the variable contents of a MC680XY data register named in parentheses following the effective address (this register number is encoded into the extension field of the binary machine code instruction):

FMOVE.P   FP1,(A1)(D3)

The opclass encoding of 011 is used for a packed decimal real number with k digits to the right of the implied decimal point specified as a constant in the parentheses following the effective address (this k-factor is encoded into the extension field):

FMOVE.P   FP1,(A1)(#−5)

In both cases, the *k*-factor has the following meaning:

> −64 to 0: # significant digits to right of decimal point (FORTRAN "F" format)
>
> +1 to +17: # significant digits in mantissa (FORTRAN "E" format)

Move system control register to/from CPU instructions (opclass = 101/100). This class of instructions within the general instruction type includes:

$$\left.\begin{array}{ccc} \text{FPControlR} & \xrightarrow{\text{store}} & \text{CPURm} \\ \text{FPControlR} & \xrightarrow{\text{store}} & \text{Memory} \end{array}\right\} \quad \text{Opclass 101}$$

$$\left.\begin{array}{ccc} \text{CPURm} & \xrightarrow{\text{load}} & \text{FPControlR} \\ \text{Memory} & \xrightarrow{\text{load}} & \text{FPControlR} \end{array}\right\} \quad \text{Opclass 100}$$

where the control registers are specified in bits 10–12 of the command field as follows: bit 10, FPIAR (instruction address register); bit 11, FPSR (status register); bit 12, FPCR (control register). The order of movement is always first FPCR, then FPSR, and finally FPIAR. The FMOVE.L instruction involves a single control register; the FMOVEM.L instruction involves up to three control registers and can only involve system memory (not a MC680XY register). The syntax is:

```
FMOVE.L        FPIAR,(A3)
FMOVEM.L       FPIAR/FPSR/FPCR,(A3)
```

Move multiple data registers to/from memory instructions (opclass = 111/110). This class of instructions within the general instruction type includes:

$$\begin{array}{lcl} \text{FPRm/ . . . /FPRn} & \longrightarrow & -(\text{CPUAddressRi})\} \text{ Opclass 111} \\ (\text{CPUAddressRi})+ & \longrightarrow & \text{FPRn/ . . . /FPRm}\} \text{ Opclass 110} \end{array}$$

where the register list is mask encoded in bits 0 through 7 of the command word (bit 11 of command word = 0) or where the register is mask encoded in bits 0 through 7 of the MC680XY data register (bit 11 of command word = 1 and bits 4 through 6 = MC680XY data register). Bit 12 of the command field specifies the order of register movement (1 means FP0, FP1, . . . , FP7; 0 means FP7, FP6, . . . , FP0).

Conditional Type (Type = 001, 010, 011)
Coprocessor Instructions

This group of instruction types exactly corresponds to the equivalent program flow-of-control instructions of the MC680XY CPU. The conditions that are checked are given in Figure 10.8, and the instruction formats are shown in Figure 10.15. The action of three of the four instructions are:

```
IF <condition>
      THEN perform action — FBcc  – branch to label
                             FTRAPcc – save PC, branch to label with immediate
                                datum available
                             FScc – set byte = FFhex and continue

      ELSE perform action — FBcc and FTRAPcc – continue
                             FScc – set byte = 00hex and continue
```

The action for the floating decrement and branch on condition instruction is:

```
IF <condition>
      THEN continue
      ELSE decrement MC680XY CPU data register
            IF <CPUDR  ≠ −1>
                  THEN branch to label
                  ELSE continue
```

Save/Restore Context Type (Type = 100/101) Coprocessor Instructions

These two instructions have inverse actions, and because of the speed of execution desired by the Motorola designers, each is assigned a complete type and occupies only one word of storage. They are designed to allow a multiprogramming operating system to suspend execution temporarily in such a way as to be able to resume correctly later. In the meantime, another (or several other) program(s) will be taking its (their) turn in using a time slice. Therefore, the saving-for-later restoration of the entire processor state of the MC680XY and the MC68881 in the programs private memory is necessary. In an effort to minimize state saving storage space and also to minimize state frame information transfer time to/from memory, the MC68881 has three state frame formats available. Note that the FSAVE instruction must use a control alterable mode or the address register indirect with predecrement memory addressing mode. Similarly, the FRESTORE instruction must use a control alterable mode or the address register indirect with postincrement memory addressing mode. The algorithm involved in choosing which state frame format to use approximates:

```
IF MC68881 save CIR ≠ ready
      THEN signal MC680XY to try again
      ELSE IF MC68881 has not been used since RESET
                  THEN use NULL state frame (FRESTORE caused RESET)
                  ELSE IF MC68881 not busy
```

Floating Branch on Condition   (Word, Long)
FBcc.x   label

15	14	13	12	11	10	9	8	7	6	5	4	3	2	1	0
1	1	1	1	Coprocessor ID			0	1	Size	Conditional Predicate					
16-bit Displacement, or Most Significant Word of 32-bit Displacement															
Least Significant Word of 32-bit Displacement (if needed)															

Size Field — Specifies the size of the twos complement displacement:
Size = 0 — Displacement is 16-bits and will be sign extended.
Size = 1 — Displacement is 32-bits.

Floating Trap on Condition   (Word, Long)
FTRAPcc.x   Immediate

15	14	13	12	11	10	9	8	7	6	5	4	3	2	1	0
1	1	1	1	Coprocessor ID			0	0	1	1	1	1	Mode		
0	0	0	0	0	0	0	0	0	0	Conditional Predicate					
16-bit Operand or Most Significant Word of 32-bit Operand (if needed)															
Least Significant Word of 32-bit Operand (if needed)															

Mode Field — Secifies the form of the instruction:
010 — The instruction is followed by a 16-bit operand.
011 — The instruction is followed by a 32-bit operand.
100 — The instruction has no operand following it.

Floating Decrement and Branch on Condition
FDBcc   CPUDR, label

15	14	13	12	11	10	9	8	7	6	5	4	3	2	1	0
1	1	1	1	Coprocessor ID			0	0	1	0	0	1	Count Register		
0	0	0	0	0	0	0	0	0	0	Conditional Predicate					
16-bit Displacement															

Count Register Field — Specifies the main processor data register to be decremented.

Floating Set Byte on Condition   (Byte)
FScc.B   ⟨ea⟩

15	14	13	12	11	10	9	8	7	6	5	4	3	2	1	0
1	1	1	1	Coprocessor ID			0	0	1	Effective Address Mode Register					
0	0	0	0	0	0	0	0	0	0	Conditional Predicate					

Figure 10.15 The floating-point program flow-of-control instruction formats. (The conditions are given in Figure 10.8.)

Floating-Save Program Context of MC6881 (privileged)
FSAVE ⟨ea⟩

15	14	13	12	11	10	9	8	7	6	5	4	3	2	1	0
1	1	1	1	Coprocessor ID			1	0	0	Effective Address Mode			Register		

Floating Restore Program Context of MC6881 (privileged)
FRESTORE ⟨ea⟩

15	14	13	12	11	10	9	8	7	6	5	4	3	2	1	0
1	1	1	1	Coprocessor ID			1	0	1	Effective Address Mode			Register		

MC68881 State Frame Formats

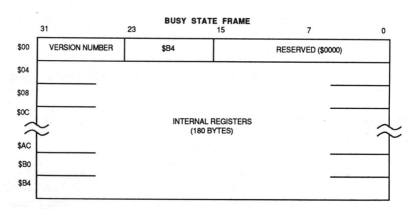
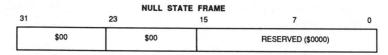
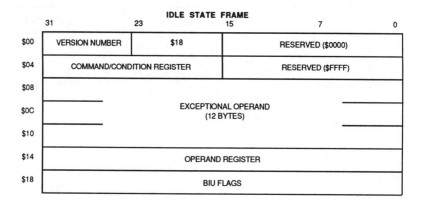

Figure 10.16 The instructions FSAVE and FRESTORE are privileged and result in the correct state frame being stored in or loaded from system memory. (Courtesy of Motorola, Inc.)

THEN use idle state frame
ELSE IF   time to save all information greater
                 than time to complete current instruction
            THEN complete current instruction
                       and use idle state frame
            ELSE use busy state frame

The FSAVE instruction causes immediate entry into the above algorithm. The co-processor context is saved in system memory. Note that this instruction does not save the eight 96-bit floating-point data registers or the three 32-bit control registers. If the idle or busy state frame occurs, the operating system should then employ the FMOVEM.X and FMOVEM.L instructions to move the necessary members of these 11 registers to system memory. Similarly, the FRESTORE instruction immediately suspends any action of the MC68881 and proceeds to load (restore the previous) co-processor internal state frame from system memory. Again, the operating system will also have to restore the MC68881 FPCP data and control registers. The instruction formats and state frame formats are shown in Figure 10.16.

EXCEPTIONS AND INTERRUPTS

As in all processors, exception detection allows the MC68881 to report programming and/or data errors via an interrupt so as to allow specialized and responsive correction actions or to allow default corrective actions with subsequent resumption of execution. In addition, the detection of exceptions can be employed to implement software extensions to the MC68881 processor system.

As noted earlier and shown in Figure 10.15, each type of MC68881 exception has a flag and a flag mask. The occurrence of an exception causes the appropriate associated flag to be set, following which the subsequent action depends on the flag mask.

Bits 8 through 15 of the floating-point status register (FPSR) contain a bit for each of the eight floating-point exceptions that may have occurred during execution of the previous instruction. (This bit is cleared at the start of each MC68881 operation except FMOVE control register, FMOVEM, and very few others that cannot generate exceptions.) If the corresponding bit of the control register (FPCR) is set ON and an operation results in an exception (thus setting the bit in the FPSR), a branch will be taken to the appropriate exception service routine. The FPSR and FPCR are shown in Figure 10.5. The pertinent information is summarized in Figure 10.17.

MC68881-detected exceptions fall into two classes: those related to communications with the MC680XY CPU (F-line traps and protocol violations) and those related to the execution of floating-point instructions (such as divide by zero and the FTRAPcc instruction). For the purpose of reporting and servicing exceptions, the MC68881 coprocessor is logically considered a portion of the main MC680XY

Bit Position FPCR & FPSR	Flag ID.	Vector Number (Decimal)	Vector Offset (Hexadecimal)	Assignment
—	—	7	$01C	FTRAPcc Instruction
—	—	11	$02C	F-Line Emulator
—	—	13	$034	Coprocessor Protocol Violation
15	BSUN	48	$0C0	Branch or Set on Unordered Condition
8 & 9	INEX182	49	$0C4	Inexact Result
10	DZ	50	$0C8	Floating-Point Divide by Zero
11	UNFL	51	$0CC	Underflow
13	OPERR	52	$0D0	Operand Error
12	OVFL	53	$0D4	Overflow
14	SNAN	54	$0D8	Signaling NAN

Figure 10.17   Floating-point exception vector numbers. (Courtesy of Motorola, Inc.)

CPU. All exception processing is uniformly treated for the system as a whole by the MC680XY CPU. Thus, MC68881 exception processing of a floating-point exception involves the following seven steps:

1. Detect an exception. The corresponding bits in both the FPSR (reporting the exception) and the FPCR (allowing the detection) are both ON.
2. Determine the exception vector number and report the exception to the MC680XY.
3. If the MC680XY is in user state, change the state to supervisor.
4. Save the context of the presently executing program of the MC680XY in system memory.
5. Load the exception processing context into the MC680XY from the memory address contained in the exception vector table.
6. Execute the exception handler routine. This may or may not involve saving the present context of the MC68881 in system memory for later restoration.
7. At the conclusion of exception processing, restore the old program context from system memory and continue execution. In some cases, the exception handler may determine that the exception is fatal to further program execution and may terminate the program instead of restoring the old context.

The basic protocol followed in response to an MC68881-detected exception is as follows:

1. The MC68881 encodes the appropriate take-exception primitive (pre- or mid-instruction), along with the vector number, in the response CIR.
2. The MC68020 reads the response CIR (usually in an attempt to initiate the next instruction) and receives the take-exception request.

3. The MC68020 acknowledges the request by writing an exception acknowledge to the control CIR. The appropriate stack frame is then stored in memory, and control is transferred to the exception handler routine.

4. In response to the exception acknowledge, the MC68881 clears all pending exceptions and enters the idle state.

The main processor coordinates all exception processing. Therefore, when the MC68881 detects an exception, it cannot always force exception processing immediately but must wait until the main processor is ready to start exception processing. The main processor is always prepared to process an exception when it attempts to initiate a new MC68881 instruction. Thus, if an MC68881-detected exception occurs during the calculation phase of an instruction, it is held pending within the MC68881 until the next write to the command or condition coprocessor interface register (CIR). Then, instead of returning the first primitive of the dialog for the new instruction, the MC68881 returns the take preinstruction exception primitive to start exception processing for the previous instruction.

When the exception handler completes execution, a return from exception (RTE) instruction is executed, and the previously interrupted program resumes execution at one of the following points:

1. The beginning of the instruction that was preempted by an exception detected by or reported to the MC68020 (preinstruction exception).
2. The point where the exception occurred during the execution of an instruction (mid-instruction exception).
3. The beginning of the instruction immediately following the instruction that caused or detected the exception (postinstruction exception).

The following subsections describe the exceptions in some detail.

Branch/set on unordered (BSUN).   The BSUN exception may occur only on MC68881 conditional instructions with the IEEE nonaware branch condition predicates. The MC68881 detects a BSUN exception if the conditional predicate is one of the IEEE nonaware branches, and the NAN condition code bit is set. When this exception is detected, the BSUN bit in the FPSR exception status byte is set.

Trap-Disabled Results.   The MC68881 evaluates the condition and reports "true" or "false" to the MC68020 in the response CIR.

Trap-Enabled Results.   The MC68881 reports a preinstruction exception with the BSUN vector number to the MC68020 in lieu of a "true" or "false" report. The BSUN exception is unique in that the trap is taken before the requested conditional predicate is evaluated. Furthermore, the instruction that caused the BSUN exception is re-executed upon return from the BSUN trap handler. Therefore, it is the responsibility of the trap handler to modify the floating-point condition codes so that when the trap handler returns, the conditional instruction does not continue to take the BSUN trap. The trap handler, by modifying the condition codes, determines whether the "true" or "false" report is indicated to the MC68020 when the conditional instruction is re-executed. This allows the trap handler to determine how the unordered condition is to be handled.

Signaling not-a-number (SNAN).   SNANs are used as an escape mechanism for user-defined, non-IEEE data types. The MC68881 never creates a SNAN as a result of an operation; NANs created by operand error exceptions are always nonsignaling NANs. When a SNAN is an operand involved in an arithmetic instruction, the SNAN bit is set in the FPSR exception byte. Since the FMOVEM, FMOVE FPcr, and FSAVE instructions do not modify the status bits, they cannot generate exceptions. Therefore, these instructions are useful for manipulating SNANs.

Trap-Disabled Results.   If the SNAN bit in the NAN is set to 1 and the resulting nonsignaling NAN is transferred to the destination, no bits other than the SNAN bit of the NAN are modified, although the input NAN is truncated if necessary.

Trap-Enabled Results.   For memory or MC680XY data register destinations, the result is written in the same manner as if the traps were disabled; then a mid-instruction exception is signaled. If desired, the trap handler can overwrite the result.

For floating-point data register destinations, instruction execution is terminated and the floating-point data registers are not modified. In this case, the SNAN trap handler should supply the result. To enable the trap handler to return a result, the MC680XY and the MC68881 supply the following:

1. The address of the instruction where the error occurred (in the FPIAR). By examining the instruction, the trap handler may determine the operation being performed, the value of the second operand (for dyadic instructions), and the destination location.
2. The address of the destination, if in memory, in the mid-instruction stack frame (at offset +$10). This allows the trap handler to overwrite the NAN, if necessary, without recalculating the effective address.
3. The FSAVE instruction that places the exceptional operand in a stack frame. The exceptional operand is the source input argument converted to extended precision.

Note that the trap handler should use only the FMOVEM instruction to read or write the floating-point data registers, since FMOVEM can not generate further exceptions. Also, the only way that a SNAN can be written into a floating-point data register is via the FMOVEM instruction.

Operand error (OPERR).   Operand errors encompass problems that arise in a variety of operations; they cover those errors not frequent or important enough to merit a specific exception condition. Basically, an operand error occurs when an operation has no mathematical interpretation for the given operands.

Trap-Disabled Results.   For a memory or MC68020 data register destination, several possible results can be generated, depending on the destination size and error type. If traps are disabled and the destination is a floating-point data register, then an extended precision nonsignaling NAN is stored in the destination floating-point data register.

Trap-Enabled Results.   For memory or MC680XY data register destinations, the destination operand is written as if the trap were disabled; then a take-exception primitive is returned to the MC68020. If the destination is a floating-point data register, the register is not modified by the MC68881. In this case, the trap handler should generate the appropriate results. Note that the trap handler should use only the FMOVEM instruction to read or write to the floating-point data registers, since FMOVEM will not generate further exceptions or change the condition codes.

Overflow (OVFL).   Overflow is the condition that exists when an arithmetic operation creates a floating-point intermediate result that is too large to be represented in a floating-point data register or, in a store to memory, when the contents of the source floating-point data register are too large to be represented in the destination format. Overflow is detected for a given data format and operation when the result exponent is greater than or equal to the maximum exponent value of the format. Overflow can only occur when the destination is in the S, D, or X formats. Overflows when converting to the B, W, or L integer and packed decimal formats are included as operand errors. At the end of any operation that could potentially overflow, and before the result is stored to the destination, the intermediate result is checked for underflow, then rounded, and then checked for overflow. If overflow occurs, the OVFL bit is set in the FPSR exception byte. An overflow can occur when the destination is a floating-point data register even if the intermediate result is small enough to be represented as an extended precision number. This can happen when the selected rounding precision is single or double, the intermediate result is rounded to that precision (both the mantissa and the exponent), and then the rounded result is stored in extended precision format. If the magnitude of the intermediate result exceeds the range of the selected rounding precision format, an overflow will occur.

Trap-Disabled Results.   The following values are stored at the destination, based on the current rounding mode:

Rounding Mode	Result
RN	Infinity, with the sign of the intermediate result
RZ	Largest magnitude number, with the sign of the intermediate result
RM	For positive overflow, largest positive number
	For negative overflow, minus infinity
RP	For positive overflow, plus infinity
	For negative overflow, largest negative number

Trap-Enabled Results. The result stored in the destination is the same as the result stored when the trap is disabled, and a take-exception primitive is returned to the MC68020. If the destination is memory or an MC68020 data register, the operand is stored; then a take mid-instruction exception primitive is issued. If the destination is a floating-point data register, a take pre-instruction exception primitive is returned when the MC68020 attempts to initiate the next MC68881 instruction.

The address of the instruction that causes the overflow is available to the trap handler in the FPIAR. By examining the instruction, the exception type and operand location(s) may be determined. Additional information is available to the trap handler by executing the FSAVE instruction. Note that the trap handler should use only the FMOVEM instructions to read or write to the floating-point data registers, since FMOVEM will not generate further exceptions or change the condition codes.

Underflow (UNFL). Underflow is the condition that occurs when an arithmetic operation creates an intermediate result that is too small to be represented in a floating-point data register using the selected rounding precision or, in a store to memory, when the contents of the source floating-point data register are too small to be represented in the destination format as a normalized result. Underflow is detected for a given data format and operation when the intermediate result exponent is less than or equal to the minimum exponent value of the destination format. At the end of any operation that could potentially underflow, the intermediate result is checked for underflow, rounded, and checked for overflow before it is stored to the destination. If an underflow occurs, the UNFL bit is set in the FPSR exception status byte. An underflow can occur when the destination is a floating-point data register, even if the intermediate result is large enough to be represented as an extended precision number. This can happen when the selected rounding precision is single or double, the intermediate result is rounded to that precision (both the mantissa and the exponent), and then the rounded result is stored in extended precision format. If the magnitude of the intermediate result is too small to be represented in the selected rounding precision format, an underflow will occur.

Trap-Disabled Results. The result that is stored in the destination is either a denormalized number or 0. If, in the process of denormalizing the intermediate result, all of the significant bits are shifted off to the right, then the following values are stored at the destination, based on the current rounding mode:

Rounding Mode	Result
RN	Zero, with the sign of the intermediate result
RZ	Zero, with the sign of the intermediate result
RM	For positive underflow, plus zero
	For negative underflow, smallest denormalized negative number
RP	For positive underflow, smallest denormalized positive number
	For negative overflow, minus zero

Trap-Enabled Results. The result stored in the destination is the same as the result stored when traps are disabled, and a take-exception primitive is returned to the MC68020. The address of the instruction that caused the underflow is available to the trap handler in the FPIAR. By examining the instruction, the operation type and operand location(s) may be determined. Additional information is available to the trap handler by executing a FSAVE instruction. Note that the trap handler should use only the FMOVEM instructions to read or write to the floating-point data registers, since FMOVEM can not generate further exceptions or change the condition codes.

Divide by zero (DZ). This exception occurs when a zero divisor occurs in a division or when a transcendental function is asymptotic, with infinity as the asymptote. When a divide by zero is detected, the DZ bit is set in the FPSR exception status byte.

Trap Disabled Results. Store the following results in the destination floating-point data register: (1) for the FDIV and FSGLDIV instructions, return an infinity with the sign set to the exclusive OR of the signs of the input operands; (2) for the FTAN instruction, return infinity with the sign of the source operand; (3) for the FLOGx instructions, return minus infinity.

Trap-Enabled Results. The destination floating-point data register is not modified, and a take preinstruction exception primitive is returned when the MC680XY attempts to initiate the next MC68881 instruction. The trap handler must generate a result to store in the destination. To assist the trap handler in this function, the MC68881 supplies the following:

1. The address of the instruction where the divide by zero occurred (in the FPIAR). By examining this instruction, the trap handler can determine the op-

eration being performed, the value of the source operand (for dyadic instructions), and the destination floating-point register number.

2. The FSAVE instruction that places the exceptional operand in a stack frame. The exceptional operand is the source input argument converted to extended precision.

Note that the trap handler should use only the FMOVEM instruction to read or write the floating-point registers, since FMOVEM can not generate further exceptions or change the condition codes.

Inexact result (INEX2).   In a general sense, inexact result 2 (INEX2) is the condition that exists when any operation, except the input of a packed decimal number, creates a floating-point intermediate result whose infinitely precise mantissa has too many significant bits to be represented exactly in the current rounding precision or in the destination precision. If this condition occurs, the INEX2 bit is set in the status register EXC byte and the infinitely precise result is rounded as described below. The MC68881 provides two inexact bits (INEX1 and INEX2) to help distinguish between inexact results generated by decimal input (INEX1) and other inexacts (INEX2). This is useful in such instructions as

FADD.P #6.023E+24,FP3

where both types of inexacts can occur. In this case, the conversion of the immediate source operand from packed decimal to extended precision causes an inexact error to occur, which is signaled as INEX1. Furthermore, the subsequent add might also produce an inexact result and may cause INEX2 to be set. Note that only one inexact exception vector number is generated by the MC68881. If either of the two inexact exceptions is enabled, the inexact exception vector is fetched by the MC680XY and the exception handler routine is initiated.

Trap-Disabled Results.   The rounded result is delivered to the destination.

Trap-Enabled Results.   The rounded result is delivered to the destination, and an exception is reported to the MC68020. The address of the instruction that generated the inexact result is available to the trap handler in the FPIAR. By examining the instruction, the location of the operand(s) may be determined. In the case of a memory destination, the evaluated effective address of the operand is available in the MC68020 mid-instruction stack frame. Unlike the other exceptions, when an FSAVE is executed by an inexact trap handler, the value of the exceptional operand in the stack frame is not defined. If an inexact condition is the only exception that occurred during the execution of an instruction, the value of the exceptional operand is invalid. If multiple exceptions occur during an instruction, the operand value that caused the exception is related to the other, higher-priority exceptions. Note that the trap handler should use only the FMOVEM instruction to read or write the floating-point data registers, since FMOVEM can not generate further exceptions or change the condition codes.

Inexact result on decimal input (INEX1).   In a general sense, inexact result 1 (INEX1) is the condition that exists when a packed decimal operand cannot be converted exactly to extended precision in the current rounding mode. If this condition occurs, the INEX1 bit is set in the FPSR exception status byte, and the infinitely precise result is rounded as previously described. As noted earlier, the MC68881 provides two inexact bits (INEX1 and INEX2) to help distinguish between inexact results generated by decimal input (INEX1) and other inexact results (INEX2).

Trap-Disabled Results.   If the instruction is an FMOVE to a floating-point data register, the rounded result is stored in the floating-point data register. If the instruction is not an FMOVE, the rounded result is used in the calculation.

Trap-Enabled Results.   The result is generated in the same manner as if traps were disabled, except that a take preinstruction exception primitive is returned to the MC68020 when it attempts to initiate the next MC68881 instruction. The address and other information needed by the trap handler follow the rules given above for INEX2.

Multiple exceptions.   Dual and triple instruction exceptions may be generated by a single instruction in a few cases. When multiple exceptions occur with traps enabled for more than one exception class, only the highest-priority exception trap is taken; the other enabled exceptions cannot cause a trap. The higher-priority trap handler must check for multiple exceptions. The priorities of the traps are as follows:

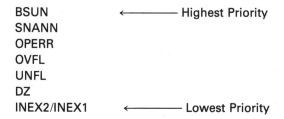

```
BSUN              ←———————— Highest Priority
SNANN
OPERR
OVFL
UNFL
DZ
INEX2/INEX1       ←———————— Lowest Priority
```

The multiple instruction exceptions that can occur are as follows:

```
SNAN and INEX1
OPERR and INEX2
OPERR and INEX1
OVFL and INEX2 and/or INEX1
UNFL and INEX2 and/or INEX1
```

IEEE Exception and Trap Compatibility

The IEEE Standard defines only five exceptions. The MC68881 FPSR AEXC byte contains bits representing these five exceptions, which are defined to function exactly as the IEEE Standard specifies the exceptions. However, it may be more useful to differentiate the IEEE required exceptions into the eight exceptions represented in the FPSR EXC byte. Since the MC68881 uses the bits in the FPSR EXC byte and the FPCR enable byte to determine when to trap, seven possible instruction traps are defined (INEX1 and INEX2 share a trap vector) instead of the five defined by the IEEE Standard. If it is necessary to write an application program that supports only the five IEEE-specified traps, the BSUN, SNAN, and OPERR trap vectors should be set to point to the same trap handler. This allows the MC68881 to support the invalid operation exception defined in the IEEE Standard, which is represented by the valid operation (IOP) bit in the AEXC byte.

Illegal Command Words

Illegal coprocessor commands are coprocessor command work bit patterns that are not implemented by the MC68881. The MC68881 reports illegal coprocessor commands as preinstruction exceptions, using the F-line emulator vector number.

Detected Protocol Violation

All interprocessor communications in the coprocessor interface occur as standard MC680XY bus cycles. A failure in this communication results in the MC68881 reporting a mid-instruction exception with the coprocessor protocol violation vector number. Once a protocol violation has been detected by the MC68881, the response CIR is encoded to the take preinstruction exception primitive so that the next read of the response CIR by the main processor will terminate the dialog. The MC68881 signals a protocol violation when unexpected accesses of the command, condition, register select, or operand CIRs occur. A protocol violation is the highest-priority MC68881-detected exception. It is also considered to be a fatal exception, since the MC680XY acknowledgement of the protocol violation exception clears any pending MC68881 instruction exceptions or illegal instructions.

Recovery from Exceptions

When an MC68881-detected exception occurs, enough information is made available to the trap handler to perform the necessary corrective action and then resume execution of the program that caused the exception. Of course, in some instances it may not be valid to resume execution of the program; and for protocol violations, recovery is not possible. If an exception handler is required to execute any MC68881 instruction other than a FMOVEM, a FSAVE should be the first MC68881 instruction to be executed. This assures that an exception handler cannot generate any exceptions related to, or modify the context of, the program that caused the exception. It should also be noted that the FPIAR value must be saved before any instruction other than the FMOVEM is executed, so that the address of the instruction that caused the exception is not lost. When the exception handler completes the error recover and is prepared to return to the suspended program, a FRESTORE instruction is executed as the last MC68881 instruction; this restores the previous context of the program that caused the exception.

Trace Exceptions

To aid in program development, the MC680XY includes a facility to allow instruction-by-instruction tracing. In the single-step trace mode, after each instruction is executed, the MC68020 takes a postinstruction exception, using the trace vector number. This allows a debug program in the trace exception handler to monitor the execution of a program under test. The first and last MC68881 instructions that should be executed by a trace exception handler are the FSAVE and FRESTORE instructions, respectively. By executing the FSAVE instruction before any other floating-point instruction, any pending exceptions are saved in a state frame and then cleared internally; thus, an exception generated by the main program cannot be reported while the trace exception handler is executing. After the FSAVE instruction is executed, the FMOVEM instruction can be used to save the user-visible portion of the MC68881 context; then the trace handler is free to utilize the coprocessor as desired, without affecting the main program context. When the trace handler is ready to return to the main program, the FMOVEM instruction is used to restore the user-visible context, followed by a FRESTORE instruction to reinstate the exact context of the MC68881 prior to the trace exception processing. Note that because the MC68020 is forced to wait until the completion of an MC68881 instruction before processing a pending trace exception, the execution of the FSAVE instruction by the trace handler will always result in an idle state frame being saved, and the user-visible registers will reflect the results of the last floating-point instruction. This is not the case if the trace exception handler is allowed to begin execution before the MC68881 instruction is completed. Processors other than the MC68020 must implement the trace synchronization mechanism in software (by polling the PF bit) to assure these conditions.

CONTEXT SWITCHING

In most types of multitasking systems, it is often necessary to take control from one program and give control to another program. This requires that the operating system extract (from the MC68881) data corresponding to one program context and load the context corresponding to the next program to be executed. The information that must be exchanged is divided into two categories:

1. Programmer's model: consists of data accessible by the programmer, using nonprivileged instructions. These data are saved and restored using the FMOVEM instructions.

2. Internal state: consists of various internal flags and registers that the application program need not be concerned with but that are vital in restoring the MC68881 to the proper state. These internal flags and registers are accessed by the privileged FSAVE and FRESTORE instructions.

The basic mechanism for performing a context switch on the MC68881 is provided through the FSAVE amd FRESTORE instructions. These instructions provide a logical extension to the instruction continuation mechanism that is used by the MC68010 and MC68020 processors to support virtual memory. Depending on the state of the MC68881 when an FSAVE instruction is executed, the format of the internal state information written to memory may be in one of three forms. The three state frame formats that are generated by the MC68881 are shown in Figure 10.15.

To perform a complete context save or restore operation, three MC68881 instructions are required:

```
SAVE OLD CONTEXT:
          FSAVE       -(An)                    ; SAVE MC68881 STATE FRAME
          TST.B       (An)                     ; CHECK FOR NULL FRAME
          BEQ         NULL_SV                  ; SKIP PROGRAMMER'S MODEL SAVE IF NULL
          FMOVEM      FP0-FP7,-(An)            ; ELSE, SAVE DATA REGISTERS
          FMOVEM      FPCR/FPSR/FPIAR,-(An)   ; AND SAVE CONTROL REGISTERS
          ST          -(An)                    ; PLACE NOT-NULL FLAG ON STACK
NULL_SV   ...

RESTORE NEXT CONTEXT:
          TST.B       (An)                     ; CHECK FOR NULL FRAME OR NOT-NULL FLA
          BEQ         NULL_RST                 ; SKIP PROGRAMMER'S MODEL RESTORE IF N
          ADDQ.L      #2,An                    ; ELSE, THROW AWAY THE NOT-NULL FLAG
          FMOVEM      (An)+,FPCR/FPSR/FPIAR   ; RESTORE THE CONTROL REGISTERS
          FMOVEM      (An)+,FP0-FP7           ; RESTORE THE DATA REGISTERS
NULL_RST  FRESTORE    (An)+                    ; RESTORE THE MC68881 STATE FRAME
```

EXERCISES

10.1. Design, implement, test, and document a subprocedure to accept a floating-point number in one of the following MC68881 formats and then to print the value in all three formats:

    (a) MC68881 internal format expressed in base 16.

    (b) Base 10 scientific notation.

    (c) Conventional decimal form.

10.2. Perform a series of tests and report the different results for various floating-point arithmetic operations using a large number of input values under the four different (available) rounding rules.

10.3. Design, implement, test, and document a subprocedure to initialize a floating-point array of specified dimensionality and size to NANs, with the significand of each array element set to the value of the element index.

10.4. Devise an adequate test to assure that you fully understand the need for MC680XY/ MC68881 program synchronization and the adequacy of the FNOP solution given in the text. Report your results and defend the adequacy of your test.

10.5. (Project) Design, implement, test, and document a package of subroutines to perform multiple-precision integer arithmetic with complete accuracy. Include (at least) addition, subtraction, multiplication, and division.

10.6. (Project) Design, implement, test, and document a package of subroutines to perform pure rational arithmetic with the results always in the lowest form allowed for complete accuracy. Include (at least) addition, subtraction, multiplication, division, and cancellation. (*Note:* this is a major project).

10.7. (Project) Design, implement, test, and document a package of subroutines to perform fixed-point arithmetic of a specified range and a specified accuracy. Include (at least) addition, subtraction, multiplication, and division.

10.8. (Project) Design, implement, test, and document a package of subroutines to perform interval arithmetic. Include (at least) addition, subtraction, multiplication, and division. Carry three values through all calculations: high, low, and most likely (round to nearest).

Bibliography

BARRON, D. W. *Assemblers and Loaders,* 2nd ed. New York: Elsevier, 1972.

BECK, L. L. *System Software: An Introduction to Systems Programming.* Reading, MA: Addison-Wesley, 1985.

BOHM, C., and G. JACOPINI. Flow Diagrams, Turing Machines, and Languages with Only Two Formation Rules. *Commun. ACM* 9(5):366–371, 1966.

BRAUN, E., and S. MACDONALD. *Revolution in Miniature.* New York: Cambridge University Press, 1978.

CALINGAERT, P. *Assemblers, Compilers, and Program Translation.* Rockville, Md.: Computer Science Press, 1979.

CICHELLI, R. J. Minimal Perfect Hash Functions Made Simple. *Commun. ACM* 23(1):17–19, 1980.

CLARK, W. A. From Electron Mobility to Logical Structures: A View of Integrated Circuits. *Comput. Surv.* 12(3):325–356, 1980.

COFFMAN, Jr., E. G., and P. J. DENNING. *Operating System Theory.* Englewood Cliffs, N.J.: Prentice-Hall, 1973.

COLWELL, R. P., C. Y. HITCHCOCK III, and E. D. JENSEN. Peering Through the RISC/CISC Fog: An Outline of Research. *Computer Architecture News* 11(1):44–50, 1983.

COOK, C. R., and R. R. OLDEHOEFT. A Letter Oriented Minimal Perfect Hashing Function. *SIGPLAN Notic (ACM)* and 17(9):18–27, 1982.

COONEN, J. T. Underflow and Denormalized Numbers. *Computer* 14:75–87, March 1981.

COONEN, J. T., W. KAHAN, J. PALMER, T. PITTMAN, and D. STEVENSON. A Proposal Standard for Binary Floating Point Arithmetic. *SIGNUM Newslett. (ACM),* Special Issue, pp. 4–12, October 1979.

DEITEL, H. M. *An Introduction to Operating Systems*. Reading, Mass.: Addison-Wesley, 1982.

DENNING, P. J. Virtual Memory. *Computer Surv.* 2(3):153–189, 1970. Corrected: *Computer Surveys* 4(1):1–3, 1972.

———. Third Generation Computer Systems. *Computer Surveys* 3(4):175–216, 1971.

DONOVAN, J. J. *Systems Programming*. New York: McGraw-Hill, 1972.

EIN-DOR, P. Grosch's Law Re-revisited: CPU Power and the Cost of Computation. *Commun. ACM* 28(2):142–151, 1985.

EL-ASFOURI, S., O. JOHNSON, and W. K. KING. *Computer Organization and Programming: VAX-11*. Reading, Mass: Addison-Wesley, 1984.

FAIRLEY, R. E. *Software Engineering Concepts*. New York: McGraw-Hill, 1985.

GIBSON, G., and Y. LIU. *Microcomputers for Engineers and Scientists*. Englewood Cliffs, N.J.: Prentice-Hall, 1980.

GILMORE, J. Suggested Enhancements to the Motorola MC68000. Comp. Arch. News (ACM) 8(7):8–14, December 1980.

GORSLINE, G. W. *Modern Microcomputers: The Intel 18086 Family*. Englewood Cliffs, N.J.: Prentice-Hall, 1985.

———. *Computer Organization: Hardware/Software*, 2nd ed. Englewood Cliffs, N.J.: Prentice-Hall, 1986.

GREENFIELD, S. E. *The Architecture of Microcomputers*. Cambridge, Mass: Winthrop, 1980.

HARMON, T. L., and B. LAWSON. *The Motorola MC68000 Microprocessor Family, Assembly Language, Interface Design, and System Design*. Englewood Cliffs, N.J.: Prentice-Hall, 1985.

HARPER, K. *A Terminal Interface, Printer Interface, and Background Printing for an MC68000-Based System Using the MC68681 DUART*. AN899. Austin, Tex.: Motorola Semiconductor Products, Inc., 1984.

KORNERUP, P., and D. M. MATULA. *A Feasibility Analysis of Fixed-Slash Rational Arithmetic*. Tech. Rep. CS7810, Computer Science Department, Southern Methodist University, Dallas, July 1976. (Also presented at the 4th IEEE Symp. Comput. Arith., Santa Monica, Calif., October 1978.)

LEMONE, K. A., and M. E. KALISKI. *Assembly Language Programming for the VAX-11*. Boston: Little, Brown, 1983.

McWHORTER, E. W. The Small Electronic Calculator. *Sci. Am.*, pp. 86–98, May 1976.

MOORE, R. E. *Methods and Applications of Interval Analysis*. SIAM Studies in Applied Mathematics. Philadelphia: SIAM, 1979.

Motorola. *M68000 8-/16-/32-Bit Microprocessors: Programmer's Reference Manual*, 5th ed. Englewood Cliffs, N.J.: Prentice-Hall, 1986.

———. *MC68020 32-Bit Microprocessor User's Manual*, 2nd ed. Englewood Cliffs, N.J.: Prentice-Hall, 1985.

———. *MC68120-MC68121 Intelligent Peripheral Controller*. Austin, Tex.: Motorola Semiconductor Products, Inc., 1981.

———. *MC68450 Technical Summary-Direct Memory Access Controller (DMAC)*. Austin, Tex.: Motorola Semiconductor Products, Inc., 1985.

———. *MC68451 Memory Management Unit*. Austin, Tex.: Motorola Semiconductor Products, Inc., 1983.

———. *MC688851 Floating-Point Coprocessor User's Manual*. Chicago: Motorola, Inc., 1985.

MYERS, G. J. *Advances in Computer Architecture*, 2nd ed. New York: Wiley-Interscience, 1982.

NASH, JO, and M. SPAK, Hardware and Software Tools for the Development of a Microprogrammed Microprocessor. *Proc. 12th Ann. Microprogramming Workshop. ACM SIG-MICRO Newsletter* 10(4):73–83, 1979.

NASSI, I., and B. SCHNEIDERMAN. Flowchart Techniques for Structured Programming. *SIG-PLAN Notic. (ACM)* 8:12–16, August 1973.

ORGANICK, E. I. *Computer System Organization—The B 5700/B 6700 Series*. New York: Academic Press, 1973.

PALMER, J. F. The Intel 8087 Numeric Data Processor. *AFIPS Conf. Proc., 1980*, pp. 983–987. National Computer Conference, Anaheim, Calif., May 1980.

PARNAS, D. On the Criteria to Be Used in Decomposing Systems into Modules. *Commun. ACM* 15(12):1053–1058, 1972.

PETERSON, J., and A. SILBERSCHATZ. *Operating Systems Concepts*. Reading, Mass.: Addison-Wesley, 1983.

REIMS, R. *The MC68010 and Virtual Memory*. Austin, Tex.: Motorola Semiconductor Products, Inc. (undated).

ROSIN, R. F. Contemporary Concepts of Microprogramming and Emulation. *Comput. Surv.* 1 (4):197–212, 1969.

STEVENSON, D. A Proposed Standard for Binary Floating Point Arithmetic: Draft 8.0 IEEE Task P754. *Computer* 14:51–62, March 1981.

STRITTER, J., and N. TREDENNICK. Microprogrammed Implementation of a Single Chip Microprocessor. *Proc. 11th Annual Microprogramming Workshop, ACM SIGMICRO Newsletter* 9(4):8–16, 1978.

THACKER, W. I. Rational as an Alternative to Floating-Point Arithmetic. Unpublished M.S. thesis, Virginia Polytechnic Institute and State University, May 1978. (Also reported in the 17th Annu. Natl. Bur. Standards Symp., *Tools for Improving Computing in the 80's,* June 1978, p. 242.)

TOBIAS, J. R. LSI/VLSI Building Blocks. *Computer* 14(8):83–101, 1981.

TRIEBEL, W. A, and A. SINGH. *The 68000 Microcomputer: Architecture, Software, and Interfacing Techniques*. Englewood Cliffs, N.J.: Prentice-Hall, 1986.

Appendix:
The Instruction Set
of the MC680XY
Processor Family

The MC680XY family includes the following:

MC68008

MC68000

MC68010

MC68012

MC68020

MC68881

The following definitions are used for the operation description in the details of the instruction set.

OPERANDS:

An	— address register
Dn	— data register
Rn	— any data or address register
PC	— program counter
SR	— status register
CCR	— condition codes (lower order byte of status register)
SSP	— supervisor stack pointer
USP	— user stack pointer
SP	— active stack pointer (equivalent to A7)
X	— extend operand (from condition codes)
Z	— zero condition code
V	— overflow condition code
Immediate Data	— immediate data from the instruction
d	— address displacement
Source	— source contents
Destination	— destination contents
Vector	— location of exception vector
ea	— any valid effective address

SUBFIELDS AND QUALIFIERS:

<bit>OF<operand>	selects a single bit of the operand
<ea>{offset:width}	selects a bit field
(<operand>)	the contents of the referenced location
<operand>$_{10}$	the operand is binary coded decimal; operations are to be performed in decimal.
(<address register>)	the register indirect operator which indicates that the
−(<address register>)	operand register points to the memory location of the instruc-
(<address register>)+	tion operand. The optional mode qualifiers are −, +, (d) and (d, ix).
#xxx or #<data>	immediate data located with the instruction is the operand.

MC68000/08/10/12 Effective Addressing Mode Categories

Address Modes	Mode	Register	Data	Memory	Control	Alterable	Assembler Syntax
Data Register Direct	000	reg. no.	X	–	–	X	Dn
Address Register Direct	001	reg. no.	–	–	–	X	An
Address Register Indirect	010	reg. no.	X	X	X	X	(An)
Address Register Indirect with Postincrement	011	reg. no.	X	X	–	X	(An) +
Address Register Indirect with Predecrement	100	reg. no.	X	X	–	X	– (An)
Address Register Indirect with Displacement	101	reg. no	X	X	X	X	(d_{16},An) or $d_{16}(An)$
Address Register Indirect with Index	110	reg. no.	X	X	X	X	(d_8,An,Xn) or $d_8(An,Xn)$
Absolute Short	111	000	X	X	X	X	(xxx).W
Absolute Long	111	001	X	X	X	X	(xxx).L
Program Counter Indirect with Displacement	111	101	X	X	X	–	(d_{16},PC) or $d_{16}(PC)$
Program Counter Indirect with Index	111	011	X	X	X	–	(d_8,PC,Xn) or $d_8(PC,Xn)$
Immediate	111	100	X	X	–	–	#<data>

MC68020 Effective Addressing Mode Categories

Address Modes	Mode	Register	Data	Memory	Control	Alterable	Assembler Syntax
Data Register Direct	000	reg. no.	X	–	–	X	Dn
Address Register Direct	001	reg. no.	–	–	–	X	An
Address Register Indirect	010	reg. no.	X	X	X	X	(An)
Address Register Indirect with Postincrement	011	reg. no.	X	X	–	X	(An) +
Address Register Indirect with Predecrement	100	reg. no.	X	X	–	X	– (An)
Address Register Indirect with Displacement	101	reg. no	X	X	X	X	(d_{16},An)
Address Register Indirect with Index (8-Bit Displacement)	110	reg. no.	X	X	X	X	(d_8,An,Xn)
Address Register Indirect with Index (Base Displacement)	110	reg. no.	X	X	X	X	(bd,An,Xn)
Memory Indirect Post-Indexed	110	reg. no.	X	X	X	X	([bd,An],Xn,od)
Memory Indirect Pre-Indexed	110	reg. no.	X	X	X	X	([bd,An,Xn],od)
Absolute Short	111	000	X	X	X	X	(xxx).W
Absolute Long	111	001	X	X	X	X	(xxx).L
Program Counter Indirect with Displacement	111	010	X	X	X	–	(d_{16},PC)
Program Counter Indirect with Index (8-Bit Displacement)	111	011	X	X	X	–	(d_8,PC,Xn)
Program Counter Indirect with Index (Base Displacement)	111	011	X	X	X	–	(bd,PC,Xn)
PC Memory Indirect Post-Indexed	111	011	X	X	X	–	([bd,PC],Xn,od)
PC Memory Indirect Pre-Indexed	111	011	X	X	X	–	([bd,PC,Xn],od)
Immediate	111	100	X	X	–	–	#<data>

ABCD

Add Decimal with Extend

Operation: Source$_{10}$ + Destination$_{10}$ + X → Destination

Assembler   ABCD Dy,Dx
Syntax: ABCD − (Ay), − (Ax)

Attributes: Size = (Byte)

Description: Add the source operand to the destination operand along with the extend bit, and store the result in the destination location. The addition is performed using binary coded decimal arithmetic. The operands may be addressed in two different ways:
1. Data register to data register: The operands are contained in the data registers specified in the instruction.
2. Memory to memory: The operands are addressed with the predecrement addressing mode using the address registers specified in the instruction.

This operation is a byte operation only.

Condition Codes:

X	N	Z	V	C
*	U	*	U	*

N   Undefined.
Z   Cleared if the result is non-zero. Unchanged otherwise.
V   Undefined.
C   Set if a carry (decimal) was generated. Cleared otherwise.
X   Set the same as the carry bit.

NOTE

Normally the Z condition code bit is set via programming before the start of an operation. This allows successful tests for zero results upon completion of multiple-precision operations.

ADD

Add

Operation: Source + Destination → Destination

Assembler   ADD <ea>,Dn
Syntax: ADD Dn,<ea>

Attributes: Size = (Byte, Word, Long)

Description: Add the source operand to the destination operand using binary addition, and store the result in the destination location. The size of the operation may be specified to be byte, word, or long. The mode of the instruction indicates which operand is the source and which is the destination as well as the operand size.

Condition Codes:

X	N	Z	V	C
*	*	*	*	*

N   Set if the result is negative. Cleared otherwise.
Z   Set if the result is zero. Cleared otherwise.
V   Set if an overflow is generated. Cleared otherwise.
C   Set if a carry is generated. Cleared otherwise.
X   Set the same as the carry bit.

ADDA   Add Address

Operation: Source + Destination → Destination

**Assembler
Syntax:**   ADDA <ea>,An

Attributes: Size = (Word, Long)

Description: Add the source operand to the destination address register, and store the
result in the address register. The size of the operation may be specified to be word or
long. The entire destination address register is used regardless of the operation size.

Condition Codes: Not affected.

ADDI   Add Immediate

Operation: Immediate Data + Destination → Destination

**Assembler
Syntax:**   ADDI #<data>,<ea>

Attributes: Size = (Byte, Word, Long)

Description: Add the immediate data to the destination operand, and store the result in
the destination location. The size of the operation may be specified to be byte, word,
or long. The size of the immediate data matches the operation size.

Condition Codes:

X	N	Z	V	C
*	*	*	*	*

N   Set if the result is negative. Cleared otherwise.
Z   Set if the result is zero. Cleared otherwise.
V   Set if an overflow is generated. Cleared otherwise.
C   Set if a carry is generated. Cleared otherwise.
X   Set the same as the carry bit.

ADDQ   Add Quick

Operation: Immediate Data + Destination → Destination

Assembler
Syntax: ADDQ #<data>,<ea>

Attributes: Size = (Byte, Word, Long)

Description: Add the immediate data to the operand at the destination location. The data range is from 1 to 8. The size of the operation may be specified to be byte, word, or long. Word and long operations are also allowed on the address registers, in which case the condition codes are not affected. When adding to address registers, the entire destination address register is used, regardless of the operation size.

Condition Codes:

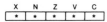

X	N	Z	V	C
*	*	*	*	*

  N   Set if the result is negative. Cleared otherwise.
  Z   Set if the result is zero. Cleared otherwise.
  V   Set if an overflow is generated. Cleared otherwise.
  C   Set if a carry is generated. Cleared otherwise.
  X   Set the same as the carry bit.

The condition codes are not affected if the destination is an address register.

ADDX   Add Extended

Operation: Source + Destination + X → Destination

Assembler   ADDX Dy,Dx
Syntax: ADDX −(Ay), −(Ax)

Attributes: Size = (Byte, Word, Long)

Description: Add the source operand to the destination operand along with the extend bit and store the result in the destination location. The operands may be addressed in two different ways:
1. Data register to data register: the operands are contained in data registers specified in the instruction.
2. Memory to memory: the operands are addressed with the predecrement addressing mode using the address registers specified in the instruction.
The size of the operation may be specified to be byte, word, or long.

Condition Codes:

X	N	Z	V	C
*	*	*	*	*

  N   Set if the result is negative. Cleared otherwise.
  Z   Cleared if the result is non-zero. Unchanged otherwise.
  V   Set if an overflow is generated. Cleared otherwise.
  C   Set if a carry is generated. Cleared otherwise.
  X   Set the same as the carry bit.

NOTE
Normally the Z condition code bit is set via programming before the start of an operation. This allows successful tests for zero results upon completion of multiple-precision operations.

AND   AND Logical

Operation: Source∧Destination → Destination

Assembler   AND <ea>,Dn
Syntax: AND Dn,<ea>

Attributes: Size = (Byte, Word, Long)

Description: AND the source operand to the destination operand and store the result in
the destination location. The size of the operation may be specified to be byte, word,
or long. The contents of an address register may not be used as an operand.

Condition Codes:

X	N	Z	V	C
—	*	*	0	0

    N   Set if the most significant bit of the result is set. Cleared otherwise.
    Z   Set if the result is zero. Cleared otherwise.
    V   Always cleared.
    C   Always cleared.
    X   Not affected.

ANDI   AND Immediate

Operation: Immediate Data∧Destination → Destination

Assembler
Syntax: ANDI #<data>,<ea>

Attributes: Size = (Byte, Word, Long)

Description: AND the immediate data to the destination operand and store the result in
the destination location. The size of the operation may be specified to be byte, word,
or long. The size of the immediate data matches the operation size.

Condition Codes:

X	N	Z	V	C
—	*	*	0	0

    N   Set if the most significant bit of the result is set. Cleared otherwise.
    Z   Set if the result is zero. Cleared otherwise.
    V   Always cleared.
    C   Always cleared.
    X   Not affected.

ANDI
to CCR   AND Immediate to Condition Codes

Operation:　Source ∧ CCR → CCR

**Assembler
Syntax:**　ANDI #<data>,CCR

Attributes:　Size = (Byte)

Description:　AND the immediate operand with the condition codes and store the result
in the low-order byte of the status register.

Condition Codes:

X	N	Z	V	C
*	*	*	*	*

N　Cleared if bit 3 of immediate operand is zero. Unchanged otherwise.
Z　Cleared if bit 2 of immediate operand is zero. Unchanged otherwise.
V　Cleared if bit 1 of immediate operand is zero. Unchanged otherwise.
C　Cleared if bit 0 of immediate operand is zero. Unchanged otherwise.
X　Cleared if bit 4 of immediate operand is zero. Unchanged otherwise.

ANDI
to SR   AND Immediate to the Status Register
           (Privileged Instruction)

Operation:　If supervisor state
　　　then Source ∧ SR → SR
　　　else TRAP

**Assembler
Syntax:**　ANDI #<data>,SR

Attributes:　Size = (Word)

Description:　AND the immediate operand with the contents of the status register and
store the result in the status register. All bits of the status register are
affected.

Condition Codes:

X	N	Z	V	C
*	*	*	*	*

N　Cleared if bit 3 of immediate operand is zero. Unchanged otherwise.
Z　Cleared if bit 2 of immediate operand is zero. Unchanged otherwise.
V　Cleared if bit 1 of immediate operand is zero. Unchanged otherwise.
C　Cleared if bit 0 of immediate operand is zero. Unchanged otherwise.
X　Cleared if bit 4 of immediate operand is zero. Unchanged otherwise.

ASL, ASR   Arithmetic Shift

Operation: Destination Shifted by <count> → Destination

Assembler ASd Dx,Dy
Syntax: ASd #<data>,Dy
               ASd <ea>
               where d is direction, L or R

Attributes: Size = (Byte, Word, Long)

Description: Arithmetically shift the bits of the operand in the direction (L or R)
specified. The carry bit receives the last bit shifted out of the operand. The shift
count for the shifting of a register may be specified in two different ways:
1. Immediate: the shift count is specified in the instruction (shift range, 1-8).
2. Register: the shift count is contained in a data register specified in the instruction
   (shift count is modulo 64).
The size of the operation may be specified to be byte, word, or long. The content of
memory may be shifted one bit only, and the operand size is restricted to a word.

For ASL, the operand is shifted left; the number of positions shifted is the shift
count. Bits shifted out of the high order bit go to both the carry and the extend bits;
zeroes are shifted into the low order bit. The overflow bit indicates if any sign
changes occur during the shift.

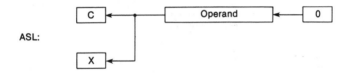

ASL:

For ASR, the operand is shifted right; the number of positions shifted is the shift
count. Bits shifted out of the low order bit go to both the carry and the extend bits;
the sign bit (MSB) is replicated into the high order bit.

ASR:

Condition Codes:

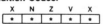

X	N	Z	V	X
*	*	*	*	*

N   Set if the most significant bit of the result is set. Cleared otherwise.
Z   Set if the result is zero. Cleared otherwise.
V   Set if the most significant bit is changed at any time during the shift opera-
    tion. Cleared otherwise.
C   Set according to the last bit shifted out of the operand. Cleared for a shift
    count of zero.
X   Set according to the last bit shifted out of the operand. Unaffected for a shift
    count of zero.

Bcc   **Branch Conditionally**

Operation: If (condition true) then PC + d → PC

Assembler
Syntax: Bcc <label>

Attributes: Size = (Byte, Word, Long)—Long on MC68020 only

Description: If the specified condition is met, program execution continues at location
(PC) + displacement. The displacement is a twos complement integer which counts
the relative distance in bytes. The value in the PC is the sign-extended instruction
location plus two. If the 8-bit displacement in the instruction word is zero, then the
16-bit displacement (word immediately following the instruction) is used. If the 8-bit
displacement in the instruction word is all ones ($FF), then the 32-bit displacement
(long word immediately following the instruction) is used. "cc" may specify the
following conditions:

CC	carry clear	0100	$\overline{C}$		LS	low or same	0011	$C + Z$
CS	carry set	0101	C		LT	less than	1101	$N \cdot \overline{V} + \overline{N} \cdot V$
EQ	equal	0111	Z		MI	minus	1011	N
GE	greater or equal	1100	$N \cdot V + \overline{N} \cdot \overline{V}$		NE	not equal	0110	$\overline{Z}$
GT	greater than	1110	$N \cdot V \cdot \overline{Z} + \overline{N} \cdot \overline{V} \cdot \overline{Z}$		PL	plus	1010	$\overline{N}$
HI	high	0010	$\overline{C} \cdot \overline{Z}$		VC	overflow clear	1000	$\overline{V}$
LE	less or equal	1111	$Z + N \cdot \overline{V} + \overline{N} \cdot V$		VS	overflow set	1001	V

Condition Codes: Not affected.

BCHG   **Test a Bit and Change**

Operation: ~(<bit number> of Destination) → Z;
                  ~(<bit number> of Destination) → <bit number> of Destination

Assembler   BCHG Dn,<ea>
Syntax: BCHG #<data>,<ea>

Attributes: Size = (Byte, Long)

Description: A bit in the destination operand is tested and the state of the specified bit
is reflected in the Z condition code. After the test, the state of the specified bit is
changed in the destination. If a data register is the destination, then the bit numbering is modulo 32 allowing bit manipulation on all bits in a data register. If a memory
location is the destination, a byte is read from that location, the bit operation is performed using the bit number, modulo 8, and the byte is written back to the location.
In all cases, bit zero refers to the least significant bit. The bit number for this operation may be specified in two different ways:
1. Immediate — the bit number is specified in a second word of the instruction.
2. Register — the bit number is contained in a data register specified in the instruction.

Condition Codes:

X	N	Z	V	C
—	—	*	—	—

N   Not affected.
Z   Set if the bit tested is zero. Cleared otherwise.
V   Not affected.
C   Not affected.
X   Not affected.

BCLR
Test a Bit and Clear

Operation: ~(<bit number> of Destination)→Z;
                0→<bit number> of Destination

Assembler   BCLR Dn,<ea>
Syntax: BCLR #<data>,<ea>

Attributes: Size = (Byte, Long)

Description: A bit in the destination operand is tested and the state of the specified bit
is reflected in the Z condition code. After the test, the specified bit is cleared in the
destination. If a data register is the destination, then the bit numbering is modulo 32
allowing bit manipulation on all bits in a data register. If a memory location is the
destination, a byte is read from that location, the bit operation performed using the
bit number, modulo 8, and the byte written back to the location. In all cases, bit zero
refers to the least significant bit. The bit number for this operation may be specified
in two different ways:
1. Immediate — the bit number is specified in a second word of the instruction.
2. Register — the bit number is contained in a data register specified in the instruction.

Condition Codes:

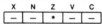

X	N	Z	V	C
—	—	*	—	—

N   Not affected.
Z   Set if the bit tested is zero. Cleared otherwise.
V   Not affected.
C   Not affected.
X   Not affected.

BFCHG
Test Bit Field and Change (MC68020 only)

Operation: ~(<bit field> of Destination)→<bit field> of Destination

Assembler
Syntax: BFCHG <ea> {offset:width}

Attributes: Unsized

Description: Complement a bit field at the specified effective address location. The condition codes are set according to the value in the field before it is changed.

The field selection is specified by a field offset and field width. The field offset
denotes the starting bit of the field. The field width determines the number of bits to
be included in the field.

Condition Codes:

X	N	Z	V	C
—	*	*	0	0

N   Set if the most significant bit of the field is set. Cleared otherwise.
Z   Set if all bits of the field are zero. Cleared otherwise.
V   Always cleared.
C   Always cleared.
X   Not affected.

BFCLR   Test Bit Field and Clear (MC68020 only)

Operation: 0 → <bit field> of Destination

**Assembler
Syntax:**   BFCLR <ea> {offset:width}

Attributes: Unsized

Description: Clear a bit field at the specific effective address location. The condition codes are set according to the value in the field before it is cleared.

The field selection is specified by a field offset and field width. The field offset denotes the starting bit of the field. The field width determines the number of bits to be included in the field.

Condition Codes:

X	N	Z	V	C
—	*	*	0	0

N   Set if the most significant bit of the field is set. Cleared otherwise.
Z   Set if all bits of the field are zero. Cleared otherwise.
V   Always cleared.
C   Always cleared.
X   Not affected.

BFEXTS   Extract Bit Field Signed (MC68020 only)

Operation: <bit field> of Source → Dn

**Assembler
Syntax:**   BFEXTS <ea> {offset:width},Dn

Attributes: Unsized

Description: Extract a bit field from the specified effective address location, sign extend to 32 bits, and load the result into the destination data register.

The field selection is specified by a field offset and field width. The field offset denotes the starting bit of the field. The field width determines the number of bits to be included in the field.

Condition Codes:

X	N	Z	V	C
—	*	*	0	0

N   Set if the most significant bit of the field is set. Cleared otherwise.
Z   Set if all bits of the field are zero. Cleared otherwise.
V   Always cleared.
C   Always cleared.
X   Not affected.

BFEXTU   **Extract Bit Field Unsigned (MC68020 only)**

Operation: < bit field > of Source → Dn

**Assembler
Syntax:**   BFEXTU <ea> {offset:width},Dn

Attributes: Unsized

Description: Extract a bit field from the specified effective address location, zero extend
to 32 bits, and load the results into the destination data register.

The field selection is specified by a field offset and field width. The field offset
denotes the starting bit of the field. The field width determines the number of bits to
be included in the field.

Condition Codes:

X	N	Z	V	C
—	*	*	0	0

N   Set if the most significant bit of the source field is set. Cleared otherwise.
Z   Set if all bits of the field are zero. Cleared otherwise.
V   Always cleared.
C   Always cleared.
X   Not affected.

BFFFO   **Find First One in Bit Field (MC68020 only)**

Operation: < bit field > of Source Bit Scan → Dn

**Assembler
Syntax:**   BFFFO <ea> {offset:width},Dn

Attributes: Unsized

Description: The source operand is searched for the most significant bit position that
contains a set bit. The bit offset (the original bit offset plus the offset of the first set
bit) of that bit is then placed in Dn. If no bit of the bit field is set, the value placed in
Dn is the field offset plus field width. The condition codes are set according to the
bit field operand.

The field selection is specified by a field offset and field width. The field offset
denotes the starting bit of the field. The field width determines the number of bits to
be included in the field.

Condition Codes:

X	N	Z	V	C
—	*	*	0	0

N   Set if the most significant bit of the field is set. Cleared otherwise.
Z   Set if all bits of the field are zero. Cleared otherwise.
V   Always cleared.
C   Always cleared.
X   Not affected.

BFINS   Insert Bit Field (MC68020 only)

Operation: Dn → <bit field> of Destination

**Assembler
Syntax:**   BFINS Dn,<ea> {offset:width}

Attributes: Unsized

Description: Move a bit field from the low-order bits of the specified data register to a bit
field at the specified effective address location. The condition codes are set according to the inserted value.

The field selection is specified by a field offset and field width. The field offset
denotes the starting bit of the field. The field width determines the number of bits to
be included in the field.

Condition Codes:

X	N	Z	V	C
—	*	*	0	0

N   Set if the most significant bit of the field is set. Cleared otherwise.
Z   Set if all bits of the field are zero. Cleared otherwise.
V   Always cleared.
C   Always cleared.
X   Not affected.

BFSET   Set Bit Field (MC68020 only)

Operation: 1s → <bit field> of Destination

**Assembler
Syntax:**   BFSET <ea> {offset:width}

Attributes: Unsized

Description: Set all bits of a bit field at the specified effective address location. The condition codes are set according to the value in the field before it is set.

The field selection is specified by a field offset and field width. The field offset
denotes the starting bit of the field. The field width determines the number of bits to
be included in the field.

Condition Codes:

X	N	Z	V	C
—	*	*	0	0

N   Set if the most significant bit of the field is set. Cleared otherwise.
Z   Set if all bits of the field are zero. Cleared otherwise.
V   Always cleared.
C   Always cleared.
X   Not affected.

BFTST   Test Bit Field (MC68020 only)

Operation: < bit field > of Destination

**Assembler
Syntax:**   BFTST < ea > {offset:width}

Attributes: Unsized

Description: Extract a bit field from the specified effective address location, and set the
condition codes according to the value in the field.

The field selection is specified by a field offset and field width. The field offset
denotes the starting bit of the field. The field width determines the number of bits to
be included in the field.

Condition Codes:

X	N	Z	V	C
—	*	*	0	0

N   Set if the most significant bit of the field is set. Cleared otherwise.
Z   Set if all bits of the field are zero. Cleared otherwise.
V   Always cleared.
C   Always cleared.
X   Not affected.

BKPT   Breakpoint

Operation: If breakpoint vector acknowledged
then execute returned operation word
else Trap as Illegal instruction

**Assembler
Syntax:**   BKPT #< data >

Attributes: Unsized

Description: This instruction is used to support the program breakpoint function for
debug monitors and real-time hardware emulators, and the operation will be dependent on the implementation. Execution of this instruction will cause the MC680XY to
run a breakpoint acknowledge bus cycle, with the immediate data (value 0-7)
presented on address lines A2, A3, and A4, and zeros on address lines A0 and A1.
Two responses are permitted: normal and exception.

The normal response to the MC68020 is an operation word (typically an instruction,
originally replaced by the breakpoint instruction) on the data lines with the DSACKx
signal asserted. This operation word will then be executed in place of the breakpoint
instruction.

For the exception response, a bus error signal will cause the MC68020 to take an illegal instruction exception.

Condition Codes: Not affected.

BRA
Branch Always

Operation: PC + d → PC

Assembler
Syntax: BRA < label >

Attributes: Size = (Byte, Word, Long)—Long on MC68020 only

Description: Program execution continues at location (PC) + displacement. The displacement is a twos complement integer, which counts the relative distance in bytes. The value in the PC is the instruction location plus two. If the 8-bit displacement in the instruction word is zero, then the 16-bit displacement (word immediately following the instruction) is used. If the 8-bit displacement in the instruction word is all ones ($FF), then the 32-bit displacement (long word immediately following the instruction) is used.

Condition Codes: Not affected.

BSET
Test a Bit and Set

Operation: ~(< bit number > of Destination) → Z;
                1 → < bit number > of Destination

Assembler   BSET Dn, < ea >
Syntax: BSET # < data >, < ea >

Attributes: Size = (Byte, Long)

Description: A bit in the destination operand is tested, and the state of the specified bit is reflected in the Z condition code. After the test, the specified bit is set in the destination. If a data register is the destination, then the bit numbering is modulo 32, allowing bit manipulation on all bits in a data register. If a memory location is the destination, a byte is read from that location, the bit operation performed using the bit number, modulo 8, and the byte written back to the location. Bit zero refers to the least significant bit. The bit number for this operation may be specified in two different ways:
1. Immediate — the bit number is specified in a second word of the instruction.
2. Register — the bit number is contained in a data register specified in the instruction.

Condition Codes:

X	N	Z	V	C
—	—	*	—	—

N   Not affected.
Z   Set if the bit tested is zero. Cleared otherwise.
V   Not affected.
C   Not affected.
X   Not affected.

BSR   Branch to Subroutine

Operation: SP – 4 → SP; PC → (SP); PC + d → PC

Assembler
Syntax: BSR < label >

Attributes: Size = (Byte, Word, Long)—Long on MC68020 only

Description: The long word address of the instruction immediately following the BSR instruction is pushed onto the system stack. Program execution then continues at
location (PC) + displacement. The displacement in a twos complement integer which
counts the relative distances in the bytes. The value in the PC is the instruction location plus two. If the 8-bit displacement in the instruction word is zero, then the 16-bit
displacement (word immediately following the instruction) is used. If the 8-bit
displacement in the instruction word is all ones ($FF), then the 32-bit displacement
(long word immediately following the instruction) is used.

Condition Codes: Not affected.

BTST   Test a Bit

Operation: ~(< bit number > of Destination) → Z;

Assembler   BTST Dn,< ea >
Syntax: BTST #< data >,< ea >

Attributes: Size = (Byte, Long)

Description: A bit in the destination operand is tested, and the state of the specified bit
is reflected in the Z condition code. If a data register is the destination, then the bit
numbering is modulo 32, allowing bit manipulation on all bits in a data register. If a
memory location is the destination, a byte is read from that location, and the bit
operation performed using the bit number, modulo 8, with zero referring to the least
significant bit. The bit number for this operation may be specified in two different
ways:
1. Immediate — the bit number is specified in a second word of the instruction.
2. Register — the bit number is contained in a data register specified in the
instruction.

Condition Codes:

X	N	Z	V	C
–	–	*	–	–

   N   Not affected.
   Z   Set if the bit tested is zero. Cleared otherwise.
   V   Not affected.
   C   Not affected.
   X   Not affected.

CALLM
CALL Module (MC68020 only)

Operation: Save current module state on stack;
Load new module state from destination

**Assembler
Syntax:** CALLM #<data>,<ea>

Attributes: Unsized

Description: The effective address of the instruction is the location of an external module descriptor. A module frame is created on the top of the stack, and the current module state is saved in the frame. The immediate operand specifies the number of bytes of arguments to be passed to the called module. A new module state is loaded from the descriptor addressed by the effective address. Additional information is presented in Appendix D.

Condition Codes: Not affected.

CAS
CAS2
Compare and Swap with Operand (MC68020 only)

Operation: CAS Destination — Compare Operand → cc;
if Z, Update_Operand → Destination
else Destination → Compare_Operand

CAS2 Destination 1 — Compare 1 → cc;
if Z, Destination 2 — Compare 2 → cc
if Z, Update 1 → Destination 1 Update 2 → Destination 2
else Destination 1 → Compare 1 Destination 2 → Compare 2

Assembler CAS Dc,Du,<ea>
Syntax: CAS2 Dc1:Dc2,Du1:Du2,(Rn1):(Rn2)

Attributes: Size = (Byte*, Word, Long)

Description: The Effective Address operand(s) is fetched and compared to the compare operand data register(s). If the operands match, the update operand data register(s) is (are) written to the destination location(s); otherwise, the memory operand location is left unchanged and the compare operand is loaded with the memory operand. The operation is indivisible (using a read-modify-write memory cycle) to allow synchronization of several processors. Additional information is presented in Appendix D.

Condition Codes:

X	N	Z	V	C
—	*	*	*	*

N Set if the result is negative. Cleared otherwise.
Z Set if the result is zero. Cleared otherwise.
V Set if an overflow is generated. Cleared otherwise.
C Set if a carry is generated. Cleared otherwise.
X Not affected.

CHK
Check Register Against Bounds

Operation: If Dn <0 or Dn> Source then TRAP

**Assembler
Syntax:** CHK <ea>,Dn

Attributes: Size = (Word, Long)—Long on MC68020 only

Description: The content of the data register specified in the instruction is examined and compared to the upper bound. The upper bound is a twos complement integer. If the register value is less than zero or greater than the upper bound, then the processor initiates exception processing. The vector number is generated to reference the CHK instruction exception vector.

Condition Codes:

X	N	Z	V	C
—	*	U	U	U

N   Set if Dn< 0; cleared if Dn> Source. Undefined otherwise.
Z   Undefined.
V   Undefined.
C   Undefined.
X   Not affected.

CHK2
Check Register Against Bounds (MC68020 only)

Operation: If Rn<Source—lower-bound or
                   Rn>Source—upper-bound
               Then TRAP

**Assembler
Syntax:** CHK2 <ea>,Rn

Attributes: Size = (Byte, Word, Long)

Description: Check the value in Rn against the bounds pair at the effective address location. The lower bound is at the address specified by the effective address, with the upper bound at that address plus the operand length. For signed comparisons, the arithmetically smaller value should be the lower bound, while for unsigned comparison, the logically smaller value should be the lower bound.

The size of the data to be checked, and the bounds to be used, may be specified as byte, word, or long. If the checked register is a data register and the operation size is byte or word, only the appropriate low-order part of Rn is checked. If the checked register is an address register and the operation size is byte or word, the bounds operands are sign-extended to 32 bits and the resultant operands compared against the full 32 bits of An.

If the upper bound equals the lower bound, then the valid range is a single value. If the register operand is out of bounds, the processor initiates exception processing. The vector number is generated to reference the CHK instruction exception vector. Otherwise, the next instruction is executed.

Condition Codes:

X	N	Z	V	C
—	U	*	U	*

N   Undefined.
Z   Set if Rn is equal to either bound. Cleared otherwise.
V   Undefined.
C   Set if Rn is out of bounds. Cleared otherwise.
X   Not affected.

CLR
Clear an Operand

Operation: 0 → Destination

**Assembler
Syntax:**   CLR <ea>

Attributes: Size = (Byte, Word, Long)

Description: The destination is cleared to all zero. The size of the operation may be
specified to be byte, word, or long.

Condition Codes:

X	N	X	V	C
—	0	1	0	0

N   Always cleared.
Z   Always set.
V   Always cleared.
C   Always cleared.
X   Not affected.

CMP
Compare

Operation: Destination — Source

**Assembler
Syntax:**   CMP <ea>,Dn

Attributes: Size = (Byte, Word, Long)

Description: Subtract the source operand from the specified data register and set the
condition codes according to the result; the data register is not changed. The size of
the operation may be byte, word, or long.

Condition Codes:

X	N	Z	V	C
—	*	*	*	*

N   Set if the result is negative. Cleared otherwise.
Z   Set if the result is zero. Cleared otherwise.
V   Set if an overflow is generated. Cleared otherwise.
C   Set if a borrow is generated. Cleared otherwise.
X   Not affected.

CMPA   **Compare Address**

Operation: Destination – Source

**Assembler
Syntax:**   CMPA < ea >,An

Attributes: Size = (Word, Long)

Description: Subtract the source operand from the destination address register and set
the condition codes according to the result; the address register is not changed. The
size of the operation may be specified to be word or long. Word length source
operands are sign extended to 32-bit quantities before the operation is done.

Condition Codes:

X	N	Z	V	C
—	*	*	*	*

N   Set if the result is negative. Cleared otherwise.
Z   Set if the result is zero. Cleared otherwise.
V   Set if an overflow is generated. Cleared otherwise.
C   Set if a borrow is generated. Cleared otherwise.
X   Not affected.

CMPI   **Compare Immediate**

Operation: Destination – Immediate Data

**Assembler
Syntax:**   CMPI #< data >,< ea >

Attributes: Size = (Byte, Word, Long)

Description: Subtract the immediate data from the destination operand and set the condition codes according to the result; the destination location is not changed. The
size of the operation may be specified to be byte, word, or long. The size of the immediate data matches the operation size.

Condition Codes:

X	N	Z	V	C
—	*	*	*	*

N   Set if the result is negative. Cleared otherwise.
Z   Set if the result is zero. Cleared otherwise.
V   Set if an overflow is generated. Cleared otherwise.
C   Set if a borrow is generated. Cleared otherwise.
X   Not affected.

CMPM

Compare Memory

Operation: Destination − Source

**Assembler
Syntax:**   CMPM (Ay) + ,(Ax) +

Attributes: Size = (Byte, Word, Long)

Description: Subtract the source operand from the destination operand, and set the condition codes according to the results; the destination location is not changed. The operands are always addressed with the postincrement addressing mode, using the address registers specified in the instruction. The size of the operation may be specified to be byte, word, or long.

Condition Codes:

X	N	Z	V	C
−	*	*	*	*

N   Set if the result is negative. Cleared otherwise.
Z   Set if the result is zero. Cleared otherwise.
V   Set if an overflow is generated. Cleared otherwise.
C   Set if a borrow is generated. Cleared otherwise.
X   Not affected.

CMP2

Compare Register Against Bounds (MC68020 only)

Operation: Compare Rn < Source—lower-bound or
Rn > Source—upper-bound
and Set Condition Codes

**Assembler
Syntax:**   CMP2 < ea >,Rn

Attributes: Size = (Byte, Word, Long)

Description: Compare the value in Rn against the bounds pair at the effective address location and set the condition codes accordingly. The lower bound is at the address specified by the effective address, with the upper bound at that address plus the operand length. For signed comparisons, the arithmetically smaller value should be the lower bound, while for unsigned comparison, the logically smaller value should be the lower bound.

The size of the data to be compared, and the bounds to be used, may be specified as byte, word, or long. If the compared register is a data register and the operation size is byte or word, only the appropriate low-order part of Dn is checked. If the checked register is an address register and the operation size is byte or word, the bounds operands are sign-extended to 32 bits and the resultant operands compared against the full 32 bits of An.

If the upper bound equals the lower bound, then the valid range is a single value.

NOTE: This instruction is analogous to CHK2, but avoids causing exception processing to handle the out-of-bounds case.

Condition Codes:

X	N	Z	V	C
−	U	*	U	*

N   Undefined.
Z   Set if Rn is equal to either bound. Cleared otherwise.
V   Undefineo.
C   Set if Rn is out of bounds. Cleared otherwise.
X   Not affected.

cpBcc   Branch on Coprocessor Condition (MC68020 only)

Operation: If cpcc true then PC + d → PC

Assembler Syntax: cpBcc <label>

Attributes: Size = (Word, Long)

Description: If the specified coprocessor condition is met, program execution continues at location (PC) + displacement. The displacement is a twos complement integer which counts the relative distance in bytes. The value in the PC is the address of the displacement word(s). The displacement may be either 16 bits or 32 bits. The coprocessor determines the specific condition from the condition field in the operation word.

Condition Codes: Not affected.

cpDBcc   Test Coprocessor Condition Decrement and Branch (MC68020 only)

Operation: If cpcc false then (Dn − 1 → Dn; If Dn ≠ − 1 then PC + d → PC)

Assembler Syntax: cpDBcc Dn, <label>

Attributes: Size = (Word)

Description: If the specified coprocessor condition is met, execution continues with the next instruction. Otherwise, the low order word in the specified data register is decremented by one. If the result is equal to − 1, execution continues with the next instruction. If the result is not equal to − 1, execution continues at the location indicated by the current value of PC plus the sign extended 16-bit displacement. The value in the PC is the address of the displacement word. The coprocessor determines the specific condition from the condition word which follows the operation word.

Condition Codes: Not affected.

cpGEN   Coprocessor General Function (MC68020 only)

Operation: Pass Command Word to Coprocessor

Assembler Syntax: cpGEN <parameters as defined by coprocessor>

Attributes: Unsized

Description: This instruction is the form used by coprocessors to specify the general data processing and movement operations. The coprocessor determines the specific operation from the command word which follows the operation word. Usually a coprocessor defines specific instances of this instruction to provide its instruction set.

Condition Codes: May be modified by coprocessor. Unchanged otherwise.

cpRESTORE   Coprocessor Restore Functions (MC68020 only)
(Privileged Instruction)

Operation: Restore Internal State of Coprocessor

**Assembler
Syntax:**   cpRESTORE < ea >

Attributes: Unsized

Description: This instruction is used to restore the internal state of a coprocessor.

Condition Codes: Not affected.

cpSAVE   Coprocessor Save Function (MC68020 only)
(Privileged Instruction)

Operation: Save Internal State of Coprocessor

**Assembler
Syntax:**   cpSAVE < ea >

Attributes: Unsized

Description: This instruction is used to save the internal state of a coprocessor.

Condition Codes: Not affected.

cpScc   Set on Coprocessor Condition (MC68020 only)

Operation: If cpcc true then 1s → Destination
else 0s → Destination

**Assembler
Syntax:**   cpScc < ea >

Attributes: Size = (Byte)

Description: The specified coprocessor condition code is tested; if the condition is true, the byte specified by the effective address is set to TRUE (all ones), otherwise that byte is set to FALSE (all zeros). The coprocessor determines the specific condition from the condition word which follows the operation word.

Condition Codes: Not affected.

cpTRAPcc   Trap on Coprocessor Condition (MC68020 only)

Operation: If cpcc true then TRAP

Assembler   cpTRAPcc
Syntax: cpTRAPcc #<data>

Attributes: Unsized or Size = (Word, Long)

Description: If the selected coprocessor condition is true, the processor initiates exception processing. The vector number is generated to reference the cpTRAPcc exception vector, the stacked program counter is the address of the next instruction. If the selected condition is not true, no operation is performed, and execution continues with the next instruction. The coprocessor determines the specific condition from the condition word which follows the operation word. Following the condition word is a user-defined data operand specified as immediate data data, to be used by the trap handler.

Condition Codes: Not affected.

DBcc   Test Condition, Decrement, and Branch

Operation: If condition false then (Dn − 1 → Dn; If Dn ≠ − 1 then PC + d → PC)

Assembler
Syntax: DBcc Dn, <label>

Attributes: Size = (Word)

Description: This instruction is a looping primitive of three parameters: a condition, a counter (data register), and a displacement. The instruction first tests the condition to determine if the termination condition for the loop has been met, and if so, no operation is performed. If the termination condition is not true, the low order 16 bits of the counter data register are decremented by one. If the result is − 1, the counter is exhausted and execution continues with the next instruction. If the result is not equal to − 1, execution continues at the location indicated by the current value of the PC plus the sign-extended 16-bit displacement. The value in the PC is the current instruction location plus two.

"cc" may specify the following conditions:

CC	carry clear	0100	$\overline{C}$		LS	low or same	0011	C + Z
CS	carry set	0101	C		LT	less than	1101	$N \cdot \overline{V} + \overline{N} \cdot V$
EQ	equal	0111	Z		MI	minus	1011	N
F	never true	0001	0		NE	not equal	0110	$\overline{Z}$
GE	greater or equal	1100	$N \cdot V + \overline{N} \cdot \overline{V}$		PL	plus	1010	$\overline{N}$
GT	greater than	1110	$N \cdot V \cdot \overline{Z} + \overline{N} \cdot \overline{V} \cdot \overline{Z}$		T	always true	0000	1
HI	high	0010	$\overline{C} \cdot \overline{Z}$		VC	overflow clear	1000	$\overline{V}$
LE	less or equal	1111	$Z + N \cdot \overline{V} + \overline{N} \cdot V$		VS	overflow set	1001	V

Condition Codes: Not affected.

Notes: 1. The terminating condition is like that defined by the UNTIL loop constructs of high-level languages. For example: DBMI can be stated as "decrement and branch until minus".

2. Most assemblers accept DBRA for DBF for use when no condition is required for termination of a loop.

3. There are two basic ways of entering a loop: at the beginning or by branching to the trailing DBcc instruction. If a loop structure terminated with DBcc is entered at the beginning, the control index count must be one less than the number of loop executions desired. This count is useful for indexed addressing modes and dynamically specified bit operations. However, when entering a loop by branching directly to the trailing DBcc instruction, the control index should equal the loop execution count. In this case, if a zero count occurs, the DBcc instruction will not branch, causing a complete bypass of the main loop.

DIVS
DIVSL

Signed Divide (All processors)
(MC68020 only)

Operation: Destination/Source → Destination

Assembler DIVS.W<ea>,Dn   32/16 → 16r:16q
Syntax: DIVS.L<ea>,Dq   32/32 → 32q ⎫
DIVS.L<ea>,Dr:Dq   64/32 → 32r:32q ⎬ MC68020 only
DIVSL.L<ea>,Dr:Dq   32/32 → 32r:32q ⎭

Attributes: Size = (Word, Long)—long on MC68020 only.

Description: Divide the destination operand by the source and store the result in the destination. The operation is performed using signed arithmetic.

The instruction has a word form and three long forms. For the word form, the destination operand is a long word and the source operand is a word. The result is 32-bits, such that the quotient is in the lower word (least significant 16 bits) of the destination and the remainder is in the upper word (most significant 16 bits) of the destination. Note that the sign of the remainder is the same as the sign of the dividend.

For the first long form, the destination operand is a long word and the source operand is a long word. The result is a long quotient, and the remainder is discarded.

For the second long form, the destination operand is a quad word, contained in any two data registers, and the source operand is a long word. The result is a long word quotient and a long word remainder.

For the third long form, the destination operand is a long word and the source operand is a long word. The result is a long word quotient and a long word remainder.

Two special conditions may arise during the operation:
1. Division by zero causes a trap.
2. Overlow may be detected and set before completion of the instruction. If overflow is detected, the condition is flagged but the operands are unaffected.

Condition Codes:

X	N	Z	V	C
—	*	*	*	0

N   Set if the quotient is negative. Cleared otherwise. Undefined if overflow or divide by zero.
Z   Set if the quotient is zero. Cleared otherwise. Undefined if overflow or divide by zero.
V   Set if division overflow is detected. Cleared otherwise.
C   Always cleared.
X   Not affected.

DIVU
DIVUL

Unsigned Divide   (All processors)
(MC68020 only)

Operation: Destination/Source → Destination

Assembler DIVU.W<ea>,Dn   32/16 → 16r:16q
Syntax: DIVU.L<ea>,Dq   32/32 → 32q
                 DIVU.L<ea>,Dr:Dq   64/32 → 32r:32q } MC68020 only
                 DIVUL.L<ea>,Dr:Dq   32/32 → 32r:32q

Attributes: Size = (Word, Long)—long on MC68020 only

Description: Divide the destination operand by the source and store the result in the destination. The operation is performed using unsigned arithmetic.

The instruction has a word from and three long forms. For the word form, the destination operand is a long word and the source operand is a word. The result is 32-bits, such that the quotient is in the lower word (least significant 16 bits) of the destination and the remainder is in the upper word (most significant 16 bits) of the destination. Note that the sign of the remainder is the same as the sign of the dividend.

For the first long form, the destination operand is a long word and the source operand is a long word. The result is a long word quotient, and the remainder is discarded.

For the second long form, the destination operand is a quad word, contained in any two data registers, and the source operand is a long word. The result is a long word quotient and a long word remainder.

For the third long form, the destination operand is a long word and the source operand is a long word. The result is a long word quotient and a long word remainder.

Two special conditions may arise:
1. Division by zero causes a trap.
2. Overlow may be detected and set before completion of the instruction. If overflow is detected, the condition is flagged but the operands are unaffected.

Condition Codes:

X	N	Z	V	C
—	*	*	*	0

N   Set if the quotient is negative. Cleared otherwise. Undefined if overflow or divide by zero.
Z   Set if the quotient is zero. Cleared otherwise. Undefined if overflow or divide by zero.
V   Set if division overflow is detected. Cleared otherwise.
C   Always cleared.
X   Not affected.

EOR   **Exclusive OR Logical**

Operation: Source ⊕ Destination → Destination

Assembler
Syntax: EOR Dn,<ea>

Attributes: Size = (Byte, Word, Long)

Description: Exclusive OR the source operand to the destination operand and store the
result in the destination location. The size of the operation may be specified to be
byte, word, or long. This operation is restricted to data registers as the source
operand. The destination operand is specified in the effective address field.

Condition Codes:

X	N	Z	V	C
—	*	*	0	0

N   Set if the most significant bit of the result is set. Cleared otherwise.
Z   Set if the result is zero. Cleared otherwise.
V   Always cleared.
C   Always cleared.
X   Not affected.

EORI   **Exclusive OR Immediate**

Operation: Immediate Data ⊕ Destination → Destination

Assembler
Syntax: EORI #<data>,<ea>

Attributes: Size = (Byte, Word, Long)

Description: Exclusive OR the immediate data to the destination operand and store the
result in the destination location. The size of the operation may be specified to be
byte, word, or long. The immediate data matches the operation size.

Condition Codes:

X	N	Z	V	C
—	*	*	0	0

N   Set if the most significant bit of the result is set. Cleared otherwise.
Z   Set if the result is zero. Cleared otherwise.
V   Always cleared.
C   Always cleared.
X   Not affected.

EORI
to CCR   Exclusive OR Immediate to Condition Code

Operation: Source ⊕ CCR → CCR

Assembler
Syntax: EORI #<data>,CCR

Attributes: Size = (Byte)

Description: Exclusive OR the immediate operand with the condition codes and store the result in the low-order byte of the status register.

Condition Codes:

X	N	Z	V	C
*	*	*	*	*

    N   Changed if bit 3 of immediate operand is one. Unchanged otherwise.
    Z   Changed if bit 2 of immediate operand is one. Unchanged otherwise.
    V   Changed if bit 1 of immediate operand is one. Unchanged otherwise.
    C   Changed if bit 0 of immediate operand is one. Unchanged otherwise.
    X   Changed if bit 4 of immediate operand is one. Unchanged otherwise.

EORI
to SR   Exclusive OR Immediate to the Status Register
(Privileged Instruction)

Operation: If supervisor state
             then Source ⊕ SR → SR
             else TRAP

Assembler
Syntax: EORI #<data>,SR

Attributes: Size = (Word)

Description: Exclusive OR the immediate operand with the contents of the status register and store the result in the status register. All bits of the status register are affected.

Condition Codes:

X	N	Z	V	C
*	*	*	*	*

    N   Changed if bit 3 of immediate operand is one. Unchanged otherwise.
    Z   Changed if bit 2 of immediate operand is one. Unchanged otherwise.
    V   Changed if bit 1 of immediate operand is one. Unchanged otherwise.
    C   Changed if bit 0 of immediate operand is one. Unchanged otherwise.
    X   Changed if bit 4 of immediate operand is one. Unchanged otherwise.

EXG
Exchange Registers

Operation: Rx ↔ Ry

Assembler   EXG Dx,Dy
Syntax: EXG Ax,Ay
   EXG Dx,Ay

Attributes: Size = (Long)

Description: Exchange the contents of two registers. This exchange is always a long (32 bit) operation. Exchange works in three modes:
1. Exchange data registers.
2. Exchange address registers.
3. Exchange a data register and an address register.

Condition Codes: Not affected.

EXT
EXTB
Sign Extend   **(All processors)**
(MC68020 only)

Operation: Destination Sign-extended → Destination

Assembler   EXT.W Dn   extend byte to word
Syntax: EXT.L Dn   extend word to long word
   EXTB.L Dn   extend byte to long word—MC68020 only

Attributes: Size = (Word, Long)

Description: Extend the sign bit of a data register from a byte to a word, from a word to a long word, or from a byte to a long word operand, depending on the size selected. If the operation is word, bit [7] of the designated data register is copied to bits [15:8] of that data register. If the operation is long, bit [15] of the designated data register is copied to bits [31:16] of the data register. The EXTB form copies bit [7] of the designated register to bits [31:8] of the data register.

Condition Codes:

X	N	Z	V	C
—	*	*	0	0

N   Set if the result is negative. Cleared otherwise.
Z   Set if the result is zero. Cleared otherwise.
V   Always cleared.
C   Always cleared.
X   Not affected.

FABS   Absolute Value (MC68881 or software)

Operation: Absolute Value of Source → FPn

Assembler   FABS.<fmt>   <ea>,FPn
Syntax: FABS.X   FPm,FPn
                  FABS.X   FPn

Attributes: Format = (Byte, Word, Long, Single, Double, Extended, Packed)

Description: Convert the source operand to extended precision (if necessary) and store the absolute
value of that operand into the destination floating-point data register.

FACOS   Arc Cosine (MC68881 or software)

Operation: Arc Cosine of Source → FPn

Assembler   FACOS.<fmt>   <ea>,FPn
Syntax: FACOS.X   FPm,FPn
                  FACOS.X   FPn

Attributes: Format = (Byte, Word, Long, Single, Double, Extended, Packed)

Description: Convert the source operand to extended precision (if necessary) and calculate the arc
cosine of that value. Return the result to the destination floating-point data register. The function is
not defined for source operands outside of the range [-1...+1]; if the source is not in the correct
range, a NAN is returned as the result and the OPERR bit is set in the FPSR. If the source is in the
correct range, the result will have a value in the range of $[0...\pi]$.

FADD   Add (MC68881 or software)

Operation: Source + FPn → FPn

Assembler   FADD.<fmt>   <ea>,FPn
Syntax: FADD.X   FPm,FPn

Attributes: Format = (Byte, Word, Long, Single, Double, Extended, Packed)

Description: Convert the source operand to extended precision (if necessary) and add that number to
the number contained in the destination floating-point data register. The result is stored in the
destination floating-point data register

FASIN   Arc Sine (MC68881 or software)

Operation: Arc Sine of the Source → FPn

Assembler   FASIN.<fmt>   <ea>,FPn
Syntax: FASIN.X   FPm,FPn
                  FASIN.X   FPn

Attributes: Format = (Byte, Word, Long, Single, Double, Extended, Packed)

Description: Convert the source operand to extended precision (if necessary) and calculate the arc
sine of the number. The result is stored in the destination floating-point data register. The function
is not defined for source operands outside of the range [-1...+1]; if the source in not in the correct
range, a NAN is returned as the result and the OPERR bit is set in the FPSR. If the source is in the
correct range, the result will have a value in the range of $[-\pi/2...+\pi/2]$.

FATAN

Arc Tangent (MC68881 or software)

Operation: Arc Tangent of Source → FPn

Assembler FATAN.<fmt>   <ea>,FPn
Syntax: FATAN.X   FPm,FPn
FATAN.X   FPn

Attributes: Format = (Byte, Word, Long, Single, Double, Extended, Packed)

Description: Convert the source operand to extended precision (if necessary) and calculate the arc tangent of that value. Return the result to the destination floating-point data register. The result will have a value in the range of [$-\pi/2...+\pi/2$].

FATANH

Hyperbolic Arc Tangent (MC68881 or software)

Operation: Hyperbolic Arc Tangent of Source → FPn

Assembler FATANH.<fmt>   <ea>,FPn
Syntax: FATANH.X   FPm,FPn
FATANH.X   FPn

Attributes: Format = (Byte, Word, Long, Single, Double, Extended, Packed)

Description: Convert the source operand to extended precision (if necessary) and calculate the hyperbolic arc tangent of that value. Return the result to the destination floating-point data register. The function is not defined for source operands outside of the range (-1...+1), with the result equal to -infinity or + infinity if the source is equal to +1 or -1, respectively. If the source is outside of the range [-1...+1], a NAN is returned as the result and the OPERR bit is set in the FPSR.

FBcc

Branch Conditionally (MC68881 or software)

Operation: If condition true, then PC + d →PC

Assembler
Syntax: FBcc.<size>   <label>

Attributes: Size = (Word, Long)

Description: If the specified floating-point condition is met, program execution continues at the location (PC) + displacement. The displacement is a twos complement integer which counts the relative distance in bytes. The value of the PC used to calculate the destination address is the address of the branch instruction plus two. If the displacement size is word, then a 16-bit displacement is stored in the word immediately following the instruction operation code. If the displacement size is long word, then a 32-bit displacement is stored in the two words immediately following the instruction operation code.

The conditional specifier "cc" may specify any one of the 32 floating-point conditional tests.

FCMP

Compare (MC68881 or software)

Operation: FPn - Source

Assembler FCMP.<fmt>   <ea>,FPn
Syntax: FCMP.X   FPm,FPn

Attributes: Format = (Byte, Word, Long, Single, Double, Extended, Packed)

Description: Convert the source operand to extended precision (if necessary) and subtract that number from the destination floating-point data register. The result of the subtraction is not retained, but it is used to set the floating-point condition codes.

FCOS

Cosine (MC68881 or software)

Operation: Cosine of Source → FPn

Assembler   FCOS.\<fmt\>   \<ea\>,FPn
Syntax: FCOS.X   FPm,FPn
                FCOS.X   FPn

Attributes: Format = (Byte, Word, Long, Single, Double, Extended, Packed)

Description: Convert the source operand to extended precision (if necessary) and calculate the cosine of that value. Return the result to the destination floating-point data register. The function is not defined for source operands of ±infinity. If the source operand is not in the range of $[-2\pi...+2\pi]$, then the argument will be reduced to within that range before the cosine is calculated. However, large arguments may lose accuracy during reduction, and very large arguments (greater than approximately 10^{20}) will lose all accuracy. The result will be in the range of $[-1...+1]$.

FCOSH

Hyperbolic Cosine (MC68881 or software)

Operation: Hyperbolic Cosine of Source → FPn

Assembler   FCOSH.\<fmt\>   \<ea\>,FPn
Syntax: FCOSH.X   FPm,FPn
                FCOSH.X   FPn

Attributes: Format = (Byte, Word, Long, Single, Double, Extended, Packed)

Description: Convert the source operand to extended precision (if necessary) and calculate the hyperbolic cosine of that value. Return the result to the destination floating-point data register.

FDBcc

Test Condition, Decrement, and Branch (MC68881 or software)

Operation: If condition true then no operation;
              else Dn - 1 → Dn;
                if Dn ≠ -1
                    then PC + d → PC

Assembler   FDBcc   Dn,\<label\>
Syntax:

Attributes: Unsized

Description: This instruction is a looping primitive of three parameters: a floating-point condition, a counter (an MC68020 data register) and a 16-bit displacement. The instruction first tests the condition to determine if the termination condition for the loop has been met, and if so, the main processor proceeds to execute the next instruction in the instruction stream. If the termination condition is not true, the low order 16-bits of the counter register are decremented by one. If the result is -1, the counter is exhausted and execution continues with the next instruction. If the result is not equal to -1, execution continues at the location specified by the current value of the PC plus the sign-extended 16-bit displacement. The value of the PC used in the branch address calculation is the address of the FDBcc instruction plus two.

The conditional specifier "cc" may specify any one of the 32 floating-point conditional tests.

FDIV

Divide (MC68881 or software)

Operation: FPn + Source → FPn

Assembler FDIV.<fmt> <ea>,FPn
Syntax: FDIV.X FPm,FPn

Attributes: Format = (Byte, Word, Long, Single, Double, Extended, Packed)

Description: Convert the source operand to extended precision (if necessary) and divide that number into the number contained in the destination floating-point data register. The result is stored in the destination floating-point data register

FETOX

e^x (MC68881 or software)

Operation: $e^{(Source)}$ → FPn

Assembler FETOX.<fmt> <ea>,FPn
Syntax: FETOX.X FPm,FPn
   FETOX.X FPn

Attributes: Format = (Byte, Word, Long, Single, Double, Extended, Packed)

Description: Convert the source operand to extended precision (if necessary) and calculate e to the power of that number. The result is stored in the destination floating-point data register

FETOXM1

$e^x - 1$ (MC68881 or software)

Operation: $e^{(Source)} - 1$ → FPn

Assembler FETOXM1.<fmt> <ea>,FPn
Syntax: FETOXM1.X FPm,FPn
   FETOXM1.X FPn

Attributes: Format = (Byte, Word, Long, Single, Double, Extended, Packed)

Description: Convert the source operand to extended precision (if necessary) and calculate e to the power of that number, then subtract one from that value. The result is stored in the destination floating-point data register

FGETEXP

Get Exponent (MC68881 or software)

Operation: Exponent of Source → FPn

Assembler FGETEXP.<fmt> <ea>,FPn
Syntax: FGETEXP.X FPm,FPn
   FGETEXP.X FPn

Attributes: Format = (Byte, Word, Long, Single, Double, Extended, Packed)

Description: Convert the source operand to extended precision (if necessary) and extract the binary exponent. Convert the extracted exponent to an extended precision floating-point number, remove the exponent bias and store the result in the destination floating-point data register.

FGETMAN

Get Mantissa (MC68881 or software)

Operation: Mantissa of Source → FPn

Assembler   FGETMAN.<fmt>   <ea>,FPn
Syntax: FGETMAN.X   FPm,FPn
               FGETMAN.X   FPn

Attributes: Format = (Byte, Word, Long, Single, Double, Extended, Packed)

Description: Convert the source operand to extended precision (if necessary) and extract the
mantissa. Convert the mantissa to an extended precision value and store the result in the
destination floating-point data register. The result will be in the range [1.0...2.0), with the sign of the
source mantissa, zero, or a NAN.

FINT

Integer Part (MC68881 or software)

Operation: Integer Part of Source → FPn

Assembler   FINT.<fmt>   <ea>,FPn
Syntax: FINT.X   FPm,FPn
               FINT.X   FPn

Attributes: Format = (Byte, Word, Long, Single, Double, Extended, Packed)

Description: Convert the source operand to extended precision (if necessary), extract the integer part,
and convert it to an extended precision floating-point number. Store the result in the destination
floating-point data register. The integer part is extracted by rounding the extended precision
number to an integer using the current rounding mode selected in the FPCR Control byte. Thus,
the integer part returned is the number that is to the left of the radix point when the exponent is
zero, after rounding. For example, the integer part of 137.57 is 137.0 for the round-to-zero and
round-to-minus infinity modes, and 138.0 for the round-to-nearest and round-to-plus infinity modes.
Note that the result of this operation is a floating-point number.

FINTRZ

Integer Part, Round-to-Zero (MC68881 or software)

Operation: Integer Part of Source → FPn

Assembler   FINTRZ.<fmt>   <ea>,FPn
Syntax: FINTRZ.X   FPm,FPn
               FINTRZ.X   FPn

Attributes: Format = (Byte, Word, Long, Single, Double, Extended, Packed)

Description: Convert the source operand to extended precision (if necessary), extract the integer part,
and convert it to an extended precision floating-point number. Store the result in the destination
floating-point data register. The integer part returned is the number that is to the left of the radix
point when the exponent is zero. The integer part is extracted by rounding the extended precision
number to an integer using the round-to-zero mode, regardless of the current rounding mode
selected in the FPCR Control byte (making it useful for FORTRAN assignments). For example, the
integer part of 137.57 is 137.0; the integer part of 0.1245×10^2 is 12.0. Note that the result of this
operation is a floating-point number.

FLOG10

Log$_{10}$ (MC68881 or software)

Operation: Log$_{10}$ of Source -> FPn

Assembler	FLOG10.<fmt>	<ea>,FPn
Syntax:	FLOG10.X	FPm,FPn
	FLOG10.X	FPn

Attributes: Format = (Byte, Word, Long, Single, Double, Extended, Packed)

Description: Convert the source operand to extended precision (if necessary) and calculate its logarithm using base 10 arithmetic. Store the result in the destination floating-point data register. This function is not defined for input values less than zero.

FLOG2

Log$_2$ (MC68881 or software)

Operation: Log$_2$ of Source $\rightarrow$ FPn

Assembler	FLOG2.<fmt>	<ea>,FPn
Syntax:	FLOG2.X	FPm,FPn
	FLOG2.X	FPn

Attributes: Format = (Byte, Word, Long, Single, Double, Extended, Packed)

Description: Convert the source operand to extended precision (if necessary) and calculate its logarithm using base 2 arithmetic. Store the result in the destination floating-point data register. This function is not defined for input values less than zero.

FLOGN

Log$_e$ (MC68881 or software)

Operation: Log$_e$ of Source $\rightarrow$ FPn

Assembler	FLOGN.<fmt>	<ea>,FPn
Syntax:	FLOGN.X	FPm,FPn
	FLOGN.X	FPn

Attributes: Format = (Byte, Word, Long, Single, Double, Extended, Packed)

Description: Convert the source operand to extended precision (if necessary) and calculate the natural logarithm of that number. Store the result in the destination floating-point data register. This function is not defined for input values less than zero.

FLOGNP1

Log$_e$(x+1) (MC68881 or software)

Operation: Log$_e$ of (Source + 1) $\rightarrow$ FPn

Assembler	FLOGNP1.<fmt>	<ea>,FPn
Syntax:	FLOGNP1.X	FPm,FPn
	FLOGNP1.X	FPn

Attributes: Format = (Byte, Word, Long, Single, Double, Extended, Packed)

Description: Convert the source operand to extended precision (if necessary), add 1 to that value, and calculate the natural logarithm of the intermediate result. Store the final result in the destination floating-point data register. This function is not defined for input values less than -1.

FMOD

Modulo Remainder (MC68881 or software)

Operation: Modulo remainder of (FPn + Source) → FPn

Assembler   FMOD.<fmt>   <ea>,FPn
Syntax: FMOD.X   FPm,FPn

Attributes: Format = (Byte, Word, Long, Single, Double, Extended, Packed)

Description: Convert the source operand to extended precision (if necessary) and calculate the modulo remainder of the destination floating-point data register, using the source value as the modulus. The result is stored in the destination floating-point data register, and the seven least significant quotient bits and the sign of the quotient are stored in the FPSR quotient byte (where the quotient is the result of FPn + Source). The modulo remainder function is defined as:

$$FPn - (Source \times N)$$

where N = INT(FPn + Source) in the round-to-zero mode

The FMOD function is not defined for a source operand equal to zero or for a destination operand equal to infinity. Note that this function is not the same as the FREM instruction, which uses the round-to-nearest mode and thus returns the remainder that is required by the *IEEE Specification for Binary Floating-Point Arithmetic.*

FMOVE

Move Floating-Point Data Register (MC68881 or software)

Operation: Source → Destination

Assembler   FMOVE.<fmt>   <ea>,FPn
Syntax: FMOVE.<fmt>   FPm,<ea>
                  FMOVE.P   FPm,<ea>{Dn}
                  FMOVE.P   FPm,<ea>{#k}

Attributes: Format = (Byte, Word, Long, Single, Double, Extended, Packed)

Description: Move the contents of the source operand to the destination operand. Although the primary function of this instruction is data movement, it is also considered an arithmetic instruction, since conversions from the source operand format to the destination operand format are performed implicitly during the move operation. Also, the source operand will be rounded according to the selected rounding precision and mode.

Unlike the M68000 Family integer data movement instruction, the floating-point move instruction does not support a memory-to-memory format (for such transfers, it is much faster to utilize the M68000 Family integer MOVE instruction to transfer the floating-point data than to use the FMOVE instruction). The FMOVE instruction only supports memory-to-register, register-to-register, and register-to-memory operations (in this context, "memory" may refer to an MC68020 data register if the data format is byte, word, long or single). In fact, these two operations use distinctly different command word encodings, and are described separately below.

Memory-to-Register Operation:
The source operand is converted to an extended precision floating-point number (if necessary) and stored in the destination floating-point data register. Depending on the source data format and the rounding precision, some operations may produce an inexact result. In the following table, combinations that can produce an inexact result are marked with a dot (•), while all other combinations will produce an exact result.

		Source Format:	B	W	L	S	D	X	P
Rounding	Single				•		•	•	•
Precision:	Double						•	•
	Extended							•

Register-to-Memory Operation:
The source operand is rounded, if necessary, to the specified size and stored at the destination effective address. If the format of the destination is packed decimal, then a third operand is required to specify the format of the resultant string. This operand, called the k-factor, is a 7-bit signed integer (twos complement) and may be specified as an immediate value or in a main processor data register. If a data register contains the k-factor, only the least significant 7-bits are used, and the rest of the register is ignored.

FMOVE
Move System Control Register (MC68881 or software)

Operation: Source → Destination

Assembler   FMOVE.L   \<ea>,FPcr
Syntax: FMOVE.L   FPcr,\<ea>

Attributes: Size = (Long)

Description: Move the contents of a floating-point system control register into or out of the MC68881 (the control registers are the FPCR, FPSR and FPIAR). The external register image may be located in memory or an MC68020 register. A 32-bit transfer is always performed, even though the system control register may not have 32 implemented bits. Unimplemented bits of a control register are read as zeros and are ignored during writes (but must be zero for compatability with future devices).

This instruction will not cause a pending exception to be reported to the main processor. Further - more, a write to the FPCR exception enable byte or the FPSR exception status byte will not generate a new exception, regardless of the value written.

Status Register: Will be changed only if the destination is the FPSR; in which case all bits will be modified to reflect the value of the source operand.

FMOVECR
Move Constant ROM (MC68881 or software)

Operation: ROM Constant → FPn

Assembler   FMOVECR.X   #ccc,FPn
Syntax:

Attributes: Format = (Byte, Word, Long, Single, Double, Extended, Packed)

Description: Move an extended precision constant from the MC68881 on-chip ROM, round it to the precision specified by the FPCR, and store it in the destination floating-point data register. A constant value is specified by a predefined offset into the constant ROM. The constants contained in the ROM are shown in the table below.

Offset	Constant	Offset	Constant
$00	π	$35	10^4
$0B	$Log_{10}(2)$	$36	10^8
$0C	e	$37	10^{16}
$0D	$Log_2(e)$	$38	10^{32}
$0E	$Log_{10}(e)$	$39	10^{64}
$0F	0.0	$3A	10^{128}
$30	$ln(2)$	$3B	10^{256}
$31	$ln(10)$	$3C	10^{512}
$32	10^0	$3D	10^{1024}
$33	10^1	$3E	10^{2048}
$34	10^2	$3F	10^{4096}

Other constants are contained in the on-chip ROM, but are useful only to the on-chip microcode routines. The values contained at offsets other than those defined above are reserved for the use of Motorola, and may be different on various mask sets of the MC68881.

FMOVEM   Move Multiple Data Registers (MC68881 or software)

Operation: Register List → Destination
                  Source → Register List

Assembler   FMOVEM.X   <list>,<ea>
Syntax: FMOVEM.X   Dn,<ea>
                  FMOVEM.X   <ea>,<list>
                  FMOVEM.X   <ea>,Dn

                <list> A list of any combination of the eight floating-point data registers, with individual register names separated by a slash, "/"; and/or contiguous blocks of registers specified by the first and last register names separated by a dash, "-".

Attributes: Format = (Extended)

Description: Move one or more extended precision values to or from a list of floating-point data registers. No conversion or rounding is performed during this operation, and the FPSR is not affected by the instruction. This instruction will not cause a pending exception to be reported to the main processor.

Any combination of the eight floating-point data registers may be transferred, with the selected registers specified by a user-supplied mask. This mask is an 8-bit number, where each bit corresponds to one register; if a bit is set in the mask, that register will be moved. The register select mask may be specified as a static value contained in the instruction, or a dynamic value in the least significant 8-bits of an MC68020 data register (the upper 24-bits of the register are ignored).

FMOVEM allows three types of addressing modes: the control modes, the predecrement mode, or the postincrement mode. If the effective address is one of the control addressing modes, the registers are transferred between the MC68881 and memory starting at the specified address and up through higher addresses. The order of the transfer is from FP0 through FP7.

If the effective address is the predecrement mode, only a register to memory operation is allowed. The registers are stored starting at the address contained in the address register and down through lower addresses. Before each register is stored, the address register is decremented by 12 (the size of an extended precision number in memory) and the floating-point data register is then stored at the resultant address. When the operation is complete, the address register points to the image of the last floating-point data register stored. Each register is stored in the format described in section **2.2 Operand Data Types and Formats**, such that the most significant byte of the register image is stored at the lowest address, and the least significant byte at the highest address. The order of the transfer is from FP7 through FP0.

If the effective address is the postincrement mode, only a memory to register operation is allowed. The registers are loaded starting at the specified address and up through higher addresses. After each register is stored, the address register is incremented by 12 (the size of an extended precision number in memory). When the operation is complete, the address register points to the byte immediately following the image of the last floating-point data register loaded. The order of the transfer is the same as for the control addressing modes, FP0 through FP7.

Status Register:
Not Affected. Note that the FMOVEM instruction provides the only mechanism for moving a floating-pointdata item between the MC68881 and memory without performing any data conversions or affecting the condition code and exception status bits.

Programming Note: This instruction provides a very useful feature, dynamic register list specification, that can significantly enhance system performance. If the calling conventions used for procedure calls utilize the dynamic register list feature, the number of floating-point data registers saved and restored can be reduced. Since a save or restore of a floating-point data register requires at least 6 bus cycles (more if the memory address is not long word aligned), then if a register does not need to be saved and restored, a minimum of 36 clock cycles will be eliminated from the procedure call and return overhead for each register not saved unnecessarily.

In order to utilize the dynamic register selection feature of the FMOVEM instruction, both the calling and the called procedures must be written to communicate information about register usage. When one procedure calls another procedure, a register mask should be passed to the called procedure that indicates which registers must not be altered upon return to the calling procedure. The called procedure can then save only those registers that will be modified *and* are already in use. There are several techniques that can be used to utilize this mechanism, and an example is given below.

In this example, a convention is defined where each called procedure is passed a word mask in D7 which identifies all floating-point registers in use by the calling procedure. Bits 15 though 8 identify the registers in the order FP0 through FP7, while bits 7 through 0 identify the registers in the order FP7 through FP0 (the two masks are required due to the different transfer order used by the pre - decrement and postincrement addressing modes). The code used by the calling procedure consists of simply moving the mask (which is generated at compile time) for the floating-point data registers currently in use into D7:

```
Calling procedure...
    MOVE.W      #ACTIVE_NOW,D7      Load the list of FP registers that are in use
    BSR         PROC_2
```

The entry code for all other procedures computes two masks. The first mask identifies the registers in use by the calling procedure that will be used by the called procedure (and therefore saved and restored by the called procedure). The second mask identifies the registers in use by the calling procedure that will not be used by the called procedure (and therefore not saved on entry). The appropriate registers are then stored along with the two masks:

```
Called procedure...
    MOVE.W      D7,D6                Copy the list of active registers
    AND.W       #WILL_USE,D7         Generate the list of doubly-used registers
    FMOVEM      D7,-(A7)             Save those registers
    MOVE.W      D7,-(A7)             Save the register list
    EOR.W       D7,D6                Generate the list of not saved active registers
    MOVE.W      D6,NOT_SAVED(A7)     Save it for later use
```

If the second procedure must call a third procedure, a register mask must be passed to the third procedure that will indicate which registers must not be altered by the third procedure. This mask must identify any registers in the list from the first procedure that were not saved by the second procedure, plus any registers used by the second procedure that must not be altered by the third procedure. An example of the calculation of this mask is:

```
Nested calling sequence...
    MOVE.W      NOT_SAVED(A7),D7     Load the list of active registers not saved at entry
    OR.W        #ACTIVE_NOW,D7       Combine with those active at this time
    BSR         PROC_3
```

Upon return from a procedure, the restoration of the necessary registers follows the same convention, and the register mask generated during the save operation on entry can be used to restore the required floating-point data registers:

```
Return to caller...
    MOVE.B      (A7)+,D7             Get the register list (pop a word, use high byte)
    FMOVEM      (A7)+,D7             Restore the registers
        .
        .
        .
    RTS                              Return to the calling routine
```

FMOVEM
Move Multiple Control Registers (MC68881 or software)

Operation: Register List → Destination
Source → Register List

Assembler FMOVEM.L   <list>,<ea>
Syntax: FMOVEM.L   <ea>,<list>

    <list> A list of any combination of the three floating-point system control registers (FPCR, FPSR and FPIAR), with individual register names separated by a slash, "/".

Attributes: Size = (Long)

Description: Move one or more 32-bit values into or out of the specified system control registers. Any combination of the three system control registers may be selected. The registers are always moved in the same order, regardless of the addressing mode used; with the FPCR moved first, followed by the FPSR, and the FPIAR moved last (if a register is not selected for the transfer, the relative order of the transfer of the other registers is the same). The first register is transferred between the MC68881 and the specified address, with successive registers located up through higher addresses.

When more than one register is moved, the memory or memory alterable addressing modes are allowed as shown below. If the addressing mode is predecrement, the address register is first decremented by the total size of the register images to be moved (ie, 4 times the number of registers) and then the registers are transferred starting at the resultant address. For the postincrement addressing mode, the selected registers are transferred to or from the specified address, and then the address register is incremented by the total size of the register images that were transferred. If a single system control register is selected, the data register direct addressing mode may be used; or, if the selected register is the FPIAR, then the address register direct addressing mode may be used. Note that if a single register is selected, the opcode generated is the same as for the FMOVE single system control register instruction.

Status Register: Will be changed only if the destination list includes the FPSR; in which case all bits will be modified to reflect the value of the source register image.

FMUL
Multiply (MC68881 or software)

Operation: Source x FPn → FPn

Assembler FMUL.<fmt>   <ea>,FPn
Syntax: FMUL.X   FPm,FPn

Attributes: Format = (Byte, Word, Long, Single, Double, Extended, Packed)

Description: Convert the source operand to extended precision (if necessary) and multiply that number by the value in the destination floating-point data register. Store the result in the destination floating-point data register.

FNEG
Negate (MC68881 or software)

Operation: -(Source) → FPn

Assembler FNEG.<fmt>   <ea>,FPn
Syntax: FNEG.X   FPm,FPn
              FNEG.X   FPn

Attributes: Format = (Byte, Word, Long, Single, Double, Extended, Packed)

Description: Convert the source operand to extended precision (if necessary), invert the sign of the mantissa, and store the result in the destination floating-point data register.

FNOP
No Operation (MC68881 or software)

Operation: None

Assembler FNOP
Syntax:

Attributes: Unsized

Description: This instruction does not perform any explicit operation. It is useful, however, to force synchronization of the MC68881 with a main processor, or to force processing of pending exceptions. The syncronization function is inherent in the way that the MC68881 uses the M68000 Family Coprocessor Interface. For most MC68881 instructions, the main processor is allowed to continue with the execution of the next instruction once the MC68881 has any operands needed for an operation; thus supporting concurrent execution of floating-point and integer instructions. However, if the main processor attempts to initiate the execution of a new instruction in the MC68881 before the previous one is completed, then the main processor will be forced to wait until that instruction execution is done before proceeding with the new instruction. FNOP is treated in the same way as other instructions, and thus cannot be executed until the previous floating-point instruction is completed and the main processor is "synchronized" with the MC68881.

The FNOP can also be used to force the processing of pending exceptions from the execution of previous instructions. This is also inherent in the way that the MC68881 utilizes the M68000 Family Coprocessor Interface. Once the MC68881 has received an input operand for an arithmetic instruction, it will **always** release the main procesor to execute the next instruction (regardless of whether or not concurrent execution is prevented for the instruction due to tracing) without reporting the exception during the execution of that instruction. Then, when the main processor attempts to initiate the execution of the next MC68881 instruction, a pre-instruction exception will be reported that starts exception processing for the exception that occurred during the previous instruction. By using the FNOP instruction, the user can force any pending exceptions to be processed without performing any other operations.

FREM
IEEE Remainder (MC68881 or software)

Operation: IEEE Remainder of (FPn + Source) → FPn

Assembler FREM.<fmt> <ea>,FPn
Syntax: FREM.X FPm,FPn

Attributes: Format = (Byte, Word, Long, Single, Double, Extended, Packed)

Description: Convert the source operand to extended precision (if necessary) and calculate the IEEE remainder of the destination floating-point data register using the source value as the divisor. The result is stored in the destination floating-point data register, and the seven least significant quotient bits and the sign of the quotient are stored in the FPSR quotient byte (where the quotient is the result of FPn + Source). The IEEE remainder function is defined as:

$$FPn - (Source \times N)$$

$$where\ N = INT(FPn + Source)\ in\ the\ round-to-nearest\ mode$$

The FREM function is not defined for a source operand equal to zero or for a destination operand equal to infinity. Note that this function is not the same as the FMOD instruction, which uses the round-to-zero mode and thus returns a remainder that is different from the remainder required by the *IEEE Specification for Binary Floating-Point Arithmetic.*

FRESTORE

Restore Internal State (MC68881 or software)
(Privileged Instruction)

Operation: If in supervisor state
                   then MC68881 State Frame → Internal State
                   else trap

Assembler
Syntax: FRESTORE   <ea>

Attributes: Unsized, privileged.

Description: The MC68881 aborts any execution of any operation that it was performing, and a new internal state is loaded from the state frame located at the effective address. The first word at the specified address is the format word of the state frame, which specifies the size of the frame and the revision number of the MC68881 that created it. The MC68020 will write the first word to the MC68881 Restore CIR to initiate the restore operation, and then read the Response CIR to verify that the MC68881 recognizes the format word as valid. If the format word is invalid for this MC68881 (either because the size of the frame is not recognized, or the revision number does not match the revision of this processor), then the MC68020 is instructed to take a format exception and the MC68881 enters the IDLE state. If the format word is valid, the appropriate state frame is loaded, starting at the specified location and up through higher addresses.

The FRESTORE does not normally affect the programmer's model registers of the MC68881 (except for the NULL state size, as described below); but, rather, is used only to restore the non-user visible portion of the machine. The FRESTORE instruction may be used with the FMOVEM instruction to perform a full context restoration of the MC68881, including the floating-point data registers and system control registers. In order to accomplish such a restoration, the FMOVEM instructions are first executed to load the programmer's model, followed by the FRESTORE instruction to load the internal state and continue any previously suspended operation.

NULL: This state frame is four bytes long, with a format word of $0000. An FRESTORE with this size state frame is identical to a hardware reset of the MC68881. The programmer's model is set to the reset state, with non-signalling NANs in the floating-point data registers and zero in the FPCR, FPSR and FPIAR (thus, the programmer's model does not need to be loaded after this operation).

IDLE: This state frame is 28 ($1C) bytes long. An FRESTORE with this size state frame causes the MC68881 to restore itself to an idling condition, waiting for the initiation of the next instruction. Any exceptions that were pending at the time of the previous FSAVE will be pending after the FRESTORE. The programmer's model is not affected by the loading of this type of a state frame (although the completion of the suspended instruction after the restore is executed may modify the programmer's model).

BUSY: This state frame is 184 ($B8) bytes long. An FRESTORE with this size state frame causes the MC68881 to restore itself to the busy state, executing the instruction that was previously suspended by an FSAVE. The programmer's model is not affected by the loading of this type of a state frame.

FSAVE

Save Internal State   (MC68881 or software)
(Privileged Instruction)

Operation: If in supervisor state
                 then MC68881 Internal State → State Frame
                 else trap

Assembler
Syntax: FSAVE   <ea>

Attributes: Unsized, privileged.

Description: The MC68881 suspends the execution of any operation that it was performing, and saves its internal state in a state frame located at the effective address. After the save operation, the MC68881 is in the idle state, waiting for the execution of the next instruction. The first word written to the state frame is the format word, which specifies the size of the frame and the revision number of this MC68881. The MC68020 initiates the FSAVE instruction by reading the MC68881 Save CIR, which will be encoded with a format word that indicates the appropriate action to be taken by the main processor. The current implementation of the MC68881 will always return one of five responses in the Save CIR:

Value	Definition
$0018	Save NULL state frame
$0118	Not Ready, come again
$0218	Illegal, take Format exception
$1F18	Save IDLE state frame
$1FB4	Save BUSY state frame

The Not Ready format word indicates that the MC68881 is not prepared to perform a state save and that the MC68020 should process interrupts, if necessary, and then re-read the Save CIR. The MC68881 uses this format word to cause the main processor to wait while an internal operation is completed, if possible, in order to allow an IDLE frame to be saved rather than a BUSY frame. The Illegal format word is used to abort an FSAVE operation that is attempted while the MC68881 was previously executing an FSAVE operation. All other format words cause the MC68020 to save the indicated state frame at the specified address. These state frames are defined as follows

NULL: This state frame is four bytes long. An FSAVE of this size state frame indicates that the MC68881 state has not been modified since the last FRESTORE with a NULL state frame, or hardware reset. This indicates that programmer's model is in the reset state, with non-signalling NANs in the floating-point data registers and zero in the FPCR and FPSR (thus, it is not necessary to perform a save of the programmer's model).

IDLE: This state frame is 28 ($1C) bytes long. An FSAVE of this size state frame indicates that the MC68881 was in an idle condition, waiting for the initiation of the next instruction. Any exceptions that were pending are saved in the frame, and are then cleared internally. Thus, the pending exceptions will not be reported until after a subsequent FRESTORE of the state frame. In addition to being used for context switching, this frame may be used by exception handler routines, since it contains the value of the operand that caused the last floating-point exception to be taken.

BUSY: This state frame is 184 ($B8) bytes long. An FSAVE of this size state frame indicates that the MC68881 was at a point within an instruction where it was necessary to save the entire internal state of the processor. This frame size is only used when absolutely necessary, because of the large size of the frame and the amount of time required to transfer it. The action of the MC68881 when this state frame is saved is same as for the IDLE state frame.

The FSAVE does not save the programmer's model registers of the MC68881; but, rather, is used only to save the non-user visible portion of the machine. The FSAVE instruction may be used with the FMOVEM instruction to perform a full context save of the MC68881, including the floating-point data registers and system control registers. In order to accomplish such a save, the FSAVE instruction is first executed to suspend the current operation and save the internal state, followed by the FMOVEM instructions to store the programmer's model.

FSCALE

Scale Exponent (MC68881 or software)

Operation: FPn x INT(2^{Source}) → FPn

Assembler   FSCALE.<fmt>   <ea>,FPn
Syntax: FSCALE.X   FPm,FPn

Attributes: Format = (Byte, Word, Long, Single, Double, Extended, Packed)

Description: Convert the source operand to an integer (if necessary) and add it to the destination exponent. Save the result in the destination floating-point data register. This function has the effect of multiplying the destination by 2^{Source}, but is much faster than multiplying the destination by 2^{Source} when the source is an integer value.

The MC68881 assumes that the scale factor is already an integer value before the operation. If not, the factor will be chopped (ie, rounded using the round-to-zero mode) to an integer before being added to the exponent. When the absolute value of the source operand is $\geq 2^{16}$, an overflow or underflow will always result.

FScc

Set According to Condition (MC68881 or software)

Operation: If (condition true)
                  then 1s → Destination
                  else 0s → Destination

Assembler
Syntax: FBcc.<size>   <ea>

Attributes: Size= (Byte)

Description: If the specified floating-point condition is true, set the byte integer operand at the destination to TRUE (all ones), otherwise set the byte to FALSE (all zeroes). The condition code may be any of the 32 floating-point conditional tests

FSGLDIV

Single Precision Divide (MC68881 or software)

Operation: FPn + Source → FPn

Assembler   FSGLDIV.<fmt>   <ea>,FPn
Syntax: FSGLDIV.X   FPm,FPn

Attributes: Format = (Byte, Word, Long, Single, Double, Extended, Packed)

Description: Convert the source operand to extended precision (if necessary) and divide the destination floating-point data register by that value. Store the result in the destination floating-point data register. The result will be rounded to single precision.

Both the source and the destination operands are assumed to be representable as single precision values. If either operand requires more than 24 bits of mantissa to be accurately represented, the accuracy of the result is not guaranteed. This function is undefined for 0/0 and infinity/infinity.

FSGLMUL   Single Precision Multiply (MC68881 or software)

Operation: Source x FPn → FPn

Assembler   FSGLMUL.<fmt>   <ea>,FPn
Syntax: FSGLMUL.X   FPm,FPn

Attributes: Format = (Byte, Word, Long, Single, Double, Extended, Packed)

Description: Convert the source operand to extended precision (if necessary) and multiply the destination floating-point data register by that value. Store the result in the destination floating-point data register. The result will be rounded to single precision.

Both the source and the destination operands are assumed to be representable as single precision values. Both operands are chopped to 24 bits of mantissa before the multiplication is performed.

FSIN   Sine (MC68881 or software)

Operation: Sine of Source → FPn

Assembler   FSIN.<fmt>   <ea>,FPn
Syntax: FSIN.X   FPm,FPn
                FSIN.X   FPn

Attributes: Format = (Byte, Word, Long, Single, Double, Extended, Packed)

Description: Convert the source operand to extended precision (if necessary) and calculate the sine of that value. Return the result to the destination floating-point data register. The function is not defined for source operands of ±infinity. If the source operand is not in the range of $[-2\pi...+2\pi]$, then the argument will be reduced to within that range before the sine is calculated. However, large arguments may lose accuracy during reduction, and very large arguments (greater than approximately 10^{20}) will lose all accuracy. The result will be in the range of [-1...+1].

FSINCOS   Simultaneous Sine and Cosine (MC68881 or software)

Operation: Sine of Source → FPs
                 Cosine of Source → FPc

Assembler   FSINCOS.<fmt>   <ea>,FPc:FPs
Syntax: FSINCOS.X   FPm,FPc:FPs

Attributes: Format = (Byte, Word, Long, Single, Double, Extended, Packed)

Description: Convert the source operand to extended precision (if necessary) and calculate both the sine and the cosine of that value. Both functions are calculated simultaneously, thus, this instruction is significantly faster than performing a separate FSIN and FCOS instruction. The sine result is loaded into the destination floating-point data register FPs; and the cosine result is loaded into the destination floating-point data register FPc. The condition code bits are set according to the sine result. If FPs and FPc are specified to be the same register, the cosine result is first loaded into the register, and then is over written with the sine result. The function is not defined for source operands of ±infinity.

If the source operand is not in the range of $[-2\pi...+2\pi]$, then the argument will be reduced to within that range before the sine and cosine are calculated. However, large arguments may lose accuracy during reduction, and very large arguments (greater than approximately 10^{20}) will lose all accuracy. The results will be in the range of [−1...+1].

FSINH

Hyperbolic Sine (MC68881 or software)

Operation: Hyperbolic Sine of Source → FPn

Assembler   FSINH.<fmt>, <ea>,FPn
Syntax: FSINH.X   FPm,FPn
                 FSINH.X   FPn

Attributes: Format = (Byte, Word, Long, Single, Double, Extended, Packed)

Description: Convert the source operand to extended precision (if necessary) and calculate the hyper -
bolic sine of that value. Return the result to the destination floating-point data register.

FSQRT

Square Root (MC68881 or software)

Operation: Square Root of Source → FPn

Assembler   FSQRT.<fmt> <ea>,FPn
Syntax: FSQRT.X   FPm,FPn
                 FSQRT.X   FPn

Attributes: Format = (Byte, Word, Long, Single, Double, Extended, Packed)

Description: Convert the source operand to extended precision (if necessary) and calculate the
square root of that number. Store the result in the destination floating-point data register. This
function is not defined for negative source operands.

FSUB

Subtract (MC68881 or software)

Operation: FPn – Source → FPn

Assembler   FSUB.<fmt>   <ea>,FPn
Syntax: FSUB.X   FPm,FPn

Attributes: Format = (Byte, Word, Long, Single, Double, Extended, Packed)

Description: Convert the source operand to extended precision (if necessary) and subtract that
number from the number in the destination floating-point data register. The result is stored in the
destination floating-point data register.

FTAN

Tangent (MC68881 or software)

Operation: Tangent of Source → FPn

Assembler   FTAN.<fmt>   <ea>,FPn
Syntax: FTAN.X   FPm,FPn
                 FTAN.X   FPn

Attributes: Format = (Byte, Word, Long, Single, Double, Extended, Packed)

Description: Convert the source operand to extended precision (if necessary) and calculate the
tangent of that number. Store the result in the destination floating-point data register. The function
is not defined for source operands of ±infinity. If the source operand is not in the range of
$[-\pi/2...+\pi/2]$, then the argument will be reduced to within that range before the tangent is
calculated. However, large arguments may lose accuracy during reduction, and very large
arguments (greater than approximately 10^{20}) will lose all accuracy.

FTANH   **Hyperbolic Tangent (MC68881 or software)**

Operation: Hyperbolic Tangent of Source $\rightarrow$ FPn

Assembler   FTANH.<fmt>   <ea>,FPn
Syntax: FTANH.X   FPm,FPn
                 FTANH.X   FPn

Attributes: Format = (Byte, Word, Long, Single, Double, Extended, Packed)

Description: Convert the source operand to extended precision (if necessary) and calculate the
                 hyperbolic tangent of that number. Store the result in the destination floating-point data register.

FTENTOX   **10^x (MC68881 or software)**

Operation: $10^{Source} \rightarrow$ FPn

Assembler   FTENTOX.<fmt>   <ea>,FPn
Syntax: FTENTOX.X   FPm,FPn
                 FTENTOX.X   FPn

Attributes: Format = (Byte, Word, Long, Single, Double, Extended, Packed)

Description: Convert the source operand to extended precision (if necessary) and calculate 10 to the
                 power of that number. Store the result in the destination floating-point data register.

FTRAPcc   **Trap Conditionally (MC68881 or software)**

Operation: If condition true, then TRAP

Assembler   FTRAPcc
Syntax: FTRAPcc.W   #<data>
                 FTRAPcc.L   #<data>

Attributes: Size = (Word, Long)

Description: If the selected condition is true, the main processor initiates exception processing. The
                 vector number is generated to reference the TRAPcc exception vector. The stacked program
                 counter points to the next instruction. If the selected condition is not true, no operation is
                 performed, and execution continues with the next instruction in sequence. The immediate data
                 operand is placed in the next word(s) following the conditional predicate word and is available for
                 user definition for use within the trap handler. The conditional test may be any one of the 32
                 conditional tests

FTST   **Test Operand (MC68881 or software)**

Operation: Test Source Operand and Set the Floating-Point Condition Codes

Assembler   FTST.<fmt>   <ea>
Syntax: FTST.X   FPm

Attributes: Format = (Byte, Word, Long, Single, Double, Extended, Packed)

Description: Convert the source operand to extended precision (if necessary) and set the condition
                 codes according to that number.

FTWOTOX   2^x (MC68881 or software)

Operation: $2^{\text{Source}} \rightarrow \text{FPn}$

Assembler   FTWOTOX.<fmt>   <ea>,FPn
Syntax: FTWOTOX.X   FPm,FPn
                  FTWOTOX.X   FPn

Attributes: Format = (Byte, Word, Long, Single, Double, Extended, Packed)

Description: Convert the source operand to extended precision (if necessary) and calculate 2 to the power of that number. Store the result in the destination floating-point data register.

ILLEGAL   Take Illegal Instruction Trap

Operation: SSP – 2 → SSP; Vector Offset → (SSP);
                  SSP – 4 → SSP; PC → (SSP);
                  SSP – 2 → SSP; SR → (SSP);
                  Illegal Instruction Vector Address → PC

Assembler
Syntax: ILLEGAL

Attributes: Unsized

Description: This bit pattern causes an illegal instruction exception. All other illegal instruction bit patterns are reserved for future extension of the instruction set.

Condition Codes: Not affected.

JMP   Jump

Operation: Destination Address → PC

Assembler
Syntax: JMP <ea>

Attributes: Unsized

Description: Program execution continues at the effective address specified by the instruction. The address is specified by the control addressing modes.

Condition Codes: Not affected.

JSR

Jump to Subroutine

Operation: $SP - 4 \rightarrow SP$; $PC \rightarrow (SP)$
Destination Address $\rightarrow PC$

**Assembler
Syntax:**   JSR <ea>

Attributes: Unsized

Description: The long word address of the instruction immediately following the JSR instruction is pushed onto the system stack. Program execution then continues at the
address specified in the instruction.

Condition Codes: Not affected.

LEA

Load Effective Address

Operation: <ea> $\rightarrow$ An

**Assembler
Syntax:**   LEA <ea>,An

Attributes: Size = (Long)

Description: The effective address is loaded into the specified address register. All 32
bits of the address register are affected by this instruction.

Condition Codes: Not affected.

LINK

Link and Allocate

Operation: $SP - 4 \rightarrow SP$; $An \rightarrow (SP)$;
$SP \rightarrow An$; $SP + d \rightarrow SP$

**Assembler
Syntax:**   LINK An, #<displacement>

Attributes: Size = (Word, Long)—Long for MC68020 only

Description: The current content of the specified address register is pushed onto the
stack. After the push, the address register is loaded from the updated stack pointer.
Finally, the displacement operand is added to the stack pointer. For word size operation, the displacement is the sign-extended word following the operation word. For
long size operation, the displacement is the long word following the operation word.
The content of the address register occupies one long word on the stack. A negative
displacement is specified to allocate stack area.

Condition Codes: Not affected.

LSL, LSR   Logical Shift

Operation: Destination Shifted by<count> → Destination

Assembler   LSd Dx,Dy
Syntax: LSd #<data>,Dy
    LSd <ea>
    where d is direction, L or R

Attributes: Size = (Byte, Word, Long)

Description: Shift the bits of the operand in the direction (L or R) specified. The carry bit receives the last bit shifted out of the operand. The shift count for the shifting of a register may be specified in two different ways:
1. Immediate — the shift count is specified in the instruction (shift range 1-8).
2. Register — the shift count is contained in a data register specified in the instruction (shift count modulo 64).
The size of the operation may be specified to be byte, word, or long. The content of memory may be shifted one bit only, and the operand size is restricted to a word.

For LSL, the operand is shifted left; the number of positions shifted is the shift count. Bits shifted out of the high order bit go to both the carry and the extend bits; zeroes are shifted into the low order bit.

LSL:

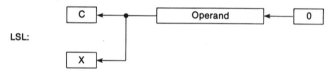

For LSR, the operand is shifted right; the number of positions shifted is the shift count. Bits shifted out of the low order bit go to both the carry and the extend bits; zeroes are shifted into the high order bit.

LSR:

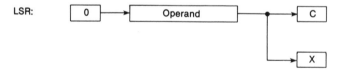

Condition Codes:

X	N	Z	V	C
*	*	*	0	*

N   Set if the result is negative. Cleared otherwise.
Z   Set if the result is zero. Cleared otherwise.
V   Always cleared.
C   Set according to the last bit shifted out of the operand. Cleared for a shift count of zero.
X   Set according to the last bit shifted out of the operand. Unaffected for a shift count of zero.

MOVE   Move Data from Source to Destination

Operation: Source → Destination

**Assembler
Syntax:**   MOVE < ea >,< ea >

Attributes: Size = (Byte, Word, Long)

Description: Move the content of the source to the destination location. The data is examined as it is moved, and the condition codes set accordingly. The size of the operation may be specified to be byte, word, or long.

Condition Codes:

X	N	Z	V	C
—	*	*	0	0

 N Set if the result is negative. Cleared otherwise.
 Z Set if the result is zero. Cleared otherwise.
 V Always cleared.
 C Always cleared.
 X Not affected.

MOVE
from CCR   Move from the (MC68010/12/20)
Condition Code Register

Operation: CCR → Destination

**Assembler
Syntax:**   MOVE CCR,< ea >

Attributes: Size = (Word)

Description: The content of the status register is moved to the destination location. The source operand is a word, but only the low order byte contains the condition codes. The upper byte is all zeroes.

Condition Codes: Not affected.

MOVE
to CCR   Move to Condition Codes

Operation: Source → CCR

**Assembler
Syntax:**   MOVE < ea >,CCR

Attributes: Size = (Word)

Description: The content of the source operand is moved to the condition codes. The source operand is a word, but only the low order byte is used to update the condition codes. The upper byte is ignored.

Condition Codes:

X	N	Z	V	C
*	*	*	*	*

 N Set the same as bit 3 of the source operand.
 Z Set the same as bit 2 of the source operand.
 V Set the same as bit 1 of the source operand.
 C Set the same as bit 0 of the source operand.
 X Set the same as bit 4 of the source operand.

MOVE
from SR

Move from the Status Register (MC68000/08)
(Privileged Instruction)

Operation: If supervisor state
                 then SR→Destination
                 else TRAP;

Assembler
Syntax: MOVE SR,< ea >

Attributes: Size = (Word)

Description: The content of the status register is moved to the destination location. The
operand size is a word.

Condition Codes: Not affected.

MOVE
from SR

Move from the Status Register (MC68010/12/20)
(Privileged Instruction)

Operation: If supervisor state
                 then SR → Destination
                 else TRAP

Assembler
Syntax: MOVE SR,< ea >

Attributes: Size = (Word)

Description: The content of the status register is moved to the destination location. The
operand size is a word.

Condition Codes: Not affected.

MOVE
to SR

Move to the Status Register
(Privileged Instruction)

Operation: If supervisor state
                 then Source→SR
                 else TRAP

Assembler
Syntax: MOVE < ea >,SR

Attributes: Size = (Word)

Description: The content of the source operand is moved to the status register. The
source operand is a word and all bits of the status register are affected.

Condition Codes: Set according to the source operand.

MOVE
USP

Move User Stack Pointer
(Privileged Instruction)

Operation: If supervisor state
             then USP → An or An → USP
             else TRAP

Assembler   MOVE USP,An
Syntax: Move An,USP

Attributes: Size = (Long)

Description: The contents of the user stack pointer are transferred to or from the specified address register.

Condition Codes: Not affected.

MOVEA
Move Address

Operation: Source → Destination

Assembler
Syntax: MOVEA <ea>,An

Attributes: Size = (Word, Long)

Description: Move the content of the source to the destination address register. The size of the operation may be specified to be word or long. Word size source operands are sign extended to 32 bit quantities before the operation is done.

Condition Codes: Not affected.

MOVEC
Move Control Register (MC6810/12/20)
(Privileged Instruction)

Operation: If supervisor state
             then Rc → Rn or Rn → Rc
             else TRAP

Assembler   MOVEC Rc,Rn
Syntax: MOVEC Rn,Rc

Attributes: Size = (Long)

Description: Copy the contents of the specified control register (Rc) to the specified general register or copy the contents of the specified general register to the specified control register. This is always a 32-bit transfer even though the control register may be implemented with fewer bits. Unimplemented bits are read as zeros.

Condition Codes: Not affected.

MOVEM   **Move Multiple Registers**

Operation: Registers → Destination
Source → Registers

Assembler MOVEM register list,< ea >
Syntax: MOVEM < ea >,register list

Attributes: Size = (Word, Long)

Description: Selected registers are transferred to or from consecutive memory locations starting at the location specified by the effective address. A register is transferred if the bit corresponding to that register is set in the mask field. The instruction selects how much of each register is transferred; either the entire long word can be moved or just the low order word. In the case of a word transfer to the registers, each word is sign-extended to 32 bits (including data registers) and the resulting long word loaded into the associated register.

MOVEM allows three forms of address modes: the control modes, the predecrement mode, or the postincrement mode. If the effective address is in one of the control modes, the registers are transferred starting at the specified address and up through higher addresses. The order of transfer is from data register 0 to data register 7, then from address register 0 to address register 7.

If the effective address is the predecrement mode, only a register to memory operation is allowed. The registers are stored starting at the specified address minus the operand length (2 or 4) and down through lower addresses. The order of storing is from address register 7 to address register 0, then from data register 7 to data register 0. The decremented address register is updated to contain the address of the last word stored.

If the effective address is the postincrement mode, only a memory to register operation is allowed. The registers are loaded starting at the specified address and up through higher addresses. The order of loading is the same as for the control mode addressing. The incremented address register is updated to contain the address of the last word loaded plus the operand length (2 or 4).

Condition Codes: Not affected.

MOVEP   **Move Peripheral Data**

Operation: Source → Destination

Assembler   MOVEP Dx,(d,Ay)
Syntax: MOVEP (d,Ay)Dx

Attributes: Size = (Word, Long)

Description: Data is transferred between a data register and alternate bytes of memory, starting at the location specified and incrementing by two. The high order byte of the data register is transferred first and the low order byte is transferred last. The memory address is specified using the address register indirect plus 16-bit displacement addressing mode. This instruction is designed to work with 8-bit peripherals on a 16-bit data bus. If the address is even, all the transfers are made on the high order half of the data bus; if the address is odd, all the transfers are made on the low order half of the data bus. On an 8- or 32-bit bus, the instruction still accesses every other byte.

Example: Long transfer to/from an even address.

Byte organization in register

31	24 23	16 15	8 7	0
Hi-Order	Mid-Upper	Mid-Lower	Low-Order	

Byte organization in memory (low address at top)

15	8	7	0
Hi-Order			
Mid-Upper			
Mid-Lower			
Low-Order			

Example: Word transfer to/from an odd address.

Byte organization in register

31	24 23	16 15	8 7	0
		Hi-Order	Low-Order	

Byte organization in memory (low address at top)

15	8	7	0
		Hi-Order	
		Low-Order	

MOVEQ   Move Quick

Operation: Immediate Data → Destination

**Assembler
Syntax:** MOVEQ #<data>,Dn

Attributes: Size = (Long)

Description: Move immediate data to a data register. The data is contained in an 8-bit field within the operation word. The data is sign-extended to a long operand and all 32 bits are transferred to the data register.

Condition Codes:

X	N	Z	V	C
—	*	*	0	0

N   Set if the result is negative. Cleared otherwise.
Z   Set if the result is zero. Cleared otherwise.
V   Always cleared.
C   Always cleared.
X   Not affected.

MOVES   Move Address Space   (MC68010/12/20)
                          (Privileged Instruction)

Operation: If supervisor state
    then Rn → Destination [DFC] or Source [SFC] → Rn
    else TRAP

**Assembler   MOVES Rn,<ea>
Syntax:**   MOVES <ea>,Rn

Attributes: Size = (Byte, Word, Long)

Description: Move the byte, word, or long operand from the specified general register to a location within the address space specified by the destination function code (DFC) register. Or, move the byte, word, or long operand from a location within the address space specified by the source function code (SFC) register to the specified general register.

If the destination is a data register, the source operand replaces the corresponding low-order bits of that data register. If the destination is an address register, the source operand is sign-extended to 32 bits and then loaded into that address register.

Condition Codes: Not affected.

MULS   **Signed Multiply**

Operation: Source*Destination → Destination

Assembler   MULS.W<ea>,Dn   16 × 16 → 32
Syntax: MULS.L<ea>,Dl   32 × 32 → 32 ⎫
                 MULS.L<ea>,Dh:Dl   32 × 32 → 64 ⎭ MC68020 only

Attributes: Size = (Word, Long)—Long for MC68020 only

Description: Multiply two signed operands yielding a signed result. The operation is performed using signed arithmetic.

The instruction has a word form and a long form. For the word form, the multiplier and multiplicand are both word operands and the result is long word operand. A register operand is taken from the low order word, the upper word is unused. All 32 bits of the product are saved in the destination data register.

For the long form, the multiplier and multiplicand are both long word operands and the result is either a long word or a quad word. The long word result is the low order 32 bits of the quad word result.

Condition Codes:

X	N	Z	V	C
—	*	*	*	0

N   Set if the result is negative. Cleared otherwise.
Z   Set if the result is zero. Cleared otherwise.
V   Set if overflow. Cleared otherwise.
C   Always cleared.
X   Not affected.

MULU   **Unsigned Multiply**

Operation: Source*Destination → Destination

Assembler   MULU.W<ea>,Dn   16 × 16 → 32
Syntax: MULU.L<ea>,Dl   32 × 32 → 32 ⎫
                 MULU.L<ea>,Dh:Dl   32 × 32 → 64 ⎭ MC68020 only

Attributes: Size = (Word, Long)—Long for MC68020 only

Description: Multiply two unsigned operands yielding a unsigned result. The operation is performed using unsigned arithmetic.

The instruction has a word form and a long form. For the word form, the multiplier and multiplicand are both word operands and the result is a long word operand. A register operand is taken from the low order word, the upper word is unused. All 32 bits of the product are saved in the destination data register.

For the long form, the multiplier and multiplicand are both long word operands and the result is either a long word or a quad word. The long word result is the low order 32 bits of the quad word result.

Condition Codes:

X	N	Z	V	C
—	*	*	*	0

N   Set if the result is negative. Cleared otherwise.
Z   Set if the result is zero. Cleared otherwise.
V   Set if overflow. Cleared otherwise.
C   Always cleared.
X   Not affected.

NBCD   Negate Decimal with Extend

Operation: $0 - \text{Destination}_{10} - X \rightarrow \text{Destination}$

**Assembler
Syntax:**   NBCD <ea>

Attributes: Size = (Byte)

Description: The operand addressed as the destination and the extend bit are subtracted from zero. The operation is performed using decimal arithmetic. The result is
saved in the destination location. This instruction produces the tens complement of
the destination if the extend bit is clear, the nines complement if the extend bit is
set. This is a byte operation only.

Condition Codes:

X	N	Z	V	C
*	U	*	U	*

N   Undefined.
Z   Cleared if the result is non-zero. Unchanged otherwise.
V   Undefined.
C   Set if a borrow (decimal) was generated. Cleared otherwise.
X   Set the same as the carry bit.

NOTE

Normally the Z condition code bit is set via programming before the start of
an operation. This allows successful tests for zero results upon completion of
multiple precision operations.

NEG   Negate

Operation: $0 - \text{Destination} \rightarrow \text{Destination}$

**Assembler
Syntax:**   NEG <ea>

Attributes: Size = (Byte, Word, Long)

Description: The operand addressed as the destination is subtracted from zero. The
result is stored in the destination location. The size of the operation may be
specified to be byte, word, or long.

Condition Codes:

X	N	Z	V	C
*	*	*	*	*

N   Set if the result is negative. Cleared otherwise.
Z   Set if the result is zero. Cleared otherwise.
V   Set if an overflow is generated. Cleared otherwise.
C   Cleared if the result is zero. Set otherwise.
X   Set the same as the carry bit.

NEGX

Negate with Extend

Operation: 0 − (Destination) − X → Destination

**Assembler
Syntax:**   NEGX <ea>

Attributes: Size = (Byte, Word, Long)

Description: The operand addressed as the destination and the extend bit are subtracted from zero. The result is stored in the destination location. The size of the
operation may be specified to be byte, word, or long.

Condition Codes:

X	N	Z	V	C
*	*	*	*	*

N   Set if the result is negative. Cleared otherwise.
Z   Cleared if the result is non-zero. Unchanged otherwise.
V   Set if an overflow is generated. Cleared otherwise.
C   Set if a borrow is generated. Cleared otherwise.
X   Set the same as the carry bit.

NOTE

Normally the Z condition code bit is set via programming before the start of
an operation. This allows successful tests for zero results upon completion of
multiple-precision operations.

NOP

No Operation

Operation: None

**Assembler
Syntax:**   NOP

Attributes: Unsized

Description: No operation occurs. The processor state, other than the program counter,
is unaffected. Execution continues with the instruction following the NOP instruction. The NOP instruction does not complete execution until all pending bus cycles
are completed. This allows synchronization of the pipeline to be accomplished, and
prevents instruction overlap.

Condition Codes: Not affected.

NOT
Logical Complement

Operation: ~ Destination → Destination

Assembler
Syntax: NOT <ea>

Attributes: Size = (Byte, Word, Long)

Description: The ones complements of the destination operand is taken and the result is stored in the destination location. The size of the operation may be specified to be byte, word, or long.

Condition Codes:

X	N	Z	V	C
—	*	*	0	0

     N   Set if the result is negative. Cleared otherwise.
     Z   Set if the result is zero. Cleared otherwise.
     V   Always cleared.
     C   Always cleared.
     X   Not affected.

OR
Inclusive OR Logical

Operation: Source v Destination → Destination

Assembler   OR <ea>,Dn
Syntax: OR Dn,<ea>

Attributes: Size = (Byte, Word, Long)

Description: Inclusive OR the source operand to the destination operand and store the result in the destination location. The size of the operation may be specified to be byte, word, or long. The contents of an address register may not be used as an operand.

Condition Codes:

X	N	Z	V	C
—	*	*	0	0

     N   Set if the most significant bit of the result is set. Cleared otherwise.
     Z   Set if the result is zero. Cleared otherwise.
     V   Always cleared.
     C   Always cleared.
     X   Not affected.

ORI   Inclusive OR Immediate

Operation: Immediate Data v Destination → Destination

Assembler
Syntax: ORI #<data>,<ea>

Attributes: Size = (Byte, Word, Long)

Description: Inclusive OR the immediate data to the destination operand and store the
result in the destination location. The size of the operation may be specified to be
byte, word, or long. The size of the immediate data matches the operation size.

Condition Codes:

X	N	Z	V	C
—	*	*	0	0

N   Set if the most significant bit of the result is set. Cleared otherwise.
Z   Set if the result is zero. Cleared otherwise.
V   Always cleared.
C   Always cleared.
X   Not affected.

ORI
to CCR   Inclusive OR Immediate
                  to Condition Codes

Operation: Source v CCR → CCR

Assembler
Syntax: ORI #<data>,CCR

Attributes: Size = (Byte)

Description: Inclusive OR the immediate operand with the condition codes and store the
result in the low-order byte of the status register.

Condition Codes:

X	N	Z	V	C
*	*	*	*	*

N   Set if bit 3 of immediate operand is one. Unchanged otherwise.
Z   Set if bit 2 of immediate operand is one. Unchanged otherwise.
V   Set if bit 1 of immediate operand is one. Unchanged otherwise.
C   Set if bit 0 of immediate operand is one. Unchanged otherwise.
X   Set if bit 4 of immediate operand is one. Unchanged otherwise.

ORI
to SR
Inclusive OR Immediate to the Status Register
(Privileged Instruction)

Operation: If supervisor state
                    then Source v SR → SR
                    else TRAP

Assembler
Syntax: ORI #<data>,SR

Attributes: Size = (Word)

Description: Inclusive OR the immediate operand with the contents of the status register and store the result in the status register. All bits of the status register are affected.

Condition Codes:

X	N	Z	V	C
*	*	*	*	*

N   Set if bit 3 of immediate operand is one. Unchanged otherwise.
Z   Set if bit 2 of immediate operand is one. Unchanged otherwise.
V   Set if bit 1 of immediate operand is one. Unchanged otherwise.
C   Set if bit 0 of immediate operand is one. Unchanged otherwise.
X   Set if bit 4 of immediate operand is one. Unchanged otherwise.

PEA
Push Effective Address

Operation: SP − 4 → SP; EA → (SP)

Assembler
Syntax: PEA <ea>

Attributes: Size = (Long)

Description: The effective address is computed and pushed onto the stack. A long word address is pushed onto the stack.

Condition Codes: Not affected.

RESET
Reset External Devices
(Privileged Instruction)

Operation: If supervisor state
                    then Assert RESET Line
                    else TRAP

Assembler
Syntax: RESET

Attributes: Unsized

Description: The reset line is asserted, causing all external devices to be reset. The processor state, other than the program counter, is unaffected and execution continues with the next instruction.

Condition Codes: Not affected.

PACK

Pack (MC68020 only)

Operation: Source (Unpacked BCD) + adjustment → Destination (Packed BCD)

Assembler   PACK − (Ax), − (Ay),#< adjustment >
Syntax: PACK Dx,Dy,#< adjustment >

Attributes: Unsized

Description: The low four bits of each of two bytes are adjusted and packed into a single byte.

When both operands are data registers, the adjustment is added to the value contained in the source register. Bits [11:8] and [3:0] of the intermediate result are concatenated and placed in bits [7:0] of the destination register. The remainder of the destination register is unaffected.

Source:

	15	14	13	12	11	10	9	8	7	6	5	4	3	2	1	0
Dx	x	x	x	x	a	b	c	d	x	x	x	x	e	f	g	h

Add Adjustment Word:

15	14	13	12	11	10	9	8	7	6	5	4	3	2	1	0
							16-Bit Extension								

Resulting in:

15	14	13	12	11	10	9	8	7	6	5	4	3	2	1	0
x′	x′	x′	x′	a′	b′	c′	d′	x′	x′	x′	x′	e′	f′	g′	h′

Destination:

	15	14	13	12	11	10	9	8	7	6	5	4	3	2	1	0
Dy	u	u	u	u	u	u	u	u	a′	b′	c′	d′	e′	f′	g′	h′

When the addressing mode specified is predecrement, two bytes from the source are fetched, adjusted, and concatenated. The extension word is added to the concatenated bytes. Bits [3:0] of each byte are extracted. These eight bits are concatenated to form a new byte which is then written to the destination.

Source:

	7	6	5	4	3	2	1	0
	x	x	x	x	a	b	c	d
	x	x	x	x	e	f	g	h
(Ax)								

Concatenated Word:

15	14	13	12	11	10	9	8	7	6	5	4	3	2	1	0
x	x	x	x	a	b	c	d	x	x	x	x	e	f	g	h

Add Adjustment Word:

15	14	13	12	11	10	9	8	7	6	5	4	3	2	1	0
							16-Bit Extension								

Destination:

	7	6	5	4	3	2	1	0
	a′	b′	c′	d′	e′	f′	g′	h′
(Ay)								

Condition Codes: Not affected.

ROL
ROR

Rotate (Without Extend)

Operation: Destination Rotated by <count> → Destination

Assembler ROd Dx,Dy
Syntax: ROd #<data>,Dy
ROd <ea>
where d is direction, L or R

Attributes: Size = (Byte, Word, Long)

Description: Rotate the bits of the operand in the direction (L or R) specified. The extend bit is not included in the rotation. The rotate count for the rotation of a register may be specified in two different ways:
1. Immediate — the rotate count is specified in the instruction (rotate range, 1-8).
2. Register — the rotate count is contained in a data register specified in the instruction.
The size of the operation may be specified to be byte, word, or long. The content of memory may be rotated by one bit only and the operand size is restricted to a word.

For ROL, the operand is rotated left; the number of positions rotated is the rotate count. Bits rotated out of the high order bit go to both the carry bit and back into the low order bit. The extend bit is not modified or used.

ROL: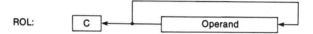

For ROR, the operand is rotated right; the number of positions rotated is the rotate count. Bits shifted out of the low order bit go to both the carry bit and back into high order bit. The extend bit is not modified or used.

ROR: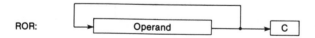

Condition Codes:

X	N	Z	V	C
—	*	*	0	*

N Set if the most significant bit of the result is set. Cleared otherwise.
Z Set if the result is zero. Cleared otherwise.
V Always cleared.
C Set according to the last bit rotated out of the operand. Cleared for a rotate count of zero.
X Not affected.

ROXL
ROXR

Rotate with Extend

Operation: Destination Rotated with X by <count> → Destination

Assembler ROXd Dx,Dy
Syntax: ROXd #<data>,Dy
ROXd <ea>

Attributes: Size = (Byte, Word, Long)

Description: Rotate the bits of the destination operand in the direction specified. The extend bit (X) is included in the rotation. The rotate count for the rotation of a register may be specified in two different ways:
1. Immediate — the rotate count is specified in the instruction (rotate range, 1-8).
2. Register — the rotate count (modulo 64) is contained in a data register specified in the instruction.
The size of the operation may be specified to be byte, word, or long. The content of memory may be rotated one bit only and the operand size is restricted to a word.

For ROXL, the operand is rotated left; the number of positions rotated is the rotate count. Bits rotated out of the high order bit go to both the carry and extend bits; the previous value of the extend bit is rotated into the low order bit.

ROXL: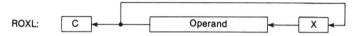

For ROXR, the operand is rotated right; the number of positions shifted is the rotate count. Bits rotated out of the low order bit go to both the carry and extend bits; the previous value of the extend bit is rotated into the high order bit.

ROXR: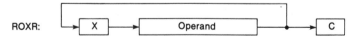

Condition Codes:

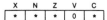

X	N	Z	V	C
*	*	*	0	*

N Set if the most significant bit of the result is set. Cleared otherwise.
Z Set if the result is zero. Cleared otherwise.
V Always cleared.
C Set according to the last bit rotated out of the operand. Set to the value of the extend bit for a rotate count of zero.
X Set according to the last bit rotated out of the operand. Unaffected for a rotate count of zero.

RTD
Return and Deallocate Parameters (MC68010/12/20)

Operation: (SP) → PC; SP + 4 + d → SP

**Assembler
Syntax:**   RTD #< displacement >

Attributes: Unsized

Description: The program counter is pulled from the stack. The previous program counter value is lost. After the program counter is read from the stack, the displacement value (16 bits) is sign-extended to 32 bits and added to the stack pointer.

Condition Codes: Not affected.

RTE
**Return from Exception
(Privileged Instruction)**

Operation: If supervisor state
  then (SP) → SR; SP + 2 → SP; (SP) → PC; SP + 4 → SP;
    restore state and deallocate
    stack according to (SP)
  else TRAP

**Assembler
Syntax:**   RTE

Attributes: Unsized

Description: The processor state information in the exception stack frame on top of the stack is loaded into the processor. The stack format field in the format/offset word is examined to determine how much information must be restored.

Condition Codes: Set according to the content of the word on the stack.

RTM
Return from Module (MC68020 only)

Operation: Reload Saved Module State from Stack

**Assembler
Syntax:**   RTM Rn

Attributes: Unsized

Description: A previously saved module state is reloaded from the top of stack. After the module state is retrieved from the top of the stack, the caller's stack pointer is incremented by the argument count value in the module state.

Condition Codes: Set according to the content of the word on the stack.

RTR
Return and Restore Condition Codes

Operation: $(SP) \rightarrow CCR; SP + 2 \rightarrow SP;$
$(SP) \rightarrow PC; SP + 4 \rightarrow SP$

**Assembler
Syntax:** RTR

Attributes: Unsized

Description: The condition codes and program counter are pulled from the stack. The previous condition codes and program counter are lost. The supervisor portion of the status register is unaffected.

Condition Codes: Set according to the content of the word on the stack.

RTS
Return from Subroutine

Operation: $(SP) \rightarrow PC; SP + 4 \rightarrow SP$

**Assembler
Syntax:** RTS

Attributes: Unsized

Description: The program counter is pulled from the stack. The previous program counter is lost.

Condition Codes: Not affected.

SBCD
Subtract Decimal with Extend

Operation: $Destination_{10} - Source_{10} - X \rightarrow Destination$

**Assembler
Syntax:** SBCD Dx,Dy
SBCD $-(Ax), -(Ay)$

Attributes: Size = (Byte)

Description: Subtract the source operand from the destination operand with the extend bit and store the result in the destination location. The subtraction is performed using decimal arithmetic. The operands may be addressed in two different ways:
1. Data register to data register: The operands are contained in the data registers specified in the instruction.
2. Memory to memory: The operands are addressed with the predecrement addressing mode using the address registers specified in the instruction.
This operation is a byte operation only.

Condition Codes:

X	N	Z	V	C
*	U	*	U	*

N   Undefined.
Z   Cleared if the result is non-zero. Unchanged otherwise.
V   Undefined.
C   Set if a borrow (decimal) is generated. Cleared otherwise.
X   Set the same as the carry bit.

NOTE
Normally the Z condition code bit is set via programming before the start of an operation. This allows successful tests for zero results upon completion of multiple-precision operations.

Scc

Set According to Condition

Operation: If Condition True
                 then 1s → Destination
                 else 0s → Destination

**Assembler
Syntax:**   Scc <ea>

Attributes: Size = (Byte)

Description: The specified condition code is tested; if the condition is true, the byte specified by the effective address is set to TRUE (all ones), otherwise that byte is set to FALSE (all zeroes). "cc" may specify the following conditions:

CC	carry clear	0100	$\overline{C}$
CS	carry set	0101	C
EQ	equal	0111	Z
F	never true	0001	0
GE	greater or equal	1100	$N \cdot V + \overline{N} \cdot \overline{V}$
GT	greater than	1110	$N \cdot V \cdot \overline{Z} + \overline{N} \cdot \overline{V} \cdot \overline{Z}$
HI	high	0010	$\overline{C} \cdot \overline{Z}$
LE	less or equal	1111	$Z + N \cdot \overline{V} + \overline{N} \cdot V$

LS	low or same	0011	$C + Z$
LT	less than	1101	$N \cdot \overline{V} + \overline{N} \cdot V$
MI	minus	1011	N
NE	not equal	0110	$\overline{Z}$
PL	plus	1010	$\overline{N}$
T	always true	0000	1
VC	overflow clear	1000	$\overline{V}$
VS	overflow set	1001	V

Condition Codes: Not affected.

STOP

**Load Status Register and Stop
(Privileged Instruction)**

Operation: If supervisor state
                 then Immediate Data → SR; STOP
                 else TRAP

**Assembler
Syntax:**   STOP #<data>

Attributes: Unsized

Description: The immediate operand is moved into the entire status register; the program counter is advanced to point to the next instruction and the processor stops fetching and executing instructions. Execution of instructions resumes when a trace, interrupt, or reset exception occurs. A trace exception will occur if the trace state is on when the STOP instruction begins execution. If an interrupt request is asserted with a priority higher than the priority level set by the immediate data, an interrupt exception occurs, otherwise, the interrupt request has no effect. If the bit of the immediate data corresponding to the S-bit is off, execution of the instruction will cause a privilege violation. External reset will always initiate reset exception processing.

Condition Codes: Set according to the immediate operand.

SUB   Subtract Binary

Operation: Destination − Source → Destination

Assembler   SUB < ea >,Dn
Syntax: SUB Dn,< ea >

Attributes: Size = (Byte, Word, Long)

Description: Subtract the source operand from the destination operand and store the result in the destination. The size of the operation may be specified to be byte, word, or long. The mode of the instruction indicates which operand is the source and which is the destination as well as the operand size.

Condition Codes:

X	N	Z	V	C
*	*	*	*	*

  N   Set if the result is negative. Cleared otherwise.
  Z   Set if the result is zero. Cleared otherwise.
  V   Set if an overflow is generated. Cleared otherwise.
  C   Set if a borrow is generated. Cleared otherwise.
  X   Set the same as the carry bit.

SUBA   Subtract Address

Operation: Destination − Source → Destination

Assembler
Syntax: SUBA < ea >,An

Attributes: Size = (Word, Long)

Description: Subtract the source operand from the destination address register and store the result in the address register. The size of the operation may be specified to be word or long. Word size source operands are sign extended to 32 bit quantities before the operation is done.

Condition Codes: Not affected.

SUBI
Subtract Immediate

Operation: Destination − Immediate Data → Destination

**Assembler
Syntax:**   SUBI #<data>,<ea>

Attributes: Size = (Byte, Word, Long)

Description: Subtract the immediate data from the destination operand and store the result in the destination location. The size of the operation may be specified to be byte, word, or long. The size of the immediate data matches the operation size.

Condition Codes:

X	N	Z	V	C
*	*	*	*	*

    N   Set if the result is negative. Cleared otherwise.
    Z   Set if the result is zero. Cleared otherwise.
    V   Set if an overflow is generated. Cleared otherwise.
    C   Set if a borrow is generated. Cleared otherwise.
    X   Set the same as the carry bit.

SUBQ
Subtract Quick

Operation: Destination − Immediate Data → Destination

**Assembler
Syntax:**   SUBQ #<data>,<ea>

Attributes: Size = (Byte, Word, Long)

Description: Subtract the immediate data from the destination operand. The data range is from 1-8. The size of the operation may be specified to be byte, word, or long. Word and long operations are also allowed on the address registers and the condition codes are not affected. When subtracting from address registers, the entire destination address register is used, regardless of the operation size.

Condition Codes:

X	N	Z	V	C
*	*	*	*	*

    N   Set if the result is negative. Cleared otherwise.
    Z   Set if the result is zero. Cleared otherwise.
    V   Set if an overflow is generated. Cleared otherwise.
    C   Set if a borrow is generated. Cleared otherwise.
    X   Set the same as the carry bit.

SUBX
Subtract with Extend

Operation: Destination − Source − X → Destination

**Assembler
Syntax:** SUBX Dx,Dy
SUBX − (Ax), − (Ay)

Attributes: Size = (Byte, Word, Long)

Description: Subtract the source operand from the destination operand along with the extend bit and store the result in the destination location. The operands may be addressed in two different ways:
1. Data register to data register: The operands are contained in data registers specified in the instruction.
2. Memory to memory. The operands are contained in memory and addressed with the predecrement addressing mode using the address registers specified in the instruction.
The size of the operand may be specified to be byte, word, or long.

Condition Codes:

X	N	Z	V	C
*	*	*	*	*

N   Set if the result is negative. Cleared otherwise.
Z   Cleared if the result is non-zero. Unchanged otherwise.
V   Set if an overflow is generated. Cleared otherwise.
C   Set if a carry is generated. Cleared otherwise.
X   Set the same as the carry bit.

NOTE
Normally the Z condition code bit is set via programming before the start of an operation. This allows successful tests for zero results upon completion of multiple-precision operations.

SWAP
Swap Register Halves

Operation: Register [31:16] ↔ Register [15:0]

**Assembler
Syntax:** SWAP Dn

Attributes: Size = (Word)

Description: Exchange the 16-bit halves of a data register.

Condition Codes:

X	N	Z	V	C
—	*	*	0	0

N   Set if the most significant bit of the 32-bit result is set. Cleared otherwise.
Z   Set if the 32-bit result is zero. Cleared otherwise.
V   Always cleared.
C   Always cleared.
X   Not affected.

TAS
Test and Set an Operand

Operation: Destination Tested → Condition Codes; 1 → bit 7 of Destination

**Assembler
Syntax:** TAS <ea>

Attributes: Size = (Byte)

Description: Test and set the byte operand addressed by the effective address field. The current value of the operand is tested and N and Z are set accordingly. The high order bit of the operand is set. The operation is indivisible (using a read-modify-write memory cycle) to allow synchronization of several processors.

Condition Codes:

X	N	Z	V	C
—	*	*	0	0

  N   Set if the most significant bit of the operand was set. Cleared otherwise.
  Z   Set if the operand was zero. Cleared otherwise.
  V   Always cleared.
  C   Always cleared.
  X   Not affected.

TRAP
Trap

Operation: SSP − 2 → SSP; Format/Offset → (SSP);
SSP − 4 → SSP; PC → (SSP); SSP − 2 → SSP;
SR → (SSP); Vector Address → PC

**Assembler
Syntax:** TRAP #<vector>

Attributes: Unsized

Description: The processor initiates exception processing. The vector number is generated to reference the TRAP instruction exception vector specified by the low order four bits of the instruction. Sixteen TRAP instruction vectors (0-15) are available.

Condition Codes: Not affected.

TRAPcc   **Trap on Condition (MC68020 only)**

Operation: If cc then TRAP

Assembler
Syntax: TRAPcc
                    TRAPcc.W #<data>
                    TRAPcc.L #<data>

Attributes: Unsized or Size = (Word, Long)

Description: If the selected condition is true, the processor initiates exception processing. The vector number is generated to reference the TRAPcc exception vector. The
stacked program counter points to the next instruction. If the selected condition is
not true, no operation is performed, and execution continues with the next instruction in sequence. The immediate data operand(s) is placed in the next word(s) following the operation word and is (are) available for user definition for use within the
trap handler. "cc" may specify the following conditions.

CC	carry clear	0100	$\overline{C}$
CS	carry set	0101	C
EQ	equal	0111	Z
F	never true	0001	0
GE	greater or equal	1100	$N \cdot V + \overline{N} \cdot \overline{V}$
GT	greater than	1110	$N \cdot V \cdot \overline{Z} + \overline{N} \cdot \overline{V} \cdot \overline{Z}$
HI	high	0010	$\overline{C} \cdot \overline{Z}$
LE	less or equal	1111	$Z + N \cdot \overline{V} + \overline{N} \cdot V$

LS	low or same	0011	$C + Z$
LT	less than	1101	$N \cdot \overline{V} + \overline{N} \cdot V$
MI	minus	1011	N
NE	not equal	0110	$\overline{Z}$
PL	plus	1010	$\overline{N}$
T	always true	0000	1
VC	overflow clear	1000	$\overline{V}$
VS	overflow set	1001	V

Condition Codes: Not affected.

TRAPV   **Trap on Overflow**

Operation: If V then TRAP

Assembler
Syntax: TRAPV

Attributes: Unsized

Description: If the overflow condition is set, the processor initiates exception
processing. The vector number is generated to reference the TRAPV exception vector. If the overflow condition is clear, no operation is performed and execution continues with the next instruction in sequence.

Condition Codes: Not affected.

TST   Test an Operand

Operation: Destination Tested → Condition Codes

**Assembler
Syntax:**   TST <ea>

Attributes: Size = (Byte, Word, Long)

Description: Compare the operand with zero. No results are saved; however, the condition codes are set according to results of the test. The size of the operation may be specified to be byte, word, or long.

Condition Codes:

X	N	Z	V	C
—	*	*	0	0

N   Set if the operand is negative. Cleared otherwise.
Z   Set if the operand is zero. Cleared otherwise.
V   Always cleared.
C   Always cleared.
X   Not affected.

UNLK   Unlink

Operation: An → SP; (SP) → An; SP + 4 → SP

**Assembler
Syntax:**   UNLK An

Attributes: Unsized

Description: The stack pointer is loaded from the specified address register. The address register is then loaded with the long word pulled from the top of the stack.

Condition Codes: Not affected.

UNPK

Unpack BCD (MC68020 only)

Operation: Source (Packed BCD) + adjustment → Destination (Unpacked BCD)

Assembler   UNPACK − (Ax), − (Ay),#<adjustment>
Syntax: UNPK Dx,Dy,#<adjustment>

Attributes: Unsized

Description: In the unpack operation, two BCD digits within the byte source operand are separated into two bytes with the BCD digit residing in the lower nibble and 0 in the upper nibble. The adjustment is then added to this unpacked value without affecting the condition codes.

When both operands are data registers, the source register contents are unpacked, the extension word is added, and the result is placed in the destination register. The high word of the destination register is unaffected.

Source:

	15	14	13	12	11	10	9	8	7	6	5	4	3	2	1	0
Dx	u	u	u	u	u	u	u	u	a	b	c	d	e	f	g	h

Intermediate Expansion:

15	14	13	12	11	10	9	8	7	6	5	4	3	2	1	0
0	0	0	0	a	b	c	d	0	0	0	0	e	f	g	h

Add Adjustment Word:

15	14	13	12	11	10	9	8	7	6	5	4	3	2	1	0
16-Bit Extension															

Destination:

	15	14	13	12	11	10	9	8	7	6	5	4	3	2	1	0
Dy	v	v	v	v	a′	b′	c′	d′	w	w	w	w	e′	f′	g′	h′

When the addressing mode specified is predecrement, two BCD digits are extracted from a byte at the source address. After adding the extension word, two bytes are then written to the destination address.

Source:

	7	6	5	4	3	2	1	0
	a	b	c	d	e	f	g	h
(Ax)								

Intermediate Expansion:

15	14	13	12	11	10	9	8	7	6	5	4	3	2	1	0
0	0	0	0	a	b	c	d	0	0	0	0	e	f	g	h

Add Adjustment Word:

15	14	13	12	11	10	9	8	7	6	5	4	3	2	1	0
16-Bit Extension															

Destination:

	7	6	5	4	3	2	1	0
	v	v	v	v	a′	b′	c′	d′
	w	w	w	w	e′	f′	g′	h′
(Ay)								

Condition Codes: Not affected.

Index